D1716121

KANSAS CITY CHIEFS ENCYCLOPEDIA

BY
MARK STALLARD

SP
SPORTS PUBLISHING L.L.C.

www.SportsPublishingLLC.com

Senior Graphic Designer: Kenneth J. O'Brien
Interior layout: Kenneth J. O'Brien and Greg Hickman
Coordinating Editor: Erin M. Linden-Levy
Copy Editor: Cynthia L. McNew

Back cover photos:
Hank Stram: Transcendental Graphics
Stadium: *Kansas City Star*
Len Dawson: *Topeka Capital-Journal*
Priest Holmes: Susan Walsh, AP/Wide World Photos
Tony Gonzalez, Derrick Thomas, Joe Montana, Marcus Allen: Alan Barzee

Hard back edition
ISBN: 1-58261-129-7

Leather edition
ISBN: 1-58261-275-7

We have made every effort to trace the ownership of copyrighted photos. If we have failed to give adequate credit, we will be pleased to make changes in future printings.

Sports Publishing L.L.C.
www.SportsPublishingLLC.com

To Merrie Jo,
who still makes all things possible

Table of Contents

Acknowledgements

This was a project I thoroughly enjoyed working on. It seemed, however, that the more information I gathered or found on the Chiefs, the more I needed. In pursuit of that information, I asked for—and got—a lot of help.

First, I want to thank the excellent people at Sports Publishing, specifically Mike Pearson, who gave me the initial go-ahead on this project. Erin Linden-Levy, Kenny O'Brien, Greg Hickman and Cindy McNew helped make the book a reality, and put up with my endless stream of calls and concerns. I'd also like to thank Joe Bannon, Jr.

The Kansas City Chiefs assisted me a great deal, and I especially want to thank Morgan Shaw and Janet Feltham for answering numerous questions and providing many different items used in the book. Their contributions were invaluable.

A special thanks to Otis Taylor, a true Hall-of-Famer in my eyes.

Thanks to the Pro Football Hall of Fame Research Library in Canton, specifically Saleem Choudhry, who answered questions, supplied me with a great deal of material, and pointed me in the right direction to find other items.

A very big thank you to Bob Carroll for allowing me to use his excellent drawings.

Keith Zimmerman once again helped me, and Jim Chappelle supplied several items for use in the book.

Thanks to Mike Webber, who provided some valuable editing expertise, and Roger Gordon, who listened when I needed him to.

A belated thanks to Pola Firestone for much needed guidance.

Others I want to thank include: Jim Donovan, for his excellent advice; Alan Barzee, who's exceptional photos are spread throughout the book, and Keith Fogliani for his overall photographic advice; former Chiefs' players Tommy Brooker, Chris Burford, Ed Budde, Gloster Richardson, Jim Kearney and Ed Podolak.

I'd also like to thank everyone at the University of Kansas Archives and Spencer Research Library, the *Topeka Capital-Journal*, *Kansas City Star*, *Wichita Eagle*, John Dodderidge and the San Diego Chargers Media Relations department.

Thanks to my friends whose encouragement and support kept me going: Steve Ediger, Kevin Murphy, Dan Consolver, Mike O'Connell, Bob Estabrook and Lloyd Johnson.

And of course, thanks to my wife Merrie Jo, who now knows more about the Chiefs and pro football than she ever thought possible—or wanted to know. I couldn't have completed this book without her help.

KANSAS CITY CHIEFS
Foreword by Otis Taylor

The path that brought me to the Chiefs may sound unbelievable. In 1965, the NFL and AFL were in the middle of their now-famous bidding wars over top college prospects, and I got caught in the middle.

Kansas City and a few NFL teams were interested in my services. When I completed my senior season at Prairie View A&M, the Cowboys, acting for the NFL, invited me to spend the Thanksgiving Day weekend in Dallas. Their intent was to keep me away from the AFL, and they ended up "baby-sitting" me in a Dallas motel. Chiefs' scout Lloyd Wells hunted me down and slipped me a note through room service promising me a red Thunderbird if I would play for them. When the scouts were distracted, I climbed out the window, went to the airport with Wells and flew to Kansas City. It was a snap decision, but becoming a Chief turned out to be a very good idea.

Playing for the Kansas City Chiefs was special, primarily because of the tremendous fan support. The organization gave me the opportunity to excel as a person, to maximize my playing ability, and become a world champion. I might have had similar chances had I opted to play for an NFL team, but coming to Kansas City just felt right. That is why it is still my home.

With the Chiefs, I had the benefit of playing with some of the greatest football players of the day: Buck Buchanan, Willie Lanier, Bobby Bell, Len Dawson, Mike Garrett, Emmitt Thomas, Jim Kearney, and Ed Budde to name few. We were a team, in every sense of the word. I felt a closeness to those guys, and that was as important to me as the success we achieved on the football field.

One-on-one talent-wise, I think the Chiefs were the best team in pro football in the late 1960s and early 1970s. Some might question my call, but man-for-man, we had the ability and the toughness. We won two AFL championships and a Super Bowl; we should have won twice as many.

The difference between our two Super Bowl appearances was like night and day. In the first Super Bowl against the Packers, we had lost before even taking the field. I really believe we were scared of Green Bay, intimidated by the color of their uniforms. We were playing against legendary players, and of course Vince Lombardi. It was too much for many of us to conceive that we really belonged on the same field with that great team. We probably did, but in our minds that day, we didn't. Several of my teammates didn't come to play that day and the result was obvious. We took the loss to the Green Bay Packers in Super Bowl I hard, and felt we had let down the other teams in the AFL, as well as the fans in Kansas City.

Conversely, winning Super Bowl IV meant so much to the team, and so much to me. It took a little longer than we thought or had planned on to return to the Super Bowl, but the result was the highlight of my career. We wanted to win and prove to the country we were a championship-quality team. When I scored the final touchdown against the Vikings and heard my mother calling my name through the loud cheers of the crowd, I can't describe how overwhelmingly special it was. The one regret that I have about both games is that I didn't contribute more. I would have liked to have caught more passes and been more of an offensive weapon than I was.

We had our share of heartbreaking losses on the Chiefs. Losing to the Dolphins in the 1971 double-overtime playoff game was difficult to accept, and I've never really gotten over it. That loss was tougher than losing Super Bowl I.

Of course there was the game against the Raiders in 1970 in which I attacked big Ben Davidson after he tried to hurt Lenny with a dirty, cheap shot. And I'd do it again today. Nobody hurts our quarterback, especially when it's Dawson, but my penalty cost us a win and maybe the division championship.

One of our greatest moments as a team came against the Chicago Bears in a 1967 preseason game. To this day, I still consider it the greatest game ever played by the Chiefs, as do many of my teammates. Hungry to beat an NFL team, we destroyed Chicago at Municipal Stadium, 66-24. We were emotionally charged and angry. We scored on the Bears in every way possible, and afterwards Papa Bear himself, George Halas, walked off the field crying. It was sweet payback for the loss to the Packers, and to the NFL in general, for the lack of respect we got before and after Super Bowl I.

A lot of people have asked me about my relationship with Hank Stram, my head coach with the Chiefs for all but one season. Coach was a hands-on type of guy, running everybody's business. The best way to explain my relationship with him is that it was a love/hate sort of thing. I used to hate him on Thursdays before a game, but on Sundays I would gladly jump over the goal posts for him. He loved to boss people, make us run 10 sets of 100-yards sprints, and then make us run them again until we dropped. There would be 50 players wanting to kill him, but after it was all over, especially if it was a difficult practice, he'd invariably have beer and ribs ready for the entire team. He really knew how to work your mind.

My position coach on the Chiefs was Pete Brewster, and I owe him a big thank you for all he taught me. He helped me through many hard times and was a big part of the successes I enjoyed with the Chiefs. My teammates had a lot to do with my personal success as well. It always helps when you've got a great offensive line, plus a Hall-of-Fame quarterback throwing to you.

The Chiefs have a rich history, and the teams I played with are only a small part of it. Their history is closely tied to the formation of the AFL and Lamar Hunt's huge contribution to the world of pro football. It became a better game because of his innovative commitment to form a new league. Dick Vermeil is the team's new head coach, and his commitment and talent will go a long way toward restoring championship glory in Kansas City. I'll be cheering harder than ever for the Chiefs to finally return to the Super Bowl.

I'll always consider myself a Kansas City Chief. I was so proud to wear the red and gold uniform, proud to play for the Chiefs, and proud to say that Kansas City is my home.

May 2002

Otis Taylor leaps to take a pass from quarterback Len Dawson on the 7-yard line to set up Kansas City's only touchdown in Super Bowl I. (Kansas Collection, U. of Kansas)

INTRODUCTION

Think about it.

If the Dallas football community had embraced the Dallas Texans the way they should have, if following a winner had been more important than following an NFL team and if championships meant something, the Kansas City Chiefs might not exist today.

Lamar Hunt, your average, everyday, 26-year-old multi-millionaire, wanted his own pro football team, and he wanted one in Dallas. Shut out by the NFL's establishment, he altered his pursuit to the formation of a new league, and gave birth to the American Football League in 1960. Many booby-traps were laid by the NFL as the new league and its group of owners tried to gain firm footing in the sports world, the worst trap being the placement of an NFL expansion team in Dallas. It was competition Hunt's Texans hadn't expected.

In the end, the Texans won all the battles against the NFL's Cowboys—they had better players, a better team, and won a championship—but lost the war. Allegiance to the two teams was split unevenly in Dallas, and the Cowboys, losers on the field, were the winners off of it.

Hunt looked for another city, and found the perfect home for his financially-floundering franchise: Kansas City. Heavily wooed by Kansas City Mayor H. Roe Bartle and the promise of 25,000 season tickets, Hunt officially announced that the Texans were moving in May, 1963.

After three mediocre seasons and poor attendance, the Chiefs exploded for the franchise's second AFL championship and a berth in the first Super Bowl. From 1966 to today, the Chiefs have held the city's affection, and rightly so. The Chiefs organization was the major player in making the Truman Sports Complex (Arrowhead and Kauffman Stadiums) a reality, and they brought the city its first major championship of any kind when they defeated the Minnesota Vikings in Super Bowl IV. The perception of Kansas City as a winning city started with the Chiefs, and led by Hunt, General Manager Jack Steadman, Head Coach Hank Stram, and quarterback Len Dawson, the team won 43 games between 1966 and 1969.

By the end of the 1960s, the ten-year-old franchise was the best in the world, and the AFL was gone forever, merged into the NFL. Five years later, the Chiefs had one of the worst teams in the league, and the only coach the franchise had ever had, Hank Stram, was fired. The Chiefs fielded poor teams for more than a decade—losing begets losing—posting winning seasons just twice between 1974 and 1986. They failed to qualify for the playoffs for 15 straight years.

The organization changed directions in 1989 when Hunt named Carl Peterson as the team's new President/General Manager. Peterson hired Marty Schottenheimer as the team's new coach, and after almost two decades of lifeless, losing teams, winning football returned to Kansas City.

The last ten seasons have been the best-ever in the team's 40-year history; six straight playoff appearances, three AFC West championships, nine winning seasons, and 76 consecutive soldout games at Arrowhead. The only thing missing was a return trip to the Super Bowl, something of which every Chiefs fan is painfully aware.

The Chiefs' history is full of men who made a difference in the fortunes of the club; six men from the organization are in the Pro Football Hall of Fame. But the men who played like winners on losing teams are just as important. Art Still, Gary Barbaro, Lloyd Burruss, J. T. Smith, Tony Reed, and many more played hard when there was truly nothing to play for.

Arrowhead Stadium, used to half-capacity crowds for years, has swelled, rocked and screamed with joyous, thundering fans for the past decade. These fans are the envy of the entire league, and while the facility is almost 30 years old, Arrowhead is still one of the finest stadiums in the NFL. It is truly the "Home of the Chiefs."

Forty-two years of history, memories and numbers are in this book: Abner Haynes calling the overtime coin toss in the 1962 AFL championship game; Mack Lee Hill ripping through would-be tacklers; Len Dawson tossing a perfect pass to Chris Burford; Curtis McClinton scoring a touchdown in Super Bowl I; Otis Taylor making a marvelously athletic 46-yard touchdown reception in Super Bowl IV; the 1971 playoff game with the Dolphins; the first win at Arrowhead against the Raiders; Art Still sacking a quarterback; Deron Cherry picking off a pass; the Chiefs' defeat of the Steelers to make the 1986 playoffs; Joe Montana leading the Chiefs to two come-from-behind wins in the 1993 playoffs; and Marcus Allen scoring the 100th rushing touchdown of his career.

The Kansas City Chiefs have been to the top of the pro football world and languished at the bottom. Some of the game's greatest players have donned the red and gold of the Chiefs, and been involved in many great games. Lamar Hunt's dream of owning a pro football team ultimately transformed Kansas City into a football town. From the small amount of paying customers during the early years of the franchise, to winning the Super Bowl, to countless seasons of losing, and finally, a glorious return to victory, the Chiefs have endured.

Carl Peterson finally got the coach he had always wanted when Dick Vermeil came to Kansas City to lead the Chiefs in 2001. An upbeat mood immediately fell over the team and city—the promise of winning looms in the future. A return to the Super Bowl remains an unmet expectation, but like every other obstacle and goal placed before this team throughout its history, it's an objective that should be met.

MS
May 2002

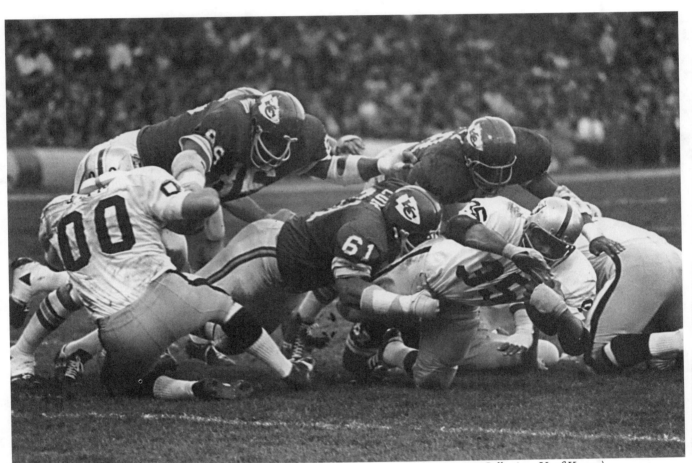

Buck Buchanan, Curly Culp and Bobby Bell stop the Raiders' Hewritt Dixon in 1969. (Kansas Collection, U. of Kansas)

KANSAS CITY CHIEFS
His Own Team

LAMAR HUNT

He is a true revolutionary, although the word doesn't seem to fit his persona. Lamar Hunt wanted his own professional football team, and using his ample resources, as well as his intelligence, business sense, and determination, he got one. Of course, in getting one, he had to invent a new football league, sustain a few financial losses, and even move his franchise from his beloved Dallas.

He also managed to change the face of professional football forever.

The son of one of the wealthiest men in the world, Lamar Hunt attended Southern Methodist University, played football for the Mustangs—although he didn't actually play very much—and earned a degree in geology. Quiet and soft-spoken by nature, Hunt was also a great sports enthusiast, and in 1958, at the age of 26, he began his quest to obtain a professional football franchise.

Starting with the Chicago Cardinals (who eventually moved to St. Louis in 1960, and from St. Louis to Arizona in 1988), Hunt hoped to purchase the team and move it to Dallas, but after many fruitless meetings with the Cardinals' owners, found the team wasn't for sale. He then talked to NFL officials—including commissioner Bert Bell—about an expansion franchise for Dallas, and was again turned down. The NFL, he was told, was not interested in expansion.

Hunt then got the idea of a lifetime—starting a new pro football league. He became the owner of the American Football League's Dallas Texans and the leading architect for the revolutionary changes that took place in pro football throughout the next four decades. Unfortunately for Hunt, the NFL added an expansion team in Dallas shortly after the AFL was formed. Unable to make a go of it against the Cowboys, Hunt moved his Texans to Kansas City and renamed them the Chiefs.

A major player in the merger of the AFL and NFL in 1966, Hunt not only helped conceive the Super Bowl, he also named it. Today, it is the world's largest single-day sporting event. Since 1984, the championship trophy for the AFC has been called the "Lamar Hunt Trophy."

Hunt's interest in sports doesn't stop with the Chiefs. He owns teams in the MLS (soccer league), is a minority owner of the Chicago Bulls of the NBA, and also started the North American Soccer League and World Championship Tennis, both defunct.

His contributions to pro football were recognized in 1972 when he was the first AFL figure to be inducted into the Pro Football Hall of Fame in Canton, Ohio. His induction represents everything he fought for throughout the development of the AFL, the changes he helped to orchestrate in the NFL (the merger, the Super Bowl, rule changes, etc.), and the success of the Kansas City Chiefs.

"My selection is symbolic of all the general managers, coaches, and players who worked for the growth of the American Football League," Hunt said at his induction.

"It was an era when the game of pro football was really ready to grow. Also, the United States had a lot of markets that didn't have pro football. There were only 11 cities in America that had NFL teams. It was very focused in the northeast part of the country, plus the two on the West Coast in Los Angeles and San Francisco. So there were a lot of markets that didn't have teams."
—Lamar Hunt

*At the 1971 National Football League annual meeting, Lamar Hunt, right, meets with
George Halas, left, and NFL comissioner Pete Rozelle. Hunt was the president of the AFC. (AP/Wide World Photos)*

Forty-two years after the "new" league was started, Lamar Hunt remains a part of the game, still the owner of the Kansas City franchise. He has seen his club in two Super Bowls, and has experienced many great victories and a lot of painful losses. In the past decade, he watched as Arrowhead Stadium became one of the most feared places to play in the NFL.

Hunt has been honored by the Missouri Sports Hall of Fame and the Texas Sports Hall of Fame.

*Hunt before the start of Super Bowl IV at
Tulane Stadium in New Orleans. (Topeka Capital-Journal)*

At Arrowhead Stadium in 2000 (Alan Barzee)

The sportsman. Lamar Hunt had a hand in several different sports ventures. In addition to the Chiefs, he has owned interest in baseball, soccer, basketball and tennis teams. (Bettmann/CORBIS)

KANSAS CITY CHIEFS
Franchise History

An Overview of the Kansas City Chiefs

That they were born as another team in another city seems somehow appropriate today. Charting the course of the Kansas City Chiefs' franchise history requires trips through Chicago and Dallas, Los Angeles and New Orleans, and most recently, San Francisco and St. Louis. Many cities contributed in the lifetime of the franchise to build and enhance what is one of today's premier NFL clubs—Chicago to see about an NFL team, Dallas with the new AFL team, Los Angeles and New Orleans for Super Bowls, San Francisco for quarterbacks, and St. Louis for a head coach.

The Chiefs were the winningest team in the AFL's 10-year history, and they produced the third-most wins in the 1990s, dominating play in the tough AFC West. Kansas City has played in two Super Bowls and won one orld championship. The Chiefs' owner was so instrumental in the development of the AFL and subsequent changes that occurred in pro football that the AFC championship trophy bears his name.

All of which makes it hard to believe the Chiefs are the product of failure. Two failures, in fact. Lamar Hunt, a 26-year-old graduate of Southern Methodist University—who also happened to be a multimillionaire—wanted his own professional football franchise in Dallas. He failed to get the NFL franchise, but started a new league instead. His team in the new league, the Dallas Texans, failed financially and left Texas for Kansas City.

Hunt's franchise made the most of its second chance in a new city, but not without enduring a few financial and personal obstacles. After three mediocre seasons, the franchise began to thrive—winning on the field and with gate receipts—and peaked in time to represent the AFL in the first Super Bowl. This was a franchise that refused to fail. Lamar Hunt's dream to own a pro football team seems rather tame compared to the histories of some of today's enterprises. But no new professional sports league had succeeded before the AFL, and no league has succeeded since. The AFL forever changed the game of pro football, on and off the field. And Kansas City, through the collected "failures" of Hunt's pursuit, has benefited as much as any city can from the venture of a pro football team.

The World Champs. Holding the Super Bowl IV trophy at a celebration rally following the Chiefs' win over the Vikings are, from the left: Lamar Hunt, Otis Taylor, Hank Stram, Len Dawson and Bill Grigsby. (Kansas Collection, U. of Kansas)

The Foolish Club and the Birth of the AFL

Lamar Hunt began his attempt to bring professional football to Dallas in 1958. Even though an NFL franchise had failed in the Texas city as recently as 1952, Hunt was convinced that the time was right and that Dallas was ready for pro football. Given the right circumstances, he felt a new NFL team could flourish in Texas.

He was unsuccessful in purchasing an existing franchise (he tried in vain to acquire the Chicago Cardinals), and talks with NFL commissioner Bert Bell about expansion went nowhere. Returning from a final meeting with the Cardinals' ownership, Hunt struck upon the idea for a new league.

> *"It was sort of like a light bulb coming on. I got to thinking . . . maybe there was enough interest nationwide to form a new league."* — Lamar Hunt, on starting the AFL

"I was flying back from what had been the last meeting with Mr. and Mrs. Wolfner," Hunt said. "Mrs. Wolfner was the owner of the [Cardinals] and her husband was the general manager. . . . I was just there making some notes, and all of a sudden here came this light bulb over my head. 'Hey, why not try to form a second league?'

"I thought, 'Why wouldn't a second league work?' There was an American and National League in baseball, why not in football?" Hunt said. "All the basic information I needed had been supplied by the Wolfners in the four or five months we had tried to negotiate a sale. They had dropped the names of Bud Adams in Houston, Max Winter in Minneapolis, Bob Howsam in Denver. Here were a bunch of people on the outside waiting. So why not start a new league?"

> *"No new league had succeeded since the turn of the century. Hunt was not, however, the sort of man to abandon a dream just because no one was selling what he wanted to buy."* —Joe Foss, the AFL's first commissioner

Starting with Adams, Winter, and Howsam, Hunt assembled a group of owners, and the American Football League was born. The original six owners were Bud Adams in Houston, Cal Kunz in Denver, Lamar Hunt in Dallas, Harry Wismer in New York, Chet Soda and his group in Oakland, and Barron Hilton in Los Angeles. Oakland had replaced the Minneapolis group (which defected to the NFL), and Billy Sullivan in Boston and Ralph Wilson in Buffalo were later added to the league. This was the group of men known as "The Foolish Club."

Foolish or not, the timing for the new league couldn't have been better.

"It was an era when the game of pro football was really ready to grow," Hunt said of starting the AFL. "There were only 11 cities in America that had NFL teams. . . . So there were a lot of markets that didn't have teams. We began with that: Dallas,

> *"It was actually Wayne Valley [one of the Oakland group] who gave us the name. I sort of picked up on it. I had a montage of eight photographs (from the 1960 season), each three-by-five, showing each team in action, and I sent them out as Christmas gifts one year. At the top was the hand-lettered phrase, 'The Foolish Club.'"* —Lamar Hunt

Houston, Denver, Minneapolis, Buffalo." The Minneapolis group would later be used by the NFL in a sabotage attempt on the AFL; when offered a franchise in the NFL, they jumped ship. They would be replaced by Oakland at the 11th hour, before the 1960 season started. With eight teams in place for the new league, Hunt focused on his franchise, the Dallas Texans (which was also the name of the failed 1952 NFL franchise). Hank Stram, a little-known assistant coach at the University of Miami, was selected as the team's head coach. Stram would coach the team for 15 seasons, develop many innovations on both offense and defense, and lead the franchise to some of its greatest moments.

Hunt felt that stocking his team with as much local talent as possible would create strong local interest, as well as foster team identity with the fans. The Texans were loaded with players from the Lone Star state. Abner Haynes, a speedster from North Texas State, quickly became the team's—and league's—marquee player. Other top Texas players added to the roster the first couple of seasons included Jack Spikes, E.J. Holub, Sherrill Headrick, and Jerry Mays.

> *"I met Hank and was impressed. He had that good reputation of having an offensive mind, and gosh, he was ready to do it. It was an awfully lucky choice. I can't believe how fortunate it was."* —Lamar Hunt

In late 1959, the NFL announced it was expanding into Dallas; Hunt was even offered the Dallas franchise if he would abandon the AFL. Hunt, committed to the new league, refused.

"We were committed to the AFL people, and they were committed to us," he said of the proposed jump to the NFL. "We just couldn't pull out."

It was clear to everyone, though, that the NFL was out to squash the upstart league. The move to put a team in Dallas, coupled with the reversal by the Minnesota group, hurt the AFL before it ever got started. Hunt, who had tried early on to have an amiable relationship with the older league, dropped his gloves and started swinging. The war between the two leagues began. "This is an effort to sabotage us that will be apparent to 170 million people," Hunt said of the NFL's tactics. Maybe he knew even then that Dallas simply wasn't big enough to be a two-team town.

The AFL, in an effort to distinguish itself from the NFL, added several innovations, many of them simple things taken for granted by today's fans. They added the players' names on the backs of their jerseys and also provided the two-point option on PATs.

"The NFL did everything it could to stop the AFL," Chiefs and Texans' running back Curtis McClinton said. "It took a man of great courage to survive and allow it to thrive, and that was Lamar Hunt. The AFL was a class act.

Pro Football in Dallas

Chris Burford (88) was one of the first stars on the Texans. Here he pulls in a 26-yard touchdown pass against the Broncos in 1961. (Kansas Collection, U. of Kansas)

"We helped make pro football a national game. You have to remember, the NFL had 12 teams then, two on the West Coast. We opened the gates and the battle caught public imagination." —Lamar Hunt

The AFL began play in the fall of 1960 with eight teams. The Dallas Texans started that first season with a loss to the Chargers, 21-20, but notched their first-ever win against the Raiders at Oakland, 34-16. It was an exciting year for the Texans, and the team remained in the title hunt throughout the year. But they lost too many close games. Despite the star quality and outstanding play of Abner Haynes, the Texans finished their inaugural campaign with an 8-6 record. The team fell to 6-8 in 1961, floundering on both offense and defense. But a big change in the Texans' fortunes, on the field at least, loomed on the horizon.

A little-used quarterback in the NFL arrived to play for Dallas for the 1962 season, and he would become the franchise player of the team for the next 14 seasons. Len Dawson was exactly what the team needed to push it to the championship level.

The Texans, behind Dawson's passing and leadership, won their first Western Division title in 1962, finishing with an 11-3 record. They met the Oilers in Houston for the AFL championship, a game that was to become a classic and one of the AFL's early claims to legitimacy. The two teams battled into a second overtime period before Dallas won on a 25-yard field goal by Tommy Brooker. The Texans were champions, but the same money problems persisted. The team was still losing money, and the reality of the situation couldn't be ignored.

Despite winning the 1962 championship, the Texans were in obvious financial trouble. Hunt made a hard decision; he didn't want to compete with the NFL's Cowboys anymore. The Texans would move. After making a preliminary statement in February 1963, he made it official in May—the Dallas Texans were going to move to Kansas City. The announcement shocked both the players and the coaches.

"It was a very difficult situation. During that time, Texans games did not draw flies, frankly. The year we won the championship, we averaged 10,100 paid per game." —Lamar Hunt

"We had been so wrapped up in trying to win football games," Texans coach Hank Stram said, "that most of us had never given any thought to the possibility of the team being moved."

"One of the things that attracted me was that it was geographically close to Dallas, only an hour to an hour and a half away by airline," Hunt said of Kansas City. "And there was no competition in the city from college football."

Goin' to Kansas City

"I was impressed with Mayor Bartle. He spoke highly of Kansas City....We were looking for a home where we would be welcome, and he just made me feel that we could do well in Kansas City." —Lamar Hunt

The franchise was moving to Kansas City, and Hunt made it known that he very much wanted to keep the name Texans for the team. He felt there wasn't a decision to make and was determined to keep the name.

"Hank Stram and I wanted to keep the same name that we had in Dallas," Hunt said. "We wanted to call the team the Kansas City Texans. We reasoned that we had won the championship, and like the Lakers when they left Minneapolis, they didn't rename the team just because they took them to Los Angeles."

Hunt came to the realization, or maybe to his senses, that a team called the Texans must reside in the Lone Star state. After listening to the sound reasoning of general manager Jack Steadman, Hunt relented and gave up on the idea of calling the team the Kansas City Texans.

The *Kansas City Star* ran a name contest for the city's new franchise, and from hundreds of different options, which included Mules, Stars, Royals, and Steers, the name "Chiefs" was selected.

"When it came down to it, we wanted a distinctive name," Hunt said of the selection. "We didn't want to be a second team called the Bears or the Tigers. A lot of the new names that have crept into American sports over the last 40 years didn't exist at the time. We wanted something distinctive to the area. Certainly there was a heritage related to the Indians and the Indians' background in this part of the world. We felt the word "Chiefs" signified "tops" and "best" and "high quality." It also tied very closely to the name of the man who was most instrumental in our moving here, the Big Chief, Roe Bartle. That's why we picked the name 'Chiefs.'" Most of the Texans' players resented the move from Dallas. As the defending AFL champs, they couldn't understand why the Texans were leaving instead of the then-lowly NFL Cowboys. Attendance figures for both teams were similarly low, but it was apparent that when the Cowboys started winning, they would take over the city.

Kansas City got a championship team, and with more than 15,000 season tickets sold, the city promised to bring good for-

Len Dawson throws a pass in front of empty stands at Municipal Stadium in 1963. (Topeka Capital-Journal)

The death of star fullback Mack Lee Hill, who died during routine knee surgery at the end of the 1965 season, was the biggest blow to the team. Already established as a powerful, pounding runner, Hill looked like a player whose best years were ahead of him. The Chiefs won their final game of the 1965 season—dedicated to Hill—and finished with a 7-5-2 record, the best since the team moved from Dallas. Nothing indicated that the Chiefs were ready to step up in competition, especially without Hill, but 1966 saw the beginning of great success for Kansas City.

"He was probably the most unselfish player I ever coached. He was completely dedicated to the team—football was his life."—Hank Stram, on Mack Lee Hill

tune to the club. The initial part of the move went smoothly, and the Chiefs were looking forward to defending their championship in their new home. But a string of tragedies and problems was in the offing, and nothing could have prepared the Chiefs for what was going to happen over the course of the next three years. In the final exhibition game of the 1963 season, Chiefs rookie flanker from Grambling Stone Johnson broke his neck and died less than two weeks later. It was a tremendous shock to his teammates. Johnson was extremely likable and had the potential to be a star.

"It is the most tragic thing that has happened to us since we started the organization," Chiefs general manager Jack Steadman said of Johnson's death. "Johnson was a great athlete and a fine gentleman."

Kansas City destroyed the Broncos in their first game as the Chiefs, but that game was the high point of the 1963 season, as the team finished 5-7-2. More misfortune and tragedy would soon strike the club. Guard Ed Budde suffered a fractured skull and Fred Arbanas lost vision in his left eye. Both players' careers were in doubt, but both were able to resume them.

The Merger & Super Bowl I

By the end of the 1965 season, the AFL had shown it was going to be around for a while. Big money was being paid out to collegiate stars—Joe Namath received more than $400,000 from the New York Jets—and the two leagues, especially the NFL, saw that salaries were only going to go up. Merger talks, something that would have been unheard of in 1960, were started.

"From the long-range standpoint, the AFL's TV contract was the biggest single factor in bringing the two leagues together," Hunt said of the AFL's merger with the NFL. "It was the most dramatic single development with regard to impact. It was also important when the Jets established that two teams could do well in New York. The biggest stumbling block was the personal antagonism—if that's the right word—that had gone on for seven years."

Tex Schramm, left, NFL commissioner Pete Rozelle, center, and Lamar Hunt announce the merger between the NFL and AFL in 1966. (Bettmann/CORBIS)

Kansas City's Hank Stram and Green Bay's Vince Lombardi pose with the World Professional Football Championship trophy in Los Angeles before the first AFL-NFL title game in 1967. The game was not yet known as the Super Bowl. (Bettmann/CORBIS)

The merger of the two leagues took place over a period of four years, and starting in 1970, the AFL teams officially became a part of the NFL. The merger brought about a common draft between the two leagues, shared television revenues, and most importantly, an interleague championship game.

"It was the sensible thing to do. Our goal when we brought the American Football League into existence was to build a successful entity. We weren't trying to build something that was in a perpetual war, a perpetual fight. . . . The merger made a great deal of sense for everyone in pro football, including the stability of the league. The thing I'm proudest of is that all eight teams survived and it was the only league that went forward together as a group." —Lamar Hunt

The Chiefs hit their stride in 1966 and dominated the rest of the AFL, finishing with a record of 11-2-1. More importantly, the Chiefs were finally and forever taken to the hearts of Kansas City's fans. And when the Chiefs defeated the Buffalo Bills, 31-7, in the 1966 AFL title game, they earned the right to play the NFL-champion Green Bay Packers in the first-ever AFL vs. NFL World Professional Football Championship Game (not yet officially called the Super Bowl) in Los Angeles.

Lamar Hunt, part of the merger committee that paved the way for the AFL to join the NFL, attached a name to what would soon become the biggest sporting event in the United States.

"It was one of those accidental things," Hunt said of naming the Super Bowl. "It's not a name you would ever sit down and do an analysis and figure out that it's a good name. It had to be accidental and it truly was."

While meeting with the merger committee, Hunt casually referred to the new championship between the AFL and NFL as the "super bowl." The rest of the committee knew exactly what he was talking about, and soon they were calling the game the Super Bowl.

"The media liked that immediately," Hunt said, "even though Pete Rozelle [the NFL commissioner] felt it was an undignified name."

And where did Hunt get the name?

"I don't know where the term came from except that my daughter Sharon had a 'Super Ball,' a little rubber ball with phenomenal bouncing ability. It would literally bounce over a house. I've never seen anything like it. So it must have come from that."

The first Super Bowl matchup between the AFL and the NFL presented something new to America's sporting public, but it was not embraced as a great showcase for football. Green Bay was heavily favored, and unbelievably, 30,000 seats went unsold at the Los Angeles Coliseum. Because they belonged to a league called the "Mickey Mouse League" by the NFL, the Chiefs had the opportunity to prove all of the AFL's critics wrong. The Chiefs stayed with the Packers in the first half, but a costly interception early in the third period turned the tide for the Packers, and they waltzed to a 35-10 win. "I sincerely felt we could win," Stram said after the game. "And I think our people felt that way."

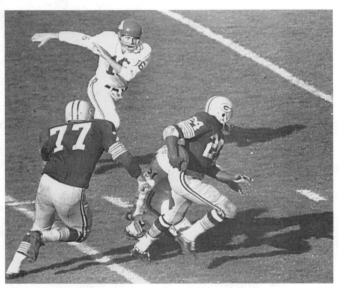

Willie Wood's interception and return of a Len Dawson pass early in the third quarter was the critical turning point of Super Bowl I. (Kansas Collection, U. of Kansas)

The loss haunted Kansas City throughout the offseason, and invariably there were the accusations that the Chiefs and the entire AFL were weak and inferior. When Kansas City faced the Chicago Bears in a 1967 preseason game, the frustration and pain of the Super Bowl loss were unleashed on the unsuspecting NFL team.

"The Bears never had a clue," Dawson said of the '67 exhibition game against Chicago, which Kansas City easily won, 66-24. "They came in here expecting a scrimmage, but we had lost the Super Bowl and were considered the stupid stepchild. Like Rodney Dangerfield, we got no respect. Well, we had to listen to that crap for seven months and we were ready. It may have been an exhibition for the Bears, but it was our Super Bowl. It was a chance for us to get some respect."

Kansas City absolutely destroyed the Bears, 66-24

That game proved to be the highlight of the 1967 season. The Chiefs did not repeat as champions, their record falling to 9-5. Stram rebounded his troops for a great season in 1968, and the Chiefs finished at 12-2, tied for first place in the AFL West with the Oakland Raiders. In the divisional playoff, the Raiders humiliated the Chiefs, 41-6, to advance to the AFL championship game against the New York Jets (originally the Titans).

1969: Super Chiefs

Kansas City's defense, shown here racking up a Houston runner, was super throughout the 1969 season. (Topeka Capital-Journal)

"When we got there, the Raiders had their bags packed to go to New Orleans for the Super Bowl." —Jerry Mays, on the 1969 AFL championship game at Oakland

The Chiefs were again heavy underdogs when they took the field at Tulane Stadium in New Orleans for Super Bowl IV against Minnesota. But unlike the way the players felt before the game against the Packers, this time they felt they would win. Len Dawson shook off false gambling accusations and played a superb game to capture MVP honors.

"I was more confident playing the Vikings than I was the Raiders," Willie Lanier said of the Super Bowl IV matchup.

"I felt that if we played Minnesota ten times, we'd beat them ten times," Dave Hill said. "We knew their offense didn't have a prayer against our defense."

Jan Stenerud booted three field goals for Kansas City, Mike Garrett scored a touchdown, and Otis Taylor put the game away with a spectacular 46-yard scoring reception. The Chiefs dominated the Vikings from start to finish, and won Super Bowl IV in convincing fashion, 23-7.

"It was wonderful to get the satisfaction of winning the final game between the AFL and the NFL. It was also very satisfying to beat the Vikings because the Viking ownership had been one of the six founding clubs in the AFL and had backed out of it after we had our draft the first year." —Lamar Hunt, on winning Super Bowl IV

After two years of rebuilding and reshaping his team, Stram had the Chiefs ready to make another realistic run at the Super Bowl in 1969. There was no bad aftertaste from the devastating playoff loss to the Raiders that ended the 1968 season, and the Chiefs' players—as well as Hank Stram—felt they had the kind of team that could return to the Super Bowl. Jim Marsalis, the club's top draft pick in 1969, took over the left cornerback spot and immediately improved the secondary on an already strong defense.

"We have a lot to be proud of. Looking back over the years we've spent in the AFL, we've won three league championships. That's more than any other team." —Lamar Hunt

Overcoming injuries, specifically Len Dawson's knee problems, became the theme of the '69 season. Mike Livingston, a second-year quarterback from SMU, took over for Dawson and performed very well, winning all six games he started.

"Mike was a big part of our success in 1969," Otis Taylor said. "We couldn't have won it all without him."

By the end of the season, Stram was extremely pleased with his defense. The Chiefs would give up just 177 points in the regular season. Kansas City's scatback running backs were also successful, with Mike Garrett, Wendell Hayes and Robert Holmes all gaining at least 500 yards on the ground.

A 10-6 loss at Oakland in the final game of the year left the Chiefs with an 11-3 record and another second-place finish in the division. But because of a one-time-only playoff format implemented by the AFL for its final season, the Chiefs were still in the hunt for the Super Bowl. To make it to New Orleans for the big game, the Chiefs had to beat the defending world-champion Jets in New York, and if they accomplished that, defeat the Raiders in Oakland. Willie Lanier and the defense led the way in New York as the Chiefs fought through the bitter cold and beat the Jets, 13-6. Two weeks later, the team defied the odds and surprised the football world, as well as the Raiders, winning the final AFL championship in Oakland, 17-7, and returning to the Super Bowl.

Otis Taylor bounced back from his injury-plagued '68 season to catch 41 passes, seven for touchdowns, in 1969. (Kansas Collection, U. of Kansas)

"The good thing about this game is that we don't have to answer for it for the next three years as we did the last time." —Len Dawson, after the Chiefs won Super Bowl IV

Losing the Crown

With the conclusion of Super Bowl IV, the AFL existed no more. The final stage of the two leagues' merger was completed when Baltimore, Pittsburgh, and Cleveland joined the 10 AFL teams to form the new American Football Conference (AFC). The other 13 teams made up the National Football Conference (NFC), and the two conferences made up the 26-team NFL.

As the defending world champs, Stram vowed his Chiefs would be better than ever in 1970.

"We'll be better this season than last," Stram said before the season started. "We've won three championships and one world championship. We want to repeat as world champions. Our program is geared to harder work to achieve that goal."

It was a goal, however, that was not within the team's reach.

Kansas City easily disposed of the College All-Stars before the season started. But with their first regular-season game in 1970—a rematch against the Vikings that they lost—it was apparent there was something missing, an intangible motivator that had driven the team the previous four years. By the time Oakland came to Kansas City for the seventh game of the season, =the Chiefs were 3-3 and had played mediocre football. The resulting 17-17 tie with the Raiders—a late, controversial penalty helped Oakland achieve the tie—proved to be the game of the year. Kansas City sputtered through the rest of its schedule finishing a disappointing 7-5-2, that kept them out of the playoffs.

Len Dawson (Topeka Capital-Journal)

"Our team learned many lessons during the course of the 1970 season," Stram said. "We must constantly be on the attack, offensively, defensively, and with our specialty teams. . . . The nucleus for a championship team is there, but we must constantly strive for perfection. . . ."

"I think it was because we didn't play anywhere near the level we were capable of playing," Taylor said of the disappointing 1970 season. "I don't know if it was injuries, lack of leadership, or other things. We just didn't have the fire we usually had. It was a nonchalant-type season. We seemed to have 'we will play it and let it go and not worry about it' attitudes the whole year."

The Longest Game

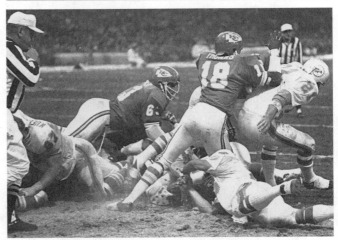

Miami's Jim Kiick slides past the Chiefs' Emmitt Thomas and falls into the end zone for a Dolphins' touchdown during the 1971 divisional playoff game at Municipal Stadium in Kansas City. (Kansas Collection, U. of Kansas)

Hank Stram coaxed one more great season out of his veterans in 1971, and the Chiefs had one of their finest regular seasons en route to the AFC Western Division title. Stram's much-ballyhooed "Offense of the Seventies" had its last great season, and on December 25, 1971, the Chiefs hosted the Miami Dolphins in a divisional playoff game. Today the game is considered a classic—one of the greatest playoff games of all time—and for the second time in the Chiefs' history, the team battled in a double-overtime marathon.

"In 1971, we had the best team we ever had," Jim Kearney said. "We had a better team than we had the year we won the Super Bowl. Going into the playoff game [with Miami] we had no doubt. We knew the Dolphins had a good team, but we had such good camaraderie and team chemistry that we felt like we could beat anybody.

After more than 82 minutes of playing time, Miami finally won the longest game in NFL history, 27-24. The game not only marked the end of Municipal Stadium, but the beginning of rough times for the Chiefs.

"I have the worst feeling anyone could have. I have no idea what I'm going to do now. I feel like hiding. I don't feel like playing football. It's a shame guys play like hell, like our team did, and lose because of a missed field goal. It's unbearable. It's totally unbearable." —Jan Stenerud, after the Chiefs lost to the Dolphins in double overtime in the 1971 playoffs

"That sudden death is horrifying. One bad break and you're out of it." —Len Dawson, after the same loss

The Chiefs began to play in Arrowhead Stadium in 1972 and lost again to the Dolphins in the first-ever regular season game at the new venue. After going 7-0 at Municipal in 1971, the Chiefs could do no better than a 3-4 record at Arrowhead, and they finished 1972 with an 8-6 mark. While it wasnt' apparent at the time, the Chiefs' run as one of the leagues powerhouse teams was over.

Bottom of the Heap

Kansas City challenged for the division title in 1973, but the Raiders crushed them, 37-7, late in the season to end any playoff hopes the team had. When the Chiefs finished with a losing record in 1974, the team's first since 1963, Hunt and Steadman made a move they never expected to make. Hank Stram was fired.

"Our downfall was because of a mistake I made in the early 1970s. Hank [Stram] wanted to run the whole operation . . . but it was just too much for one man to handle. I made the mistake of letting him tend in that direction. There was a period when we didn't do a good enough job of scouting. We didn't do a good job of bringing in players." —Lamar Hunt, on the Chiefs' decline in the 1970s

"There was very likely a letdown after the 1971 season. Most of the players were in their thirties at that time, and not letting fresh blood on the team was probably a mistake. — Otis Taylor

The move ignited a chain reaction that had been building for three or four seasons, and the Chiefs quickly fell to the bottom of the NFL. Losing became the standard at Arrowhead Stadium. After winning their division in 1971 and posting winning records in 1972-73, Kansas City won just 23 games from 1975 through 1979. Paul Wiggin, Stram's successor, took over the team in 1975 and posted back-to-back 5-9 seasons.

The Chiefs started so poorly in 1977 that Hunt fired Wiggin in the middle of the season. The Chiefs finished with the franchise's worst-ever record at 2-12. Marv Levy took the head coaching position next, and while he was able to bring a mediocre respectability to the Chiefs, he was fired after five up-and-down seasons.

"Football is a game. It should be fun, and that's the way I intend to pursue it." —Paul Wiggin

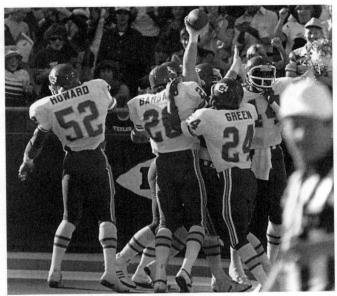

A happy moment for the Chiefs' defense in the late 1970's. (Kansas Collection, U. of Kansas)

"He's the greatest guy I've ever played for and it's just a shame we didn't perform better for him. They should have fired us instead of him." —Mike Livingston, on the firing of Paul Wiggin

"In our evaluation of the team, coaching leadership was the thing we were lacking. We didn't have the coaching leadership to get over the top." —Lamar Hunt, on the firing of Marv Levy

From 1974 through 1985, the Chiefs posted just one winning season, a 9-7 mark in 1981. Joe Delaney, a sensational rookie running back, led the Chiefs that year in rushing and promised to be one of the best runners in the franchise's history. But tragedy struck the club again following the 1982 season when Delaney drowned while trying to rescue three young boys from a pond near his home in Monroe, Louisiana. His death left a huge void on the Chiefs and took a hefty emotional toll on the team's mental outlook.

Kansas City finished with a 3-6 record in the strike-shortened 1982 season, and Hunt once again made a coaching change, hoping to restore the lost glory of the Chiefs' winning days in the 1960s.

Mike Livingston guided the Chiefs' offense for most of the 1970s. (Kansas Collection, U. of Kansas)

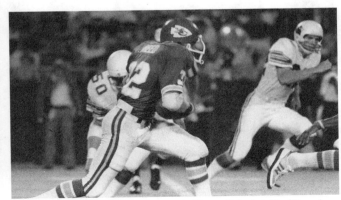

Tony Reed ran for 1,053 yards in 1978. (Kansas Collection, U. of Kansas)

"Everyone knew Delaney was a great football player. But that was only a small part of what made him so special to us. As a young rookie, he played with cracked ribs, a broken wrist, a sprained knee. Then he had the courage to come back in his second year after detached retinas in both of his eyes, knowing that there was a chance he could lose his sight. When those little kids needed help, he gave up his life trying to save them. He wasn't a swimmer. . . . The man had a tremendous heart— he was special." —Tom Condon

Nick Lowery, left, and Steve Fuller celebrate following a game-winning field goal. (Kansas Collection, U. of Kansas)

Return to Respectability

John Mackovic took over for Levy in 1983 and, despite the loss of Delaney, rebuilt the team into a contender. Kansas City went 6-10 in 1983, 8-8 in 1984, and 6-10 again in 1985. It seemed the team was spinning its wheels. But in 1986 Mackovic's hard work paid off with a playoff berth, as the Chiefs finished 10-6, winning many games because of the spectacular play of their special teams (11 blocked kicks and six touchdown returns). It was the club's first postseason appearance in 15 years, and despite losing in the first round to the Jets, more playoff spots in the future seemed a certainty. Unfortunately, the success of the '86 team was short-lived.

Albert Lewis (29) became a starter in the Chiefs' defensive backfield in 1984 and was named to four Pro Bowls during his career with Kansas City. (Kansas Collection, U. of Kansas)

Lloyd Burruss and Kevin Ross (Kansas Collection, U. of Kansas)

A series of complaints and secret maneuvers between a handful of players, management and assistant coaches convinced Hunt and Steadman that Mackovic wasn't the right man to be the Chiefs' head coach. He was replaced by his special teams coach, Frank Gansz, who was extremely popular with the players. At the time, Gansz's hiring was ballyhooed as the right move to push the Chiefs deeper and farther into the playoffs.

Instead, the Chiefs fell fast and hard.

"We're going to get there [Super Bowl] as fast as we can. We're going to pursue that. That's going to be our objective. That's what our players want to do and that's what I want to do. I'm not going to be content with making the playoffs." — Frank Gansz, 1987

The team's number one draft pick in 1983, Todd Blackledge, was a disappointment at quarterback for the Chiefs. (Topeka Capital-Journal)

Joe Delaney rushed for 1,121 yards in 1981 and was selected for the Pro Bowl. (Topeka Capital-Journal)

Raiders Rivalry

It is one of the fiercest rivalries in pro football, and perhaps in all of sports. The Chiefs and Raiders have been warring against one another for more than 40 seasons, playing some of the best football games in that time period. The tactics both sides use can vary—scratching, clawing, biting, and kicking—and neither side is likely to give up. From 1966 through 1969, the Raiders defeated the Chiefs seven out of nine times, yet it was the Chiefs who won the final AFL championship game, exacting revenge. The Raiders then dominated the series through the 1980s, but Kansas City was virtually unbeatable against its top rival throughout the 1990s. Top games in the series include the Chiefs' 1968 win at Municipal Stadium, the 1969 AFL championship game, the 1970 tie game, Kansas City's division-clinching win in 1971, the Chiefs' first-ever regular-season win at Arrowhead Stadium in 1972, and any one of the Chiefs' numerous victories throughout the 1990s.

"I've hated the Raiders since 1963," Chiefs great Ed Budde said of the rivalry. "It's a tradition that's been handed down over time. I think

Derrick Thomas zeroes in on the Raiders' Rich Gannon. (Alan Barzee)

all of Kansas City hated the Raiders. It's as true today as it was 30 years ago."

Many times fights and penalties prevailed throughout the contests. Big Ben Davidson, one of the all-time Raider greats, and fullback Marv Hubbard, are two Raiders who were particularly hated by Kansas City followers. Inevitably, both teams were locked in a fight for the division title, and even in the Chiefs' down years, they still held their own against the Raiders.

"Each game has always been a monumental one," Willie Lanier said of the rivalry. "If they [Raiders] beat us twice, they'd damn near gotten the league wrapped up. And if we beat them twice, we'd done the same thing."

Oakland has had the most recent satisfaction in the series, denying Kansas City a spot in the 1999 playoffs with a come-from-behind 41-38 overtime win in the season's final game. The new millennium has seen the series momentum swing back to the Raiders, who have won five straight meetings through the end of the 2001 season. The rivalry lives on.

Marcus Allen runs against his former team. (Alan Barzee)

"There was so much hate between teams [Chiefs and Raiders], but there was also so much respect. —Otis Taylor

"I don't like the Chiefs, and I hope they hear what I'm saying. I have an intense hatred for them." —Marv Hubbard, Raiders fullback, 1969-75

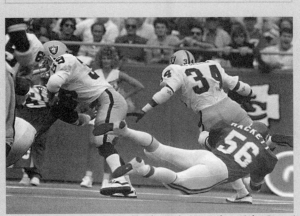

The Chiefs' Dino Hackett tackles the Raiders' Bo Jackson. (Alan Barzee)

Daryle Lamonica (3) terrorized Kansas City's defense with his long bombs and accurate passing. (Kansas Collection, U. of Kansas)

Marty Ball and the Nigerian Nightmare

Gansz's promotion to head coach proved to be a bust, and the Chiefs won only eight games in the 1987-88 season. Once again, Hunt moved to make major changes on the team. He started by replacing Jack Steadman with Carl Peterson, who became the new president/general manager/CEO of the team and was given complete control of operations. Peterson's first order of business was to fire Gansz and name Marty Schottenheimer the team's new head coach. "I believe the opportunity is there with this football team to once again approach that great tradition of the Kansas City Chiefs," Schottenheimer said after he was named head coach. "My principal reason for selecting this opportunity is that I believe we can win—and win very, very quickly."

The Chiefs—true to Schottenheimer's word—began to win consistently for the first time in almost two decades.

Led by Christian Okoye, the NFL's top rusher, the Chiefs improved to 8-7-1 in 1989 and just missed a playoff spot. They posted an 11-5 mark in 1990 and made the playoffs, the first of six consecutive trips to postseason play for Kansas City. The downside of this new success was the Chiefs' poor playoff performance; they won just one of four playoff games from 1990 through 1992.

Christian Okoye (Kansas Collection, U. of Kansas)

Superstars in Kansas City

Joe Montana (Alan Barzee)

Hoping the addition of a couple top players would lead them to the Super Bowl, the Chiefs traded for legendary quarterback Joe Montana and signed free-agent running back Marcus Allen prior to the 1993 season. Both superstars were near the end of their careers, but coming to Kansas City revitalized them. With Montana's passing and leadership and Allen's all-around offensive skills, Kansas City captured the 1993 AFC Western Division title with an 11-5 record and two victories in come-from-behind playoff games. Appearing in their first-ever AFC championship game, at Buffalo, the Chiefs, unable to rally after Montana had to leave the game with a concussion early in the third quarter, lost 30-13.

Marty Schottenheimer (Alan Barzee)

"The best way to establish a position of excellence in the National Football League is first to expect it. I've always felt the worst thing you can ever do is arbitrarily set a goal that might well be beneath what you are capable of achieving."
—Marty Schottenheimer

Derrick Thomas (Alan Barzee)

The Front Office

A successful sports franchise is much more than its players and coaches. The men off the field play a large role in the fortunes of their team, and the Chiefs' front office leadership has always been crucial in the accomplishments of the club. A mostly hands-off owner, Lamar Hunt has trusted the daily operation of the Chiefs to a couple of men who have helped build the foundation of the Chiefs' winning tradition.

Jack Steadman has been with the Chiefs' franchise since the beginning in Dallas. The original General Manager for the club, Steadman was promoted to Executive Vice President and General Manager in 1966. When a major reorganization was called for within the overall structure of the Chiefs in the mid-1970s, he was named President of the Chiefs in charge of all operating operations, passing his GM duties to Jim Schaff. In 1989 Steadman was named Chairman of the Board, the position he still holds. Of his numerous contributions to the Chiefs' organization, Steadman's best is without a doubt the role he played (the idea was largely his) in Kansas City building the Harry S Truman Sports Complex, home of the Chiefs' Arrowhead Stadium, and the Royals' Kauffman Stadium. The complex, now 30 years old, remains one of the best in the world.

"In my opinion, the success of any business is directly related to the quality and dedication of the people who make up the organization," Steadman said in 1977. I am proud of the fact that Lamar has provided us with everything necessary to build the finest organization in all of pro sports."

When the Chiefs again needed to shake things up, Hunt brought in Carl Peterson, who has been the President/GM/CEO since December, 1988. When Peterson took over the Chiefs, the club was losing on the field and off. He hired Mary Schottenheimer as the team's head coach, and the Chiefs went ten years before experiencing a losing season. The winning success on the field meant winning in the stands as well, and the Chiefs have enjoyed some of the best home fans in the NFL for the past decade.

"My administrative philosophy is very simple," Peterson said of his working style. "Hire the most talented, most creative, most innovative people possible. Give them a goal and all the support possible. Then get out of the way and let them do what they do best. Overall, my job is to create an environment that is conducive to allowing individual and collective excellence to emerge."

Carl Peterson (Alan Barzee)

"Under Carl's leadership, the Chiefs have achieved a high level of respect as one of the leaders in the NFL," Lamar Hunt said. "This respect has been measured in several principle areas, including development and guidance of a quality organization in every phase - front office, scouting, coaching and team."

In 1993, Peterson who pulled off the biggest trade in Chiefs history, obtaining Hall of Fame quarterback Joe Montana from the 49ers. Peterson also made one of the best acquisitions in the history of unrestricted free agency that same year when he inked future Hall of Famer, running back Marcus Allen to a contract. Peterson was also responsible for drafting Derrick Thomas, Tony Gonzalez and John Tait. His favorite acquisition, though, has to be when he urged his longtime friend Dick Vermeil to come out of retirement and coach the Chiefs.

"I've had one goal since I came here and I know that Dick now shares that goal with me. That goal is to hand the trophy that bears Lamar Hunt's name (AFC Championship trophy) to him at the conclusion of the season. Hopefully that will happen soon."

Tony Richardson (Alan Barzee)   Andre Rison (Alan Barzee)

Marcus Allen (Alan Barzee)

Kansas City returned to the playoffs in 1994, but Montana retired following the season, leaving Steve Bono with the quarterbacking duties. The 1995 Chiefs had an incredible season and posted an NFL-best record of 13-3. The playoffs once again proved to be the club's downfall, and the Chiefs suffered an embarrassing upset loss at home to the Colts. In 1996 the Chiefs failed to make the playoffs for the first time in seven years.

Elvis in the House

Kansas City once again looked west for a quarterback following the 1996 season and signed Elvis Grbac from San Francisco, hoping he could become the long-term quarterback the club hadn't had in almost 20 years. Grbac was the third straight quarterback to come to the Chiefs from the 49ers, following Montana and Bono. The 1997 Chiefs matched the 1995 team's 13-3 record, went undefeated at Arrowhead, and then spurred by a close 24-22 win over the Broncos at Arrowhead, again captured home-field advantage for the playoffs, as they won the AFC West. But like the '95 club, the '97 Chiefs faltered in the playoffs. They dropped a close contest in the divisional playoff to the Broncos, 14-10, ending an otherwise brilliant season.

Elvis Grbac (Alan Barzee)

The 1998 season started well for the Chiefs, and after easily defeating the Raiders in the season opener, they raced to a 4-1 record and appeared to be one of the top teams in the conference. The season took an abrupt about-face, though, and a 40-10 thrashing at the hands of the Patriots exposed many weaknesses on the team. Kansas City dropped six games in a row and finished the season 7-9, Schottenheimer's first losing season ever as a head coach in the NFL. The real shocker came on January 11, 1999, when Schottenheimer announced he was retiring.

Gunther Takes Over

Carl Peterson and Gunther Cunningham were all smiles at the press conference announcing Cunningham as the Chiefs' new head coach. (Kansas City Star)

Less than two weeks after Schottenheimer resigned, Peterson hired Chiefs defensive coordinator Gunther Cunningham as the team's eighth head coach, and a new era of Chiefs football began. Cunningham returned the team to its winning ways in 1999, and only a final-game loss to the Raiders in overtime kept the Chiefs from making the playoffs. They finished with a 9-7 record, and looked to the 2000 season as the opportunity to return to the playoffs and reestablish the Chiefs as one of the NFL's elite teams.

Elvis Grbac embraces Bam Morris after the big back scored during the 1999 season. (Alan Barzee)

The 2000 season promised to be another good year, but a mental breakdown by Cunningham (the coach contemplated resigning and shared his feelings with the team) following the Chiefs' opening-day loss set the tone for the season. The coach never really controlled the team again, and despite the infusion of a pass-oriented offense—Grbac finished the season with 4,169 yards passing—the Chiefs floundered in the second half of the season and lost five in a row at one point. They finished with a 7-9 mark.

On January 5, 2001, Gunther Cunningham was fired.

Vermeil Comes to Kansas City

"I'm looking forward to that challenge. I have a lot of energy left. A lot of energy left. I'm not concerned about age. You know the one thing I learned in the one year off going to corporations and speaking, I learned a lot from some bright people. The only place that they worry about age is the National Football League. There are so many outstanding people in their late sixties and seventies working very hard, running major corporations, billion-dollar outfits." —Dick Vermeil

Chiefs Vice President/GM Carl Peterson could hardly contain his boy-like glee. The man he revered more than any other in the coaching world, the man he wanted to hire in 1989 instead of Marty Schottenheimer, the man who was one of his closest friends, had agreed to coach the Chiefs starting in 2001.

"It gives me great pleasure to, quite candidly, do something that I wanted to do 12 years ago," Peterson said at the press conference announcing Dick Vermeil as the Chiefs' new head man. "Twelve years ago, Lamar Hunt and his family gave me an opportunity to run this franchise. And at that time, there was only one person on my mind I would like to be the head coach of the Kansas City Chiefs."

"Until the opportunity and possibility to hire Dick Vermeil presented itself, I was definitely thinking of not making a change. Of course, that was when I was in the process of still evaluating this past season. That process went on for a period of time. It's a very difficult business. Timing and opportunity are key. Obviously, we went through that process and came to this decision. While the process that we had to go through with the Commissioner prolonged this decision, I can say unequally that we are thrilled about the future and we're moving ahead from this point on." —Carl Peterson

Pro Bowler Will Shields (Alan Barzee)

Trent Green (Alan Barzee)

So after a one-year retirement from coaching, Vermeil, who had led the St. Louis Rams to a Super Bowl triumph in 1999, was ready for another challenge.

"Sooner or later, it was probably going to happen that Carl and I would be back together again, rejoined and initiate a new crusade," Vermeil said of the reunion with his old friend. "Every time we've done it, we've been successful, from a Rose Bowl Championship to an NFC Championship to a loss in the Super Bowl."

Dick Vermeil (Alan Barzee)

Vermeil had a somewhat tough road ahead of him. Following the 2000 season, the Chiefs needed to replace Elvis Grbac, James Hasty, and Chester McGlockton, as well as shore up needs on other areas of the team. But Vermeil showed he could make effective changes in St. Louis, and if ever a coach was worth two draft picks and half a million dollars (the compensation paid to the Rams by the Chiefs) it was Vermeil.

One of the first things Vermeil did was to obtain Trent Green from the Rams. Still in the final stages of rehabbing an injured knee when the Chiefs acquired him, Green knew the offense Vermeil was implementing. Another big move was to sign free agent running back Priest Holmes from the Baltimore Ravens. Holmes's addition to the Chiefs' offense proved to be one of the best signings in the history of the club. Greg Robinson, longtime defensive coordinator for the Denver Broncos, was added to the coaching staff.

The Chiefs floundered a bit the first half of the 2001 season, winning just one of their first seven games. But there were bright spots. Holmes was showing each week that he not only could be a top back in the NFL, he was *the* best all-around back in the league at the end of the year. Green, unfortunately, struggled with his new team most of the season and finished with a league-high 24 interceptions. On the upside, he threw for almost 3,800 yards and the defense was much improved by season's end, too. The Chiefs finished on a strong note, winning three of their final four games to post a 6-10 record for the year.

If the past is any reflection of the future, Vermeil's coaching stint in Kansas City should ultimately be a success.

Tony Gonzalez was selected for his third consecutive Pro Bowl in 2001. (Alan Barzee)

The NFL's top rusher in 2001, Priest Holmes also caught 62 passes and scored 10 touchdowns. (Alan Barzee)

KANSAS CITY CHIEFS
Season-by-Season Review

1960 Head Coach: Hank Stram

The American Football League was off and running, and the Texans' inagural season was a successful venture as the team was a winner on the field, and also showed signs of becoming a solid franchise off the field as well. But despite the star running power of Abner Haynes and one of the top defenses in the league, Dallas fell short in their bid to capture the Western Division title. Three close losses, 21-20 to the Chargers, 37-35 to the Titans, and 20-19 to the Raiders, kept the team from capturing division honors and playing in the AFL title game. Haynes became the fledgling league's first true superstar, rushing for 875 yards and scoring 12 touchdowns. Coach Stram's defense, led by Mel Branch, Sherrill Headrick and Dave Webster, posted three shutouts. The team's final record of 8 wins and 6 losses was good enough for a second place finish behind the San Diego Chargers. The Texans averaged 24,500 fans per home game—tops in the AFL—but, the attendance numbers throughout the season were greatly exagerated. Tough times, at least financially, awaited the franchise.

Key Dates in 1960:

July 8—The Dallas Texans open their first training camp.

July 31—The Texans play their first game ever, an exhibition win over the Raiders, 20-13.

September 10—In their first league game, the Texans lose to the Chargers in Los Angeles, 21-20.

November 24—Abner Haynes racks up 157 yards rushing against the Titans in New York, but the Texans still lose, 41-35.

December 18—The Texans defeat Buffalo, 24-7, ending their first season with an 8-6 record and second-place finish in the Western Division. Abner Haynes wins the rushing title and is named Rookie of the Year, as well as Outstanding Player in the AFL.

Big Game of 1960:

September 25 at Dallas

Dallas 17, Los Angeles 0

Playing before an estimated crowd of 42,000 fans, the Dallas Texans won their first regular season home game behind the passing and kicking of Cotton Davidson, who helped send the Los Angeles Chargers home on the short end of a 17-0 score. Davidson hit Johnny Robinson with six-yard scoring strike in the second quarter, and booted an 11-yard field goal with just three minutes remaining in the game to lead the way for Dallas. Los Angeles, the eventual Western Divsion champs, missed three field goals and were victimized throughout the game by the Dallas defense, which picked off four passes and recovered two fumbles. Davidson finished the game with 167 yards passing, and Curley Johnson scored the Texans' other touchdown in the fourth quarter on a one-yard run. The win proved the Texans could compete with—and defeat—any team in the AFL.

The Texans' Abner Haynes became the star of the AFL in its first season. (St. Louis Mercantile Library)

Preseason
Record: 6-0

7/31	W	20-13	at Oakland	13,000
8/6	W	27-10	Houston (Tulsa, OK)	12,000
8/14	W	24-14	at Boston	11,000
8/20	W	38-14	N.Y. Titans (Abilene, TX)	8,000
8/27	W	48-0	Denver (Little Rock, AR)	5,500
9/2	W	24-3	HOUSTON	51,000

Regular Season
Record: 8-6

9/10	L	20-21	at L.A. Chargers (Sat.) (N)	17,724
9/16	W	34-16	at Oakland (Fri.) (N)	8,021
9/25	W	17-0	L.A. CHARGERS	42,000
10/2	L	35-37	N.Y. TITANS	37,500
10/9	L	19-20	OAKLAND	21,000
10/16	L	10-20	at Houston	19,026
10/30	W	17-14	at Denver	13,102
11/6	W	45-28	at Buffalo	19,610
11/13	W	34-7	DENVER	21,000
11/18	L	14-42	at Boston (Fri.) (N)	14,721
11/24	L	35-41	at N.Y. Titans	14,344
12/4	W	24-0	HOUSTON	20,000
12/11	W	34-0	BOSTON	12,000
12/18	W	24-7	BUFFALO	18,000

Individual Statistics

Passing

	Att.	Cmp.	Yds.	Pct.	TD	INT	LG	Rating
Davidson	379	179	2474	47.2	15	16	74	64.5
Enis	54	30	357	55.6	1	2	39	66.9
Haynes	1	0	0	0.0	0	0	0	39.6
Robinson	1	0	0	0.0	0	1	0	0.0
Texan Totals	435	209	2831	48.0	16	19	74	63.2
Opp. Total	406	209	2703	51.5	11	27	53	83.8

Receiving

	No.	Yds.	Avg.	LG	TD
Haynes	55	576	10.5	34	3
Burford	46	789	17.2	57	5
Robinson	41	611	14.9	74	4
Boydston	29	357	12.3	25	3
Spikes	11	158	14.4	25	0
Johnson	10	174	17.4	36	1
Bernet	4	49	12.3	15	0
Dickinson	3	38	12.7	21	0
Davidson	1	-1	-1.0	-1	0
Texans Totals	209	2831	13.5	74	16
Opp. Totals	261	3002	11.5	—	19

Rushing

	No.	Yds.	Avg.	LG	TD
Haynes	156	875	5.6	67	9
Robinson	98	458	4.7	49	4
Spikes	115	457	4.0	36	5
Johnson	23	43	1.9	8	1
*Enis	12	-12	-1.0	11	3
*Davidson	31	-122	-3.9	7	1
Texans Totals	483	1814	3.8	67	24
Opp. Totals	421	980	2.3	—	14

*Yards lost attempting to pass (sack yards) were counted as negative rushing yards during the AFL's inaugural season.

Team Statistics

	Texans	Opp.
Total First Downs	272	253
Rushing	119	76
Passing	136	147
Penalty	17	30

Total Net Yards	4645	3982
Avg. Per Game	331.8	284.4
Total Plays	918	924
Avg. Per Play	5.1	4.3
Net Yards Rushing	1814	980
Avg. Per Game	129.6	70.0
Total Rushes	483	421
Avg. Per Play	3.8	2.3
*Net Yards Passing	2634	2644
Avg. Per Game	188.1	188.9
Yards Lost Att. to Pass	197	358
Gross Yards	2831	3002
Attempts/Completions	435/209	503/261
Pct. of Completions	48.0	51.9
Had Intercepted	19	32
Punts/Average	61/39.3	79/36.9
Punt Returns/Yards	33/496	27/151
Kickoff Returns/Yards	41/845	55/1330
Penalties/Yards	80/743	59/569
Fumbles/Lost	30/18	34/16
Touchdowns	46	35
Rushing	24	14
Passing	16	19
Returns	6	2
Safeties	0	0

Score By Periods	1	2	3	4	Total
Texans Total	61	106	68	127	362
Opp. Total	69	68	59	57	253

*Reflects yards lost attempting to pass.

Regular Starters

	Offense		Defense
WR	Chris Burford	LE	Paul Miller
LT	Charlie Diamond	LT	Walter (Buffalo) Napier
LG	Sid Fournet	RT	Ray Collins
C	Jim Barton	RE	**Mel Branch**
RG	**Bill Krisher**	LLB	E.J. Holub
RT	Jerry Cornelison	MLB	**Sherrill Headrick**
TE	Bob Bryant	RLB	Smokey Stover
	Max Boydstrum		Walt Corey
QB	Cotton Davidson	LCB	Duane Wood
LHB	**Abner Haynes**	RCB	David Webster
FB	Jack Spikes	LS	Don Flynn
RHB	Johnny Robinson	RS	Jimmy Harris
K	Jack Spikes	P	Cotton Davidson

ALL-AFL as selected by *The Sporting News* in Bold

No AFL All-Star game was played in 1960.

Team Leaders

Scoring: Jack Spikes — 103 pts; 5 TD, 34 PATs, 13 FGs
INTs: David Webster — 6-156 yds., 2 TDs
Punting: Cotton Davidson — 58-2287 yds., 39.4 avg., 62 LG
Punt Returns: Abner Haynes — 14-215 yds., 15.4 avg., 0 TDs
Kickoff Returns: Abner Haynes — 19-434 yds., 22.8 avg., 0 TDs

1960 AFL Standings

Western Division

	W	L	T	Pct.
L.A. Chargers	10	4	0	.714
Dallas	8	6	0	.571
Oakland	6	8	0	.429
Denver	4	9	1	.308

Eastern Division

	W	L	T	Pct.
Houston	10	4	0	.714
N.Y. Titans	7	7	0	.500
Buffalo	5	8	1	.385
Boston	5	9	0	.357

AFL Championship: HOUSTON 24, L.A. Chargers 16

1961 Head Coach: Hank Stram

The Texans bolstered their roster considerably before the 1961 season, signing several blue chip prospects that included E.J. Holub, Jim Tyrer, and Jerry Mays. These players would contribute greatly to the franchise for the next decade. A mid-season six-game losing streak dropped the team out of contention for the division title, and the high expectations for the club at the beginning of the season—they won three of their first four games—vanished. The Texans' running game, again led by All Star Abner Haynes, was superb and the best in the league. Quarterback Cotton Davidson suffered through an inconsistent year, and injuries to key personnel on both offense and defense took their toll on both sides of the ball. The Texans finished with a disappointing 6-8 record and a second place finish in the AFL West.

Key Dates in 1961:

September 10—The Texans lose the season opener at home to the Chargers, 26-10.

October 8—The Texans win their third game in a row at Denver, 19-12.

November 26—The Texans end their six-game losing streak and humble the Raiders, 43-11, at the Cotton Bowl. Abner Haynes sets a team record by scoring five touchdowns, four of them rushing.

December 17—The Texans end a disappointing season by defeating the Titans at the Cotton Bowl, 35-24.

Big Game of 1961:

November 3, 1961 at Boston
Boston 28, Dallas 21

In one of the most bizarre endings ever to a game, the Boston Patriots, with the help of an over-zealous hometown fan, stopped the Texans bid to tie the score on the game's final play. After surrendering a 91-yard kickoff return late in the fourth quarter to fall behind 28-21, Cotton Davidson and Chris Burford hooked up on a 72-yard pass play that put the ball on the Patriots' three-yard line. Davidson's last-chance pass into the end zone on the game's final play was knocked down by a spectator, who had run onto field during the play. Surprisingly, the officials let the play stand and the Texans took the loss, 28-21. It was the team's fourth defeat in a row and dropped them from contention for the AFL West title.

The Texans lost their next two games, running the the losing streak to six games before stopping the Raiders at the Cotton Bowl. The franchise wouldn't lose six in a row again until the 1977 season in Kansas City.

Cotton Davidson (19) watches as Abner Haynes (28) dives in for a touchdown during the 1961 season. Note the mostly empty stands in the background. (Transcendental Graphics)

Preseason　　　　　　　　　　Record: 4-1

8/5	W	39-28	N.Y. Titans (Cobb Stadium, Dallas)	20,500
8/12	W	31-13	Denver (Midland, TX)	10,000
8/18	W	35-26	at Buffalo	33,376
8/25	W	29-27	Denver (Ft. Worth, TX)	20,000
9/3	L	10-31	at San Diego	15,232

Regular Season　　　　　　　　Record: 6-8

9/10	L	10-26	SAN DIEGO	24,500
9/24	W	42-35	at Oakland	6,700
10/1	W	26-21	HOUSTON	28,000
10/8	W	19-12	at Denver	14,500
10/15	L	24-27	at Buffalo	20,678
10/22	L	7-38	at Houston	23,228
10/29	L	17-18	BOSTON	20,500
11/3	L	21-28	at Boston (Fri.) (N)	25,063
11/12	L	20-30	BUFFALO	15,000
11/19	L	14-24	at San Diego	33,788
11/26	W	43-11	OAKLAND	14,500
12/3	L	7-28	at N.Y. Titans	14,117
12/10	W	49-21	DENVER	8,000
12/17	W	35-24	N.Y. TITANS	12,500

Individual Statistics

Passing

	Att.	Cmp.	Yds.	Pct.	TD	INT	LG	Rating
Davidson	330	151	2445	45.8	17	23	—	59.3
Duncan	67	25	361	37.3	1	3	—	41.9
Jackson	2	1	9	50.0	0	1	—	22.9
Texan Totals	399	177	2576	44.4	18	27	—	52.7
Opp. Total	439	219	2777	49.9	20	25	—	61.6

Receiving

	No.	Yds.	Avg.	LG	TD
Burford	51	850	16.7	54	5
Robinson	35	601	17.2	71	5
Haynes	34	558	16.4	69	3
Dickinson	14	209	14.9	48	2
Jackson	13	171	13.2	52	2
Boydston	12	167	13.9	24	1
Spikes	8	136	17.0	46	0
Romeo	7	89	12.7	20	0
Pricer	2	21	10.5	11	0
Barnes	1	13	13.0	13	0
Texans Totals	177	2815	14.6	71	18
Opp. Totals	219	2777	12.7	—	20

Rushing

	No.	Yds.	Avg.	LG	TD
Haynes	179	841	4.7	59	9
Jackson	65	386	5.9	49	3
Spikes	39	334	8.6	74	5
Dickinson	71	263	3.7	65	3
Robinson	52	200	3.9	45	2
Davidson	21	123	5.9	40	1
Duncan	5	42	8.5	19	0
Pricer	5	13	2.6	5	0
Gilliam	1	-6	-6.0	-6	0
Burford	1	-13	-13.0	-13	0
Texans Totals	439	2183	4.9	74	23
Opp. Totals	410	1525	3.7	—	18

Team Leaders

Scoring: Jack Spikes	54 pts: 5 TDs, 10 PATs, 4 FGs
INTs: David Webster	5-50 yds., 0 TDs
Punting: Cotton Davidson	61-2479 yds., 40.6 avg., 62 LG
Punt Returns: Abner Haynes	19-196 yds., 10.3 avg., 0 TDs
Kickoff Returns: Dave Grayson	16-453 yds., 28.3 avg., 0 TDs

Team Statistics

	Texans	Opp.
Total First Downs	247	248
Rushing	112	89
Passing	122	139
Penalty	13	20
Total Net Yards	4759	4302
Avg. Per Game	339.9	307.3
Total Plays	862	884
Avg. Per Play	5.5	4.9
Net Yards Rushing	2183	1525
Avg. Per Game	155.9	108.9
Total Rushes	439	410
Avg. Per Play	5.0	3.7
Net Yards Passing	2576	3077
Avg. Per Game	184.0	219.8
Sacked/Yards Lost	24/239	34/300
Gross Yards	2815	3377
Attempts/Completions	399/177	439/219
Pct. of Completions	44.4	49.9
Had Intercepted	27	25
Punts/Average	62/40.0	63/41.7
Punt Returns/Yards	26/219	17/176
Kickoff Returns/Yards	53/1465	65/1249
Penalties/Yards	89/875	62/619
Fumbles/Lost	32/18	31/18
Touchdowns	45	44
Rushing	23	18
Passing	18	21
Returns	4	5
Safeties	0	0

Score By Periods	1	2	3	4	Total
Texans Total	77	87	87	83	334
Opp. Total	36	127	41	139	343

Regular Starters

	Offense		Defense
WR	**Chris Burford**	LE	Paul Miller
LT	Charlie Diamond	LT	**Paul Rochester**
LG	Sid Fournet	RT	Ray Collins
C	Jim Barton	RE	**Mel Branch**
RG	**Bill Krisher**	LLB	**E.J. Holub**
RT	Jerry Cornelison	MLB	**Sherrill Headrick**
TE	Max Boydstrum	RLB	Smokey Stover
			Walt Corey
QB	**Cotton Davidson**	LCB	Duane Wood
LHB	**Abner Haynes**	RCB	**David Webster**
FB	Jack Spikes	LS	Don Flynn
RHB	Johnny Robinson	RS	Jimmy Harris
K	Jack Spikes	P	Cotton Davidson

AFL ALL-STARS in Bold*

1961 AFL Standings

Western Division

	W	L	T	Pct.
San Diego	12	2	0	.857
Dallas	6	8	0	.429
Denver	3	11	0	.214
Oakland	2	12	0	.143

Eastern Division

	W	L	T	Pct.
Houston	10	3	1	.769
Boston	9	4	1	.692
N.Y. Titans	7	7	0	.500
Buffalo	6	8	0	.429

AFL Championship: Houston 10, SAN DIEGO 3

1962 Head Coach: Hank Stram

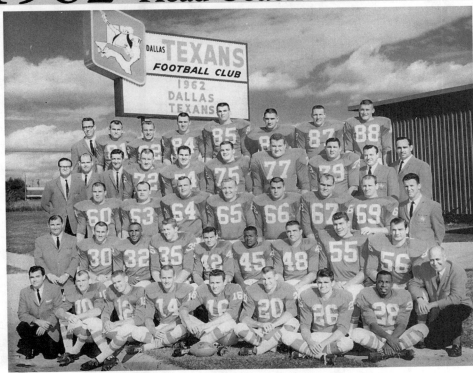

(Tommy Brooker)

Len Dawson came to the Texans as a seldom used NFL quarterback and led the Texans to the AFL Championship. He passed for 2,759 yards and 29 touchdowns and provided the consistency at quarterback that the Texans had lacked in their previous two seasons. Abner Haynes was again super and had his best season, rushing for 1,049 yards and scoring a team-record 19 touchdowns. The defense was revitalized and became one of the best in the league. Chris Burford caught 12 touchdown passes, rookie fullback Curtis McClinton rushed for 604 yards, and tight end Fred Arbanas caught 39 passes. Jerry Mays, E.J. Holub, and Sherrill Headrick were key players on the defense; Dave Grayson led a much improved secondary. The Texans finished with an 11-3 record, and then defeated the Oilers in a double-overtime classic to capture the franchise's first championship.

Key Dates in 1962:

September 8—The Texans start the season with a 42-28 win over Boston in Dallas.

September 30—Abner Haynes rushes for 164 yards on 16 carries in the Texans 41-21 win over the Bills.

October 12—Len Dawson passes for 302 yards and two touchdowns as the Texans beat the Patriots, 27-7, in Boston. Chris Burford catches 10 passes for 171 receiving yards.

November 18—Len Dawson and Tommy Brooker hook up on a 92-yard touchdown pass as the Texans beat the Broncos in Denver, 24-3.

December 1—Using the draft choice they received from Oakland in the Cotton Davidson trade, the Texans choose Buck Buchanan of Grambling College as the No. 1 pick in the AFL draft and sign him immediately.

December 16—Dallas wins the season finale, beating the Chargers, 26-17, at the Cotton Bowl and finishing with an 11-3 record and first place in the AFL West.

December 23—The Texans win an exciting double-overtime game against the Houston Oilers and claim their first league championship, 20-17. Tommy Brooker's 25-yard field goal ended what was at that time pro football's longest game at 77 minutes and 54 seconds. Texans back Jack Spikes rushed for 77 yards to earn game MVP honors. Abner Haynes scored two touchdowns.

Big Game of 1962:

November 25 at Dallas
Dallas 35, Oakland 7

The Texans clinched a tie for the AFL West Division by routing the Raiders at the Cotton Bowl. Len Dawson tossed a couple of touchdown passes, and Abner Haynes ran at will against the leaky Raider defense. In all, the Texans compiled 281 yards rushing and 129 yards passing. Haynes also returned eight punts for 112 yards. The Chargers loss to the Oilers clinched the tie for Dallas. The only disappointing thing about the win was the small crowd of 13,557 spectators at the Cotton Bowl; despite the winning team and prospect of a division championship, the Texans were still losing the attendence war with the NFL's Cowboys.

Al Reynolds leads the way for Curtis McClinton during the 1962 AFL Championship game against Houston. (Chris Burford)

Jerry Mays, Frank Jackson and Jerry Cornelison came to the Texans from SMU, and were major contributors to the franchise's early success. (Jim Chappelle)

Preseason   Record: 2-3

8/4	W	13-3	Oakland (American Field, Atlanta)	8,000
8/11	L	0-17	at San Diego	28,555
8/18	W	22-6	Oakland (Midland, TX)	10,000
8/24	L	*24-27	Denver (Ft. Worth, TX)	18,000
8/31	L	31-34	Houston (Orange Bowl, Miami)	27,530

Regular Season   Record: 11-3

9/8	W	42-28	Boston (Sat.) (N)	32,000
9/23	W	26-16	at Oakland	12,500
9/30	W	41-21	BUFFALO	25,500
10/7	L	28-32	at San Diego	23,092
10/12	W	27-7	at Boston (Fri.) (N)	23,874
10/21	W	20-17	N.Y. TITANS	17,814
10/28	W	31-7	at Houston	31,750
11/4	L	6-14	HOUSTON	29,017
11/11	W	52-31	at N.Y. Titans	13,275
11/18	W	24-3	at Denver	23,523
11/25	W	35-7	OAKLAND	13,557
12/2	L	14-23	at Buffalo	35,261
12/9	W	17-10	DENVER	19,137
12/16	W	26-17	SAN DIEGO	18,384
AFL Championship Game:				
12/23	W	**20-17	at Houston	37,981

Individual Statistics

Passing

	Att.	Cmp.	Yds.	Pct.	TD	INT	LG	Rating
Dawson	310	189	2759	61.0	29	17	92	98.4
Wilson	11	6	65	54.5	0	0	22	72.1
Haynes	1	0	0	0.0	0	0	0	39.6
Texan Totals	322	195	2455	60.6	29	17	92	92.3
Opp. Total	469	239	2701	51.0	13	32	—	49.6

Receiving

	No.	Yds.	Avg.	LG	TD
Burford	45	645	14.4	49	12
Haynes	39	573	14.7	78	6
Arbanas	29	469	16.2	47	6
McClinton	29	333	11.5	24	0
Miller	23	277	12.0	39	0
Jackson	10	177	17.7	62	1
Spikes	10	132	13.2	35	1
Saxton	5	64	12.8	33	0
Brooker	4	138	34.5	92	3
Robinson	1	16	16.0	16	0
Texans Totals	195	2824	14.5	92	29
Opp. Totals	239	2701	11.3	—	13

Rushing

	No.	Yds.	Avg.	LG	TD
Haynes	221	1049	4.8	71	13
McClinton	111	604	5.4	69	2
Dawson	38	252	6.6	22	3
Jackson	47	251	5.3	35	3
Spikes	57	232	4.1	17	0
Burford	1	13	13.0	13	0
Wilson	1	5	5.0	5	0
Saxton	3	1	0.3	9	0
Texans Totals	479	2407	5.0	71	21
Opp. Totals	351	1250	3.6	—	16

Team Leaders

Scoring: Abner Haynes — 114 pts: 19 TDs, 0 PATs
INTs: Bobby Hunt — 8-101 yds., 0 TDs
Punting: Eddie Wilson — 47-1691 yds., 36.0 avg., 52 LG
Punt Returns: Frank Jackson — 11-117 yds., 10.6 avg., 0 TDs
Kickoff Returns: Dave Grayson — 18-535 yds., 29.7 avg., 0 TDs

Team Statistics

	Texans	Opp.
Total First Downs	259	239
Rushing	119	76
Passing	125	143
Penalty	15	20
Total Net Yards	4862	3951
Avg. Per Game	347.3	282.2
Total Plays	840	848
Avg. Per Play	5.8	4.7
Net Yards Rushing	2407	1250
Avg. Per Game	171.9	89.3
Total Rushes	479	351
Avg. Per Play	5.0	3.6
Net Yards Passing	2455	2701
Avg. Per Game	175.4	192.9
Sacked/Yards Lost	37/369	27/252
Gross Yards	2824	2953
Attempts/Completions	322/195	469/239
Pct. of Completions	60.6	51.0
Had Intercepted	17	32
Punts/Average	54/36.1	55/41.1
Punt Returns/Yards	27/236	26/219
Kickoff Returns/Yards	37/955	72/1592
Penalties/Yards	66/644	74/650
Fumbles/Lost	26/14	32/17
Touchdowns	50	29
Rushing	21	14
Passing	29	13
Returns	0	2
Safeties	28/14	28/11

Score By Periods	1	2	3	4	Total
Texans Total	103	96	61	129	389
Opp. Total	45	72	59	57	233

Regular Starters

	Offense		Defense
WR	Chris Burford	LE	Curt Merz
LT	Jim Tyrer	LT	Paul Rochester
LG	**Marvin Terrell**	RT	**Jerry Mays**
C	Jon Gilliam	RE	**Mel Branch**
RG	Al Reynolds	LLB	**E.J. Holub**
RT	Charlie Diamond	MLB	**Sherrill Headrick**
TE	**Fred Arbanas**	RLB	Walt Corey
WR	Frank Jackson	QB	**Len Dawson**
LCB	Duane Wood	RB	**Abner Haynes**
RCB	**Dave Grayson**	RB	**Curtis McClinton**
LS	Bobby Hunt	RS	Johnny Robinson
K	Tommy Brooker	P	Jerrel Wilson

AFL ALL-STARS in Bold

1962 AFL Standings

Western Division

	W	L	T	Pct.
Dallas	11	3	0	.786
Denver	7	7	0	.500
San Diego	4	10	0	.286
Oakland	1	13	0	.071

Eastern Division

	W	L	T	Pct.
Houston	11	3	0	.786
Boston	9	4	1	.692
Buffalo	7	6	1	.583
N.Y. Titans	5	9	0	.357

AFL Championship: Dallas 20, HOUSTON 17 (double overtime)

1963 Head Coach: Hank Stram

Despite the club's first AFL Championship in 1962, the stands at the Cotton Bowl remained relatively empty. Texans' owner Lamar Hunt made the decision to move the team, and in May 1963, it was announced that the Texans were going to Kansas City and would be renamed the Chiefs. The franchise was warmly received by its new city, and a decent fan base was established. But the first season in K.C. proved bittersweet in many respects. Rookie Stone Johnson died as the result of neck injuries in a preseason game, the team fell far below it's expectations as the defending AFL champs, and for the second time in three years, the club finished with a losing record. Rookies Buck Buchanan and Bobby Bell starred on defense, and Dave Grayson and Johnny Robinson were all-AFL performers in the secondary. After winning the opener against the Broncos in convincing style, the Chiefs won just once in their next ten games. They finished the season 5-7-2.

Key Dates in 1963:

May 14—The Texans announce they are moving to Kansas City. The team is renamed the Kansas City Chiefs.

August 9—The Chiefs debut at Municipal Stadium before a small crowd of 5,721 fans, beating Buffalo, 17-13, in an exhibition game.

August 31—In their final preseason game in Wichita, Kansas, the Chiefs lose to Houston, 23-17. In the game, Stone Johnson, a rookie flanker from Grambling, injures his neck and is paralyzed. He dies on September 8, a tragedy that affects the team for the rest of the season.

October 6—The Chiefs defeat the Oilers, 28-7, before a home opener crowd of 27,801.

December 22—The Chiefs beat the Jets, 48-0, ending their first season in Kansas City with a disappointing record of 5-7-2.

Big Game of 1963:

September 7 at Denver
Kansas City 59, Denver 7

Before their first game in Kansas City uniforms, head coach Hank Stram delivered a short pep talk to his team. "There's no mystery to this game," he said. "Just hit and win. You're the Yankees of the AFL."

And that's what they did. In their debut as a Kansas City team, the Chiefs scored first, fast, and often as they routed the Broncos in Denver, 59-7, amassing a point total that is still the most ever by a Chiefs team in a regular-season game. Fullback Curtis McClinton scored the game's first touchdown, and later threw a touchdown pass to Chris Burford. Dave Grayson ran a kickoff back 99 yards for a score, Len Dawson threw four touchdown passes, and Tommy Brooker added eight extra points and a field goal. It was, in short, a massacre.

"The greatest performance by the Chiefs in their four years," Stram said following the game. "What a great way to start the season."

The Chiefs racked up 458 yards passing and 120 yards rushing. The defense was just as dominating, intercepting five Bronco passes—linebacker Sherrill Headrick ran one back for a score. The defending AFL champs showed they had what it takes to defend their title, at least in this one game.

Jack Spikes continued to play well for the club in Kansas City. He rushed for 257 yards and two touchdowns in 1963. (Topeka Capital-Journal)

Preseason   Record: 3-2

Date		Score	Opponent	Attendance
8/3	L	14-26	at San Diego	25,862
8/9	W	7-13	BUFFALO	5,721
8/17	W	35-21	Oakland (Seattle, WA)	13,500
8/23	W	30-16	DENVER	6,865
8/30	L	17-23	Houston	11,000

Regular Season   Record: 5-7-2

Date		Score	Opponent	Attendance
9/7	W	59-7	at Denver (Sat.) (N)	21,115
9/22	T	27-27	at Buffalo	33,487
9/29	L	10-24	at San Diego	22,654
10/6	W	28-7	HOUSTON	27,801
10/13	L	26-35	BUFFALO	25,519
10/20	L	17-38	SAN DIEGO	30,107
10/27	L	7-28	at Houston	26,331
11/3	L	7-10	at Oakland	18,919
11/8	L	7-22	OAKLAND (Fri.) (N)	24,897
11/17	T	24-24	at Boston	17,270
12/1	L	0-17	at N.Y. Jets	18,824
12/8	W	52-21	DENVER	17,443
12/14	W	35-3	BOSTON (Sat.)	12,598
12/22	W	48-0	N.Y. JETS	12,202

Individual Statistics

Passing	Att.	Cmp.	Yds.	Pct.	TD	INT	LG	Rating
Dawson	352	190	2389	54.0	26	19	82	77.6
E. Wilson	82	39	537	47.6	3	2	48	71.4
McClinton	2	1	33	50.0	1	0	33	135.4
Haynes	2	1	24	50.0	0	0	24	93.8
Spikes	1	0	0	0.0	0	1	0	0.0
Chiefs Totals	439	231	2651	52.6	30	22	82	72.9
Opp. Total	428	218	2629	50.9	18	26	—	58.7

Receiving	No.	Yds.	Avg.	LG	TD
Burford	68	824	12.1	69	9
Jackson	50	785	15.7	82	8
Arbanas	34	373	11.0	40	6
Haynes	33	470	14.2	73	2
McClinton	27	301	11.1	46	3
Spikes	11	125	11.4	30	1
Coan	2	35	17.5	31	0
Brooker	2	32	16.0	16	0
J. Wilson	2	21	10.5	15	0
D. Johnson	2	17	8.5	11	1
Chiefs Totals	231	2983	12.9	82	30
Opp. Totals	218	2629	12.1	—	18

Rushing	No.	Yds.	Avg.	LG	TD
McClinton	142	568	4.0	36	3
Haynes	99	352	3.6	46	4
Dawson	37	272	7.4	43	2
Spikes	84	257	3.1	15	2
Coan	17	100	5.9	51	0
Jackson	3	52	17.3	25	1
E. Wilson	8	45	5.6	21	0
J. Wilson	9	41	4.6	12	0
Burford	1	10	10.0	10	0
Chiefs Totals	400	1697	4.2	51	12
Opp. Totals	397	1558	3.9	—	12

Team Leaders

Scoring: Chris Burford — 56 pts: 9 TDs, 1 PAT (2 pt)
INTs: Bobby Hunt — 6-228 yds., 0 TDs
Punting: Jerrel Wilson — 77-3292 yds., 42.7 avg., 70 LG
Punt Returns: Frank Jackson — 11-95 yds., 8.6 avg., 0 TD
Kickoff Returns: Dave Grayson — 20-564 yds., 28.2 avg., 1 TD

Team Statistics

	Chiefs	Opp.
Total First Downs	250	228
Rushing	94	83
Passing	141	130
Penalty	15	15
Total Net Yards	4348	4187
Avg. Per Game	310.6	299.1
Total Plays	872	856
Avg. Per Play	5.0	4.9
Net Yards Rushing	1697	1558
Avg. Per Game	121.2	111.3
Total Rushes	400	397
Avg. Per Play	4.2	3.9
Net Yards Passing	2651	2629
Avg. Per Game	189.4	187.8
Sacked/Yards Lost	34/332	35/300
Gross Yards	2983	2629
Attempts/Completions	439/231	428/218
Pct. of Completions	52.6	50.9
Had Intercepted	22	26
Punts/Average	62/43.1	70/40.2
Punt Returns/Yards	26/259	32/345
Kickoff Returns/Yards	47/1166	55/1322
Penalties/Yards	52/605	47/411
Fumbles/Lost	27/16	29/19
Touchdowns	46	33
Rushing	12	12
Passing	30	18
Returns	4	3
Safeties	1	2

Score By Periods	1	2	3	4	Total
Chiefs Total	79	72	109	87	347
Opp. Total	29	107	51	76	263

Regular Starters

	Offense		Defense
WR	Chris Burford	LE	Bobby Bell
LT	**Jim Tyrer**	LT	Buck Buchanan
LG	Marvin Terrell		Paul Rochester
C	Jon Gilliam	RT	Jerry Mays
RG	Al Reynolds	RE	**Mel Branch**
	Curt Merz	LLB	E.J. Holub
RT	Dave Hill	MLB	Sherrill Headrick
	Charlie Diamond	RLB	**Walt Corey**
TE	**Fred Arbanas**	LCB	Duane Wood
WR	Frank Jackson	RCB	**Dave Grayson**
QB	Len Dawson	LS	Bobby Hunt
RB	Abner Haynes	RS	**Johnny Robinson**
RB	Curtis McClinton	P	Jerrel Wilson
K	Tommy Brooker		

AFL ALL-STARS in Bold

1963 AFL Standings

Western Division

	W	L	T	Pct.
San Diego	11	3	0	.786
Oakland	10	4	0	.714
Kansas City	5	7	2	.417
Denver	2	11	1	.154

Eastern Division

	W	L	T	Pct.
Boston	7	6	1	.583
Buffalo	7	6	1	.583
Houston	6	8	0	.429
N.Y. Jets	5	8	1	.385

AFL Championship: SAN DIEGO 51, Boston 10

1964 Head Coach: Hank Stram

KANSAS CITY CHIEFS FOOTBALL CLUB

The Chiefs played roller coaster football throughout the season, posting impressive wins against the Chargers and Jets, then losing to the lowly Broncos, the worst team in the AFL. Coach Stram got stellar performances on offense from Len Dawson, who threw 30 touchdown passes, rookie fullback Mack Lee Hill, Curtis McClinton and Chris Burford. The defense was again led by Jerry Mays, Buck Buchanan, Bobby Bell and Johnny Robinson. But the team never put it all together—injuries were also costly—and despite sending 12 players to the AFL All-Star game, Kansas City could produce no better than a 7-7 record. Average attendance for the season was just 18,126, which was even more disappointing than the team's final record.

Key Dates in 1964:

March 6—Chiefs offensive guard Ed Budde is severely injured in a fight and suffers a fractured skull. He is able to return and play when training camp opens.

September 13—The Chiefs win at Buffalo, 34-17, to open the season.

November 1—Len Dawson passes for a club-record 435 yards and six touchdowns, as the Chiefs down the Broncos, 49-39, at Municipal Stadium. Dawson hit on 23 of 38 pass attempts.

December 13—The Chiefs embarrass the Chargers in San Diego, 49-6.

December 20—The Chiefs lose to the Jets at Municipal Stadium, 24-7. Kansas City finishes the disappointing season with a 7-7 record, second in the AFL West.

December—Chiefs tight end Fred Arbanas suffers major damage to his left eye when he is attacked by a mugger. Despite losing almost all vision in the eye, Arbanas returns the following year and continues his career.

Big Game of 1964:

November 8 at Kansas City
Kansas City 42, Oakland 7

In a textbook performance, the Chiefs humiliated the Oakland Raiders at Municipal Stadium in what was easily their best overall game of the season. Dawson threw four touchdown passes, and the defense held Oakland to 169 total yards and recovered four fumbles. Head coach Hank Stram cackled with delight following the game.

"How sweet it is, when you win," Stram said.

Consistency was the key. The Chiefs had been unable to put together complete games from their offense and defense throughout the season. They finally found a way to get the best from both units.

"Now we are showing signs of great progress," Stram continued with his analysis of the game. "We should continue to get better from here on in."

The Chiefs finished with 164 rushing yards and 186 passing yards. They only attempted 19 passes. The win put the Chiefs' record at 4-4, leaving them an outside shot at the division title. Losses in three of the next four games eliminated any chance Kansas City had to win the division.

Rookie Mack Lee Hill pounded opposing defenses for 567 returning yards in 1964. (Topeka Capital-Journal)

Preseason
Record: 4-1

8/9	W	21-14	at Oakland		11,118
8/14	W	24-21	at Buffalo		17,738
8/22	L	14-26	SAN DIEGO		28,653
8/28	W	14-10	Denver (Wichita, KS)		19,500
9/3	W	27-17	at Houston		17,450

Regular Season
Record: 7-7

9/13	L	17-34	at Buffalo	30,157
9/27	W	21-9	at Oakland	18,163
10/4	W	28-7	HOUSTON	22,727
10/11	L	27-33	at Denver	16,285
10/18	L	22-35	BUFFALO	20,904
10/23	L	7-24	at Boston (Fri.) (N)	27,400
11/1	W	49-39	DENVER	15,053
11/8	W	42-7	OAKLAND	21,023
11/15	L	14-28	SAN DIEGO	19,792
11/22	W	28-19	at Houston	17,782
11/29	L	14-27	at N.Y. Jets	38,135
12/6	L	24-31	BOSTON	13,166
12/13	W	49-6	at San Diego	26,562
12/20	L	24-7	N.Y. JETS	14,316

Individual Statistics

Passing	Att.	Cmp.	Yds.	Pct.	TD	INT	LG	Rating
Dawson	354	199	2879	56.2	30	18	72	89.9
E. Wilson	47	25	392	53.2	1	1	55	79.4
Beathard	9	4	50	44.4	1	2	22	59.7
Haynes	1	0	0	0.0	0	0	0	39.6
Spikes	1	0	0	0.0	0	0	0	39.6
Chiefs Totals	412	228	2871	55.3	32	21	72	82.0
Opp. Total	443	218	2620	49.2	25	28	—	65.3

Receiving	No.	Yds.	Avg.	LG	TD
Jackson	62	943	15.2	72	9
Burford	51	675	13.2	55	7
Haynes	38	562	14.8	59	3
Arbanas	34	686	20.2	68	8
M. Hill	19	144	7.6	34	2
McClinton	13	221	17.0	66	2
Spikes	5	17	3.4	6	0
Carolan	3	54	18.0	25	1
Coan	2	8	4.0	4	0
J. Wilson	1	11	11.0	11	0
Chiefs Totals	228	3321	14.5	72	32
Opp. Totals	218	2620	12.0	—	25

Rushing	No.	Yds.	Avg.	LG	TD
Haynes	137	713	5.2	80	5
M. Hill	105	567	5.4	71	4
McClinton	72	252	3.5	30	1
Spikes	34	113	3.3	13	0
Dawson	39	95	2.4	18	2
Coan	11	56	5.1	37	2
Beathard	4	43	10.8	41	0
Jackson	2	5	2.5	12	0
E. Wilson	6	5	0.8	8	0
J. Wilson	1	-10	-10.0	-10	0
Chiefs Totals	411	1839	4.5	80	14
Opp. Totals	387	1315	3.4	—	9

Team Leaders

Scoring: Tommy Brooker — 70 pts: 46 PATs, 8 FGs
INTs: Dave Grayson — 7-187 yds., 0 TDs
Bobby Hunt — 7-133 yds., 1 TD
Punting: Jerrel Wilson — 60-2628 yds., 43.8 avg., 72 LG
Punt Returns: Willie Mitchell — 18-167 yds., 9.3 avg., 0 TDs
Kickoff Returns: Dave Grayson — 30-679 yds., 22.6 avg., 0 TDs

Team Statistics

	Chiefs	Opp.
Total First Downs	244	204
Rushing	88	76
Passing	142	117
Penalty	14	11
Total Net Yards	4710	3935
Avg. Per Game	336.4	281.1
Total Plays	871	856
Avg. Per Play	5.4	4.6
Net Yards Rushing	1839	1315
Avg. Per Game	131.4	93.9
Total Rushes	411	387
Avg. Per Play	4.5	3.4
Net Yards Passing	2871	2620
Avg. Per Game	205.1	187.1
Sacked/Yards Lost	44/450	28/279
Gross Yards	3321	2899
Attempts/Completions	412/228	443/218
Pct. of Completions	55.3	49.2
Had Intercepted	21	28
Punts/Average	78/42.6	78/40.7
Punt Returns/Yards	40/377	32/242
Kickoff Returns/Yards	58/1244	62/1449
Penalties/Yards	56/604	47/460
Fumbles/Lost	37/19	30/19
Touchdowns	49	38
Rushing	14	9
Passing	32	25
Returns	3	4
Safeties	0	0

Score By Periods	1	2	3	4	Total
Chiefs Total	60	106	106	94	366
Opp. Total	70	72	84	80	306

Regular Starters

	Offense		Defense
WR	Chris Burford	LE	**Bobby Bell**
LT	**Jim Tyrer**	LT	**Jerry Mays**
LG	Ed Budde	RT	**Buck Buchanan**
C	Jon Gilliam	RE	Mel Branch
RG	Al Reynolds	LLB	**E.J. Holub**
	Curt Merz	MLB	Sherrill Headrick
RT	Dave Hill	RLB	Walt Corey
TE	**Fred Arbanas**	LCB	Duane Wood
WR	Frank Jackson	RCB	**Dave Grayson**
QB	**Len Dawson**	SS	**Bobby Hunt**
RB	**Mack Lee Hill**	FS	**Johnny Robinson**
	Jack Spikes	P	Jerrel Wilson
RB	Curtis McClinton		
K	**Tommy Brooker**		

AFL ALL-STARS in Bold

1964 AFL Standings

Western Division

	W	L	T	Pct.
San Diego	8	5	1	.615
Kansas City	7	7	0	.500
Oakland	5	7	2	.471
Denver	2	11	1	.154

Eastern Division

	W	L	T	Pct.
Buffalo	12	2	0	.857
Boston	10	3	1	.769
N.Y. Jets	5	8	1	.385
Houston	4	10	0	.286

AFL Championship: BUFFALO 20, San Diego 7

1965 Head Coach: Hank Stram

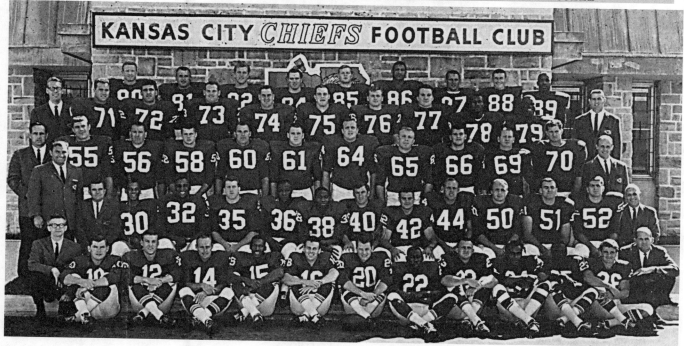

The cloak of tragedy found the Chiefs again at the end of the 1965 season when Mack Lee Hill died suddenly during routine knee surgery. The big fullback had injured his knee against Buffalo in the next-to-last game of the season. His death darkened and ruined an otherwise good season for Kansas City, a year that saw the team post its first winning record since departing Dallas. As in previous seasons in Kansas City, inconsistency plagued the team and they routinely lost to lesser opponents. Rookie wide out Otis Taylor greatly strengthened the offensive fire power, and the defense was supported by its returning veterans; Buchanan, Mays, Holub, Headrick, Bell, and Robinson. Quarterback Len Dawson's numbers dropped a bit as backup quarterback Pete Beathard got more playing time behind center. Curtis McClinton led the rushers, and Hill was right behind him. Despite a final record of 7-5-2, the Chiefs still seemed unable to take the big step forward and seriously challenge for the division title.

Key Dates in 1965:

October 3—Kansas City defeats the Patriots at Municipal Stadium, 27-17, in the team's home opener.

October 31—The Chiefs beat Oakland at Municipal Stadium, 14-7, improving the team's record to 4-3-1.

November 28—Mack Lee Hill runs for 119 yards as the Chiefs smash the Oilers, 52-21.

December 14—Mack Lee Hill, the Chiefs' star second-year fullback, dies during knee surgery. He injured the knee against Buffalo two days earlier and died when his body temperature soared to 108 degrees during the surgery. His death devastates the team.

Big Game of 1965

December 19 at Kansas City
Kansas City 45, Denver 35

Filled with sorrow and brimming with overloaded emotions, the Chiefs dedicated the final game of the 1965 season to their fallen fullback, Mack Lee Hill, and turned away the Denver Broncos at Municipal Stadium.

"There was a lot of emotion in this game. I know I tried a lot," Jerry Mays said following the Chiefs' 45-35 win. "We were trying to get it for Mack." Hill had died suddenly 5 days before during knee surgery.

Curtis McClinton took over Hill's fullback spot and played a terrific game, catching five passes for 213 yards.

"I played Mack's position and I tried to play it the way he would," McClinton said after the game. "We got together before the game and dedicated this one to Mack, and I dedicated myself to playing one that would make Mack proud."

"Curtis showed super-human effort," Dawson said of McClinton. "You could tell he wanted this one badly."

The defense was a little sloppy, but only because they were over-charged. Stram knew his players desperately wanted to win for Hill.

"I was concerned before the game because I had no way of judging what we would do."

Rookie wide receiver Otis Taylor caught 26 passes for 446 yards and five touchdowns in 1965. (Topeka Capital-Journal)

Preseason — Record: 3-2

Date	W/L	Score	Opponent	Attendance
8/7	W	30-24	at Denver	17,077
8/15	L	10-31	SAN DIEGO	13,132
8/22	L	6-23	at Oakland	13,592
8/28	W	18-16	Buffalo (Wichita, KS)	8,630
9/4	W	34-7	BOSTON	15,157

Regular Season — Record: 7-5-2

Date	W/L	Score	Opponent	Attendance
9/12	L	10-37	at Oakland	18,659
9/18	W	14-10	at N.Y. Jets (Sat.) (N)	53,658
9/26	T	10-10	at San Diego	28,126
10/3	W	27-17	BOSTON	26,773
10/10	W	31-23	at Denver	31,001
10/17	L	7-23	BUFFALO	26,941
10/24	L	36-38	at Houston	34,670
10/31	W	14-7	OAKLAND	18,354
11/7	L	10-13	N.Y. JETS	25,523
11/14	W	31-7	SAN DIEGO	21,968
11/21	T	10-10	at Boston	13,056
11/28	W	52-21	HOUSTON	16,459
12/12	L	25-34	at Buffalo	40,298
12/19	W	45-35	DENVER	14,421

Individual Statistics

Passing	Att.	Cmp.	Yds.	Pct.	TD	INT	LG	Rating
Dawson	305	163	2262	53.4	21	14	67	81.3
Beathard	89	36	632	40.5	1	6	73	41.1
McClinton	15	0	0	0	0	0	0	39.6
Chiefs Totals	395	199	2543	50.4	22	20	73	68.3
Opp. Total	438	203	2457	46.3	18	20	—	58.6

Receiving	No.	Yds.	Avg.	LG	TD
Burford	47	575	12.2	57	6
McClinton	37	590	15.9	69	3
Jackson	28	440	15.7	73	1
Taylor	26	446	17.2	48	5
Arbanas	24	418	17.4	67	4
Hill	21	264	12.6	46	1
Coan	9	85	9.4	23	2
Carolan	6	65	10.8	14	0
Pitts	1	11	11.0	11	0
Chiefs Totals	199	2894	14.5	73	22
Opp. Totals	203	2457	12.1	—	18

Rushing	No.	Yds.	Avg.	LG	TD
McClinton	175	661	3.8	48	6
Hill	125	627	5.0	66	2
Dawson	43	142	3.3	40	2
Coan	45	137	3.0	21	1
Beathard	25	138	5.5	26	4
Taylor	2	17	8.5	15	0
Jackson	1	26	26.0	26	0
Wilson	2	4	2.0	3	0
Chiefs Totals	418	1752	4.2	66	15
Opp. Totals	383	1366	3.6	—	14

Team Leaders

Scoring: Tommy Brooker — 76 pts: 37 PATs, 13 FGs
INTs: Fred Williamson — 6-89 yds., 0 TDs
Punting: Jerrel Wilson — 68-3132 yds., 46.1 avg., 64 LG
Punt Returns: Willie Mitchell — 19-242 yds., 12.7 avg., 1 TD
Kickoff Returns: Bert Coan — 19-479 yds., 25.2 avg., 0 TDs

Team Statistics

	Chiefs	Opp.
Total First Downs	228	200
Rushing	101	67
Passing	119	112
Penalty	8	24
Total Net Yards	4290	3749
Avg. Per Game	306.4	267.8
Total Plays	833	847
Avg. Per Play	5.2	4.4
Net Yards Rushing	1736	1366
Avg. Per Game	124.0	97.6
Total Rushes	417	383
Avg. Per Play	4.2	3.6
Net Yards Passing	2554	2457
Avg. Per Game	182.4	175.5
Sacked/Yards Lost	343	299
Gross Yards	2897	2756
Attempts/Completions	409/200	438/203
Pct. of Completions	48.9	46.3
Had Intercepted	20	20
Punts/Average	72/44.6	82/44.3
Punt Returns/Yards	35/422	29/14.9
Kickoff Returns/Yards	46/1043	55/1182
Penalties/Yards	70/728	60/623
Fumbles/Lost	33/21	25/13
Touchdowns	40	34
Rushing	15	14
Passing	22	18
Returns	3	2
Safeties	0	0

Score By Periods	1	2	3	4	Total
Chiefs Total	90	81	37	114	322
Opp. Total	33	64	76	112	285

Regular Starters

	Offense		Defense
WR	Chris Burford	LE	**Jerry Mays**
LT	**Jim Tyrer**	LT	Ed Lothamer
LG	Ed Budde	RT	**Buck Buchanan**
C	Jon Gilliam	RE	Mel Branch
RG	Curt Merz	LLB	**Bobby Bell**
RT	Dave Hill	MLB	**Sherrill Headrick**
TE	**Fred Arbanas**	RLB	**E.J. Holub**
WR	**Frank Jackson**	LCB	Fred Williamson
QB	Len Dawson	RCB	Willie Mitchell
RB	Mack Lee Hill	LS	Bobby Hunt
RB	Curtis McClinton	RS	**Johnny Robinson**
K	Tommy Brooker	P	Jerrel Wilson

AFL ALL-STARS in Bold

1965 AFL Standings

Western Division

	W	L	T	Pct.
San Diego	9	2	3	.818
Oakland	8	5	1	.615
Kansas City	7	5	2	.583
Denver	4	10	0	.286

Eastern Division

	W	L	T	Pct.
Buffalo	10	3	1	.769
N.Y. Jets	5	8	1	.385
Boston	4	8	2	.333
Houston	4	10	0	.286

AFL Championship: Buffalo 23, SAN DIEGO 0

1966 Head Coach: Hank Stram

The Chiefs put all the pieces of their talent together and swept through the AFL to win the franchise's second championship, and its first in Kansas City. Heisman Trophy winner Mike Garrett received a lot of money to play for the Chiefs instead of for an NFL team, and the speedy back added another dimension to an already strong offense, running for 801 yards. Otis Taylor had a great season, catching 58 passes for 1,297 yards and eight touchdowns. Chris Burford also hauled 58 receptions, and Len Dawson tossed 26 touchdown passes. Buck Buchanan and Bobby Bell were the mainstays on defense. The Chiefs won eight of their first ten games and wrapped up the division title with two games left. Their 11-2-1 record was the best ever for the club. Kansas City met Buffalo on January 1, 1967, for the AFL Championship, and the right to meet the NFL's Green Bay Packers in the first Super Bowl. The Chiefs handily defeated the Bills, 31-7, but were overwhelmed by the Packers two weeks later in Los Angeles, 35-10.

Key Dates in 1966:

October 23—The Chiefs dismantle the Broncos at Denver, 56-10. This convincing win improves the team's mark to 5-2.

October 30—Otis Taylor catches five passes for 187 yards as the Chiefs roll to a 48-23 win over Houston at Municipal.

December 18—The Chiefs end the regular season with a 27-17 win at San Diego and finish with an 11-2-1 record.

January 1, 1967—Playing in frigid conditions, the Chiefs roll past the Bills in Buffalo, 31-7, and capture the AFL championship. Mike Garrett scores two touchdowns and Len Dawson throws a couple of touchdown passes to lead the offense.

January 15, 1967—The Chiefs take their place in history as the first AFL representative in what is now called Super Bowl I. They are beaten convincingly by the Green Bay Packers, 35-10. Trailing 14-10 at the half, Kansas City is unable to solve Green Bay's blitzing tactics and fails to move the ball with any consistency the rest of the game. Dawson hit Curtis McClinton on a seven-yard pass for the Chiefs' only touchdown in the losing effort.

Big Game of 1966:

November 27 at New York
Kansas City 32, New York 24

Finally. The Chiefs reached back for a little extra in the fourth quarter and held on to defeat the New York Jets and claim their first Western Division title as a Kansas City team. It wasn't easy. The Jets staged a comeback in the final quarter, as Joe Namath threw two touchdown passes to pull the Jets within five points at 29-24. The Chiefs responded, and on their next possession banged out a six-minute drive that ended with a Mike Mercer field goal, his fourth of the game. Willie Mitchell intercepted a Namath pass on the Jets' next possession, and the Chiefs held on for the win, 32-24, and the division championship.

Chiefs' head coach Hank Stram refused to talk about the AFL championship game, or their opponent, the Buffalo Bills.

"Frankly, we just want to be in the game (AFL championship) ourselves."

The team learned they were outright division champs during the flight back to Kansas City. A wild celebration followed and, for 30 minutes, liquids were thrown, poured, and consumed. Congratulations also flowed freely, and the joyous team celebrated during the entire flight, or at least until the beer ran out.

Mike Garrett (21) takes off on a busted play during the 1966 AFL championship game at Buffalo. Len Dawson is the improbable interference. (Topeka Capital-Journal)

Len Dawson, far right, watches as Ed Budde (on the ground) makes just enough room for Mike Garrett to squeeze across the goal line in the second half of the 1966 AFL Championship game. (Topeka Capital-Journal)

Preseason Record: 4-0

Date	Result	Score	Opponent	Attendance
8/6	W	32-30	at Denver	17,771
8/12	W	33-0	at Miami	34,277
8/20	W	31-21	San Diego (Anaheim, CA)	36,038
8/27	W	31-20	HOUSTON	25,270

Regular Season Record: 11-2-1

Date	Result	Score	Opponent	Attendance
9/11	W	42-20	at Buffalo	42,023
9/18	W	32-10	at Oakland	50,746
9/25	W	43-24	at Boston	22,641
10/2	L	14-29	BUFFALO	43,885
10/8	W	37-10	DENVER (Sat.) (N)	33,929
10/16	L	13-34	OAKLAND	33,057
10/23	W	56-10	at Denver	26,196
10/30	W	48-23	HOUSTON	31,676
11/6	W	24-14	SAN DIEGO	40,986
11/13	W	34-16	MIAMI	34,063
11/20	T	27-27	BOSTON	41,475
11/27	W	32-24	at N.Y. Jets	60,318
12/11	W	19-18	at Miami	17,881
12/18	W	27-17	at San Diego	28,348

Individual Statistics

Passing	Att.	Cmp.	Yds.	Pct.	TD	INT	LG	Rating
Dawson	284	159	2527	56.0	26	10	89	101.9
Beathard	90	394	578	43.3	4	4	77	61.3
Coan	1	1	18	100.0	1	0	18	158.3
Garrett	1	0	0	0.0	0	0	0	39.6
Taylor	1	0	0	0.0	0	1	0	0.0
Chiefs Totals	377	199	3123	52.8	31	15	89	91.3
Opp. Total	494	226	2616	45.8	18	33	—	46.3

Receiving	No.	Yds.	Avg.	LG	TD
Taylor	58	1297	22.4	89	8
Burford	58	758	13.1	38	8
Arbanas	22	305	13.9	36	4
McClinton	19	285	15.0	68	5
Coan	18	131	7.3	20	2
Garrett	15	175	11.7	36	1
Carolan	7	154	22.0	45	3
Pitts	1	11	11.0	11	0
Wilson	1	7	7.0	7	0
Chiefs Totals	199	3123	14.2	89	31
Opp. Totals	226	2614	11.5	—	18

Rushing	No.	Yds.	Avg.	LG	TD
Garrett	147	801	5.5	77	6
McClinton	140	540	3.9	49	4
Coan	96	521	5.4	57	7
Dawson	24	167	7.0	18	0
Beathard	20	152	7.6	52	1
G. Thomas	7	53	7.6	28	1
Taylor	2	33	16.5	19	0
Wilson	3	7	2.3	5	0
Chiefs Totals	439	2274	5.2	77	19
Opp. Totals	353	1356	3.8	—	10

Team Leaders

Scoring: Mike Mercer — 93 pts: 33 PATs, 20 FG
INTs: Johnny Robinson — 10-136 yds., 1 TD
Bobby Hunt — 10-113 yds., 0 TDs
Punting: Jerrel Wilson — 61-2715 yds., 44.5 avg., 69 LG
Punt Returns: Mike Garrett — 17-139 yds., 8.2 avg., 1 TD
Kickoff Returns: Emmitt Thomas — 29-673 yds., 23.2 avg., 0 TDs

Team Statistics

	Chiefs	Opp.
Total First Downs	266	222
Rushing	106	75
Passing	140	125
Penalty	20	22
Total Net Yards	5114	3970
Avg. Per Game	365.3	283.6
Total Plays	846	873
Avg. Per Play	6.0	4.6
Net Yards Rushing	2274	1356
Avg. Per Game	162.4	96.9
Total Rushes	439	353
Avg. Per Play	5.2	3.8
Net Yards Passing	2840	2614
Avg. Per Game	202.9	186.7
Sacked/Yards Lost	30/283	26/262
Gross Yards	3123	2616
Attempts/Completions	377/199	494/226
Pct. of Completions	52.8	45.8
Had Intercepted	15	33
Punts/Average	62/43.8	69/41.3
Punt Returns/Yards	31/276	36/359
Kickoff Returns/Yards	54/114	84/2045
Penalties/Yards	61/680	56/592
Fumbles/Lost	21/16	21/8
Touchdowns	55	32
Rushing	19	10
Passing	31	18
Returns	5	4
Safeties	0	0

Score By Periods	1	2	3	4	Total
Chiefs Total	158	80	94	116	448
Opp. Total	33	115	50	78	276

Regular Starters

	Offense		Defense
WR	Chris Burford	LE	**Jerry Mays**
LT	**Jim Tyrer**	LT	Andy Rice
LG	**Ed Budde**		Ed Lothamer
C	Jon Gilliam	RT	**Buck Buchanan**
	Wayne Frazier	RE	Chuck Hurston
RG	Curt Merz	LLB	**Bobby Bell**
RT	Dave Hill	MLB	**Sherrill Headrick**
TE	Fred Arbanas	RLB	**E.J. Holub**
WR	Otis Taylor	LCB	Fred Williamson
QB	**Len Dawson**	RCB	Willie Mitchell
RB	**Mike Garrett**	SS	Bobby Hunt
RB	**Curtis McClinton**	FS	**Johnny Robinson**
K	Mike Mercer	P	Jerrel Wilson
	Tommy Brooker		

AFL ALL-STARS in Bold

1966 AFL Standings

Western Division

	W	L	T	Pct.
Kansas City	11	2	1	.846
Oakland	8	5	1	.615
San Diego	7	6	1	.538
Denver	4	10	0	.286

Eastern Division

	W	L	T	Pct.
Buffalo	9	4	1	.692
Boston	8	4	2	.667
N.Y. Jets	6	6	2	.500
Houston	3	11	0	.214
Miami	3	11	0	.214

AFL Championship: Kansas City 31, BUFFALO 7
Super Bowl I: Green Bay 35, Kansas City 10

1967 Head Coach: Hank Stram

As the defending AFL champs, the Chiefs were never able to regain the form that had carried them to the first Super Bowl the previous year. A series of injuries, bad luck, and sloppy play kept Kansas City from repeating, but the team was still able to forge a respectable 9-5 record and second place in the division. On the up side, several rookies played key positions on the team; Willie Lanier and Jim Lynch took over two of the linebacking spots, tiny Nolan Smith was spectacular as the team's return specialist, and soccer-style place-kicker Jan Stenerud booted footballs farther than anyone imagined possible. The offense was led by Mike Garrett, who ran for 1,087 yards, Otis Taylor, and Len Dawson. Bobby Bell and Buck Buchanan were solid on defense. The Chiefs won their final three games of the season, giving them reason to believe 1968 held better things in store for the team.

Key Dates in 1967:

August 23—It might have been the greatest game the Chiefs have ever played. Forget that it was a preseason game, because when Kansas City took the field to play the Chicago Bears, they had one goal: exacting revenge on the NFL. It was time for payback, and the Bears were the victims. With the force of a chainsaw, the Chiefs unleashed seven months of emotions from their loss in the first Super Bowl and ripped through George Halas's team, 66-24. "This proves we're capable of winning any time we play anyone," said Stram after the game.

October 8—The Chiefs play their first home game of the season and crush the Dolphins, 41-0.

November 5—Mike Garrett runs for 193 yards in the Chiefs' 42-18 win over the Jets.

December 17—Noland "Super Gnat" Smith returns a kickoff an NFL record 106 yards against the Broncos in Denver as the Chiefs win, 38-24. The team finishes the season with a 9-5 record, good for second place the AFL West.

The Bears' defense tries in vain to bring down Mike Garrett during the Chiefs' 66-24 preseason rout of Chicago. (Topeka Capital-Journal)

Big Game in 1967:

October 1, 1967 at Oakland
Oakland 23, Kansas City 21

Missed opportunities by the Chiefs was the story of this game. Kansas City repeatedly fought back throughout the game, overcoming big plays by the Raiders and their own mistakes, but fell short in the end. Big plays decided the outcome, maybe none bigger than the third-and-44 play by the Raiders early in the fourth quarter. A personal foul was called on the Chiefs' defense, and instead giving up the ball, the Raiders continued their drive. Bobby Bell intercepted a pass early in the second half that looked like a sure three points for Kansas City. Instead, they got nothing.

"You make a couple of plays, or you don't, that will change the complexion of the ball game," Stram said after the loss. "Make no mistake about it. Oakland plays well."

The costliest big-play miss by Kansas City occured with two minutes remaining in the game. The Chiefs trailed, 23-21, and from deep in their own teritory, Dawson threw 1 on 2 to Otis Taylor, who had beaten his man by a couple of steps. The ball hit Taylor in the hands, and he dropped it.

"If I had caught it, I'd have been the hero," Taylor said. "If I missed it, I'd become the goat. So I'm the goat. ...This is not going to end my career."

How did he drop the ball?

"I overran it. I was going full speed. It was under thrown some," Taylor said of the play. "I guess I kind of kicked it out of my hands, I don't know. If I had caught it, I don't think I'd have gone all the way. But if I had caught it, we would have had excellent field position."

Oakland held on and won the game, moving into a first-place tie with the Chargers. The Chiefs fell back to third place and never recovered as serious contenders in the race for the Western Division title.

Preseason   Record: 4-1

Date		Score	Opponent	Attendance
8/5	W	24-9	at Houston	36,362
8/12	W	30-17	N.Y. Jets (Birmingham, AL)	53,109
8/19	W	48-0	Oakland (Portland, OR)	13,352
8/23	W	66-24	CHICAGO	33,041
9/1	L	24-44	at L.A. Rams	73,990

Regular Season   Record: 9-5

Date		Score	Opponent	Attendance
9/9	W	25-20	at Houston (Sat.) (N)	28,003
9/24	W	24-0	at Miami	36,272
10/1	L	21-23	at Oakland	50,268
10/8	W	41-0	MIAMI	45,291
10/15	L	31-45	at San Diego	45,365
10/22	L	19-24	HOUSTON	46,365
10/29	W	52-9	DENVER	44,002
11/5	W	42-18	N.Y. JETS	46,642
11/12	W	33-10	at Boston	23,010
11/19	L	16-17	SAN DIEGO	46,738
11/23	L	22-44	OAKLAND (Thur.)(Thanksgiving)	44,020
12/3	W	23-13	BUFFALO	41,948
12/10	W	21-7	at N.Y. Jets	62,891
12/17	W	38-24	at Denver	31,660

Individual Statistics

Passing	Att.	Cmp.	Yds.	Pct.	TD	INT	LG	Rating
Dawson	357	206	2651	57.7	24	17	71	83.5
Lee	19	6	105	31.6	1.	2	29	29.6
Garrett	4	1	17	25.0	1	0	17	84.4
Chiefs Totals	382	213	2773	55.8	26	26	71	73.2
Opp. Total	462	229	2536	49.6	13	31	—	47.7

Receiving	No.	Yds.	Avg.	LG	TD
Taylor	59	958	16.2	71	11
Garrett	46	261	5.7	34	1
McClinton	26	219	8.4	25	1
Burford	25	389	15.6	55	3
Arbanas	20	295	14.8	43	5
G. Thomas	13	99	7.6	27	2
Richardson	12	312	26.0	56	2
Coan	5	41	8.2	24	0
Pitts	4	131	32.8	59	1
Carolan	2	26	13.0	23	0
N. Smith	1	42	42.0	42	0
Chiefs Totals	213	2773	13.0	71	26
Opp. Totals	229	2536	11.1	—	13

Rushing	No.	Yds.	Avg.	LG	TD
Garrett	236	1087	4.6	58	9
McClinton	97	392	4.0	34	2
Coan	63	275	4.4	38	4
G. Thomas	35	133	3.8	19	1
Dawson	20	68	3.4	24	0
Taylor	5	29	5.8	24	1
Pitts	3	19	6.3	15	1
Wilson	1	10	10.0	10	0
N. Smith	1	8	8.0	8	0
Lee	1	-3	-3.0	-3	0
Chiefs Totals	462	2018	4.5	58	18
Opp. Totals	343	1408	4.1	—	10

Team Leaders

Scoring: Jan Stenerud   108 pts: 45 PATs, 21 FGs
INTs: Fletcher Smith   6-150 yds., 0 TDs
Punting: Jerrel Wilson   41-1739 yds., 42.4 avg., 59 LG
Punt Returns: Noland Smith   26-212 yds., 8.2 avg., 0 TDs
Kickoff Returns: Noland Smith   41-1148 yds., 28.0 avg., 1 TD

Team Statistics

	Chiefs	Opp.
Total First Downs	251	221
Rushing	116	73
Passing	117	132
Penalty	18	16
Total Net Yards	4490	3944
Avg. Per Game	320.7	281.7
Total Plays	872	843
Avg. Per Play	5.1	4.7
Net Yards Rushing	2018	1408
Avg. Per Game	144.1	100.6
Total Rushes	462	343
Avg. Per Play	4.4	4.1
Net Yards Passing	2472	2536
Avg. Per Game	176.6	181.1
Sacked/Yards Lost	32/301	38/354
Gross Yards	2773	2536
Attempts/Completions	382/213	462/229
Pct. of Completions	55.8	49.6
Had Intercepted	19	31
Punts/Average	61/41.3	60/42.3
Punt Returns/Yards	33/245	31/331
Kickoff Returns/Yards	53/1245	55/1207
Penalties/Yards	68/680	76/747
Fumbles/Lost	28/8	27/11
Touchdowns	49	30
Rushing	18	10
Passing	26	13
Returns	5	7
Safeties	1	0

Score By Periods	1	2	3	4	Total
Chiefs Total	87	143	83	95	408
Opp. Total	61	91	6	66	254

Regular Starters

	Offense		Defense
WR	Chris Burford	LE	**Jerry Mays**
LT	Jim Tyrer	LT	Andy Rice
LG	**Ed Budde**		Ed Lothamer
C	Jon Gilliam	RT	**Buck Buchanan**
		RE	Chuck Hurston
RG	Curt Merz	LLB	**Bobby Bell**
RT	Dave Hill	MLB	Sherrill Headrick
TE	**Fred Arbanas**	RLB	E.J. Holub
WR	Gloster Richardson	LCB	Emmitt Thomas
	Otis Taylor	RCB	Willie Mitchell
QB	**Len Dawson**	LS	Bobby Hunt
RB	**Mike Garrett**	RS	**Johnny Robinson**
RB	**Curtis McClinton**	P	Jerrel Wilson
K	Jan Stenerud		Wayne Walker

AFL ALL STARS in Bold

1967 AFL Standings

Western Division

	W	L	T	Pct.
Oakland	13	1	0	.929
Kansas City	9	5	0	.643
San Diego	8	5	1	.615
Denver	3	11	0	.214

Eastern Division

	W	L	T	Pct.
Houston	9	4	1	.692
N.Y. Jets	8	5	1	.615
Buffalo	4	10	0	.286
Miami	5	8	1	.385
Boston	3	10	1	.231

AFL Championship: OAKLAND 40, Houston 7
Super Bowl II: Green Bay 33, Oakland 14

1968 Head Coach: Hank Stram

The Chiefs fought through injuries on both sides of the ball and bounced back from their 1967 slump to tie for the AFL Western division title. The defense led the way, allowing the fewest points in the league (170, the lowest ever by a Chiefs team), picking off 37 passes and recovering 12 fumbles. On offense, rookie running back Robert Holmes led the team in rushing, gaining 866 yards and scoring seven touchdowns. Dawson passed for 2,109 yards and 17 touchdowns, and Mike Garrett was the leading receiver with just 33 receptions. The team's 12-2 record in the regular season is still the top mark in the history of the franchise.

Key Dates in 1968:

September 9—The Chiefs defeat the Oilers at Houston, 26-21, to start the season.

September 15—The Chiefs lose, 20-19, to the Jets at home. Jets quarterback Joe Namath controls the ball for the final five and a half minutes of the game to seal the win for New York.

November 3—The Raiders easily defeat the Chiefs at Oakland, 38-21. One of the few highlights for Kansas City was when Len Dawson and Gloster Richardson hooked up for a 92-yard touchdown pass.

December 14—The Chiefs wrap up the regular season with a 30-7 win at Denver, finishing with a 12-2 record. Oakland also finishes with a 12-2 mark, and a divisional playoff is setup the following week.

December 22—The Raiders humiliate the Chiefs, 41-6, to win the Western Division and the right to play the New York Jets for the AFL championship. The Raiders score 21 points in the first quarter to put the game away early. At the time it is the Chiefs' worst defeat ever.

Fullback Wendell Hayes rips through the Raiders' line. (Kansas Collection, U. of Kansas)

Big Game in 1968

October 20 at Kansas City
Kansas City 24, Oakland 10

Hank Stram pulled a few pages from football's past and installed a T-formation running attack into his offense that helped the Chiefs literally run over the Raiders at Municipal Stadium, 24-10. With his receiver corps crippled by injuries—Otis Taylor and Gloster Richardson were both out—Stram felt the overemphasis on the running game would work, and he was right. Mike Garrett and Robert Holmes lined up at the two halfback spots, and Wendell Hayes settled in at fullback. The Chiefs also employed two tight ends.

"All I was concerned with was winning, and I thought this was the best way for us to win," Stram said after the game. "Give the credit for this game to the people it belongs to, the people up front who blocked and tackled, and to our entire squad. It was a team effort."

Garrett ran for 109 yards, Robert Holmes for 95 yards, and Wendell Hayes for 89 yards, as the Chiefs totaled 294 yards rushing on 60 attempts. Len Dawson threw just three passes, an AFL record for fewest attempts in a game. Hayes scored two of the touchdowns on runs of one and 11 yards.

"I was pleased with the guys today," offensive tackle Jim Tyrer said. "I'm partial to the offensive line, of course, but everybody did the job."

The defense was solid, too. Raider quarterback Daryle Lamonica faced a ferocious defensive line throughout the game.

"It was a helluva pass rush," Lamonica said. "Maybe it's the best I've faced up to now."

"You have to do what you think is best when your squad situation is the way it was," Stram said of the game plan. "The win moved the Chiefs one and a half games ahead of the Raiders in the standings.

Preseason — Record: 4-1

Date	W/L	Score	Opponent	Attendance
8/3	W	38-14	at Cincinnati	21,682
8/10	W	13-10	at Minnesota	46,228
8/17	W	13-10	ST. LOUIS	47,462
8/24	W	31-21	OAKLAND	43,769
8/31	L	16-36	at L.A. Rams	54,323

Regular Season — Record: 12-2

Date	W/L	Score	Opponent	Attendance
9/9	W	26-21	at Houston (Mon.) (N)	45,083
9/15	L	19-20	N.Y. JETS	48,871
9/22	W	34-2	DENVER	45,821
9/28	W	48-3	at Miami (Sat.) (N)	28,501
10/5	W	18-7	at Buffalo (Sat.) (N)	40,748
10/13	W	13-3	CINCINNATI	47,096
10/20	W	24-10	OAKLAND	50,015
10/27	W	27-20	SAN DIEGO	50,344
11/3	L	21-38	at Oakland	53,357
11/10	W	16-9	at Cincinnati	25,537
11/17	W	31-17	BOSTON	48,271
11/28	W	24-10	HOUSTON (Thur.)(Thanksgiving)	48,493
12/8	W	40-3	at San Diego	51,174
12/14	W	30-7	at Denver (Sat.)	38,463

Individual Statistics

Passing	Att.	Cmp.	Yds.	Pct.	TD	INT	LG	Rating
Dawson	224	131	2109	58.5	17	9	92	98.8
Lee	45	25	383	55.6	3	1	61	97.1
Garrett	1	0	0	0.0	0	1	0	0.0
Chiefs Totals	270	156	2492	57.8	20	11	92	96.3
Opp. Total	461	214	3562	46.4	14	37	—	49.6

Receiving	No.	Yds.	Avg.	LG	TD
Garrett	33	359	10.9	43	3
Pitts	30	655	21.8	90	6
Richardson	22	494	22.5	92	6
Taylor	20	420	21.0	67	4
Holmes	19	201	10.6	43	0
Hayes	12	108	9.0	22	1
Arbanas	11	189	17.2	48	0
McClinton	3	-4	-1.3	5	0
Carolan	2	26	13.0	19	0
Coan	2	15	7.5	12	0
Wilson	1	14	14.0	14	0
Smith	1	15	15.0	15	0
Chiefs Totals	156	2492	16.0	92	20
Opp. Totals	214	3562	16.6	—	14

Rushing	No.	Yds.	Avg.	LG	TD
Holmes	174	866	5.0	76	7
Garrett	164	564	3.4	37	3
Hayes	85	340	4.0	25	4
Coan	40	160	4.0	24	1
Pitts	11	107	9.7	28	0
McClinton	24	107	4.5	19	0
Taylor	5	41	8.2	30	1
Dawson	28	40	2.0	22	0
Arbanas	3	14	4.7	8	0
Livingston	2	2	1.0	3	0
Wilson	5	1	0.2	1	0
Smith	2	-2	-1.0	1	0
Richardson	1	-3	-3.0	-3	0
Lowe	1	-10	-10.0	-10	0

Team Leaders

Scoring: Jan Stenerud — 129 pts: 39 PATs, 30 FGs
INTs: Johnny Robinson — 6-40 yds., 0 TDs
Punting: Jerrel Wilson — 63-2841 yds., 45.1 avg., 70 LG
Punt Returns: Noland Smith — 18-270 yds., 15.0 avg., 1 TD
Kickoff Returns: Noland Smith — 23-549 yds., 23.9 avg., 0 TDs

Team Statistics

	Chiefs	Opp.
Total First Downs	223	215
Rushing	123	52
Passing	89	140
Penalty	11	23
Total Net Yards	4503	4089
Avg. Per Game	321.6	292.1
Total Plays	831	900
Avg. Per Play	5.4	4.5
Net Yards Rushing	2227	1266
Avg. Per Game	159.1	90.4
Total Rushes	537	365
Avg. Per Play	4.1	3.5
*Net Yards Passing	2276	2823
Avg. Per Game	162.6	201.6
Sacked/Yards Lost	24/216	45/439
Gross Yards	2492	3562
Attempts/Completions	270/156	461/214
Pct. of Completions	57.8	46.4
Had Intercepted	11	37
Punts/Average	65/45.3	63/41.8
Punt Returns/Yards	31/450	31/220
Kickoff Returns/Yards	38/736	54/1044
Penalties/Yards	66/650	62/555
Fumbles/Lost	26/16	22/12
Touchdowns	40	18
Rushing	16	4
Passing	20	14
Returns	4	0
Safeties	1	1

Score By Periods	1	2	3	4	Total
Chiefs Total	90	111	74	96	371
Opp. Total	46	57	40	27	170

Regular Starters

	Offense		Defense
WR	Frank Pitts	LE	**Jerry Mays**
LT	**Jim Tyrer**	LT	Ed Lothamer
LG	**Ed Budde**	RT	**Buck Buchanan**
C	E.J. Holub	RE	Aaron Brown
RG	Mo Moorman	LLB	Bobby Bell
RT	Dave Hill	MLB	**Willie Lanier**
TE	Fred Arbanas	RLB	**Jim Lynch**
WR	Gloster Richardson	LCB	**Emmitt Thomas**
	Otis Taylor	RCB	Willie Mitchell
QB	**Len Dawson**	LS	Jim Kearney
RB	Mike Garrett	RS	**Johnny Robinson**
RB	Robert Holmes	P	Jerrel Wilson
K	**Jan Stenerud**		

AFL ALL-STARS IN Bold

1968 AFL Standings

Western Division

	W	L	T	Pct.
Oakland	12	2	0	.857
Kansas City	12	2	0	.857
San Diego	9	5	0	.643
Denver	5	9	0	.357
Cincinnati	3	11	0	.214

Eastern Division

	W	L	T	Pct.
N.Y. Jets	11	3	0	.786
Houston	7	7	0	.500
Miami	5	8	1	.385
Boston	4	10	0	.286
Buffalo	1	12	1	.077

Western Division Playoff: OAKLAND 41, Kansas City 6
AFL Championship: N.Y. JETS 27, Oakland 23
Super Bowl III: N.Y. Jets 16, Baltimore 7

KANSAS CITY *CHIEFS* FOOTBALL CLUB

Despite losing to the Raiders twice and finishing second in the AFL West, the Chiefs took advantage of the league's one-time-only playoff system—the second-place teams in each division played the first-place teams in the other division—and ran the table of opponents to win pro football's world championship. Like so many seasons before, the Chiefs fought off adversity, mainly the knee injury to quarterback Len Dawson, and maintained a high level of play. Second-year man Mike Livingston took over for Dawson, and the team won four in a row with him at the helm. The running game was again superb, with Garrett, Holmes, Hayes, and Warren McVea alternating equally in Stram's "scatback" offense. Otis Taylor rebounded from his injury-prone season the previous year, catching 41 passes for 696 yards and seven touchdowns. The defense, greatly bolstered by the addition of Jim Marsalis in the secondary, was the best in pro football at the season's end. Curley Culp, Buck Buchanan, Bobby Bell, Willie Lanier, and Johnny Robinson were the other big stars on defense. After losing to the Raiders 10-6 in the regular season's final game, the Chiefs traveled to New York to face Joe Namath and the Jets in the first round of the playoffs. Kansas City won a hard-fought defensive battle in bitterly cold conditions, 13-6. Two weeks later they exacted revenge on the Raiders and won the final AFL Championship game, 17-7. When the Chiefs played the Minnesota Vikings a week later in New Orleans, they entered the game a big underdog, but left the field at the game's end with a 23-7 victory and the world championship.

Key Dates in 1969:

September 21—Kansas City defeats the Patriots in Boston, 31-0, but Dawson suffers an injury to his left knee. He misses several games throughout the season.

September 28—Dawson's backup, Jacky Lee, goes down for the season, leaving the quarterback duties to Mike Livingston, a little-used second-year quarterback from SMU. The offense sputters, and the Chiefs are defeated by the Bengals in Cincinnati, 24-19.

October 19—The Chiefs beat the Dolphins, 17-10. Mike Livingston, Otis Taylor, and Robert Holmes combine for a unique 93-yard touchdown pass play; Taylor caught the initial pass from Livingston, then lateraled to Holmes, who carried the ball into the end zone.

November 2—Len Dawson returns to the lineup, and the Chiefs defeat the Bills in Buffalo, 29-7.

November 16—Kansas City destroys the defending world champion New York Jets, 34-16, at Shea Stadium. The win is the seventh in a row for the team.

November 23—The winning streak ends as the Chiefs fall to the Raiders at home, 27-24. The Chiefs outplay the Raiders statistically, but miscues and turnovers prove too much to overcome.

December 7—The Chiefs squeak by the Bills at Municipal Stadium, 22-19. Jan Stenerud hits five field goals for Kansas City.

December 13—Once again the Chiefs fall to Oakland, 10-6, and the Raiders clinch the AFL Western Division title. Kansas City attempts only six passes throughout the game and finishes the season with an 11-3 mark. But the playoffs lie ahead, thanks to the AFL's special one-year-only playoff system setup.

December 20—Using a ferocious goal-line stand in the fourth quarter, the Chiefs defeat the Jets, 13-6, to advance to the AFL Championship game. Dawson passes for 201 yards and a touchdown, and Jim Marsalis picks off two passes to lead the Chiefs.

January 4, 1970—Back to the Super Bowl. The Chiefs rode their defense to the title in the last AFL game ever, defeating the Raiders in Oakland, 17-7. Wendell Hayes and Robert Holmes each scored a touchdown, and Jan Stenerud kicked a field goal late in the fourth quarter to seal the win. Emmitt Thomas picked off a couple of passes to lead a stingy defense.

January 11, 1970—The Chiefs win the Super Bowl. Representing the AFL in the league's last game, Kansas City won a decisive victory over the Minnesota Vikings, 23-7, in Super Bowl IV in New Orleans. Despite being a two-touchdown underdog, Kansas City never trailed in the game. Jan Stenerud booted three field goals, the longest from 48 yards, and Mike Garrett pranced into the end zone on a five-yard run to put the Chiefs up 16-0 at the half. Otis Taylor scored on a spectacular 46-yard pass play to close out the scoring in the third period, and the defense manhandled the Vikings' quarterback, Joe Kapp, the rest of the game. Len Dawson, ignoring false gambling allegations that were made against him earlier in the week, played brilliantly and was named the game's MVP.

Big Game of 1969:

October 5 at Denver
Kansas City 26, Denver 13

On a soggy, rain-soaked field, the Chiefs outslugged a lesser Denver team and earned a 26-13 victory. Second-year quarterback Mike Livingston, thrust into the starting lineup because of injuries to Len Dawson and Jacky Lee, connected on 14 of 27 passes for 214 yards. His performance proved he was capable of leading the Chiefs, and division title hopes, dashed somewhat the week before when Dawson went down, were re-ignited.

"Mike did a great job," Hank Stram said of his young quarterback. "He had great poise, great play selection. He did a great job of keeping their defense off balance."

"You have to believe you can do the job," Livingston said of his play. "I did. After the first couple of plays I got my confidence, and I started zipping the balls in there."

Jan Stenerud kicked four field goals, one from 54 yards, and safety Jim Kearney returned an interception 60 yards for a touchdown. Buck Buchanan, the Chiefs' big defensive tackle, knew Livingston and the rest of the offense would do well.

"I never worry about the offense," Buchanan said. "I know they're gonna do their job."

The bad thing to come out of the game was the barrage of ice and snowballs the Bronco fans pelted the Chiefs with as they left the field after the game. Stram took a shot in the ear, and strength coach Alvin Roy was hit in the back of the head. The players kept their helmets on and avoided any serious hits.

The win moved the Chiefs' record to 3-1, and placed them back in the thick of the AFL Western Division race Livingston was more than an adaquate replacement for the injured Dawson, and the Chiefs did not lose any of the games in which he started.

Jan Stenerud led the Chiefs in scoring in 1969 with 119 points. (Kansas Collection, U. of Kansas)

The addition of Jim Marsalis (40) to the Chiefs' secondary greatly bolstered the defense in 1969. (Kansas Collection, U. of Kansas)

Preseason

Record: 6-0

Date	Result	Score	Opponent	Attendance
8/2	W	23-17	Oakland (Birmington, AL)	21,000
8/9	W	38-13	DETROIT	38,027
8/16	W	23-7	Cincinnati (Jackson, MS)	24,513
8/23	W	42-14	at L.A. Rams	58,306
8/28	W	31-21	at St. Louis	48,006
9/6	W	14-10	ATLANTA	37,273

Regular Season

Record: 11- 3

Date	Result	Score	Opponent	Attendance
9/14	W	27-9	at San Diego	47,988
9/21	W	31-0	at Boston	22,002
9/28	L	19-24	at Cincinnati	27,812
10/5	W	26-13	at Denver	50,564
10/12	W	24-0	HOUSTON	45,805
10/19	W	17-10	MIAMI	49,809
10/26	W	42-22	CINCINNATI	50,934
11/2	W	29-7	at Buffalo	45,844
11/9	W	27-3	SAN DIEGO	51,104
11/16	W	34-16	at N.Y. Jets	63,849
11/23	L	24-27	OAKLAND	51,982
11/27	W	31-17	DENVER (Thur.) (Thanksgiving)	48,773
12/7	W	22-19	BUFFALO	47,112
12/13	L	6-10	at Oakland (Sat.)	54,443

Individual Statistics

Passing	Att.	Cmp.	Yds.	Pct.	TD	INT	LG	Rating
Dawson	166	98	1323	59.0	9	13	55	70.0
Livingston	161	84	1123	52.2	4	6	93	67.6
Lee	20	12	109	60.0	1	1	31	70.6
McVea	3	1	50	33.0	1	0	50	121.5
Flores	1	1	33	100.0	1	0	33	158.3
Chiefs Totals	351	196	2638	55.8	16	20	93	71.5
Opp. Total	426	200	2491	46.9	10	32	—	42.0

Receiving	No.	Yds.	Avg.	LG	TD
Garrett	43	432	10.0	41	2
Taylor	41	696	17.0	79	7
Pitts	31	470	15.8	50	2
Holmes	26	266	10.2	33	3
Richardson	23	381	16.6	39	2
Arbanas	16	258	16.1	44	0
Hayes	9	64	7.1	17	0
McVea	7	71	10.1	22	0
Chiefs Totals	196	2638	12.1	79	16
Opp. Totals	200	2491	12.5	80	10

Rushing	No.	Yds.	Avg.	LG	TD
Garrett	168	732	4.4	34	6
Holmes	150	612	4.1	25	2
McVea	106	500	4.7	80	7
Hayes	62	208	3.4	11	4
Livingston	15	102	6.8	39	0
Lowe	10	33	3.3	18	0
Pitts	5	28	5.6	11	0
Dawson	1	3	3.0	3	0
Lee	1	3	3,0	3	0
Arbanas	1	1	1.0	1	0
Flores	1	0	0.0	0	0
Taylor	2	-2	-1.0	10	0
Chiefs Totals	522	2220	4.3	80	19
Opp. Totals	314	1091	3.5	50	8

Team Leaders

Scoring: Jan Stenerud — 119 pts: 38 PATs, 27 FGs
INTs: Johnny Robinson — 8-158 yds., 0 TDs
Punting: Jerrel Wilson — 68-3022 yds., 44.4 avg., 62 LG
Punt Returns: Noland Smith — 9-107 yds., 11.9 avg., 0 TDs
Kickoff Returns: Warren McVea — 13-318 yds., 24.5 avg., 0 TDs

Team Statistics

	Chiefs	Opp.
Total First Downs	258	181
Rushing	129	53
Passing	125	111
Penalty	4	17
Total Net Yards	4607	3163
Avg. Per Game	329.1	225.9
Total Plays	899	808
Avg. Per Play	5.1	3.9
Net Yards Rushing	2220	1091
Avg. Per Game	158.6	77.9
Total Rushes	522	316
Avg. Per Play	4.3	3.5
Net Yards Passing	2387	2072
Avg. Per Game	170.5	148.0
Sacked/Yards Lost	26/251	48/419
Gross Yards	2638	2491
Attempts/Completions	351/196	426/200
Pct. of Completions	55.8	46.9
Had Intercepted	20	32
Punts/Average	68/44.4	94/42.6
Punt Returns/Yards	33/242	43/509
Kickoff Returns/Yards	41/1090	59/1431
Penalties/Yards	62/757	39/434
Fumbles/Lost	34/19	25/15
Touchdowns	40	19
Rushing	19	6
Passing	16	10
Returns	5	3
Safeties	0	1

Regular Starters

	Offense		Defense
WR	Frank Pitts	LE	Jerry Mays
LT	**Jim Tyrer**	LT	**Curley Culp**
LG	**Ed Budde**	RT	**Buck Buchanan**
C	E.J. Holub	RE	Aaron Brown
RG	Mo Moorman	LLB	Bobby Bell
RT	Dave Hill	MLB	**Willie Lanier**
TE	Fred Arbanas	RLB	Jim Lynch
WR	Gloster Richardson	LCB	**JimMarsalis**
	Otis Taylor	RCB	Emmitt Thomas
QB	**Len Dawson**	LS	Jim Kearney
	Mike Livingston	RS	Johnny Robinson
RB	Mike Garrett	P	Jerrel Wilson
RB	**Robert Holmes**		
K	**Jan Stenerud**		

AFL ALL-STARS IN Bold

1969 AFL Standings

Western Division

	W	L	T	Pct.
Oakland	12	1	1	.923
Kansas City	11	3	0	.786
San Diego	8	6	0	.571
Denver	5	8	1	.385
Cincinnati	4	9	1	.308

Eastern Division

	W	L	T	Pct.
N.Y. Jets	10	4	0	.714
Houston	6	6	2	.500
Boston	4	10	0	.286
Buffalo	4	10	0	.286
Miami	3	10	1	.231

AFL Divisional Playoffs: OAKLAND 56, Houston 7; Kansas City 13, NEW YORK JETS 6
AFL Championship: Kansas City 17, OAKLAND 7
Super Bowl IV: Kansas City 23, Minnesota 7

Robert Holmes gained 612 yards rushing in 1969. (Kansas Collection, U. of Kansas)

1970 Head Coach: Hank Stram

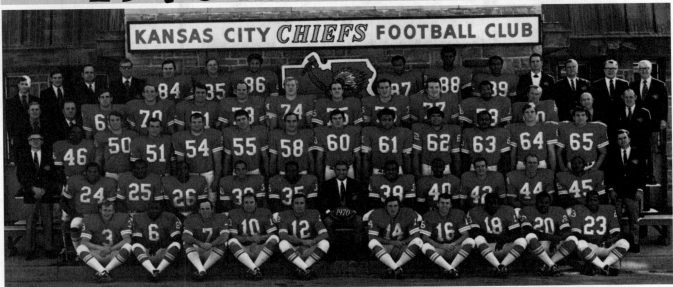

KANSAS CITY *CHIEFS* FOOTBALL CLUB

As the defending Super Bowl champions, the Chiefs were never able to regain the form that led them to the Super Bowl in 1969. The big-play tendencies on offense and defense were absent. Mike Garrett was traded to San Diego, and Ed Podolak took over the main running back duties; for the first time since 1965, the team failed to rush for more than 2,000 yards. Len Dawson threw more interceptions than touchdowns, and Otis Taylor caught just 34 passes to lead the receivers. Only Jan Stenerud had a good year, kicking 30 field goals and scoring 116 points. The defense was almost as good as it had been in previous seasons, but gave up the big play too much; their opponents scored 244 points. A mid-season tie with the Raiders hurt the Chiefs, and when they lost to the Raiders in the next-to-last game of the year, they were eliminated from the playoffs. Nine Chiefs were selected for the Pro Bowl.

Key Dates in 1970:

July 31—As the defending world champions, the Chiefs represent the NFL against the College All-Stars in Chicago and win easily, 24-3.

September 20—Minnesota exacts revenge on the Chiefs and defeats them, 27-10, in the season opener.

September 28—The Chiefs make their first appearance on "*Monday Night Football*" and easily beat the Colts in Baltimore, 44-24.

October 4—Jan Stenerud boots a 55-yard field goal in Denver, but the Chiefs lose, 26-13.

October 15—Mike Garrett is traded to the Chargers for a second-round pick in the 1971 draft. Ed Podolak takes over the starting halfback position.

December 12—The Chiefs are eliminated from the playoffs as they lose to the Raiders in Oakland, 20-6.

December 20—Kansas City loses the final game of the season at San Diego, 31-13, and finishes with a 7-5-2 record.

Big Game of 1970

November 1 at Kansas City
Kansas City 17, Oakland 17

Controversy swirled with the wind at Municipal Stadium, and after 60 minutes of typically rugged, slug-it-out football between Kansas City and Oakland, the Raiders walked away with a stolen 17-17. No loss could have hurt more than this.

With 1:08 left in the game and the Chiefs leading 17-14, Len Dawson ran an unlikely 19-yard bootleg to the Oakland 29 that should have clinched the game. Raider Ben Davidson hit Dawson after the play, drawing an unnecessary roughness penalty. Chiefs receiver Otis Taylor then hit Davidson after play, a protection retaliation. Both benches emptied, and confusion took over. When the flags and players were cleared away, the Raiders were penalized 15 yards and Taylor was ejected from the game. But the Raiders argued that if Taylor was thrown out, the Chiefs should also be penalized. After a long discussion, the refs agreed, refused to give Kansas City the important first down, called it a continuous play penalty, and stipulated the rules say the down must be replayed. The Chiefs contended that if Davidson was guilty of piling on, as he was called for, then the play was already over. The ball was moved back to the original line of scrimmage (actually one yard farther back, the officials messed that up, too), and the Chiefs had to replay the down. They failed to make the first down and punted. Raider quarterback Daryle Lamonica moved his team to the Chiefs' 41, and George Blanda then kicked a 48-yard field with eight seconds left to tie the game.

"I've never been more proud of a 40-man squad," Hank Stram said of his team after the game. "They played with great effort and purpose. It's just a shame they were deprived of an opportunity to win the football game."

"Lenny deserves all the protection we can give him," Taylor said of his assault on Davidson. "He (Davidson) could have hurt Lenny."

The Chiefs had outfought the Raiders throughout the game, and with a win would have moved into first place in the AFC West. The tie, however, moved Oakland into first place and dropped Kansas City to third place.

"It's an emotional game," Stram said. "You fight for your lives. It's team play. And I think it's what wins it for you in the end."

Except for this game.

The Chiefs floundered the rest of the season, and when they lost to the Raiders in the next-to-last-game of the year in Oakland, were officially eliminated from making the playoffs.

Ed Podolak became the Chiefs' main running back after Mike Garrett was dealt to San Diego. (Kansas Collection, U. of Kansas)

Preseason

Record: 4-3

7/31	W	24-3	College All-Stars (Chicago, IL)	69,940
8/8	W	30-17	at Detroit	55,032
8/14	L	3-17	BALTIMORE	38,341
8/22	W	16-13	Cleveland (Memphis, TN)	31,532
8/29	L	17-22	at Atlanta	56,990
9/5	W	13-0	at Dallas	69,055
9/12	L	24-34	at St. Louis	50,661

Regular Season

Record: 7-5-2

9/20	L	10-27	at Minnesota	47,900
9/28	W	44-24	at Baltimore (Mon.) (N)	53,911
10/4	L	13-26	at Denver	50,705
10/11	W	23-10	BOSTON	50,698
10/18	W	27-19	at Cincinnati	57,265
10/25	L	16-27	DALLAS	51,158
11/1	T	17-17	OAKLAND	51,334
11/8	W	24-9	HOUSTON	49,810
11/15	W	31-14	at Pittsburgh	50,081
11/22	T	6-6	ST. LOUIS	50,711
11/29	W	26-14	SAN DIEGO	50,315
12/6	w	16-0	DENVER	50,454
12/12	L	6-20	at Oakland (Sat.)	54,596
12/20	L	13-31	at San Diego	41,379

Individual Statistics

Passing	Att.	Cmp.	Yds.	Pct.	TD	INT	LG	Rating
Dawson	262	141	1876	53.8	13	14	61T	71.3
Livingston	22	11	122	5.0.0	0	1	31	48.1
Podolak	2	2	40	100.0	0	0	24	118.8
Huarte	2	0	0	0.0	0	1	0	0.0
McVea	1	0	0	0.0	0	0	0	39.6

Receiving	No.	Yds.	Avg.	LG	TD
Taylor	34	618	18.2	59t	3
Podolak	26	307	11.8	59t	1
Hayes	26	219	8.3	28	0
Holmes	23	173	7.5	31	1
Pitts	11	172	15.6	54	2
Arbanas	8	108	14.5	26	1
Cannon	7	125	17.8	45	2
Richardson	5	171	34.2	61	2
McVea	5	26	5.2	15	0
Garrett	4	4	1.0	5	0
Stroud	4	86	24.5	50	1
Porter	1	29	29.0	29	0

Rushing	No.	Yds.	Avg.	LG	TD
Podolak	168	749	4.5	65t	3
Hayes	109	381	3.5	22	5
McVea	61	260	4.3	34	0
Holmes	63	206	3.3	22	3
Pitts	5	84	16.8	42	0
Garrett	21	62	3.2	18	0
Dawson	11	46	4.2	21	0
Livingston	3	26	8.7	16	0
Porter	2	21	10.5	21	0
Taylor	3	13	4.3	7	0
Cannon	1	10	10.0	10	0
Richardson	1	4	4.0	4	0

Team Leaders

Scoring: Jan Stenerud — 116 pts: 26 PATs, 30 FGs
INTs: Johnny Robinson — 10-155 yds., 1 TD
Punting: Jerrel Wilson — 76-3415 yds., 44.9 avg., 68 LG
Punt Returns: Ed Podolak — 23-311 yds., 13.5 avg., 0 TDs
Kickoff Returns: Robert Holmes — 19-535 yds., 28.2 avg., 0 TDs

Team Statistics

	Chiefs	Opp.
Total First Downs	183	226
Rushing	83	83
Passing	86	111
Penalty	14	32
Total Net Yards	3577	3667
Avg. Per Game	255.5	261.9
Total Plays	775	861
Avg. Per Play	4.6	4.3
Net Yards Rushing	1858	1657
Avg. Per Game	132.7	118.4
Total Rushes	448	418
Avg. Per Play	4.1	4.0
Net Yards Passing	1719	2010
Avg. Per Game	122.8	143.6
Sacked/Yards Lost	38/319	35/270
Gross Yards	2038	2280
Attempts/Completions	289/154	408/195
Pct. of Completions	53.3	47.8
Had Intercepted	16	31
Punts/Average	76/44.9	77/41.5
Punt Returns/Yards	31/371	51/414
Penalties/Yards	83/888	71/817
Fumbles/Lost	26/15	22/12
Touchdowns	26	26
Rushing	11	10
Passing	13	15
Returns	2	1
Safeties	0	0

Score By Periods	1	2	3	4	Total
Chiefs Total	53	98	46	75	272
Opp. Total	32	77	51	84	244

Regular Starters

	Offense		Defense
WR	Frank Pitts	LE	Jerry Mays
LT	**Jim Tyrer**	LT	**Curley Culp**
LG	**Ed Budde**	RT	**Buck Buchanan**
C	Jack Rudnay	RE	Aaron Brown
	E.J. Holub	LLB	Bobby Bell
RG	Mo Moorman	MLB	**Willie Lanier**
RT	Dave Hill	RLB	Jim Lynch
TE	Fred Arbanas	LCB	Jim Marsalis
	Morris Stroud	RCB	**Emmitt Thomas**
WR	**Otis Taylor**	LS	Jim Kearney
QB	Len Dawson	RS	Johnny Robinson
RB	Mike Garrett	P	**Jerrel Wilson**
	Ed Podolak		
RB	Wendell Hayes		
K	**Jan Stenerud**		

PRO-BOWLERS in Bold

1970 AFC Standings

Western Division

	W	L	T	Pct.
Oakland	8	4	2	.667
Kansas City	7	5	2	.583
San Diego	5	6	3	.455
Denver	5	8	1	.385

Central Division

	W	L	T	Pct.
Cincinnati	8	6	0	.571
Cleveland	7	7	0	.500
Pittsburgh	5	9	0	.357
Houston	3	10	1	.231

Eastern Division

	W	L	T	Pct.
Baltimore	11	2	1	.846
Miami +	10	4	0	.714
N.Y. Jets	4	10	0	.286
Buffalo	3	10	1	.231
Boston	2	12	0	.143

AFC Championship: BALTIMORE 27, Oakland 17
Super Bowl V: Baltimore 16, Dallas 13

In the 1970 game against the Raiders at Municipal Stadium, a late penalty against Otis Taylor nullified what might have been a game winning scramble by Len Dawson.

1. Dawson is tripped up and about to go down.

2. Oakland's Ben Davidson spears Dawson in the back after the Kansas City quarterback was already down.

3. Otis Taylor grabs Davidson

4. —and wrestles him to the ground.

Taylor was called for the penalty, and when the officials ruled the infraction as a continuing play foul, the Chiefs had to run the down over again—failing to make a first down. The Raiders kicked a game-tying field goal in the final seconds of the game. (Otis Taylor)

1971 Head Coach: Hank Stram

The Chiefs returned to championship-caliber play and captured the AFC Western division title. Propelled by the offense—Otis Taylor led the NFL with 1,110 receiving yards and eight touchdowns, Len Dawson threw for 2,504 yards, and the team compiled 1,843 yards rushing—Kansas City snuck past the Raiders for the title. The team's outstanding linebacker trio of Willie Lanier, Bobby Bell, and Jim Lynch led a somewhat aging, but still outstanding defense. Taylor's season was especially spectacular, as he routinely made big receptions, many of the circus variety, to again establish himself as one of the league's best receivers. Ed Podolak was the top rusher. Emmitt Thomas picked off eight passes, and Jerrell Wilson averaged almost 45 yards per punt. In all, 11 Chiefs were selected for the Pro Bowl. Rookie wide receiver Elmo Wright was as popular—he danced a high step in the end zone after scoring touchdowns—as he was good. Hopes for a return to the Super Bowl died on Christmas day, however, when the Miami Dolphins outfought Kansas City in the longest game ever played in the history of the NFL. The playoff loss was especially hard to take, because Jan Stenerud had failed on two different chances to win the game at the end of regulation and in overtime.

Key Dates in 1971:

September 19—The Chiefs start the season with a loss at San Diego, 21-14.

October 18—The Chiefs easily defeat the Steelers on "*Monday Night Football*", 38-16.

October 31—Oakland kicks a late field goal to come from behind and tie Kansas City, 20-20.

December 12—Jan Stenerud kicks a late field goal set up by a Raiders' interference penalty, and the Chiefs' defeat Oakland, 16-14, to clinch the AFC West. It is the Chiefs' first division championship since 1966.

December 25—The Chiefs lose to the Dolphins in the first round of the AFC playoffs in the longest pro football game ever played, 27-24. Miami placekicker Garo Yepremian boots a 37-yard field goal to end the double-overtime marathon after more than 82 minutes of playing time. Kansas City's Ed Podolak accumulated 350 all-purpose yards. Chiefs kicker Jan Stenerud had a tough game, missing a field-goal attempt at the end of regulation that would have won the game, and another that was blocked in overtime. It was the last time the Chiefs played at Municipal Stadium.

Big Game of 1971

October 24 at Kansas City
Kansas City 27, Washington 20

Displaying the heart of a championship team, the Chiefs rallied from a 17-6 halftime deficit to defeat the Washington Redskins. The win was the fifth in a row for Kansas City and kept them tied with the Raiders atop the AFC West. The Redskins were undefeated coming into the game.

"What a great win," Hank Stram said after the game. "What a great, great, great win."

The Chiefs scored three second-half touchdowns to claim the victory, the game-winner on a spectacular, one-handed catch by Otis Taylor from 28 yards out. Redskins defensive back Pat Fischer was all over Taylor on the play.

"It really is tough to come back when you're down by 11 points," Taylor said afterwards. "We didn't do at all what we wanted to do in the first half. In the second half, we went after them with good, straight football."

"I thought it might be intercepted," Len Dawson said of the game-winning touchdown pass. He was knocked down after the throw. "Then I heard the roar of the crowd, and since we were playing in Kansas City, I assumed something good had happened."

The Chiefs' defense held off the Redskins the final 3:59 of the game to secure the win. Ed Podolak also starred, running for 110 yards.

"We didn't do a good job (in the first half), and we were in desperate trouble," Stram continued in his analysis of the game. "But we came back, and we came back because we have 40 great people on this team."

The win catapulted the Chiefs through the rest of their season. They clinched the AFC West on December 12 when they defeated the Raiders at home, 16-14.

Preseason

Record: 4-1-1

8/7	W	10-7	at Baltimore		16,771
8/14	W	12-10	ATLANTA		37,403
8/21	W	27-7	at New Orleans		70,459
8/30	W	21-16	N.Y. JETS		37,650
9/4	T	17-17	ST. LOUIS		36,743
9/11	L	17-24	at Dallas		74,035

Regular Season

Record: 10-3-1

9/19	L	14-21	at San Diego	54,061
9/26	W	20-16	at Houston	46,498
10/3	W	16-3	at Denver	51,200
10/10	W	31-10	SAN DIEGO	50,514
10/18	W	38-16	PITTSBURGH (Mon.) (N)	49,533
10/24	W	27-20	WASHINGTON	51,989
10/31	T	20-20	at Oakland	54,715
11/7	L	10-13	at N.Y. Jets	62,812
11/14	W	13-7	CLEVELAND	50,388
11/21	W	28-10	DENVER	49,945
11/25	L	21-32	at Detroit (Thur.) (Thanksgiving)	54,418
12/6	W	26-17	at San Francisco (Mon.) (N)	45,306
12/12	W	16-14	OAKLAND	51,215
12/19	W	22-9	BUFFALO	48,121

Individual Statistics

Passing

	Att.	Cmp.	Yds.	Pct.	TD	INT	LG	Rating
Dawson	301	167	2504	55.2	15	13	82	81.8
Livingston	28	12	130	42.9	0	0	36	57.2
Huarte	6	2	18	33.3	0	0	26	42.3
Podolak	2	2	42	100.0	0	0	23	118.8
Chiefs Totals	337	183	2694	54.3	15	13	82	74.9
Opp. Total	418	209	2703	50.0	11	27	53	83.8

Receiving

	No.	Yds.	Avg.	LG	TD
Taylor	57	1110	19.5	82	7
Podolak	36	306	8.5	23	0
Wright	26	524	20.3	69t	3
Stroud	22	454	20.6	54	1
Hayes	16	163	10.2	26t	1
Otis	12	74	6.2	26	2
McVea	5	-3	-0.6	10	0
Homan	3	47	9.0	9	0
Frazier	2	41	20.5	23	0
Holmes	2	16	8.0	12	0
Smith	1	12	12.0	12	0
Adamle	1	6	6.0	6t	1
Chiefs Totals	183	2694	14.7	82	15
Opp. Totals	209	2703	12.9	53	11

Rushing

	No.	Yds.	Avg.	LG	TD
Podolak	184	708	3.8	25	9
Hayes	132	541	4.1	27	1
McVea	68	286	4.2	19	3
Otis	49	184	3.8	11	0
Adamle	13	43	3.3	3	0
Taylor	1	25	25.0	25t	1
Dawson	12	24	2.0	8	0
Holmes	21	35	1.7	6	0
Livingston	5	11	2.2	3	0
Frazier	1	-2	-2.0	-2	0
Wright	1	-10	-10.0	-10	0
Chiefs Totals	487	1843	3.8	27	14
Opp. Totals	367	1337	3.7	28	6

Team Statistics

	Chiefs	Opp.
Total First Downs	240	223
Rushing	108	73
Passing	119	125
Penalty	13	25
Total Net Yards	4190	3770
Avg. Per Game	29.3	269.3
Total Plays	836	813
Avg. Per Play	5.0	4.6
Net Yards Rushing	1843	1337
Avg. Per Game	131.6	95.5
Total Rushes	462	367
Avg. Per Play	4.0	3.7
Net Yards Passing	2347	2506
Avg. Per Game	167.6	179.0
Sacked/Yards Lost	35/347	28/235
Gross Yards	2694	2741
Attempts/Completions	337/183	406/209
Pct. of Completions	54.3	51.5
Had Intercepted	13	27
Punts/Average	64/44.3	67/39.3
Punt Returns/Yards	32/150	38/286
Penalties/Yards	72/734	72/752
Fumbles/Lost	23/13	16/7
Touchdowns	32	21
Rushing	14	9
Passing	15	11
Returns	3	1
Safeties	0	1

Score By Periods	1	2	3	4	Total
Chiefs Total	61	124	48	70	302
Opp. Total	41	71	22	74	208

Regular Starters

	Offense		Defense
WR	Elmo Wright	LE	Marvin Upshaw
LT	**Jim Tyrer**	LT	**Curley Culp**
LG	**Ed Budde**	RT	**Buck Buchanan**
C	Jack Rudnay	RE	Aaron Brown
RG	Mo Moorman	LLB	**Bobby Bell**
RT	Dave Hill	MLB	**Willie Lanier**
TE	Morris Stroud	RLB	Jim Lynch
WR	**Otis Taylor**	LCB	Jim Marsalis
QB	**Len Dawson**	RCB	**Emmitt Thomas**
RB	Ed Podolak	LS	Jim Kearney
RB	Wendell Hayes	RS	Johnny Robinson
K	**Jan Stenerud**	P	**Jerrel Wilson**

PRO-BOWLERS in Bold

Team Leaders

Scoring: Jan Stenerud — 110 pts: 32 PATs, 26 FGs
INTs: Emmitt Thomas — 8-145 yds., 1 TD
Punting: Jerrel Wilson — 64-2865 yds., 44.8 avg., 68 LG
Punt Returns: Ed Podolak — 13-84 yds., 6.5 avg., 0 TDs
Kickoff Returns: Kerry Reardon — 12-308 yds., 25.7 avg., 0 TDs

1971 AFC Standings

Western Division

	W	L	T	Pct.
Kansas City	10	3	1	.769
Oakland	8	4	2	.667
San Diego	6	8	0	.429
Denver	4	9	1	.308

Central Division

	W	L	T	Pct.
Cleveland	9	5	0	.643
Pittsburgh	6	8	0	.429
Houston	4	9	1	.308
Cincinnati	4	10	0	.286

Eastern Division

	W	L	T	Pct.
Miami	10	3	1	.769
Baltimore +	10	4	0	.714
New England	6	8	0	.429
N.Y. Jets	6	8	0	.429
Buffalo	1	13	0	.071

AFC Championship: MIAMI 21, Baltimore 0
Super Bowl VI: Dallas 24, Miami 3

Chief's rookie Elmo Wright made a big splash in Kansas City and around the league with his high-stepping dance after he scored touchdowns. (Kansas Collection, U. of Kansas)

This improbable catch by Otis Taylor against the Redskins gave the Chiefs a 27-20 win at Municipal Stadium. (Otis Taylor)

1972 Head Coach: Hank Stram

The Chiefs opened a new era and a new stadium at the start of the season. After playing in Municipal Stadium since moving to Kansas City in 1963, the Chiefs moved into Arrowhead Stadium, the much-anticipated showcase football palace. In addition to the new stadium, owner Lamar Hunt was inducted into the Pro Football Hall of Fame in July. If only the team's play on the field could have matched the modern convenience of Arrowhead and the honor bestowed upon Hunt. The Chiefs won just three games at their new stadium, as age and poor draft selections began to eat away at the power of the team. Len Dawson was finally slowing down, the offensive line was old, and safety Johnny Robinson had retired. The result was a season of more downs than ups for the Chiefs, despite the fact they finished with an 8-6 record. Otis Taylor, Jerrell Wilson, Emmitt Thomas, Bobby Bell, and Willie Lanier were selected for the Pro Bowl, but it was evident at season's end that the Chiefs' powerhouse team of the past six seasons had dropped from the rank of challengers for the league title.

Key Dates in 1972:

July 29—Lamar Hunt is inducted into the Pro Football Hall of Fame in Canton, Ohio.

August 12—Arrowhead Stadium is dedicated in a preseason game against the St. Louis Cardinals. The Chiefs win the game, 24-14.

September 17—In the first regular-season game played at Arrowhead, the Chiefs lose to Miami, 20-10.

November 5—82,094 fans cram into Arrowhead Stadium and watch the Chiefs defeat the Raiders, 27-14, the team's first win at the new stadium. It is still the largest home crowd ever in Chiefs history.

December 17—The Chiefs beat the Falcons in Atlanta, 17-14, finishing the season at 8-6 and in second place in the AFC West.

Big Game of 1972

October 22 at Kansas City
Philadelphia 21, Kansas City 20

This was surely one of the most embarassing losses ever suffered by the Kansas City Chiefs. Facing a winless Philadelphia Eagles team in the rain-soaked gloom of Arrowhead Stadium, the Chiefs somehow walked off the field as 21-20 losers, still winless in their new stadium.

"There were crazy things things happening," Hank Stram said after the game. "Bizarre plays."

The Eagles scored their first touchdown when cornerback Jim Marsalis and safety Mike Sensibaugh batted the ball away from Eagle receiver Po James, only to have it strike Sensibaugh's leg and bound into the arms of Eagle receiver Ben Hawkins. He scored easily, and before the Chiefs could get their offense moving, they found themselves trailing, 21-0.

The Chiefs rallied, scoring the final 20 points of the game, but it wasn't enough.

"We had to have a couple of big plays," Stram lamented. "We didn't get them."

The loss dropped the Chiefs' record to 3-3, putting them in chase mode for the division title. Maybe Willie Lanier, Kansas City's Pro Bowl linebacker, summed up the loss best.

"It's disgusting," he said.

Otis Taylor had another Pro Bowl season in 1972, catching 57 passes for 821 yards and six touchdowns. (Kansas Collection, U. of Kansas)

Preseason   Record: 5-2

7/29	W	23-17	N.Y. Giants (Canton, OH)	19,304
8/5	W	24-10	Chicago (Notre Dame, IN)	32,391
8/12	W	24-14	ST. LOUIS	78,190
8/21	L	17-23	BALTIMORE	76,882
8/27	W	19-13	L.A. RAMS	77,764
9/2	W	20-10	DALLAS	79,592
9/9	L	0-20	at Green Bay (Milwaukee, WI)	47,281

Regular Season   Record: 8-6

9/17	L	10-20	MIAMI	79,829
9/25	W	20-17	at New Orleans (Mon.) (N)	70,793
10/1	W	45-24	at Denver	51,656
10/8	W	31-7	at Cleveland	83,819
10/15	L	16-23	CINCINNATI	79,068
10/22	L	20-21	PHILADELPHIA	78,389
1029	W	26-14	at San Diego	54,533
11/5	W	27-14	OAKLAND	82,094
11/12	L	7-16	at Pittsburgh	50,350
11/19	L	17-27	SAN DIEGO	79,011
11/26	L	3-26	at Oakland	54,801
12/3	W	24-21	DENVER	66,725
12/10	W	24-10	BALTIMORE	44,175
12/17	W	17-14	at Atlanta	58,850

Individual Statistics

Passing

	Att.	Cmp.	Yds.	Pct.	TD	INT	LG	Rating
Dawson	305	175	1835	57.4	13	12	44	73.1
Livingston	78	41	480	52.6	7	8	36	62.0
Wilson	1	1	20	100.0	0	0	20	118.8
Chiefs Totals	384	217	2335	56.5	20	20	44	70.2
Opp. Total	368	186	2483	50.5	17	24	67t	60.6

Receiving

	No.	Yds.	Avg.	LG	TD
Taylor	57	821	14.4	44	6
Podolak	46	345	7.5	27t	2
Hayes	31	295	9.5	29t	3
Adamle	15	76	5.1	11	0
Frazier	13	172	13.2	35	5
Homan	12	135	11.3	38	1
Otis	12	76	6.3	13	0
Wright	11	81	7.4	14	0
West	9	165	18.3	42t	2
Stroud	4	80	20.0	44	1
Kinney	4	45	11.2	19	0
Jankowski	2	24	12.0	18	0
Allen	1	20	20.0	20	0
Chiefs Totals	217	2335	10.8	44	20
Opp. Totals	186	2483	13.3	67t	17

Rushing

	No.	Yds.	Avg.	LG	TD
Podolak	171	615	3.6	30	4
Hayes	128	536	4.2	28	0
Adamle	73	536	4.2	19	1
Livingston	14	133	9.5	51	0
Kinney	38	122	3.2	16	1
Otis	29	92	3.2	12	0
Dawson	15	75	5.0	20	0
Wright	1	24	24.0	24	0
Taylor	5	13	2.6	11	0
West	2	2	1.0	10	0
Chiefs Totals	476	1915	4.0	51	6
Opp. Totals	453	1805	4.0	45	12

Team Statistics

	Chiefs	Opp.
Total First Downs	245	227
Rushing	121	90
Passing	116	116
Penalty	11	18
Total Net Yards	3956	4027
Avg. Per Game	282.6	287.6
Total Plays	894	853
Avg. Per Play	4.4	4.7
Net Yards Rushing	1915	1805
Avg. Per Game	136.8	128.9
Total Rushes	476	453
Avg. Per Play	4.0	4.0
*Net Yards Passing	2041	2222
Avg. Per Game	145.8	158.7
Sacked/Yards Lost	34/297	32/261
Gross Yards	2335	2483
Attempts/Completions	384/217	368/186
Pct. of Completions	56.5	50.5
Had Intercepted	20	24
Punts/Average	66/44.8	61/40.4
Punt Returns/Yards	29/126	40/296
Penalties/Yards	69/653	66/643
Fumbles/Lost	23/12	35/19
Touchdowns	32	30
Rushing	6	12
Passing	20	17
Returns	6	1
Safeties	0	0

Score By Periods	1	2	3	4	Total
Chiefs Total	20	90	85	92	287
Opp. Total	55	98	37	64	254

Regular Starters

	Offense		Defense
WR	Dennis Homan	LE	Marvin Upshaw
	Robert West	LT	Curley Culp
LT	Jim Tyrer	RT	Buck Buchanan
LG	Ed Budde	RE	Wilbur Young
C	Jack Rudnay	LLB	**Bobby Bell**
RG	Mo Moorman	MLB	**Willie Lanier**
RT	Dave Hill	RLB	Jim Lynch
TE	Morris Stroud	LCB	Jim Marsalis
	Willie Frazier	RCB	**Emmitt Thomas**
WR	**Otis Taylor**	LS	Jim Kearney
QB	Len Dawson	RS	Mike Sensibaugh
RB	Ed Podolak	P	**Jerrel Wilson**
RB	Wendell Hayes		
K	Jan Stenerud		

PRO-BOWLERS in Bold

Team Leaders

Scoring: Jan Stenerud	95 pts: 32 PATs, 21 FGs
INTs: Mike Sensibaugh	8-65 yds., 0 TDs
Punting: Jerrel Wilson	66-2960 yds., 44.8 avg., 69 LG
Punt Returns: Larry Marshall	18-103 yds., 5.7 avg., 0 TDs
Kickoff Returns: Larry Marshall	23-651 yds., 28.3 avg., 0 TDs

1972 AFC Standings

Western Division

	W	L	T	Pct.
Oakland	10	3	1	.750
Kansas City	8	6	0	.571
Denver	5	9	0	.357
San Diego	4	9	1	.321

Central Division

	W	L	T	Pct.
Pittsburgh	11	3	0	.786
Cleveland	10	4	0	.714
Cincinnati	8	6	0	.571
Houston	1	13	0	.071

Eastern Division

	W	L	T	Pct.
Miami	14	0	0	1.00
N.Y. Jets	7	7	0	.500
Baltimore	5	9	0	.357
Buffalo	4	9	1	.321
New England	3	11	0	.214

AFC Championship: Miami 21, PITTSBURGH 17
Super Bowl VII: Miami 14, Washington 7

Hank Stram couldn't shake his team's overall mediocrity throughout the 1972 season. The Chiefs finished with a disappointing 8-6 record. (Kansas Collection, U. of Kansas)

1973 Head Coach: Hank Stram

As the Chiefs' primary quarterback in 1973, Mike Livingston passed for 916 yards and six touchdowns. (Kansas Collection, U. of Kansas)

Slowed by age and injuries, the Chiefs made a push for the playoffs—they were actually in first place in late November—but a late season loss to the Broncos and a humiliating 37-7 beating from the Raiders ended any chance Kansas City had to play in the postseason. Len Dawson was hobbled by injuries throughout the season, and after experimenting with Pete Beathard at quarterback, Stram went back to Mike Livingston, the perennial backup. The Chiefs' quarterbacks threw just ten touchdown passes for the entire season, but the running game, led by Ed Podolak and Willie Ellison, made up for the passing deficiency. Willie Lanier again led the defense—he was joined in the Pro Bowl by Jerrell Wilson and Jack Rudnay—but it was obvious at season's end that most of the Chiefs' best seasons were behind them. Kansas City finished third in the AFC West with a 7-5-2 record

Key Dates in 1973:

September 16—The Chiefs lose their season opener for the fourth straight year, falling 23-13 to the Rams at Arrowhead.

November 18—The Chiefs defeat the Oilers at home, 38-14, improving their record to 6-3-1.

December 16—Kansas City handily beats the Chargers, 33-6, at Arrowhead, but it's too late. The Chiefs finish the season with a 7-5-2 mark, tied for second in the division.

January 20, 1974—The Chiefs and Arrowhead Stadium play host to the Pro Bowl. The AFC wins, 15-13 as Miami's Garo Yepremian boots five field goals for the winners.

Big Game of 1973

December 8 at Oakland
Oakland 37, Kansas City 7

It was supposed to be a battle for the AFC West, but while the Raiders came heavily armed, the Chiefs came without weapons. The result was a staggering, brutal beating.

"It's the worst athletic defeat I've ever suffered," Chiefs' running back Ed Podolak said after the game. How bad was it? The Chiefs gained a paltry 24 yards rushing, compared to the Raiders' 259. And that was the story of the game. When Podolak fumbled early in the first quarter, Oakland took command and left no prisoners. It was 20-0 at the half, and the Chiefs were never in the game.

"We just beat 'em up front," Raiders running back Pete Banaszak said after the game. "We dominated 'em."

The Raiders tallied 24 first downs, the Chiefs had eight. Oakland ran an incredible 83 offensive plays, the Chiefs just 36.

"It's pretty hard to describe," Hank Stram said of the lopsided loss. "It's just an unbelievable feeling, and you can't understand how anything like this could happen to you."

The loss eliminated Kansas City from the playoffs and left their record at 6-5-2. The team ended the season with a 33-7 win over San Diego the following week.

Preseason

Record: 2-4

Date		Score	Opponent	Attendance
8/4	W	12-6	NEW ORLEANS	67,216
8/13	L	16-17	DETROIT	67,624
8/18	L	10-13	MINNESOTA	72,676
8/26	L	16-21	GREEN BAY	75,231
9/1	L	16-27	at Dallas	57,468
9/7	W	16-7	at St. Louis	49,486

Regular Season

Record: 7-5-2

Date		Score	Opponent	Attendance
9/16	L	13-23	L.A. RAMS	62,315
9/23	W	10-7	at New England	57,918
9/30	W	16-3	OAKLAND	72,631
10/7	W	16-14	DENVER	71,414
10/14	T	10-10	at Green Bay (Milwaukee, WI)	47,265
10/21	L	6-14	at Cincinnati	56,397
10/29	L	14-23	at Buffalo (Mon.) (N)	76,071
11/4	W	19-0	at San Diego	52,035
11/12	W	19-7	CHICAGO (Mon.)	70,664
11/18	W	38-14	HOUSTON	68,444
11/25	L	10-14	at Denver	51,706
12/2	T	20-20	CLEVELAND	70,296
12/8	L	7-37	at Oakland (Sat.)	53,061
12/16	W	33-6	SAN DIEGO	43,755

Individual Statistics

Passing

	Att.	Cmp.	Yds.	Pct.	TD	INT	LG	Rating
Livingston	145	75	916	51.7	6	7	48	65.2
Dawson	101	66	725	65.3	2	5	48	72.3
Beathard	64	31	389	48.4	2	1	44	71.4
Wilson	1	1	9	100.0	0	0	9	104.2
Podolak	1	0	0	0	0	0	0	39.6
Keyes	1	0	0	0	0	0	0	39.6
Chiefs Totals	313	173	2039	55.2	10	13	48	68.5
Opp. Total	324	157	1942	48.5	11	21	62t	47.7

Receiving

	No.	Yds.	Avg.	LG	TD
Podolak	55	445	8.1	25	0
Taylor	34	536	15.8	46	4
Hayes	18	134	7.4	13	0
Wright	16	252	15.8	44	2
Stroud	12	216	18.0	48	2
Kinney	11	126	11.5	25	0
Ellison	9	64	7.1	17	0
Butler	8	124	15.5	23	2
West	4	65	16.3	23	0
Hamilton	2	35	17.5	20	0
Smith	2	20	10.0	17	0
Moorman	1	-1	-1.0	-1	0
Keyes	1	-6	-6	-6	0
Chiefs Totals	173	2039	11.8	48	10
Opp. Totals	157	1942	12.4	62t	11

Rushing

	No.	Yds.	Avg.	LG	TD
Podolak	210	721	3.4	25	3
Ellison	108	411	3.8	19	2
Hayes	95	352	3.7	27	2
Kinney	50	128	2.6	8	1
Livingston	19	94	4.9	28	2
Dawson	6	39	6.5	13	0
Wright	5	29	5.8	13	0
Beathard	6	16	2.7	11	1
Butler	2	10	5.0	9	0
Taylor	4	-14	-1.1	-19	0
McVea	4	5	1.3	2	0
Keyes	2	1	0.5	2	0
Chiefs Totals	511	1793	3.5	28	11
Opp. Totals	493	1956	4.0	72	11

Team Statistics

	Chiefs	Opp.
Total First Downs	208	209
Rushing	106	90
Passing	93	95
Penalty	9	24
3RD Down: Made/Att.	72/204	69/206
3rd Down Pct.	35.3	33.5
Total Net Yards	3536	3575
Avg. Per Game	252.6	255.4
Total Plays	863	856
Avg. Per Play	4.1	4.2
Net Yards Rushing	1793	1956
Avg. Per Game	128.1	139.7
Total Rushes	511	493
Avg. Per Play	3.5	4.0
Net Yards Passing	1743	1619
Avg. Per Game	124.5	115.6
Sacked/Yards Lost	39/296	38/323
Gross Yards	2039	1942
Attempts/Completions	313/173	324/157
Pct. of Completions	55.3	48.6
Had Intercepted	13	21
Punts/Average	80/45.5	87/41.4
Penalties/Yards	83/797	63/649
Fumbles/Lost	36/18	33/18
Touchdowns	23	22
Rushing	11	11
Passing	10	11
Returns	2	0
Safeties	0	0

Score By Periods	1	2	3	4	Total
Chiefs Total	40	57	53	81	231
Opp. Total	30	71	35	56	192

Regular Starters

	Offense		Defense
WR	Elmo Wright	LE	Marvin Upshaw
LT	Jim Tyrer	LT	Curley Culp
LG	Ed Budde	RT	Buck Buchanan
C	**Jack Rudnay**	RE	Wilbur Young
RG	Mo Moorman	LLB	Bobby Bell
RT	Francis Peay	MLB	**Willie Lanier**
	Dave Hill	RLB	Jim Lynch
TE	Morris Stroud	LCB	Nate Allen
WR	Otis Taylor	RCB	Emmitt Thomas
QB	Mike Livingston	LS	Jim Kearney
	Len Dawson	RS	Mike Sensibaugh
RB	Ed Podolak	P	**Jerrel Wilson**
RB	Wendell Hayes		
	Willie Ellison		
K	Jan Stenerud		

PRO-BOWLERS in Bold

Team Leaders

Scoring: Jan Stenerud   93 pts: 21 PATs, 24 FGs
INTs: Emmitt Thomas,   Tied with 3
    Mike Sensibaugh, Willie Lanier,
    Jim Kearney
Punting: Jerrel Wilson   280-3942 yds., 45.5 avg., 68 LG
Punt Returns: Larry Marshall   29-180 yds., 6.2 avg., 0 TDs
Kickoff Returns: Larry Marshall   14-391 yds., 27.9 avg., 0 TDs

1973 AFC Standings

Western Division

	W	L	T	Pct.
Oakland	9	4	1	.679
Denver	7	5	2	.571
Kansas City	7	5	2	.571
San Diego	2	11	1	.179

Central Division

	W	L	T	Pct.
Cincinnati	10	4	0	.714
Pittsburgh +	10	4	0	.714
Cleveland	7	5	2	.571
Houston	1	13	0	.071

Eastern Division

	W	L	T	Pct.
Miami	12	2	0	.857
Buffalo	9	5	0	.643
New England	5	9	0	.357
Baltimore	4	10	0	.286
N.Y. Jets	4	10	0	.286

AFC Championship: MIAMI 27, Oakland 10
Super Bowl VIII: Miami 24, Minnesota 7

Jerrel Wilson enjoyed another Pro Bowl season as the Chiefs' punter in 1973. (Kansas Collection, U. of Kansas)

1974 Head Coach: Hank Stram

With 43 interceptions, Ed Podolak was the top receiver for the Chiefs in 1974. (Kansas Collection, U. of Kansas)

Age finally slammed the door on the Chiefs, and for the first time since 1963, Kansas City finished the season with a losing record. The poor showing by the team was the cumulative result of aging veterans, poor draft choices, and the inability to regenerate talent. Injuries also hurt the team, but the fact was that the Chiefs' days as a power in the AFC West were gone. Rookie running back Woody Green made a nice splash with 509 yards rushing, but Len Dawson threw just seven touchdown passes, and the defense allowed 60 more points than the offense scored. It was a dismal season. Willie Lanier and Emmitt Thomas were again the stars of the team, and Jack Rudnay was chosen for his second Pro Bowl. The losing season prompted Lamar Hunt to fire Hank Stram, the only head coach the Chiefs had ever had, after the season was completed. Kansas City finished with a 5-9 record.

Key Dates in 1974:

September 15—Kansas City opens the season with a win over the Jets, 24-16, at Arrowhead.

October 20—The Chiefs lose a heartbreaker to Miami, 9-3.

December 14—The Vikings easily defeat the Chiefs in Minnesota, 35-15. Kansas City ends the season with a disappointing 5-9 record.

December 27—Hank Stram is fired.

Big Game of 1974

December 1 at St. Louis
Kansas City 17, St. Louis 13

Somebody forgot to tell the Chiefs this wasn't their game to win, and somebody forgot to tell the St. Louis Cardinals they would actually have to play the game in order to win. Fighting wind and snow, the Chiefs held off a late Cardinals rally and upset their cross-state rival, 17-13. It was a big win in an otherwise disappointing season for Kansas City, and despite the loss, the Cardinals still clinched a playoff berth.

The big star for the Chiefs was Cleophus Miller, subbing for the injured Woody Green. Miller ran for 95 yards on 15 carries. Jeff Kinney scored on a four-yard touchdown pass, and Wendell Hayes earned six points on one-yard run. The Chiefs' much-maligned defense played brilliantly throughout the game, and held off the Cardinals' last-ditch attempt to win in their final drive of the game.

"We were using more slot and double-wing formations," Hank Stram said of the Chiefs' offensive success as he clutched the Governor's Cup. "The other thing is that we were provided with good field position and scored both times."

"We were in a zone defense most of the day," Mike Sensibaugh said of the Chiefs' effective pass coverage against the Cardinals. "(Jim) Hart (the Cardinals' quarterback) was trying to keep us in a zone all day."

The win improved the Chiefs record to 5-7, and was last game the Chiefs won with Hank Stram as the head coach of the Chiefs. Kansas City finished the season with losses to Oakland and Minnesota.

Preseason
Record: 3-3

8/5	W	20-12	DETROIT	35,521
8/12	L	21-35	BUFFALO	39,248
8/17	L	16-58	at L.A. Rams	48,828
8/24	W	26-7	SAN FRANCISCO	46,548
8/31	L	16-25	at Dallas	43,492
9/6	W	21-16	ST. LOUIS	46,067

Regular Season
Record: 5-9

9/15	W	24-16	N.Y. JETS	74,854
9/22	L	7-27	at Oakland	48,108
9/29	W	17-7	at Houston	28,538
10/6	L	14-17	DENVER	67,298
10/13	L	24-34	PITTSBURGH	65,517
10/20	L	3-9	at Miami	67,779
10/27	W	24-14	at San Diego	34,371
11/3	L	27-33	N.Y. GIANTS	61,437
11/10	L	7-14	SAN DIEGO	48,551
11/18	W	42-34	at Denver (Mon.) (N)	50,236
11/24	L	6-33	at Cincinnati	49,777
12/1	W	17-13	at St. Louis	41,863
12/8	L	6-7	OAKLAND	60,577
12/14	L	15-35	MINNESOTA (Sat.)	35,480

Individual Statistics

Passing

	Att.	Cmp.	Yds.	Pct.	TD	INT	LG	Rating
Dawson	235	138	1573	58.7	7	13	84t	66.0
Livingston	141	66	732	46.8	4	10	48	42.5
Carlson	15	7	1116	46.7	0	1	34	45.3
Jaynes	2	0	0	0.0	0	1	0	0.0
Wilson	2	0	0	0.0	0	0	0	39.6
Chiefs Totals	395	211	2421	53.4	11	25	84t	55.2
Opp. Total	408	206	2838	50.5	22	28	—	50.0

Receiving

	No.	Yds.	Avg.	LG	TD
Podolak	43	306	7.1	26	1
Pearson	27	387	14.3	48	1
Green	26	247	9.5	69t	1
Taylor	24	375	15.6	64	2
Brunson	22	374	17.0	84t	2
Kinney	18	105	5.8	16	1
Miller	14	149	10.6	34	0
Wright	13	209	16.1	51	1
Stroud	12	141	11.8	25	2
Ellison	5	64	12.8	26	0
Hayes	3	23	7.7	9	0
Hamilton	2	25	12.5	19	0
Strada	1	16	16.0	16	0
Chiefs Totals	211	2421	11.5	84t	11
Opp. Totals	206	2838	13.8	71t	22

Rushing

	No.	Yds.	Avg.	LG	TD
Green	135	509	3.8	43	3
Podolak	101	386	3.8	14	2
Kinney	63	249	4.0	21	0
Hayes	57	206	3.6	19	2
Miller	40	184	4.6	47	0
Ellison	37	114	3.1	11	2
Dawson	11	28	2.5	10	0
Livingston	9	28	3.1	9	0
Wright	3	26	8.7	12t	1
Carlson	2	17	8.5	11	0
Taylor	1	6	6.0	6	0
Pearson	1	0	0.0	0	0
Jaynes	1	0	0.0	0	0
Thomas	3	-4	-1.3	0	0
Brunson	5	-29	-5.8	4	0
Chiefs Totals	469	1720	3.67	47	10
Opp. Totals	502	1801	3.59	53	16

Team Statistics

	Chiefs	Opp.
Total First Downs	224	267
Rushing	92	107
Passing	113	141
Penalty	19	19
3rd Down: Made Att.	67/197	72/200
3rd Down Pct.	34.0	36.0
Total Net Yards	3828	4464
Avg. Per Game	273.4	318.9
Total Plays	901	936
Avg. Per Play	4.3	4.8
Net Yards Rushing	1720	1801
Avg. Per Game	122.9	128.6
Total Rushes	3.7	3.6
Avg. Per Play	469	502
Net Yards Passing	2108	2663
Avg. Per Game	150.6	190.2
Sacked/Yards Lost	37/313	26/175
Gross Yards	2421	2838
Attempts/Completions	395/211	408/20
Pct. of Completions	53.4	50.5
Had Intercepted	25	28
Punts/Average	83/41.7	80/40.1
Penalties/Yards	70/515	83/811
Fumbles/Lost	29/13	34/16
Touchdowns	26	40
Rushing	10	16
Passing	11	22
Returns	5	2
Safeties	1	1

Score By Periods	1	2	3	4	OT	Total
Chiefs Total	30	73	53	77	0	233
Opp. Total	57	110	34	92	0	293

Regular Starters

Offense		Defense	
WR	Elmo Wright	LE	Marvin Upshaw
LT	Charlie Getty	LT	Tom Keating
LG	Ed Budde	RT	Buck Buchanan
C	**Jack Rudnay**	RE	Wilbur Young
RG	George Daney	LLB	Bobby Bell
RT	Jim Nicholson	MLB	**Willie Lanier**
TE	Morris Stroud	RLB	Jim Lynch
WR	Otis Taylor	LCB	Nate Allen
QB	Mike Livingston	RCB	**Emmitt Thomas**
	Len Dawson	LS	Jim Kearney
RB	Ed Podolak	RS	Mike Sensibaugh
RB	Woody Green	P	Jerrel Wilson
	Wendell Hayes		
K	Jan Stenerud		

PRO-BOWLERS in Bold

Team Leaders

Scoring: Jan Stenerud	75 pts: 24 PATs, 17 FGs
INTs: Emmitt Thomas	12-214 yds., 2 TDs
Sacks: Marvin Upshaw	9.5 (-49.0 yds.)
Punting: Jerrel Wilson	83-3462 yds., 41.7 avg., 64 LG
Punt Returns: Ed Podolak	15-134 yds., 8.9 avg., 0 TDs
Kickoff Returns: Bill Thomas	25-571 yds., 22.8 avg., 0 TDs

1974 AFC Standings

Western Division

	W	L	T	Pct.
Oakland	12	2	0	.857
Denver	7	6	1	.536
Kansas City	5	9	0	.357
San Diego	5	9	0	.357

Central Division

	W	L	T	Pct.
Pittsburgh	10	3	1	.750
Cincinnati	7	7	0	.500
Houston	7	7	0	.500
Cleveland	4	10	0	.286

Eastern Division

	W	L	T	Pct.
Miami	11	3	0	.786
Buffalo	9	5	0	.643
New England	7	7	0	.500
N.Y. Jets	7	7	0	.500
Baltimore	2	12	0	.143

AFC Championship: Pittsburgh 24, OAKLAND 13
Super Bowl IX: Pittsburgh 16, Minnesota 6

Hank Stram, the Chiefs' all-time greatest coach and Len Dawson, the club's best-ever quarterback, teamed up one last season in 1974. Stram was fired after the season ended. Dawson retired following the 1975 season. (Kansas Collection, U. of Kansas)

1975 Head Coach: Paul Wiggin

A new era started in Kansas City, and for the first time in the franchise's history, someone other than Hank Stram served as the Chiefs' head coach. Paul Wiggen took over the coaching duties in January. Unfortunately for Wiggen, the cupboard had been left relatively bare by Stram, and with a shortage of talented players, the Chiefs suffered through another losing season and once again finished with a 5-9 record. Kansas City did struggle for respectability midway through the season, and at one time held a 5-5 record. Victories over the Raiders and Cowboys were the highlights of the

Key Dates in 1975:

January 23—Paul Wiggin is named as the Chiefs' new head coach.

September 21—The Chiefs lose a close contest in the season opener at Denver, 37-33.

October 12—Paul Wiggin's first victory as the Chiefs' head coach is a rout. The Chiefs humble the Raiders at Arrowhead, 42-10.

November 10—Kansas City upsets the Cowboys on *Monday Night Football*, 34-31.

December 7—Len Dawson's season—and career—ends when he fractures his right thumb. Playing in his last game ever for Kansas City, Dawson can't help his team, and the Chiefs lose to the Chargers at Arrowhead, 28-20.

December 21—Oakland beats the Chiefs, 28-20, in the final game of the season. Kansas City finishes the year with a 5-9 record.

Big Game of 1975

October 12 at Kansas City

Kansas City 42, Oakland 10

The Chiefs were 0-3, hobbled by injuries, and who was in town? The Raiders, who seemed primed to send the Chiefs to the football boneyard and nail shut the coffin. But a funny thing happened to the Raiders once they arrived at Arrowhead Stadium. Kansas City had found some of its greatness of the past, and when the final gun sounded, they had delivered a major whipping to the Raiders, handing the Bay Bandits their worst loss in 15 years. The win was the first-ever for Chiefs coach Paul Wiggin.

"I don't drink champagne, but I'm going to have some tonight," a smiling Wiggin said after the game. "Where do you get it, at the grocery store?"

While the Raiders scored the first three points of the game, Kansas City scored the next 42, cashing in on turnovers and making big plays throughout the rout. Mike Livingston hit Walter White with a 48-yard bomb for the Chiefs' first touchdown, and interceptions by Kerry Reardon and Emmitt Thomas set up the next two scores, to make it 21-3, Kansas City. The Raiders also lost three fumbles and another interception in the lopsided game.

"The turnovers were in such a way it helped them along," said Raiders coach John Madden. "We couldn't get back control of the game."

Before the game, many of the Chiefs' players were questioning their ability and the quality of the team.

"I felt it was a do-or-die thing," Livingston said of his feelings before the game. "We were getting in such a rut. ...I think some of the guys felt like we weren't supposed to win."

Woody Green rushed for 101 yards and Livingston passed for 170. And the defense came away with six turnovers, obviously the biggest contribution to the win.

"It was a combination today of offense and defense, and I think that's what was missing," Wiggin said. "I was confident going into the game that at least I'd walk off the field feeling proud."

When he did leave the field, the Chiefs were big winners, and he raised a clenched fist, celebrating the big victory.

Kansas City won four of its next six games, but when they lost the rematch with the Raiders in the final game of the year, their record stood at 5-9.

Preseason   Record: 3-3

8/9	L	3-10	ST. LOUIS	40,081
8/18	W	26-20	DALLAS	35,630
8/23	L	24-27	at Detroit	62,094
8/30	L	6-14	L.A. RAMS	36,814
9/6	W	13-3	GREEN BAY	35,543
9/12	W	9-7	at Buffalo	48,691

Regular Season   Record:5-9

9/21	L	33-37	at Denver	51,858
9/28	L	24-30	N.Y. JETS	74,169
10/5	L	3-20	SAN FRANCISCO	54,590
10/12	W	42-10	OAKLAND	60,425
10/19	W	12-10	at San Diego	26,657
10/26	W	26-13	DENVER	70,043
11/2	L	13-17	HOUSTON	62,989
11/10	W	34-31	at Dallas (Mon.) (N)	63,539
11/16	L	3-28	at Pittsburgh	48,803
11/23	W	*24-21	DETROIT	55,161
11/30	L	14-28	at Baltimore	42,122
12/7	L	20-28	SAN DIEGO	46,888
12/14	L	14-20	at Cleveland	44,368
12/21	L	20-28	at Oakland	48,604

Individual Statistics

Passing

	Att.	Cmp.	Yds.	Pct.	TD	INT	LG	Rating
Dawson	140	93	1095	66.4	5	4	51	89.9
Livingston	176	88	1245	50.0	8	6	69	74.1
Adams	77	36	445	46.8	2	4	32	52.2
Podolak	1	0	0	0.0	0	1	0	0.0
White	1	0	0	0.0	0	0	0	39.6
Chiefs Totals	395	217	2785	54.9	15	16	69	72.8
Opp. Total	325	186	2520	57.2	18	20	90	74.6

Receiving

	No.	Yds.	Avg.	LG	TD
Podolak	37	332	9.0	21	2
Pearson	36	608	16.9	45	3
Lane	25	202	8.1	32	0
Masters	24	314	13.1	32	3
White	23	559	24.3	69t	3
Brunson	23	398	17.3	36	2
Green	23	215	9.3	28	1
Kinney	21	148	7.0	15	0
Dressler	2	7	3.5	4	1
Craig	1	10	10.0	10	0
LaGrand	1	-1	-1.0	0	0
Adams	1	-7	-7.0	0	0
Chiefs Totals	217	2785	12.8	69t	15
Opp. Totals	186	2520	13.5	90t	18

Rushing

	No.	Yds.	Avg.	LG	TD
Green	167	611	3.7	42	5
Podolak	102	351	3.4	25	3
Lane	79	311	3.9	39	2
Kinney	85	304	3.6	20	2
Brunson	2	89	44.5	65	0
Livingston	13	68	5.2	28	1
Adams	8	42	5.3	16	0
LaGrand	13	38	2.9	11	1
Miller	7	20	2.9	10	0
Dressler	3	16	5.3	11	0
Dawson	5	7	1.4	9	0
White	4	-10	-2.5	0	0
Chiefs Totals	488	1847	3.8	65	14
Opp. Totals	562	2712	4.8	50	24

Team Statistics

	Chiefs	Opp.
Total First Downs	261	289
Rushing	110	149
Passing	128	121
Penalty	23	19
3rd Down: Made Att.	83/215	83/190
3rd Down Pct.	38.6	43.7
Total Net Yards	4207	5224
Avg. Per Game	300.5	373.1
Total Plays	933	915
Avg. Per Play	4.5	5.7
Net Yards Rushing	1847	2712
Avg. Per Game	131.9	193.7
Total Rushes	488	562
Avg. Per Play	3.8	4.8
Net Yards Passing	2360	2512
Avg. Per Game	168.6	179.4
Sacked/Yards Lost	53/425	28/179
Gross Yards	2785	2520
Attempts/Completions	395/217	325/186
Pct. of Completions	54.9	57.2
Had Intercepted	16	20
Punts/Average	72/39.3	61/40.6
Penalties/Yards	82/668	98/929
Fumbles/Lost	38/18	40/22
Touchdowns	31	44
Rushing	14	24
Passing	15	18
Returns	2	2
Safeties	0	2

Score By Periods	1	2	3	4	OT	Total
Chiefs Total	64	86	47	82	3	282
Opp. Total	48	93	98	102	0	342

Regular Starters

	Offense		Defense
WR	Barry Pearson	LE	John Matuszak
LT	Charlie Getty	LT	Marvin Upshaw
LG	Rocky Rasley	RT	Buck Buchanan
C	**Jack Rudnay**	RE	Wilbur Young
RG	Tom Condon	LLB	Bill Peterson
RT	Jim Nicholson	MLB	**Willie Lanier**
TE	Billy Masters	RLB	Jim Lynch
WR	Larry Brunson	LCB	Kerry Reardon
QB	Mike Livingston	RCB	**Emmitt Thomas**
	Len Dawson	LS	Jim Kearney
RB	Woody Green	RS	Mike Sensibaugh
RB	MacArthur Lane	P	Jerrel Wilson
	Jeff Kinney		
K	**Jan Stenerud**		

PRO-BOWLERS in Bold

Team Leaders

Scoring: Jan Stenerud	96 pts: 30 PATs, 22 FGs
INTs: Emmitt Thomas	6-119 yds., 0 TDs
Sacks: Wilbur Young	9.5 (-73.0 yds.)
Punting: Jerrel Wilson	54-2233 yds., 41.4 avg., 64 LG
Punt Returns: Charlie Thomas	12-112 yds., 9.3 avg., 0 TDs
Kickoff Returns: Reggie Craig	10-247 yds., 24.7 avg., 0 TDs

1975 AFC Standings

Western Division

	W	L	T	Pct.
Oakland	11	3	0	.786
Denver	6	8	0	.429
Kansas City	5	9	0	.357
San Diego	2	12	0	.143

Central Division

	W	L	T	Pct.
Pittsburgh	12	2	0	.857
Cincinnati +	11	3	0	.786
Houston	10	4	0	.714
Cleveland	3	11	0	.214

Eastern Division

	W	L	T	Pct.
Baltimore	10	4	0	.714
Miami	10	4	0	.714
Buffalo	8	6	0	.571
New England	3	11	0	.241
N.Y. Jets	3	11	0	.214

AFC Championship: PITTSBURGH 16, Oakland 10
Super Bowl X: Pittsburgh 21, Dallas 17

Paul Wiggin (Kansas Collection, U. of Kansas)

Emmitt Thomas was at the top of his game again in 1975, earning another spot on the AFC Pro Bowl roster. (Kansas Collection, U. of Kansas)

1976 Head Coach: Paul Wiggin

The Chiefs were once again mired in mediocrity. Mike Livingston led the NFL's second-best passing attack, but a porous defense, the second worst in the league, couldn't keep the Chiefs in very many games. Running back MacArthur Lane led the NFL in pass receptions with 66, and also ran for 542 yards. An aging Ed Podolak added 371 yards and five touchdowns to the ground attack, and Livingston, in one of his finest seasons, threw for 2,682 yards and 12 touchdowns. The defense gave up 376 points for the year. Safety Gary Barbaro was one of the few bright spots on defense and won the Mack Lee Hill Award as the team's top rookie in 1976. The Chiefs lost their first four games of the season, making any kind of playoff run an impossibility. Jack Rudnay was the Chiefs' lone position player elected to the Pro Bowl.

Key Dates in 1976:

September 12—The Chiefs lose the season opener to the Chargers, 30-16.

September 20—Kansas City loses a close one at Arrowhead to the Raiders on *Monday Night Football*, 24-21.

November 7—The Steelers thrash the Chiefs at home, 45-0.

December 12—Kansas City beats the Browns easily, 39-14, finishing the season with their third-straight 5-9 record.

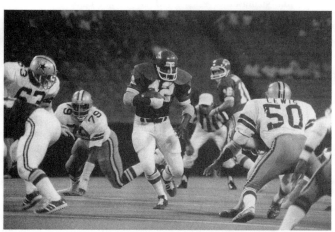

MacArthur Lane led the NFL in pass receptions with 66. (Kansas Collection, U. of Kansas)

Big Game of 1976

October 3 at Buffalo
Buffalo 50, Kansas City 17

Offensive mistakes coupled with the NFL's worst defense usually mean one thing: a blowout loss. The Chiefs traveled to Buffalo with hopes of righting their sinking ship, and instead took a direct torpedo hit. The Bills blew Kansas City off the field, racking up an easy 50-17 win.

"I really feel we defeated ourselves," a sullen Paul Wiggin said after the game. "The turnovers killed us, but we met a team that was trying to get itself untracked and I have to give them credit."

But he wasn't fooling anyone. The Chiefs were bad, and the 50 points scored by Buffalo was the most ever given up by the franchise in its history. Six turnovers led to the rout, but the Bills also amassed 266 yards on the ground—130 by O.J. Simpson—and another 180 in the air. The Chiefs had 321 yards passing and 181 yards rushing, but this is clearly a case of statistics lying.

"I don't think the Chiefs have a bad team," Buffalo quarterback Joe Ferguson said after the game. "They're just young and are going to make mistakes."

Still, Wiggin tried to remain upbeat about his team.

"What now? The more adversity you have to face, the tougher it is to get your momentum back. We're just going to get up tomorrow morning . . . and see if we can pick up the pieces."

The Chiefs' record after the game was 0-4.

Preseason

Record: 2-4

8/2	W	9-3	HOUSTON	30,006
8/7	L	10-13	MINNESOTA	32,851
8/15	L	13-21	at San Francisco	36,101
8/21	W	23-20	WASHINGTON	30,014
8/28	L	21-23	DETROIT	27,410
9/3	L	14-31	at St. Louis	42,997

Regular Season

Record: 5-9

9/12	L	16-30	SAN DIEGO	53,133
9/20	L	21-24	OAKLAND (Mon.) (N)	60,884
9/26	L	17-27	NEW ENGLAND	53,918
10/3	L	17-50	at Buffalo	51,909
10/10	W	33-30	at Washington	53,060
10/17	W	20-17	at Miami	43,325
10/24	L	26-35	DENVER	57,961
10/31	W	28-19	at Tampa Bay	41,779
11/7	L	0-45	PITTSBURGH	71,516
11/14	L	10-21	at Oakland	48,859
11/21	L	24-27	CINCINNATI	46,259
11/28	W	23-21	at San Diego	29,272
12/5	L	16-17	at Denver	58,170
12/12	W	39-14	CLEVELAND	34,340

Individual Statistics

Passing

	Att.	Cmp.	Yds.	Pct.	TD	INT	LG	Rating
Livingston	338	189	2682	55.9	12	13	57	77.9
Adams	71	36	575	50.7	3	4	49	68.8
Nott	10	4	46	40.0	0	0	23	54.6
Lane	0	0	0	0.0	0	0	0	0.0
Chiefs Totals	419	229	3303	54.6	15	17	57	75.4
Opp. Total	375	215	2684	57.3	25	23	—	76.6

Receiving

	No.	Yds.	Avg.	LG	TD
Lane	66	686	10.4	44	1
White	47	808	17.2	41	7
Brunson	33	656	19.9	57	1
Marshall	28	443	15.8	31t	2
Masters	18	269	14.9	30	3
Podolak	13	156	12.0	23	0
Reamon	10	136	13.6	49t	1
Green	9	100	11.1	31	0
McNeil	2	33	16.5	18	0
Harrison	1	12	12.0	12	0
Williams	1	9	9.0	9	0
Getty	1	-5	-5.0	0	0
Chiefs Totals	229	3303	14.4	57	15
Opp. Totals	215	2684	12.5	57	25

Rushing

	No.	Yds.	Avg.	LG	TD
Lane	162	542	3.3	20	5
Podolak	88	371	4.2	22t	5
Green	73	322	4.4	27	1
Reamon	103	314	3.1	14	4
Marshall	5	101	20.2	59t	1
Livingston	31	89	2.9	19	2
Adams	5	46	9.2	21	0
Harrison	16	41	2.6	7	0
McNeil	8	26	3.3	7	0
White	2	15	7.5	8	0
Kinney	1	7	7.0	7	0
Brunson	3	-1	-0.3	5	0
Stenerud	1	0	0.0	0	0
Chiefs Totals	498	1873	3.76	59t	18
Opp. Totals	555	2861	5.15	77t	24

Team Statistics

	Chiefs	Opp.
Total First Downs	275	309
Rushing	104	161
Passing	151	133
Penalty	20	15
3rd Down: Made Att.	79/210	78/184
3rd Down Pct.	37.6	42.4
Total Net Yards	4804	5359
Avg. Per Game	343.1	382.8
Total Plays	959	899
Avg. Per Play	5.0	6.0
Net Yards Rushing	1873	2861
Avg. Per Game	133.8	204.4
Total Rushes	498	555
Avg. Per Play	3.8	5.2
Net Yards Passing	2929	2496
Avg. Per Game	209.2	178.3
Sacked/Yards Lost	42/374	22/188
Gross Yards	3303	2684
Attempts/Completions	419/229	375/215
Pct. of Completions	54.6	57.3
Had Intercepted	17	23
Punts/Average	67/41.7	63/39.7
Net Punting Avg.	33.7	30.3
Penalties/Yards	97/789	88/762
Fumbles/Lost	31/16	35/20
Touchdowns	33	51
Rushing	18	24
Passing	15	25
Returns	0	2
Safeties	1	0

Score By Periods	1	2	3	4	OT	Total
Chiefs Total	49	95	71	72	3	290
Opp. Total	95	71	83	127	0	376

Regular Starters

	Offense		Defense
WR	Henry Marshall	LE	Whitney Paul
LT	Matt Herkenhoff	LT	James Wolf
LG	Charlie Getty	RT	Keith Simons
C	**Jack Rudnay**	RE	Wilbur Young
RG	Tom Condon	LLB	Billy Andrews
RT	Jim Nicholson	MLB	Willie Lanier
TE	Billy Masters	RLB	Jim Lynch
WR	Larry Brunson	LCB	Kerry Reardon
QB	Mike Livingston	RCB	Emmitt Thomas
RB	Woody Green	LS	Tim Gray
	Ed Podolak	RS	Gary Barbaro
	Tommy Reamon	P	Jerrel Wilson
RB	MacArthur Lane		
K	**Jan Stenerud**		

PRO-BOWLERS in Bold

Team Leaders

Scoring: Jan Stenerud   90 pts: 21 PATs, 27 FGs
INTs: Kerry Reardon   5-26 yds., 0 TDs
Sacks: Lawrence Estes   5.0 (-52.0 yds.)
Punting: Jerrel Wilson   65-2729 yds., 42.0 avg., 62 LG
Punt Returns: Larry Brunson   31-387 yds., 12.5 avg., 0 TDs
Kickoff Returns: Lawrence Williams   26-688 yds., 27.6 avg., 0 TDs

1976 AFC Standings

Western Division

	W	L	T	Pct.
Oakland	13	1	0	.929
Denver	9	5	0	.643
San Diego	6	8	0	.429
Kansas City	5	9	0	.357
Tampa Bay	0	14	0	.000

Central Division

	W	L	T	Pct.
Pittsburgh	10	4	0	.714
Cincinnati	10	4	0	.714
Cleveland	9	5	0	.643
Houston	5	9	0	.357

Eastern Division

	W	L	T	Pct.
Baltimore	11	3	0	.786
New England	11	3	0	.786
Miami	6	8	0	.429
N.Y. Jets	3	11	0	.214
Buffalo	2	12	0	.143

AFC Championship: OAKLAND 24, Pittsburgh 7
Super Bowl XI: Oakland 32, Minnesota 14

Henry Marshall (Kansas Collection, U. of Kansas)

1977 Head Coaches: Paul Wiggin (1-6), Tom Bettis (1-6)

It was the worst season in the history of the Chiefs franchise; losses piled up, and for the first and only time, a Kansas City head coach was fired in the middle of the season. How bad were these Chiefs? They had an anemic, mistake-prone offense that scored just 225 points and a leaky defense that allowed 349 points. After the Browns whipped the Chiefs in midseason, Lamar Hunt fired Paul Wiggin. Tom Bettis led the team to one inspired win in his first game as the head man, but the Chiefs dropped their last six games of the season, finished 2-12, and settled into last place in the AFC West. The veteran Ed Podolak led the team in rushing with 550 yards; Walter White caught 48 passes and scored five touchdowns. Gary Barbaro was one of the few standouts on defense, picking off eight passes. Jack Rudnay was the team's lone Pro Bowler.

Defeat weighed heavily on Gary Barbaro and the rest of the Chiefs throughout the 1977 season. (Kansas Collection, U. of Kansas)

Key Dates in 1977:

September 18—The Chiefs suffer a 21-17 season-opening loss to the Patriots.

October 31—Paul Wiggin is fired. Tom Bettis takes over the head coaching duties for the Chiefs on an interim basis, coaching the team for the remaining seven games of the season.

November 6—Tom Bettis gets his first and only win as Kansas City's head coach when the Chiefs play an inspired game and defeat the Packers, 20-10.

December 11—Gary Barbaro returns an interception for a team-record 102 yards and a touchdown in the Chiefs' 34-31 loss to the Seahawks at Arrowhead Stadium.

December 18—Oakland squeaks out a 21-20 win over the Chiefs in the season's final game. The loss leaves KC with a record of 2-12, the worst in the club's history.

December 20—Marv Levy is hired as the Chiefs' new head coach.

Big Game of 1977

October 30 at Cleveland
Cleveland 44, Kansas City 7

Just midway through the season, and it's hard to imagine a Chiefs team sinking any lower than they did in this game. Cleveland dominated Kansas City in virtually every aspect of the game and rolled to an embarrassingly easy 44-7 win.

"We didn't play well at any one point," Chiefs coach Paul Wiggin said after the game. "It was a total disaster. This game was a source of embarrassment."

Kansas City committed six turnovers. They gave up 322 yards rushing. Cleveland passed for 204 yards. The Chiefs ran for just 17 yards, passed for only 119.

"The offense, as a group, broke down," Wiggin continued. "The defense, as a group, broke down and the kicking game, which we rely on to give us some breaks, hasn't been there all year."

"It was a total disaster for us."

The loss put the Chiefs at 1-6 and left them hopeless and helpless, the prospect of going the rest of the year without winning another game looming over their heads.

It was only a mild shock when Paul Wiggin was fired the next day. Tom Bettis was given the job of interim head coach, and the Chiefs won their first game under his control before dropping the final six games of the season.

Preseason
Record: 3-3

Date	W/L	Score	Opponent	Attendance
8/6	L	0-17	at Detroit	52,309
8/13	W	23-21	PITTSBURGH	28,584
8/18	L	7-13	at Washington	33,263
8/27	W	27-19	L.A. RAMS	34,975
9/5	L	16-24	ATLANTA	22,748
9/10	W	20-37	ST. LOUIS	35,954

Regular Season
Record: 2-12

Date	W/L	Score	Opponent	Attendance
9/18	L	17-21	at New England	58,185
9/25	L	7-23	SAN DIEGO	56,146
10/3	L	28-37	OAKLAND (Mon.) (N)	60,684
10/9	L	7-23	at Denver	74,878
10/16	L	6-17	BALTIMORE	63,076
10/23	W	21-16	at San Diego	33,010
10/30	L	7-44	at Cleveland	60,631
11/6	W	20-10	GREEN BAY	62,687
11/13	L	27-28	at Chicago	49,543
11/20	L	7-14	DENVER	54,050
11/27	L	20-34	at Houston	42,934
12/4	L	7-27	CINCINNATI	38,488
12/11	L	31-34	SEATTLE	22,262
12/18	L	20-21	at Oakland	50,304

Individual Statistics

Passing

	Att.	Cmp.	Yds.	Pct.	TD	INT	LG	Rating
Livingston	282	143	1823	50.7	9	15	49	59.8
Adams	92	47	691	51.1	2	11	63	43.7
Chiefs Totals	374	190	2514	50.8	11	26	63	52.9
Opp. Total	333	175	2244	52.6	15	21	48	62.8

Receiving

	No.	Yds.	Avg.	LG	TD
White	48	674	14.0	48t	5
Podolak	32	313	9.8	23	0
Marshall	20	445	19.3	49	4
Brunson	20	295	14.8	63	0
Brockington	19	222	11.7	48	1
Bailey	17	206	12.1	47t	1
Reed	12	125	10.4	20	0
Williams	7	94	13.4	27	0
Samuels	5	65	13.0	32	0
Lane	3	40	13.3	21	0
Morgado	2	21	10.5	12	0
McKnight	1	11	11.0	11	0
Beckman	1	3	3.0	3	0
Chiefs Totals	190	2514	13.2	63	11
Opp. Totals	175	2244	12.8	48	15

Rushing

	No.	Yds.	Avg.	LG	TD
Podolak	133	550	4.1	41	5
Reed	126	505	4.0	59	5
Bailey	66	266	4.0	37t	2
Brockington	54	161	3.0	12	2
Lane	25	79	3.2	9	1
Livingston	19	78	4.1	13	1
McKnight	11	74	6.7	19	1
Burks	1	51	51.0	51	0
Williams	2	30	15.0	17	0
Adams	5	21	4.2	8	1
Morgado	3	12	4.0	9	0
Marshall	7	11	1.6	5	0
Brunson	2	8	4.0	11	0
White	2	-3	-0.7	3	0
Chiefs Totals	456	1843	4.0	59	13
Opp. Totals	634	2971	4.7	78t	23

Team Statistics

	Chiefs	Opp.
Total First Downs	228	304
Rushing	95	169
Passing	110	113
Penalty	23	22
3rd Down: Made Att.	64/196	83/202
3rd Down Pct.	32.7	41.1
Total Net Yards	3936	4993
Avg. Per Game	281.1	356.7
Total Plays	878	992
Avg. Per Play	4.5	5.0
Net Yards Rushing	1843	2971
Avg. Per Game	131.6	211.8
Total Rushes	456	634
Avg. Per Play	4.0	4.7
Net Yards Passing	2093	2022
Avg. Per Game	149.5	144.4
Sacked/Yards Lost	48/421	25/222
Gross Yards	2514	2244
Attempts/Completions	374/190	333/175
Pct. of Completions	50.8	52.6
Had Intercepted	26	21
Punts/Average	89/39.4	63/41.0
Net Punting Avg.	30.8	35.7
Penalties/Yards	82/706	105/930
Fumbles/Lost	32/21	39/23
Touchdowns	29	42
Rushing	13	23
Passing	11	15
Returns	5	4
Safeties	0	0

Score By Periods	1	2	3	4	OT	Total
Chiefs Total	73	50	23	79	0	225
Opp. Total	92	99	79	79	0	349

Regular Starters

	Offense		Defense
WR	Henry Marshall	LE	Whitney Paul
LT	Matt Herkenhoff	LT	Willie Lee
LG	Bobby Simmons	RT	Keith Simons
C	**Jack Rudnay**	RE	Wilbur Young
RG	Tom Condon	LLB	Billy Andrews
RT	Jim Nicholson	MLB	Willie Lanier
TE	Walter White	RLB	Jim Lynch
WR	Larry Williams	LCB	Gary Green
QB	Mike Livingston	RCB	Emmitt Thomas
RB	Tony Reed		Tim Collier
	Ed Podolak	LS	Tim Gray
RB	Mark Bailey	RS	Gary Barbaro
	John Brockington	P	Jerrel Wilson
K	Jan Stenerud		

PRO-BOWLERS in Bold

Team Leaders

Scoring: Jan Stenerud — 51 pts: 27 PATs, 8 FGs
INTs: Gary Barbaro — 8-165 yds., 1 TD
Tackles: Willie Lanier — 132 (88 solo)
Sacks: Wilbur Young — 5.5 (-51.5 yds.)
Punting: Jerrel Wilson — 85-3394 yds., 39.9 avg., 59 LG
Punt Returns: Gary Green — 14-115 yds., 8.2 avg., 0 TDs
Kickoff Returns: Ted McKnight — 12-305 yds., 25.4 avg., 0 TDs

1977 AFC Standings

Western Division

	W	L	T	Pct.
Denver	12	2	0	.857
Oakland	11	3	0	.786
San Diego	7	7	0	.500
Seattle	5	9	0	.357
Kansas City	2	12	0	.143

Central Division

	W	L	T	Pct.
Pittsburgh	9	5	0	.643
Houston	8	6	0	.571
Cincinnati	8	6	0	.571
Cleveland	6	8	0	.429

Eastern Division

	W	L	T	Pct.
Baltimore	10	4	0	.714
Miami	10	4	0	.714
New England	9	5	0	.643
N.Y. Jets	3	11	0	.214
Buffalo	3	11	0	.214

AFC Championship: DENVER 20, Oakland 17
Super Bowl XII: Dallas 27, Denver 10

Tom Bettis took over as the Chiefs' head coach after Paul Wiggin was fired. (Kansas Collection, U. of Kansas)

1978 Head Coach: Marv Levy

Chiefs' quarterback Mike Livingston discusses strategy with his new head coach, Marv Levy.
(Kansas Collection, U. of Kansas)

The arrival of Marv Levy as the Chiefs' new head coach brought about major housecleaning in Kansas City. The final pieces of the Chiefs' past Super Bowl glory were gone; Ed Podolak, Willie Lanier, Jim Lynch, and Jerrell Wilson were no longer on the team. Art Still, Gary Spani, and Sylvester Hicks became main players on the defense, and Levy installed a winged-T running attack on offense. The Chiefs showed major improvement from the year before, but still only won four games. The running attack offense compiled high numbers as the team ran for 2,986 yards and 19 touchdowns. Tony Reed led the Chiefs with 1,053 yards rushing and Ted McKnight added 627. Gary Spani racked up 144 tackles and Art Still added 6.5 sacks. It was a good rebuilding year for the Chiefs, and with late-season wins over San Diego and Buffalo, the future—for the first time in many years—looked bright.

Key Dates in 1978:

September 3—The Chiefs' win the season opener at Cincinnati, 24-23, Marv Levy's first victory as the Chiefs' head coach.

October 15—The Chiefs lose their sixth straight game, this time to Oakland, 28-6.

November 26—The Chiefs defeat the Chargers, 23-0, for just their third win of the season.

December 17—Seattle beats the Chiefs, 23-19. Kansas City ends the year with a 4-12 record, last in the AFC West.

Big Game of 1978

September 24 at Kansas City
Denver 23, Kansas City 17 OT

For 70 minutes the Chiefs played even with the defending AFC Champion Broncos, but in the end they couldn't contain Denver's running game. Bronco rookie Dave Preston scored from the one-yard line with 4:32 left in overtime, and Denver escaped the Chiefs' bid for a major upset.

"Any time you stay with a team like Denver you have to have hope for the rest of the season," Chiefs safety Gary Barbaro said after the game. "You know you must be doing some things right. Sure we were up for Denver. If you're not, you'll get blown out of the park."

Both teams missed opportunities to win in regulation, both teams had costly mistakes. Mike Livingston's intercepted pass in the end zone cost the Chiefs a sure three points, and Denver's Jim Turner missed a 41-yard field goal with 21 seconds remaining in regulation.

"You just want to cry," said Chiefs linebacker Dave Rozumek. "This is one of the worst feelings you can ever have. I really believe that."

Tony Reed led the Chiefs with 79 yards rushing and scored on a 15-yard run. The Kansas City defense yielded 228 yards rushing to the Broncos, but effectively shut down their passing game, limiting them to just 29 yards through the air.

"I'm sure there are good things you can point to as being good, but right now it's just a very bitter—very bitter—disappointment to have lost this game," Marv Levy said after the game. "I feel very bad for our players. They have tried so darn hard."

The loss was the third in a row after Kansas City won the season opener against the Bengals. They would lose three more before finally defeating Cleveland for their seond win.

Preseason
Record: 2-2

8/5	W	17-14	at Green Bay	54,453
8/12	W	17-13	MINNESOTA	41,092
8/20	L	7-24	at New England	39,043
8/26	L	7-12	ST. LOUIS	40,884

Regular Season
Record:4-12

9/3	W	24-23	at Cincinnati	41,810
9/10	L	17-20	HOUSTON	40,213
9/17	L	10-26	at N.Y. Giants	70,546
9/24	L	*17-23	DENVER	60,593
10/1	L	13-28	at Buffalo	47,310
10/8	L	13-30	TAMPA BAY	38,201
10/15	L	6-28	at Oakland	50,759
10/22	W	17-3	CLEVELAND	41,157
10/29	L	23-27	at Pittsburgh	48,185
11/5	L	10-20	OAKLAND	75,418
11/12	L	*23-29	at San Diego	41,395
11/19	L	10-13	SEATTLE	35,252
11/26	W	23-0	SAN DIEGO	26,248
12/3	W	14-10	BUFFALO	25,781
12/10	L	3-24	at Denver	74,149
12/17	L	19-23	at Seattle	58,490

Individual Statistics

Passing

	Att.	Cmp.	Yds.	Pct.	TD	INT	LG	Rating
Livingston	290	159	1573	54.8	5	13	44	57.3
Adams	79	44	415	55.7	2	3	26	62.9
White	1	1	44	100.0	0	0	44	118.8
Chiefs Totals	370	204	2032	55.1	7	16	44	59.3
Opp. Total	365	219	2820	60.0	17	21	57t	75.8

Receiving

	No.	Yds.	Avg.	LG	TD
Reed	48	483	10.1	44	1
White	42	340	8.1	24	1
Lane	36	279	7.8	44	0
H. Marshall	26	433	16.7	40	2
McKnight	14	83	5.9	19	1
Belton	11	88	8.0	22	0
Dorsey	9	169	18.8	33	2
Morgado	7	47	6.7	15	0
Samuels	6	97	16.2	38	0
Bailey	5	13	2.6	15	0
Chiefs Totals	204	2032	9.7	44	7
Opp. Totals	219	2820	12.9	57t	17

Rushing

	No.	Yds.	Avg.	LG	TD
Reed	206	1053	5.1	62t	6
McKnight	104	627	6.0	41t	5
Morgado	160	593	3.7	18	7
Bailey	83	298	3.6	17	0
Lane	52	277	5.3	30	0
Belton	24	79	3.3	8	0
Livingston	23	49	2.1	18	1
Adams	9	15	1.7	6	0
Andrusyshyn	1	0	0.0	0	0
Marshall	1	-5	-5.0	-5	0
Chiefs Totals	663	2986	4.5	62t	19
Opp. Totals	601	2389	4.0	55	21

Team Statistics

	Chiefs	Opp.
Total First Downs	287	284
Rushing	160	138
Passing	98	122
Penalty	29	24
3rd Down: Made Att.	102/247	98/225
3rd Down Pct.	41.3	43.6
Total Net Yards	4820	4971
Avg. Per Game	301.3	310.7
Total Plays	1054	995
Avg. Per Play	4.6	5.0
Net Yards Rushing	2986	2389
Avg. Per Game	213.3	149.3
Total Rushes	663	601
Avg. Per Play	4.5	4.0
Net Yards Passing	1834	2582
Avg. Per Game	114.6	161.4
Sacked/Yards Lost	21/198	29/238
Gross Yards	2032	2820
Attempts/Completions	370/204	365/219
Pct. of Completions	55.1	60.0
Had Intercepted	16	21
Punts/Average	80/40.6	76/39.9
Net Punting Avg.	32.1	30.9
Penalties/Yards	110/1048	100/938
Fumbles/Lost	32/18	30/14
Touchdowns	26	42
Rushing	19	21
Passing	7	17
Returns	0	4
Safeties	1	0

Score By Periods	1	2	3	4	OT	Total
Chiefs Total	42	70	62	69	0	243
Opp. Total	64	113	47	91	12	327

Regular Starters

	Offense		Defense
WR	Henry Marshall	LE	Art Still
LT	Matt Herkenhoff	NT	Don Parrish
LG	Bobby Simmons	RE	Sylvester Hicks
C	Jack Rudnay	LOLB	Whitney Paul
RG	Tom Condon	LILB	Billy Andrews
RT	Charlie Getty	MLB	Dave Rozumek
TE	Walter White	RILB	Gary Spani
QB	Mike Livingston	ROLB	Thomas Howard
LHB	Tony Reed	LCB	Gary Green
FB	Mark Bailey	ROLB	Emmitt Thomas
	Arnold Morgado		Tim Collier
RHB	Ted McKnight	SS	Tim Gray
K	Jan Stenerud	FS	Gary Barbaro
		P	Zenon Zndrusyshyn

PRO-BOWLERS in Bold

Team Leaders

Scoring: Jan Stenerud	85 pts: 25 PATs, 20 FGs
INTs: Tim Gray	6-118 yds., 0 TDs
Tackles: Gary Spani	144 (102 solo)
Sacks: Art Still	6.5 (-59.0 yds.)
Punting: Zenon Andrusyshyn	79-3247 yds., 41.1 avg., 61 LG
Punt Returns: Eddie Payton	32-364 yds., 11.4 avg., 2 TDs
Kickoff Returns: Eddie Payton	30-775 yds., 25.8 avg., 0 TDs

1978 AFC Standings

Western Division

	W	L	T	Pct.
Denver	10	6	0	.625
Oakland	9	7	0	.563
Seattle	9	7	0	.563
San Diego	9	7	0	.563
Kansas City	4	12	0	.250

Central Division

	W	L	T	Pct.
Pittsburgh	14	2	0	.875
Houston	10	6	0	.625
Cleveland	8	8	0	.500
Cincinnati	4	12	0	.250

Eastern Division

	W	L	T	Pct.
New England	11	5	0	.688
Miami	11	5	0	.688
N.Y. Jets	8	8	0	.500
Buffalo	5	11	0	.313
Baltimore	5	11	0	.313

AFC Championship: PITTSBURGH 34, Houston 5
Super Bowl XIII: Pittsburgh 35, Dallas 31

Art Still had a good rookie season for Kansas City, leading the Chiefs with 6.5 sacks. (Alan Barzee)

1979 Head Coach: Mary Levy

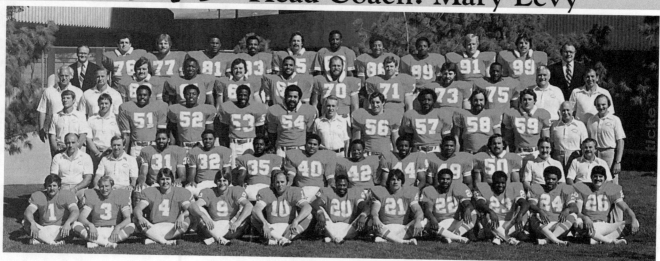

With the first stage of rebuilding finished for the Chiefs, Marv Levy and his staff saw considerable advances in the play of their squad. Kansas City won seven games, the most by the team since 1973. The defense, which had been one of the worst in the league just two seasons earlier, was greatly improved. Rookie Steve Fuller saw most of the action at quarterback and despite throwing only six touchdown passes showed promise for the future. The running game was still the focus of the offense, however, and it wasn't as strong as it had been the previous year. Ted McKnight led the team with 755 yards and eight touchdowns. Gary Spani and Art Still were again brilliant, and rookie punter Bob Grupp led the NFL in punting and was selected for the Pro Bowl. J. T. Smith was spectacular at returning kicks. The Chiefs' record of 7-9 was still not good enough to get them out of last place in the tough AFC West, but opposing teams no longer looked forward to an easy win against Kansas City.

Key Dates in 1979:

September 2—Kansas City starts the season at Arrowhead and beats the Colts, 14-0.

September 23—J.T. Smith returns a punt for a franchise-record 88 yards against the Raiders, helping the Chiefs to an easy win, 35-7.

September 30—Chiefs running back Ted McKnight rips off an 84-yard touchdown run, a franchise record, and the Chiefs beat the Seahawks in Seattle, 24-6.

November 4—Punter Bob Grupp launches a punt for a team-record 74 yards in the Chiefs' 20-14 loss to San Diego.

Big Game of 1979

December 16 at Tampa Bay
Tampa Bay 3, Kansas City 0

The Chiefs fought the rain, wind, and mud more than the Tampa Bay Buccaneers, and were washed away in the impossible playing conditions, 3-0. Everything about the weather, coupled with the Bucs' defense, stymied Kansas City's attack. When Tampa Bay kicker Neil O'Donoghue kicked a 19-yard field goal six minutes into the fourth quarter, the Chiefs were beaten. They ran only three offensive plays the entire fourth quarter.

"If anybody had told me we'd come down here and lose 3-0, I'd say they were a liar," Chiefs cornerback Gary Green said afterwards.

Kansas City could muster just 80 yards of total offense, a new team record for fewest yards in a game. The Bucs had trouble also, but still pounded out 269 yards and held the ball more than 40 minutes of the game. The win clinched the NFC central division title for Tampa Bay.

"We wanted to come in the game and finish up strong," Art Still said. "It's the end of the season, and some people think about going home. We came down here to be 8-8."

But despite the loss and 7-9 record, the Chiefs would look forward to next season and the hope of continuing the modest successes gained in 1979.

Preseason
Record: 3-1

8/4	L	10-14	at Green Bay	53,994
8/9	W	24-21	PHILADELPHIA	33,578
8/18	W	20-3	ST. LOUIS	43,214
8/23	W	25-0	at Minnesota	39,578

Regular Season
Record: 7-9

9/2	W	14-0	BALTIMORE	50,442
9/9	L	24-27	CLEVELAND	42,181
9/16	L	6-20	at Houston	45,684
9/23	W	35-7	OAKLAND	67,281
9/30	W	24-6	at Seattle	61,169
10/7	W	10-7	at Cincinnati	40,041
10/14	L	10-24	DENVER	74,292
10/21	L	17-21	N.Y. GIANTS	45,742
10/28	L	3-20	at Denver	74,908
11/4	L	14-20	SAN DIEGO	59,353
11/11	L	3-30	PITTSBURGH	70,132
11/18	W	24-21	at Oakland	53,596
11/25	L	7-28	at San Diego	50,078
12/2	W	37-21	SEATTLE	42,160
12/9	W	10-7	at Baltimore	25,684
12/16	L	0-3	at Tampa Bay	63,624

Individual Statistics

Passing

	Att.	Cmp.	Yds.	Pct.	TD	INT	LG	Rating
Fuller	270	146	1484	54.1	6	14	40	55.8
Livingston	90	44	469	48.9	1	4	38	49.9
Grupp	1	0	0	0.0	0	0	0	39.6
Chiefs Totals	361	190	1953	52.6	7	18	40	54.0
Opp. Total	528	296	3404	56.1	22	23	56	71.4

Receiving

	No.	Yds.	Avg.	LG	TD
McKnight	38	226	6.0	24	0
Reed	34	352	10.4	40	0
J.T. Smith	33	444	13.5	34	3
Marshall	21	332	15.8	38t	1
Williams	16	129	8.1	25	2
Gant	15	101	6.7	26	0
Samuels	14	147	10.5	30	0
Morgado	5	55	11.0	22	0
Gaunty	5	87	17.4	23	1
Belton	4	44	11.0	23	0
White	3	15	5.0	12	0
Beckman	2	21	10.5	12	0
Chiefs Totals	190	1953	10.3	40	7
Opp. Totals	296	3404	11.5	56	22

Rushing

	No.	Yds.	Avg.	LG	TD
McKnight	153	755	4.9	84t	8
Reed	113	446	4.0	23	1
Fuller	50	264	5.3	49	1
Williams	69	261	3.8	22	1
Morgado	75	231	3.1	19	4
Gant	56	196	3.5	16	1
Belton	44	134	3.0	19	1
Marshall	2	34	17.0	23	1
Livingston	3	2	0.7	5	0
Haslip	2	1	0.5	1	0
Manumaleuga	1	-3	-3.0	-3	0
Rome	1	-5	-5.0	5	0
Chiefs Totals	569	2316	4.07	84t	18
Opp. Totals	522	1847	3.53	41	8

Team Statistics

	Chiefs	Opp.
Total First Downs	241	297
Rushing	122	102
Passing	91	169
Penalty	28	26
3rd Down: Made Att.	76/235	108/259
3rd Down Pct.	32.3	41.7
Total Net Yards	3976	4971
Avg. Per Game	248.5	310.7
Total Plays	972	1088
Avg. Per Play	4.1	4.6
Net Yards Rushing	2316	1847
Avg. Per Game	144.8	115.4
Total Rushes	569	522
Avg. Per Play	4.1	3.5
Net Yards Passing	1660	3124
Avg. Per Game	103.8	195.3
Sacked/Yards Lost	42/293	38/280
Gross Yards	1953	3404
Attempts/Completions	361/190	528/296
Pct. of Completions	52.6	56.1
Had Intercepted	18	23
Punts/Average	90/43.1	88/38.8
Net Punting Avg.	37.2	30.5
Penalties/Yards	108/971	127/1012
Fumbles/Lost	31/18	34/14
Touchdowns	29	32
Rushing	18	8
Passing	7	22
Returns	4	2
Safeties	0	0

Score By Periods	1	2	3	4	OT	Total
Chiefs Total	52	53	40	93	0	238
Opp. Total	64	55	64	79	0	262

Regular Starters

	Offense		Defense
WR	Henry Marshall	LE	Art Still
LT	Charlie Getty	NT	Don Parrish
LG	Bobby Simmons	RE	Sylvester Hicks
C	Jack Rudnay	LOLB	Whitney Paul
RG	Tom Condon	LILB	Frank Manumaleuga
RT	Jim Nicholson	RILB	Gary Spani
TE	Walter White	ROLB	Thomas Howard
WR	J.T. Smith	LCB	Gary Green
QB	Steve Fuller	RCB	Tim Collier
TE	Tony Samuels		M.L. Carter
RB	Tony Reed	SS	Jerry Reese
RB	Ted McKnight		Herb Christopher
K	Jan Stenerud	FS	Gary Barbaro
		P	**Bob Grupp**

PRO-BOWLERS in Bold

Team Leaders

Scoring: Jan Stenerud	64 pts: 23 PATs, 12 FGs
INTs: Gary Barbaro	7-142 yds., 1 TD
Tackles: Gary Spani	157 (115 solo)
Sacks: Art Still	8.5 (-63.5 yds.)
Punting: Bob Grupp	89-3883 yds., 43.6 avg., 74 LG
Punt Returns: J.T. Smith	58-612 yds., 10.6 avg., 2 TDs
Kickoff Returns: Horace Belton	22-463 yds., 21.0 avg., 0 TDs

1979 AFC Standings

Western Division

	W	L	T	Pct.
San Diego	12	4	0	.750
Denver	10	6	0	.625
Seattle	9	7	0	.563
Oakland	9	7	0	.563
Kansas City	7	9	0	.438

Central Division

	W	L	T	Pct.
Pittsburgh	12	4	0	.750
Houston	11	5	0	.688
Cleveland	9	7	0	.563
Cincinnati	4	12	0	.250

Eastern Division

	W	L	T	Pct.
Miami	10	6	0	.625
New England	9	7	0	.563
N.Y. Jets	8	8	0	.500
Buffalo	7	9	0	.438
Baltimore	5	11	0	.313

AFC Championship: PITTSBURGH 27, Houston 13
Super Bowl XIV: Pittsburgh 31, Los Angeles 19

With two touchdowns and 10.6 yards averaged, J.T. Smith was one of the NFL's top punt returners in 1979. (Kansas Collection, U. of Kansas)

Ted McKnight led the Chiefs in rushing yards and receptions in 1979. (Kansas Collection, U. of Kansas)

1980 Head Coach: Marv Levy

Nick Lowery replaced Jan Stenerud as the Chiefs' placekicker, ending an era in Kansas City. Finally, things were looking up for the team. Led by a strong defense that was consistent throughout the season, the Chiefs finally escaped the AFC West cellar, and for the first time since 1973, finished with a non-losing record. Kansas City dropped its first four games of the season, in part because of an injury-ravaged offensive line, but finished strongly to forge an 8-8 record. Marv Levy's defensive unit was again led by Pro Bowlers Art Still and Gary Barbaro, with help from Gary Green and Gary Spani. Bill Kenney led the team at the end of the season, showing the ability to be a starting quarterback in the NFL. J.T. Smith was again outstanding returning kicks and was selected for the Pro Bowl, and Ted McKnight led the team in rushing. Levy had turned the corner on the rebuilding the team, and good things appeared to be on the horizon for the Chiefs.

Key Dates in 1980:

September 7—The Chiefs open the season at home and lose to the Raiders, 27-14.

September 14—Nick Lowery booms a 57-yard field goal in the Chiefs' 17-16 loss to the Seahawks at Arrowhead Stadium.

October 5—The Chiefs defeat the Raiders, 31-17, snapping a four-game losing streak for their first win of the season.

October 12—Chiefs quarterback Steve Fuller runs 38 yards for the winning touchdown late in the game as Kansas City upsets the Oilers, 21-20.

October 26—The Chiefs win their fourth game in a row, defeating Detroit at Arrowhead, 20-17.

J.T. Smith and Henry Marshall (Kansas Collection, U. of Kansas)

Big Game of 1980

December 21 at Baltimore
Kansas City 38, Baltimore 28

The Chiefs blew a 21-point lead in the first half and went to the locker room trailing, 28-21. In past seasons the team would have completed the fold and lost. Marv Levy, finishing his third season as the Chiefs' head coach, didn't let that happen.

"I said I was embarrassed for them," Levy said of his angry halftime address. "I told them we were manhandled worse by the Colts more than any team this season." His message got through.

Led by the passing of Bill Kenney, Kansas City came back, took control of the game in the third quarter and won it in the fourth. Kenney threw touchdown passes of 23 and 75 yards to Henry Marshall.

"I think we all knew what we had to do," Kenney said of the comeback. "We knew we'd be all right if we had a little more time to throw, because our receivers were running good routes."

Marshall caught nine passes for 176 yards, and Kenney racked up 316 yards passing and three touchdown passes. J. T. Smith returned a punt 53 yards for a score in the first quarter.

The win put the Chiefs' final record at 8-8, the first non-losing season for Kansas City since 1973.

"It was a big barrier to cross for this team to get to .500," Levy said. "I was very proud of the way it was done today, with a lot of players who were not starters and people being out of position."

Preseason — Record: 3-1

Date		Score	Opponent	Attendance
8/9	W	42-0	CLEVELAND	38,055
8/18	W	24-10	MINNESOTA	39,879
8/23	W	20-10	at St. Louis	41,687
8/30	L	21-31	San Francisco (Tucson, AZ)	27,000

Regular Season — Record: 8-8

Date		Score	Opponent	Attendance
9/7	L	14-27	OAKLAND	54,269
9/14	L	16-17	SEATTLE	42,403
9/21	L	13-20	at Cleveland	63,614
9/28	L	7-24	SAN DIEGO	45,161
10/5	W	31-17	at Oakland	40,153
10/12	W	21-20	HOUSTON	75,048
10/19	W	23-17	at Denver	74,459
10/26	W	20-17	DETROIT	59,391
11/2	L	24-31	BALTIMORE	52,383
11/9	W	31-30	at Seattle	58,976
11/16	L	7-20	at San Diego	50,248
11/23	W	21-13	at St. Louis	42,871
11/30	L	6-20	CINCINNATI	41,594
12/7	W	31-14	DENVER	40,237
12/14	L	16-21	at Pittsburgh	50,013
12/21	W	38-28	at Baltimore	16,941

Individual Statistics

Passing

	Att.	Cmp.	Yds.	Pct.	TD	INT	LG	Rating
Fuller	320	193	2250	60.3	10	12	77	76.1
Kenney	69	37	542	53.6	5	2	75t	91.4
Clements	12	7	77	58.3	0	0	18	77.4
Chiefs Totals	401	237	2869	59.1	15	14	77t	78.9
Opp. Total	523	278	3394	53.2	25	28	62	67.0

Receiving

	No.	Yds.	Avg.	LG	TD
Marshall	47	799	17.0	75t	6
J.T. Smith	46	655	14.2	77	2
Reed	44	422	9.6	34	1
McKnight	38	320	8.4	26	0
Hadnot	15	97	6.5	18	0
Gant	9	68	7.6	33	0
Samuels	8	110	13.8	34	2
Dixon	7	115	16.4	32	1
Belton	5	94	18.8	55	0
Morgado	5	27	5.4	10	1
Rome	3	58	19.3	33	0
Garcia	3	27	9.0	10	1
Williams	2	9	4.5	6	1
Chiefs Totals	237	2869	12.1	77	15
Opp. Totals	278	3394	12.2	63	25

Rushing

	No.	Yds.	Avg.	LG	TD
McKnight	206	693	3.4	25	3
Fuller	60	274	4.5	38	4
Belton	68	273	4.0	14	2
Hadnot	76	244	3.2	11	2
Reed	68	180	2.6	24	0
Morgado	47	120	2.6	11	4
Carson	2	41	20.5	37	0
Gant	9	32	3.6	11	0
Marshall	3	22	7.3	9	0
Kenney	8	8	1.0	4	0
Clements	2	0	0.0	0	0
Grupp	3	-14	-4.7	-4	0
Chiefs Totals	552	1873	3.39	38	15
Opp. Totals	536	2201	4.12	57	17

Team Statistics

	Chiefs	Opp.
Total First Downs	270	328
Rushing	130	136
Passing	122	179
Penalty	18	13
3rd Down: Made Att.	93/230	109/231
3rd Down Pct.	40.4	47.2
Total Net Yards	4321	5315
Avg. Per Game	270.1	332.2
Total Plays	1009	1096
Avg. Per Play	4.2	4.9
Net Yards Rushing	1873	2206
Avg. Per Game	117.1	137.9
Total Rushes	552	536
Avg. Per Play	3.4	4.1
Net Yards Passing	2448	3109
Avg. Per Game	153.0	194.3
Sacked/Yards Lost	57/241	37/284
Gross Yards	2869	3394
Attempts/Completions	401/237	523/278
Pct. of Completions	59.1	53.2
Had Intercepted	14	28
Punts/Average	85/390	67/41.6
Net Punting Avg.	33.7	31.4
Penalties/Yards	74/698	82/617
Fumbles/Lost	42/16	26/15
Touchdowns	37	42
Rushing	15	17
Passing	15	25
Returns	7	0
Safeties	0	0

Score By Periods

	1	2	3	4	OT	Total
Chiefs Total	58	105	75	81	0	319
Opp. Total	62	109	80	85	0	336

Regular Starters

	Offense		Defense
WR	Henry Marshall	LE	**Art Still**
LT	Matt Herkenhoff	NT	Don Parrish
LG	Bobby Simmons	RE	Dave Lindstrom
C	Jack Rudnay	LOLB	Thomas Howard
RG	Tom Condon	LILB	Frank Manumaleuga
RT	Charlie Getty	RILB	Gary Spani
	Jim Rourke	ROLB	Whitney Paul
TE	Mike Williams	LCB	Gary Green
WR	**J.T. Smith**	RCB	Eric Harris
QB	Steve Fuller	SS	Herb Christopher
RB	Tony Reed	FS	**Gary Barbaro**
	James Hadnot	P	Bob Grupp
RB	Ted McKnight		
K	Nick Lowery		

PRO-BOWLERS in Bold

Team Leaders

Scoring: Nick Lowery	97 pts: 37 PATs, 20 FGs
INTs: Gary Barbaro	10-163 yds., 0 TDs
Tackles: Gary Spani	149 (96 solo)
Sacks: Art Still	14.5 (-115 yds.)
Punting: Bob Grupp	84-3317 yds., 39.5 avg., 57 LG
Punt Returns: J.T. Smith	40-581 yds., 14.5 avg., 2 TDs
Kickoff Returns: Carlos Carson	40-917 yds., 22.9 avg., 0 TDs

1980 AFC Standings

Western Division

	W	L	T	Pct.
San Diego	11	5	0	.688
Oakland +	11	5	0	.688
Kansas City	8	8	0	.500
Denver	8	8	0	.500
Seattle	4	12	0	.250

Central Division

	W	L	T	Pct.
Cleveland	11	5	0	.688
Houston +	11	5	0	.688
Pittsburgh	9	7	0	.963
Cincinnati	6	10	0	.375

Eastern Division

	W	L	T	Pct.
Buffalo	11	5	0	.688
New England	10	6	0	.625
Miami	8	8	0	.500
Baltimore	7	9	0	.438
N.Y. Jets	4	12	0	.250

AFC Championship: Oakland 34, SAN DIEGO 27
Super Bowl XV: Oakland 27, Philadelphia 10

Gary Barbaro (26) and Charles Jackson (51) close in on a St. Louis runner. (Kansas Collection, U. of Kansas)

Ted McKnight follows four-time Pro Bowl center Jack Rudnay. McKnight was the Chiefs' leading rusher again in 1980. (Kansas Collection, U. of Kansas)

1981 Head Coach: Marv Levy

The Chiefs' defense smothers a Chicago runner. (Kansas Collection, U. of Kansas)

It was a breakthrough season by all accounts for the Chiefs, as they competed for a playoff spot late into the schedule and eventually finished with the team's first winning record, 9-7, since 1973. Coach Marv Levy's defense was blossoming into one of the league's best, and when rookie running back Joe Delaney burst into the lineup for the offense, Kansas City had the kind of explosive back missing from its backfield since the days of Abner Haynes and Mike Garrett. Delaney averaged 4.8 yards per carry and topped the 1,000-yard rushing mark for the season, despite not starting until a third of the season was gone. The Chiefs weren't eliminated from the playoff race until a crushing 17-7 loss to the Dolphins in the next-to-last game of the year. Bill Kenney stepped in at quarterback for the injured Steve Fuller and was adequate. J. T. Smith caught 63 passes to lead the receivers. Despite the five-game absence of Pro Bowler Art Still, the defense was solid throughout, led by the Chiefs' other defensive Pro Bowlers, Gary Barbaro and Gary Green. Gary Spani also contributed greatly, making 153 tackles. Delaney and kicker Nick Lowery were also chosen for the Pro Bowl.

Key Dates in 1981:

September 6—Kansas City travels to Pittsburgh and opens the season with a 37-33 victory.

October 25—Kansas City improves its record to 6-2 by defeating the Raiders for the second time in three weeks, 28-17.

November 15—Joe Delaney rushes for 193 yards against the Oilers at Arrowhead. The Chiefs win, 23-10.

November 26—Kansas City loses to Detroit on Thanksgiving Day 27-10, dropping their record to 8-5.

December 20—The Chiefs conclude the season with a 10-6 win at Minnesota. For the first time since 1973 they post a winning record, a 9-7 mark.

Big Game of 1981

October 18 at Kansas City
Kansas City 28, Denver 14

It is a role the Chiefs have coveted for many seasons, one that is usually out of reach by this point of the season—that of the playoff contender.

By overcoming various mistakes and defeating a good Broncos team, 28-14, the Chiefs stepped into a world they had desired, but hadn't achieved in several seasons. Now tied for first place in the AFC West, Kansas City can legitimately claim a spot in the race for the playoffs.

"Evidence of a good team is the ability to overcome mistakes," Marv Levy said after the game.

Kansas City turned the ball over five times, allowed more than 300 yards passing, and made mental mistakes throughout the contest. But they made the plays necessary to hold off Denver and now stand with an impressive 5-2 record.

"We found a way to win," Jack Rudnay said of the team's effort. "We made a lot of mistakes, but we still won. ... Maybe in years past when we fumbled the ball away like that, we would have folded our tents and gone home. But this club has a lot of inner confidence."

Rookie sensation Joe Delaney led the offense with 149 yards rushing, including an electrifying 82-yard run for the Chiefs' final score. Chiefs quarterback Bill Kenney threw just 12 times and completed six for 100 yards. His biggest toss was to Henry Marshall for 64 yards and a touchdown. It was the defense that won this game, though, and Levy knew it.

"They did a superb job," Levy boasted of his defensive unit. "They kept coming up with the big plays to bail us out. They played with verve and played a dogged-type of game.

"What do you say? It feels great."

Even though the Chiefs would win just four more games the rest of the season, 1981 was truly a turn-the-corner year.

Preseason
Record: 1-3

Date	W/L	Score	Opponent	Attendance
8/7	L	10-16	at Washington	32,488
8/15	W	13-0	CHICAGO	41,099
8/22	L	3-16	ST. LOUIS	42,550
8/28	L	7-31	at Miami	36,896

Regular Season
Record: 9-7

Date	W/L	Score	Opponent	Attendance
/6	W	37-33	at Pittsburgh	53,305
9/13	W	19-10	TAMPA BAY	50,555
9/20	L	31-42	SAN DIEGO	63,866
9/27	W	20-14	at Seattle	59,255
10/4	L	17-33	at New England	55,931
10/11	W	27-0	OAKLAND	76,543
10/18	W	28-14	DENVER	74,672
10/25	W	28-17	at Oakland	42,914
11/1	L	20-22	at San Diego	51,307
11/8	L	*13-16	CHICAGO	60,605
11/15	W	23-10	HOUSTON	73,984
11/22	W	40-13	SEATTLE	49,002
11/26	L	10-27	at Detroit (Thur.) (Thanksgiving)	76,735
12/6	L	13-16	at Denver	74,744
12/13	L	7-17	MIAMI	57,407
12/20	W	10-6	at Minnesota	41,110

Individual Statistics

Passing

	Att.	Cmp.	Yds.	Pct.	TD	INT	LG	Rating
Kenney	274	147	1983	53.6	9	16	64t	63.8
Fuller	134	77	934	57.5	3	4	53	73.9
Marshall	1	0	0	0.0	0	1	0	0.0
Hadnot	1	0	0	0.0	0	1	0	0.0
Chiefs Totals	410	224	2917	54.6	12	22	64t	64.4
Opp. Total	567	291	3821	51.3	16	26	86t	63.1

Receiving

	No.	Yds.	Avg.	LG	TD
J.T. Smith	63	852	13.5	42	2
Marshall	38	620	16.3	64t	4
Dixon	29	356	12.3	48	2
Hadnot	23	215	9.3	20	0
Delaney	22	246	11.2	61	0
Rome	17	203	11.9	23	1
McKnight	8	77	9.6	23	0
Carson	7	179	25.6	53	1
B. Jackson	6	31	5.2	10	1
Scott	5	72	14.4	26	1
Bledsoe	3	27	9.0	17	0
Murphy	2	36	18.0	22	0
Williams	1	3	3.0	3	0
Chiefs Totals	224	2917	13.0	64t	12
Opp. Totals	291	3821	13.1	86	16

Rushing

	No.	Yds.	Avg.	LG	TD
Delaney	234	1121	4.8	82t	3
Hadnot	140	603	4.3	30	3
B. Jackson	111	398	3.6	31	10
McKnight	54	195	3.6	26	5
Fuller	19	118	6.2	27	0
Kenney	24	89	3.7	21	1
Marshall	3	69	23.0	34	0
Bledsoe	20	65	3.3	13	0
Williams	2	0	0.0	3	0
Carson	1	-1	-1.0	-1	0
Dixon	1	-5	-5.0	-5	0
Grupp	1	-19	-19.0	-19	0
Chiefs Totals	610	2633	4.3	82t	22
Opp. Totals	507	1747	3.5	30	17

Team Statistics

	Chiefs	Opp.
Total First Downs	315	316
Rushing	160	112
Passing	132	177
Penalty	23	27
3rd Down: Made Att.	91/217	93/238
3rd Down Pct.	41.9	39.1
Total Net Yards	5273	5373
Avg. Per Game	329.6	335.8
Total Plays	1057	1102
Avg. Per Play	5.0	4.9
Net Yards Rushing	2633	1747
Avg. Per Game	164.6	109.2
Total Rushes	610	507
Avg. Per Play	4.3	3.4
Net Yards Passing	2640	3626
Avg. Per Game	165.0	226.6
Sacked/Yards Lost	37/277	27/195
Gross Yards	2917	3821
Attempts/Completions	410/224	567/291
Pct. of Completions	54.6	51.3
Had Intercepted	22	26
Punts/Average	70/38.5	80/38.9
Net Punting Avg.	33.2	30.8
Penalties/Yards	96/920	88/723
Fumbles/Lost	36/24	42/21
Touchdowns	38	34
Rushing	22	17
Passing	12	16
Returns	4	1
Time of Possession	31:01	28:59

Score By Periods

	1	2	3	4	OT	Total
Chiefs Total	85	69	85	104	0	343
Opp. Total	82	97	51	57	3	290

Regular Starters

	Offense		Defense
WR	Henry Marshall	LE	**Art Still**
LT	Matt Herkenhoff	NT	Don Parrish
LG	Brad Budde		Ken Kremer
C	Jack Rudnay	RE	Mike Bell
RG	Tom Condon	LOLB	Thomas Howard
RT	Charlie Getty	LILB	Jerry Blanton
TE	Al Dixon	RILB	Gary Spani
WR	J.T. Smith	ROLB	Charles Jackson
QB	Bill Kenney	LCB	**Gary Green**
RB	**Joe Delaney**	RCB	Eric Harris
RB	James Hadnot	SS	Lloyd Burruss
K	**Nick Lowery**	FS	**Gary Barbaro**
		P	Bob Grupp

PRO-BOWLERS in Bold

Team Leaders

Scoring: Nick Lowery	115 pts: 37 PATs, 26 FGs	
INTs: Eric Harris	7-109 yds., 1 TD	
Tackles: Gary Spani	153 (104 solo)	
Sacks: Ken Kremer	8.0 (-57.5 yds.)	
Punting: Bob Grupp	41-1556 yds., 38.0 avg., 5 ln 20, 57 LG	
Punt Returns: J.T. Smith	50-528 yds., 10.6 avg., 0 TDs	
Kickoff Returns: James Murphy	20-457 yds., 22.9 avg., 0 TDs	

1981 AFC Standings

Western Division

	W	L	T	Pct.
San Diego	10	6	0	.625
Denver	10	6	0	.625
Kansas City	9	7	0	.563
Oakland	7	9	0	.438
Seattle	6	10	0	.375

Central Division

	W	L	T	Pct.
Cincinnati	12	4	0	.750
Pittsburgh	8	8	0	.500
Houston	7	9	0	.438
Cleveland	5	11	0	.313

Eastern Division

	W	L	T	Pct.
Miami	11	4	1	.719
N.Y. Jets +	10	5	1	.656
Buffalo +	10	6	0	.625
Baltimore	2	14	0	.125
New England	2	14	0	.125

AFC Championship: CINCINNATI 27, San Diego 7
Super Bowl XVI: San Francisco 26, Cincinnati 21

Nick Lowry led the Chiefs with 115 points. (Alan Barzee)

J.T. Smith returns a punt against the Bears. (Kansas Collection, U. of Kansas)

1982 Head Coach: Marv Levy

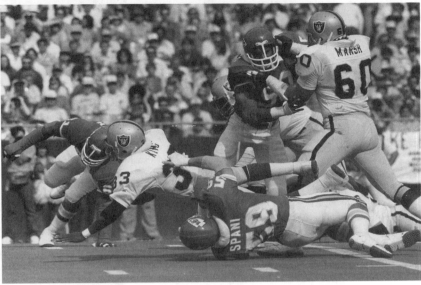

Gary Spani pulls down Raider running back Kenny King. (Kansas Collection, U. of Kansas)

After four years of rebuilding, it appeared at the outset of the season that Marv Levy had prepared the Chiefs to make the playoffs for the first time in more than a decade. Kansas City split its first two games of the season, and then the NFL Players Association called a players strike. By the time the strike ended and play resumed in late November, seven games were lost from the schedule, and the Chiefs were incapable of restoring their early-season fire. They lost their first four games after coming back and once again sat on the outside looking in when the playoffs began. The offense was inconsistent and the defense never lived up to its preseason expectations. Joe Delaney led the offense with just 380 yards rushing and was hampered much of the season by an eye injury. Bill Kenney and Steve Fuller alternated at quarterback, but Nick Lowery performed well in the short season, scoring 74 points. On defense, Gary Green and Gary Barbaro were once again named to the Pro Bowl. Veteran center Jack Rudnay called it quits after the season concluded. Fan interest in the team fell considerably during the short season, partly because of the strike, but mainly because of the team's losing record. Marv Levy was fired two days after the season ended.

Key Dates in 1982:

September 12—Kansas City loses the season opener in Buffalo, 14-9.

September 19—The Chiefs defeat the Chargers at home, 19-12, and even their record at 1-1. The NFL Players Association went on strike following the second week of play. Seven games were lost from the schedule.

November 21—Kansas City loses at New Orleans in their return game from the strike, 27-17.

December 12—The Raiders come to Arrowhead to hand Kansas City their fourth loss in a row, 21-16.

December 19—The Chiefs rout the Broncos in Denver, 37-16.

January 2, 1983—The Chiefs cruise to an easy win over the Jets, 37-13. A small crowd of only 11,902 fans show up for the season finale of the strike-plagued campaign. The Chiefs finish with a 3-6 record.

January 4, 1983—Marv Levy is fired.

Big Game of 1982

November 21 at New Orleans
New Orleans 27, Kansas City 17

The Saints returned from the players strike ready to play football. The Chiefs just returned. Playing lackadaisical on offense, defense, and particularly special teams, the Chiefs fell to New Orleans, 27-17, at the Superdome.

"It is absolutely the most galling thing to have happen to you," Marv Levy said of the Chiefs' special teams performance. "To have the thing that you count on being your strength be the cause of the defeat is absolutely galling."

The biggest play for New Orleans came after the Chiefs pulled to within three points in the fourth quarter on Steve Fuller's 13-yard touchdown pass to Al Dixon. Saint return man Wayne Wilson took the following kickoff on his own seven-yard line and returned to the Kansas City 18. The Saints scored a touchdown four plays later.

"It's obvious the layoff hurt us," Gary Barbaro said of the Chiefs' poor performance. "Just the points we gave up are an indication. ... We didn't play our own game, so the layoff hurt us, it really did."

The Chiefs could muster just 44 yards rushing and made two turnovers. The Saints ran for 149 yards.

"We just couldn't put together anything consistent," Steve Fuller said. "We made a big play here, then had a couple of breakdowns, then a big play."

The loss put the Chiefs at 1-2 and in ninth place in the AFC. Eight teams ultimately qualified for the playoffs in the strike-shortened format, but the Chiefs and their 3-6 overall record weren't one of the clubs.

Preseason

Record: 2-1-1

Date		Score	Opponent	Attendance
8/13	W	26-10	CINCINNATI	39,815
8/21	L	3-6	at New Orleans	46,585
8/28	T	17-17	MIAMI	42,290
9/4	W	10-6	at St. Louis	39,926

Regular Season

Record: 3-6

Date		Score	Opponent	Attendance
9/12	L	9-14	at Buffalo	79,383
9/19	W	19-12	SAN DIEGO	60,514
11/21	L	17-27	at New Orleans	39,341
11/28	L	14-20	at L.A. Rams	45,793
12/5	L	14-35	at Pittsburgh	52,090
12/12	L	16-21	L.A. RAIDERS	26,307
12/19	W	37-16	at Denver	74,192
12/26	L	13-26	SAN FRANCISCO	24,319
1/2	W	37-13	N.Y. JETS	11,902

*Season shortened to nine games due to NFLPA strike

Individual Statistics

Passing

	Att.	Cmp.	Yds.	Pct.	TD	INT	LG	Rating
Kenney	169	95	1192	56.2	7	6	51	77.0
Fuller	93	49	665	52.7	3	2	51	77.3
Gagliano	1	1	7	100.0	0	0	7	95.8
Marshall	1	0	0	0.0	0	0	0	39.6
Chiefs Totals	264	145	1864	54.9	10	8	51	77.4
Opp. Total	262	155	1787	59.2	12	12	74t	76.0

Receiving

	No.	Yds.	Avg.	LG	TD
Marshall	40	549	13.7	44t	3
Carson	27	494	18.3	51	2
Dixon	18	251	13.9	37	2
Hadnot	14	96	6.9	28	0
Delaney	11	53	4.8	13	0
Smith	10	168	16.8	51	0
Scott	8	49	6.1	13	1
Hancock	7	116	16.6	41t	1
B. Jackson	5	41	8.2	13	0
Rome	2	25	12.5	16	0
Gaines	2	17	8.5	7	0
Bledsoe	1	5	5.0	5	0
Chiefs Totals	145	1864	12.9	51	10
Opp. Totals	155	1787	11.5	74t	12

Rushing

	No.	Yds.	Avg.	LG	TD
Delaney	95	380	4.0	36	0
B. Jackson	86	243	2.8	18	3
Hadnot	46	172	3.7	25	0
Fuller	10	56	5.6	12	0
Kenney	13	40	3.1	12	0
Marshall	3	25	8.3	16	0
Bledsoe	10	20	2.0	5	0
Thompson	4	7	1.8	4	0
Gaines	1	0	0.0	0	0
Studdard	1	0	0.0	0	0
Chiefs Totals	269	943	3.5	6	3
Opp. Totals	279	1066	3.8	24	7

Team Statistics

	Chiefs	Opp.
Total First Downs	163	170
Rushing	71	69
Passing	79	92
Penalty	13	9
3rd Down: Made Att.	48/126	65/123
3rd Down Pct.	38.1	52.8
4th Down: Made Att.	7/12	2/4
4th Down Pct.	58.3	50.0
Total Net Yards	2498	2733
Avg. Per Game	277.6	303.7
Total Plays	573	556
Avg. Per Play	4.4	4.9
Net Yards Rushing	943	1066
Avg. Per Game	104.8	118.4
Total Rushes	269	279
Avg. Per Play	3.5	3.8
Net Yards Passing	1555	1667
Avg. Per Game	172.8	185.2
Sacked/Yards Lost	40/309	15/120
Gross Yards	1864	1787
Attempts/Completions	264/145	262/155
Pct. of Completions	54.9	59.2
Had Intercepted	8	12
Punts/Average	38/40.5	38/38.6
Net Punting Avg.	29.0	32.1
Penalties/Yards	43/372	59/476
Fumbles/Lost	13/4	23/10
Touchdowns	17	22
Rushing	3	7
Passing	10	19
Returns	4	3
Time of Possession	30:11	29:49

Score By Periods	1	2	3	4	OT	Total
Chiefs Total	33	63	16	64	0	176
Opp. Total	40	55	31	58	0	184

Regular Starters

	Offense		Defense
WR	Henry Marshall	LE	**Art Still**
LT	Matt Herkenhoff	NT	Ken Kremer
LG	Brad Budde	RE	Mike Bell
C	Jack Rudnay		Dave Lindstrom
RG	Tom Condon	LOLB	Thomas Howard
RT	Charlie Getty	LILB	Jerry Blanton
TE	Al Dixon	RILB	Gary Spani
WR	Carlos Carson	ROLB	Charles Jackson
QB	Bill Kenney	LCB	**Gary Green**
RB	Joe Delaney	RCB	Eric Harris
RB	Billy Jackson	SS	Lloyd Burruss
K	Nick Lowery	FS	**Gary Barbaro**
		P	Jeff Gossett

PRO-BOWLERS in Bold

Team Leaders

Scoring: Nick Lowery	74 pts: 17 PATs, 19 FGs	
INTs: Eric Harris	3-66 yds., 1 TD	
Gary Barbaro	3-48 yds., 1 TD	
Tackles: Art Still	68 (44 solo)	
Sacks: Art Still	3.5 (-30.5 yds.)	
Punting: Jeff Gossett	33-1366 yds., 41.1 avg., 56 LG	
Punt Returns: Anthony Hancock	12-103 yds., 8.6 avg., 0 TDs	
Kickoff Returns: Anthony Hancock	27-609 yds., 22.6 avg., 0 TDs	

1982 AFC Standings

	W	L	T	Pct.
L.A. Raiders	8	1	0	.889
Miami	7	2	0	.778
Cincinnati	7	2	0	.778
Pittsburgh	6	3	0	.667
San Diego	6	3	0	.667
N.Y. Jets	6	3	0	.667
New England	5	4	0	.556
Cleveland	4	5	0	.444
Buffalo	4	5	0	.444
Seattle	4	5	0	.444
Kansas City	3	6	0	.333
Denver	2	7	0	.222
Houston	1	8	0	.111
Baltimore	0	8	1	.056

AFC Championship: MIAMI 14, N.Y. Jets 0
Super Bowl XVII: Washington 27, Miami 17

Joe Delaney, who died tragically in the summer of 1983, led the Chiefs in rushing the two years he played. (Kansas Collection, U. of Kansas)

1983 Head Coach: John Mackovic

The Chiefs' superstar running back Joe Delaney died tragically in the summer, leaving a large void in his teammates' hearts. Delaney drowned while trying to rescue three children from a park pond. The Chiefs' new head coach was John Mackovic, and he was given the unenviable task of building the Chiefs' offense without Delaney. But surprisingly, it was the lack of consistent defensive play that hurt Kansas City throughout the season; they lost six games by a total of 18 points. Bill Kenney became the starting quarterback and thrived, passing for 4,348 yards and 24 touchdowns in Mackovic's new passing offense. Billy Jackson and Theotis Brown took over the running duties, but the Chiefs ran for just 1,254 yards as a team. Carlos Carson had a Pro Bowl season, catching 80 passes for 1,351 and seven touchdowns. Gary Barbaro left the Chiefs for the USFL, and while Deron Cherry took his place and performed well, the leadership role Barbaro had filled for several seasons was missing. Kenney, Cherry and Gary Green represented the Chiefs in the Pro Bowl. Kansas City outscored their opponents for the season but still finished with a losing record, 6-10.

Key Dates in 1983:

February 3—John Mackovic is chosen as the Chiefs' new head coach. Club President Jack Steadman said, "He's one of the brightest young men I have ever met at any age. I had tremendous recommendation on him."

June 29—Joe Delaney, the Chiefs' young superstar running back, drowns while trying to rescue three children from a park pond in Monroe, Louisiana. Only 24, Delaney promised to become one of the franchise's greatest running backs.

July 30—Bobby Bell becomes the first Chiefs player inducted into the Pro Football Hall of Fame in Canton, Ohio.

September 18—Nick Lowery kicks a club-record 58-yard field goal in the Chiefs' 27-12 loss to Washington.

December 11—Bill Kenney completes 31 of 41 passes for 411 yards and four touchdowns against the Chargers in San Diego. The Chiefs still lose, 41-38.

December 18—For the second year in a row, a small crowd of less than 12,000 specators attends the Chiefs' final game of the season. Kansas City destroys the playoff-bound Broncos, 48-17, finishing at 6-10 and tying for fourth in the division.

Big Game of 1983

November 27 at Seattle
Seattle 51, Kansas City 48 (OT)

Exhausting and unbelievable. After four-plus hours of play, almost 1,000 yards of offense, and a total of 99 points scored between the two teams, Kansas City succumbed to the Seattle Seahawks and lost a game they shouldn't have in overtime, 51-48.

"Losing, just flat losing this is just a game that has me boggled," Chiefs coach John Mackovic said afterward. "There are a lot of things about this game that have me bothered."

Here's what bothered Mackovic: the 51 points scored by Seattle are the most ever against the Chiefs; Seahawks running back Curt Warner ran for 207 yards; the Chiefs had leads of 14, 11, and three points, but lost them all; and Nick Lowery missed an extra point.

"You just don't lose a game like that," Chiefs running back Theotis Brown said. "You have to win that game; you just have to win it."

The Chiefs took their final lead of the game, 48-45, with 1:30 left to play on a 21-yard touchdown pass from Kenney to Brown. But Seattle quickly moved the into field-goal range and tied the score with two seconds left in regulation. When the Seahawks won the toss, they essentially won the game. Seattle kicker Norm Johnson booted the game-winner just 1:46 into the extra period.

"We've been down so long, and we have so many guys who want to win so much—this is so frustrating," Kenney said of the loss. "Sometimes you wonder if we know how to win. It is sickening."

"You've got to learn to endure, keep your character, and persevere," Chiefs defensive back Lucious Smith said. "Hard times won't last forever, but tough people will." The Chiefs are still searching for that toughness. The loss dropped their record to 5-8.

Bill Kenney had a great season in 1983, passing for 4,348 yards and 24 touchdowns. (Kansas Collection, U. of Kansas)

Preseason   Record: 2-2

Date	W/L	Score	Opponent	Attendance
8/6	W	24-7	at Cincinnati	42,662
8/13	L	13-17	DETROIT	32,885
8/20	W	17-16	ST. LOUIS	34,070
8/27	L	17-20	at Chicago	56,311

Regular Season   Record: 6-10

Date	W/L	Score	Opponent	Attendance
9/4	W	17-13	SEATTLE	42,531
9/12	L	14-17	SAN DIEGO (Mon.) (N.)	62,150
9/18	L	12-27	at Washington	52,610
9/25	L	6-14	at Miami	50,785
10/2	W	38-14	ST. LOUIS	58,975
10/9	L	20-21	at L.A. Raiders	40,492
10/16	W	38-17	N.Y. GIANTS	55,449
10/23	W	13-10	at Houston	39,462
10/30	L	24-27	at Denver	76,640
11/6	L	20-28	L.A. RAIDERS	75,497
11/13	W	20-15	CINCINNATI	46,711
11/20	L	21-41	at Dallas	64,102
11/27	L	48-51	at Seattle	56,793
12/4	L	9-14	BUFFALO	27,104
12/11	L	38-41	at San Diego	35,510
12/18	W	48-17	DENVER	11,377

Individual Statistics

Passing

	Att.	Cmp.	Yds.	Pct.	TD	INT	LG	Rating
Kenney	603	346	4348	57.4	24	18	53	80.8
Blackledge	34	20	259	58.8	3	0	43	112.3
J. Thomas	2	1	18	50	1	1	18t	81.3
Carson	1	1	48	100.0	1	0	48	158.3
Brown	1	1	11	100.0	0	0	11	112.5
Marshall	0	0	0	0.0	0	0	0	0.0
Chiefs Totals	641	369	4684	57.6	29	19	53	83.2
Opp. Total	500	261	3361	52.2	21	30	58	62.6

Receiving

	No.	Yds.	Avg.	LG	TD
Carson	80	1351	16.9	50t	7
Marshall	50	788	15.8	52	6
Brown	47	418	8.9	53	2
Hancock	37	584	15.8	50	1
B. Jackson	32	243	7.6	29	0
Paige	30	528	17.6	43	6
K. Thomas	30	254	8.5	25	1
Scott	29	247	8.5	22	6
Beckman	13	130	10.0	20	0
J. Thomas	8	33	4.1	7	0
J.T. Smith	7	85	12.1	18	0
Ricks	3	5	1.7	7	0
Hadnot	2	18	9.0	16	0
Kenney	1	0	0.0	0	0
Chiefs Totals	369	4684	12.7	53	29
Opp. Totals	261	3361	12.9	58	21

Rushing

	No.	Yds.	Avg.	LG	TD
B. Jackson	152	499	3.3	19	2
Brown	124	467	3.8	49t	8
J. Thomas	44	115	2.6	11	0
Kenney	23	59	2.6	11	3
K. Thomas	15	55	3.7	28	0
Ricks	21	28	1.3	10	0
Carson	2	20	10.0	18	0
Hadnot	4	10	2.5	7	0
Scott	1	1	1.0	1	0
Blackledge	1	0	0.0	0	0
Chiefs Totals	387	1254	3.2	49t	13
Opp. Totals	554	2275	4.1	60	19

Team Statistics

	Chiefs	Opp.
Total First Downs	314	319
Rushing	83	136
Passing	208	158
Penalty	23	25
3rd Down: Made Att.	93/234	83/221
3rd Down Pct.	39.7	39.6
4th Down: Made Att.	4/9	7/12
4th Down Pct.	44.4	58.3
Total Net Yards	5595	5386
Avg. Per Game	349.7	336.6
Total Plays	1074	1089
Avg. Per Play	5.2	4.9
Net Yards Rushing	1254	2275
Avg. Per Game	78.4	142.2
Total Rushes	387	554
Avg. Per Play	3.2	4.1
Net Yards Passing	4341	3111
Avg. Per Game	271.3	194.4
Sacked/Yards Lost	46/343	35/250
Gross Yards	4684	3361
Attempts/Completions	641/369	500/261
Pct. of Completions	57.6	52.2
Had Intercepted	19	30
Punts/Average	93/39.9	85/41.2
Net Punting Avg.	32.6	33.8
Penalties/Yards	113/911	105/837
Fumbles/Lost	30/19	34/21
Touchdowns	45	44
Rushing	13	19
Passing	29	21
Returns	3	4
Time of Possession	28:35	31:07

Score By Periods	1	2	3	4	OT	Total
Chiefs Total	86	96	85	116	3	386
Opp. Total	57	89	88	130	3	367

Regular Starters

	Offense		Defense
WR	**Carlos Carson**	LE	Art Still
LT	Matt Herkenhoff	NT	Dino Mangiero
LG	Brad Budde	RE	Mike Bell
C	Bob Rush	LOLB	Thomas Howard
RG	Tom Condon	LILB	Jerry Blanton
	Bob Simmons	RILB	Gary Spani
RT	Dave Lutz	ROLB	Calvin Daniels
TE	Willie Scott	LCB	**Gary Green**
WR	Anthony Hancock	RCB	Lucious Smith
	Henry Marshall	SS	Lloyd Burruss
QB	**Bill Kenney**	FS	**Deron Cherry**
TE	Ed Beckman	P	Jim Arnold
RB	Theotis Brown		
RB	Billy Jackson		
K	Nick Lowery		

PRO-BOWLERS in Bold

Team Leaders

Scoring: Nick Lowery — 116 pts: 44 PATs, 24 FGs
INTs: Deron Cherry — 7-100 yds., 0 TDs
Tackles: Jerry Blanton — 136 (83 solo)
Sacks: Mike Bell — 10.0 (-62.0 yds.)
Punting: Jim Arnold — 93-3710 yds., 39.9 avg.,
21 ln 10, 64 LG
Punt Returns: J.T. Smith — 26-210 yds., 8.1 avg., 0 TDs
Kickoff Returns: Theotis Brown — 15-301 yds., 20.1 avg., 0 TDs

1983 AFC Standings

Western Division

	W	L	T	Pct.
L.A. Raiders	12	4	0	.750
Seattle +	9	7	0	.563
Denver +	9	7	0	.563
San Diego	6	10	0	.375
Kansas City	6	10	0	.375

Central Division

	W	L	T	Pct.
Pittsburgh	10	6	0	.625
Cleveland	9	7	0	.563
Cincinnati	7	9	0	.483
Houston	2	14	0	.125

Eastern Division

	W	L	T	Pct.
Miami	12	4	0	.750
New England	8	8	0	.500
Buffalo	8	8	0	.500
Baltimore	7	9	0	.438
N.Y. Jets	7	9	0	.438

AFC Championship: L.A. RAIDERS 30, Seattle 14
Super Bowl XVII: L.A. Raiders 38, Washington 9

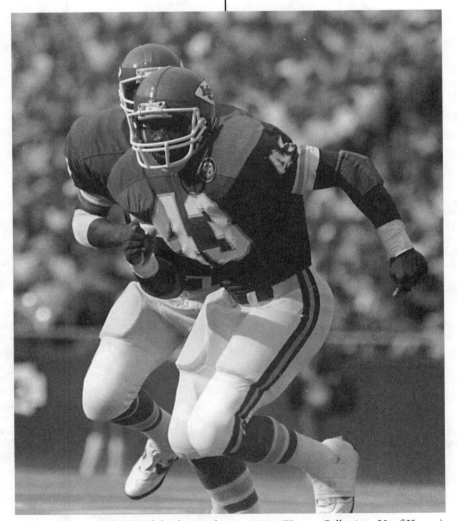

Billy Jackson was the Chiefs' leading rusher in 1983. (Kansas Collection, U. of Kansas)

1984 Head Coach: John Mackovic

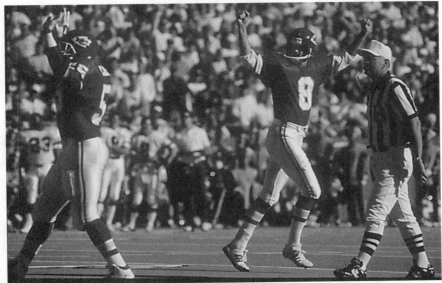

Nick Lowery led the Chiefs in scoring with 104 points. (Kansas Collection, U. of Kansas)

More preseason hopes, more regular-season disappointment. The Chiefs thought they would be in position to challenge for the playoffs during the season, but a preseason injury to Bill Kenney, an ineffective running game, and the loss of Gary Green on the defense led to an unimpressive 8-8 record. Second-year quarterback Todd Blackledge struggled until Kenney returned, and a four-game losing streak late in the season dashed any playoff chances. Henry Marshall enjoyed one of his finest seasons ever, catching 62 passes for 912 yards and four touchdowns. Herman Heard was the top running back with 684 yards. The defense was led by Pro Bowler Art Still, who had 14.5 sacks, Bill Maas, and Deron Cherry, who was selected for the Pro Bowl, too. As they had in the past, Kansas City had trouble with close contests and lost four games by a total of five points. Three straight wins at the end of the season evened the club's record, but it was obvious the Chiefs had played below their potential again.

Key Dates in 1984:

September 2—Kansas City opens with a 37-27 win over the Steelers.

October 14—Wide receiver Carlos Carson catches seven passes for 165 yards in the Chiefs' 31-13 win over the Chargers.

November 4—The Chiefs are humiliated in Seattle, 45-0.

December 9—The Chiefs avenge their earlier loss to the Seahawks and beat them at Arrowhead, 34-7.

December 16—An easy win over San Diego, 42-21, closes out the season for Kansas City. The Chiefs finish with a record of 8-8.

Big Game of 1984

December 2 at Kansas City
Kansas City 16, Denver 13

What a way to end a losing streak. It wasn't a big play, a defensive stop, or even a turnover. Kansas City defeated the Broncos because of an upright on the goal post. Denver's Rich Karlis clanked a potential game-tying kick off the right upright on the goalpost in the waning seconds of the fourth quarter, allowing Kansas City to escape with a 16-13 win. The four-game losing streak was history.

"I thought he was going to miss it," Chiefs guard Tom Condon said. "His foot (Karlis kicks barefooted) had to be freezing then. I was all bundled up, and I was cold."

Where Karlis failed, Nick Lowery succeeded. Trailing 13-7 going into the fourth quarter, Kansas City's kicking specialist booted three field goals, the last with less than two to go in the game.

"I've been waiting a long time for a kick like that," Lowery said of his second field goal, which hit the upright before going through. "They'll only remember that it went through, that it was good, and that I made the third one for the win."

The Chiefs' offense fought to find a rhythm most of the game.

"This was the most inconsistent game I have had with the Chiefs," Kenney said of his passing. He hit 20 of 38 passes for 281 yards. "Never have I hit so many big plays and missed the five and six yarders." Herman Heard added 84 yards rushing.

The win improved the Chiefs' record to 6-8, and they closed out the year with impressive wins over Seattle and San Diego to finish fourth in the division.

Preseason   Record: 1-3

8/4	L	20-34	NEW ORLEANS	34,230
8/10	L	10-14	at St. Louis	30,233
8/18	W	31-13	CLEVELAND	33,074
8/24	L	7-36	at New England	22,721

Regular Season   Record: 8-8

9/2	W	37-27	at Pittsburgh	56,709
9/9	W	27-22	at Cincinnati	47,111
9/16	L	20-22	L.A. RAIDERS	75,111
9/23	L	0-21	at Denver	74,263
9/30	W	10-6	CLEVELAND	40,785
10/7	L	16-17	N.Y. JETS	53,167
10/14	W	31-13	SAN DIEGO	67,465
10/21	L	7-28	at N.Y. Jets	76,891
10/28	W	24-20	TAMPA BAY	41,710
11/4	L	0-45	at Seattle	64,915
11/11	L	16-17	HOUSTON	44,464
11/18	L	7-17	at L.A. Raiders	48,575
11/25	L	27-28	at N.Y. Giants	74,383
12/2	W	16-13	DENVER	38,949
12/9	W	34-7	SEATTLE	34,855
12/16	W	42-21	at San Diego	40,211

Individual Statistics

Passing

	Att.	Cmp.	Yds.	Pct.	TD	INT	LG	Rating
Kenney	282	151	2098	53.5	15	10	65t	80.7
Blackledge	294	147	1707	50.0	6	11	46t	59.2
Osiecki	17	7	64	41.2	0	1	19	27.6
Chiefs Totals	593	305	3869	51.4	21	22	65t	68.5
Opp. Total	586	329	4009	56.1	19	30	80t	67.3

Receiving

	No.	Yds.	Avg.	LG	TD
Marshall	62	912	14.7	37	4
Carson	57	1078	18.9	57	4
Brown	38	236	6.2	17	0
Paige	30	541	18.0	65t	4
Scott	28	253	9.0	27	3
Heard	25	223	8.9	17	0
B. Jackson	15	101	6.7	11	1
Lacy	13	87	6.7	20	2
W. Arnold	11	95	8.6	15	1
Hancock	10	217	21.7	46t	1
Smith	8	69	9.4	16	0
Beckman	7	44	6.3	9	1
Little	1	13	13.0	13	0
Chiefs Totals	305	3869	12.7	65t	21
Opp. Totals	329	4009	12.2	80t	19

Rushing

	No.	Yds.	Avg.	LG	TD
Heard	65	684	4.1	69t	4
Brown	97	337	3.5	25	4
B. Jackson	50	225	4.5	16	1
Lacy	46	165	3.6	24t	2
Blackledge	18	102	5.7	26	1
Paige	3	19	6.3	9	0
Gunter	15	12	0.8	4	0
Ricks	2	1	0.5	1	0
W. Arnold	1	0	0.0	0	0
Osiecki	1	-2	-2.0	-2	0
Kenney	9	-8	-0.9	1	0
Carson	1	-8	-8.0	-8	0
Chiefs Totals	408	1527	3.7	69t	12
Opp. Totals	523	1982	3.8	52	10

Team Statistics

	Chiefs	Opp.
Total First Downs	295	335
Rushing	88	121
Passing	178	192
Penalty	29	22
3rd Down: Made Att.	73/221	89/246
3rd Down Pct.	33.0	36.2
4th Down: Made Att.	1/6	9/24
4th Down Pct.	16.7	37.5
Total Net Yards	5095	5625
Avg. Per Game	318.4	351.6
Total Plays	1034	1159
Avg. Per Play	4.9	4.9
Net Yards Rushing	1527	1982
Avg. Per Game	95.4	123.9
Total Rushes	408	523
Avg. Per Play	3.7	3.8
Net Yards Passing	3568	3645
Avg. Per Game	223.0	227.8
Sacked/Yards Lost	33/301	50/364
Gross Yards	3869	4009
Attempts/Completions	593/305	586/329
Pct. of Completions	51.4	56.1
Had Intercepted	22	30
Punts/Average	98/44.9	91/40.0
Net Punting Avg.	37.5	33.6
Penalties/Yards	99/806	108/951
Fumbles/Lost	34/15	18/11
Touchdowns	35	38
Rushing	12	10
Passing	21	19
Returns	2	9
Time of Possession	27:25	32:25

Score By Periods	1	2	3	4	OT	Total
Chiefs Total	57	105	61	91	0	314
Opp. Total	37	127	73	87	0	324

Regular Starters

	Offense		Defense
WR	Carlos Carson	LE	**Art Still**
LT	Matt Herkenhoff	NT	Bill Maas
LG	Brad Budde	RE	Mike Bell
C	Bob Rush	LOLB	Ken McAlister
RG	Tom Condon	LILB	John Zamberlin
RT	Dave Lutz		Jerry Blanton
	Jim Rourke	RILB	Gary Spani
TE	Willie Scott	ROLB	Calvin Daniels
WR	Henry Marshall	LCB	Albert Lewis
QB	Bill Kenney	RCB	Kevin Ross
	Todd Blackledge	SS	Lloyd Burruss
RB	Billy Jackson	FS	**Deron Cherry**
K	Nick Lowery	P	Jim Arnold

PRO-BOWLERS in Bold

Team Leaders

Scoring: Nick Lowery	104 pts: 35 PATs, 23 FGs
INTs: Deron Cherry	7-140 yds., 0 TDs
Tackles: Art Still	131 (107 solo)
Sacks: Art Still	14.5 (-86.0 yds.)
Punting: Jim Arnold	98-4397 yds., 44.9 avg., 63 LG
Punt Returns: J.T. Smith	39-332 yds., 8.5 avg., 0 TDs
Kickoff Returns: J.T. Smith	19-391 yds., 20.6 avg., 0 TDs

1984 AFC Standings

Western Division

	W	L	T	Pct.
Denver	13	3	0	.813
Seattle	12	4	0	.750
L.A. Raiders	11	5	0	.688
Kansas City	8	8	0	.500
San Diego	7	9	0	.438

Central Division

	W	L	T	Pct.
Pittsburgh	9	7	0	.563
Cincinnati	8	8	0	.500
Cleveland	5	11	0	.313
Houston	3	13	0	.188

Eastern Division

	W	L	T	Pct.
Miami	14	2	0	.875
New England	9	7	0	.563
N.Y. Jets	7	9	0	.438
Indianapolis	4	12	0	.250
Buffalo	2	14	0	.125

AFC Championship: MIAMI 45, Pittsburgh 28
Super Bowl XIX: San Francisco 38, Miami 16

Theotis Brown rushed for 337 yards and four touchdowns in 1984. (Kansas Collection, U. of Kansas)

1985 Head Coach: John Mackovic

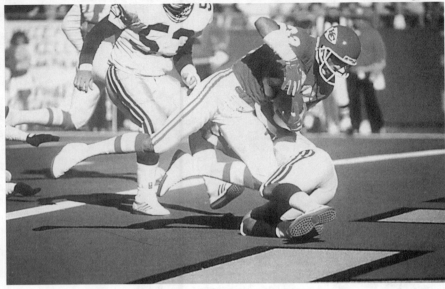

Stephone Paige had 10 touchdown receptions in 1985. (Kansas Collection, U. of Kansas)

The Chiefs were riddled with injuries throughout the season, and, as a result, had a poor running game, couldn't effectively stop the run, and suffered a seven-game losing streak in the middle of the season. Quarterback Bill Kenney almost missed playing time, which shortened what promised to be one of his best seasons. Backup Todd Blackledge was a poor replacement, throwing 14 interceptions and just six touchdowns passes. Injuries were everywhere. Art Still missed seven games, and the offensive line was hampered throughout the season. Herman Heard led the running game with 595 yards, and as a team, Kansas City averaged just 3.5 yards per rushing attempt. One of the few highlights of the season came in the final game when Stephone Paige broke the NFL record for the most receiving yardage in one game, 309 yards on eight receptions. Deron Cherry was again chosen for the Pro Bowl. But no matter how coach John Mackovic shuffled and planned, he couldn't prevent the Chiefs from missing the postseason for the 14th straight year.

Key Dates in 1985:

September 8—Bill Kenney passes for 397 yards and three touchdowns as the Chiefs smother the Saints in New Orleans, 47-27.

September 12—Nick Lowery kicks the second 58-yard field goal of his career as the Chiefs whip the Raiders at home, 36-20.

September 29—Chiefs free safety Deron Cherry ties an NFL record with four interceptions against the Seahawks at Arrowhead, and Kansas City wins, 28-7.

November 17—The Chiefs lose to the 49ers, 31-3, their seventh loss in a row.

December 22—Wide receiver Stephone Paige has eight receptions and racks up 309 receiving yards, a then-NFL record, as the Chiefs close out the season by beating San Diego, 38-34. The team still finishes in last place with a 6-10 record.

Big Game of 1985

October 6 at Los Angeles Raiders
Los Angeles Raiders 19, Kansas City 10

When the Chiefs lost their starting offensive tackles, they lost the game. Starting tackles Matt Herkenhoff and David Lutz were both out of the game before the first quarter was over, and any chance the Chiefs had to remain competitive against the Raiders left with them. Kansas City lost to the silver and black, 19-10.

"We are just breaking down in different places each week," Chiefs quarterback Bill Kenney said. "When we lost our tackles, our running game went downhill, and our passing game didn't click. We had a tough time. ... There just wasn't enough time to throw the ball."

The Raiders' defensive line toyed with the Chiefs the rest of the game, shutting off Kansas City's running game and sustaining a fierce pass rush that caused Kenney to hurry throws. They sacked him six times.

"A combination of things in the game didn't work in our favor," Chiefs coach John Mackovic said. "They (the Raiders) pressured the passer very well in the middle part of the game." Kansas City gained just 81 yards rushing and threw for 181 yards.

The defense was up, though, and kept the Chiefs in the game until the end.

"I really thought we were going to win it," Chiefs defensive end Mike Bell said. "I thought we would come back and win it 17-16 right at the end of the game."

The loss dropped the Chiefs record to 3-2, and was the first of what would turn into a seven-game losing streak. The Chiefs didn't win again until November 24, almost two months later.

Preseason   Record: 3-1

8/10	W	35-27	at Cincinnati	41,115
8/17	L	13-31	NEW ENGLAND	35,162
8/24	W	24-19	at Houston	36,501
8/31	W	17-13	ST. LOUIS	38,618

Regular Season   Record: 6-10

9/8	W	47-27	at New Orleans	57,760
9/12	W	36-20	L.A. RAIDERS (Thur.) (N)	72,686
9/22	L	0-31	at Miami	69,791
9/29	W	28-7	SEATTLE	50,485
10/6	L	10-19	at L.A. Raiders	55,133
10/13	L	20-31	at San Diego	50,067
10/20	L	0-16	L.A. RAMS	64,474
10/27	L	10-30	DENVER	68,248
11/3	L	20-23	at Houston	41,238
11/10	L	28-36	PITTSBURGH	46,126
11/17	L	3-31	at San Francisco	56,447
11/24	W	20-7	INDIANAPOLIS	21,762
12/1	L	6-24	at Seattle	52,655
12/8	W	38-10	ATLANTA	18,199
12/14	L	13-14	at Denver (Sat.)	69,209
12/22	W	38-34	SAN DIEGO	18,178

Individual Statistics

Passing

	Att.	Cmp.	Yds.	Pct.	TD	INT	LG	Rating
Kenney	338	181	2536	53.6	17	9	84t	83.6
Blackledge	172	86	1190	50.0	6	14	70	50.5
Horton	1	0	0	0	0	0	0	39.6
Chiefs Totals	511	267	3726	52.3	23	23	84t	72.3
Opp. Total	576	332	3752	57.6	22	27	56	70.3

Receiving

	No.	Yds.	Avg.	LG	TD
Carson	47	843	17.9	37t	4
Paige	43	943	21.9	84t	10
Heard	31	257	8.3	27	2
W. Arnold	28	339	12.1	38	1
Horton	28	185	6.6	22	1
Marshall	25	446	17.8	50	0
Smith	18	157	8.7	45t	2
Hancock	15	286	19.1	48	2
King	7	45	6.4	8	0
Pruitt	7	43	6.1	9	0
Scott	5	61	12.2	21	0
Holston	5	51	10.2	17	0
Hayes	5	39	7.8	12	1
Jones	3	31	10.3	15	0
Chiefs Totals	267	3726	14.0	84t	23
Opp. Totals	332	3752	11.3	56t	22

Rushing

	No.	Yds.	Avg.	LG	TD
Heard	164	595	3.6	33	4
Pruitt	105	366	3.5	54	2
Horton	48	146	3.0	19t	3
Smith	30	118	3.9	27	0
Blackledge	17	97	5.7	25	0
King	28	83	3.0	9	0
Carson	3	25	8.3	13	0
Lacy	6	21	3.5	6	0
Jones	12	19	1.6	7	0
Paige	1	15	15.0	15	0
Kenney	14	1	0.1	5	1
Chiefs Totals	428	1486	3.5	54	10
Opp. Totals	513	2169	4.2	50	18

Team Statistics

	Chiefs	Opp.
Total First Downs	258	336
Rushing	79	129
Passing	158	184
Penalty	21	23
3rd Down: Made Att.	76/224	99/239
3rd Down Pct.	33.9	41.4
4th Down: Made Att.	7/15	11/21
4th Down Pct.	46.7	52.4
Total Net Yards	4877	5658
Avg. Per Game	304.8	353.6
Total Plays	982	1126
Avg. Per Play	5.0	5.0
Net Yards Rushing	1486	2169
Avg. Per Game	92.9	135.6
Total Rushes	428	513
Avg. Per Play	3.5	4.2
Net Yards Passing	3391	3489
Avg. Per Game	211.9	218.1
Sacked/Yards Lost	43/335	37/263
Gross Yards	3726	3752
Attempts/Completions	511/267	576/332
Pct. of Completions	52.3	57.6
Had Intercepted	23	27
Punts/Average	95/40.3	75/41.2
Net Punting Avg.	32.3	34.2
Penalties/Yards	87/666	85/720
Fumbles/Lost	22/11	25/14
Touchdowns	35	41
Rushing	10	18
Passing	23	22
Returns	2	1
Time of Possession	28:06	31:54

Score By Periods	1	2	3	4	OT	Total
Chiefs Total	77	111	66	63	0	317
Opp. Total	39	135	65	121	0	360

Regular Starters

	Offense		Defense
WR	Carlos Carson	LE	Art Still
LT	Matt Herkenhoff	NT	Bill Maas
LG	Brad Budde	RE	Mike Bell
	Scott Auer	LOLB	Calvin Daniels
C	Bob Rush	LILB	Scott Radecic
RG	Bob Olderman	RILB	Gary Spani
RT	Dave Lutz	ROLB	Ken Jolly
TE	Walt Arnold	LCB	Albert Lewis
WR	Henry Marshall	RCB	Kevin Ross
	Stephone Paige	SS	Lloyd Burruss
QB	Bill Kenney	FS	**Deron Cherry**
	Todd Blackledge	P	Jim Arnold
RB	Herman Heard		
RB	Mike Pruitt		
	Bruce King		
K	Nick Lowery		

PRO-BOWLERS in Bold

Team Leaders

Scoring: Nick Lowery — 107 pts: 35 PATs, 24 FGs
INTs: Albert Lewis — 8-59 yds., 0 TDs
Tackles: Deron Cherry — 134 (85 solo)
Sacks: Bill Maas — 7.0 (-51.0 yds.)
Punting: Jim Arnold — 93-3827 yds., 41.2 avg., 62 LG
Punt Returns: Garcia Lane — 43-381 yds., 8.9 avg., 0 TDs
Kickoff Returns: Jeff Smith — 33-354 yds., 19.8 avg., 0 TDs

1985 AFC Standings

Western Division

	W	L	T	Pct.
L.A. Raiders	12	4	0	.750
Denve	11	5	0	.688
Seattle	8	8	0	.500
San Diego	8	8	0	.500
Kansas City	6	10	0	.375

Central Division

	W	L	T	Pct.
Cleveland	8	8	0	.500
Cincinnati	7	9	0	.438
Pittsburgh	7	9	0	.438
Houston	5	11	0	.313

Eastern Division

	W	L	T	Pct.
Miami	12	4	0	.750
N.Y. Jets	11	5	0	.688
New England	11	5	0	.688
Indianapolis	5	11	0	.313
Buffalo	2	14	0	.125

AFC Championship: New England 31, MIAMI 14
Super Bowl XX: Chicago 46, New England 10

Stephone Paige, Anthony Hancock and Willie Scott (Kansas Collection, U. of Kansas)

1986 Head Coach: John Mackovic

Kansas City had a swarming defense throughout the year, as shown here against the Chargers. (Kansas Collection, U. of Kansas)

The Chiefs returned to postseason play for the first time in 15 seasons. Led by the special teams, Kansas City won its final three games to finish at 10-6 and snag a playoff berth. Led by Albert Lewis' four blocked kicks, the special teams blocked a total of 11 kicks and had six returns for touchdowns through the course of the season. Never was the dominance of this unit more apparent than against the Steelers in the playoff-clinching game, when they were responsible for all three of the Chiefs' touchdowns. Despite losing convincingly to the Jets, Kansas City appeared ready to once again become a yearly threat in the AFC West. But the success of the team clouded the management's judgment, and in an ugly, silly move, head coach John Macokovic was fired and replaced by special teams coach Frank Gansz less than two weeks after the playoff game. Bill Kenney passed for 1,922 yards and 13 touchdowns, and Mike Pruitt led the rushers with 448 yards. Art Still led the defense with 10.5 sacks, and Bill Maas, Lloyd Burruss, and Deron Cherry were named to the Pro Bowl.

Key Dates in 1986:

August 2—Willie Lanier is inducted into the Pro Football Hall of Fame in Canton, Ohio.

September 7—Kansas City starts the season with a 24-14 win over the Bengals at Arrowhead.

October 19—The Chiefs win a close one over the Chargers at home, 42-41, improving the team's record to 4-3.

November 9—The Chiefs gain a victory against the Seahawks, 27-7. After ten games, Kansas City's record is 7-3.

November 30—The Chiefs lose their third game in a row to Buffalo at Arrowhead 17-14. They appear to be out of the chase for a playoff spot.

December 14—The Chiefs win against the Raiders in Los Angeles, 20-17, and keep their playoff hopes alive.

December 28—AFC wildcard playoff game. The Chiefs travel to New York for their first playoff game in 15 years. Starting quarterback Bill Kenney is injured and misses the game. As a result, the offense plays poorly, and the Chiefs lose to the Jets, 35-15. Kansas City took an early 6-0 lead on Jeff Smith's one-yard touchdown run, but the Jets score 28 straight points to put the game away.

Big Game of 1986

December 21 at Pittsburgh
Kansas City 24, Pittsburgh 19

No more waiting, no more looking to next year. Fifteen years of frustration, losing and apathy were wiped away. The Kansas City Chiefs were going back to the NFL playoffs.

"I don't know how many times we've been written off," Chiefs coach John Mackovic said after the game. "This is the greatest group of guys you'd ever want to be associated with. When you hear for so long about not being able to get into the playoffs and you come so close . . . it's gratifying to see these guys play this way."

It wasn't an easy win, and the Chiefs had to flex their special teams muscle to get the job done. Kansas City scored three first-half touchdowns off a blocked punt, a kickoff return, and a blocked field goal. The defense, despite giving up more than 500 yards in total offense, made the scores stand up, and the Chiefs had the win they needed.

"We did the way we have done it all year," Mackovic said, "with special teams and defense. Our offense wasn't that good today."

Kansas City gained a meager 171 yards of total offense and just eight first downs. They made their 24-7 halftime lead hold up, though.

"It means respect, it means acceptance," Nick Lowery said of the playoff berth. "Not so much acceptance from other people, but acceptance on our own part when you've been through so many years with people saying you're not worth anything. This proves something nobody can take away from us."

"This is wonderful," Chiefs owner Lamar Hunt said in the locker room after the game. "It's hard as heck to make it into the playoffs, just as we've proven for so long."

Preseason

Record: 2-2

Date		Score	Opponent	Attendance
8/9	W	20-0	CINCINNATI	30,067
8/16	W	27-26	at St. Louis	30,305
8/23	L	6-13	BUFFALO	39,911
8/30	L	10-13	at New Orleans	47,945

Regular Season

Record: 10-6

Date		Score	Opponent	Attendance
9/7	W	24-14	CINCINNATI	43,430
9/14	L	17-23	at Seattle	64,947
9/21	W	27-13	HOUSTON	43,699
9/28	W	20-17	at Buffalo	67,555
10/5	L	17-24	L.A. RAIDERS	74,430
10/12	L	7-20	at Cleveland	72,304
10/19	W	42-41	SAN DIEGO	55,767
10/26	W	27-20	TAMPA BAY	36,230
11/2	W	24-23	at San Diego	44,518
11/9	W	27-7	SEATTLE	53,268
11/16	L	17-38	at Denver	75,745
11/23	L	14-23	at St. Louis	29,680
11/30	L	14-17	BUFFALO	31,492
12/7	W	37-10	DENVER	47,019
12/14	W	20-17	at L.A. Raiders	68,771
12/21	W	24-19	at Pittsburgh	47,150

Individual Statistics

Passing

	Att.	Cmp.	Yds.	Pct.	TD	INT	LG	Rating
Kenney	308	161	1922	52.3	13	11	56	70.8
Blackledge	211	96	1200	45.5	10	6	70t	67.6
Green	1	0	0	0	0	1	0	0.0
Marshall	1	0	0	0	0	0	0	39.6
Chiefs Totals	521	257	3122	49.3	23	18	70t	68.5
Opp. Total	569	303	3555	53.3	21	31	51	62.1

Receiving

	No.	Yds.	Avg.	LG	TD
Paige	52	829	15.9	51	11
Marshall	46	652	14.2	31	1
J. Smith	33	230	7.0	18	3
Carson	21	497	23.7	70t	4
Arnold	20	169	8.5	27	1
Green	19	137	7.2	17	0
Heard	17	83	4.9	13	0
Coffman	12	75	6.3	10	2
Harry	9	211	23.4	53	1
Hayes	8	69	8.6	16	0
Pruitt	8	56	7.0	13	0
Moriarty	7	51	7.3	19	0
Hancock	4	63	15.8	25	0
Kenney	1	0	0.0	0	0
Chiefs Totals	257	3122	12.1	70t	23
Opp. Totals	303	3555	11.7	51	21

Rushing

	No.	Yds.	Avg.	LG	TD
Pruitt	139	448	3.2	16	2
Green	90	314	3.5	27	3
Heard	71	295	4.2	40	2
J. Smith	54	238	4.4	32	3
Moriarty	35	115	3.3	11	0
Blackledge	23	60	2.6	14	0
Kenney	18	0	0.0	9	0
Paige	2	-2	-1.0	12	0
Chiefs Totals	432	1468	3.4	40	10
Opp. Totals	485	1739	3.6	411	13

Team Statistics

	Chiefs	Opp.
Total First Downs	264	310
Rushing	83	111
Passing	152	173
Penalty	29	26
3rd Down: Made Att.	74/220	80/224
3rd Down Pct.	33.6	35.7
4th Down: Made Att.	5/9	7/16
4th Down Pct.	55.6	43.8
Total Net Yards	4218	4934
Avg. Per Game	263.6	308.4
Total Plays	1003	1098
Avg. Per Play	4.2	4.5
Net Yards Rushing	1468	1739
Avg. Per Game	91.8	108.7
Total Rushes	432	485
Avg. Per Play	3.4	3.6
Net Yards Passing	2750	3195
Avg. Per Game	171.9	199.7
Sacked/Yards Lost	50/372	44/360
Gross Yards	3122	3555
Attempts/Completions	521/257	569/303
Pct. of Completions	49.3	53.3
Had Intercepted	18	31
Punts/Average	99/40.7	83/37.0
Net Punting Avg.	33.7	30.9
Penalties/Yards	96/824	114/965
Fumbles/Lost	27/17	26/18
Touchdowns	43	38
Rushing	10	13
Passing	23	21
Returns	10	4
Time of Possession	28:29	31:31

Score By Periods	1	2	3	4	OT	Total
Chiefs Total	67	113	83	95	0	358
Opp. Total	49	121	90	66	0	326

Regular Starters

	Offense		Defense
WR	Carlos Carson	LE	Art Still
	Henry Marshall	NT	**Bill Maas**
LT	Irv Eatman	RE	Pete Koch
LG	Brad Budde	LOLB	Louis Cooper
C	Rick Donnalley	LILB	Dino Hackett
RG	Mark Adickes	RILB	Scott Radecic
RT	Dave Lutz	ROLB	Tim Cofield
TE	Walt Arnold	LCB	Albert Lewis
WR	Stephone Paige	RCB	Kevin Ross
QB	Todd Blackledge	SS	**Lloyd Burruss**
	Bill Kenney	FS	**Deron Cherry**
RB	Herman Heard	P	Lewis Colbert
RB	Mike Pruitt		
K	Nick Lowery		

PRO-BOWLERS in Bold

Team Leaders

Scoring: Nick Lowery — 100 pts: 43 PATs, 19 FGs
INTs: Deron Cherry — 9-150 yds., 0 TDs
Tackles: Dino Hackett — 140 (78 solo)
Sacks: Art Still — 10.5 (-77.0 yds.)
Punting: Lewis Colbert — 99-4033 yds., 40.7 avg., 56 LG
Punt Returns: Jeff Smith — 29-245 yds., 8.4 avg., 0 TDs
Kickoff Returns: Boyce Green — 10-254 yds., 25.4 avg., 1 TD

1986 AFC Standings

Western Division

	W	L	T	Pct.
Denver	11	5	0	.688
Kansas City	10	6	0	.625
Seattle	10	6	0	.625
L.A. Raiders	8	8	0	.500
San Diego	4	12	0	.250

Central Division

	W	L	T	Pct.
Cleveland	12	4	0	.750
Cincinnati	10	6	0	.625
Pittsburgh	6	10	0	.325
Houston	5	11	0	.313

Eastern Division

	W	L	T	Pct.
New England	11	5	0	.688
N.Y. Jets	10	6	0	.625
Miami	8	8	0	.500
Buffalo	4	12	0	.250
Indianapolis	3	13	0	.188

AFC Wildcard Playoff: Kansas City 15, N.Y. JETS 35
AFC Championship: Denver 23, CLEVELAND 20 (overtime)
Super Bowl XXI: N.Y. Giants 39, Denver 20

Albert Lewis and Lloyd Burruss (Kansas Collection, U. of Kansas)

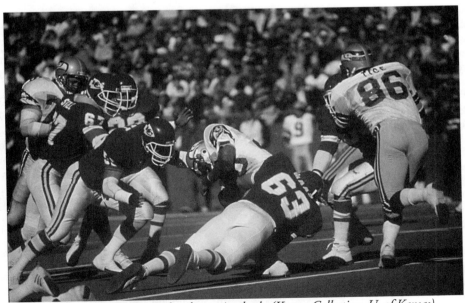

Bill Maas wraps up a Seahawk running back. (Kansas Collection, U. of Kansas)

1987 Head Coach: Frank Gansz

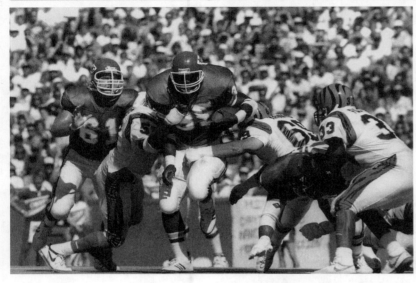

Christian Okoye burst into the Chiefs lineup and led the team in rushing yards.
(Kansas Collection, U. of Kansas)

The firing of John Mackovic was a coup of sorts, led by a few players and misguided management. He was replaced by his special teams coach, Frank Gansz. All Mackovic had done was lead the Chiefs back to the promised land of the playoffs; Gansz led the Chiefs back to last place. The league once again went through a players strike, but unlike 1982, the owners retaliated with "replacement players," and three weeks of non-NFL players suited up for the Chiefs. To make matters worse, the Chiefs' replacement players lost all three of their games, which were ridiculously counted in the standings, dooming the team's season and springing it to a franchise-record nine-game losing streak. The defense slipped badly from the year before, and despite the impressive debut of rookie Christian Okoye in the Chiefs' backfield, the offense was also sub-par. However, Carlos Carson had a stellar season, gaining 1,044 yards receiving on 55 receptions, earning a spot in the Pro Bowl. Bill Maas, Albert Lewis, and Deron Cherry were also given Pro Bowl honors.

Key Dates in 1987:

January 8—Despite leading the Chiefs into the playoffs for the first time in 15 years, John Mackovic is fired. The move leaves a lot of people perplexed.

January 10—Frank Gansz, special teams coach under Mackovic, is named head coach of the Chiefs.

August 8—Len Dawson is inducted into the Pro Football Hall of Fame in Canton, Ohio.

September 13—The Chiefs win the season opener at Arrowhead against the Chargers, 20-13. Two rookies, Paul Palmer and Christian Okoye, star in the win. Palmer returns a kickoff for a touchdown, and Okoye rushes for 105 yards.

September 27—Because of the players' strike, the Chiefs' game with the Vikings is cancelled. All NFL teams put together "replacement" teams, and league games resumed the following week.

October 18—The Chiefs' replacement team loses its third straight game, 26-17, to the Broncos, dropping the team's record to 1-4.

October 25—San Diego easily beats the "real" Chiefs in their return game from the strike, 42-21. Carlos Carson has 197 receiving yards in the loss.

November 22—The Chiefs lose a team-record ninth game in a row. Green Bay wins at Arrowhead, 23-3.

December 27—Kansas City defeats Seattle, 41-20, and finishes with a 4-11 record, last in the AFC West.

Big Game of 1987

October 4 at Los Angeles Raiders
Los Angeles 35, Kansas City 17

The uniforms were the same, but the names and faces were different. Masquerading as pro football players, the Kansas City Chiefs fielded their squad of "replacement" players against the Raiders' replacement players, and the result was ugly. The Chiefs were whipped, 35-17, in a mostly empty L.A. Coliseum.

"We weren't the Kansas City Chiefs," replacement linebacker Bob Harris said after the game. "No way were we the Kansas City Chiefs defense. . . We were just trying to show individually that we have the skills to play."

"These are very spirited guys," Chiefs coach Frank Gansz said of his replacement team. "They have tried very, very hard under very, very difficult circumstances to say the least."

Led by quarterback Vince Evans, the Raiders ran up 500 yards of total offense and led 21-0 at the half. At one point Kansas City cut the lead to 28-14 when Chiefs quarterback Matt Stevens hit Rod Jones on a four-yard touchdown pass. The Raiders scored at the beginning of the fourth quarter to put the game away.

"I play to win," Stevens said of the replacements' performance. "Coach Gansz is a super man, and I feel really disappointed that I let him down."

The loss dropped the Chiefs' record to 1-2 and sent the team into last place in the AFC West. This replacement game, like the two that followed, counted in the standings. This game was also the second loss in the Chiefs' franchise record nine-game losing streak. The regular players returned October 25th for the San Diego game.

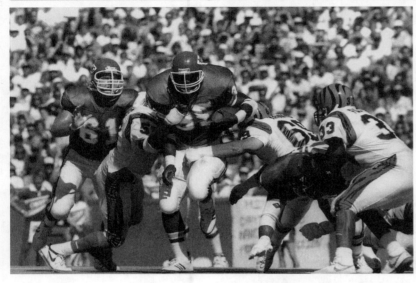

Preseason   Record: 4-1

8/8	L	7-20	San Francisco (Canton, OH)	23,826
8/13	W	32-20	at Houston	30,147
8/22	W		ATLANTA	39,164
8/29	W		BUFFALO	43,887
9/6	W	*13-10	St. Louis (Memphis, TN)	62,353

Regular Season   Record: 4-11

9/13	W	20-13	SAN DIEGO	56,940
9/20	L	14-43	at Seattle	61,667
9/27			MINNESOTA	(Cancelled/Strike)
10/4	L	17-35	*at L.A. Raiders	10,708
10/11	L	0-42	* at Miami	25,867
10/18	L	17-26	* DENVER	20,296
10/25	L	21-42	at San Diego	47,972
11/1	L	28-31	at Chicago	63,498
11/8	L	16-17	PITTSBURGH	45,249
11/15	L	9-16	N.Y. JETS	40,718
11/22	L	3-23	GREEN BAY	34,611
11/26	W	27-20	at Detroit (Thur.)	43,820
12/6	L	27-30	at Cincinnati	46,489
12/13	W	16-10	L.A. RAIDERS	63,834
12/19	L	17-20	at Denver (Sat.)	75,053
12/27	W	41-20	SEATTLE	20,370

- Replacement Games

Individual Statistics

Passing	Att.	Cmp.	Yds.	Pct.	TD	INT	LG	Rating
Kenney	273	154	2107	56.4	15	9	81t	85.8
Seuer	55	26	340	47.3	0	4	33	36.9
Blackledge	31	15	154	48.4	1	1	19	60.4
Palmer	1	0	0	0.0	0	0	0	39.6
Others	72	41	384	56.9	1	3	23	42.2
Chiefs Totals	432	236	2985	54.6	17	17	81t	73.1
Opp. Total	484	279	3473	57.6	25	11	44	87.8

Receiving	No.	Yds.	Avg.	LG	TD
Carson	55	1044	19.0	81t	7
Paige	43	707	16.4	51	4
Okoye	24	169	7.0	22	3
Hayes	21	272	13.0	33	2
Heard	14	118	8.4	15	0
Marshall	10	126	12.6	19	0
Moriarty	10	37	3.7	8	1
Coffman	5	42	8.4	13t	1
Palmer	4	27	6.8	10	0
Arnold	3	26	8.7	10	0
D. Colbert	3	21	7.0	9	0
Keel	2	9	4.5	7	0
Adickes	1	3	3.0	3t	1
Others	41	384	9.4	23	1
Chiefs Totals	236	2985	12.6	81t	17
Opp. Totals	279	3473	12.4	44	25

Rushing	No.	Yds.	Avg.	LG	TD
Okoye	157	660	4.2	43t	3
Heard	82	466	5.7	64t	3
Palmer	24	155	6.5	35	0
Moriarty	30	107	3.6	11	0
Seurer	9	33	3.7	11	0
Blackledge	5	21	4.2	11	0
Goodburn	1	16	16.0	16	0
Clemons	2	7	3.5	7	0
Kenney	12	-2	-0.2	6	0
Carson	1	-7	-7.0	-7	0
Others	96	343	3.6	17	1
Chiefs Totals	419	1799	4.3	64t	7
Opp. Totals	535	2333	4.4	48	16

Team Statistics

	Chiefs	Opp.
Total First Downs	265	344
Rushing	97	139
Passing	141	172
Penalty	27	33
3rd Down: Made Att.	77/192	92/206
3rd Down Pct.	40.1	44.7
4th Down: Made Att.	4/10	5/15
4th Down Pct.	40.0	33.3
Total Net Yards	4418	5639
Avg. Per Game	294.5	375.9
Total Plays	899	1045
Avg. Per Play	4.9	5.4
Net Yards Rushing	1799	2333
Avg. Per Game	119.9	155.5
Total Rushes	419	535
Avg. Per Play	4.3	4.7
Net Yards Passing	2619	3306
Avg. Per Game	174.6	220.4
Sacked/Yards Lost	48/366	26/167
Gross Yards	2985	3473
Attempts/Completions	432/236	484/279
Pct. of Completions	54.6	57.6
Had Intercepted	17	11
Punts/Average	69/40.4	56/40.4
Net Punting Avg.	32.3	31.7
Penalties/Yards	108/861	112/936
Fumbles/Lost	41/24	24/17
Touchdowns	30	45
Rushing	7	16
Passing	17	25
Returns	6	4
Time of Possession	27:10	32:50

Score By Periods	1	2	3	4	OT	Total
Chiefs Total	55	88	74	56	0	273
Opp. Total	88	116	93	88	3	388

Regular Starters

	Offense		Defense
WR	**Carlos Carson**	LE	Art Still
LT	John Alt	NT	**Bill Maas**
LG	Rich Baldinger	RT	Pete Koch
C	Tom Baugh	RE	Mike Bell
	Rick Donnalley	OLB	Louis Cooper
RG	Mark Adickes		Aaron Pearson
RT	Dave Lutz	ILB	Aaron Pearson
	Irv Eatman	MLB	Dino Hackett
TE	Jonathan Hayes	OLB	Tim Cofield
WR	Stephone Paige		Jack Del Rio
QB	Bill Kenney	LCB	**Albert Lewis**
RB	Christian Okoye	RCB	Kevin Ross
RB	Herman Heard	SS	Lloyd Burruss
K	Nick Lowery	FS	**Deron Cherry**
		P	Kelly Goodburn

Does not include replacement players
PRO-BOWLERS in Bold

Team Leaders

Scoring: Nick Lowery — 83 pts: 26 PATs, 19 FGs
INTs: Deron Cherry — 3-58 yds., 0 TDs
    Kevin Ross — 3-40 yds., 0 TDs
Tackles: Dino Hackett — 103 (74 solo)
Sacks: Mike Bell — 6.5 (-44.0 yds.)
Punting: Kelly Goodburn — 76-3059 yds., 40.3 avg., 55 LG
Punt Returns: Kitrick Taylor — 29-187 yds., 6.4 avg., 0 TDs
Kickoff Returns: Kenny Gamble — 15-291 yds., 19.4 avg., 0 TDs

1987 AFC Standings

Western Division

	W	L	T	Pct.
Denver	10	4	1	.700
Seattle	9	6	0	.600
San Diego	8	7	0	.533
L.A. Raiders	5	10	0	.333
Kansas City	4	11	0	.267

Central Division

	W	L	T	Pct.
Cleveland	10	5	0	.667
Houston	9	6	0	.600
Pittsburgh	8	7	0	.533
Cincinnati	4	11	0	.267

Eastern Division

	W	L	T	Pct.
Indianapolis	9	6	0	.600
New England	8	7	0	.533
Miami	8	7	0	.533
Buffalo	7	8	0	.467
N.Y. Jets	6	9	0	.400

AFC Championship: DENVER 38, Cleveland 33
Super Bowl XXII: Washington 42, Denver 10

Frank Gansz (Kansas Collection, U. of Kansas)

1988 Head Coach: Frank Gansz

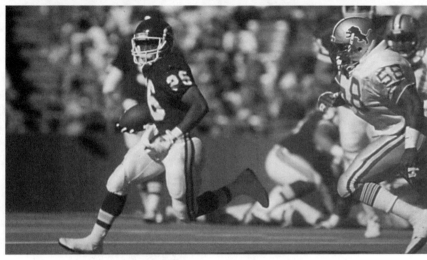

Paul Palmer (Kansas Collection, U. of Kansas)

Same old story for the Chiefs. Injuries riddled the team and they sank to last place. Coach Frank Gansz tried to right his floundering team, but couldn't. Quarterback Steve DeBerg, acquired from Tampa Bay, became the starter and passed for 2,935 yards, but an inconsistent running game hampered the offense throughout the season. The Chiefs suffered through a seven-game non-winning streak in the middle of the year. Christian Okoye fought the injury bug and rushed for just 473 yards to lead the team. Paul Palmer and Herman Heard each ran for more than 400 yards to pick up the slack. Stephone Paige caught 61 passes for 902 to lead the receiving corps. On defense, Deron Cherry, Albert Lewis and Dino Hackett had good seasons and were named to the Pro Bowl. But Bill Maas missed half the season and the Chiefs had problems stopping the run when he was out of the lineup. A 4-11-1 record was the result of Kansas City's poor play. Tired of losing, Lamar Hunt finally made some major changes. The first was to make Carl Peterson the President/General Manager and CEO of the team.

Key Dates in 1988:

September 4—Kansas City loses the season opener at home to Cleveland, 6-3.

September 18—The Chiefs defeat the Broncos at Arrowhead, 20-13.

November 13—The Chiefs end their seven-game non-winning streak by defeating the Bengals, 31-28.

December 18—The Chiefs lose at San Diego, 24-13, finishing the season with a record of 4-11-1, and again in last place in the AFC West.

December 19—Carl Peterson is named president/general manager/CEO of the Chiefs.

Big Game of 1988

October 4 at Kansas City
San Diego 24, Kansas City 23

A controversial penalty cost the Chiefs. A penalty that everyone, except the official, thought didn't happen. The result led to defeat for Kansas City, and San Diego left Arrowhead Stadium with a 24-23 win.

With 1:10 left in the game and the Chargers at the Chiefs' nine-yard line, San Diego quarterback Babe Laufenberg was hit by Kansas city linebacker Tim Cofield as he released a pass over the middle. The ball fluttered and was picked off by Dino Hackett. Cofield was called for roughing the passer, negating the interception. Two plays later Laufenberg threw a nine-yard touchdown pass to win the game.

"I couldn't believe it," Cofield said of the roughing penalty. "I didn't hit him with my head . . . I didn't hit him in the head . . . I didn't hit him late.

"I made contact with him as he threw the ball. I thought the ball was still in his hands. It's crazy to lose a game like that."

After the game, Laufenberg agreed with Cofield. "It wasn't a late hit," he said.

Kansas City held a 23-14 lead going into the fourth quarter, after trailing 14-0 early in the game. Steve DeBerg had thrown three touchdown passes, and it appeared with Hackett's interception they were going to escape with a win.

"I'm going to say I feel like we were robbed," Deron Cherry said of the penalty. "We made some mistakes out there that (if avoided) maybe wouldn't have put us in that situation."

The loss dropped the Chiefs 1-3, and they wouldn't win again until November 13 against the Bengals.

Preseason
Record: 2-1-1

8/6	W	34-21	CINCINNATI	31,947
8/13	W	27-13	at Atlanta	23,369
8/19	T	21-21	at Green Bay (Milwaukee, WI)	32,361
8/25	L	21-41	PHOENIX	36,883

Regular Season
Record: 4-11-1

9/4	L	3-6	CLEVELAND	55,654
9/11	L	10-31	at Seattle	61,512
9/18	W	20-13	DENVER	63,268
9/25	L	23-24	SAN DIEGO	45,498
10/2	T	17-17	at N.Y. Jets	66,110
10/9	L	6-7	at Houston	39,134
10/16	L	17-27	L.A. RAIDERS	77,078
10/23	L	6-7	DETROIT	66,926
10/30	L	10-17	at L.A. Raiders	36,103
11/6	L	11-17	at Denver	74,227
11/13	W	31-28	CINCINNATI	34,614
11/20	W	27-24	SEATTLE	33,152
11/27	L	10-16	at Pittsburgh	42,057
12/4	W	38-34	N.Y. JETS	30,059
12/11	L	12-28	at N.Y. Giants	69,809
12/18	L	13-24	at San Diego	26,339

Individual Statistics

Passing

	Att.	Cmp.	Yds.	Pct.	TD	INT	LG	Rating
DeBerg	414	224	2935	54.1	16	16	80t	73.5
Kenney	114	58	549	50.9	0	5	25	46.3
Chiefs Totals	528	282	3484	53.4	16	21	80t	67.6
Opp. Total	410	214	2591	52.2	12	18	42t	63.4

Receiving

	No.	Yds.	Avg.	LG	TD
Paige	61	902	14.8	49	7
Palmer	53	611	11.5	71t	4
Carson	46	711	15.5	80t	3
Harry	26	362	13.9	38	1
Hayes	22	233	10.6	25	1
Heard	20	198	9.9	32	0
Saxon	19	177	9.3	22	0
Roberts	10	104	10.4	20	0
Taylor	9	105	11.7	36	0
Okoye	8	51	6.4	12	0
Moriarty	6	40	6.7	12	0
Colbert	1	-3	-3.0	-3	0
Gamble	1	-7	-7.0	-7	0
Chiefs Totals	282	3484	12.4	80t	16
Opp. Totals	214	2591	12.1	42t	12

Rushing

	No.	Yds.	Avg.	LG	TD
Okoye	105	473	4.5	48	3
Palmer	134	452	3.4	26t	2
Heard	106	438	4.1	20	0
Saxon	60	236	3.9	14	2
Moriarty	20	62	3.1	9	0
DeBerg	18	30	1.7	13	1
Goodburn	1	15	15.0	15	0
Kenney	2	4	2.0	2	0
Taylor	1	2	2.0	2	0
Carson	1	1	1.0	1	0
Chiefs Totals	448	1713	3.8	48	8
Opp. Totals	609	2592	4.3	36	23

Team Statistics

	Chiefs	Opp.
Total First Downs	289	318
Rushing	104	162
Passing	161	136
Penalty	24	20
3rd Down: Made Att.	88/224	94/209
3rd Down Pct.	39.3	45.0
4th Down: Made Att.	12/18	6/13
4th Down Pct.	66.7	46.2
Total Net Yards	4844	5026
Avg. Per Game	302.8	314.1
Total Plays	1019	1042
Avg. Per Play	4.8	4.8
Net Yards Rushing	1713	2592
Avg. Per Game	107.1	162.0
Total Rushes	448	609
Avg. Per Play	3.8	4.3
Net Yards Passing	3131	2434
Avg. Per Game	195.7	152.1
Sacked/Yards Lost	43/353	23/157
Gross Yards	3484	2591
Attempts/Completions	528/282	410/214
Pct. of Completions	53.4	52.2
Had Intercepted	21	18
Punts/Average	76/40.3	63/40.2
Net Punting Avg.	31.9	34.2
Penalties/Yards	85/636	106/854
Fumbles/Lost	21/12	30/13
Touchdowns	24	39
Rushing	8	23
Passing	16	12
Returns	0	4
Time of Possession	28:31	31:29

Score By Periods	1	2	3	4	OT	Total
Chiefs Total	51	74	47	82	0	254
Opp. Total	77	118	52	73	0	320

Regular Starters

	Offense		Defense
WR	Carlos Carson	LE	Leonard Griffin
LT	John Alt		Neil Smith
LG	Rich Baldinger	NT	Bill Maas
C	Tom Baugh	RE	Mike Bell
RG	Mark Adickes	LOLB	Jack Del Rio
RT	Irv Eatman	LILB	Aaron Pearson
TE	Alfredo Roberts	RILB	**Dino Hackett**
	Jonathan Hayes	ROLB	Tim Cofield
WR	Stephone Paige	LCB	**Albert Lewis**
QB	Steve DeBerg	RCB	Kevin Ross
RB	Christian Okoye	SS	Lloyd Burruss
RB	Paul Palmer		Kevin Porter
K	Nick Lowery	FS	**Deron Cherry**
		P	Kelly Goodburn

PRO-BOWLERS in Bold

Team Leaders

Scoring: Nick Lowery	104 pts: 23 PATs, 27 FGs
INTs: Deron Cherry	7-51 yds., 0 TDs
Tackles: Deron Cherry	151 (90 solo)
Sacks: Bill Maas	4.0 (-34.0 yds.)
Punting: Kelly Goodburn	76-3059 yds., 40.3 avg., 59 LG
Punt Returns: Kitrick Taylor	29-187 yds., 6.4 avg., 0 TDs
Kickoff Returns: Kenny Gamble	15-291 yds., 19.4 avg., 0 TDs

1988 AFC Standings

Western Division

	W	L	T	Pct.
Seattle	9	7	0	.563
Denver	8	8	0	.500
L.A. Raiders	7	9	0	.438
San Diego	6	10	0	.375
Kansas City	4	11	1	.281

Central Division

	W	L	T	Pct.
Cincinnati	12	4	0	.750
Cleveland	10	6	0	.625
Houston	10	6	0	.625
Pittsburgh	5	11	0	.313

Eastern Division

	W	L	T	Pct.
Buffalo	12	4	0	.750
Indianapolis	9	7	0	.563
New England	9	7	0	.563
N.Y. Jets	8	7	1	.531
Miami	6	10	0	.375

AFC Championship: CINCINNATI 21, Buffalo 10
Super Bowl XXIII: San Francisco 20, Cincinnati 16

Irv Eatman (Kansas Collection, U. of Kansas)

Christian Okoye led the NFL in rushing with 1,480 yards. (Kansas Collection, U. of Kansas)

The Chiefs had changed coaches before, but never had the organization gone through the complete overhaul it did between the 1988 and 1989 seasons. Lamar hired Carl Peterson as the team's new President/General Manager. Peterson wasted no time in making changes—he fired head coach Frank Gansz two weeks after taking over. Less than three weeks after that he hired Marty Schottenheimer as the club's new head coach. Schottenheimer also cleaned house and with Peterson's help made several roster changes. The Chiefs started the season slowly, winning just one of their first four games. But then they started to win. Schottenheimer featured running back Christian Okoye in the offense, and the big back responded with a great season. He gained 1,480 yards to led the NFL, and also scored 12 touchdowns. Steve DeBerg passed for 2,529 yards, and Stephone Paige led the receivers with 44 receptions. Rookie linebacker Derrick Thomas made 10 sacks and with two weeks left in the season Kansas City looked like a playoff team. A disheartening loss to San Diego put an end to the Chiefs postseason hopes, but they finished at 8-7-1, good for second place in the AFC West. In addition to Okoye, Thomas, Albert Lewis and Kevin Ross from the defense were named to the Pro Bowl. This season proved to be a prelude of good things in the future.

Key Dates in 1989:

January 5—Carl Peterson fires Frank Gansz.

January 24—Marty Schottenheimer is hired as the Chiefs' head coach.

September 10—Schottenheimer loses his first game as the Chiefs' head coach at Denver, 34-20.

September 17—Kansas City downs the Raiders at Arrowhead, 24-19, Schottenheimer's first win as the Chiefs' head coach.

October 22—Christian Okoye carries the ball 33 times for 170 rushing yards as the Chiefs defeat the Cowboys at Arrowhead, 36-28.

November 26—Kansas City cruises past the Oilers, 34-0.

December 24—The Chiefs defeat the Dolphins for the second time in the season, 27-24, but still miss the playoffs. They finish with a winning record, 8-7-1, second in the AFC West.

Big Game of 1989

December 17 at Kansas City
San Diego 20, Kansas City 13

Using a bruising running game and a smothering defense, the San Diego Chargers marched into Arrowhead Stadium and crushed the Chiefs' playoff dreams. They bulldozed their way to 219 yards rushing, 176 by Marion Butts, and won, 20-13. The loss virtually eliminated the Chiefs from any chance of making the playoffs.

"They physically manhandled us today," Chiefs cornerback Albert Lewis said of the Chargers' running game.

"They kept us mixed up all day long," Chiefs linebacker Dino Hackett said of the Chargers' attack. "They ran a lot of misdirection rushing attempts, lots of pulling linemen. When we got in the 4-1 defense, they tried cutback runs." Everything seemed to work for the Chargers. For the Chiefs' vaunted running game, very little did.

Christian Okoye constantly found his path blocked, holes jammed. Chiefs quarterback Steve DeBerg was ineffective because of the chilling 18-degree weather and completed just 14 of 33 passes.

"If you get into situations where you have to throw against San Diego," Chiefs coach Marty Schottenheimer said, "you can bet that you're going to get your quarterback hit, and you're to get sacked."

The Chiefs had one final opportunity to tie the game, driving from their own 36 yard line to the San Diego 19. DeBerg's next pass into the end zone was intercepted, ending the Chiefs' chances and the game.

"It's very disappointing; it's a goal a lot of people in this room have been shooting for for a long time," Hackett said of the Chiefs' elimination from the playoffs. "When you get these opportunities, you have to take advantage of them.

"We had it in our grasp."

Preseason   Record: 1-3

Date	Result	Score	Opponent	Attendance
8/12	L	13-23	Minnesota (Memphis, TN)	63,528
8/20	L	7-45	N.Y. GIANTS	36,820
8/27	W	22-17	at Chicago	56,343
9/1	L	13-15	N.Y. JETS	41,105

Regular Season   Record: 8-7-1

Date	Result	Score	Opponent	Attendance
9/10	L	20-34	at Denver	74,284
9/17	W	24-19	L.A. RAIDERS	71,741
9/24	L	6-21	at San Diego	40,128
10/1	L	17-21	CINCINNATI	61,165
10/8	W	20-16	at Seattle	60,715
10/15	L	14-20	at L.A. Raiders	40,453
10/22	W	36-28	DALLAS	76,841
10/29	L	17-23	at Pittsburgh	54,194
11/5	W	20-10	SEATTLE	54,489
11/12	L	13-16	DENVER	76,245
11/19	T	10-10	at Cleveland	77,922
11/26	W	34-0	HOUSTON	51,342
12/3	W	25-21	MIAMI	54,610
12/10	W	21-3	at Green Bay	56,694
12/17	L	13-20	SAN DIEGO	40,623
12/24	W	27-24	at Miami	43,612

Individual Statistics

Passing

	Att.	Cmp.	Yds.	Pct.	TD	INT	LG	Rating
DeBerg	324	196	2529	60.5	11	16	50	75.8
Jaworski	61	36	385	59.0	2	5	32	54.3
Pelluer	47	26	301	55.3	1	0	24	82.0
Elkins	2	1	5	50.0	0	1	5	16.7
Saxon	1	0	0	0.0	0	1	0	0.0
Chiefs Totals	435	259	3220	59.5	14	23	50	71.2
Opp. Total	471	236	2821	50.1	16	15	64t	66.8

Receiving

	No.	Yds.	Avg.	LG	TD
Paige	44	759	17.3	50	2
Mandley	35	476	13.6	44	1
McNair	34	372	10.9	24	1
Harry	33	430	13.0	25	2
Heard	25	246	9.8	27	1
Weathers	17	192	11.3	27	0
Hayes	18	229	12.7	23	2
Saxon	11	86	7.8	18	0
Dressel	9	136	15.1	49t	1
R. Thomas	8	58	7.3	12	2
Roberts	8	55	6.9	25	1
Carson	7	95	13.6	28	1
Worthen	5	69	13.8	21	0
Okoye	2	12	6.0	8	0
Gamble	2	2	1.0	6	0
Carruth	1	3	3.0	3	0
Chiefs Totals	259	3220	12.4	50	14
Opp. Totals	236	2821	12.0	64t	16

Rushing

	No.	Yds.	Avg.	LG	TD
Okoye	370	1480	4.0	59	12
Saxon	58	233	4.0	19	3
Heard	63	216	3.4	28	0
Pelluer	17	143	8.4	27	2
McNair	23	121	5.3	25	0
Gamble	6	24	4.0	20	1
Harry	1	9	9.0	9	0
Jaworski	4	5	1.3	4	0
Agee	1	3	3.0	3	0
Mandley	2	1	0.5	8	0
DeBerg	14	-8	-0.6	15	0
Chiefs Totals	559	2227	4.0	59	18
Opp. Totals	445	1766	4.0	63t	9

Team Statistics

	Chiefs	Opp.
Total First Downs	304	252
Rushing	120	92
Passing	165	140
Penalty	19	20
3rd Down: Made Att.	88/208	81/211
3rd Down Pct.	42.3	38.4
4th Down: Made Att.	6/9	8/15
4th Down Pct.	66.7	53.3
Total Net Yards	5265	4293
Avg. Per Game	329.1	268.3
Total Plays	1017	952
Avg. Per Play	5.2	4.5
Net Yards Rushing	2227	1766
Avg. Per Game	139.2	110.4
Total Rushes	559	445
Avg. Per Play	4.0	4.0
Net Yards Passing	3038	2527
Avg. Per Game	189.9	157.9
Sacked/Yards Lost	23/182	36/294
Gross Yards	3220	2821
Attempts/Completions	435/259	471/236
Pct. of Completions	59.5	50.1
Had Intercepted	23	15
Punts/Average	67/40.1	82/39.1
Net Punting Avg.	33.8	32.9
Penalties/Yards	116/878	102/797
Fumbles/Lost	32/18	32.18
Touchdowns	35	32
Rushing	18	9
Passing	14	16
Returns	3	7
Time of Possession	32:35	27:25

Score By Periods	1	2	3	4	OT	Total
Chiefs Total	67	137	53	61	0	318
Opp. Total	74	83	47	82	0	286

Regular Starters

	Offense		Defense
WR	Pete Mandley	LE	Neil Smith
LT	John Alt	NT	Bill Maas
LG	Mark Adickes		Dan Saleaumua
C	Mike Webster	RE	Mike Bell
RG	Dave Lutz		Leonard Griffin
RT	Irv Eatman	LOLB	Chris Martin
TE	Jonathan Hayes	LILB	Walker Lee Ashley
WR	Stephone Paige	RILB	Dino Hackett
QB	Steve DeBerg	ROLB	**Derrick Thomas**
RB	**Christian Okoye**	LCB	**Albert Lewis**
RB	Herman Heard	RCB	**Kevin Ross**
K	Nick Lowery	SS	Kevin Porter
		FS	Mark Adickes
		P	Bryan Barker

PRO-BOWLERS in Bold

Team Leaders

Scoring: Nick Lowery		106 pts: 34 PATs, 24 FGs
INTs: Albert Lewis		4-37 yds., 0 TDs
Kevin Ross		4-29 yds., 0 TDs
Tackles: Deron Cherry		87 (45 solo)
Sacks: Derrick Thomas		10.0 (-95.5 yds.)
Punting: Kelly Goodburn		67-2688 yds., 40.1 avg., 54 LG
Punt Returns: Pete Mandley		19-151 yds., 7.9 avg., 0 TDs
Kickoff Returns: Danny Copeland		26-466 yds., 17.9 avg., 0 TDs

1989 AFC Standings

Western Division

	W	L	T	Pct.
Denver	11	5	0	.688
Kansas City	8	7	1	.531
L.A. Raiders	8	8	0	.500
Seattle	7	9	0	.438
San Diego	6	10	0	.375

Central Division

	W	L	T	Pct.
Cleveland	9	6	1	.594
Houston	9	7	0	.563
Pittsburgh	9	7	0	.563
Cincinnati	8	8	0	.500

Eastern Division

	W	L	T	Pct.
Buffalo	9	7	0	.563
Indianapolis	8	8	0	.500
Miami	8	8	0	.500
New England	5	11	0	.313
N.Y. Jets	4	12	0	.250

AFC Championship: BUFFALO 51, L.A. Raiders 3
Super Bowl XXIV: N.Y. Giants 20, Buffalo 19

Steve DeBerg (Kansas Collection, U. of Kansas)

Marty Schottenheimer (Alan Barzee)

1990 Head Coach: Marty Schottenheimer

Steve DeBerg and Barry Word had superb seasons as the Chiefs returned to the playoffs for the first time in four years. (Kansas Collection, U. of Kansas)

The successes of the 1989 season carried into 1990, and the Chiefs put together a super season to return to the playoffs for just the second time since 1971. Marty Schottenheimer's smashmouth offense was consistent throughout the season, but it was the opportunistic defense that carried the team; they compiled 60 quarterback sacks, recovered 25 fumbles, picked off 20 passes, and blocked six punts. Defensive stars included Pro Bowler Derrick Thomas, who had a great season with 20 sacks, while Albert Lewis and Kevin Ross starred in the secondary. Quarterback Steve DeBerg had his finest season as a pro, passing for 3,444 yards and 23 touchdowns. Newcomer Barry Word topped the 1,000-yard mark in rushing, and Stephone Paige caught 65 passes for 1,021 yards. Kicker Nick Lowery scored 139 points and was also selected for the Pro Bowl. All put together, it was a great year for Kansas City, easily the best the club had had since the 1971 season.

Key Dates in 1990:

August 4—Buck Buchanan, Chiefs defensive tackle, is inducted into the Pro Football Hall of Fame in Canton, Ohio.

September 17—Stephone Paige catches ten passes for 206 yards, but the Chiefs still lose in Denver, 24-23, on Monday Night Football.

October 14—Barry Word rushes for a team-record 200 yards against Detroit at Arrowhead. Kansas City wins, 43-24.

November 11—Derrick Thomas sacks Seattle quarterback Dave Krieg an NFL-record seven times, but it's not enough. On the game's last play, Krieg eludes Thomas's grasp and throws a game-winning touchdown pass. The Seahawks win at Arrowhead, 17-16.

December 29—The Chiefs close out the regular season with a 21-10 win at Chicago. Kansas City finishes with an 11-5 mark, the club's best record since 1969. The Chiefs make the playoffs as a wild-card entry.

January 5, 1991—The Chiefs suffer a heart-wrenching loss to the Dolphins, 17-16, in the AFC wild card game. Leading 16-3 in the fourth quarter, the Chiefs gave up two touchdowns, but were driving for a game-winning score when a questionable holding call brought back a long run by Christian Okoye. Lowery's 52-yard field-goal attempt to win the game fell short.

Big Game of 1990

December 9 at Kansas City
Kansas City 31, Denver 20

Two big fourth-down calls, two big touchdowns. Chiefs coach Marty Schottenheimer let his team make two big plays that ultimately led to Kansas City's 31-20 win over the Denver Broncos and clinched a playoff spot.

"If you want to set high goals and expectations, you'd better give your team an opportunity to do it, and not make decisions that might compromise that opportunity," Schottenheimer said of his two decisions to go for it on fourth down. "My feeling was that we could make it."

The first play was a fourth-and-goal at the Denver one-yard line, and Barry Word carried the ball into the end zone to give the Chiefs a 17-13 lead. The second fourth-down attempt resulted in a 27-yard touchdown pass from Steve DeBerg to Rob Thomas and put the game away in the fourth quarter. DeBerg passed for 254 yards and three touchdowns in the game, and wasn't surprised by Schottenheimer's confidence in the team.

"I think that he addressed us with that challenge and gave us the opportunity to see if were ready to be champions," DeBerg said of his coach.

Kansas City trailed 13-10 at the half, but scored 21 second-half points to take control of the game.

"This is about as good as it gets," DeBerg said of the offense and the win. "It's a very good mix of play calling."

The win clinched at least a wild-card spot in the playoffs for Kansas City and improved their record to 9-4. The Chiefs won two of their final three games to finish at 11-5, the team's best record since 1971.

Preseason
Record: 1-3

8/11	L	3-19	L.A. Rams (Berlin, Germany)	55,429
8/18	L	0-20	N.Y. JETS	40,448
8/24	L	21-35	at Detroit	50,293
8/31	W	27-14	GREEN BAY	42,806

Regular Season
Record: 11-5

9/9	W	24-21	MINNESOTA	68,363
9/17	l	23-24	at Denver (Mon.) (N)	75,277
9/23	W	17-3	at Green Bay	58,817
9/30	W	34-0	CLEVELAND	75,462
10/7	L	19-23	at Indianapolis	54,950
10/14	W	43-24	DETROIT	74,312
10/21	L	7-19	at Seattle	60,358
11/4	W	9-7	L.A. RAIDERS	70,951
11/11	L	16-17	SEATTLE	71,285
11/18	W	27-10	SAN DIEGO	63,717
11/25	W	27-24	at L.A. Raiders	65,710
12/2	W	37-7	at New England	26,280
12/9	W	31-20	DENVER	74,347
12/16	L	10-27	HOUSTON	61,756
12/23	W	24-21	at San Diego	45,135
12/29	W	21-10	at Chicago (Sat.)	60,262

Individual Statistics

Passing

	Att.	Cmp.	Yds.	Pct.	TD	INT	LG	Rating
DeBerg	444	258	3444	58.1	23	4	90t	96.3
Pelluer	5	2	14	40.0	0	1	11	8.3
Chiefs Totals	449	260	3458	57.9	23	5	90t	94.9
Opp. Total	512	267	3662	52.1	16	20	87t	69.5

Receiving

	No.	Yds.	Avg.	LG	TD
Paige	65	1021	15.7	86t	5
R. Thomas	41	545	13.3	47t	4
Harry	41	519	12.7	60	2
McNair	40	507	12.7	65	2
B. Jones	19	137	7.2	19	5
Birden	15	352	23.5	90t	3
Roberts	11	119	10.8	27	0
Hayes	9	83	9.2	21	1
Mandley	7	97	13.9	24	0
Word	4	28	7.0	10	0
Okoye	4	23	5.8	8	0
Whitaker	2	17	8.5	16	1
F. Jones	1	5	5.0	5	0
Saxon	1	5	5.0	5	0
Chiefs Totals	260	3458	13.3	90t	23
Opp. Totals	267	3662	13.7	87t	16

Rushing

	No.	Yds.	Avg.	LG	TD
Word	204	1015	5.0	53t	4
Okoye	245	805	3.3	32	7
McNair	14	61	4.4	13	0
B. Jones	10	47	4.7	14	0
Saxon	3	15	5.0	8	0
Pelluer	5	6	1.2	5	0
Goodburn	1	5	5.0	5	0
F. Jones	1	-1	-1.0	-1	0
DeBerg	21	-5	-0.2	6	0
Chiefs Totals	504	1948	3.9	53t	11
Opp. Totals	373	1640	4.4	42	2

Team Statistics

	Chiefs	Opp.
Total First Downs	280	268
Rushing	115	85
Passing	142	164
Penalty	23	19
3rd Down: Made Att.	91/222	81/204
3rd Down Pct.	41.0	39.7
4th Down: Made Att.	7/10	3/15
4th Down Pct.	70.0	20.0
Total Net Yards	5215	4881
Avg. Per Game	325.9	305.1
Total Plays	975	945
Avg. Per Play	5.3	5.2
Net Yards Rushing	1948	1640
Avg. Per Game	121.8	102.5
Total Rushes	504	373
Avg. Per Play	3.9	4.4
Net Yards Passing	3267	3241
Avg. Per Game	204.2	202.6
Sacked/Yards Lost	22/191	60/421
Gross Yards	3458	3662
Attempts/Completions	449/260	512/267
Pct. of Completions	57.9	52.1
Had Intercepted	5	20
Punts/Average	81/38.7	72/37.0
Net Punting Avg.	32.9	32.3
Penalties/Yards	111/886	122/859
Fumbles/Lost	30/14	38/25
Touchdowns	38	30
Rushing	11	12
Passing	23	16
Returns	4	2
Time of Possession	31:30	28:30

Score By Periods	1	2	3	4	OT	Total
Chiefs Total	86	123	71	89	0	369
Opp. Total	48	66	62	81	0	257

Regular Starters

	Offense		Defense
WR	Robb Thomas	LE	Neil Smith
LT	John Alt	NT	Dan Saleaumua
LG	Frank Winters	RE	Mike Bell
	Dave Szott	LOLB	Chris Martin
C	Mike Webster	LILB	Percy Show
	Tim Grunhard	RILB	Dino Hackett
RG	Dave Lutz	ROLB	**Derrick Thomas**
RT	Rich Baldinger	LCB	**Albert Lewis**
TE	Alfredo Roberts	RCB	**Kevin Ross**
	Jonathan Hayes	SS	Kevin Porter
WR	Stephone Paige	FS	Jeff Donaldson
QB	Steve DeBerg		Deron Cherry
RB	Christian Okoye	P	Bryan Barker
K	**Nick Lowery**		Kelly Goodburn

PRO-BOWLERS in Bold

Team Leaders

Scoring: Nick Lowery   139 pts: 37 PATs, 34 FGs
INTs: Kevin Ross   5-97 yds., 0 TDs
Tackles: Dino Hackett   95 (53 solo)
Sacks: Derrick Thomas   20.0 (-150.0 yds.)
Punting: Bryan Barke   64-2479 yds., 38.7 avg., 56 LG
Punt Returns: Naz Worthen   25-180 yds., 7.2 avg., 0 TDs
Kickoff Returns: Todd McNair   14-227 yds., 16.2 avg., 0 TDs

1990 AFC Standings

Western Division

	W	L	T	Pct.
L.A. Raiders	12	4	0	.750
Kansas City	11	5	0	.688
Seattle	9	7	0	.563
San Diego	6	10	0	.375
Denver	5	11	0	.313

Central Division

	W	L	T	Pct.
Cincinnati	9	7	0	.563
Houston	9	7	0	.563
Pittsburgh	9	7	0	.563
Cleveland	3	13	0	.188

Eastern Division

	W	L	T	Pct.
Buffalo	13	3	0	.813
Miami	12	4	0	.750
Indianapolis	7	9	0	.438
N.Y. Jets	6	10	0	.375
New England	1	15	0	.063

AFC Championship: BUFFALO 51, L.A. Raiders 3
Super Bowl XXV: N.Y. Giants 20, Buffalo 19

Dan Saleaumua (Alan Barzee)

Christian Okoye (Kansas Collection, U. of Kansas)

For the first time in the franchise's history, the Chiefs made the playoffs two years in a row. The season itself was not what Kansas City had hoped for, though, and despite advancing to the second round of the playoffs for the first time since 1969, it was apparent that the Chiefs weren't yet ready to make the final step toward the Super Bowl. After his dream season in 1990, Steve DeBerg's consistency dropped, and the Chiefs relied a little more on the running game than they wanted. Pro Bowler Christian Okoye topped the 1,000-yard mark in rushing, Barry Word was productive, and rookie Harvey Williams was outstanding in limited playing time. The defense was again led by Derrick Thomas, and he was joined by Neil Smith on the Pro Bowl team. The Chiefs got by the Raiders in the first round of the playoffs, but met a Buffalo stampede in the second round.

Key Dates in 1991:

July 27—Jan Stenerud is inducted into the Pro Football Hall of Fame in Canton, Ohio.

September 16—The Chiefs lose to Houston on *Monday Night Football*, 17-7.

October 7—The Chiefs trounce the Bills at Arrowhead Stadium on *Monday Night Football*, 33-6. It's the Chiefs' first home *Monday Night Football* game in eight years.

October 13—The Chiefs toy with the Dolphins and win easily, 42-7. Christian Okoye stars in the game, running for 153 yards.

October 28—Kansas City comes from behind on *Monday Night Football* to beat the Raiders, 24-21. The win puts the team's record at 6-3.

December 28—The Chiefs win their first postseason game since Super Bowl IV, edging the Raiders, 10-6, in the first-ever playoff game at Arrowhead Stadium. The Chiefs' defense forces six Raider turnovers.

January 5, 1992—The Buffalo Bills pound the Chiefs in the second round of the playoffs, 37-14.

Big Game of 1991

December 22 at Los Angeles Raiders
Kansas City 27, Los Angeles Raiders 21

Christmas came early for the Chiefs and their fans. By playing brilliantly and holding off the Raiders in the end, they left Los Angeles with a 27-21 win. The victory gave the Chiefs a home playoff game against the Raiders. A loss would have meant playing in Los Angeles again the following week. It will be the first playoff game in Kansas City in 20 years.

"I can't tell you how delighted this organization is—from Lamar (Hunt) on down through the entire football squad," Chiefs coach Marty Schottenheimer said after the win. "I think it's great."

The offense was superb. Quarterback Steve DeBerg completed 14 of 20 passes for 227 yards and 2 touchdowns. Barry Word rushed for 152 yards, and J. J. Birden caught eight passes for 188 yards and two touchdowns. Even more impressive was that the Chiefs didn't have to punt in the game.

"Overall it was a performance that may well have been our best of the season offensively," Schottenheimer said. Kansas City held the ball for almost 40 minutes.

The Chiefs led 17-7 at the half, and after the Raiders scored with just under four minutes left in the game to pull within 27-21, the Chiefs ran out the clock to secure the win.

Preseason   Record: 2-2

8/3	L	14-24	DALLAS	56,038
8/10	W	19-10	N.Y. Jets (St. Louis, MO)	52,935
8/17	W	38-14	DETROIT	57,320
8/23	L	7-20	at Tampa Bay	33,996

Regular Season   Record: 10-6

9/1	W	14-3	ATLANTA	74,246
9/8	L	10-17	NEW ORLEANS	74,816
9/16	L	7-17	at Houston (Mon.) (N)	61,058
9/22	W	20-13	SEATTLE	71,789
9/29	W	14-13	at San Diego	44,907
10/7	W	33-6	BUFFALO (Mon.) (N)	76,120
10/13	W	42-7	MIAMI	76,021
10/20	L	16-19	at Denver	75,866
10/28	W	24-21	L.A. RAIDERS (Mon.) (N)	77,111
11/10	W	27-20	at L.A. Rams	52,511
11/17	L	20-24	DENVER	74,661
11/24	L	15-20	at Cleveland	63,991
12/1	W	19-6	at Seattle	57,248
12/8	W	20-17	SAN DIEGO	73,330
12/14	L	14-28	at San Francisco (Sat.)	62,672
12/22	W	27-21	at L.A. Raiders	65,144

Individual Statistics

Passing

	Att.	Cmp.	Yds.	Pct.	TD	INT	LG	Rating
DeBerg	434	256	2965	59.0	17	14	63	79.3
Vlasic	44	28	316	63.6	2	0	30	100.2
Williams	1	0	0	0.0	0	0	0	39.6
Chiefs Totals	479	284	3281	59.3	19	14	63	81.1
Opp. Total	471	279	3532	59.2	17	15	71t	81.5

Receiving

	No.	Yds.	Avg.	LG	TD
R. Thomas	43	494	11.5	39	1
Barnett	41	564	13.8	63	5
McNair	37	342	9.2	36	1
Harry	35	431	12.3	36	3
Birden	27	465	17.2	57t	2
Hayes	19	208	10.9	23	2
Williams	16	147	9.2	17	2
B. Jones	14	97	6.9	14	1
Holohan	13	113	8.7	26	2
Paige	9	111	12.3	26	0
Stradford	9	91	10.1	17	0
F. Jones	8	85	10.6	23	0
Saxon	6	55	9.2	22	0
Okoye	3	34	11.3	13	0
Anders	2	30	15.0	17	0
Word	2	13	6.5	8	0
Chiefs Totals	284	3281	11.6	63	19
Opp. Totals	279	3532	12.7	71t	17

Rushing

	No.	Yds.	Avg.	LG	TD
Okoye	225	1031	4.6	48	9
Word	160	684	4.3	37	4
Williams	97	447	4.6	21	1
McNair	10	51	5.1	11	0
Saxon	6	13	2.2	8	0
Stradford	1	7	7.0	7	0
Vlasic	1	-1	-1.0	-1	0
DeBerg	21	-15	-0.7	0	0
Chiefs Totals	521	2217	4.3	48	14
Opp. Totals	417	1770	4.2	60t	8

Team Statistics

	Chiefs	Opp.
Total First Downs	322	275
Rushing	127	88
Passing	172	168
Penalty	23	19
3rd Down: Made Att.	92/205	76/191
3rd Down Pct.	44.9	39.8
4th Down: Made Att.	12/20	11/18
4th Down Pct.	60.0	61.1
Total Net Yards	5321	4998
Avg. Per Game	332.6	312.4
Total Plays	1021	927
Avg. Per Play	5.2	5.4
Net Yards Rushing	2217	1770
Avg. Per Game	138.6	110.6
Total Rushes	521	417
Avg. Per Play	4.3	4.2
Net Yards Passing	3104	3228
Avg. Per Game	194.0	201.8
Sacked/Yards Lost	21/177	39/304
Gross Yards	3281	3532
Attempts/Completions	479/284	471/279
Pct. of Completions	59.3	59.2
Had Intercepted	14	15
Punts/Average	57/40.4	60/42.5
Net Punting Avg.	35.0	36.5
Penalties/Yards	94/724	110/827
Fumbles/Lost	22/8	27/18
Touchdowns	35	27
Rushing	14	9
Passing	19	17
Returns	2/0	2/0
Time of Possession	31:16	28:44

Score By Periods	1	2	3	4	OT	Total
Chiefs Total	44	91	79	105	3	322
Opp. Total	58	85	50	59	0	252

Regular Starters

	Offense		Defense
WR	Robb Thomas	LE	**Neil Smith**
LT	John Alt	NT	Dan Saleaumua
LG	Dave Szott	RE	Bill Maas
C	Tim Grunhard	LOLB	Chris Martin
RG	Dave Lutz	LILB	Tracy Simien
RT	Rich Baldinger	RILB	Dino Hackett
TE	Jonathan Hayes	ROLB	**Derrick Thomas**
WR	Tim Barnett	LCB	Jayice Pearson
QB	Steve DeBerg		Albert Lewis
FB	Bill Jones	RCB	Kevin Ross
RB	**Christian Okoye**	SS	Kevin Porter
K	Nick Lowery	FS	Deron Cherry
		P	Bryan Barker

PRO-BOWLERS in Bold

Team Leaders

Scoring: Nick Lowery   110 pts: 35 PATs, 25 FGs
INTs: Deron Cherry   4-31 yds., 0 TDs
Tackles: Deron Cherry   116 (59 solo)
Sacks: Derrick Thomas   13.5 (-112.0 yds.)
Punting: Bryan Barker   57-2303 yds., 40.4 avg.,
                              11 ln 20, 57 LG
Punt Returns: Troy Stradford   22-150 yds., 6.8 avg., 0 TDs
Kickoff Returns: Harvey Williams   24-524 yds., 21.8 avg., 0 TDs

1991 AFC Standings

Western Division

	W	L	T	Pct.
Denver	12	4	0	.750
Kansas City +	10	6	0	.625
L.A. Raiders +	9	7	0	.563
Seattle	7	9	0	.438
San Diego	4	12	0	.250

Central Division

	W	L	T	Pct.
Houston	11	5	0	.688
Pittsburgh	7	9	0	.438
Cleveland	6	10	0	.375
Cincinnati	3	13	0	.188

Eastern Division

	W	L	T	Pct.
Buffalo	13	3	0	.813
N.Y. Jets +	8	8	0	.500
Miami	8	8	0	.500
New England	6	10	0	.375
Indianapolis	1	15	0	.063

AFC First Round Playoff: KANSAS CITY 10, L.A. Raiders 6
AFC Divisional Playoff: BUFFALO 37, Kansas City 14
AFC Championship: BUFFALO 10, Denver 7
Super Bowl XXVI: Washington 37, Buffalo 24

Neil Smith (Alan Barzee)

Dan Saleaumua and Deron Cherry (Kansas Collection, U. of Kansas)

1992 Head Coach: Marty Schottenheimer

Dave Krieg took over Kansas City's quarterbacking duties in 1992. (Kansas Collection, U. of Kansas)

Derrick Thomas (Alan Barzee)

The Chiefs made the playoffs for the third straight year, but it was still a season of disappointment. Dave Krieg came from Seattle to stabilize the offense, and he had a decent year, passing for 3,115 yards. But the running game dissolved, and Kansas City gained almost 700 fewer rushing yards than they did in 1991. Barry Word was the leading rusher with 607 yards. Neil Smith and Derrick Thomas were the top dogs on defense, both men recording 14.5 sacks. The Chiefs went into the final month of the season with an 8-4 record, but needed a final game win over Denver to make the playoffs. Kansas City finished with a 10-6 record and in second place in the AFC West. Despite defeating the Chargers twice in the regular season, the Chiefs had to travel to San Diego for their first-round playoff game. They came home losers, as the Chargers shut them out, 17-0.

Key Dates in 1992:

September 6—Kansas City beats the Chargers on opening day, 24-10.

September 28—The Raiders come to Arrowhead for *Monday Night Football* and lose to the Chiefs for the sixth straight time, 27-7.

October 25—The Chiefs are embarrassed by the Steelers at Arrowhead, 27-3. The loss leaves Kansas City's record at 4-4.

November 29—The Chiefs beat the Jets, 23-7, for their fourth win in a row.

December 27—With the season and a playoff berth on the line, the Chiefs rise to the occasion and bury the Broncos at Arrowhead, 42-20. The Chiefs finish at 10-6 and will play at San Diego in the first round of the playoffs.

January 2, 1993—Kansas City exits quickly and quietly from the playoffs, losing to the Chargers, 17-0, in San Diego.

Big Game of 1992

December 19 at New York Giants
New York Giants 35, Kansas City 21

The Chiefs' division championship hopes took a major blow, and their involvement in the postseason party came into question. Kansas City was simply not ready to play and was easily defeated by the Giants, 35-21. New York had lost five games in a row.

"I don't know if we were flat," Chiefs Coach Marty Schottenheimer said. "We didn't play very well."

A victory would have assured the Chiefs of their third straight playoff berth and given them complete control over the AFC West race. Instead, they had to rely on other teams' losses.

"I wish I could find a way of summing this up," Chiefs defensive end Neil Smith said following the game. "We were very flat. We have been flat the last three or four weeks. Somewhere the aggressiveness of this team has been lost."

The Giants scored on five consecutive possessions from the end of the first quarter through the middle of the third quarter to lead at one point, 35-7. Kansas City, which had come from behind in previous games during the season, had dug a hole they couldn't get out of this time. The Giants ran up 348 yards of total offense and controled the ball for almost 35 minutes.

"This is probably the worst we have played all year," Chiefs cornerback Kevin Ross said. "The fact is that we kissed the game away, the home-field advantage—even if we get in now."

Preseason   Record: 1-3

8/8	L	13-21	at Green Bay	54,322
8/15	L	0-30	at Minnesota	38,132
8/24	W	35-0	BUFFALO	71,481
8/28	L	10-21	INDIANAPOLIS	65,557

Regular Season   Record: 10-6

9/6	W	24-10	at San Diego	45,024
9/13	W	26-7	SEATTLE	75,125
9/20	L	20-23	at Houston	60,955
9/28	W	27-7	L.A. RAIDERS (Mon.) (N)	77,486
10/4	L	19-20	at Denver	75,629
10/11	W	24-17	PHILADELPHIA	76,626
10/18	L	10-17	at Dallas	64,115
10/25	L	3-27	PITTSBURGH (N)	76,175
11/8	W	16-14	SAN DIEGO	72,826
11/15	W	35-16	WASHINGTON	75,238
11/22	W	24-14	at Seattle (N)	49,867
11/29	W	23-7	at N.Y. Jets	57,375
12/6	L	7-28	at L.A. Raiders	45,227
12/13	W	27-20	NEW ENGLAND	52,208
12/19	L	21-35	at N.Y. Giants (Sat.)	53,427
12/27	W	42-20	DENVER	76,240

Individual Statistics

Passing

	Att.	Cmp.	Yds.	Pct.	TD	INT	LG	Rating
Krieg	413	230	3115	55.7	15	12	77t	79.9
Chiefs Totals	413	230	3115	55.7	15	12	77t	79.9
Opp. Total	458	253	2928	55.2	19	24	62	66.7

Receiving

	No.	Yds.	Avg.	LG	TD
McNair	44	380	8.6	36	1
Birden	42	644	15.3	72t	3
Davis	36	756	21.0	74t	3
Barnett	24	442	18.4	77t	4
F. Jones	18	265	14.7	56	0
Hargain	17	205	12.1	25	0
Cash	12	113	9.4	19	2
Word	9	80	8.9	22	0
Hayes	9	77	8.6	21	2
Anders	5	65	13.0	28	0
Harry	5	46	9.2	13	0
Williams	5	24	4.8	12	0
B. Jones	2	6	3.0	5	0
Dyal	1	7	7.0	7	0
Okoye	1	5	5.0	5	0
Chiefs Totals	230	3115	13.5	77t	15
Opp. Totals	253	2928	11.6	62	19

Rushing

	No.	Yds.	Avg.	LG	TD
Word	163	607	3.7	44t	4
Okoye	144	448	3.1	22	6
Williams	78	262	3.4	11	1
McNair	21	124	5.9	30	1
Krieg	37	74	2.0	17	2
Harry	1	27	27.0	27	0
Anders	1	1	1.0	1	0
Davis	1	-11	-11.0	-11	0
Chiefs Totals	446	1532	3.4	44t	14
Opp. Totals	441	1787	4.1	40t	12

Team Statistics

	Chiefs	Opp.
Total First Downs	246	256
Rushing	87	97
Passing	134	145
Penalty	25	14
3rd Down: Made Att.	71/207	73/205
3rd Down Pct.	34.3	35.6
4th Down: Made Att.	5/14	6/11
4th Down Pct.	35.7	54.5
Total Net Yards	4324	4324
Avg. Per Game	270.3	270.3
Total Plays	907	949
Avg. Per Play	4.8	4.6
Net Yards Rushing	1532	1787
Avg. Per Game	95.8	111.7
Total Rushes	446	441
Avg. Per Play	3.4	4.1
Net Yards Passing	2792	2537
Avg. Per Game	174.5	158.6
Sacked/Yards Lost	48/323	50/391
Gross Yards	3115	2928
Attempts/Completions	413/230	458/253
Pct. of Completions	55.7	55.2
Had Intercepted	12	24
Punts/Average	86/42.2	80/43.1
Net Punting Avg.	35.4	36.0
Penalties/Yards	82/675	124/959
Fumbles/Lost	28/9	34/15
Touchdowns	40	34
Rushing	14	12
Passing	15	19
Returns	8/3	1/2
Time of Possession	29:37	30:23

Score By Periods	1	2	3	4	OT	Total
Chiefs Total	53	128	66	101	0	348
Opp. Total	68	57	64	90	3	282

Regular Starters

	Offense		Defense
WR	J.J Birden	LE	**Neil Smith**
LT	**John Alt**	NT	Dan Saleaumua
LG	Dave Szott	DT	Joe Phillips
C	Tim Grunhard	RE	Leonard Grifin
RG	Dave Lutz	LOLB	Chris Martin
RT	Rich Baldinger	LILB	Ervin Randle
TE	Jonathan Hayes	MLB	Tracy Simien
WR	Willie Davis	ROLB	**Derrick Thomas**
QB	Dave Krieg	LCB	Kevin Ross
TE	Keith Cash	RCB	Albert Lewis
RB	Barry Wood		Dale Carter
RB	Bill Jones	SS	Martin Bayless
K	**Nick Lowery**	FS	Charles Mincy
		P	Bryan Barker

PRO-BOWLERS in Bold

Team Leaders

Scoring: Nick Lowery	105 pts: 39 PATs, 22 FGs
INTs: Dale Carter	7-65 yds., 1 TD
Tackles: Tracy Simien	97 (56 solo)
Sacks: Neil Smith	14.5 (-114.5 yds.)
Derrick Thomas	14.5 (-113.0 yds.)
Punting: Bryan Barker	75-3245 yds., 43.3 avg., 65 LG
Punt Returns: Dale Carter	38-398 yds., 10.5 avg., 2 TDs
Kickoff Returns: Harvey Williams	21-405 yds., 19.3 avg., 0 TDs

1992 AFC Standings

Western Division

	W	L	T	Pct.
San Diego	11	5	0	.699
Kansas City +	10	6	0	.625
Denver	8	8	0	.500
L.A. Raiders	7	9	0	.438
Seattle	2	14	0	.125

Central Division

	W	L	T	Pct.
Pittsburgh	11	5	0	.688
Houston +	10	6	0	.352
Cleveland	7	9	0	.438
Cincinnati	5	11	0	.313

Eastern Division

	W	L	T	Pct.
Miami	11	5	0	.688
Buffalo +	11	5	0	.688
Indianapolis	9	7	0	.563
N.Y. Jets	4	12	0	.250
New England	2	14	0	.125

AFC First Round Playoff: SAN DIEGO 17, Kansas City 0
AFC Championship: Buffalo 29, MIAMI 10
Super Bowl XXVII: Dallas 52, Buffalo 17

Dave Krieg (Alan Barzee)

1993 Head Coach: Marty Schottenheimer

Marcus Allen and Joe Montana
(Kansas Collection, U. of Kansas)

Kansas City acquired two superstar veterans to bolster their sagging offense, and for the first time since 1971, they won the AFC West and eventually advanced to the AFC Championship game. Joe Montana and Marcus Allen provided something that had been lacking on previous playoff teams—winning leadership. Montana missed five games during the season because of various nagging injuries, but played very well when in the lineup. He passed for 2,144 yards and 13 touchdowns, and was selected for the Pro Bowl. Marcus Allen ran for 764 yards and scored 15 touchdowns, was named NFL Comeback Player of the Year, and was also selected for the Pro Bowl. Other offensive stars on the team included receivers Willie Davis and J. J. Birden. Offensive tackle John Alt was named to his second consecutive Pro Bowl. The defense was led by Pro Bowlers Neil Smith and Derrick Thomas, as the two combined for 23 sacks. Kansas City finshed the regular season with an 11-5 record. A nice run in the playoffs that included come-from-behind wins over Pittsburgh and Houston brought the Chiefs to the doorstep of the Super Bowl, but they couldn't handle the Buffalo Bills in the AFC championship game and fell just short of the big game.

Key Dates in 1993:

April 20—The Chiefs trade a first-round pick in the 1993 draft to the San Francisco 49ers for Joe Montana. Kansas City also gets safety David Whitmore and a third-round pick in the trade.

June 9—Marcus Allen signs with the Chiefs.

September 5—The Montana-Allen era of Kansas City football begins with a 27-3 win over the Tampa Bay Bucs.

September 20—Denver visits Arrowhead on. The Chiefs' offense is ineffective most of the game, but they prevail, on the strength of five Nick Lowery field goals as the Chiefs down the Broncos on *Monday Night Football*, 15-7.

October 3—Marcus Allen scores the 100th touchdown of his career against his former team, the Raiders. The Chiefs win, 24-9.

October 17—Kansas City nips San Diego, 17-14, improving their record to 5-1.

November 28—The Chiefs defeat the Buffalo Bills at Arrowhead, 23-7

December 26—The Chiefs play poorly and lose to the Vikings, 30-10.

January 8, 1994—AFC Wild Card game. A fourth-down touchdown pass from Joe Montana ties the game with 46 seconds left, and Lowery hits a 32-yard field in overtime, as the Chiefs beat the Steelers at Arrowhead, 27-24.

January 16, 1994—The Chiefs' top the heavily favored Houston Oilers in the Astrodome, 28-20, and advance to the AFC championship game for the first time ever.

January 23, 1994—The Chiefs' playoff run ends as Buffalo wins their fourth straight AFC championship, downing Kansas City, 30-13.

Big Game of 1993

December 19 at Kansas City
Kansas City 28, San Diego 24

Joe Montana's first pass of the game was picked off, Marcus Allen fumbled on the Chiefs' next possession, and after the Chargers scored on the first play of the second quarter, Kansas City trailed, 17-0. Instead of giving up, the Chiefs sucked it up and played a gritty, resolved game the rest of the way to win, 28-24.

"The game today was not won by talent," Chiefs coach Marty Schottenheimer said afterward. "It was not won by coaching, certainly. It was won by people with determination. Something in their hearts said, 'I am not going to be denied.'"

While the offense methodically worked the Chiefs back into the game, the defense shut down the Chargers. Twice in the fourth quarter the Chargers were stopped short of scoring.

"There was no alarm on the sideline," Chiefs running back Marcus Allen said of the early 17-0 deficit. "Nobody was worried. There's no question that having that experience, to be in adverse conditions and come back to win, is a great teacher." Allen rushed for just 16 yards, but scored the Chiefs' first touchdown in the second quarter. Joe Montana threw for 168 yards and two touchdowns.

"I felt confident we could get back into it," Schottenheimer continued. "I wasn't convinced we could get it all back right away, but that really wasn't the purpose."

The victory put the Chiefs at 10-4 and in first place in the AFC West. Winning both of their remaining two games would have assured the team a bye in the first round of playoffs, but Kansas City was decisively defeated by the Vikings in Minneapolis. The Chiefs defeated Seattle in the final game to win the West, but the club still had to play in the first round of the playoffs.

Preseason

Record: 3-1

Date		Score	Opponent	Attendance
8/7	W	29-21	at Green Bay (Milwaukee, WI)	51,655
8/12	L	7-30	BUFFALO	73,550
8/21	W	27-20	MINNESOTA	73,080
8/27	W	27-20	at New England	46,501

Regular Season

Record: 11-5
(1st – AFC West)

Date		Score	Opponent	Attendance
9/5	W	27-3	at Tampa Bay	63,378
9/12	L	0-30	at Houston	59,780
9/20	W	15-7	DENVER (Mon.) (N)	78,453
10/3	W	24-9	L.A. RAIDERS	77,395
10/10	W	17-15	CINCINNATI	75,394
10/17	W	17-14	at San Diego	60,729
10/31	L	10-30	at Miami	67,765
11/8	W	23-16	GREEN BAY (Mon.) (N)	76,742
11/14	W	31-20	at L.A. Raiders	66,553
11/21	L	17-19	CHICAGO	76,872
11/28	W	23-7	BUFFALO	74,452
12/5	W	31-16	at Seattle	58,551
12/12	L	21-27	at Denver	75,882
12/19	W	28-24	SAN DIEGO	74,778
12/26	L	10-30	at Minnesota (N)	59,236
1/2	W	34-24	SEATTLE	72,136

Individual Statistics

Passing

	Att.	Cmp.	Yds.	Pct.	TD	INT	LG	Rating
Montana	298	181	2144	60.7	13	7	50t	87.4
Krieg	189	105	1238	55.6	7	3	66t	81.4
Blundin	3	1	2	33.3	0	0	2	42.4
Anders	0	0	0	0.0	0	0	0	-1.0
Chiefs Totals	490	287	3384	58.6	20	10	66t	84.8
Opp. Total	525	312	3379	59.4	18	21	77t	73.2

Receiving

	No.	Yds.	Avg.	LG	TD
Davis	52	909	17.5	66t	7
Birden	51	772	14.1	50t	2
Anders	40	326	8.2	27	1
Allen	34	238	7.0	18t	3
Hayes	24	33t	13.8	49	1
Cash	24	242	10.1	24	4
Barnett	17	182	10.7	25	1
McNair	10	74	7.4	24	0
F. Jones	9	111	12.3	19	0
H. Jones	7	91	13.0	22	0
Dyal	7	83	11.9	31	0
H. Williams	7	42	6.0	14	0
E. Thompson	4	33	8.3	13	0
Valerio	1	1	1.0	1t	1
Chiefs Totals	287	3384	11.8	66t	20
Opp. Totals	312	3379	10.8	77t	18

Rushing

	No.	Yds.	Avg.	LG	TD
Allen	206	764	3.7	39	12
Anders	75	291	3.9	18	0
McNair	51	278	5.5	47	2
H. Williams	42	149	3.5	19	0
Montana	25	64	2.6	17	0
F. Jones	5	34	6.8	13	0
E. Thompson	11	28	2.5	14	0
Krieg	21	24	1.1	20	0
J. Stephens	6	18	3.0	7	0
Barnett	1	3	3.0	3	0
Carter	1	2	2.0	2	0
Cash	1	0	0.0	0	0
Chiefs Totals	445	1655	3.1	39	14
Opp. Totals	453	1620	3.6	38	11

Team Statistics

	Chiefs	Opp.
Total First Downs	300	300
Rushing	94	103
Passing	180	161
Penalty	26	36
3rd Down: Made Att.	82/203	86/210
3rd Down Pct.	40.4	41.0
4th Down: Made Att.	4/9	3/13
4th Down Pct.	44.4	23.1
Total Net Yards	4835	4771
Avg. Per Game	302.2	298.2
Total Plays	970	1013
Avg. Per Play	5.0	4.7
Net Yards Rushing	1655	1620
Avg. Per Game	103.4	101.3
Total Rushes	445	453
Avg. Per Play	3.7	3.6
Net Yards Passing	3180	3151
Avg. Per Game	198.8	196.9
Sacked/Yards Lost	35/204	35/228
Gross Yards	3384	3379
Attempts/Completions	490/287	525/312
Pct. of Completions	58.6	59.4
Had Intercepted	10	21
Punts/Average	77/42.1	68/44.6
Net Punting Avg.	35.4	37.8
Penalties/Yards	122/969	127/1015
Fumbles/Lost	28/18	30/17
Touchdowns	37	30
Rushing	14	1.1
Passing	20	18
Returns	2/1	1/0
Time of Possession	29:29	30:31

Score By Periods	1	2	3	4	OT	Total
Chiefs Total	71	108	82	67	0	328
Opp. Total	51	86	50	104	0	291

Regular Starters

	Offense		Defense
WR	J.J Birden	LE	**Neil Smith**
LT	**John Alt**	NT	Joe Phillips
LG	Dave Szott	RT	Dan Saleaumua
C	Tim Grunhard	RBK	**Derrick Thomas**
RG	Will Shields	LOLB	Tracy Rogers
RT	Ricky Siglar	MLB	Tracy Simien
WR	Willie Davis	ROLB	Lonnie Marts
QB	**Joe Montana**	LCB	Albert Lewis
FB	Kimble Anders	RCB	Kevin Ross
RB	**Marcus Allen**		Dale Carter
K	Nick Lowery	SS	Doug Terry
			Martin Bayless
		FS	David Whitmore
			Kevin Ross
		P	Bryan Barker

PRO-BOWLERS in Bold

Team Leaders

Scoring: Nick Lowery — 106 pts: 37 PATs, 23 FGs
INTs: Albert Lewis — 6-61 yds., 0 TDs
Tackles: Tracy Simien — 105 (68 solo)
Sacks: Neil Smith — 15.0 (-127.0 yds.)
Punting: Bryan Barker — 76-3240 yds., 42.6 avg., 59 LG
Punt Returns: Dale Carter — 27-247 yds., 9.1 avg., 0 TDs
Kickoff Returns: Danan Hughes — 14-266 yds., 19.0 avg., 0 TDs

1993 AFC Standings

Western Division

	W	L	T	Pct.
Kansas City	11	5	0	.688
L.A. Raiders	10	6	0	.625
Denver	9	7	0	.563
San Diego	8	8	0	.500
Seattle	6	10	0	.375

Central Division

	W	L	T	Pct.
Houston	12	4	0	.750
Pittsburgh	9	7	0	.563
Cleveland	7	9	0	.438
Cincinnati	3	13	0	.188

Eastern Division

	W	L	T	Pct.
Buffalo	12	4	0	.750
Miami	9	7	0	.563
N.Y. Jets	8	8	0	.500
New England	5	11	0	.313
Indianapolis	4	12	0	.250

AFC First Round Playoff: KANSAS CITY 27, Pittsburgh 24
AFC Divisional Playoff: KANSAS CITY 28, Houston 20

AFC Championship: BUFFALO 30, Kansas City 13
Super Bowl XXVIII: Dallas 30, Buffalo 13

Todd McNair rushed for 278 yards and 2 touchdowns for Kansas City in 1993. (Kansas Collection, U. of Kansas)

1994 Head Coach: Marty Schottenheimer

Greg Hill (Alan Barzee)

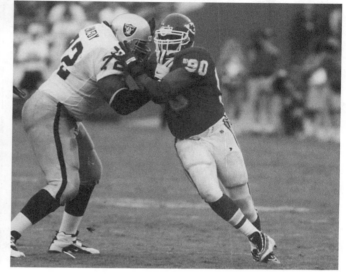

Neil Smith (Alan Barzee)

After the great success of the 1993 season, anything short of another trip to the AFC Championship game would make for a disappointing season, and 1994 was just that. The Chiefs played just well enough throughout the year to ensure a return trip to the playoffs, but nothing more. A three-game losing streak toward the end of the season almost kept the Chiefs out of the playoffs, but wins over Houston and the Raiders in the season's final two games secured a wild-card entry in postseason play. Joe Montana had good numbers, 3,283 yards passing and 16 touchdowns, but overall, the offense lacked the aggressiveness and spark from the previous year. Marcus Allen ran for 709 yards, and rookie Greg Hill totaled 574 rushing yards. Fullback Kimble Anders was the leading receiver with 67 receptions. The defense showed flashes of brilliance, and as had become the standard, was led by perennial Pro Bowlers Derrick Thomas and Neil Smith. Defensive back Dale Carter had a superb year and was also chosen for the Pro Bowl. The Chiefs finished second in the AFC West with a 9-7 record and lost to the Dolphins in the first round of the playoffs.

Key Dates in 1994:

September 11—Facing his former team, Joe Montana leads the Chiefs to a 24-17 win over the San Francisco 49ers at Arrowhead.

December 24—Marcus Allen gains 132 yards rushing as the Chiefs beat the Raiders in Los Angeles, 19-9. The win secures a fifth-straight playoff spot for the Chiefs. Kansas City finishes with a 9-7 record.

December 31—The Chiefs lose to the Dolphins in the first round of the playoffs, 27-17.

Big Game of 1994

October 17 at Denver
Kansas City 31, Denver 28

A six-yard pass and a tightrope run into the end zone ended the Chiefs' 11-year drought in Mile High Stadium. Joe Montana led a methodical, 75-yard drive in the game's final 82 seconds to bring Kansas City back from a four-point defecit and defeat the Broncos, 31-28.

"You don't like to be in those two-minute situations very often, but it's all a part of it," Montana said of the game-winning drive. "It's nerve-racking. But it's a lot of fun. We felt we had a good chance there."

"They played off me in a zone," Chiefs receiver Willie Davis said of his game-winning reception. "I was the third receiver on the play. Joe threw it to where it had to be on the outside." Eight seconds remained in the game when Davis scored.

The final drive took nine plays, all of which were Montana passes except one run of ten yards by Marcus Allen. For the game, Montana hit 34 of 54 pass attempts for 393 yards and three touchdowns. The Chiefs improved their record to 4-2 with the win and thrust themselves back into the playoff hunt.

"The fact that it was in Denver . . . I won't lie to you and say it didn't cross my mind, because it certainly did," Chiefs Coach Marty Schottenheimer said of his personal seven-game losing streak in Mile High Stadium. "But the victory was the important thing from our perspective."

The game was tied 14-14 at the half. Lin Elliott's field goal with 4:08 left in the game temporarily put the Chiefs ahead 24-21. An Allen fumble set up the Broncos' final touchdown. In the end, it was Montana and his inspiring confidence that resulted in the comeback.

"(The victory was) at least as important psychologically as mathematically," Schottenheimer concluded of the win. Most importantly, the Chiefs showed they are capable of playing to their potential, something they've haven't done with any consistency this season.

Preseason   Record: 2-3

7/31	W	24-17	HOUSTON	70,732
8/7	L	9-17	Minnesota (Tokyo, Japan)	49,555
8/12	W	17-14	at Washington	40,778
8/22	L	18-21	CHICAGO	75,114
8/26	L	3-24	at Buffalo	46,166

Regular Season   Record: 9-7

9/4	W	30-17	at New Orleans	69,362
9/11	W	24-17	SAN FRANCISCO	79,907
9/18	W	30-10	at Atlanta (N)	67,357
9/25	L	0-16	L.A. RAMS	78,184
10/9	L	6/20	at San Diego	62,923
10/17	W	31-28	at Denver (Mon.) (N)	75,151
10/23	W	38-23	SEATTLE	78,847
10/30	L	10-44	at Buffalo	79,501
11/6	W	13-3	L.A. RAIDERS (N)	78,709
11/13	L	13-14	SAN DIEGO	78,997
11/20	W	20-13	CLEVELAND	69,121
11/27	L	9-10	at Seattle	54,120
12/4	L	*17-20	DENVER	77,831
12/12	L	28-45	at Miami (Mon.) (N)	71,578
12/18	W	31-9	HOUSTON	74,474
12/24	W	19-9	at L.A. Raiders (Sat.)	64,130

Individual Statistics

Passing

	Att.	Cmp.	Yds.	Pct.	TD	INT	LG	Rating
Montana	493	299	3283	60.6	16	9	57t	83.6
Bono	117	66	796	56.4	4	4	62t	74.6
Blundin	5	1	13	20.0	0	1	13	0.0
Chiefs Totals	615	366	4092	59.5	20	14	62t	80.8
Opp. Total	504	300	3500	59.5	23	12	72t	85.9

Receiving

	No.	Yds.	Avg.	LG	TD
Anders	67	525	7.8	30	1
W. Davis	51	822	16.1	62t	5
Birden	48	637	13.3	44	4
Allen	42	349	8.3	38	0
Dawson	37	537	14.5	50	2
D. Walker	36	382	10.6	57t	2
Martin	21	307	14.6	61	1
Cash	19	192	10.1	31	2
Hill	16	92	5.8	21	0
Hughes	7	80	11.4	22	0
Bennett	7	53	7.6	15	0
Greene	6	69	11.5	20	1
Penn	3	24	8.0	13	0
Dickerson	2	11	5.5	6	0
Johnson	2	7	3.5	5	0
Valerio	2	5	2.5	4t	2
Chiefs Totals	366	4092	11.2	62t	20
Opp. Totals	300	3500	11.7	72t	23

Rushing

	No.	Yds.	Avg.	LG	TD
Allen	189	709	3.8	36t	7
Hill	141	574	4.1	20	1
Anders	62	231	3.7	19	2
Bennett	46	178	3.9	17	2
Dawson	3	24	8.0	13	0
Montana	18	17	0.9	13	0
Dickerson	1	0	0.0	0	0
Bono	4	-1	-0.2	2	0
Chiefs Totals	464	1732	3.7	36t	12
Opp. Totals	446	1734	3.9	60	11

Team Statistics

	Chiefs	Opp.
Total First Downs	322	289
Rushing	97	93
Passing	211	164
Penalty	14	32
3rd Down: Made Att.	94/238	80/212
3rd Down Pct.	39.5	37.7
4th Down: Made Att.	12/23	8/14
4th Down Pct.	52.2	57.1
Total Net Yards	5692	5000
Avg. Per Game	355.8	312.5
Total Plays	1098	989
Avg. Per Play	5.2	5.1
Net Yards Rushing	1732	1734
Avg. Per Game	108.3	108.4
Total Rushes	464	446
Avg. Per Play	3.7	3.9
Net Yards Passing	3960	3266
Avg. Per Game	247.5	204.1
Sacked/Yards Lost	19/132	39/234
Gross Yards	4092	3500
Attempts/Completions	615/366	504/300
Pct. of Completions	59.5	59.5
Had Intercepted	14	12
Punts/Average	85/42.1	85/45.0
Net Punting Avg.	34.5	38.9
Penalties/Yards	127/911	119/925
Fumbles/Lost	21/12	36/26
Touchdowns	34	35
Rushing	12	1.1
Passing	20	23
Returns	1/1	1/0
Time of Possession	30:55	29:05

Score By Periods	1	2	3	4	OT	Total
Chiefs Total	52	92	79	96	0	319
Opp. Total	40	84	72	99	3	298

Regular Starters

	Offense		Defense
WR	J.J. Birden	LE	**Neil Smith**
LT	John Alt	NT	Joe Phillips
LG	Dave Szott	RT	Dan Saleaumua
C	Tim Grunhard	RE	Darren Mickell
RG	Will Shields	LOLB	**Derrick Thomas**
RT	Ricky Siglar	MLB	Tracy Simien
	Derrick Graham	ROLB	George Jamison
TE	Keith Cash	LCB	Mark Collins
	Derrick Walker	RCB	**Dale Carter**
WR	Willie Davis	SS	David Whitmore
QB	Joe Montana	FS	William White
FB	Kimble Anders	P	Louie Aguiar
RB	Marcus Allen		
K	Lin Elliot		
PRO-BOWLERS in Bold			

Team Leaders

Scoring: Lin Elliot   105 pts: 30 PATs, 25 FGs
INTs: Charles Mincy   3-49 yds., 0 TDs
Tackles: Tracy Simien   99 (65 solo)
Sacks: Neil Smith   11.5 (-89.0 yds.)
Punting: Louie Aguiar   85-3582 yds., 42.1avg., 61 LG
Punt Returns: Danan Hughes   27-192 yds., 7.1 avg., 0 TDs
Kickoff Returns: Ron Dickerson   21-472 yds., 22.5 avg., 1 TD

1994 AFC Standings

Western Division

	W	L	T	Pct.
San Diego	11	5	0	.699
Kansas City	9	7	0	.563
L.A. Raiders	9	7	0	.563
Denver	7	9	0	.438
Seattle	6	10	0	.375

Central Division

	W	L	T	Pct.
Pittsburgh	12	4	0	.750
Cleveland	11	5	0	.688
Cincinnati	3	13	0	.188
Houston	2	14	0	.125

Eastern Division

	W	L	T	Pct.
Miami	10	6	0	.625
New England	10	6	0	.625
Indianapolis	8	8	0	.500
Buffalo	7	9	0	.438
N.Y. Jets	6	10	0	.375

AFC First Round Playoff: MIAMI 27, Kansas City 17
AFC Championship: SAN DIEGO 17, Pittsburgh 13
Super Bowl XXIX: San Francisco 49, San Diego 26

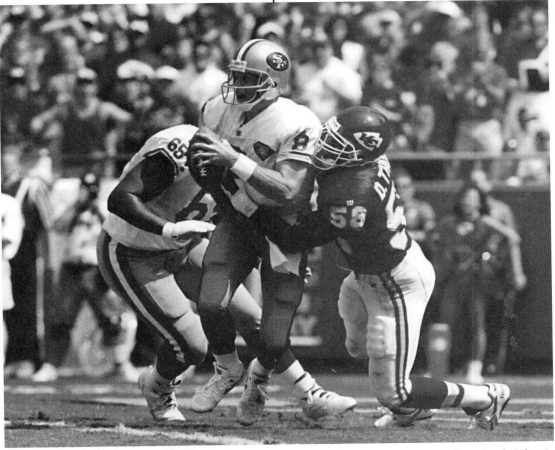

Derrick Thomas sacks the 49ers' Steve Young during the Chiefs' 24-17 win over San Francisco at Arrowhead. (Alan Barzee)

The Chiefs had one of their best regular seasons ever and posted the best record in the NFL. After missing out on the home-field advantage several times the past five seasons, Kansas City appeared ready to make a serious run to the Super Bowl within the friendly atmosphere of Arrowhead Stadium. But the great season—AFC West Champs with a 13-3 mark—will always be remembered as a huge disappointment because of the Chiefs' shocking loss to the Colts in the divisional playoff game. Quarterback Steve Bono threw three interceptions in the playoff loss, and coupled with Kicker Lin Elliott's three field goal misses, the Chiefs let their great season slip away. Marcus Allen was again a standout for the offense, gaining 890 yards rushing and scoring five touchdowns. Bono passed for 3,121 yards and 21 touchdowns in his first year as the Chiefs' starter. Kimble Anders led in pass receptions with 55. The biggest key to the team's success was the defense, and it enjoyed a great season, holding opponents to a league-low 241 points and recording 47 sacks. Cornerback Dale Carter led with four interceptions. Rookie kick returner Tamarick Vanover was also spectacular, returning two kickoffs and one punt for scores. Six Chiefs were named to the Pro Bowl: Steve Bono, Dale Carter, guard Will Shields, Neil Smith, Derrick Thomas, and Dan Saleaumua.

Key Dates in 1995:

April 19—Joe Montana announces his retirement.

Sep tember 3—Kansas City opens the season with a convincing 34-10 win over the Seahawks in Seattle.

September 17—James Hasty picks off a Jeff Hostetler pass and returns it for a touchdown in overtime as the Chiefs beat the Raiders, 23-17.

October 9—Tamarick Vanover returns a punt 86 yards in overtime to give the Chiefs a 29-23 victory over San Diego on *Monday Night Football*. It is the Chiefs' third overtime win at Arrowhead Stadium during the 1995 season.

October 22—The Chiefs beat the Broncos at Mile High Stadium, 21-7.

November 19—The Chiefs win their seventh game in a row, beating the Oilers at Arrowhead Stadium, 20-13.

December 24—Tamarick Vanover runs the opening kickoff 89 yards for a touchdown, and the Chiefs defeat the Seahawks, 26-3. They win the AFC Western Division and finish the regular season with a 13-3 record.

January 7, 1996—In bitterly cold conditions, the Chiefs fall flat, suffer an unfortunate upset loss to the Indianapolis Colts at Arrowhead Stadium, 10-7, and make an early exit from the playoffs. Kicker Lin Elliott missed a 42-yard field-goal attempt in the final seconds of the game—his third failure of the day—that would have tied the score.

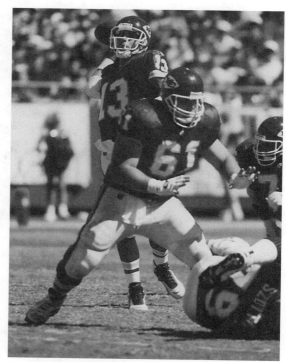

Steve Bono, shielded by Tim Grunhard, gets off a pass.
(Alan Barzee)

Big Game of 1995

September 10 at Kansas City
Kansas City 20, New York Giants 17 (OT)

Anemic and stifled, the Chiefs rose from their self-inflected doldrums and battled back from a two touchdown deficit in the fourth quarter to clip the New York Giants in overtime, 20-17.

"We could have folded," Chiefs center Tim Grunhard said of the comeback. "But this was a special victory for the fact that it showed this team has a lot of heart." The Chiefs needed that heart, because their football skills deserted them for most of the game.

A costly interception, penalties, and an ineptness on third down all led to a 17-3 Giants lead. The Chiefs didn't score a touchdown until 5:03 remained in the game. On the Chiefs' following possession, Bono hit Danan Hughes with the game-tying score after a 67-yard, 14-play drive that took just 2 minutes and 32 seconds.

"Something like this is great for the whole team," Bono said of the come-from-behind win. "The defensive guys believe in the offensive guys, and so on. It's good for everybody. It's a character builder."

Lin Elliott booted the game-winning field goal with 7:11 remaining in overtime to give the Chiefs the win. Marcus Allen led the Chiefs with 86 yards rushing and Bono passed for 187 yards. But this wasn't a game for statistics as far the Chiefs were concerned. It was about overcoming poor play and winning when they probably should have lost.

The win improved the Chiefs record to 2-0. This was the first of three overtime wins for Kansas City at Arrowhead Stadium during the 1995 season, and it set the tone for the team's ability to win tight, close games throughout the regular season.

Marcus Allen led the Chiefs in rushing again, gaining 890 yards. (Alan Barzee)

Preseason
Record: 3-1

8/5	W	37-21	WASHINGTON	70,807
8/11	L	17-22	at Arizona	37,622
8/19	W	36-10	BUFFALO	76,299
8/26	W	17-13	at Minnesota	39,349

Regular Season
Record: 13-3
(1st – AFC West)

9/3	W	34-10	at Seattle	54,062
9/10	W	*20-17	N.Y. GIANTS	77,962
9/17	W	*23-17	OAKLAND	78,696
9/24	L	17-35	at Cleveland	74,280
10/1	W	24-3	at Arizona	50,211
10/9	W	*29-23	SAN DIEGO (Mon.) (N)	79,288
10/15	W	31-26	NEW ENGLAND	77,992
10/22	W	21-7	at Denver	71,044
11/5	W	24-3	WASHINGTON	77,821
11/12	W	22-7	at San Diego	59,285
11/19	W	20-13	HOUSTON (N)	77,576
11/23	L	12-24	at Dallas (Thur.) (Thanksgiving)	64,901
12/3	W	29-23	at Oakland	53,930
12/11	L	6-13	at Miami (Mon.) (N)	70,321
12/17	W	20-17	DENVER	75,061
12/24	W	26-3	SEATTLE	75,784

Individual Statistics

Passing

	Att.	Cmp.	Yds.	Pct.	TD	INT	LG	Rating
Bono	520	293	3121	56.3	21	10	60t	79.5
Gannon	11	7	57	63.6	0	0	18	76.7
Chiefs Totals	531	300	3178	56.5	21	10	60t	79.4
Opp. Total	596	329	3569	55.2	16	16	49	70.8

Receiving

	No.	Yds.	Avg.	LG	TD
Anders	55	349	6.3	28	1
Cash	42	419	10.0	38t	1
Dawson	40	513	12.8	45t	5
Slaughter	34	514	15.1	38	4
W. Davis	33	527	16.0	60t	5
Allen	27	210	7.8	20	0
Walker	25	205	8.2	18t	1
Hughes	14	103	7.4	16	1
Vanover	11	231	21.0	57	2
Thompson	9	37	4.1	7	0
Hill	7	45	6.4	13	0
Bennett	1	12	12.0	12	0
Penn	1	12	12.0	12	0
Valerio	1	1	1.0	1t	1
Chiefs Totals	300	3178	10.6	60t	21
Opp. Totals	29	3569	10.6	49	16

Rushing

	No.	Yds.	Avg.	LG	TD
Allen	207	890	4.3	38	5
Hill	155	667	4.3	27	1
Anders	58	398	6.9	44	2
Bono	28	113	4.0	76t	5
Thompson	28	73	2.6	10	0
Vanover	6	31	5.2	13	0
Gannon	8	25	3.1	12t	1
Richardson	8	18	2.3	5	0
Bennett	7	11	1.6	11	0
Hughes	1	5	5.0	5	0
Dawson	1	-9	-9.0	-9	0
Chiefs Totals	507	2222	4.4	76t	14
Opp. Totals	404	1327	3.3	27	7

Team Statistics

	Chiefs	Opp.	
Total First Downs	295	289	
Rushing	113	83	
Passing	164	178	
Penalty	18	28	
3rd Down: Made Att.	82/231	78/229	
3rd Down Pct.	35.5	34.1	
4th Down: Made Att.	15/22	7/18	
4th Down Pct.	68.2	38.9	
Total Net Yards	5242	4549	
Avg. Per Game	327.6	284.3	
Total Plays	1059	1047	
Avg. Per Play	4.9	4.3	
Net Yards Rushing	2222	1327	
Avg. Per Game	138.9	82.9	
Total Rushes	507	404	
Avg. Per Play	4.4	3.3	
Net Yards Passing	3020	3222	
Avg. Per Game	188.8	201.4	
Sacked/Yards Lost	21/158	47/347	
Gross Yards	317.8	358.9	
Attempts/Completions	531/300	596/329	
Pct. of Completions	56.5	55.2	
Had Intercepted	10	16	
Punts/Average	91/43.8	102/41.8	
Net Punting Avg.	36.5	35.1	
Penalties/Yards	116/851	106/829	
Fumbles/Lost	17/11	35/17	
Touchdowns	42	26	
Rushing	14	7	
Passing	21	16	
Returns	4/3	5/0	
Time of Possession	31:08	28:52	

Score By Periods	1	2	3	4	OT	Total
Chiefs Total	70	120	56	97	15	358
Opp. Total	68	59	29	85	0	241

Regular Starters

	Offense		Defense
WR	Lake Dawson	LE	**Neil Smith**
	Webster Slaughter	NT	Joe Phillips
LT	John Alt	RT	**Dan Saleaumua**
LG	Dave Szott	RE	Vaughn Booker
C	Tim Grunhard		Darren Mickell
RG	**Will Shields**	LOLB	George Jamison
RT	Ricky Siglar	MLB	Tracy Simien
	Jeff Criswell	ROLB	**Derrick Thomas**
TE	Keith Cash	LCB	**Dale Carter**
	Derrick Walker	RCB	James Hasty
WR	Willie Davis	SS	Brian Washington
QB	**Steve Bono**	FS	Mark Collins
FB	Kimble Anders	P	Louie Aguiar
RB	Marcus Allen		
K	Lin Elliot		

PRO-BOWLERS in Bold

Team Leaders

Scoring: Lin Elliott — 106 pts: 34 PATs, 24 FGs
INTs: Dale Carter — 4-45 yds., 0 TDs
Tackles: Tracy Simien — 106 (75 solo)
Sacks: Neil Smith — 12.0 (-82.0 yds.)
Punting: Louie Aguiar — 91-3990 yds., 43.8 avg., 65 LG
Punt Returns: Tamarick Vanover — 51-540 yds., 10.6 avg., 1 TD
Kickoff Returns: Tamarick Vanover — 43-1095 yds., 25.5 avg., 2 TDs

1995 AFC Standings

Western Division

	W	L	T	Pct.
Kansas City	13	3	0	.813
San Diego +	9	7	0	.563
Denver	8	8	0	.500
Seattle	8	8	0	.500
Oakland	8	8	0	.500

Central Division

	W	L	T	Pct.
Pittsburgh	11	5	0	.689
Cincinnati	7	9	0	.438
Houston	7	9	0	.438
Cleveland	5	11	0	.313
Jacksonville	4	12	0	.250

Eastern Division

	W	L	T	Pct.
Buffalo	10	6	0	.625
Indianapolis +	9	7	0	.563
Miami +	9	7	0	.563
New England	6	10	0	.375
N.Y. Jets	3	13	0	.188

AFC Divisional Playoff: INDIANAPOLIS 10, Kansas City 7
AFC Championship: PITTSBURGH 20, Indianapolis 16
Super Bowl XXX: Dallas 27, Pittsburgh 17

Punter Louie Aguiar (Alan Barzee)

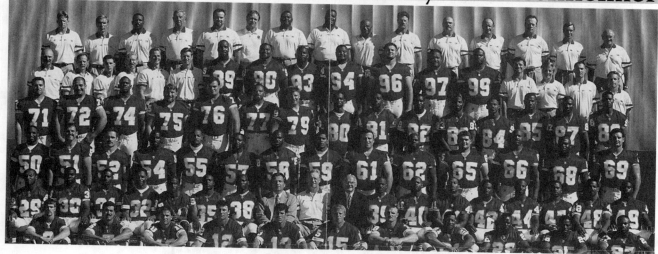

President/general manager Carl Peterson decided to stand pat with the Chiefs following 1995 season, and with the exception of replacing kicker Lin Elliott with Pete Stoyanovich, Kansas City fielded virtually the same team as it did the year before. The results were not the same, especially from the defense. The number-two unit in the NFL the year before, the Chiefs' defense fell to number 18 in 1996 and was sporadic throughout the season. Kansas City started out like gangbusters, though, winning its first four games. But the Chiefs only won five times the rest of the season. Steve Bono was ineffective at quarterback and was replaced by Rich Gannon late in the year. Still, to make the playoffs, the Chiefs just had to win one of their final three games. They lost all three. Marcus Allen ran for 830 yards, Greg Hill added 645. Bono threw for 2,572 yards, but threw more interceptions than touchdowns. Fullback Kimble Anders led in receptions with 60 catches, and was named to the Pro Bowl. Guard Will Shields, Derrick Thomas and Dale Carter were also selected for the Pro Bowl. At the end of the season, after the Chiefs had failed to make the playoffs for the first time in the 1990s, it was apparent that changes needed to be made for the team to successfully compete for postseason play again.

Key Dates in 1996:

September 1—The Chiefs win the season opener at Houston, 20-19.

September 22—Kansas City beats the Broncos, 17-14, the fourth win in a row for the Chiefs.

October 7—Pittsburgh defeats the Chiefs on *Monday Night Football*, 17-7.

November 17—Kansas City holds off the Bears and wins, 14-10, improving their record to 8-3.

November 28—Kansas City wins at Detroit on Thanksgiving Da, 28-24.

December 9—The Raiders dominate the Chiefs and beat them handily on *Monday Night Football*, 26-7.

December 15—The Colts come into Arrowhead and upset the Chiefs again, 24-19.

Big Game of 1996

December 22 at Buffalo
Buffalo 20, Kansas City 9

The Chiefs played poorly. With a chance to guarantee themselves a spot in the playoffs, they played themselves out. They gained just 249 yards total offense and committed three turnovers, but still led the game 9-6 going into the fourth-quarter. The Bills scored two fourth quarter touchdowns and locked up the game to win, 20-6.

"Maybe this capsulizes the excruciatingly disappointing season," Chiefs President Carp Peterson said of the game. "We can't even get back into the playoffs—not that we wanted to."

The loss was the third in a row for Kansas City, who at one point in the season stood at 8-3 and seemed a sure lock for the postseason. They finished the year at 9-7.

"I can't even put into words how disappointing this is," Chiefs center Tim Grunhard said. "I just hope some good can come out of this, because I really believe that some people on our team think the playoffs come for granted. It's a great honor to make the playoffs. It's not a birthright. It's an honor."

Steve Bono passed for just 138 yards, and Marcus Allen rushed for 87 yards. The defense struggled, rushing the passer the entire game. Additionally, with the Bills' two scores in the last period, the offense was unable to keep pace.

"I don't want to go home and see my mama," Chiefs linebacker Derrick Thomas said after the loss. "She'll be telling me it's all right. And it ain't all right."

"Not making the playoffs is astounding, especially when we started 4-0," Neil Smith said. "We didn't deserve to go."

Preseason   Record: 3-1

8/5	W	32-6	Dallas (Monterrey, Mexico)	45,128
8/10	W	42-6	NEW ORLEANS	65,710
8/19	L	30-34	ST. LOUIS	72,191
8/22	W	14-10	at Chicago	51,111

Regular Season   Record: 9-7

9/1	W	20-19	at Houston	27,725
9/8	W	19-3	OAKLAND	79,281
9/15	W	35-17	at Seattle	39,790
9/22	W	17-14	DENVER	79,439
9/29	L	19-22	at San Diego	59,384
10/7	L	7-17	PITTSBURGH (Mon.) (N)	79,189
10/17	W	34-16	SEATTLE (Thur.) (N)	76,057
10/22	L	7-34	at Denver	75,652
11/3	W	21-6	at Minnesota	59,552
11/10	W	27-20	GREEN BAY	79,281
11/17	W	14-10	CHICAGO	76,762
11/24	L	14-28	SAN DIEGO	69,472
11/28	W	28-24	at Detroit (Thur.) (Thanksgiving)	75,079
12/9	L	7-26	at Oakland (Mon.) (N)	57,082
12/15	L	19-24	INDIANAPOLIS	71,136
12/22	L	9-20	at Buffalo	68,671

Individual Statistics

Passing

	Att.	Cmp.	Yds.	Pct.	TD	INT	LG	Rating
Bono	438	235	2572	53.7	12	13	69	68.0
Gannon	90	54	491	60.0	6	1	25	92.4
Allen	1	0	0	0.0	0	0	0	39.6
Hughes	1	1	30	100.0	0	0	30	118.8
Chiefs Totals	530	290	3093	54.7	18	14	69	72.3
Opp. Total	536	289	3731	53.9	19	17	55	74.6

Receiving

	No.	Yds.	Avg.	LG	TD
Anders	60	529	8.8	45	2
Penn	49	628	12.8	22	5
LaChapelle	27	422	15.6	69	2
Allen	27	270	10.0	59	0
Vanover	21	241	11.5	24	1
McNair	21	181	8.6	29	1
Johnson	18	189	10.5	26	1
Hughes	17	167	9.8	26	1
Cash	14	80	5.7	20	0
Walker	9	73	8.1	24	1
Bennett	8	21	2.6	10	0
Carter	6	89	14.8	46t	1
Dawson	5	83	16.6	25	1
Hill	3	60	20.0	34t	1
Horn	2	30	15.0	21	0
Richardson	2	18	9.0	17	1
Bailey	1	12	12.0	12	0
Chiefs Totals	290	3093	10.7	69	18
Opp. Totals	289	3731	12.9	55	19

Rushing

	No.	Yds.	Avg.	LG	TD
Allen	206	830	4.0	35	9
Hill	135	645	4.8	28	4
Anders	54	201	3.7	15t	2
Bennett	36	166	4.6	34	0
Gannon	12	81	6.8	19	0
McNair	9	32	3.6	9	0
Bono	26	27	1.0	17	0
Richardson	4	10	2.5	4	0
Horn	1	8	8.0	8	0
Vanover	4	6	1.5	6	0
Carter	1	3	3.0	3	0
Chiefs Totals	488	2009	4.1	35	15
Opp. Totals	441	1666	3.8	65t	11

Team Statistics

	Chiefs	Opp.	
Total First Downs	312	296	
Rushing	111	84	
Passing	168	184	
Penalty	33	28	
3rd Down: Made Att.	77/221	92/218	
3rd Down Pct.	34.8	42.2	
4th Down: Made Att.	8/17	3/10	
4th Down Pct.	47.1	30.0	
Total Net Yards	4899	5204	
Avg. Per Game	306.2	325.3	
Total Plays	1045	1008	
Avg. Per Play	4.7	5.2	
Net Yards Rushing	2009	1666	
Avg. Per Game	125.6	104.1	
Total Rushes	488	441	
Avg. Per Play	4.1	3.8	
Net Yards Passing	2890	3538	
Avg. Per Game	180.6	221.1	
Sacked/Yards Lost	27/203	31/193	
Gross Yards	3093	3731	
Attempts/Completions	530/290	536/289	
Pct. of Completions	54.7	53.9	
Had Intercepted	14	17	
Punts/Average	88/41.7	71/41.8	
Net Punting Avg.	33.8	36.2	
Penalties/Yards	122/901	103/876	
Fumbles/Lost	17/10	23/10	
Touchdowns	35	32	
Rushing	15	11	
Passing	18	19	
Returns	1/1	1/1	
Time of Possession	30:39	29:21	

Score By Periods	1	2	3	4	OT	Total
Chiefs Total	61	108	38	90	0	297
Opp. Total	81	76	72	71	0	300

Regular Starters

	Offense		Defense
WR	Chris Penn	LE	Neil Smith
LT	John Alt	NT	Joe Phillips
LG	Dave Szott	RT	Dan Saleaumua
C	Tim Grunhard	RE	Vaughn Booker
RG	**Will Shields**	LOLB	**Derrick Thomas**
RT	Ricky Siglar	MLB	Tracy Simien
TE	Derrick Walker	ROLB	Anthony Davis
WR	Sean LaChapelle	LCB	**Dale Carter**
	Tamarick Vanover	RCB	James Hasty
QB	Steve Bono	SS	Brian Washington
FB	**Kimble Anders**	FS	Mark Collins
RB	Marcus Allen	P	Louie Aguiar
K	Pete Stoyanovich		

PRO-BOWLERS in Bold

Team Leaders

Scoring: Pete Stoyanovich — 85 pts: 34 PATs, 17 FGs
INTs: Mark Collins — 6-45 yds., 0 TDs
Tackles: Mark Collins — 119 (solo)
Sacks: Derrick Thomas — 13.0 (-109.0 yds.)
Punting: Louie Aguiar — 88-3667 yds., 41.7 avg., 68 LG
Punt Returns: Tamarick Vanover — 17-116 yds., 6.8 avg., 0 TDs
Kickoff Returns: Tamarick Vanover — 33-854 yds., 25.9 avg., 1 TD

1996 AFC Standings

Western Division

	W	L	T	Pct.
Denver	13	3	0	.813
Kansas City	9	7	0	.563
San Diego	8	8	0	.500
Oakland	7	9	0	.438
Seattle	7	9	0	.438

Central Division

	W	L	T	Pct.
Pittsburgh	10	6	0	.625
Jacksonville	9	7	0	.563
Cincinnati	8	8	0	.500
Houston	8	8	0	.500
Baltimore	4	12	0	.250

Eastern Division

	W	L	T	Pct.
New England	11	5	0	.688
Buffalo	10	6	0	.625
Indianapolis	9	7	0	.563
Miami	8	8	0	.500
N.Y. Jets	1	15	0	.063

AFC Championship: NEW ENGLAND 20, Jacksonville 6
Super Bowl XXXI: Green Bay 35, New England 21

Kimble Anders led the Chiefs with 60 pass receptions in 1996.
(Alan Barzee)

Marcus Allen (Alan Barzee)

1997 Head Coach: Marty Schottenheimer

The Chiefs had a great season: they went 13-3, won the AFC West, and secured home-field advantage for the playoffs. But because they lost to the Broncos in the divisional playoff game, 1997 can't be considered anything less than a disappointment. Like so many times throughout the 1990s, the Chiefs fell far short of their Super Bowl aspirations. After missing the playoffs for the first time in six years the season before, not much was expected of Kansas City. Twelve new starters spotted the lineup, including Elvis Grbac, the team's new quarterback. Marty Schottenheimer's team showed resolve, though, and played with a high level of consistency throughout the season. Andre Rison, the brilliant but troubled wideout, resurrected his career with the Chiefs and had an outstanding year, catching 72 passes for 1,092 yards and seven touchdowns. A group of running backs led a strong running game, with Greg Hill rushing for 550 yards and Marcus Allen gaining 505 yards. Grbac threw for 1,943 yards, and backup quarterback Rich Gannon, who played superbly, led the team to a 5-1 record during Grbac's absence because of injury, and added 1,143 yards. The defense had 54 sacks, 34 turnovers, and held their opponents to just 232 points. Despite the crushing playoff loss, many Chiefs secured well-deserved spots on the Pro Bowl roster. Rison, Will Shields, and Kimble Anders from the offense, and Derrick Thomas, Dale Carter and James Hasty from the defense all made the trip to Hawaii.

Key Dates in 1997:

August 31—The Chiefs open in Denver with a sub-par performance and lose to the Broncos, 19-3.

September 8—Elvis Grbac hit Andre Rison with three seconds left to lead the Chiefs to an improbable comeback win over the Raiders in Oakland, 28-27.

September 28—The Chiefs overcame a 10-point deficit and defeated Seattle in overtime, 20-17.

October 16—Grbac tosses two touchdown passes as the Chiefs down the Chargers, 31-3, at Arrowhead.

November 3—After falling behind, 10-0, the Chiefs battle back and win a hard-fought *Monday Night Football* game with the Steelers, 13-10. Grbac is injured and misses the next six games.

November 30—The Chiefs absolutely destroy the 49ers, romping to an incredibly easy win at Arrowhead, 44-9. Rich Gannon throws three touchdown passes, and the defense records five sacks in the dominating performance. Kansas City's record improves to 10-3.

December 7—The Chiefs hammer the Raiders, 30-0, as their defense holds Oakland to a just 93 total yards on offense.

December 21—For the second time in three years, the Chiefs win the AFC West with their 25-13 victory over the New Orleans Saints at Arrowhead. Kansas City finishes with a 13-3 record and was undefeated at Arrowhead Stadium.

January 4, 1998—The Chiefs fail to convert on a last-ditch drive and lose to the Denver Broncos in the AFC divisional playoff game at Arrowhead Stadium, 14-10. Kansas City held the Broncos to 272 yards total offense and committed no turnovers, but was unable to take advantage of their opportunities. A bad call in the end zone, a missed field goal and a poorly-timed fake field-goal attempt were problems the Chiefs couldn't overcome. In the final seconds of the game, Elvis Grbac's fourth-down pass to Lake Dawson near the end zone fell incomplete and the Broncos, not the Chiefs, moved on to the AFC title game.

Big Game of 1997

November 16 at Kansas City
Kansas City 24, Denver 22

The Chiefs made a dramatic, classic drive in the waning seconds at Arrowhead Stadium, getting just enough yardage for kicker Pete Stoyanovich to attempt an improbable 54-yarder to win the game.

"I stand up, and I'm looking and looking and waiting and waiting," holder Louis Aguiar said of Stoyanovich's kick. "Pete can't see past the line. He's looking at me 'is it good?' I didn't answer him for a while. Then I picked him up, and we all gave him a hug."

Stoyanovich's line-drive effort made it through the uprights as time expired, giving the Chiefs the win, 24-22.

"All I can tell you is that every young man in that locker room is going to battle you every step of the way," Chiefs Coach Marty Schottenheimer said of the win. "It doesn't have to be pretty. They don't give style points in our business."

And it wasn't pretty. Kansas City fell behind 13-0, as Denver scored on its first three possessions of the game. But opportunity was the name of this game, and the Chiefs converted every chance they got.

Tamarick Vanover returned a kickoff and punt into Denver territory, and a John Elway-fumble set up all three of Kansas City's touchdowns. Marcus Allen's score in the third period put the Chiefs up 21-13. Three field goals put the Broncos up 22-21. Kansas City got one last shot to pull out the game. They started at their own 27-yardline with one minute remaining in the game and had no timeouts left. They reached the Denver 42 with ten seconds left. Gannon hit Andre Rison on a quick out, and he struggled for an extra yard, foot—whatever he could get.

"I knew that every inch counted," Rison said of the play. He went out of bounds at the 37 yardline, and Stoyanovich came in for the 54-yard game-winning kick.

Statistically, the Broncos killed the Chiefs—329 yards of total offense to 202, 26 first downs to 15, and 37:25 minutes of possession to 22:35.

"The stat sheet doesn't always tell the story," Gannon said.

Derrick Thomas recorded his 100th career sack during the game, downing Denver's John Elway for the honor. Marcus Allen scored two touchdowns to lead the offense.

Derrick Thomas (Alan Barzee)

Rich Gannon (Alan Barzee)

Preseason
Record: 1-3

8/2	L	14-28	PITTSBURGH	72,726
8/9	L	7-26	at New Orleans	55,211
8/14	W	30-10	CAROLINA	76,972
8/22	L	13-14	at St. Louis	63,936

Regular Season
Record: 13-3

8/31	L	3-19	at Denver	75,600
9/8	W	28-27	at Oakland (Mon.) (N)	61,523
9/14	W	22-16	BUFFALO	78,169
9/21	W	35-14	at Carolina	67,402
9/28	W	20-17	SEATTLE	77,877
10/5	L	14-17	at Miami	71,794
10/16	W	31-3	SAN DIEGO (Thur.) (N)	77,196
10/26	W	28-20	at St. Louis	64,864
11/3	W	13-10	PITTSBURGH (Mon.) (N)	78,301
11/9	L	10-24	at Jacksonville	70,444
11/16	W	24-22	DENVER	77,963
11/23	W	19-14	at Seattle	66,264
11/30	W	44-9	SAN FRANCISCO	77,535
12/7	W	30-0	OAKLAND	76,379
12/14	W	29-7	at San Diego	54,594
12/21	W	25-13	NEW ORLEANS	66,772

Individual Statistics

Passing

	Att.	Cmp.	Yds.	Pct.	TD	INT	LG	Rating
Grbac	314	179	1943	57.6	11	6	55t	79.1
Gannon	175	98	1144	56.0	7	4	47	79.8
Tolliver	1	1	-8	100.0	0	0	-8	79.2
Allen	2	2	15	100.0	2	0	14t	137.5
Aguiar	1	1	35	100.0	0	0	35	118.8
Chiefs Totals	493	281	3129	57.0	20	10	55t	81.1
Opp. Total	507	271	3618	53.5	15	21	78	69.0

Receiving

	No.	Yds.	Avg.	LG	TD
Rison	72	1092	15.2	45	7
Anders	59	453	7.7	55t	2
Popson	35	320	9.1	21	2
Gonzalez	33	368	11.2	30	2
Dawson	21	273	13.0	27	2
Hill	12	126	10.5	39	0
Allen	11	86	7.8	18	0
Vanover	7	92	13.1	42	0
Hughes	7	65	9.3	14t	2
Bennett	7	5	0.7	4	0
Perriman	6	83	13.8	27	0
Walker	5	60	12.0	22	0
Richardson	3	6	2.0	3t	3
Horn	2	65	32.5	47	0
Lockett	1	35	35.0	35	0
Chiefs Totals	281	3129	11.1	55t	20
Opp. Totals	271	3618	13.4	78	15

Rushing

	No.	Yds.	Avg.	LG	TD
Hill	157	550	3.5	38	0
Allen	124	505	4.1	30	11
Anders	79	397	5.0	43	0
Bennett	94	369	3.9	14	1
Grbac	30	168	5.6	20	1
Gannon	33	109	3.3	13	2
Vanover	5	50	10.0	17	0
Aguiar	2	11	5.5	6	0
Richardson	2	11	5.5	6	0
Tolliver	2	-1	-0.5	0	0
Rison	1	2	2.0	2	0
Chiefs Totals	529	2171	4.1	43	15
Opp. Totals	413	1621	3.9	45	8

Team Statistics

	Chiefs	Opp.
Total First Downs	315	278
Rushing	129	94
Passing	163	158
Penalty	23	26
3rd Down: Made Att.	93/225	65/206
3rd Down Pct.	41.3	31.6
4th Down: Made Att.	5/16	4/13
4th Down Pct.	31/3	30.8
Total Net Yards	5064	4880
Avg. Per Game	316.5	305.0
Total Plays	1054	974
Avg. Per Play	4.8	5.0
Net Yards Rushing	2171	1621
Avg. Per Game	135.7	101.3
Total Rushes	529	413
Avg. Per Play	4.1	3.9
Net Yards Passing	2893	3259
Avg. Per Game	180.8	203.7
Sacked/Yards Lost	32/236	54/359
Gross Yards	3129	3618
Attempts/Completions	493/281	507/271
Pct. of Completions	57.0	53.5
Had Intercepted	10	21
Punts/Average	83/42.0	84/41.3
Net Punting Avg.	38.0	33.9
Penalties/Yards	121/1035	113/977
Fumbles/Lost	21/10	30/13
Touchdowns	42	23
Rushing	15	8
Passing	20	15
Returns	5/2	0/0
Time of Possession	31:16	28:44

Score By Periods

	1	2	3	4	OT	Total
Chiefs Total	63	149	59	101	3	375
Opp. Total	61	80	47	44	0	232

Regular Starters

	Offense		Defense
WR	**Andre Rison**	LE	Vaughn Booker
LT	Jeff Criswell	RT	Joe Phillips
LG	Dave Szott	RE	John Browning
C	Tim Grunhard	LOLB	**Derrick Thomas**
RG	**Will Shields**	ILB	Terry Wooden
RT	Glenn Parker		Wayne Simmons
TE	Ted Popson	MLB	Donnie Edwards
WR	Lake Dawson	ROLB	Anthony Davis
QB	Elvis Grbac	LCB	**Dale Carter**
FB	**Kimble Anders**	RCB	**James Hasty**
RB	Greg Hill	SS	Reggie Tongue
K	Pete Stoyanovich	FS	Jerome Woods
		P	Louie Aguiar

PRO-BOWLERS in Bold

Team Leaders

Scoring: Pete Stoyanovich — 113 pts: 35 PATs, 26 FGs
INTs: Mark McMillian — 8-274 yds., 3 TDs
Tackles: Reggie Tongue — 142 (91 solo)
Sacks: Dan Williams — 10.5 (-57.5 yds.)
Punting: Louie Aguiar — 82-3465 yds., 42.3 avg., 65 LG
Punt Returns: Tamarick Vanover — 35-383 yds., 10.9 avg., 1 TD
Kickoff Returns: Tamarick Vanover — 51-1308 yds., 25.6 avg., 1 TD

1997 AFC Standings

Western Division

	W	L	T	Pct.
Kansas City	13	3	0	.813
Denver	12	4	0	.750
Seattle	8	8	0	.500
Oakland	4	12	0	.250
San Diego	4	12	0	.250

Central Division

	W	L	T	Pct.
Pittsburgh	11	5	0	.688
Jacksonville	11	5	0	.688
Tennessee	8	8	0	.500
Cincinnati	7	9	0	.438
Baltimore	6	9	1	.406

Eastern Division

	W	L	T	Pct.
New England	10	6	0	.625
Miami	9	7	0	.563
N.Y. Jets	9	7	0	.563
Buffalo	6	10	0	.375
Indianapolis	3	13	0	.188

AFC Divisional Playoff: DENVER 14, Kansas City 10
AFC Championship: Denver 24, PITTSBURGH 21
Super Bowl XXXII: Denver 31, Green Bay 24

Elvis Grbac (Alan Barzee)

Andre Rison (Alan Barzee)

Once again starting the season with Super Bowl dreams, the Chiefs looked like they would have another good year when they won four of their first five games. A blowout loss to New England in the sixth game revealed chinks in the Chiefs' armor, however, and the team fell apart. A six-game losing streak and an ugly unsportsmanlike tirade on *Monday Night Football* left the Chiefs' season in ruins. Kansas City set NFL records for the most penalties in a season with 158, and the most penalty yardage with 1,304. They finished with a 7-9 record, the first losing season in Mary Schottenheimer's tenure as head coach of the Chiefs, and he resigned following the season. The Chiefs also endured a mild quarterback controversy between Elvis Grbac and Rich Gannon, which Grbac eventually won, even though it appeared Gannon was the more effective of the two. Without Marcus Allen, the running game suffered and never really clicked. A mid-season pickup of Bam Morris, a troubled, but talented and smashing runner bolstered the attack a little, but by the time he found his wheels, the season was lost. Kansas City rushed for less than 1,600 yards. The defense allowed a whopping 131 more points scored than in '97; their sack and turnover totals were also down from previous seasons. Offensive guard Will Shields was the team's lone selection for the Pro Bowl.

Key Dates in 1998:

April 9—Marcus Allen announces his retirement.

September 6—The Chiefs open the 1998 season with an impressive performance and easily defeat the Raiders at Arrowhead, 28-8. Kansas City sacks the Raiders' quarterbacks 10 times, with Derrick Thomas collecting six by himself.

September 13—Kansas City falls to Jacksonville on the road, 21-16.

October 4—Kansas City conquers the Seahawks and the rain at Arrowhead, 17-6. Gannon hit Andre Rison for an 80-yard touchdown pass after a 54-minute rain delay caused by a violent storm. The two teams combined for nine turnovers, five by Kansas City. The win improves the Chiefs' record to 4-1.

November 1—In another driving rainstorm, Grbac throws three interceptions, and the Chiefs blow the game against the Jets, losing 20-17.

November 16—The Chiefs unravel and display the ugliest, unsportsmanlike conduct in the franchise's history as they are easily beaten by the Broncos at Arrowhead Stadium on *Monday Night Football*, 30-7. Kansas City is flagged for five personal foul penalties—three by Derrick Thomas—during the Broncos' final touchdown drive. Derrick Thomas is suspended for one game as result of his actions.

November 22—San Diego scores 21 points in the fourth quarter to defeat the Chiefs, 38-37. It's Kansas City's sixth loss in a row, the team's longest losing streak since they dropped nine in a row in 1987.

November 29—Kansas City snaps the six-game losing streak against the Arizona Cardinals at Arrowhead Stadium, winning 34-24.

December 13—Bam Morris runs through the Dallas Cowboys defense for 137 yards and a touchdown to lead the Chiefs to a 20-17 win at Arrowhead Stadium. The win was Schottenheimer's 100th as the Chiefs' head coach.

December 26—After trailing 14-0, the Chiefs come back and defeat the Raiders in Oakland, 31-24. Grbac hit Tony Gonzalez with the game-winning touchdown late in the fourth quarter. The win leaves the Chiefs' record at 7-9, fourth in the AFC West, and is the first time Schottenheimer finishes a season with a losing mark.

Big Game of 1998

October 11 at New England
New England 40, Kansas City 10

Looking more like a last-place club than a Super Bowl contender, the Chiefs were blown out and embarrassed by the New England Patriots, 40-10. Mistakes and exposed weaknesses combined to make the game a laugher for the home team, who capitalized over and over from Kansas City's poor play.

"We made enough errors to last a season," Chiefs Coach Marty Schottenheimer said afterward. "I didn't think we could play poorly. We clearly did not play to the level we expect to play."

Here's the Chiefs' carnage left by the Patriots: 438 total yards to 134, 31 first downs to nine for Kansas City, 41 minutes and 45 seconds of possession time to the Chiefs' 18:15. New England struck quickly and held a 27-0 lead at the half. The Chiefs never challenged, and worse, apparently quit trying.

"They quit out there," New England linebacker Chris Slade said of the Chiefs' play. "They didn't play hard. They just quit. By halftime, they were out of it."

The game was so bad for Kansas City that no player can be said to have had any kind of decent performance. It was truly a team loss, and one that has Shottenheimer personally shouldering the blame.

"I've got to take responsibility for that part of it (sloppy play)," Schottenheimer said. "Those things shouldn't happen."

The loss dropped the Chiefs to 4-2, and raised serious questions about how good a team they really were.

"I've seen this happen to us before, and we bounced back," Chiefs linebacker Derrick Thomas said. "We'll bounce back from this one. . . I don't anticipate us doing anything less."

This was the first loss of the Chiefs' six-game losing streak during the season.

Rich Gannon (Alan Barzee)

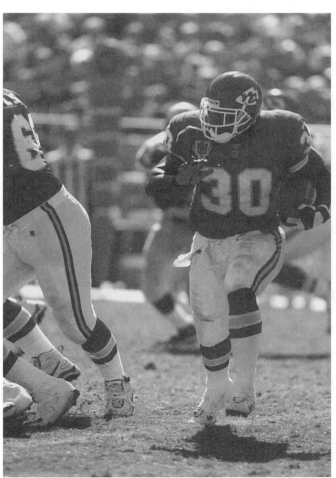

Donnell Bennett (Alan Barzee)

Preseason   Record: 2-3

8/1	L	24-27	Green Bay (Tokyo, Japan)		42,018
8/8	W	17-13	Tampa Bay (Norman, OK)		43,657
8/15	L	0-34	at Minnesota		60,995
8/22	W	22-21	JACKSONVILLE		71,079
8/28	L	6-10	ST. LOUIS		69,501

Regular Season   Record: 7-9

9/6	W	28-8	OAKLAND (N)	78,945
9/13	L	16-21	at Jacksonville	69,821
9/20	W	23-7	SAN DIEGO	73,730
9/27	W	24-21	at Philadelphia	66,675
10/4	W	17-6	SEATTLE (N)	66,418
10/11	L	10-40	at New England	59,749
10/26	L	13-20	PITTSBURGH (N)	79,431
11/1	L	17-20	N.Y. JETS	65,104
11/8	L	12-24	at Seattle	66,251
11/16	L	7-30	DENVER (Mon.) (N)	78,100
1/22	L	37-38	at San Diego	59,894
11/29	W	34-24	ARIZONA	69,613
12/6	L	31-35	at Denver	74,962
12/13	W	20-17	DALLAS	77,697
12/20	L	7-28	at N.Y. Giants	66,040
12/26	W	31-24	at Oakland (Sat.)	52,679

Individual Statistics

Passing

	Att.	Cmp.	Yds.	Pct.	TD	INT	LG	Rating
Gannon	354	206	2305	58.2	10	6	80t	80.1
Grbac	188	98	1142	52.1	5	12	65	53.1
Hughes	1	1	25	100.0	0	0	25	118.8
Chiefs Totals	543	305	3472	56.2	15	18	80t	70.9
Opp. Total	479	259	3253	52.1	17	13	58	76.0

Receiving

	No.	Yds.	Avg.	LG	TD
Anders	64	462	7.2	29	2
Gonzalez	59	621	10.5	32	2
Alexander	54	992	18.4	65	4
Rison	40	542	13.6	80t	5
Lockett	19	281	14.8	38	0
Bennett	16	91	5.7	14	1
Horn	14	198	14.1	57	1
Popson	13	90	6.9	17	0
Morris	12	95	7.9	29	0
Shehee	10	73	7.3	14	0
Richardson	2	13	6.5	15	0
Hughes	1	10	10.0	10	0
Sheilds	1	4	4.0	4	0
Chiefs Totals	305	3472	11.4	80t	15
Opp. Totals	259	3253	12.6	58	17

Rushing

	No.	Yds.	Avg.	LG	TD
Bennett	148	527	3.6	26	5
Morris	129	481	3.7	38	8
Anders	58	230	4.0	20	1
Gannon	44	168	3.8	21	3
Shehee	22	57	2.6	10	0
Richardson	20	45	2.3	6	2
Grbac	7	27	3.9	10	0
Rison	2	12	6.0	11	0
Vanover	2	1	0.5	2	0
Horn	1	0	0.0	0	0
Chiefs Totals	433	1548	3.6	38	19
Opp. Totals	491	1869	3.8	72t	22

Team Statistics

	Chiefs	Opp.
Total First Downs	289	321
Rushing	103	119
Passing	153	146
Penalty	33	56
3rd Down: Made Att.	70/220	69/204
3rd Down Pct.	31.8	33.8
4th Down: Made Att.	13/25	6/12
4th Down Pct.	52.0	50.0
Total Net Yards	4808	4854
Avg. Per Game	300.5	303.4
Total Plays	1012	1010
Avg. Per Play	4.8	4.8
Net Yards Rushing	1548	1869
Avg. Per Game	96.8	116.8
Total Rushes	433	491
Net Yards Passing	3260	2985
Avg. Per Game	203.8	186.6
Sacked/Yards Lost	36/212	40/268
Gross Yards	3472	3253
Attempts/Completions	543/305	479/259
Pct. of Completions	56.2	54.1
Had Intercepted	18	13
Punts/Average	77/42.3	77/42.2
Net Punting Avg.	77/34/3	77/36.0
Penalties/Yards	158/1304	138/1292
Fumbles/Lost	35/14	36/20
Touchdowns	35	44
Rushing	19	22
Passing	15	17
Returns	1	5
Time of Possession	29:53	30:07

Score By Periods	1	2	3	4	OT	Total
Chiefs Total	77	67	105	78	0	327
Opp. Total	101	100	65	97	0	363

Regular Starters

	Offense		Defense	
WR	Andre Rison	LE	John Browning
LT	Jeff Criswell	NT	Tom Barndt
LG	Glenn Parker	RE	Chester McGlockton
C	Tim Grunhard	FALC	Derrick Thomas
RG	**Will Shields**		Leslie O'Neal
RT	Victor Riley	ILB	Wayne Simmons
TE	Tony Gonzalez	MLB	Donnie Edwards
WR	Derrick Alexander	RLB	Anthony Davis
QB	Elvis Grbac	LCB	Dale Carter
	Rich Gannon		Mark McMillian
FB	Kimble Anders	RCB	James Hasty
RB	Donnell Bennett	SS	Reggie Tongue
K	Pete Stoyanovich	FS	Jerome Woods
		P	Louie Aguiar

PRO-BOWLERS in Bold

Team Leaders

Scoring: Pete Stoyanovich — 115 pts: 34 PATs, 27 FGs
INTs: James Hasty — 4-42 yds., 0 TDs
Tackles: Donnie Edwards — 151 (97 solo)
Sacks: Derrick Thomas — 12.0 (-79.0)
Punting: Louie Aguiar — 75-3226 yds., 43.0 avg., 59 LG
Punt Returns: Tamarick Vanover — 27-264 yds., 9.8 avg., 0 TDs
Kickoff Returns: Tamarick Vanover — 41-956 yds, 23.3 avg., 0 TDs

1998 AFC Standings

Western Division

	W	L	T	Pct.
Denver	14	2	0	.875
Oakland	8	8	0	.500
Seattle	8	8	0	.500
Kansas City	7	9	0	.438
San Diego	5	11	0	.313

Central Division

	W	L	T	Pct.
Jacksonville	11	5	0	.688
Tennessee	8	8	0	.500
Pittsburgh	7	9	0	.688
Baltimore	6	10	0	.375
Cincinnati	3	13	0	.188

Eastern Division

	W	L	T	Pct.
N.Y. Jets	12	4	0	.750
Buffalo	10	6	0	.625
Miami	10	6	0	.625
New England	9	7	0	.563
Indianapolis	3	13	0	.188

AFC Championship: DENVER 23, N.Y. Jets 10
Super Bowl XXXIII: Denver 34, Atlanta 19

All-Pro Will Shields (Alan Barzee)

1999 Head Coach: Gunther Cunningham

After the disastrous 1998 season, Marty Schottenheimer resigned and was replaced by his defensive coordinator, Gunther Cunningham. Wanting to establish a new identity for the team, Cunningham looked to the recent past and turned his team back to the smash-mouth brand of football Schottenheimer had used in the early 1990s. It worked for the most part, and despite the lack of a feature back in the offense, Kansas City once again topped the 2,000-yard mark in rushing. Elvis Grbac had a superb season at quarterback and remained injury-free for the first time in his career. He passed for 3,389 yards and 22 touchdowns, and by the end of the season, displayed many of the qualities the Chiefs had hoped for when they signed him three years earlier. Tight end Tony Gonzalez had a breakout year, catching 72 passes and scoring 11 touchdowns. The top rusher was Donnell Bennett, and Bam Morris also contributed. The defense was spectacular at times, but inconsistency and breakdowns ultimately cost the team. A three-game losing streak in the middle of the season left Kansas City with a 5-5 record, but they rebounded and won four games in a row. The Chiefs needed to win one of their last two games to make the playoffs, but lost both and again missed postseason play. The final game was especially disappointing. After leading the Raiders 17-0 in the first quarter, Kansas City ended up losing, 41-38, in overtime. The biggest problem area for the team was special teams, as short kickoffs and poor punting hurt them throughout the season. Gonzalez was rewarded for his great season with a Pro Bowl selection, and he was joined by another first-timer, center Tim Grunhard. Will Shields and James Hasty also made the AFC roster. The team again faced tragedy in the off season when Derrick Thomas was severely injured in a car accident. He died two weeks later, leaving a long legacy of excellent play, and also a huge void in the heart of the team.

Key Dates in 1999:

January 11—Marty Schottenheimer resigns as head coach of the Chiefs. His career record with Kansas City was 101-58-1, the best winning percentage in the club's history (.631). However, his playoff record with the Chiefs was a miserable 3-7. "It was a golden era of Chiefs football," Lamar Hunt said of Schottenheimer's tenure as head coach.

January 22—After looking at several candidates, Chiefs president/general manager Carl Peterson chooses Chiefs defensive coordinator Gunther Cunningham as the team's new head coach, and a new era of Chiefs football begins. Cunningham had been with the team four years. "I interviewed a lot of talented people," said Peterson, "but throughout the process, I kept coming back to Gunther Cunningham."

September 12—Gunther Cunningham loses his first game as the Chiefs' head coach, 20-17, to the Chicago Bears.

September 19—The Chiefs win impressively against the Denver Broncos at Arrowhead Stadium, 26-10, for Cunningham's first victory as head coach.

October 31—The Chiefs dominate the Chargers at Arrowhead Stadium, 34-0, improving their record to 5-2.

November 21—The Seattle Seahawks beat Kansas City at Arrowhead, 31-19. The loss drops the Chiefs' record to 5-5.

November 28—A late comeback spurs the Chiefs past the Raiders in Oakland, 37-34. Pete Stoyanivich kicks the game-winning field goal in the final seconds of play.

December 18—Kansas City dominates the Steelers at Arrowhead Stadium to win its fourth game in a row, 35-19. Their record is now 9-5.

December 26—Kansas City plays poorly and loses to the Seahawks, 23-14.

January 23, 2000—Derrick Thomas, the Chiefs' star linebacker, is severely injured in a one-car accident.

February 8, 2000—Derrick Thomas dies tragically from heart arrest. "It is a devastating tragedy to the Kansas City Chiefs family, the people of Kansas City, the fans of the National Football League, and also to me personally," Chiefs president Carl Peterson said in a statement.

Big Game of 1999

January 2, 2000 at Kansas City
Oakland 41, Kansas City 38 (OT)

So close. The Chiefs held the AFC West crown in their hands and were ready to place in on their heads, and prance into the playoffs. But the crown didn't fit, and when Oakland's Joe Nedney booted a 33-yard field goal after three minutes of overtime play, the Raiders vanquished the Chiefs from the playoffs, winning the game, 41-38.

"I felt like if we could win this game and win the AFC West, we would have made a tremendous statement about discipline, toughness, consistency," Chiefs Coach Gunther Cunningham said of the loss. "Obviously, we have a ways to go."

It appeared this was going to be the Chiefs' day. A Tamarick Vanover punt return, a James Hasty interception, and a Pete Stoyanovich field goal staked Kansas City to 17-0 lead. But the special teams, a year-long problem, came back to haunt the Chiefs once too often this season. The Raiders blocked a punt to start their comeback, and by halftime led 28-24. Kickoff specialist Jon Baker was horrible, and set up the Raiders with good field position in overtime when his kickoff went out of bounds.

"If you have any idea how much my head hurts, right about here," Cunningham said as he pointed to his head. "It says 'special teams' across that part of my forehead."

The second half went back and forth, but when Elvis Grbac led the Chiefs on a seven-play, 43-yard drive to set up a game-winning field-goal attempt at the end of regulation, it looked as if the Chiefs were going make it past the Raiders and into the playoffs. Except Stoyanovich missed the field goal.

"It looked like he just got over it a little too much, and it went left on him," Danny Pope, Stoyanovich's holder said of the missed attempt. "Everything seemed fine, it was a good snap, he just pulled it a little left."

The Chiefs' offense clicked throughout the game. Grbac threw for 243 yards and three touchdowns, and Donnell Bennett ran for 84 as Kansas City totaled 429 yards for the game. But the defense, which had bailed out the Chiefs several times during the season, couldn't stop Oakland. Rich Gannon passed for 324 yards and three touchdowns, gaining most of his yardage on screen passes.

"It's probably the most frustrating football game I've ever gone through," Cunningham said. "It's just heart sickening to have something like that happen at the end of the year."

The Chiefs finished Cunningham's first season at 9-7, and while it was an improvement over 1998, the disappointment of being so close to the playoffs and not making it was tough to take.

"You know when you have something right in your hands and you let it go?" Chiefs linebacker Donnie Edwards said. "We had it and let it go. That's the only feeling I have to help you understand."

Elvis Grbac (Alan Barzee)

Gunther Cunningham (Alan Barzee)

Preseason
Record: 2-2

8/15	W	22-20	TENNESSEE	75,152
8/21	L	7-17	TAMPA BAY	76,292
8/26	L	6-31	at Jacksonville	56,932
9/3	W	34-27	at San Diego	46,005

Regular Season
Record: 9-7

9/12	L	17-20	at Chicago	58,381
9/19	W	26-10	DENVER	78,683
9/26	W	31-21	DETROIT	78,384
10/03	L	14-21	at San Diego	58,099
10/10	W	16-14	NEW ENGLAND	78,636
10/21	W	35-8	at Baltimore	68,771
10/31	W	34-0	SAN DIEGO	78,473
11/7	L	17-25	at Indianapolis	56,689
11/14	L	10-17	at Tampa Bay	64,927
11/21	L	19-31	SEATTLE	78,714
11/28	W	37-34	at Oakland	48,632
12/05	W	16-10	at Denver	73,855
12/12	W	31-28	MINNESOTA	78,932
12/18	W	35-19	PITTSBURGH	78,697
12/26	L	14-23	at Seattle	66,332
1/2/00	L	38-41	OAKLAND	79,026

Individual Statistics

Passing

	Att.	Cmp.	Yds.	Pct.	TD	INT	LG	Rating
Grbac	499	294	3389	58.9	22	15	86T	81.7
Moon	3	1	20	33.3	0	0	20	57.6
Chiefs Totals	502	295	3409	58.8	22	15	86t	81.5
Opp. Total	578	317	3768	54.8	24	25	54	70.8

Receiving

	No.	Yds.	Avg.	LG	TD
Gonzalez	76	849	11.2	73t	11
Alexander	54	832	15.4	86t	2
Horn	35	586	16.7	76t	6
Lockett	34	426	12.5	39t	2
Richardson	24	141	5.9	29	0
Rison	21	218	10.4	20	0
Shehee	18	136	7.6	17	0
Johnson	10	98	9.8	19	1
Bennett	10	41	4.1	12	0
Morris	7	37	5.3	9	0
Cloud	3	25	8.3	12	0
Anders	2	14	7.0	9	0
Jacoby	1	6	6.0	6	0
Chiefs Totals	295	3409	11.6	86t	22
Opp. Totals	317	3768	11.9	54	24

Rushing

	No.	Yds.	Avg.	LG	TD
Bennett	161	627	3.9	44	8
Morris	120	414	3.5	24	3
Richardson	84	387	4.6	25	1
Shehee	65	238	3.7	18	1
Anders	32	181	5.7	46	0
Cloud	35	128	3.7	14	0
Alexander	2	82	41.0	82t	1
Horn	2	15	7.5	9	0
Grbac	19	10	0.5	8	0
Pope	1	0	0.0	0	0
Chiefs Totals	521	2082	4.0	82t	14
Opp. Totals	415	1557	3.8	45	10

Team Statistics

	Chiefs	Opp.
Total First Downs	282	281
Rushing	108	80
Passing	164	173
Penalty	10	28
3rd Down: Made Att.	96/243	65/215
3rd Down Pct.	39.5	30.2
4th Down: Made Att.	6/11	6/13
4th Down Pct.	54.5	46.2
Total Net Yards	5321	5039
Avg. Per Game	332.6	314.9
Total Plays	1049	1033
Avg. Per Play	5.1	4.9
Net Yards Rushing	2082	1557
Avg. Per Game	130.1	97.3
Total Rushes	521	415
Net Yards Passing	3239	3482
Avg. Per Game	202.4	217.6
Sacked/Yards Lost	26/170	40/286
Gross Yards	3409	3768
Attempts/Completions	502/295	578/317
Pct. of Completions	58.8	54.8
Had Intercepted	15	25
Punts/Average	104/40.9	98/43.5
Net Punting Avg.	104/35.1	98/35.4
Penalties/Yards	126/982	107/787
Fumbles/Lost	22/9	31/20
Touchdowns	47	38
Rushing	14	10
Passing	22	24
Returns	11	4
Time of Possession	30:20	29:40

Score By Periods	1	2	3	4	OT	Total
Chiefs Total	84	105	93	108	0	390
Opp. Total	50	133	74	62	3	322

Regular Starters

Offense		Defense	
WR	Andre Rison	LE	Eric Hicks
LT	Glenn Parker	DT	Chester McGlockton
LG	Dave Szott	DT	Tom Barndt
C	**Tim Grunhard**	RE	Leslie O'Neal
RG	**Will Shields**		Dan Williams
RT	Victor Riley	LB	Donnie Edwards
	John Tait	MLB	Marvcus Patton
TE	**Tony Gonzalez**	RLB	Derrick Thomas
WR	Derrick Alexander	LCB	Cris Dishman
QB	Elvis Grbac	RCB	**James Hasty**
RB	Bam Morris	SS	Reggie Tongue
	Rashan Shehee	FS	Jerome Woods
K	Pete Stoyanovich	P	Danny Pope
		FB	Tony Richardson

PRO-BOWLERS in Bold

Team Leaders

Scoring: Pete Stoyanovich — 108 pts: 45 PATs, 21 FGs
INTs: James Hasty — 7-98 yds., 2 TDs
Tackles: Donnie Edwards — 143 (105 solo)
Sacks: Derrick Thomas — 7.0 (-65.0)
Punting: Danny Pope — 101-4218 yds., 41.8 avg., 64 LG
Punt Returns: Tamarick Vanover — 51-627 yds., 12.3 avg., 2 TDs
Kickoff Returns: Tamarick Vanover — 44-886 yds., 20.1 avg., 0 TDs

1999 AFC Standings

Western Division

	W	L	T	Pct.
Seattle	9	7	0	.563
Kansas City	9	7	0	.563
San Diego	8	8	0	.500
Oakland	8	8	0	.500
Denver	6	10	0	.375

Central Division

	W	L	T	Pct.
Jacksonville	14	2	0	.875
Tennessee	13	3	0	.813
Baltimore	8	8	0	.500
Pittsburgh	6	10	0	.375
Cincinnati	4	12	0	.250
Cleveland	2	14	0	.125

Eastern Division

	W	L	T	Pct.
Indianapolis	13	3	0	.813
Buffalo	11	5	0	.688
Miami	9	7	0	.563
N.Y. Jets	8	8	0	.500
New England	8	8	0	.500

AFC Championship: Tennessee 33, JACKSONVILLE 14
Super Bowl XXXIV: St. Louis 23, Tennessee 16

Tamarick Vanover (Alan Barzee)

2000 Head Coach: Gunther Cunningham

The Chiefs offically dedicated their season to the memory of Derrick Thomas, the great linebacker who had tragically died in February. His loss caused changes on defense, but the team also took a different direction offensively as well. Kansas City scrapped its run-oriented offense after two quick losses at the beginning of the season, and for the first time in many years relied primarily on the pass to move the ball. Elvis Grbac responded to the new offensive philosophy and threw for more than 4,000 yards, and Tony Gonzalez broke the team record for receptions as he and Derrick Alexander both topped the 1,000 yard mark in receiving yards. But the defense was lacking in several areas, and with the exception of Eric Hicks, was mediocre at best. But the worst problem might have been the continual mental breakdown on both sides of the ball. Gunther Cunningham strangely talked about resigning to his players after the Chiefs lost their opening game. He quickly ended the notion, but never really had control of the team again. The change to a passing game helped for a while, and the Chiefs posted a 5-3 record in the first half of the season, including an impressive 54-34 win over the World Champion Rams. The season melted away to a final mark of 7-9, (including two losses to the Raiders), and even though Carl Peterson gave Cunningham a thumbs up near the end of the season, he fired the head coach in January, 2001. The Chiefs new head man, Dick Vermeil, came to Kansas City with an impressive resume—including a Super Bowl Championship at St. Louis in 1999—and a lifelong relationship with Peterson. Vermeil had a lot of rebuilding to do, as Grbac left Kansas City and signed with the Baltimore Ravens, and long-time Chiefs James Hasty, Kimble Anders and Chester McGlockton were all released.

Key Dates in 2000:

September 3—The Indianapolis Colts stop Kansas City in the season opener at Arrowhead, 27-14. After the game Gunther Cunningham talks about quitting his coaching duties with the team.

September 17—The Chargers are bombed by the Chiefs, 42-10, as Kansas City surprises San Diego with its new passing attack. Grbac throws for 235 yards and five touchdowns.

October 15—The Raiders squeak past the Chiefs at Arrowhead with a late field goal, winning 20-17. The loss drops the Chiefs' record to 3-3.

November 5—Elvis Grbac throws for 504 yards and two touchdowns, but the Raiders maul the Chiefs in Oakland anyway, 49-31.

November 26—The Chiefs lose to the lowly Chargers, 17-16. It is the Chargers' only win of the season.

December 4—New England clips Kansas City, 30-24. The loss is the fifth in a row for the Chiefs.

December 10—Kansas City defeats Carolina at Arrowhead, 15-14, to end the losing skid. Todd Peterson's 33-yard field goal with 3:28 remaining in the fourth quarter provides the winning margin.

December 24—A sloppy, unmotivated Chiefs squad loses at Atlanta, 29-13. The loss puts the team's final season record at 7-9.

January 5, 2001—Gunther Cunningham is fired.

January 12, 2001—Dick Vermeil becomes the ninth head coach in the history of the Kansas City Chiefs.

March 1, 2001—Elvis Grbac, James Hasty and Chester McGlockton are released from the Chiefs roster. Grbac later signs with the Baltimore Ravens.

Big Game of 2000

October 22, 2000 at Kansas City
Kansas City 54, St. Louis 34

For the Chiefs, this was their Super Bowl. Forget that the game was in October and their record was just 3-3. It was the undefeated Rams in Arrowhead, and a chance to show the rest of the NFL how good Kansas City really was. In the end, it wasn't close.

Kansas City 54, St. Louis 34.

"It was a scoring orgy," Chiefs center Tim Grunhard said of the game. Indeed. The Chiefs hadn't scored that many points since 1966, and the fact it was against the defending Super Bowl champs made the victory even sweeter.

"It was really the mind-set that whatever we had to do for four quarters, we had to score as many points as we could," Chiefs quarterback Elvis Grbac said after the game.

"We knew we had to be aggressive," Warren Moon added.

And the Chiefs were. It was 20-0 after the first quarter, thanks to a Frank Moreau touchdown run, two Todd Peterson field goals, and a blocked punt recovered for a touchdown. The Rams never recovered, and the Chiefs, unlike previous games this season, never let up.

"We knew we had to go after them in because Seattle and Denver scored over 30 points on them, and they got outscored at the end because the Rams' offense is so potnet," Tony Gonzalez said. "I didn't think we would score that many points on them, but I knew we could score on them."

Grbac threw for 266 yards and two touchdowns. Kimble Anders ran for 102 yards and a score. Moon even got into the action, throwing a touchdown pass to Troy Drayton after replacing Grbac because of his injured elbow.

Cunningham could hardly contain his joy over the win and heartily congratulated the players afterward. Air Kansas City had arrived, and it was an offensive philosophy the team planned on using the rest of the season.

"I hope so," Derrick Alexander said. "I hope that'll be our game plan the rest of the season."

Preseason   Record: 0-4

8/5	L	10-14	at Tennessee	68,203
8/13	L	10-33	SAN FRANCISCO	76,682
8/19	L	22-26	JACKSONVILLE	75,120
8/25	L	14-37	at Tampa Bay	64,267

Regular Season   Record: 7-9

9/3	L	14-27	INDIANAPOLIS	78,357
9/10	L	14-17	at Tennessee	68,203
9/17	W	42-10	SAN DIEGO	77,604
9/24	W	23-22	at Denver	74,596
10/2	W	24-17	SEATTLE	78,502
10/15	L	17-20	OAKLAND	79,025
10/22	W	54-34	ST. LOUIS	79,142
10/29	W	24-19	at Seattle	62,141
11/5	L	31-49	at Oakland	62,428
11/12	L	7-21	at San Francisco	68,002
11/19	L	17-21	BUFFALO	78,457
11/26	L	16-17	at San Diego	47,228
12/4	L	24-30	at New England	60,292
12/10	W	15-14	CAROLINA	77,481
12/17	W	20-7	DENVER	78,406
12/24	L	13-29	at Atlanta	41,017

Individual Statistics

Passing

	Att.	Cmp.	Yds.	Pct.	TD	INT	LG	Rating
Grbac	547	326	4169	59.6	28	14	81T	89.9
Moon	34	15	208	44.1	1	1	41	61.9
Morris	1	1	31	100.00	0	0	31	118.8
Chiefs Totals	5582	342	4408	58.8	29	15	81t	88.5
Opp. Total	549	358	3737	65.2	25	15	47	88.6

Receiving

	No.	Yds.	Avg.	LG	TD
Gonzalez	93	1203	12.9	39	9
Alexander	78	1391	17.8	81t	10
Richardson	58	468	8.1	24	3
Morris	48	678	14.1	47	3
Lockett	33	422	12.8	34t	2
Anders	15	76	5.1	12	0
Drayton	8	70	8.8	21	2
Parker	3	41	13.7	27	0
Ricks	3	35	11.7	23	0
Dunn	2	26	13.0	20	0
Bennett	2	17	8.5	13	0
Cloud	2	16	8.0	13	0
Chiefs Totals	342	4408	12.9	81t	29
Opp. Totals	358	3737	10.4	47	25

Rushing

	No.	Yds.	Avg.	LG	TD
Richardson	147	697	4.7	33	3
Anders	76	331	4.4	69	2
Moreau	67	179	2.7	22	4
Grbac	30	110	3.7	22	1
Cloud	30	84	2.8	15t	1
Alexander	3	45	15.0	26	0
Bennett	27	24	0.9	6	1
Moon	2	2	1.0	2	0
Parker	1	-7	-7.0	-7	0
Chiefs Totals	383	1465	3.8	69	12
Opp. Totals	441	1822	4.1	50	13

Team Statistics

	Chiefs	Opp.
Total First Downs	321	330
Rushing	84	103
Passing	207	201
Penalty	30	26
3rd Down: Made Att.	75/204	84/207
3rd Down Pct.	36.8	40.6
4th Down: Made Att.	4/13	8/11
4th Down Pct.	30.8	72.7
Total Net Yards	5614	5280
Avg. Per Game	350.9	330.0
Total Plays	999	1041
Avg. Per Play	5.6	5.1
Net Yards Rushing	1465	1809
Avg. Per Game	91.6	113.1
Total Rushes	383	441
Net Yards Passing	4149	3471
Avg. Per Game	259.3	216.9
Sacked/Yards Lost	34/259	51/266
Gross Yards	4408	3737
Attempts/Completions	582/342	549/358
Pct. of Completions	58.8	65.2
Had Intercepted	15	15
Punts/Average	82/44.6	78/43.1
Net Punting Avg.	82/35.8	78/36.8
Penalties/Yards	118/848	108/1020
Fumbles/Lost	23/11	19/14
Touchdowns	44	42
Rushing	12	13
Passing	29	25
Returns	13	4
Time of Possession	27:26	32:24

Score By Periods	1	2	3	4	OT	Total
Chiefs Total	50	99	82	124	0	355
Opp. Total	75	123	64	89	3	354

Regular Starters

Offense

WR	Sylvester Morris
LT	John Tait
LG	Jeff Blackshear
C	Tim Grunhard
RG	**Will Shields**
RT	Victor Riley
TE	**Tony Gonzalez**
WR	Derrick Alexander
QB	**Elvis Grbac**
FB	Tony Richardson
RB	Kimble Anders
	Frank Moreau
	Mike Cloud
K	Todd Peterson

Defense

LE	Eric Hicks
DT	Chester McGlockton
DT	John Browning
	Dan Williams
RE	Duane Clemons
LOLB	Mike Maslowski
	Lew Bush
MLB	Marcus Patton
ROLB	Donnie Edwards
LCB	Pat Dennis
RCB	James Hasty
SS	Greg Wesley
FS	Jerome Woods
P	Todd Sauerbrun

PRO-BOWLERS in Bold

Team Leaders

Scoring: Todd Peterson — 70 pts: 25 PATs, 15 FGs
INTs: James Hasty — 4-53 yds., 0 TDs
Tackles: Donnie Edwards — 151 (119 solo)
Sacks: Eric Hicks — 14.0 (-73.0)
Punting: Todd Sauerbrun — 82-3656 yds., 44.6 avg., 68 LG
Punt Returns: Kevin Lockett — 26-208 yds., 8.0 avg., 0 TDs
Kickoff Returns: Mike Cloud — 36-779 yds, 21.6 avg., 0 TDs

2000 AFC Standings

Western Division

	W	L	T	Pct.
Oakland	12	4	0	.750
Denver	11	5	0	.688
Kansas City	7	9	0	.438
Seattle	6	10	0	.375
San Diego	1	15	0	.062

Central Division

	W	L	T	Pct.
Tennessee	13	3	0	.813
Baltimore	12	4	0	.750
Pittsburgh	9	7	0	.563
Jacksonville	7	9	0	.438
Cincinnati	4	12	0	.250
Cleveland	3	13	0	.188

Eastern Division

	W	L	T	Pct.
Miami	11	5	0	.688
Indianapolis	10	6	0	.625
N.Y. Jets	9	7	0	.563
Buffalo	8	8	0	.500
New England	5	11	0	.312

AFC Championship: Baltimore 16, OAKLAND 3
Super Bowl XXXV: Baltimore 34, N.Y. Giants 7

Eric Hicks led the Chiefs with 14.0 sacks in 2000. (Alan Barzee)

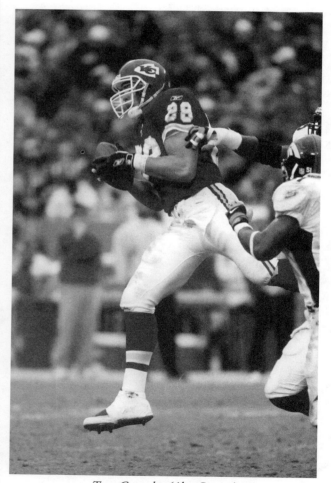

Tony Gonzalez (Alan Barzee)

2001 Head Coach: Dick Vermeil

A new era was again ushered into Arrowhead stadium when Dick Vermeil took over the head coaching duties of the Chiefs. Answering the call of his long-time friend Carl Peterson, Vermeil immediately went about the business of redesigning the Chiefs offense and defense. Trent Green was acquired from the Rams to take over at quarterback for the departed Elvis Grbac, and running back Priest Holmes was signed from the Ravens to shore up the problematic running game. Greg Robinson was hired as defensive coordinator. Green was inconsistent throughout the season, and while he threw for more than 3,700 yards, his 24 interceptions were costly. Holmes blossomed into the NFL's best back and he topped the 1,500 yard mark, the best-ever single-season rushing total in Chiefs history. He was rewarded for his outstanding season with the team MVP award and a spot in the Pro Bowl. Tony Gonzalez again enjoyed the Pro Bowl season, but his overall contributions to the offense were down from the year before. Vermeil didn't promise miracles, and the final record of 6-10 reflected as much—the Chiefs lost four games by three or less points. But the club won three of its final four games and showed signs of better things to come in the future. Will Shields continued his stellar play and was once selected to the Pro Bowl. The good news: The Chiefs, Rams and Colts were the only NFL teams to rank in the NFL's top 10 in total offense, rushing offense and passing offense in 2001. The team had only 68 penalties for the season, down from 118 the year before. Wide receiver Marvin "Snoop" Minnis was the top rookie on the team, catching 33 passes for 511. "We broke a lot of records and did some things real well starting with our running back," Vermeil said of his team's 2001 season. "I don't care how many statistics you can count, the most important stat is the difference between the points you score and points you give up." Linebacker Donnie Edwards, who was released following the season because of salary cap concerns, was again the leading tackler on the squad with 147 stops. Marvcus Patton had 138 tackles, and Eric Warfield had four interceptions. "Can we make the playoffs next year?" Vermeil asked rhetorically of his team. "I don't know. We'll go into the season with a better football team barring injuries in training camp and pre-season games. . . I firmly believe that our coaching staff will do a better job of coaching starting with me right on down in the second year. . . . I think we'll be a better football team."

Key Dates in 2001:

January 5—Chiefs head coach Gunther Cunningham is fired.

January 12—Dick Vermeil becomes the ninth head coach in the history of the Kansas City Chiefs.

March 1—Elvis Grbac, James Hasty and Chester McGlockton are released from the Chiefs roster. Grbac later signs with the Baltimore Ravens.

April 20—The Chiefs trade their 2001 first round draft pick to the St. Louis Rams for quarterback Trent Green and a fifth round draft pick.

April 21—Free agent running back Priest Holmes signs with the Chiefs. Holmes spent his first four seasons in the NFL with the Baltimore Ravens.

September 9—Dick Vermeil makes his debut as the Chiefs head coach, but the Raiders spoil his coming-out party and win the game, 27-24.

September 11—Terrorists hijack four passenger jets and crash them into the World Center in New York City and the Pentagon in Washington, D.C. Another plane crashes in a Pennsylvania field. The NFL postpones all games for the upcoming weekend.

September 16—All scheduled NFL games are postponed because of the September 11 terrorist attack.

September 23—The NFL season resumes. The Chiefs welcome the New York Giants to Arrowhead and lose, 13-3.

September 30—With their best offensive perfomance of the season, the Chiefs smash the Redskins—and former Chiefs head coach Marty Schottenheimer—45-13 in Washington. Priest Holmes is the big star for Kansas City, running for 147 yards and two touchdowns. He also has 78 receiving yards and a touchdown reception. The win is the Dick Vermeil's first as the Chiefs' head coach.

October 14—Priest Holmes rushes for 150 yards and two touchdowns, but the Chiefs can't overcome a 20-2 deficit and lose to the Steelers at Arrowhead, 20-17.

October 21—Trent Green passes for 352 yards, but the Chiefs give up three second half touchdowns and lose to the Cardinals, 24-16.

October 25—The Colts defeat the Chiefs on a Thursday night at Arrowhead, 35-28. The loss is the team's fourth in a row and drops their overall record to 1-6. Trent throws three touchdown passes—and three interception—in the game.

November 4—After blowing a 19-0 lead in the first half, the Chiefs come back with a fourth quarter touchdown and defeat the Chargers in San Diego, 25-20. Holmes runs for 181 yards as Kansas City snaps a four-game losing streak.

December 9—The Chiefs outplayed the Raiders from start to finish on offense and defense, but this game was decided by special teams. The Raiders' Tim Brown returned two kicks for touchdowns and the Raiders held off a late rally by the Chiefs to win, 28-26. The Chiefs pulled to within two points with 1:44 remaining in the game, but Trent Green was sacked on the two-point conversion attmept to seal the win for Oakland. Holmes ran for 168 yards in the losing effort for Kansas City.

January 6, 2002—The Chiefs ended the season with a 21-18 loss to the Seashawks in Seattle. The game originally scheduled for September 16, was played at the end of the regular season because of the September 11 terrorist attack on the United States. Kansas City finished the season with a 6-10 record and fourth-place in the AFC West.

February 28—The Chiefs elect not to give six-year veteran linebacker Donnie Edwards a new contract and release him.

March 25, 2002—The Chiefs acquire offensive tackle Willie Roaf from the New Orleans Saints for a 2003 fourth round draft pick. The team also signed veteran kicker Morten Andersen.

March 29, 2002—The Chiefs sign free agent wide receiver Johnnie Morton to a seven-year contract.

Big Game of 2001

December 30, 2001 at Jacksonville
Kansas City 30, Jacksonville 26

A late season win for non-playoff teams usually means little, but for the Chiefs, this one meant a lot. With just three wins in their first 12 games of the season, the Chiefs seemed destined for nothing more than a high draft pick for 2001. But with a strong showing in a losing effort against the Raiders three weeks earlier, Kansas City proved they were not packing it in early. They followed that performance with wins over Denver and San Diego, and were ready to take on the Florida jinx that had haunted the team for almost a decade.

The game with Jacksonville was a squeaker in the end, and hardly a top team performance. But it was a win in the Sunshine state, and the Chiefs' first-ever regular season victory against the Jaguars.

Final score: Kansas City 30, Jacksonville 26.

The win snapped an 11-game overall losing streak in the state of Florida, dating back to a 27-3 victory over Tampa Bay on September 5, 1993.

"I don't know if it's the best win (of the year), but it's a great win," a happy Dick Vermeil said after the game. "Denver was a great win. Any win is a great win. But to come down here, I could say it's our best win. It's a heck of an accomplishment, it really is."

The two teams were tied at 17-17 at the end of the first half. Todd Peterson kicked a 40-yard field early in the third quarter, and Tony Gonzalez scored on a 12-yard hookup with Trent Green—his second touchdown of the game—to put the Chiefs up 27-17.

"It was a great win for the team," Gonzalez said. "Three in a row and for us to put it together against a team like Jacksonville. They won three games in a row and we knew it was going to be a test to that end and it certainly was."

Peterson kicked his third field goal of the day with five minutes remaining in the game to put the Chiefs up 30-24. Kansas City took an intentional safety with 46 seconds remaining in the game, then held off the Jaguars last-ditch attempt to win the game. Jacksonville quarterback Mark Brunell's pass into the end zone fell incomplete as the clock ran out.

Inconsistent most of the season, Green completed 26 of 35 passes for 294 yards and two touchdowns. Priest Holmes ran for 91 yards, Gonzalez caught eight passes for 78 yards and two touchdowns, and Eddie Kennison caught six passes for 121 yards.

Despite losing to the Seahawks in Seattle (the makeup game from September 16) the following week, the Chiefs were happy with their late season turn around. Winning three of their final four games filled the team with high hopes for the 2002 season.

"You never want to talk about next season too soon, but we eliminated ourselves from the playoffs early on," Green said. "We then began focusing on establishing what we were going to be as a team and organization next year. When you go into the tank as early as we did, you can find guys that give up, and we haven't had any of that."

Chiefs' defensive coordinator Greg Robinson and Dick Vermeil discuss strategy before a game at Arrowhead. (Alan Barzee)

Preseason

Record: 2-2

8/12	W	20-0	WASHINGTON
8/18	W	10-9	CHICAGO
8/23	L	23-28	at Jacksonville
8/31	L	17-21	at St. Louis

Regular Season

Record: 6-10

9/9	L	24-27	OAKLAND
9/16	POSTPONED		at Seattle (game played 1/6/02)
9/23	L	3-13	NEW YORK GIANTS
9/30	W	45-13	at Washington
10/7	L	6-20	at Denver
10/14	L	17-20	PITTSBURGH
10/21	L	16-24	at Arizona
10/25	L	28-35	INDIANAPOLIS
11/4	W	25-20	at San Diego
11/11	L	7-27	at New York Jets
11/25	W	19-7	SEATTLE
11/29	L	10-23	PHILADELPHIA
12/9	L	26-28	at Oakland
12/16	W	*26-23	DENVER
12/23	W	20-17	SAN DIEGO
12/30	W	30-26	at Jacksonville
1/6	L	18-21	at Seattle

Individual Statistics

Passing

	Att.	Cmp.	Yds.	Pct.	TD	INT	LG	Rating
Green	523	296	3783	56.6	17	24	67T	71.1
Collins	4	3	40	75.0	0	0	26	106.3
Gonzalez	1	1	40	100.00	0	0	40	118.8
Chiefs Totals	528	300	3863	56.8	17	24	67t	71.7
Opp. Total	491	296	3403	60.3	19	13	49	83.1

Pass Receiving

	No.	Yds.	Avg.	LG	TD
Gonzalez	73	917	12.6	36	6
Holmes	62	614	9.9	67t	2
Minnis	33	511	15.5	56	1
Kennison	16	322	20.1	65	0
Richardson	30	265	8.8	47	0
Alexander	27	470	17.4	46	3
Thomas	19	247	13.0	28	1
Ricks	18	252	14.0	40	1
Parker	15	199	13.3	44	2
Dunn	4	54	13.5	28	1
J. Williams	2	11	5.5	9	0
Green	1	1	1.0	1	0
Chiefs Totals	300	3863	12.9	67t	17
Opp. Totals	296	3403	11.5	49	19

Rushing

	No.	Yds.	Avg.	LG	TD
Holmes	327	1555	4.8	41	8
Richardson	66	191	2.9	19	7
Green	35	158	4.5	16	0
Cloud	7	54	7.7	16	1
Kennison	2	13	6.5	14	0
Alexander	2	16	8.0	15	0
Hall	2	10	5.0	6	0
Collins	2	6	3.0	7	0
Gonzalez	1	9	9.0	9	0
Parker	3	6.0	2.0	7	0
Stryzinski	1	-10	-10.0	-10	0
Chiefs Totals	448	2008	4.5	41	16
Opp. Totals	481	2140	4.4	77t	15

Team Statistics

	Chiefs	Opp.
Total First Downs	324	296
Rushing	119	111
Passing	178	167
Penalty	27	18
3rd Down: Made Att.	70/195	86/218
3rd Down Pct.	35.9	39.4
4th Down: Made Att.	5/16	5/8
4th Down Pct.	31.3	62.5
Total Net Yards	5673	5304
Avg. Per Game	354.6	331.5
Total Plays	1015	1003
Avg. Per Play	5.6	5.3
Net Yards Rushing	2008	2140
Avg. Per Game	125.5	133.8
Total Rushes	448	481
Net Yards Passing	3665	3164
Avg. Per Game	229.1	197.8
Sacked/Yards Lost	39/198	31/239
Gross Yards	3863	3403
Attempts/Completions	528/300	491/296
Pct. of Completions	56.8	60.3
Had Intercepted	24	13
Punts/Average	75/40.5	79/41.0
Net Punting Avg.	75/35.3	79/35.6
Penalties/Yards	68/602	87/761
Fumbles/Lost	19/9	23/13
Touchdowns	34	37
Rushing	16	15
Passing	17	19
Returns	1	3
Time of Possession	29:07	30:53

Score By Periods	1	2	3	4	OT	Total
Chiefs Total	56	92	64	105	3	320
Opp. Total	43	115	103	83	0	344

Regular Starters

Regular Starters

Offense

WR	Marvin Minnis
LT	John Tait
LG	Marcus Spears
	Donald Willis
	Brian Waters
C	Casey Wiegmann
RG	**Will Sheilds**
RT	Victor Riley
	Marcus Spears
TE	**Tony Gonzalez**
WR	Derrick Alexander
	Larry Parker
QB	Trent Green
FB	Tony Richardson
RB	**Priest Holmes**
K	Todd Peterson

Defense

LE	Eric Hicks
NT	Derrick Ransom
LT	John Browning
RE	Duane Clemons
LOLB	Lew Bush
	Glenn Cadrez
MLB	Marvcus Patton
ROLB	Donnie Edwards
LCB	Ray Crockett
RCB	Eric Warfield
SS	Greg Wesley
FS	Jerome Woods
P	Dan Stryzinski

PRO-BOWLERS in Bold

Team Leaders

Scoring: Todd Peterson — 108 pts: 27 PATs, 27 FGs
INTs: Eric Warfield — 4-61 yds., 1 TD
Tackles: Donnie Edwards — 147 (112 solo)
Sacks: Duane Clemons — 7.0 (-68.5)
Punting: Dan Stryzinski — 73-2976 yds., 40.8 avg., 27 long
Punt Returns: Dante Hall — 32-235 yds., 7.3 avg., 0 TDs
Kickoff Returns: Dante Hall — 43-969 yds., 22.5 avg., 0 TDs

2000 AFC Standings

Western Division

	W	L	T	Pct.
Oakland	10	6	0	.625
Seattle	9	7	0	.562
Denver	8	8	0	.500
Kansas City	6	10	0	.375
San Diego	5	11	0	.312

Central Division

	W	L	T	Pct.
Pittsburgh	13	3	0	.812
Baltimore +	10	6	0	.625
Cleveland	7	9	0	.438
Tennessee	7	9	0	.438
Jacksonville	6	10	0	.375
Cincinnati	6	10	0	.375

Eastern Division

	W	L	T	Pct.
New England	11	5	0	.688
Miami +	11	5	0	.688
N.Y. Jets +	10	6	0	.563
Indianapolis	6	10	0	.375
Buffalo	3	13	0	.188

AFC Championship: New England 24, PITTSBURGH 17
Super Bowl XXXVI: New England 20, St. Louis Rams 17

Will Shields (68) leads Priest Holmes on an end sweep.
(Alan Barzee)

Trent Green (Alan Barzee)

KANSAS CITY CHIEFS
Player Biographies

The players highlighted in this section are divided into three groups: Chiefs players in the Pro Football Hall of Fame, players in the Kansas City Chiefs Hall of Fame, and Other Chiefs Greats. All Chiefs who are in the Pro Football Hall Fame are also in the Chiefs Hall of Fame.

Chiefs Players in the Pro Football Hall of Fame

Six members of the Chiefs organization have been inducted into Pro Football's Hall of Fame in Canton, Ohio. Owner Lamar Hunt was enshrined in 1972, followed by Bobby Bell, Willie Lanier, Len Dawson, Buck Buchanan, and Jan Stenerud. Joe Montana, who played two seasons with the Chiefs, was inducted into the Pro Football Hall of Fame in 2000, and Mike Webster, who also played two seasons in Kansas City, was inducted into the Hall in 1997.

Bobby Bell

Inducted at Canton in 1983

Linebacker
Chiefs Hall of Fame: 1979
College: Minnesota
Career: 1963-74 Kansas City Chiefs

Possibly the greatest athlete to ever play for the Chiefs, Bobby Bell came to Kansas City as a seventh-round pick in the 1963 AFL Draft after playing on the 1963 College All-Star team that defeated the NFL-champion Green Bay Packers. So versatile and complete were his talents that he played quarterback, linebacker, offensive center, and defensive tackle at the University of Minnesota. He was a consensus All-American tackle in 1962 and won the Outland Trophy as college football's outstanding lineman.

He was the first Chiefs player enshrined in the Pro Football Hall of Fame.

"[Bell] is the greatest athlete there ever was," Buck Buchanan said of his longtime teammate during their playing days. "He has caught passes for us. He's tried extra points and field goals. He can throw a ball 80 yards and punt it 70. He's a basketball star in our winter games. He's a great swimmer, diver, and skier."

"Bobby Bell is the greatest outside linebacker who ever played the game," Hank Stram said of Bell at his Hall of Fame induction. "He is the only player I have seen who could play any position on a team, and that team could still win."

After two seasons as a defensive end—he was an AFL All-Star in 1964—Bell settled into the left outside linebacker position and stayed there the rest of his career.

"I didn't care where I played," Bell said. "All I cared about was winning."

One of Bell's finest moments came in the 1969 AFL divisional playoff game against the New York Jets. In a critical goal-line stand, his key pass coverage on Jets running back Matt Snell on third down stopped the drive and forced New York to kick a field goal. The 13-6 victory over the Jets propelled Kansas City to its only Super Bowl triumph.

"He was the type of player you were glad to have on your side," Len Dawson said of Bell. "He was a winner, and he made everyone else around him a winner."

Bobby Bell (Kansas Collection, U. of Kansas)

Bell' had various athletic talents. He used his speed to great advantage, but his ability to read offenses, adjust during plays, and tackle ferociously made him the great linebacker he was. In 12 seasons with the Chiefs he intercepted 26 passes and returned them 479 yards, scoring nine touchdowns. He also scored one touchdown on a fumble recovery and one on a kickoff return.

Bell was selected to the AFL All-Star team and then the Pro Bowl for nine consecutive years. In addition, he was named to the AFL's all-time team by the Pro Football Hall of Fame.

"Bobby was a great linebacker because he was a great athlete," Chicago Bears great Dick Butkus said.

Bell played in a total of 168 career games for the Chiefs. He was inducted into the Chiefs Hall of Fame in 1979, and Canton opened its doors to the great linebacker in 1983.

Bell sacks Baltimore's Johnny Unitas during the Chiefs' first-ever appearance on Monday Night Football *in 1970. (Topeka Capital-Journal)*

Willie Lanier

Inducted at Canton in 1986

Linebacker
Chiefs Hall of Fame: 1984
College: Morgan State
Career: 1967-77 Kansas City Chiefs

Fierce and aggressive, robust and savvy; Willie Lanier tackled opposing ball carriers with thunderous hits—shots so hard and savage his teammates called him "Contact." His speed, quickness, durability, and size all contributed to his enormous success, but it was his heart and desire that propelled him into the Hall of Fame. Lanier became the center point of the Chiefs' great defense, providing leadership in addition to his tremendous football talent. His teammates had great affection for him, and he was also called "Bear" or "Honeybear" because of his bear-like appearance—he was friendly and playful, but dangerous to enemies.

"There's no question in my mind that he was as good as or better than any middle linebacker who ever played the game," Jim Lynch said of Lanier. "He had the smarts, the finesse, plus he had tremendous power. More strength than he realizes."

"His destiny was to be the prototype middle linebacker of his era," Chiefs owner Lamar Hunt said of Lanier.

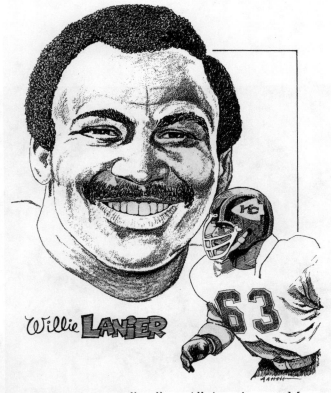

Willie LANIER

Willie Lanier (Topeka Capital-Journal)

A two-time small-college All-American at Morgan State, Lanier was selected by the Chiefs in the second round of the 1967 draft. He became the starting middle linebacker for Kansas City four games into his rookie season and wore his trademark helmet with extra padding for 11 seasons. Lanier missed just five games throughout his career.

There were numerous great moments throughout his career, but none exemplifies his heart and desire as much as the Chiefs' goal-line stand against the Jets in the 1969 divisional playoff game. Leading 6-3 in the fourth quarter, New York had a first-and-goal at the Chiefs' one-yard line after a pass interference call on Kansas City. It was then that Lanier made an emotional appeal to the rest of the Chiefs defense.

"They're not going to score!" Lanier yelled at his teammates. "They're not going to score!"

"Willie Lanier was never an extremely emotional person," Jerry Mays said of the goal-line stand against the Jets. "But something came over him, and then it came over all of us."

"He was begging us," Emmitt Thomas said. "Tears were running down his cheeks."

"Willie Lanier got us up. He fired me up," Mays continued. "It was the way he did it—tears in his eyes, teeth gnashing."

The Chiefs shut down the Jets on three straight plays and held them to a field goal. When Kansas City scored a touchdown on its next possession, the game was over. The first important step to the Super Bowl was complete.

For his career, Lanier intercepted 27 passes, returning two for touchdowns, and also recovered 15 fumbles. He was named to the AFL All-Star team and the Pro Bowl eight seasons in row, from 1968 through 1975. Lanier was named to the NFL's 75th Anniversary all-time team in 1994.

After playing in 149 games for the Chiefs, Lanier retired following the 1977 season. He was elected to the Chiefs' Hall of Fame in 1984, and to the Pro Football Hall of Fame in 1986.

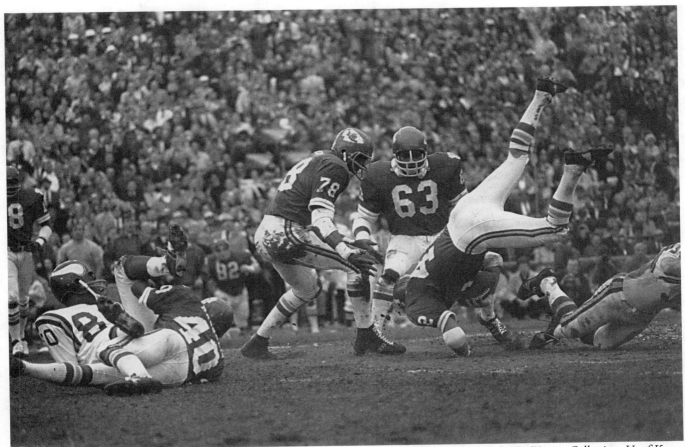

Willie Lanier (63) looks on with Bobby Bell (78) as Johnny Robinson recovers a fumble in Super Bowl IV. (Kansas Collection, U. of Kansas)

Len Dawson

Inducted at Canton in 1987

Quarterback
Chiefs Hall of Fame: 1978
Inducted: 1987
College: Purdue
Career: 1957-59 Pittsburgh Steelers, 1960-61 Cleveland Browns, 1962 Dallas Texans, 1963-75 Kansas City Chiefs

His best attribute among many, many talents, was his calm on-field demeanor, a collective reserve that never showed panic. Len Dawson was "Lenny the Cool," the Chiefs' franchise quarterback for 14 seasons. He compiled highly impressive statistics throughout his career, but he really wasn't about numbers; he was about leading, composure, stability and winning.

The defining moment for Dawson's career was Super Bowl IV and the events that transpired in the week before the game. Unfairly and unwarrantedly linked to a gambler in a federal investigation, Dawson endured the associated allegations. He made a simple statement to the press proclaiming his innocence, and the Chiefs and the league let the incident die. But the effect of the story left its mark on him.

"I know it hit him really hard," Johnny Robinson, the Chiefs' free safety and Dawson's roommate said. "It ate him up inside, and it looked to me as if he aged five years from Tuesday to Thursday [before the Super Bowl].

Dawson went about his task of leading the Kansas City offense in the Super Bowl and played an efficient, com-

posed game. He completed 12 of 17 passes for 142 yards and one touchdown as the Chiefs surprised the Minnesota Vikings and won convincingly, 23-7. Dawson was named the game's MVP.

"My teammates were definitely on my side," Dawson said of the events the week before the game, "and it might have given me an extra spark."

The road to Super Bowl MVP was a long one for Dawson.

After leading the Big Ten in passing and total offense for three seasons at Purdue, Dawson languished in the NFL with Pittsburgh and Cleveland. Originally a first-round draft pick by the Steelers in 1957, Dawson had very little playing time, throwing just 45 passes in five seasons. His skills were eroded, his confidence low. But Texans coach Hank Stram, who had been an assistant at Purdue when Dawson played there, knew there was a great quarterback waiting for the chance to prove himself. Dawson went to Dallas Texans of the AFL in the summer of 1962 and led the team to the '62 AFL Championship.

He was named the AFL's player of the year by *The Sporting News* after the '62 season, winning the passing championship as well as leading the league in completion percentage. And he threw a league-high 29 touchdown passes.

Len Dawson (Kansas Collection, U. of Kansas)

"Len Dawson was the quiet assassin," Ed Podolak said. "He could say more with a stare than most players could with words. He was the team leader, no doubt about it."

"Lenny was our man," Otis Taylor said Dawson. "He was our leader."

With Hank Stram guiding the way, Dawson became a great quarterback. He won AFL passing titles in 1964, 1966, 1968, led in completion percentage six years in a row, from 1964 through 1969, and led in touchdown passes in 1963, 1965, and 1966. The Chiefs won three AFL titles and the Super Bowl with Dawson at the helm. They also won the AFC West in 1971 and were ousted in the playoffs by the Dolphins in the infamous double-overtime contest that is still the longest game ever played in the NFL.

"There is no passer in professional football is more accurate than Lenny," Hank Stram said of his star quarterback.

Dawson led the league in completion percentage for an NFL record eight seasons, including six straight seasons from 1964-69, and finished 57.1 percent for his career. He still holds club records for the highest career quarterback rating at 83.2, most passing attempts with 3.696, completions with 2,115, and 28,507 yards. He once threw touchdown passes in 14 straight games in the 1965 and '66 seasons and finished with 237 touchdown passes. He also ran for 1,293 yards and nine scores.

Dawson was named to six AFL All-Star teams and to the Pro Bowl in 1972. He was the NFL Man of the Year in 1973, an award given to the league's outstanding pro football player-citizen. Lenny the Cool retired after the 1975 season but continues to be involved with the Chiefs and football in general. He is a member of the Chiefs' play-by-play radio broadcast team, hosts the HBO Inside the NFL show and is the sports anchor at KMBC-TV in Kansas City.

Dawson was inducted into the Chiefs' Hall of Fame in 1978 and joined the Pro Football immortals at Canton, Ohio, in 1987. The Chiefs retired his number, 16.

Len Dawson prepares to hand off during the 1966 AFL Championship game in Buffalo. (Topeka Capital-Journal)

Buck Buchanan

Inducted at Canton in 1990

Defensive tackle
Chiefs Hall of Fame: 1980
College: Grambling State
Career: 1963-75 Kansas City Chiefs

Buck **BUCHANAN**

The massive defensive lineman instilled fear in the opposing offensive lines he faced throughout his career with the Chiefs, his physical attributes so intimidating that other teams drafted bigger and faster offensive linemen specifically to block him. He was double- and triple-teamed, but many times that didn't matter. Buck Buchanan dominated play on the defensive line like no player in pro football had before him.

"He brought a new superstar dimension to our defensive line," Lamar Hunt said of Buchanan. "He was the most celebrated of our defensive linemen."

A small college All-American tackle in 1962, Buchanan played both offense and defense at Grambling State University. His legendary coach, Eddie Robinson, called him "the finest lineman I have seen." The Chiefs took Buchanan as the overall first player chosen in the 1963 AFL draft, and he was a first-round draft pick of the NFL's New York Giants as well.

A fixture on the Chiefs' defensive line for 13 seasons, Buchanan was particularly effective at intimidating and harassing passers. He knocked down 16 passes during the 1967 season.

"It was unbelievable how he could run for a big guy," Hank Stram said of Buchanan. "Some big people are quick but are not fast. Other big people are fast but not quick. He was both fast and quick. . . . He was highly motivated to be the best."

Buchanan played in six consecutive AFL All-Star Games, from 1964 through 1969, and in two Pro Bowls after the AFL and NFL merged in 1970. He was a star on both Super Bowl teams and was nothing short of spectacular in Kansas City's 23-7 win over the Vikings in Super Bowl IV. Green Bay Packers guard Jerry Kramer said that in preparing for Super Bowl I, Buchanan was the defensive player who most worried the Packers during their game preparations.

He was incredibly durable and never missed a game throughout the course of his career, playing in a total of 182 regular-season games during his 13-season professional career.

"He always played, no matter how banged up he would get," Len Dawson said. "He would play on sprained ankles so swollen, I don't know how he could have walked on them."

Buchanan retired after the 1975 season. He later served as director of the Kansas Special Olympics and as an assistant coach with the New Orleans Saints and the Cleveland Browns. He died of cancer on July 16, 1992.

"We build our sports heroes until they seem bigger than life," Chiefs president Carl Peterson said. "If anybody seemed to fit that description, it was Buck Buchanan. He was much more than the sum of his achievements. He was the personification of our sport—a hero in every way."

Buchanan was inducted into the Chiefs Hall of Fame in 1980 and enshrined at Canton in 1990.

Buck Buchanan (Bettmann/CORBIS)

Buck Buchanan (Kansas Collection, U. of Kansas)

Jan Stenerud

Inducted at Canton in 1991

Kicker
Cheifs Hall of Fame: 1991
College: Montana State
Career: 1967-79 Kansas City Chiefs, 1980-83 Green Bay Packers, 1984-85 Minnesota Vikings

Jan Stenerud began his football career in a most improbable way; the Norwegian native came to the United States on a skiing scholarship to Montana State. But in his sophomore year, he was spotted by the school's basketball coach kicking a football—booming the ball, actually—and the Montana State football coach was summoned to see the soccer-style kicks from the ski jumper. The next two seasons saw Stenerud star on the varsity team, and as a senior, he kicked a then-record 59-yard field goal and scored 82 points.

The Chiefs, who had suffered with a mediocre kicking game for a couple of seasons, selected Stenerud in the third round of the AFL's 1966 future draft. He joined the Chiefs in 1967 and was an immediate sensation, kicking 21 field goals and scoring 108 points his rookie season. He scored 129 points in 1968. Stenerud was also one of the first soccer-style kickers in the league, and the most successful in the late 1960s and throughout the 1970s.

"Jan was awesome," Chiefs running back Mike Garrett said. "We knew if we could get the ball to midfield, we could score."

Stenerud was the first pure placekicker to be inducted into the Pro Football Hall of Fame and the fifth Chiefs player to make it to Canton. He is regarded by many football historians and writers as the best placekicker in pro football history.

For 13 seasons Stenerud starred with the Chiefs. Three

times he made five field goals in a game; he also kicked at least one field goal in a string of 16 consecutive games spanning the 1969 and 1970 seasons. Stenerud owns or shares nine Chiefs records, including field goals attempted in a career (436) and a season (44), and consecutive games played (186). He opened the scoring in Super Bowl IV with a 48-yarder in the first quarter, and his three first-half field goals staked the Chiefs to a 9-0 lead in the first half of the game.

Stenerud was named to the AFL All-Star Game and Pro Bowl as a member of the Chiefs five times—he was named the outstanding offensive player in the 1972 Pro Bowl—and was the kicker on the NFL's 75th anniversary all-time team. He played a total of 19 seasons in the NFL, finishing his career with the Green Bay Packers and the Minnesota Vikings. He is the NFL's all-time leader with 373 field goals and is third on the all-time scoring list with 1,699 points.

Stenerud was inducted into the Chiefs Hall of Fame in 1991. An outstanding golfer, he has played in several celebrity tournaments since his retirement in 1985.

Jan Stenerud boots one of his three field goals in Super Bowl IV. (Topeka Capital-Journal)

Chiefs Hall of Fame

Each year, starting in 1969, the Chiefs have inducted an individual into the Chiefs Hall of Fame to honor their outstanding contributions to the organization. Owner Lamar Hunt was the first inductee. New inductees are selected by a three-person committee that represents the Chiefs Booster Club, the local media, and the Chiefs organization. The award is presented each year at the "101 Banquet."

Mack Lee Hill—1971

He was a strong, powerful runner with surprising speed, incredible balance, a huge will to succeed, and—possibly most importantly—a big heart. Mack Lee Hill's running style was far ahead of his time—he could bust it up the middle and power for yardage, but was just as effective sprinting to the outside. And in many instances, he was all but impossible to tackle.

"He just barely touched the surface of his talent," Len Dawson said of Hill. "As a professional, he was still learning. He was very raw."

Hill played just two seasons with Kansas City before he died tragically while undergoing knee surgery at the end of the 1965 season. It's safe to assume he would have been one of the Chiefs' greatest runners, and probably one of the league's best ever, too.

"He was just beginning a brilliant career," Hank Stram said of Hill. "The sky was the limit as far as what he was going to accomplish as a running back. He never had the chance to fully express that talent."

Hill came to the Chiefs as a free agent out of Southern University in 1964 and made an immediate impact on the team, rushing for 567 yards and four touchdowns on just 105 carries. He was named to the AFL All-Star Game. His bruising, unstoppable running style earned him the nickname "The Truck." He gained 627 yards his second season. For his career, Hill averaged 5.2 yards per carry, gained 1,203 yards rushing, scored nine touchdowns, and also caught 40 passes for another 408 yards.

Hill injured his knee in the next-to-last game of the season in 1965. Ironically, he was deathly afraid of hospitals, and just after surgery to repair his torn ligament had been completed, his body temperature shot up to 108 degrees. A battle to reduce his temperature followed, but the efforts were futile. He died approximately two hours later, on December 12, 1965.

"Any tragedy, you have to put it behind you, but he meant so much to the team," Buck Buchanan said of Hill. "He was a great talent. The little time he played, he did some unbelievable things."

In 1966 the Chiefs established the Mack Lee Hill Award. They present it annually to the club's outstanding rookie, to the player who "best exemplifies the spirit of the late Mack Lee Hil—the man with the giant heart and quiet way." The Chiefs also retired number 36, Hill's jersey number.

Mack Lee Hill played in only 27 games for the Chiefs, but his legacy has lived on.

"I am sure I can safely say we have never had a player whose style of play more embodied the spirit of the game of football than Mack Hill's," Lamar Hunt said after Hill's death.

Mack Lee Hill (Kansas City Chiefs)

After a great college career at SMU, Jerry Mays was selected by the Dallas Texans in the fifth round of the 1961 AFL draft, and for 10 years was a standout for the Chiefs and Texans on the defensive line.

"He gives everything he has on every play," coach Hank Stram said of his star defensive end. "He's one of the most inspirational players I've ever coached."

Mays started his career at defensive tackle and moved to end in the middle of the 1964 season.

His physical attributes were not overly impressive—he was six-foot-four and 252 pounds—but his desire and skill were overwhelming. His toughness was unmatched, and he never missed a game during his career. He was also extremely proud of the AFL, and the Chiefs' win in Super Bowl IV had great meaning for him.

"I loved the AFL," Mays said. "It was part of me . . . I was AFL from start to finish."

Conversely, he was just as disappointed by Kansas City's poor performance in Super Bowl I.

"I was personally too tight the entire ball game," Mays said. "I couldn't seem to settle down. [Losing to Green Bay] was total humiliation. But it also started us on our drive to the championship, and it helped us to gain maturity."

Mays was named to the all-time AFL team by the Pro Football Hall of Fame and was selected to play in the AFL All-Star Game six times, following the 1962 and 1964-68 seasons. He played in 140 games with the franchise, and in addition to his outstanding play on the defensive line, intercepted one pass and scored one touchdown in his career.

"He's never really satisfied with the way he performs," Stram said of Mays. "That's what makes him such a great football player."

"Football is such a great game," Mays said in 1976. "There's no other place I know of in life in which you can equal such an emotional thing . . ."

Jerry Mays died on July 17, 1994, in Lake Lewisville, Texas.

Jerry Mays (Topeka Capital-Journal)

Losing sight in one eye should be a handicap a receiver in pro football can't overcome, but for Fred Arbanas, the Chiefs' perennial all-star tight end in the 1960s, it was just an attainable goal. Arbanas was mugged in December 1964, and he suffered severe damage to his left eye, leaving it virtually blind. But for Arbanas, who had already overcome back problems, there was no question whether he would attempt to play again.

"I wanted to keep on as a player. If you want something bad enough, you can do it," Arbanas said years later of his eye problem. "So I went out that spring with Lenny Dawson when the snow was still on the ground. I was wearing an eye patch. Lenny spent hours with me [throwing passes to me]."

He made it back and continued with his stellar career.

Arbanas was a seventh-round draft pick by the Texans in 1961 following a highly successful collegiate career at Michigan State. He missed all of his rookie season follow-

ing surgery for ruptured disks in his back, an ailment he played with in college.

Despite the physical problems, Arbanas was considered one of pro football's finest tight ends during his nine seasons with the Texans/Chiefs. He caught 198 passes for 3,101 yards and 34 touchdowns. He was also an excellent, fierce blocker who was a big part of the Chiefs' running game throughout the 1960s. His presence on the field was a key ingredient for both Super Bowl teams.

"When I get on the field, I forget my problems," Arbanas said of his eye injury when he was playing. "The way I look at it, I'm just as good a receiver now as I ever was before. In fact, I might even be better. I'm trying harder now."

So complete was his return that he was named to the all-time AFL team by the Pro Football Hall of Fame. He was also a five-time All-AFL choice, selected in 1962-65 and in 1967.

"He was a real player, a guy who came to play every down," Dawson said of Arbanas.

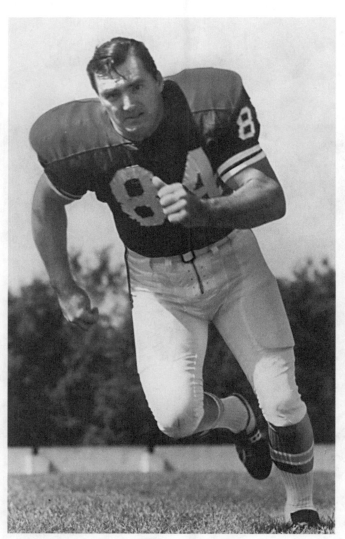

Fred Arbanas (Kansas City Star)

A standout player at LSU and a member of its 1959 national championship team, Johnny Robinson was one of the original Texans and an integral part of the team for more than a decade. He had a penchant for coming through in the clutch, invariably making game-winning and game-saving plays.

He began his career in Dallas as a halfback, teaming with Abner Haynes for two seasons. He produced good numbers on offense, rushing for 658 yards and six touchdowns on 150 carries and catching 77 passes for 1,228 yards and nine scores. Robinson moved to free safety for the 1962 season; the switch was so successful he became a perennial AFL All-Star team member and was named to the AFL's all-time team by the Pro Football Hall of Fame.

"He was a chess master, and it's a chess match out there," the Chiefs' Hall of Fame linebacker Willie Lanier said of Robinson. "You must have the mind-set of the quarterback. Johnny had that. He was intuitive. He just had the knack for the game."

Robinson finished his career as the third-leading interceptor in AFL history with 43, and had 57 career interceptions, ranking him second in team history. He led the AFL in interceptions with 10 in 1966, and was tops in the NFL in 1970 with 10.

"Coverage isn't luck, but interceptions are," Robinson said of his high pick totals. "There is no correlation between interceptions and individual ability, but there is a

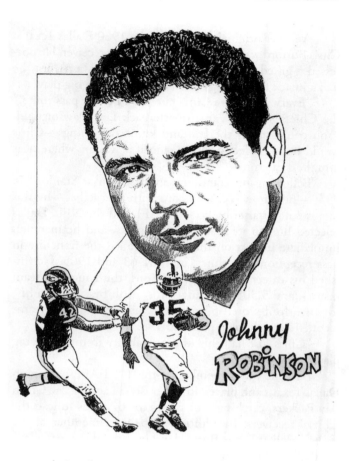

correlation between team play and interceptions. And I've been fortunate to play on a good team."

Six times he was an All-AFL selection, 1963 through 1968. Robinson's play in the secondary was one of the reasons the Chiefs enjoyed the success they did throughout the 1960s.

"Whenever you needed a big play," Len Dawson said of Robinson, "one that would break the other team's back, Johnny was there to make it."

His final game with Kansas City was the double-overtime playoff loss to the Dolphins in 1971.

Robinson played in a total of 164 games for the franchise.

Johnny Robinson (Topeka Capital-Journal)

Another original member of the 1960 Dallas Texans, Chris Burford was the franchise's first great receiver. He possessed a gifted pair of hands, and while he wasn't fast, he had a knack for getting open and making the big play.

"Every pass route Chris ran was a perfect pass route," the Chiefs' Hall of Fame quarterback Len Dawson said. "You could throw the ball and know two things—Chris would be in perfect position, and if it was anywhere near him, he'd catch it."

Following his standout senior season at Stanford in 1959—he set an NCAA record with 61 catches—he was highly sought after by both the AFL and the NFL. Dallas selected him in its first round of picks, and he made an immediate impact on the league. He led the franchise in pass reception four times, in 1961-63 and 1965. He finished his career with 391 receptions, third most in team history, and 5,505 receiving yards, fifth best in team history. Burford scored 55 touchdowns and caught a team-record 12 touchdown passes in 1962.

"Chris just had this uncanny ability to make the big play," Dawson said.

Burford was a member of the 1962 AFL-champion Dallas Texans and played in Super Bowl I against the Green Bay Packers, catching four passes for 67 yards to lead the Chiefs' receivers. In addition to being a member of the Chiefs' Hall of Fame, Burford was enshrined in the College Football Hall of Fame in 1995.

He played in a total of 103 games for the franchise.

Chris Burford (Topeka Capital-Journal)

A fiery, aggressive competitor with intense enthusiasm, E. J. Holub was the club's "Holler Guy," a name he earned for his constant yelling at his teammates and opponents. He was a fire-lighter on the team, and like so many of the men he played with, a big reason the Texans and Chiefs enjoyed major successes in the 1960s.

Holub played linebacker from 1961 through 1967, but when his knees had slowed him so much he could no longer play the position, he switched to center and played his final three seasons at that position. His linebacking play was superb, and he was named to five AFL All-Star affairs as a linebacker following the 1961-63 and 1964-66 seasons. He was the center on the Chiefs' 1969 Super Bowl champions and made a successful transition from defense to offense. His technique on the offensive line was not always perfect, but it was always effective.

"Most centers are not strong enough to man block. You have to use different types of blocks to cut the big linemen down," Holub said. "You can't just fire out at these guys all the time. They're so quick, they can get rid of you by throwing you aside."

The price he paid for his long career was steep, though, as Holub endured nine knee operations throughout the course of his playing days.

"I don't know if anyone gave more to this team than E. J.," Dawson said. "There were days he could barely walk, but when it came time to play, he was always ready."

Holub was one of the best players to come out of Texas Tech and was the Texans' first-round pick in the 1961 AFL Draft. He is also enshrined in the College Football Hall of Fame. He finished his career with nine interceptions and played in 127 games for Kansas City.

E.J. Holub (Topeka Capital-Journal)

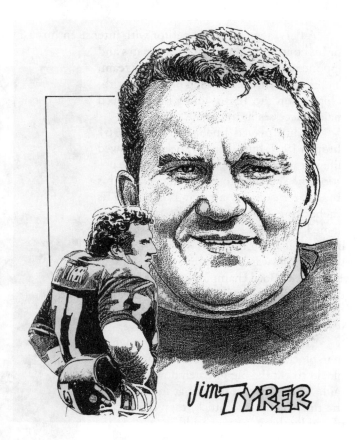

One of the best offensive tackles of his time, Jim Tyrer anchored the Chiefs' line for 13 seasons. His blocks were crushing, and the success of the Chiefs' running game during the 1960s and early 1970s was largely attributed to his play. He was selected to the AFL All-Star team and Pro Bowl nine times, and his consistent, outstanding play landed him a spot on the all-time AFL team, as selected by the Pro Football Hall of Fame.

"Being All-Pro makes me work harder," Tyrer said of his play in 1972. "The guy playing across from me expects more from me and that makes me put out more."

An All-American at Ohio State, Tyrer was chosen by the Texans in the third round of the 1961 AFL draft. He immediately moved into the starting lineup for the Texans his rookie year and was an important part of the club's three AFL championships and Super Bowl IV triumph.

"He was the best," Hank Stram said of Tyrer. "When they made Jim, they broke the mold."

He had great size, speed, and, most importantly, endurance. Tyrer played 12 seasons without missing a game.

"He made it easy," Mike Garrett said of Tyrer. "He was a big player with a big heart."

Tyrer was named AFL Offensive Lineman of the Year in 1969 and played in 180 games for the franchise. He played one season, 1974, with the Washington Redskins at the end of his career.

Tragically, Tyrer was not successful in his life after football. Following a series of business failures, he committed suicide in 1980.

Jim Tyrer (Topeka Capital-Journal)

He zigged and zagged, pranced into open holes, and was never easy to bring down. Mike Garrett arrived in Kansas City in 1966, Heisman Trophy in tow, and brought game-breaking runs to the Chiefs as well as his recognizable star power. Despite being selected in the 20th round of the 1966 AFL draft, Garrett chose the Chiefs over the NFL. Maybe more important than his running talent, Garrett brought a team-player attitude with him.

"It's not just winning games that counts; it's winning championships," Garrett said. With the mighty mite from Southern California in their backfield, the Chiefs won.

The USC star spent four and a half seasons in Kansas City and is the fourth leading rusher in Chiefs history with 3,246 yards on 736 carries. He also scored 23 touchdowns. His pass-receiving skills were just as dangerous to opposing defenses, as he hauled in 141 receptions for 1,231 yards and another seven scores.

"His power is amazing, but his best attribute may be his great sense of balance with that tricky lateral movement. He's always under control," Hank Stram said of his star halfback. "He has fantastic quickness."

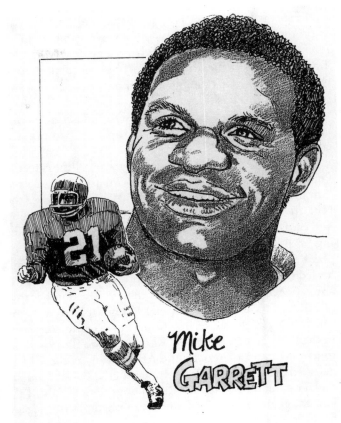

mike GARRETT

Mike Garrett (Topeka Capital-Journal)

Garrett led the Chiefs in rushing three times and had his best season in 1967, compiling 1,087 yards. He was named to the AFL All-Star Game in 1966 and again in 1967. But personal goals and statistics weren't what Garrett was about.

"I don't have goals like gaining 1,000 yards or anything like that," Garrett said. "My goal—if you can call it that—is just to play good football. If I can do that, I can contribute toward helping us win a championship."

He played on both of the Chiefs' Super Bowl teams and scored a touchdown against the Vikings in Super Bowl IV. He's also enshrined in the College Football Hall of Fame.

Garrett played in 58 games for the Chiefs. He was traded to San Diego early in the 1970 season and played three and a half seasons with the Chargers before retiring.

"Mike Garrett is a great football player," Sid Gillman, his coach at San Diego said. "All he does is kill everybody—and he's a winner."

He was big, strong, fast, acrobatic, and possessed an uncanny ability to make plays —impossible, game-winning receptions—when his team needed them the most. Otis Taylor was one of the first "modern" receivers, an exciting wideout who used his combination of size, speed, and power to transform his position.

"His catches were splendid. I just can't describe them," Hank Stram said of Taylor's receiving ability. "I don't know enough adjectives."

Highly sought after following a stellar college career at Prairie View A&M, Taylor chose the Chiefs—who selected him in the fourth round of the 1965 AFL draft—over the NFL in 1965. He had a productive rookie season, gaining 446 yards on 26 catches, but really exploded in 1966, catching 58 passes for 1,297 yards and eight touchdowns. His play helped catapult the Chiefs to the first Super Bowl. Taylor led the AFL in touchdown receptions in 1967 with 11, and, after missing a good part of the 1968 season because of injuries, returned to form in 1969 and played a major role in the Chiefs' Super Bowl run. His 35-yard reception in the third quarter propelled Kansas City to the go-ahead touchdown and eventually the AFL crown, as the Chiefs defeated the Raiders, 17-7. His magnificent 46-yard touchdown catch and run against the Vikings in Super Bowl IV iced the game for the Chiefs and established a lasting legacy for his greatness.

"I know that when they go to me on a big play, the guys in the line have the feeling that I'll do something with the ball," Taylor said. "That makes me feel pretty good. It really does."

His best overall season was in 1971, when, game after game, he made seemingly impossible plays. Taylor's jumping, one-handed touchdown catch against the Redskins late in the fourth quarter was one of his greatest plays, and it won the game for Kansas City. He finished the 1971 season with 1,110 yards receiving—tops in the NFL—57 receptions, and eight touchdowns.

"I think I can catch the ball and come up with the big play in desperate situations," Taylor said in 1971. "I've been fortunate to make the big plays."

Taylor led the Chiefs in pass receptions five times—1966-67 and 1970-72—and played in three Pro Bowls—1970-72. He owns the Chiefs' career records for receiving yards (7,306), receiving touchdowns (57), and 100-yard games (20). His 410 career receptions rank second in team history.

"Otis made my job easy," the Chiefs' Hall of Fame quarterback Len Dawson said. "If you got the pass to Otis, you knew he was going to catch it."

Taylor played in a total of 130 games for the Chiefs, and following his retirement in 1975, spent several years as a scout for the team.

Otis Taylor (Otis Taylor)

Otis Taylor (Topeka Capital-Journal)

Ed Budde—1984

A standout performer at Michigan State, Ed Budde came to Kansas City as one of the team's two first-round draft picks in 1963 (Buck Buchanan was the other). During his 14 seasons with the Chiefs, it was widely accepted throughout the league that Budde was the best offensive guard in the game. He received many awards and honors during his playing days; he was the first offensive lineman to win the AFL Offensive Player of the Week Award in 1968 for his superb run blocking.

"It's mostly mental," Budde said of offensive line play. "You're always thinking of the game, and the man you're playing against."

He was big for a guard, standing 6-foot-5 and weighing 260 most of his career. He was quick and strong, but it was his consistency and technique that made him an All-Star. He was highly proficient at both run and pass blocking.

"I don't think you ever master it," Budde said of pass blocking. "There's always somebody coming up defensively who's going to give you a new move. We all get knocked on our butt."

Budde was selected to play in the AFL All-Star Game and the Pro Bowl seven times, in 1964 and 1967-72. He

was a member of both Super Bowl teams and was always highly regarded by his teammates.

"Ed Budde stands for what pro football is all about," Ed Podolak said.

"I never saw so much love for one guy," Paul Wiggin said of the team's affection for Budde.

He played in a total of 177 games for the Chiefs. His son Brad, a first-round selection in 1980, played for Kansas City, too, giving the Chiefs a unique father-son connection.

Ed Budde (Kansas Collection, U. of Kansas)

His pass coverage was second to none throughout his career, and he had a penchant for making the big play in the big games. He was so good that opposing teams often refused to throw in his coverage area; he still made plays, still picked off passes. One of the finest cornerbacks in the history of the Chiefs, Emmitt Thomas was stationed in the Chiefs' secondary for 13 seasons and consistently displayed the skill, determination, and heart demanded by his position.

Thomas came to Kansas City in 1966 as an undrafted free agent from Bishop College in Dallas, and after playing primarily on the special teams and as a reserve for the secondary, moved into the starting right cornerback position in 1968. He was immediately successful and was named to the AFL All-Star team that season after picking off four passes as part of the Chiefs' powerful defense.

Thomas enjoyed one of his finest seasons in 1969, intercepting nine passes during the regular season to lead the AFL, and then picking off another three in the playoffs. His 62-yard interception return against the Raiders in the 1969 AFL championship game set up the game-clinching field goal as the Chiefs won the title, 17-7. He also picked off a pass in Super Bowl IV against the Vikings.

"If you want the secret to our defense, it's the ability of our cornerbacks," Johnny Robinson said. Thomas was a big part of that success.

"What you try to do is limit the opposition on crucial third-down plays and stop the long touchdown pass," Thomas said of his pass-coverage philosophy. "If you do that and we win the game, then you can say you've had a pretty good game."

He was named to the Pro Bowl from 1970-73 and 1974-75, giving him a total of six All-Star Game appearances during his career. Thomas had another big season in 1974 and led the NFL in interceptions with a team-record 12. He finished his career as Kansas City's all-time interception leader with 58, and is eighth on the NFL's all-time list. Thomas returned five interceptions for touchdowns during his career; he returned kickoffs his rookie season, averaging 23.2 yards per return. He played in 181 games for the Chiefs, tying for fifth most in the history of the team.

Thomas went into coaching following his career and recently served as the defensive coordinator for the Eagles and the Packers.

Emmitt Thomas (Kansas Collection, U. of Kansas)

Jerrell Wilson

His punts were high, booming shots that arched far down the field, potent weapons in the war for field position. Jerrel Wilson seemed to have the explosiveness of dynamite in his foot, hence the more-than-appropriate nickname of "Thunderfoot." The Southern Mississippi alum was the Chiefs' punter for 15 seasons and is considered one of the best ever to play the game.

"Jerrel Wilson made other people aware of how important the kicking game was at a time when special teams were not given special consideration," Hank Stram said. "I'm prejudiced, but he's the best punter I ever saw. He'll go down in history as the best kicker in the NFL."

Selected in the 11th round of the 1963 AFL Draft, Wilson played more seasons than any player in team history, and his 203 games played are the second most for any player in franchise history. He left behind an impressive number of records and honors earned through his kicking expertise: A franchise-record 1,014 punts during his career; highest average yardage in a career with 43.6; in a season with 46.1; and in a game with 56.5. Wilson owns the NFL record for most seasons leading the league in punting average with four, leading in 1965, 1968, and 1972-73.

"The way I attack the football, every time I hit it, I try to bust it," Wilson said of his punting technique. "Unless I'm around the 50. Then I try to hang it high."

He had four career punts over 70 yards and was named to three Pro Bowl teams.

"Basically, my power comes from everything," Wilson explained. "I try to snap everything I have in my body—my hips, knees, everything."

Wilson also played a little running back in a reserve role for the Chiefs, carrying the ball 21 times for 53 yards. He played one season for the Patriots (1978) at the end of his career.

Jerrel Wilson (Topeka Capital-Journal)

He is best remembered for his incredible performance against the Dolphins in the AFC divisional playoff game on December 25, 1971, the double-overtime loss that was so heartbreaking for the Chiefs. Ed Podolak compiled 350 yards of total offense that day, and it became the biggest moment of his career.

"If the game had never gone six quarters, no one would have known my name," Podolak said of his place in Chiefs history. He had 85 rushing yards, 110 receiving yards, and 155 on returns against Miami, but his career was much more than that one game.

"Ed embodies a lot of the things that the Chiefs have said are their ideals," Jim Lynch said of his former teammate. "He was not a selfish player at all, and a lot of things about Ed Podolak are the things that everybody should have."

The Chiefs chose the tough Iowa Hawkeye in the second round of the 1969 draft, and after spending his rookie season on special teams, Podolak became the team's top runner in 1970.

"He did not have what you call a natural athletic ability like the great running backs," former teammate Jack Rudnay said of Podolak.

Kansas City's No. 2 all-time leading rusher with 4,451 yards, Podolak also caught 288 passes for 2,456 yards. He scored 40 touchdowns.

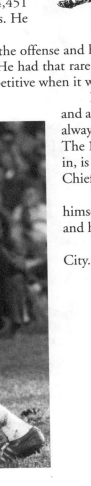

"He had an ability to understand the theory of the offense and how to make things work," Rudnay said. "He was very intense, very competitive, a very good thinker. He had that rare combination of being able to be a little laid back when he wasn't competing, but being intensely competitive when it was important to be."

Podolak led the Chiefs in rushing yardage four times and averaged 20.5 yards per kickoff return. His play was always steady and consistent, dogged and determined. The 1971 playoff game, as great a performance as he put in, is just one example of his overall contribution to the Chiefs during his career.

"Ed was a great leader who made great demands on himself," Hank Stram said. "He was a great competitor, and he did everything for this team."

Podolak played in a total of 104 games for Kansas City.

Ed Podolak (Topeka Capital-Journal)

Ed Podolak (Topeka Capital-Journal)

Jim Lynch—1990

The Chiefs' ever-reliable linebacker on the right side throughout the team's glory years of the late 1960s and early 1970s, Jim Lynch teamed with Bobby Bell and Willie Lanier to form one of the greatest linebacking trios in the history of pro football.

"I think Jim Lynch is probably one of the most consistently outstanding football players that we've had here in a long time," Stram said of his linebacker. "He plays the same way every week, and you just can't realize how very important that is."

After a notable college career at Notre Dame—he won the Maxwell Award as the nation's outstanding defensive player and has since been enshrined in the College Football Hall of Fame—Lynch joined the Chiefs as a second-round pick in the 1967 draft. Equally adept at stopping the run and defending the pass, he was solid throughout his career.

"Lynch usually has the total picture focused in his mind," Stram continued. "The other quality that makes him so valuable to our team is that he's a completely unselfish football player who's dedicated to making every personal sacrifice necessary for the team's success."

"I really like to play," Lynch said of football in 1974. "I love the game and the challenge that it presents to you as an individual and to your team."

Lynch finished his career with 17 interceptions and 14 fumble recoveries. He scored one touchdown and was selected to play in the 1968 AFL All-Star Game. Lynch was also a big part of the Chiefs' powerful defense that led the way to the 1970 Super Bowl victory over the Minnesota Vikings.

"You put in a lot of effort, time, sweat, and pain for the thrill of competing and winning," Lynch said. "You compete and lose, and it just isn't fun."

Lynch played in 151 games for Kansas City. He retired following the 1977 season.

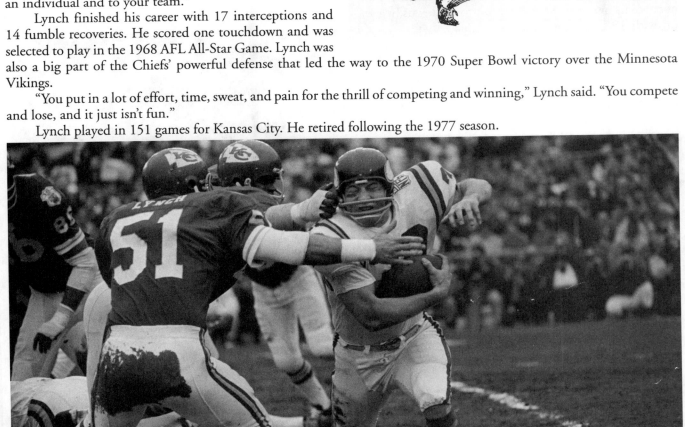

Jim Lynch (51) stops Minnesota's Bill Brown. (Bettmann/CORBIS)

The first great superstar of the franchise, Abner Haynes wasn't just the marquee player on the Dallas Texans, he was the best player in the AFL. He had incredible lateral moves, balance, and the ability to accelerate quickly once he broke into the open.

"He did it all—rushing, receiving, kickoff returns, punt returns," Hank Stram said of Haynes's talents. "He gave us the dimension we needed to be a good team in Dallas. He was a franchise player before they talked about franchise players."

Haynes joined the Texans after a standout collegiate career at North Texas; he was originally slated to play for the Raiders, but ended up with Dallas. His first three seasons were nothing short of sensational. He ran for a league-leading 875 yards and scored nine touchdowns in 1960 and was selected as the AFL's first Player of the Year. Haynes gained 841 yards rushing in 1961 and then exploded in the 1962 championship season with 1,049 yards rushing and 19 touchdowns.

"He's uncanny," Stram said. "There's no limit to what the guy can do with a football. His reflexes are as good as any I've ever seen. At times he actually seems to change direction in midair."

Haynes still owns nine franchise records, including most points in a game with 30, most touchdowns in a season with 19; most touchdowns in a game with five; the highest career average gain rushing at 4.84; most rushing touchdowns in a season with 13, and in a game with four; and the most combined yards in a career with 8,442, and in a season with 2,100. He led the club in rushing four times, 1960-62 and 1964, and was named all-AFL from 1960 through 1962. He was spectacular.

Haynes also gained notoriety for his "We'll kick to the clock" call at the coin toss before the start of overtime in the 1962 AFL championship game, a decision that put the Texans in the position of kicking into a strong wind. Luckily, his mistake didn't cost the Texans the game.

For his career, Haynes returned 55 punts for the franchise and averaged 10.9 yards per return. He returned 52 kickoffs, averaging 25.5 yards per return. He scored 56 touchdowns for the Texans/Chiefs and played in a total of 70 games for the franchise. Haynes was traded to the Broncos following the 1964 season and also played for the Jets and the Dolphins before retiring after the 1967 season.

Abner Haynes (Chris Burford)

Sherrill Headrick—1993

He was tough and wild, displaying a style of play that always amazed his coaches and teammates. He played through pain and injuries. Oh, how he played. His reckless nature and all-out disrespect for his body earned him the nickname "Psycho." The name fit perfectly, for it always seemed Sherrill Headrick was out of his mind the way he played. And if there was any doubt, he was also very good, one of the best linebackers in the AFL.

"What I really appreciate as a coach is that he gives himself fully during a game, and he plays when he's hurt," Hank Stram said of Headrick. "He has the highest pain threshold of any athlete I ever saw."

Hobbled knees, sprained ankles, broken fingers, and more. Headrick played on, always as if nothing were wrong. The former TCU star signed with the Texans as a free agent from the CFL and played in the initial AFL season. He was one of the team's first great defensive players, but he wasn't just wild energy set loose on the gridiron.

"It's true that Sherrill has great instincts for a middle linebacker," Stram said of Headrick in 1966. "But he also reads his keys very well and is highly intelligent at picking up tendencies and tips expressed by offensive teams."

Headrick was selected for five AFL All-Star Games, 1960-62, 1965, and 1966. He played on the Texans' '62 championship team and in Super Bowl I.

At every game he played for the Chiefs, Headrick left the field early during the pregame warm-ups, rushed to the locker room, and threw up. It was his special ceremony, a ritual of sorts. If he didn't throw up, he said, he didn't feel right.

"I've gotten sick before every game I've played in since college," Headrick said of his pregame practice. "It's my nervous stomach."

He had 14 interceptions during his career with the franchise—returning three for touchdowns—and played in 108 games. He played one final season for the expansion Cincinnati Bengals after leaving the Chiefs.

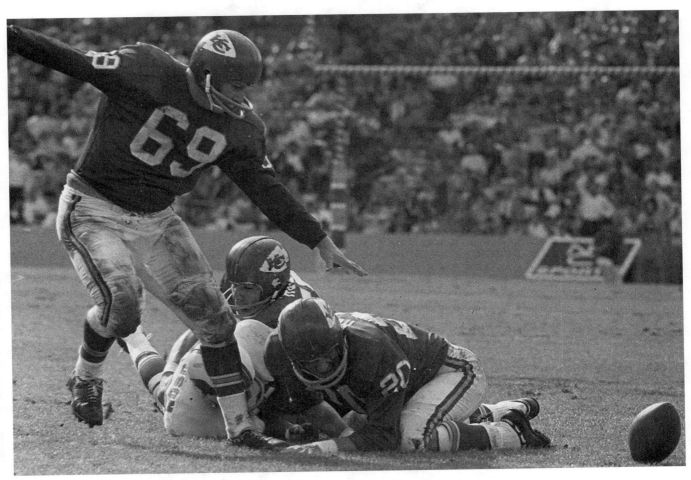

Sherrill Headrick (Topeka Capital-Journal)

Known as the "Joker" for his countless practical jokes and great sense of humor, Jack Rudnay also embodied the stuff great offensive linemen are made of and was highly regarded as one of the NFL's finest centers during the 1970s. He was tough and determined, consistent and reliable, manning the snapper's job for Kansas City for more than a decade.

After playing both center and defensive tackle at Northwestern, Rudnay was selected by the Chiefs in the fourth round of the 1969 draft. He missed the Super Bowl season after injuring his back in the College All-Star Game, but made the squad the following year and soon took over the center position from E. J. Holub.

"The second effort is always there," former Chiefs coach Marv Levy said of Rudnay. "Jack goes to the whistle on every down."

Rudnay started in the Pro Bowl four straight times, from 1973 through 1976. Beginning in 1970, he put together an impressive string, playing in 144 straight games.

"Jack is a throwback to the old days," Bill Walsh, the Chiefs' offensive line coach from 1970 to 1974, said of Rudnay. "He plays the game to the hilt. I've never seen a center come off the ball like Jack does."

And he was a winner, despite playing on some very poor teams. Rudnay never accepted losing, and he took it hard when the team played poorly or got lackadaisical.

"Jack gets very emotional after games," MacArthur Lane said. "He's a street fighter, he hates losing with a passion. He will rant and rave around the locker room if anyone dares to laugh after a loss."

He was the starting center on the Chiefs' 1971 AFC Western Division champs. Rudnay played in a total of 178 games for Kansas City, the third most by a Chiefs offensive lineman.

Jack Rudnay (Kansas Collection, U. of Kansas)

Curtis McClinton—1995

The Kansas Strongman was a powerful, hard-hitting runner, as well as an excellent receiver coming out of the backfield. Curtis McClinton rumbled for good yardage throughout his career as a fullback, then finished as a backup tight end on the Super Bowl IV championship team in 1969. He played on all three of the franchise's championship teams of the 1960s.

McClinton was selected by the Texans in the 14th round of the 1961 AFL futures draft and made a big impact during his rookie season in 1962. He ran for 604 yards and led the league with an average of 5.4 yards per carry. He also caught 29 passes for 333 yards. For his superb effort, McClinton was named AFL Rookie of the Year.

"My instincts are the same as any back," McClinton said during his playing days. "I want to carry the ball as often as possible."

The big back had another great season in 1966, running for 661 yards, catching 37 passes for 590 yards, and scoring nine touchdowns. He played in the AFL All-Star Game following the 1962 and 1966-67 seasons.

"I see to it that I am a healthy, confident football player," McClinton said. "I can play, and I know it."

McClinton was the first AFL player to score a touchdown in the Super Bowl, hauling in a seven-yard pass from Len Dawson in the second quarter of Super Bowl I against the Packers.

McClinton is the sixth-leading rusher in franchise history, finishing with 3,124 yards on 762 carries and 18 touchdowns. He also caught 154 passes for 1,945 yards and 14 scores.

McClinton played in 107 games for the Texans/Chiefs.

Curtis McClinton (Topeka Capital-Journal)

From free-agent punter to the best free safety in the AFC, Deron Cherry became one of the best players in the history of the Chiefs.

"When nobody thinks you have a chance to play because you're not big enough or strong enough or talented enough, it's tough," Cherry said. "But I've never yet seen a test that measures the size of a person's heart—or the belief that you can accomplish anything you set out to accomplish."

And Cherry accomplished a lot. The Rutgers alum failed to hook on as a punter, but quickly showed he could play in the defensive backfield and made the team in 1981.

"I knew I could play in this league," Cherry said. "The important thing for me was not to let my confidence waver, which it didn't."

"He is maybe as fine a safety as anyone who ever played the game," Schottenheimer said.

Two years later he was named to the first of six straight Pro Bowls when he picked off seven passes and displayed superior tackling and coverage skills for the Chiefs.

"The drive to be the best has been my nature for as long as I can remember," Cherry said during his playing days. "I want to be the best at my position in the NFL. I want to be a guy my teammates and coaches can depend on. I want to produce on the field. I want to be the guy who gets it done."

Cherry was so good he was selected to the Chiefs' 25-year all-time team in 1987, four years before his retirement. He had one of his best seasons in 1986, picking off nine passes to lead the AFC. Cherry also had six seasons of 100-plus tackles.

When he retired following the 1991 season, he left the numbers of a Hall of Famer: 927 career tackles, 50 interceptions (third on the Chiefs' all-time list), 15 fumble recoveries, and three touchdowns. He played in a total of 148 games for Kansas City.

Following his retirement, Cherry became part of an ownership group for the expansion Jacksonville Jaguars. But he'll always be a Chief.

"My heart will always be in Kansas City," Cherry said after joining the ownership group. "You can't play your entire career with one team and not have an emotional bond."

Deron Cherry (Kansas Collection, U. of Kansas)

Marcus Allen *(Alan Barzee)*

The Chiefs drew sellout crowds the last five seasons they played in Municipal Stadium. *(Courtesy of Jim Chappell)*

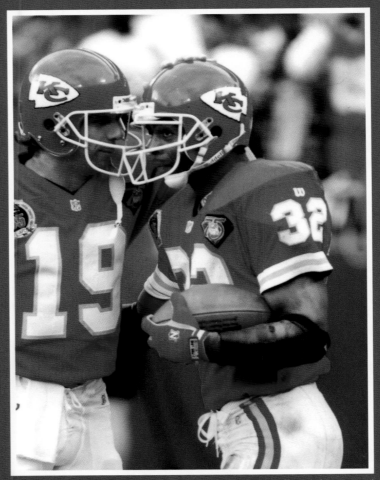

Joe Montana and Marcus Allen *(Alan Barzee)*

Nick Lowery wasn't just one of the best kickers the Chiefs ever had; he is one of the NFL's all-time greats. *(Kansas Collection, U. of Kansas)*

The Nigerian Nightmare, Christian Okoye *(Topeka Capital-Journal)*

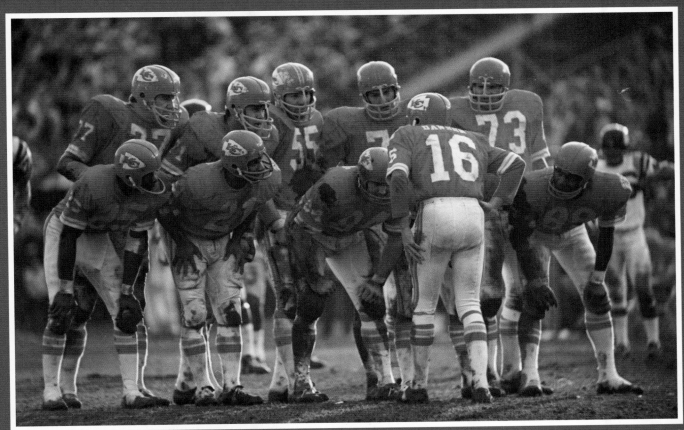

The Chiefs' famous "choir" huddle in Super Bowl IV. *(Topeka Capital-Journal)*

Jan Stenerud, the first true kicker inducted into the Pro Football Hall of Fame.
(Topeka Capital-Journal)

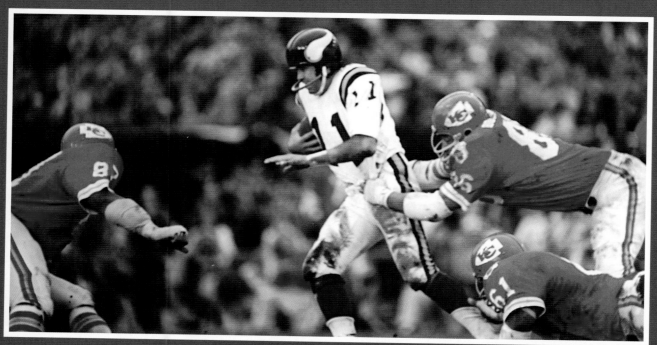

Aaron Brown (87), Buck Buchanan (86), and Curley Cope (61) sack Minnesota's Joe Kapp in Super Bowl IV.
(Topeka Capital-Journal)

Arrowhead Stadium *(Courtesy of Jim Chappell)*

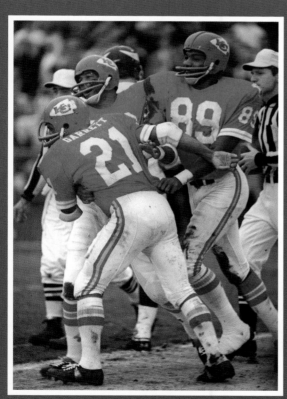

Mike Garrett, Gloster Richardson and Otis Taylor
celebrate following Garrett's touchdown in the
second quarter of Super Bowl IV.
(Topeka Capital-Journal)

Priest Holmes *(Alan Barzee)*

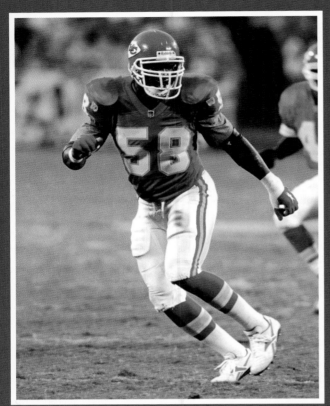

Derrick Thomas *(Alan Barzee)*

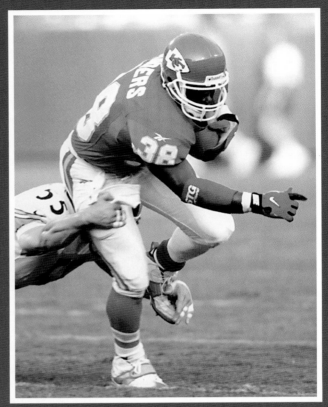

Kimble Anders *(Alan Barzee)*

Tony Gonzalez *(Phil Coale, AP/Wide World Photos)*

Super Bowl IV MVP Len Dawson
(Topeka Capital-Journal)

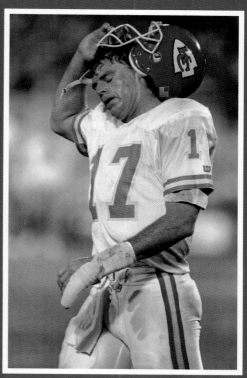

Steve DeBerg's magic 1990 season ended on a
sour note when the Chiefs lost to Miami in
the first round of the playoffs.
(Topeka Capital-Journal)

Hank Stram, center, poses with University of Kansas alums Bert Coan, left, and Curtis McClinton. *(University of Kansas Archives)*

Dick Vermeil *(Alan Barzee)*

Otis Taylor rests after scoring the Chiefs' final touchdown in
Super Bowl IV. *(Topeka Capital-Journal)*

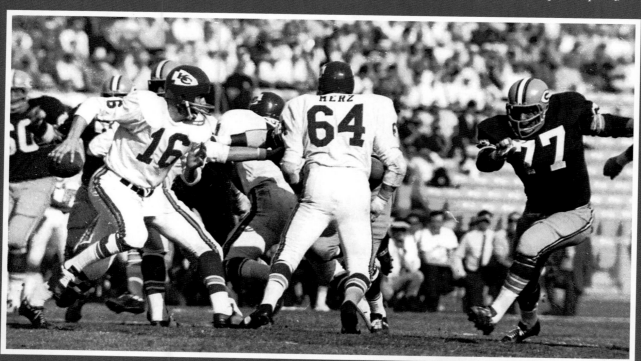

The AFL's Chiefs faced the NFL's Green Bay Packers in Super Bowl I at Los Angeles Memorial Coliseum.
(AP/ Wide World Photos)

Big Dave Hill, like so many of his contemporaries on the Chiefs, displayed superior skills at his position for more than a decade. He was one of the team's best offensive linemen ever, manning the right tackle position for 12 seasons.

As a 24th-round selection by the Chiefs in the 1963 AFL Draft, the Auburn standout was a definite long shot to make the squad. But he used his superior size—he stood 6-5 and weighed 260 pounds—in combination with his lineman skills, and was an anchor for the Chiefs' passing and running games on two AFL championship teams in 1966 and 1969; he started in both of the Chiefs' Super Bowl games. He was considered one of the best pass blockers in the game throughout his career.

"You have to think so much more in pro ball," Hill said about playing the offensive line in the NFL. "You have so many other things to worry about. They play so many different kinds of defenses."

Hill didn't miss a game for nine straight seasons and played in a total of 150 games for the Chiefs.

Dave Hill (Kansas Collection, U. of Kansas)

As a No.1 pick in the 1978 NFL draft, Art Still more than lived up to his expectations and became a defensive force for the Chiefs, shutting down running backs and rushing the passer with equal ability.

"You might get 15 sacks, and as far as the run goes, you'll be weak," Still said. "You've got to be well rounded, not just in sacks and pass rushing, but against the run."

Still was the Southeastern Conference Player of the Year as a senior at the University of Kentucky, which led to his selection in the first round by Kansas City. Although he played on some of the Chiefs' lesser teams, Still proved his worth and was selected for the Pro Bowl four times: 1980-82 and 1984.

"If you ask my evaluation of Art Still as a player," Walt Corey, Still's defensive line coach, said, "I have to say he is the best defensive end. There aren't enough adjectives to describe him."

Still led the Chiefs in sacks six times, twice registering 14.5 in a season. He finished his career with the Chiefs as the team's No. 3 all-time sack leader with 72.5, and also had 992 tackles and 11 fumble recoveries. Three times Still led the team in tackles.

"I'd like to get better," Still said in the early 1980s. "I strive to be the best. But I never want to think that, or I'll quit trying."

Still played in a total of 136 games for the Chiefs.

Kansas City traded Still to the Buffalo Bills in 1988, where he played two seasons before retiring.

Art Still (Kansas Collection, U. of Kansas)

Lloyd Burruss—1999

Coupling his hard-hitting tackles with superior pass defense, Lloyd Burruss quickly established himself as one of the top strong safeties in the NFL. A third-round pick out of Maryland in 1981, Burruss became a starter immediately and picked off four passes his rookie season. He won the Mack Lee Hill Award that season as the club's top rookie.

Burruss also showed the ability to lead his teammates.

"Lloyd has been the quiet leader," Chiefs president Carl Peterson said. "He has been the consummate professional. He's been the glue in the secondary."

The Chiefs' MVP in 1985, Burruss became the only player to win the Mack Lee Hill Award, team MVP, and be named to the Chiefs Hall of Fame. He was named to his only Pro Bowl following the 1986 season.

Burruss had a penchant for the big play, returning four of his interceptions for touchdowns. He also owns the team record for interception-return yardage in a game with 115.

He finished his career with 628 tackles, 22 interceptions, seven fumble recoveries and 3.5 sacks. Burruss played in 145 career games; he retired following the 1991 season.

"You don't replace people like Lloyd," Marty Schottenheimer said.

Lloyd Burruss (Kansas Collection, U. of Kansas)

For six seasons he rammed through defensive lines, pounding and bruising opposing defenders. He had incredible strength, amazing power, surprising speed. Christian Okoye was as dominating a running back as the NFL had ever seen. Okoye brought a presence to the Chiefs' backfield it had not had since Mack Lee Hill.

"Nobody in this league has that kind of speed and power combination," Chiefs lineman Irv Eatman said of Okoye. "There might be some guys faster, and there might be some guys out there who are nearly as strong. But none with that combination."

Tabbed the "Nigerian Nightmare," a reference to his homeland, Okoye was selected by the Chiefs in the second round of the 1987 draft. Coming from tiny Azusa Pacific College, his football skills were still raw, and he was still learning the game when he joined the Chiefs. He learned quickly and was soon dominating other teams throughout the NFL.

"I realize I have a God-given talent," Okoye said in 1989. "I know I can run with my size and my strength, so I try to utilize it to the best of my effort."

The Chiefs' all-time leading rusher, Okoye topped the 1,000-yard mark in a season twice and led the NFL in rushing in 1989 with 1,480 rushing yards, also a franchise record. He gained 1,031 yards in 1991.

"To feel the force he runs with is amazing," Eatman said. "He has slammed into my back on running plays a few times, and the only way I can describe what it feels like is to imagine standing on the street and getting hit by a car going 50 miles an hour."

A two-time Pro Bowler (1989 and 1991), Okoye finished his career with 4,987 yards rushing, 40 touchdowns, and an average of 3.9 yards per carry. His single-game best was 170 yards against Dallas in 1989. He won the Mack Lee Hill Award in 1987 as the club's top rookie, and the team MVP award in 1989.

Okoye retired following the 1992 season because of knee problems. He played in a total of 79 games for the Chiefs.

Christian Okoye (Kansas Collection, U. of Kansas)

Christian Okoye (Kansas Collection, U. of Kansas)

One of the greatest players to ever wear the red and gold of the Chiefs, Derrick Thomas terrorized quarterbacks in the NFL for 11 seasons with his quick, tenacious pass-rushing technique. Off the field, he gave of himself to the Kansas City community many times over, providing help and guidance to countless children and causes. His tragic death on February 8, 2000, left the Chiefs and the Kansas City community in a state of shock and grief.

Thomas was involved in a serious automobile accident which left his legs paralyzed. Two weeks later he suffered cardiac arrest and died. He was only 33.

"It's a devastating tragedy to the Kansas City Chiefs family, the people of Kansas City, the fans of the National Football League and to me personally," Chiefs' President Carl Peterson said. "Derrick Thomas has been such an important part of the Chiefs family for the past 11 years. He has done so much for this team and our city during his time with us. He had so much love for the game, for his teammates and for our town. Our prayers go out to Derrick's family, to his fellow teammates and to our fans who knew Derrick. A light has gone out."

Thomas joined the Chiefs as the club's first-round selection in the 1989 NFL Draft, and had a career that was highlighted with many outstanding performances, awards and honors. These are some of the deserving honors he won on and off the field: 1989 NFL Defensive Rookie of the Year; 1989 Chiefs Mack Lee Hill Award Winner; Nine consecutive Pro Bowl selections; 1993 Edge NFL Man of the Year for his community activities; and the 1995 winner of the Bryon "Whizzer" White Humanitarian Award for service to his team, his community and country.

Thomas founded "The Third and Long Foundation," in 1990, a nationally-renowned reading program for inner-city youths in Kansas City. His generous spirit and time provided the springboard to better futures for countless young students throughout the Kansas City metropolitan area. The foundation is his best legacy, and the best testament to the kind of man he was.

Thomas finished his career with a club record 126.5 sacks for the Chiefs, the ninth-highest total in NFL history. He also concluded his career with the franchise record for career safeties with three, 45 forced fumbles and 19 fumble recoveries. He ranks fifth on the club's all-time tackle chart with 728, and played in a total of 169 games for the Chiefs.

One of his best seasons was 1990, when he led the NFL with 20.0 sacks, as well as playing the game of his career when he set an NFL single-game record with 7.0 sacks against the Seattle Seahawks. Thomas just missed an eighth sack on the game's final play as Seattle quarterback Dave Krieg tossed a game-winning touchdown pass to defeat Kansas City, 17-16.

Derrick Thomas (Alan Barzee)

"It's a mind-set," Thomas said of his pass-rushing prowess. "You are going to get double-teamed, triple-teamed and you just have to do something to offset what they are doing to you and to keep going and never stop."

Thomas used his never-stop mentality to develop his philanthropic work.

"On-the-field accolades are great," Thomas said of his football awards, "but in order to reach your full potential, you have to overstep the boundaries of football and go out into the community and be an All-Pro there, too." And he did, most successfully.

An under-rated strength and robust heart propelled John Alt through 13 seasons as he became the Chiefs' cornerstone on their offensive line. A number-one draft pick out of Iowa in 1984, Alt didn't take a permanent spot in the Chiefs starting lineup until 1987. A slow start and injuries hampered him his first three seasons; he also found it difficult at times coming into a game in a reserve role.

"It takes time to get warmed up, and I have to really be into the game before I can start playing my best," he said. When he finally became a starter, the Chiefs always saw his best.

The Chiefs' running game improved in 1987, and by the time Marty Schottenheimer became head coach in 1989, Alt was ready to contribute in a big way to his new head coach's smashmouth style of football.

"I just go in and do my thing," Alt said of his playing style. "I adjust my set depending on my opponent's tactics. If he's speedy, I try to get off the ball a little quicker." Alt helped move Kansas City's running game to the top of the league, and his pass protection was also superb. The Chiefs made the playoffs five of his last six seasons with the team.

He was named to the Pro Bowl in 1992 and 1993, selected to the All-AFC first team from 1990 through 1993, and was first All-NFL in 1990 and 1991. Alt played in a total of 179 games for the Chiefs.

John Alt (Alan Barzee)

Other Chiefs Greats

Derrick Alexander (Alan Barzee)

Derrick Alexander

He's always been a steady, dependable receiver, but for one magic season, Derrick Alexander was spectacular, and one of the top receivers in the NFL. The Chiefs' single-season receiving mark was smashed by Alexander in 2000, as he gained 1,391 yards on 78 receptions. He also scored ten touchdowns to cap his best season as a pro.

"The coaches saw . . . when I get the ball, I make plays," Alexander said of his playmaking for the Chiefs. "I run routes to get open. If I'm open and catch the ball, I don't think anybody can tackle me. That's how I feel and that's how I play."

Alexander signed with the Chiefs as a free agent from Baltimore in 1998, and despite starting slowly that first season with the team because of injuries, finished in spectacular fashion. He caught 54 passes for 992 yards and four touchdowns, and provided the big plays the Chiefs were hoping for when they signed him. He ripped off an 82-yard touchdown run on a reverse against the Steelers in the '99 season, and again caught 54 passes, good for 832 yards and two touchdowns. But it was during the 2000 season that Alexander really became the kind of big play receiver the Chiefs were hoping they got when he first signed with the club. He was named the Chiefs' "Man of the Year" in 2000. He also won the Derrick Thomas Award.

The 2001 season was a disappointment for him and the Chiefs—again he fought nagging injuries—but his 27 receptions for the year moved him up to ninth place on the Chiefs all time receiving chart. He tallied 470 receiving yards and scored three touchdowns in 2001. For his career in Kansas City, Alexander has 213 receptions, has scored 19 touchdowns, and played in 60 games.

Marcus Allen (Alan Barzee)

Marcus Allen

Going from Pro Bowler to an unexplained relegation in a non-productive role in Oakland, Marcus Allen experienced a rebirth of sorts when he came to Kansas City from the Raiders, and didn't just regenerate his career, but prospered. He signed with Kansas City on June 3, 1993. His presence in the Chiefs' backfield added the multiple threat they were lacking, and his leadership provided another missing component in Kansas City's quest for an NFL championship. His running style was simple and effective and clicked well in the Chiefs' new West Coast offense.

"He kind of sits back and lets the play develop," Chiefs' center Tim Grunhard said, Allen's running. "We have a couple of plays we call slash left and slash right . . . and he kept gaining yards."

Allen joined Joe Montana on the Chiefs in 1993, and the two superstars led Kansas City to the AFC championship game. Allen was named to the Pro Bowl that season, rushing for 764 yards and scoring a total of 15 touchdowns. He scored the game-clinching touchdown against Houston in the divisional playoff on a 21-yard run that season.

Allen scored the 100th rushing touchdown of his career in 1995 and finished his career with 145 total touchdowns, 47 of those for Kansas City.

"It felt great," Allen said of his 100th rushing touchdown, which came against Denver. "I was definintely pleased. I had a great big smile on my face." He created a lot of smiles for Chiefs fans throughout his career, too.

The list of Allen's accomplishments and records is long; 12,243 yards rushing (3,698 with the Chiefs), 3,022 rushing attempts, 587 career receptions, 30 games with 100-plus yards rushing. But maybe his most important contribution to Kansas City was his champion heart and drive to win.

Allen played in 77 games for the Chiefs and started in 53.

Kimble Anders

Quiet, consistent, versatile. Kimble Anders came to Kansas City as a free agent from the University of Houston in 1991, built an impressive Pro Bowl career, and was highly regarded as one of the most complete backs in the NFL. Whether blocking, running or receiving, Anders excelled—his consistency was amazing. Starting in 1993, he caught at least 40 passes every season through 1998, and ran for at least 200 yards each season. From 1994-98, he caught 305 passes.

A fullback his entire career, Anders was switched to halfback in 1999 because of his quick, slashing runs, and was on his way to a promising season when he injured his Achilles tendon in the second game of the season. He missed the rest of the 1999 season. A valiant attempt at a comeback was made by Anders in 2000, but despite playing in 14 games and running for 331 yards, he never returned to his former level of play. The Chiefs released Anders following the 2000 season.

For his career, Anders played in 124 games for the Chiefs, rushed for 2,261 yards, caught 369 passes for 2,829 yards, and scored 18 touchdowns. He was selected to play in the Pro Bowl following the 1995, 1996 and 1997 seasons.

Kimble Anders (Alan Barzee)

Gary Barbaro

Gary Barbaro (Topeka Capital-Journal)

Coming to Kansas City as a third-round draft pick in 1976, Gary Barbaro quickly moved into the starting lineup his rookie season. Despite playing at Nichols State, Barbaro's aggressive, intelligent playing style not only left no doubt that he had what it takes to play in the NFL, but also that he could be a Pro Bowler because of it. Initially a big hitter, Barbaro eventually refined his play, settled into his free safety position, and provided the Chiefs with excellent pass coverage and team leadership.

"I figured I could knock out every running back who carried the ball and tear in half every wide receiver who came across the middle every time he touched the ball," Barbaro said in 1983. He was intimidating, standing 6-foot-4 and weighing 210 pounds. And he could hit like a linebacker. But it was his instincts as the team's "center fielder" that made him so valuable to the Chiefs.

"Gary gets around the ball and stays around it," teammate Lloyd Burruss said of Barbaro. "He knows what's happening, where it's happening, why it's happening—and then takes measures to prevent it from happening."

Barbaro compiled impressive numbers throughout his career. He picked off eight passes his second season, had a career-high 10 interceptions in 1980, and earned his first Pro Bowl selection. Twice he recorded more than 90 tackles in a season, including 96 in 1981.

"I know for a fact there are some wide receivers who look for Barbaro as much as they look for the ball when they cross the middle," Gary Green said of his secondary teammate. "Everyone knows Barbaro is going to be there—the receiver knows it, the quarterback knows it. He controls the middle." Big hits were always for those who caught the pass.

Barbaro finished his career in Kansas City with 39 interceptions, and he returned three for touchdowns. He never missed a game until his final season, 1982, and played in a total of 101 games for the Chiefs. He left Kansas City for the USFL following the 1982 season.

Mike Bell

As the Chiefs' no. 1 draft pick in 1979, Wichita native Mike Bell came to Kansas City and became one of the top defensive ends in the club's history. His size, strength, and quickness caused problems for Chiefs' opponents throughout his career. He was ferocious with his pass rush and anchored Kansas City's defensive line throughout the 1980s.

Bell was a backup his rookie season and played in just two games in 1980. He cracked the starting lineup in 1981, and stayed there the rest of his career. His first big year was 1983 when he led the team with 10 sacks and totaled 75 tackles. He followed with 13.5 sacks in 1984, the best total of his career.

Bell and his twin brother Mark were convicted of attempting to buy cocaine in June 1986. He missed the entire 1986 season, and after serving four months of a one-year sentence, Bell was released. He returned to Kansas City for the 1987 season, and putting his problems in the past, regained his starting spot on the defensive line. He played in 12 games that season, tallied 6.5 sacks, 56 tackles, and two fumble recoveries.

For his career, Bell sacked the quarterback 52 times in 135 games.

Mike Bell (Kansas Collection, U. of Kansas)

Carlos Carson

One of the most outstanding receivers in the AFC during his entire career in Kansas City, Carlos Carson was always short on notoriety, long on results. A fifth-round draft pick out of Louisiana State in 1980, Carson had his breakout season in 1983 when he caught 80 passes for 1,351 yards and seven touchdowns. His great season earned him a trip to the Pro Bowl; before 1983 he had never caught more than 27 passes in a season.

"Playing Kansas City, you have to lead the league in something," Carson said of the relatively little media attention he received throughout his career. "That's more or less what you have to do."

Carson never reached that goal, but he came close. Three times in his career he went over the 1,000-yard mark in receiving yards, and while the 80 receptions he pulled in in 1983 was his career best, he did contribute big numbers and was considered a dangerous receiver throughout the league.

"I would like to be noticed as [one] of the best receivers in the game, if not the best," Carson said in 1989. "That's what [I'm] striving for." Carson was again selected for the Pro Bowl in 1987.

For his career, he caught 352 passes for 6,360 yards and 33 touchdowns. He also threw a touchdown pass and returned 57 kickoffs early in his career. Carson played in a total of 120 games for the Chiefs and went to Philadelphia midway through the 1989 season.

Carlos Carson (Kansas Collection, U. of Kansas)

Dale Carter

One of the finest athletes to ever play for the Chiefs, Dale Carter more than surpassed the high expectations placed on him as the team's no. 1 draft choice in 1992. Arriving from the University of Tennessee, Carter did it all while he was in Kansas City: he intercepted passes, returned kicks, caught passes on offense, and was considered the finest cornerback in the AFC for several seasons. He also earned four straight trips to the Pro Bowl from 1994 through 1997.

He returned two punts for touchdowns in 1992, and also collected a career-high seven interceptions that season. Quarterbacks learned after his rookie season to stay away from his coverage, and the most he picked off after 1992 was four in 1995. But he was still the best in pass coverage, and so explosive was his speed and overall athletic ability, that the Chiefs used him as a wideout in 1996. He caught six passes and scored one touchdown for the offense that season.

For his career, Carter played in 104 games for the Chiefs, picked off 21 passes, scored four touchdowns, and returned 83 punts. Following the 1998 season, Carter left Kansas City via free agency and signed with the Denver Broncos.

Dale Carter (Alan Barzee)

Curley Culp

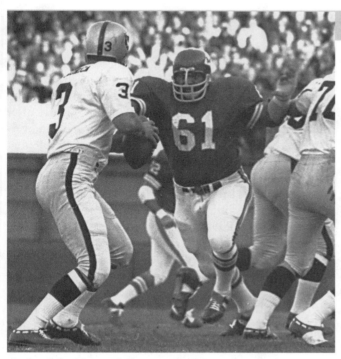

He was strong, quick, and vicious; perfect for a defensive lineman. Curley Culp, originally a second-round draft pick of the Denver Broncos in 1968, came to Kansas City later that season and once inserted into the mix of the defensive line, established himself as a powerful force in the AFL.

"I think the entire Kansas City organization at that time (1969) had the best personnel of any team I've ever been on," Culp said in 1976. "You can't compare that kind of personnel (to other teams). And he was one of the top performers.

Culp's play throughout the Chiefs' Super Bowl season in 1969 was a big reason Kansas City had one of the top defenses in pro football. He played havoc on Minnesota quarterback Joe Kapp in Super Bowl IV, and was named to the AFL All-Star game following the '69 season. He maintained his level of play for the next four years in Kansas City and was named to the Pro Bowl in 1970 and 1971. But he was all business in his attitude toward the game.

"I view football as a business. I view it completely and only as a job," Culp said. "It *is* a job, and I'd be foolish to think otherwise."

Culp played in a total of 82 games for the Chiefs.

Curley Culp (Kansas Collection, U. of Kansas)

Joe Delaney

Joe Delaney (Kansas Collection, U. of Kansas)

Two short seasons. Super Joe Delaney was the best running back the Chiefs had had in more than a decade when he broke into the starting lineup in 1981. He was fast, explosive, quick, and powerful. Delaney had the complete package to become one of the Chiefs' greatest runners. He also had a giant heart, and the complete respect of his teammates. And it was his heart that led to his tragic death.

On June 29, 1983, Delaney tried valiantly to rescue three young boys from a park pond in Monroe, Louisiana, and drowned. His death weighed heavy on his teammates; he was just 24.

"He had all the qualities and character traits that you look up to in great people," his teammate Tom Condon said of Delaney. "Courage, tenacity, honesty, loyalty."

"His pro career was brief in years," Chiefs owner Lamar Hunt said of Delaney after his death, "but his electrifying style of play and enthusiasm for life will be remembered and treasured by all in the family of the Kansas City Chiefs."

"Joe Delaney was a hero before today," John Mackovic said. "He was dedicated to his family and dedicated to his sport."

Playing in just 23 games for Kansas City, Delaney rushed for 1,501 yards, caught 33 passes, and scored three touchdowns. He was selected for the 1981 Pro Bowl.

Donnie Edwards

Donnie Edwards (Alan Barzee)

The Chiefs fourth round pick in the 1996 draft, Edwards stepped into the starting middle linebacker spot his second season with the team, and moved to the outside after Marvcus Patton joined the club. Edwards' speed and overall tenacity helped him become one of the Chiefs' premier defensive players. Although he was never selected to play in the Pro Bowl, Edwards put together five outstanding seasons in a row, and led the team in tackles four straight times, tying the team record. He made 136 tackles in 1997, 151 in 1998, 143 in 1999, 151 in 2001 and 147 in 2001, the first time in Chiefs history a player made 100 plus tackles five times in a row. Edwards has also been a big play maker, intercepting ten passes in his career (five in '99) and recovering eight fumbles. He's scored three touchdowns, one on a 79-yard fumble recovery return against Chicago in 1999, and one on a 28-yard interception return against the Chargers in 1999. Edwards also recorded 15 sacks for the Chiefs.

"He has been a model of exemplary behavior as a professional athlete and as a representative of the Chiefs in our community. Chiefs President Peterson said. "We sincerely thank him for the terrific play he gave us and our fans."

Edwards saw duty in 94 regular season games with 80 starts in six seasons for Kansas City. He was released following the 2001 season.

Tony Gonzalez

Tony Gonzalez (Alan Barzee)

Comparisons to other great tight ends in the NFL might be a bit premature at this point in Tony Gonzalez's career, but if the Chiefs' 1997 no. 1 draft pick continues to perform as he did in 1999, 2000 and 2001, his name will have to be added to the list of the NFL's all-time great tight ends.

"He's a pretty impressive guy," former Chiefs quarterback Rich Gannon said of Gonzalez. "Big guys that can run and catch like that don't come along very often."

Gonzalez earned his first trip to the Pro Bowl in 1999 after putting together a great season. He played in 15 games, caught 76 passes for 849 yards and scored 11 touchdowns. True Pro Bowl numbers, but the lost shot at the playoffs was more important to him. "I want to go to the Super Bowl and win," Gonzalez said after the season. "I think with the caliber of this team, we can do it."

The 2000 season was even better. He broke the team record for receptions in a season with 93, amassed 1,203 yards in receiving, and scored nine touchdowns en route to another trip to the Pro Bowl. "He's a competitor and a great athlete," former Chiefs coach Gunther Cunningham said of Gonzalez. "Those are the kind of guys you want on your team."

Gonzalez was selected to his third consecutive Pro Bowl following the 2001 season when he started all 16 games and led Kansas City with 73 catches for 917 yards. He also scored six touchdowns.

"We have to take advantage of his abilities in [the scoring zone]," Elvis Grbac said of Gonzalez's touchdown-scoring prowess in 1999. "Because of his size, he can fight off defensive guys in coverage down there."

"I want to go out there and make plays and be productive and win, Gonzalez said of his play. The most important thing is I want to win around here."

Trips to the Pro Bowl should be the norm for Gonzalez in the future, but the Super Bowl is his target. He has played in 79 games to date for the Chiefs, caught 334 passes for 3,958 yards, and scored 30 touchdowns. Gonzalez has amassed more receptions and receiving yardage than any other tight end in Chiefs history. He ranks seventh in franchise history in receptions and is sixth on the team's all-time chart in receiving yards.

Elvis Grbac

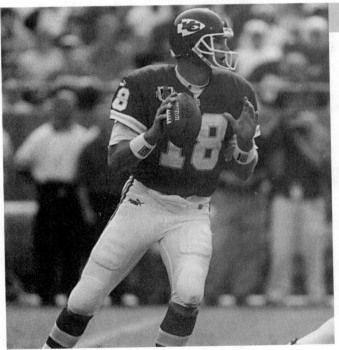

Elvis Grbac (Alan Barzee)

A victim of the injury bug his first two seasons in Kansas City, Grbac put together two complete seasons for the Chiefs—his performance in 2000 earned him an injury replacement spot in the Pro Bowl—and showed the stuff of a complete NFL quarterback. A free-agent signee from San Francisco, Grbac got caught in a quarterback controversy his first two seasons with Rich Gannon as a result of his injuries, and was never really accepted by the city or his teammates as the team leader. But he did greatly improve his quarterbacking skills.

After appearing in just 18 games his first two seasons with Kansas City, Grbac started all 16 games in 1999 and 15 games in 2000. He passed for 3,389 yards and 22 touchdowns in '99, and when the Chiefs switched to a predominantly passing-oriented offense in 2000, he produced big numbers: 326 completions out of 547 attempts, 4,169 yards passing (second highest in Chiefs history) and 28 touchdowns. His best effort came against the Raiders in Oakland when he threw for 504 yards and two touchdowns in a losing effort.

For his career in Kansas City, Grbac has played in 49 games, threw for 10,643 yards, 66 touchdowns, and 47 interceptions. He also ran for 315 yards.

Grbac signed with the Baltimore Ravens following the 2000 season.

Gary Green

The San Antonio, Texas, native brought talent, intelligence and desire to the Chiefs' secondary when he joined the team as their no. 1 draft pick in 1977 out of Baylor University. But it was his competitive spirit and drive that propelled him into the ranks of the Pro Bowlers.

"I never doubted my ability to cover every single receiver in the NFL, even as a rookie," Green said of his play. Neither did his teammates. Green went through a normal growing process his rookie season, but after his first eight games or so, he learned mental toughness was just as important as physical talent.

"The toughest thing to learn is the mental part," Green said of playing cornerback. The physical differences between the abilities of the guy on our team and a guy on the next team are so slight that you're not going to be able to dominate him, and he's not going to dominate you. You aren't invincible. You will get beat on pass coverage. You have to be able to come back and be just as mentally prepared for the next down as you were for the one on which you got burned."

Green didn't get burned often.

His interception numbers are deceptively low, simply because quarterbacks feared throwing his way. He picked off three his rookie season, twice snagged five, and collected a career-high six interceptions in 1983. He was named to the Pro Bowl three seasons in a row while with the Chiefs, 1981-83.

"After my second year, I felt I could put my performance against any of the great ones—Louis Wright, Mel Blount, Michael Haynes," Green said in 1983. "But I wasn't getting the recognition they were. Teams would line up away from me or run them away in motion. I was as good as anybody in football, but no one would throw at me."

Green picked off 24 passes in his career for the Chiefs, returning one for a touchdown. He played in a total of 100 games for Kansas City before being traded to the Los Angeles Rams following the 1983 season.

Gary Green (Kansas Collection, U. of Kansas)

Tim Grunhard

Tough, gritty, and intense, Tim Grunhard is a special breed, the offensive center, the anchor of the offensive line. Since joining the Chiefs as their second-round pick out of Notre Dame in 1990, Grunhard has become very much like the great Chiefs' centers of the past, E. J. Holub and Jack Rudnay.

"There's nothing glamorous about the center position or the entire offensive line for that matter," Grunhard said in 1997. "We're not here to get the glory, to get all the acclaim."

After ten seasons of solid line play, Grunhard received a little glory in 1999, earning his first trip to the Pro Bowl. It was a long overdue honor for the girthy center from Chicago.

An offensive guard at Notre Dame, Grunhard had never played a down at center until joining the Chiefs. Hard work, persistence, and a little tutelage from former Chiefs Mike Webster, now a Hall-of-Famer, helped Grunhard make the grade for Kansas City. Despite his great career, he yearns for a championship.

"The ring is the thing I'm playing for right now," Grunhard said two years ago.

Tim Grunhard (Alan Barzee)

"No one wants to win more than him," teammate Dave Szott said of Grunhard. "Tim is not afraid to work hard and to do what it takes to win, staying late, working hard, watching extra film."

Through the 2000 season, Grunhard has played in 169 games for the Chiefs and also appeared in 10 playoff games.

Dino Hackett

Dino Hackett (Kansas Collection, U. of Kansas)

He played each play as if it were his last, each hit on opposing runners as if his body were indestructible. Dino Hackett was a punisher, a hitter, a little wild and crazy, bringing an almost demented state of mind to the football field. A second-round pick out of tiny Appalachian State in 1986, Hackett made the starting lineup immediately and also raised the Chiefs' defense to another level.

"He's my kind of guy," teammate Bill Maas said of Hackett.

"I'd heard about guys like that," Deron Cherry said of Hackett and his playing style, "but I'd never played with one."

Hackett's rookie season was impressive, as he logged 140 tackles and created havoc for the Chiefs' opponents.

"To tell you the truth, it's nice to have people think that you're a kamikaze kind of guy," Hackett said of his play.

He started fighting injuries brought on by his big hitting, and they piled up. His reckless style, while effective, began to take a toll on his body. Hackett didn't care.

"The only way I can have any success is to go 100 percent," Hackett said of his intense playing style. "I'm a mediocre player when I'm not flying around."

Hackett was named to the Pro Bowl in 1988, but was unable to play because of a knee injury. He continued to play for the Chiefs through the 1991 season, until injuries caught up with him. He tried a brief comeback in 1993 with the Seahawks, but played in just three games for them.

Hackett played in a total of 85 games for the Chiefs, recorded nine sacks, and grabbed one interception.

James Hasty

A tenacious, hard hitter, Hasty has joined the ranks of the best ever to play in the Chiefs' secondary. A two-time Pro Bowler for Kansas City, Hasty's play was a big reason for the Chiefs' division-winning teams in 1995 and 1997. Joining Kansas City as a free agent from the New York Jets, Hasty provided a missing part to the Chiefs' defense. His level of play has not dropped at all during his tenure with the Chiefs.

Takeaways have been a big part of his game. He's picked off 17 passes through the 1999 season and recovered four fumbles. Hasty recorded a career-high 102 tackles in 1999 and also scored two big touchdowns, returning interceptions against Baltimore and Oakland. He also returned a fumble 80 yards for a score against the Raiders in 1996. Hasty was named to the Pro Bowl following the 1997 and 1999 seasons.

He's also recorded five sacks and played in a total of 78 games for the Chiefs.

James Hasty (Alan Barzee)

Priest Holmes

Priest Holmes (Alan Barzee)

The free agent running back from Baltimore more than surpassed even the highest of expectations, and put together a blockbuster 2001 season. His speed, quickness and ability to find open running space put Priest Holmes among the league's elite running backs. He finished his record-breaking first year in Kansas City with a single-season team record of 1,555 yards rushing, a team record 2,169 total yards (tops in the NFL in 2001), his first-ever Pro Bowl selection and seven 100-yard rushing games. The breakthrough season earned him the team's Derrick Thomas Award as the Chiefs' 2001 Most Valuable Player. Holmes was also the Chiefs' offensive captain.

"In this situation, he has blossomed," Chiefs coach Dick Vermeil said of his star running back. "He's a wonderful person and he has tremendous work ethic. . . . He's extremely impressive in everything he does."

In addition to leading the NFL in rushing in 2001, Holmes caught 62 passes for 614 yards, as well as scoring 10 touchdowns. He was, quite simply, the most dominating running back in a Chiefs uniform since Christian Okoye.

"Here in Kansas City I have more of a leadership role where I am standing out front, because I am getting a number of carries throughout the game," Holmes said of his big season in Kansas City. "That is the biggest change I think. That and a coaching staff believing in me and bringing me in."

A two-time AFC Offensive Player of the Week honoree in 2001, Holmes originally entered the NFL with Baltimore in 1997 out of the University of Texas. He started all 16 games for the Chiefs in 2001.

Jim Kearney

Jim Kearney (Jim Kearney)

He was the quiet man on the Chiefs' defense; intense, coiled ready. Surrounded by other players who got more attention, Jim Kearney spoke little and played big. He provided a consistency in the Chiefs' secondary for more than eight seasons, playing a big part of the team's success from 1968 through 1975.

A quarterback in college at Prarie View A & M, where his top receiver was Otis Taylor, Kearney was the Detroit Lions' 11th pick in the 1965 draft. But after two seasons in which he saw little action, the Lions dropped him. Kansas City picked him up and placed him on the taxi squad for most of the 1967 season. He became a starting strong safety in 1968, a position he held for the next eight years.

Kearney picked off three passes in 1968, his first full season with Kansas City. During the Chiefs' Super Bowl championship season in 1969, he intercepted five passes. His pass coverage was superb and was a big reason for the the success of the Chiefs' defense.

"Jim Kearney is the best man-for-man safety in the league," teammate and fellow safety Johnny Robinson said in 1971. "He really bumps them; he really covers; he doesn't let them drive deep."

Kearney put together one of his best seasons in 1972. He picked off five passes and returned four of them for touchdowns, tying an NFL record. For his career, Kearney had 23 interceptions and five touchdowns in 115 games for Kansas City.

Bill Kenney

Bill Kenney (Kansas Collection, U. of Kansas)

He was never supposed to be the Chiefs' No. 1 quarterback, but throughout his career was treated as such. Kansas City was always looking for someone to replace him, even after he made the Pro Bowl. But Bill Kenney, a free agent from Northern Colorado, possessed a great passing arm and a cool veteran persona that led the Chiefs' offense better than anyone else during his time with the club.

"It's his experience, his knowledge, not only of the league, but of our system and how we want to do things," John Mackovic, Kenny's coach from 1983 to 1986, said.

After three seasons of primarily backup play, Kenney put together one of the most prolific passing seasons in the Chiefs' history. He threw for 4,348 yards and 24 touchdowns and was named to the Pro Bowl. The yardage total is still a Chiefs record by almost 1,000 yards. And then, amazingly, Kenney's starting job was taken away from him the very next year. But when Todd Blackledge, the new starter, faltered, Kenney stepped in and took back his job. He led the Chiefs to a playoff spot in 1986 but missed the playoff game because of an injury.

But he was always made to look over his shoulder, and when Frank Gansz became the head coach in 1987, Kenney again was stripped of his starting role, this time because of an injury, but he eventually returned to the starting lineup. His career had been successful statistically, but Kenney wanted to win.

"I'd pass up a lot of statistics for victories," Kenney said. "I've had some individual success, and I went to the Pro Bowl. Ultimately, quarterbacks are judged by [their] won-lost [record], playoff victories, and Super Bowls."

For his career, Kenney passed for 17,277 yards and 105 touchdowns. He also scored five times and had a career 54 percent completion rate. He played in 123 games for the Chiefs.

Ernie Ladd

Ernie Ladd (Topeka Capital-Journal)

The "Big Cat" came to Kansas City early in the 1968 season and played in a total of just 24 games for the Chiefs. But Ernie Ladd's presence on the defensive line, when coupled with his college teammate Buck Buchanan, gave the Chiefs one of the most intimidating pairs of defensive linemen in the history of the AFL.

"When you have someone with Ladd's size and strength beside you, it makes you more reckless and able to gamble more," Buchanan said of Ladd. "Just since he's been here (1967) I've learned more about this game, little tricks of finesse."

"With the big fellow (Ladd's nickname for Buchanan) and me, it might look like the Empire State Building on the front line," Ladd said. And it did.

For two seasons, Ladd dominated the defensive line, and those playing with him also played better. Kansas City's defense in 1968 was superb, and allowed just 170 points in the regular season.

For his career with the Chiefs, Ladd had one interception with the Chiefs. He sat out the 1969 season after knee surgery, and retired to a career in pro wrestling instead of coming back to pro football.

Albert Lewis

One of the finest cornerbacks in the league during his time with the Chiefs, Lewis had extraordinary coverage skills and was so good that opposing quarterbacks rarely tested him. But as good as he was in the secondary, Lewis stood alone with his special-teams play, blocking 10 punts during his career with Kansas City. He immersed himself in the game, and the results brought many honors, specifically four trips to the Pro Bowl.

"Anyone who has mastered anything had to be consumed by it first," Lewis said of his feelings for football. "I feel bad because of how my obsession affects other people." He shouldn't.

He picked off 38 passes in 11 seasons and also recovered nine fumbles. He blocked a punt that was returned for a touchdown in the 1986 playoff game with the Jets; another three blocks during his career resulted in touchdowns for Kansas City. He was a master at making his way to the punter and almost singlehandedly raised the Chiefs' special teams to the best in the league. He went to the Pro Bowl every year from 1987 to 1990.

In addition to his 38 interceptions for Kansas City, Lewis also recorded 5.5 sacks. He played in 150 games for the Chiefs. He signed with the Raiders as a free agent in 1994.

Albert Lewis (Kansas Collection, U. of Kansas)

Mike Livingston

He waited a long time to be the no. 1 quarterback for the Chiefs, and after he had more than earned the position, it still seemed he had to prove himself every game, almost every time he threw a pass. But Mike Livingston endured the criticism, the trials, and doubt. He was the Chiefs' top quarterback and starter for six-plus seasons. Hank Stram, Livingston's first coach, always had faith in his no. 2 draft pick from SMU.

"He is unusually sure," Stram said of Livingston in 1969. "And for a young quarterback, his leadership is outstanding."

Livingston was thrust into the limelight of the Chiefs' offense in 1969 when Len Dawson injured his knee. The second-year quarterback didn't miss a beat, and neither did the Chiefs. With Livingston's guidance, the Chiefs maintained a course to the Super Bowl while Dawson recuperated.

Mike Livingston (Kansas Collection, U. of Kansas)

"If you're going to be anything in this game," Livingston said, "you have to believe in yourself, first of all." He did. And it was that belief in himself that sustained him in a backup/starter role through Len Dawson's final three seasons with the team. Finally the unchallenged incumbent, he put together his finest season in 1976, throwing for 2,682 yards and 12 touchdowns. But when Marv Levy became the Chiefs' head coach in 1978, Livingston was shelved after one season as the starter.

For his career, Livingston threw for 11,295 yards, ran for 682 yards, and tossed 56 touchdown passes. Not stellar numbers, but he was about something more than statistics. Livingston played in 91 games for the Chiefs.

Nick Lowery

Nick Lowery (Alan Barzee)

Replacing a legend isn't the best way to start a career, but that's what Nick Lowery faced when took over the Chiefs' kicking duties in 1980.

"When I first came, there was pressure to prove I belonged after they cut (Jan) Stenerud," Lowery said in 1987. He quickly proved he belonged, and while Stenerud played another six seasons with two other teams, there was never a doubt that Lowery wasn't the better kicker during that time period.

"Jan Stenerud was my hero when I started kicking," Lowery said. "He defined soccer-style kicking."

Lowery's road to kicking success was long and required a great amount of perseverance. He was cut 11 times by eight different NFL teams before making the Chiefs and ousting Stenerud. And he didn't wait very long to show he belonged, kicking a a team-record 57-yard field goal in his second game with the Chiefs. He made four field goals of 50 yards or more that season and was on his way to establishing himself as one of the greatest kickers in the NFL.

"He can do it, and he knows he can do it," former Chiefs coach Frank Ganz said of Lowery's kicking. "You hope the game comes down to the wire. Nick gives us an edge there."

His career numbers were lofty, the kind that beckon the Hall of Fame: 11 times he scored more than 100 points in a season, made 20 field goals from 50 yards or more, including the Chiefs' team record of 58 yards (he did that twice), and an astonishingly high accuracy rate, making 80 percent of his field attempts for the Chiefs. The one time missing from Lowery's impressive record is a championship.

Lowery was choosen for the Pro Bowl three times (1981, 1990, and 1992), he kicked 329 field goals for Chiefs, and scored 1,466 points for Kansas City, the all-time Chiefs record. For his total career he moved past Stenerud on the all-time scoring list, as he played his final three seasons with the Jets.

"My goal is to be considered the best kicker of all time," Lowery said during his playing days with the Chiefs. "It doesn't make any sense to me to shoot for anything less than that."

Bill Maas

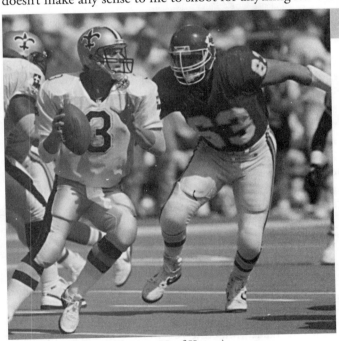

Bill Maas (Kansas Collection, U. of Kansas)

It wasn't a coincidence that the Chiefs returned to winning football shortly after Bill Maas joined the team as their no. 1 draft pick in 1984. He immediately became the starting nose tackle and brought a consistent level of intensity to the defense that had been missing in previous seasons.

"I can honestly say that on Sunday, I hate the people that line up in front of me," Maas said during his playing days. "I look at them like they killed my mother."

"He's an absolutely fierce competitor," said Frank Ganz, the Chiefs' head coach in 1987-88. "He has size, quickness, remarkable athletic skills. But it's the competitor in him that makes him outstanding."

His size matched his competitive nature. Standing 6-foot-5 and weighing between 260 and 270 pounds most of his career, Maas dominated offensive lines, shut down runners, and scared quarterbacks. He could also block field goals, which he did five times in his career.

Statistics alone can tell the story of his dominating career: 40 sacks, 396 total tackles, eight fumble recoveries, two touchdowns, and two safeties. All of which brought him a few awards.

Maas was the AP NFL Defensive Rookie of the Year in 1984, and he played in the Pro Bowl in 1986 and 1987. When he left Kansas City to play a final year in Green Bay, Maas had played in 116 games for Chiefs.

John Mackovic, Maas's first coach in Kansas City, might have said it best when asked about his pro bowl lineman in 1986: "He's the best our league (NFL) has at nose tackle."

Jim Marsalis

Jim Marsalis (Topeka Capital-Journal)

He was the first cornerback ever taken in the first round of the draft by the Chiefs, and his addition to the team was the final piece Hank Stram was looking for to solidify an already outstanding defense.

"I never thought I'd be a first-round draft choice," Jim Marsalis said in 1970. "I didn't think there was a market for a defensive back." He became a starter as a rookie and displayed a poised ability many veterans never achieve with his pass coverage.

Marsalis picked off just two passes his rookie season, a low number only because nobody threw at him. His presence in the Chiefs' secondary was so respected, his play so good, that he was selected for the AFL All-Star game as a rookie.

"I've never seen anybody quite like him," his teammate Johnny Robinson said. "Right from the beginning, he never gave an inch (in his coverage). He's relentless, aggressive, a born cornerback."

Marsalis put an exclamation point on his rookie campaign by picking off a pass in the divisional playoff against the Jets, then snagged another one in the AFL Championship game against the Raiders.

"He's got abnormal quickness," Robinson contributed in his praise for Marsalis. "He wants to shut everyone off so much, he's a problem in practice. In fact, the most difficult thing for Marsalis to learn was that he could be beaten." It was a problem the rest of the NFL endured during Marsalis's seven seasons in Kansas City.

For his career, Marsalis intercepted 14 passes and played in 78 games for Kansas City. And while he never returned to the Pro Bowl, he maintained his high level of play until injuries limited his playing time in 1973 and 1974.

Henry Marshall

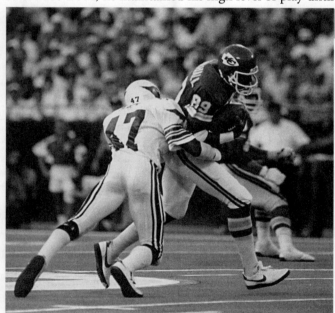

Henry Marshall (Kansas Collection, U. of Kansas)

A model of consistency throughout his career, Henry Marshall came to the Chiefs as a third-round draft pick from the University of Missouri in 1976, and stayed for 12 productive seasons. Overcoming the label of a "bad hands" receiver early on, he became Kansas City's top receiver for most of his career.

Paul Wiggin, Marshall's first coach with the Chiefs, described the wide receiver as "a super kid who can be a premier player." Marshall became just that, and by the time he called it quits, he held the Chiefs' record for the most pass receptions in a career with 416. He also gained 6,545 yards.

Marshall's climb to the top of the Chiefs' receiving records was not easy. The Chiefs had very poor teams in Marshall's first five seasons, and the most passes he caught in that time frame was just 28, and that was in his rookie season. And when Marv Levy took over the team in 1978, he installed a running offense, limiting Marshall's offensive contributions.

He had a breakout year in 1980 when the Chiefs returned to a pro-style offense. Marshall hauled in 47 receptions for 799 yards and six touchdowns and was one of the team's premier receivers through 1986. His best season was 1984 as he totaled 912 yards on 62 catches. For his career, Marshall played in 165 games for Kansas City and scored 35 touchdowns.

Joe Montana

Perhaps the greatest quarterback in the history of the NFL, Joe Montana came to Kansas City for the final two seasons of his extraordinary career in a quest for one more championship, and he came close to fulfilling that goal. The Chiefs had played musical chairs at the quarterback position for years before Montana took over, and while he produced solid numbers, his presence on the field, his winning attitude, and leadership were more important than any touchdown pass he threw.

"Watching him work the two-minute drill was like looking over the shoulder of an artist as he completes a fine painting," Marcus Allen said of Montana's quarterbacking skills. "He never gets rattled, never shows concern. There is about him an attitude that is unbelievably contagious."

Kansas City sent a first-round draft pick to the San Francisco 49ers for Montana in 1993, hoping he was the final piece to the Super Bowl puzzle. He almost was. Montana led the Chiefs to an 11-5 record and the 1993 AFC western division title, two exciting, come-from-behind play-off wins over Pittsburgh and Houston, but couldn't push Kansas City past the Buffalo Bills for the AFC championship. One of his most memorable performances in red and gold came in Denver in 1994, as he led the Chiefs to a last-second touchdown and victory against the Broncos on *Monday Night Football*.

Playing in just 25 games for the Chiefs, Montana threw for 5,427 yards and 29 touchdowns. He was also selected for the Pro Bowl in 1993 and was inducted into the Pro Football Hall of Fame in 2000.

Joe Montana (Alan Barzee)

Stephone Paige

Stephone Paige (Kansas Collection, U. of Kansas)

In a career that included many big games and big plays, one day stands alone as the defining mark of Stephone Paige's career, and sets him apart from other receivers that have played for the Chiefs. Or any other NFL team for that matter. On December 22, 1985, Paige had the game of his life, breaking the NFL record for receiving yards in Kansas City's 38-34 victory over the Chargers. He caught just eight passes that day, but amassed 309 yards, a performance that broke the four-decades record of 303 yards set by Jim Benton of the Cleveland Rams in 1945. Paige also scored two touchdowns.

"I saw it on paper, and it was unreal," Paige said of his record-breaking performance. "I still can't believe it."

That record has since been broken, but it was an unexpected achievement by Paige. He was in his third season with the Chiefs but hadn't really established himself as a premier receiver. All that changed after the San Diego game.

Paige was not a speed burner, but he also wasn't classified as a "possession receiver." He just got open.

"You put the ball in his hands or have him chase the ball or work to get open, and he runs very, very fast," Marty Schottenheimer said of Paige. "He's a big target, he runs well after the catch, and he's one of the hardest-working guys on the team."

Paige's hard work paid off. He played nine seasons for Kansas City, caught 377 passes (fourth all-time for the Chiefs) for 6,341 yards and 49 touchdowns (third all-time for the club). His best season, surprisingly, was 1990, when the Chiefs were primarily a running team. He accumulated 1,021 yards receiving that season on 65 receptions. Early in his career he also returned kickoffs.

"There's still nothing more fun than getting the long one," Paige said in 1990, "having only one guy to beat, and going the distance."

Frank Pitts

Frank Pitts *(Topeka Capital-Journal)*

Hank Stram told the play to Chiefs quarterback Len Dawson. "Listen, let's have a ... 9-0-8, 51 G-O reverse, you know." As Dawson ran back to the huddle, Stram told everyone on the sidelines, "Here comes the reverse from Tight I, it could be wide open." Dawson took the snap, faked to Wendell Hayes on the left side of the line, then turned and gave the ball to a sprinting Frank Pitts, who turned the corner and jetted down the right sideline for 20 yards. It was one of the biggest plays of the Chiefs' Super Bowl IV win over the Minnesota Vikings, and it set up Jan Stenerud's third field goal.

Pitts ran the reverse again in the third quarter and picked up a critical first down. Otis Taylor scored on the next play.

"He has the spirit of a stallion and a great attitude, Stram said of Pitts. "He is very industrious and is a complete team man who consistently expresses 100 percent."

Pitts came to the Chiefs in 1965, the team's fourth-round draft pick. He had speed and desire, but throughout the wide receiver's first three seasons in Kansas City, he acquired a "bad hands" label. He worked through the problem, and when Otis Taylor was injured in 1968, Pitts stepped in. He was a starter the next three seasons, and his end-around reverse runs became a big part of the Chiefs' offense.

In 74 games for Kansas City, Pitts caught 78 passes for 11 touchdowns and ran the ball 24 times for 238 yards and one touchdown. The Chiefs traded Pitts to the Cleveland Browns before the start of the 1971 season.

Tony Richardson

Tony Richardson *(Alan Barzee)*

One of the Chiefs' best free agent pickups, Richardson came into his own in 1999 and solidified his place in Kansas City's backfield. A devastating blocker, he finally had the opportunity to show his running talent in 1999, gaining 387 yards on the ground, which was more than four times his career total at the start of the season. But he had his best year in 2000, running for 697 yards, catching 58 passes for another 468 yards, and scoring six touchdowns. Richardson's running opportunities dropped in 2001 with the addition of Priest Holmes to the backfield, but his blocking skills propelled Holmes to a record-setting season. He was named to *Sports Illustrated's* All-Pro team in 1999 and 2000.

"Some guys try to finesse it and get around hitting, but that's the way the game was built." Richardson said. "You line up mano a mano and the toughest guy is going to win. Especially as a running back, you get hit so much that when you get a chance to hit a linebacker or a safety and put them on their back, it kind of brings energy throughout your body."

"I think he's one of the better fullbacks that I've ever been around," Coach Dick Vermeil said. "I think the great thing about him is, first, what kind of person he is, secondly, his ability to be a one-back running back also. He's not just a fullback who blocks and can carry the ball every once in a while."

For his career, Richardson has gained 1,359 yards rushing, caught 119 passes and scored 20 touchdowns. He has made 96 tackles on special teams and played in a total of 101 games for the Chiefs.

Kevin Ross

Kevin Ross (Kansas Collection, U. of Kansas)

He was called "Rock," a nickname he wasn't particularly fond of, but it fit. He was solid, dependable, loyal, intense. Kevin Ross set a standard for himself of uncompromised excellence, and went about the task of achieving it every game, every play.

"I don't think I have been around anyone quite like Kevin," Marty Schottenheimer said of Ross. "I've seen no evidence that he isn't ready to perform at any moment."

Performing was his game. The Chiefs' seventh pick in the 1984 draft, the Temple product played liked a no. 1 pick his entire career. He became a starter his rookie season and perfected a classic bump-and-run coverage that made him hard to beat in the secondary.

"I don't spend a whole lot of time trying to beat somebody up," Ross said of his bump-and-run coverage. "That is for after the ball is thrown. Then I'll try to get the ball out the best way I can. But I would rather hit a man and knock him loose from the ball. I think it has more effect."

Ross was selected for the Pro Bowl in 1989 and 1990. "I am here to be recognized," Ross said. "I want to be recognized as the best."

For his career in Kansas City, he picked off 30 passes and scored five touchdowns. Ross played in a total of 156 games for the Chiefs. He went to Atlanta as free agent before the 1994 season and later returned to play in five games in 1997.

Dan Saleaumua

Dan Saleaumua (Alan Barzee)

He came to the Chiefs as a Plan B free agent in 1989 from the Detroit Lions, but Dan Saleaumua proved to be one of the best bargins the franchise ever acquired. A defensive tackle, he was a monster force in the middle of the Chiefs' defensive line for eight seasons.

"He's very, very athletic and very, very powerful," Gunther Cunningham said of Saleaumua in 1996. "The was Danny plays, we're blowing up plays in the backfield.'

The big man dominated offensive lines and was one fo the main reasons the Chiefs enjoyed outstanding success with their defensive unit for the first part of the 1990s. Named to *Sports Illustrated*'s All Pro team in 1989 and 1990, he also garnered honors from *Pro Football Weekly* in 1990.

He totaled 531 tackles during his career with the Chiefs, made 29 sacks, recorded three interceptions, scored two touchdowns and two safeties, and blocked a field goal. Saleaumua was selected for the Pro Bowl followign the 1995 season as well as FOX's All-Madden team. Saleaumua played in a total of 125 games for Kansas City.

Will Shields (Alan Barzee)

Will Shields

Currently one of the best offensive guards in the NFL, Will Shields can rightly take his place among the great offensive linemen who have played for the Chiefs in their 40-year history. He earned his seventh consecutive trip to the Pro Bowl in 2001, and he did it with his uncanny consistency, a trademark of his play on the offensive line. Shields excells at run blocking and pass protection..

"On the football field, I'm very much a perfectionist," he said of his playing style. "I don't like to make mistakes."

A third-round draft pick out of Nebraska in 1993, Shields immediately became a starter on the offensive line at right guard, and has started in 142 consecutive games. He made his first Pro Bowl in 1995.

"There is always something you can get better on," Shields said of his play. "In your own mind, you always say I could have done this better, or done that better. If you don't, then you become complacent." This attitude should keep him returning to the Pro Bowl. He was also selected by Lamar Hunt as part of the Chiefs' 40th anniversary team.

"It's an unbelievable honor to actually be a part of that team," Shields said of his selection. "That shows some tremendous respect for what I've done."

Shields has played in 144 games for the Chiefs through the 2001 season and has also appeared in six playoff games.

Neil Smith (Alan Barzee)

Neil Smith

A powerful pass rush, a sack, a baseball swing. Neil Smith's dominating play on the Chiefs' defensive line propelled Kansas City to the top with the league's elite teams and earned him five straight appearances in the Pro Bowl.

The Chiefs' no. 1 draft pick in 1988, Smith suffered through a poor rookie season. But he fine-tuned his hard-work ethic, and produced the results Kansas City had hoped for: in addition to the Pro Bowl selections, he was named the Chiefs' MVP in 1992, led the NFL in sacks in 1993, and improved his rush defense, making him equally hard to block in passing and running situations.

His physical prowess was amazing; with an incredible 7' 1 1/2" wing span, Smith regularly knocked down passes and leveraged his way around offensive linemen. He put together consecutive seasons of outstanding sack totals, collecting 14.5 in 1992, 15 in 1993, 11.5 in 1994, and 12 in 1995. For his career, Smith tallied 86.5 sacks for the Chiefs in 138 games.

He left Kansas City following the 1996 season and signed with the Denver Broncos.

Noland Smith

Chiefs owner Lamar Hunt first saw Noland Smith during the team's 1967 training camp.

"He reminds me a lot of a gnat," Hunt said of the speedy, diminutive player. "Let's call him Super Gnat."

The smallest player in both the AFL and NFL, Smith was only 5' 6", 154 pounds—miniscule in the land of pro football giants. But he was also super, and during his time in Kansas City was highly regarded as the best return specialist in pro football. Chiefs publicist Jim Schaaf said Smith was assigned jersey No. 1 because "that's the only number that will fit on his shirt."

Kansas City selected Smith in the sixth round of the 1967 draft, and the mighty mite from Tennessee State put up big numbers his rookie season. He returned 41 kickoffs for 1,148 yards—tops in the AFL—including a league-record 106-yard return for touchdown against the Broncos in Denver. He also ran back 26 punts in 1967, averaging 8.2 yards per return.

Smith ran with long strides instead of short, choppy steps. He was clocked at 9.4 in the 100-yards dash and gave the Chiefs something they'd never really had in their short history: a break-away threat.

Noland Smith (Topeka Capital-Journal)

"I was sure he would add a new dimension to our club," Hank Stram said. "The more I saw of him in practice, the more I was impressed."

Smith's 1968 season was just as impressive as his first. He returned a punt 80 yards against the Jets for a touchdown and averaged 15 yards per punt return, tops in the AFL. He also averaged 23.9 per kickoff return.

"I'm always thinking that the next kick might be my last one of the game," Smith said in 1968. "I'm really thinking about taking it all the way." Smith was averaging 31.3 yards per kickoff return after six games in 1969, but the Chiefs traded him to San Francisco, where he finished the season. It proved to be his last.

Though he played with the Chiefs just two and a half seasons, the Super Gnat was one of the most exciting players ever to wear the red and gold. His 106-yard kickoff return remains an NFL record.

Gary Spani (Kansas Collection, U. of Kansas)

Gary Spani

Few players in the Chiefs' history have matched the overall quality and productive play that defines Gary Spani's career. A third-round draft pick in 1978 from Kansas State, Spani immediately moved into the starting lineup his rookie season and was the Chiefs' top tackler with 144 stops.

"That first go-round helps a lot for the second go-round," Spani said following his rookie campaign. "I've been learning to play with my teammates." And he learned fast, as the rest of the NFL did, too.

Through his first four seasons, Spani averaged just over 150 tackles per year and was the team leader each season. He also developed a penchant for making big plays, returning an interception against the Oilers for a touchdown in 1980 and returning a fumble 91 yards for a touchdown against the Raiders in 1981. Spani registered 100-plus tackles five seasons in a row, and finished his career with 999 tackles, 669 unassisted stops, 9.5 sacks, nine fumble recoveries, and two interceptions. He missed just 13 games over the course of his career, and played in 124 games. He had back surgery following the 1986 season and wasn't able to return.

The honor that eluded him was a Pro Bowl appearance, which seems strange, considering the excellence of his play. He has yet to be included in the Chiefs Hall of Fame, but that will surely be corrected in time. He was one of the Chiefs' greatest defensive players.

Jack Spikes

Part of Hank Stram's "elephant backfield," Jack Spikes was the Steeler's first choice in the NFL draft, but he ended up with the Texans.

"I told the Steelers I had an offer from the AFL and that I wanted to take it," Spikes said of joining the new league. "Buddy Parker, the Steeler coach, told me, 'Well, when the AFL folds, we'll be back in contact.'" Of course, Spikes never heard from them again, and he helped forge the new league to a success that no one, not even the original eight owners of the AFL, could envision.

Although plauged by injuries throughout his time in Kansas City, Spikes's contributions to the team were invaluable. He was a rugged, pounding runner and a perfect complement to the Texans' other two backs, Abner Haynes and Johnny Robinson. After rushing for 457 yards and five touchdowns in 1960, Spikes missed more than half of the 1961 season, and then another four games in 1962. He was back in time for the 1962 AFL championship game against the Oilers, and was the game's MVP after rushing for 77 yards. His run of 19 yards in the sixth quarter of the overtime contest set up the game-winning field goal.

Spikes was also a kicker, making 68 of 75 PATs, as well as 19 field goals in his career for the Chiefs. He finished with 1,392 yards rushing and 14 touchdowns before going to Houston in 1965.

Jack Spikes (Bettmann/CORBIS)

Dave Szott

An unheralded seventh-round draft selection by the Chiefs in 1990, Szott exceeded all expectations and became one of the franchise's most consistent performers on the offensive line. Known for his hardhat and lunchpail approach to the game, Szott made his presence known on the team immediately, starting 11 of 16 games his rookie season. He remained a mainstay on the Chiefs' offensive line for the next decade, and teamed with Will Shields and Tim Grunhard from 1993 to 2000 to form one of the best interior lines in the NFL.

Szott's blocking was a major reason the Chiefs enjoyed continued success with their running game throughout his tenure with the team. He consistently performed at an all-pro level but was never selected to the Pro Bowl. Szott was picked first team All-NFL by Sports Illustrated, Pro Football Weekly and Football Digest in 1997, as well as the All-Madden team.

After missing most of the 1998 season, Szott came back with a strong performance in 1999. An injury in the first game of the 2000 season ended his career with the Chiefs, but he returned in 2001 to play for the Washington Redskins. He played in 142 games for Kansas City.

Dave Szott (Alan Barzee)

Tamarick Vanover

For most of his career, Tamarick Vanover was the most consistent—and dangerous—return man in the NFL. He was a playmaker with a tremendous open-field running talent and a threat to score every time he touched the football.

Vanover had a sensational rookie season in 1995, accumulating 1,897 all-purpose yards en route to winning the Mack Lee Hill Award as the team's top first-year man. He returned a punt 86 yards for a touchdown to win an overtime contest against San Diego and also ran back two kickoffs for scores. Vanover returned one kickoff for a score in 1996 and 1997, and returned two punts for scores in 1999. In all, he's returned four punts and four kickoffs for touchdowns.

Also used as a backup receiver, Vanover caught 39 passes for 564 yards and three touchdowns during his time with the Chiefs as well. After suffering through a slump for most of the '99 season, his 80-yard punt return against Denver was a game-winner. He also ran a punt back against the Raiders in the '99 season finale.

Vanover was released by the Chiefs in April 2000 because of his admitted involvement in illegal trafficking activities.

Tamarick Vanover (Alan Barzee)

Elmo Wright

He pranced, then danced, and the Chiefs fans loved it. Opponents hated it, but in Elmo Wright, Kansas City had one of the most talented—and entertaining—wide receivers in the game.

The flamboyant wideout from the University of Houston was a smash hit his rookie season of 1971. Wright caught just 26 passes for 528 yards and three touchdowns, but it was what he did after scoring that thrust him into the national limelight.

He had the celebration dance. A high-stepping, strutting, knees-in-the-air, step-in-place dance that immediately gave him a signature, and hope for Chiefs fans everywhere that he would score, and score a lot. Others saw it as hotdogging and showboating. But his coach, the usually straight-laced Hank Stram, didn't mind.

"He said doing it was all right, because I was honest in doing it, it was an honest expression of my feelings," Wright said of Stram in 1971. "But he warned me there might be a few defensive backs in the league who might take it personally." There might have been a few who did,

Elmo Wright (Topeka Capital-Journal)

but injuries shortened Wright's playing time in Kansas City, and he only scored seven touchdowns for the Chiefs.

"As long as it's not hurting anything, why shouldn't I show my enthusiasm? People expect me to do it after I score, and I don't mind obliging them."

After playing in 45 games over four seasons and catching 66 passes, Wright went to the Oilers. His mark on Kansas City, and pro football in general, was much greater than numbers. His celebration dance was infectious, and soon after he started it, it was imitated by many.

KANSAS CITY CHIEFS
All-Time Roster

For a player to be included on the Chiefs' all-time roster, he must have been on the active list for at least one regular-season game, or active for a playoff game. Players who accrued at least one season of veteran status on the injured/reserve list are also included on this list. The one exception to the roster-qualifying rule is Stone Johnson, who received a fatal injury in the Chiefs' final 1963 preseason game. Although he never played in a regular season game (he was a rookie in 1963), the Chiefs retired his number; he deserves to be included on the all-time roster.

Abell, Bud — LB — 52 — Missouri — 1966-68

A native of Kansas City, Mo., Abell was drafted by the Chiefs as a future pick in 1964. Spent most of the 1966 season on special teams. Became the regular right linebacker in 1967 after E.J. Holub was hurt. Intercepted two passes in 1968. Played in 40 games for the Chiefs.

Acker, Bill — NT/DE — 64, 93 — Texas — 1982, 87

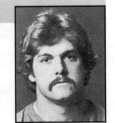

Signed with Chiefs as a free agent (from St. Louis) and was released before 1982 regular season started, but rejoined club for final three games after Mike Bell was hurt. Returned to Chiefs in 1987 as a replacement player and played in two games. Played in a total of five games for Kansas City.

Adamle, Mike — RB — 1 — Northwestern — 1971-72

A fifth-round draft pick, Adamle spent two seasons with the Chiefs before moving to the Jets, and then to the Bears. He rushed for 43 yards in 1971, and 303 in 1972. Adamle scored two touchdowns and played in 22 games for Kansas City. He moved into broadcasting following the end of his playing career in 1976.

Adams, Tony — QB — 11 — Utah State — 1975-78

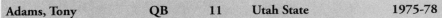

Came to the Chiefs as a free agent; Adams appeared in 50 games for Kansas City, throwing nine touchdown passes. His best effort was against Buffalo in 1976 when he completed 17 of 32 attempts for 319 yards.

Adams, Vashone — S — 26 — Eastern Michigan — 1998

Joined the Chiefs as a free agent; missed the 1998 season because of injuries.

Adickes, Mark — G — 61 — Baylor — 1986-89

The Chiefs' first pick in the 1984 supplemental draft, Adickes spent two seasons in the USFL before coming to Kansas City in 1986. Was a starter on the offensive line during his tenure with the Chiefs. Caught a touchdown pass in 1987. Played in 53 games.

Adkins, Kevin — C — 65 — Oklahoma — 1987

A replacement player during the 1987 NFL players' strike; played in two games for the Chiefs.

Agajanian, Ben — K — 3 — New Mexico — 1961

After a three-year absence from pro football, Agajanian played for the Chargers in 1960 and joined the Texans as a backup kicker for three games in the 1961 season.

Player	Position	Jersey(s) Worn	College	Year(s) Played
Agee, Tommie	RB	32	Auburn	1989

Signed as a free agent from Seattle; had one rushing attempt for three yards. Agee played in nine games for the Chiefs.

Aguiar, Louie	P	5	Utah State	1994-98

Aguiar handled the Chiefs' punting duties from 1994 through 1998. Second on the club's all-time punting list, Aguiar had 421 punts for 17,930 yards for Kansas City, an average of 42.6. Got the ball off extremely fast and also served as the team's placeholder. Played in 80 games for the Chiefs; threw one pass for 35 yards in 1997, ran the ball twice in 1997 for 11 yards.

Ale, Arnold	LB	56	UCLA	1994

Signed with the Chiefs as a free agent, coming from Seattle's practice squad. Played in two games for the Chiefs.

Alexander, Derrick	WR	82	Michigan	1998-2001

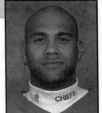

see Other Chiefs Greats

Alford, Darnell	T	72	Boston College	2000-01

Kansas City's sixth-round pick in the 2000 draft, Alford was active for four games and played in one during his rookie campaign. He appeared in two games in 2001, and has played in three total games for the Chiefs.

Allen, Marcus	RB	32	Southern California	1993-97

see Other Chiefs Greats

Allen, Nate	CB	48	Texas Southern	1971-74

An 11th-round draft pick in 1971, Allen began his career as a special-teams player before gaining playing time in the secondary. Was starter in 1973-74; intercepted three passes; played in 44 games for the Chiefs. Played for San Francisco, Minnesota, and Detroit after leaving the Chiefs.

Allen, Taje	CB	26	Texas	2001

Came to the Chiefs from the St. Louis Rams as an unrestricted free agent. Played primarily on special teams and finished the 2001 season with 11 tackles, six stops on special teams, and played in 16 games.

Allotey, Victor	T	69	Indiana	2001

Joined Chiefs as a free agent from Buffalo, Allotey was on the practice squad most of the 2001 season and on the inactive list the final game of the season.

Player	Position	Jersey(s) Worn	College	Year(s) Played

Alt, John   T   76   Iowa   1984-96

see Chiefs Hall of Fame

Anders, Kimble   RB   38   Houston   1991-2000

see Other Chiefs Greats

Anderson, Curtis   DE   90   Central State (Ohio)   1979

Signed as a free agent a third of the way into the 1979 season after Mike Bell was injured. Totaled four tackles in a reserve role. Played in six games.

Anderson, Darren   CB   44   Toledo   1994-97

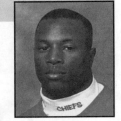

The Chiefs traded a 1995 seventh-round draft pick to Tampa Bay for Anderson. Was a key member of the special teams in 1994-96. Returned an interception 55 yards for a touchdown against the Raiders in 1997; recorded two sacks in 1997. Played in 53 games for Kansas City.

Anderson, Erick   LB   50   Michigan   1992-93

A seventh-round draft pick in 1992, Anderson spent his rookie campaign on the injured reserved list. Played in eight games in 1993, starting in one. Recorded seven special teams tackles in 1993.

Andrews, Billy   LB   53   Southwest Louisiana   1976-77

Came to the Chiefs during 1976 training camp and started all 14 games at left linebacker in 1976. Had one interception for Kansas City. Played in 28 games over two seasons.

Andrusyshyn, Zenon   P   7   UCLA   1978

The Chiefs' punter for the 1978 season, Andrusyshyn came to Kansas City after a seven-year career in the CFL. Punted 79 times with a 41.1 yard average; also performed kickoffs for the team. Played in 16 games for the Chiefs.

Ane, Charlie   C   56   Michigan State   1975-80

Won the job of long snapper for the Chiefs in 1975 and held it for six seasons. Had three career starts. His father was also a center in the NFL, playing for Detroit. Played in 90 games over six seasons for the Chiefs.

Arbanas, Fred   TE   84   Michigan State   1962-70

see Chiefs Hall of Fame

Arnold, Jim — P — 6 — Vanderbilt — 1983-85

A fifth-round draft pick in 1983, Arnold was the team's punter for three seasons. He led the league in punting attempts twice with 98 in 1984, and 93 in 1985, and led the league with a 44.9 average in 1984. Punted in 48 games for the Chiefs before going to Detroit in 1986.

Arnold, Walt — TE — 87 — New Mexico — 1984-87

Joined Kansas City before the seventh game of the 1984 season, coming from Washington; was the starting tight end through the 1986 season. Caught 62 passes for 629 yards and three touchdowns. Played in 47 games for the Chiefs.

Ashley, Walker Lee — LB — 54 — Penn State — 1989

Signed by the Chiefs before the 1989 season. Was a starter most of the season; played in 16 games with one interception.

Atkins, Larry — S — 35 — UCLA — 1999-2001

A third round draft choice in 1999, Atkins played in nine games during his rookie season, appeared in 15 games in 2000, and saw action in 12 games during 2001. Used primarily on special teams most of his career, Atkins has also played defense during goal line situations. He's made 32 tackles on special teams in three seasons and has played in a total of 36 games for Kansas City.

Auer, Scott — G/T — 68 — Michigan State — 1984-85

Drafted in the ninth round by the Chiefs in 1984. Played primarily on the special teams in 1984; returned to club before the sixth game of the 1985 season and started six games. Played in 23 games for the Chiefs.

Austin, Hise — CB — 21 — Prairie View — 1975

Joined the club late in the 1975 season, playing primarily on the special teams for three games.

Avery, Ken — LB — 53 — Southern Mississippi — 1975

Obtained from Cincinnati for a fourth-round pick in the 1975 draft, Avery started occasionally for the Chiefs during the 1975 season. Played in 14 games with Kansas City.

B

Baab, Mike — C — 60 — Texas — 1992

Brought to Kansas City to plug injury holes, Baab played in and started three games at center.

Player	Position	Jersey(s) Worn	College	Year(s) Played

Baber, Billy TE 45 Virginia 2001

The Chiefs' first of two selections in the fifth round of the 2001 draft, Baber played in one game of the 2001 season.

Bailey, Mark RB 39 Cal State (Long Beach) 1977-78

Came to the Chiefs as a fourth-round pick in the 1977 draft; rushed for 106 yards against Cincinnati in 1978; carried the ball 149 times for 564 yards in his career; scored three touchdowns; Bailey played in 27 games for the Chiefs.

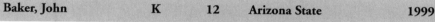

Bailey, Victor WR 85, 88 Missouri 1995-96

The Chiefs traded a 1995 second-round draft pick and a 1996 fourth-round draft pick to Philadelphia for Bailey and a 1995 fourth-round pick; was inactive for the entire 1995 season; played in two games in 1996 and caught one pass for 12 yards.

Baker, John K 12 Arizona State 1999

Played in two games as the Chiefs' kickoff specialist.

Baldinger, Gary DE 91 Wake Forest 1986-88

Selected by Kansas City in the ninth round of the 1986 draft; played as a special teams player and backup defensive lineman; brother of Rich Baldinger; played in 23 games for the Chiefs.

Baldinger, Rich T 77 Wake Forest 1983-92

A free-agent acquisition in 1983, Baldinger proved to be one of the most versatile players in the Chiefs' history, providing hard-nosed, dependable service during his time in Kansas City. Played every position on the offensive line except center (53 at right tackle, 33 at left guard, four at left tackle and two at left guard). Won the Chiefs' 1992 Ed Block Courage Award; played in 139 games for the Chiefs, starting in 92.

Barbaro, Gary S 26 Nicholls State 1976-82

see Other Chiefs Greats

Barker, Bryan P 4 Santa Clara 1990-93

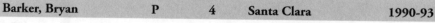

Came to Kansas City as a free agent after failing to make the Broncos and Seahawks. Took over the Chiefs' punting duties in the fourth game of the 1990 season and remained the team's punter through the 1993 season. Punted 272 time with Kansas City, averaging 41.4 yards per punt. Played in 60 games for the Chiefs.

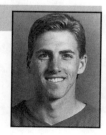

Player	Position	Jersey(s) Worn	College	Year(s) Played

Barndt, Tom — DT/G — 71 — Pittsburgh — 1996-99

A sixth-round draft pick in 1995, Barndt was originally set to play on the offensive line, but switched to defense before the 1997 season; became the starting nose tackle in 1998 and used his strength and toughness to become a pivotal part of the Chiefs' defensive line. Recorded 63 tackles, 3.5 sacks and 11 QB pressures in 1998; also recovered two fumbles. Had two sacks in 1999. Barndt has played in 61 games for the Chiefs, starting in 30.

Barnes, Charley — E — 82 — Northeast Louisiana — 1961

Picked up by the Texans after being drafted by Buffalo, Barnes played in four games and caught one pass for 13 yards.

Barnes, Lew — WR/KR — 80 — Oregon — 1989

Played in two games for the Chiefs, returning two punts for a total of 41 yards.

Barnes, Pat — QB — 17 — California — 1997

Spent most of the 1997 season on the inactive list and never played in a game.

Barnett, Tim — WR — 82 — Jackson State — 1991-93

A no. 3 pick in the 1991 draft, Barnett was known for making big plays at crucial moments in a game. His biggest catch came in the 1993 wild-card playoff game against the Steelers, a seven-yard touchdown pass from Joe Montana to send the game to overtime, which the Chiefs eventually won. Caught 82 passes for 1,188 yards and 10 touchdowns. He played in 44 games, and was a starter 11 times.

Bartee, William — CB — 24 — Oklahoma — 2000-01

The Chiefs' second round selection in the 2000 draft, Bartee racked up 12 tackles for the special teams throughout the 2000 season, and also saw duty at cornerback in 12 games, starting three times. He started five times in 2001 and made 38 total tackles for the season. He's played in a total of 32 games with 68 tackles, 23 special team tackles, and 12 passes defended.

Barton, Jim — C — 50 — Marshall — 1960

A free-agent signee, Barton was the Texans' starting center for the 1960 season. He played in 14 games.

Bartrum, Mike — TE — 87 — Marshall — 1993

Came to the Chiefs as a rookie free agent; played in three games.

Baugh, Tom — C — 58 — Southern Illinois — 1986-88

Selected in the fourth round of the 1986 draft, Baugh was the club's starting center in 1987-88. Played in 29 games for Kansas City.

Player	Position	Jersey(s) Worn	College	Year(s) Played

Bayless, Martin   S   21, 30   Bowling Green   1992-93, 1995-96

A "Plan B" free agent, Bayless signed with the Chiefs before the 1992 season and was the starting strong safety. Played with the Redskins in 1994, returned to Kansas City for the 1995 season. Intercepted three passes and made 278 tackles; played in 59 games.

Beathard, Pete   QB   10   USC   1964-67, 1973

A first-round pick by both the Chiefs and the Lions, Beathard could never oust Len Dawson from the starting quarterback, but played well enough in relief to cause a bit of a quarterback controversy. Traded to Houston midway through the 1967 season for Ernie Ladd. Threw eight touchdown passes for the Chiefs and also rushed for 349 yards. Beathard played in 51 Chiefs games.

Beckman, Ed   TE   85   Florida State   1977-84

Came to Kansas City as a free agent and was used as a blocker in short-yardage situations most of his career. Caught 23 passes for 198 yards and one touchdown. Played in 107 games.

Beisel, Monty   DE   96   Kansas State   2001

Selected in the fourth round of the 2001 draft, Beisel played in all 16 games of the 2001 season. He collected 13 total tackles on defense and added another 16 stops on special teams. Beisel also returned three kickoffs for 35 yards and forced a fumble.

Beisler, Randy   G   64   Indiana   1975

Came to Kansas City in a trade with San Francisco (Nate Allen). Became the starting left guard in the second game of the season. An injury in the third game ended his season and career. Played in three games.

Bell, Billy   CB   40   Lamar   1991

Bell played in eight games for the Chiefs and snagged one interception.

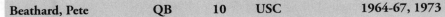

Bell, Bobby   LB   78   Minnesota   1963-74

see Chiefs in the Pro Football Hall of Fame

Bell, Mike   DE   99   Colorado State   1979-85, 1987-91

see Other Chiefs Greats

Belser, Ceasar   DB   24   Arkansas. AM&N   1968-71

A free agent, Belser moved from the taxi squad to the team. Primarily a special teams player, Belser played both safety positions, recovered four fumbles, and played in 56 games for the Chiefs.

Player	Position	Jersey(s) Worn	College	Year(s) Played

Belser, Jason S 29 Oklahoma 2001

The Chiefs' special teams captain for the 2001 season, Belser joined the club as a free agent after nine seasons with the Indianapolis Colts. A Kansas City native and son of former Chiefs' player Ceasar Belser, Jason played in 16 games in 2001 and registered 15 special team tackles.

Belton, Horace RB 35 Southeast Louisiana 1978-81

Belton rushed for 486 yards from 1978-80, averaging 3.6 yards per carry. Scored three touchdowns; returned 37 kickoffs, averaging 21.6 per return. Played in 46 games.

Bennett, Donnell RB 30 Miami (Fla.) 1994-99

The Chiefs' no. 2 draft pick in 1994, Bennett started at fullback and switched to halfback at the start of the 1998 season. A bruising runner who excels at the smashmouth style of football the Chiefs have employed for much of the past decade, he's also a excellent blocker and pass receiver. Bennett put together his best season in 1999, rushing for 627 yards and scoring eight touchdowns. His best single-game performance came against the Raiders in 1998 when he totaled 115 yards. He also had three rushing touchdowns against Philadelphia in 1998. For his career, Bennett has 1,878 yards rushing, an average of 3.9 yards per carry. He's caught 49 passes for 223 yards and one touchdown and played in 79 games for the Chiefs.

Bentley, Scott K 9 Florida State 1999

Played in two games as the Chiefs' kickoff specialist.

Bergey, Bruce TE 84 UCLA 1971

A 14th-round selection in the 1971 draft, Bergey played in six games before moving on to Houston.

Bernet, Ed E 85 SMU 1960

Bernet caught four passes for 49 yards in a backup role; played in nine games.

Bernhardt, Roger G 68 Kansas 1975

Signed as a free-agent, Bernhardt filled in for the injury-plagued offensive line in 1975. He played in four games.

Best, Keith LB 55 Kansas State 1972

A free-agent signee, Best played in six games for the Chiefs.

Biodrowski, Dennis G 61 Memphis State 1963-67

Signed as a free agent, Biodrowski added depth to the offensive line and played on the special teams. He played in 30 games.

Birden, J.J.   WR   88   Oregon   1990-94

An exciting receiver during his time in Kansas City, Birden came to the Chiefs as a free agent and moved from the practice squad to a starting wide receiver position in one season. He pulled in 183 passes for 2,819 yards and 14 touchdowns during his time in Kansas City. Occasionally returned punts; his best season was 1993 when he caught 51 passes for 721 yards and two touchdowns. He was originally drafted by Cleveland in the eighth round of the 1988 draft. Played in 71 games.

Bishop, Sonny   G   66   Fresno State   1962

A reserve lineman and special teams player for the '62 AFL Champs. Played in 14 games.

Black, James   DE   69   South Carolina State   1987

A replacement player during the 1987 NFL players' strike; played in one game for the Chiefs.

Blackledge, Todd   QB   14   Penn State   1983-87

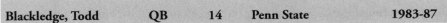
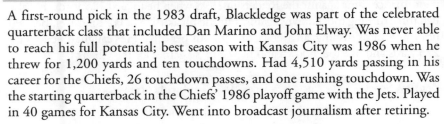

A first-round pick in the 1983 draft, Blackledge was part of the celebrated quarterback class that included Dan Marino and John Elway. Was never able to reach his full potential; best season with Kansas City was 1986 when he threw for 1,200 yards and ten touchdowns. Had 4,510 yards passing in his career for the Chiefs, 26 touchdown passes, and one rushing touchdown. Was the starting quarterback in the Chiefs' 1986 playoff game with the Jets. Played in 40 games for Kansas City. Went into broadcast journalism after retiring.

Blackshear, Jeff   G   69   NE Louisiana   2000

Signed with the Chiefs after playing seven seasons with Seattle and Baltimore. Blackshear played in all 16 games during the 2000 season for Kansas City and started in 15 of those after Dave Szott was injured.

Blakely, Robert   WR   83   North Dakota State   1982

A free-agent signee, Blakely played in two games for the Chiefs.

Blanton, Jerry   LB   57   Kentucky   1979-85

Joined Kansas City as a free agent; became a starter in 1981; led Chiefs in tackles in 1983; compiled 474 career tackles (291 unassisted); started 49 times; played in 93 games.

Bledsoe, Curtis   RB   30   San Diego State   1981-82

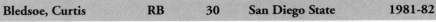

A free-agent acquisition, Bledsoe ran for 85 yards, caught four passes for 32 yards and returned six kickoffs. Played in 16 games.

Player	Position	Jersey(s) Worn	College	Year(s) Played

Blundin, Matt — QB — 14 — Virginia — 1992-95

A second-round pick in the 1992 draft, the Chiefs hoped Blundin would develop into an NFL-caliber quarterback; Blundin appeared in two games for the Chiefs and threw just eight passes.

Bolden, Juran — CB — 43 — Miss. Delta, J.C. — 1999

Played in seven games for the Chiefs and made three tackles on special teams.

Bono, Steve — QB — 13 — UCLA — 1994-96

Came to Kansas City from San Francisco for a 1995 fourth-round draft pick. Took over quarterbacking duties when Joe Montana retired and led Chiefs to a 13-3 record in 1995, passing for 3,121 yards and 21 touchdowns. Had one touchdown pass and three interceptions in playoff loss to Colts. Threw for 6,489 yards and 37 touchdowns during time with Chiefs; played in 36 games.

Booker, Vaughn — DE — 99 — Cincinnati — 1994-97

Came to Chiefs via free agency after playing two seasons in the CFL; totaled 6.5 sacks in time at Kansas City; scored a touchdown on a 14-yard fumble recovery run in 1995; had 10 tackles in two postseason games (1994-95); played in 56 games.

Bookman, John — DB — 22 — Miami (Fla.) — 1960

An original member of the Texans, Bookman played in 14 games and collected four interceptions in the club's inaugural season.

Boydston, Max — E — 81 — Oklahoma — 1960-61

The franchise's starting tight end its first two seasons, Boydston caught 41 passes for 524 yards and four touchdowns. He played in 25 games.

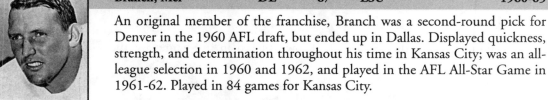

Branch, Mel — DE — 87 — LSU — 1960-65

An original member of the franchise, Branch was a second-round pick for Denver in the 1960 AFL draft, but ended up in Dallas. Displayed quickness, strength, and determination throughout his time in Kansas City; was an all-league selection in 1960 and 1962, and played in the AFL All-Star Game in 1961-62. Played in 84 games for Kansas City.

Brannon, Solomon — DB — 38 — Morris Brown — 1965-66

Made the team in 1965 after just missing out in 1964. Used primarily on kickoff returns, Brannon averaged 25.1 yards per return in 1965. Played in 13 games.

Briggs, Bob — DE — 84 — Heidelberg — 1974

Came to Kansas City from Cleveland for a no. 9 draft pick; played primarily on special teams; hurt knee and missed second half of 1974 season. Played in seven games.

Brockington, John — RB — 43 — Ohio State — 1977

The Chiefs picked up Brockington when MacArthur Lane was injured, and he filled in nicely. Ran the ball 54 times for 161 yards and one touchdown; also caught a touchdown pass. Played in 10 games for the Chiefs.

Brooker, Tommy — E/K — 81 — Alabama — 1962-66

Tommy Brooker came to the Texans as a 17th-round draft pick and immediately took over the team's kicking duties; also played tight end. His 25-yard field goal after 77 minutes and 54 seconds of play won the 1962 AFL Championship game for the Texans, 20-17. Brooker kicked 149 consecutive extra points; holds the club record for the most extra points attempted and made in a game with eight; caught six passes for 170 yards and three touchdowns; led the team in scoring in 1965 with 79 points; scored a total of 290 points in his career, adding 41 field goals to his string of extra points. Brooker played in 55 games for the franchise.

Brooks, Bucky — CB — 45 — North Carolina — 1997-98

Came to Kansas City from the Packers and saw special teams action in the club's last three games of 1997. Played in six games in 1998, a total of nine games for the Chiefs.

Brown, Aaron — DE — 87 — Minnesota — 1966-72

The Chiefs' first-round draft pick in 1966, Brown was a dominating force on the Chiefs' defensive line during their glory years. He had outstanding speed and punishing strength. His best performances came during Kansas City's run to the Super Bowl in 1969 as he dominated his offensive opponents; he had two sacks against Oakland in the 1969 AFL championship game, and dropped Minnesota quarterback Joe Kapp for 13-yard loss in Super Bowl IV. Brown played in 78 games for the Chiefs.

Brown, Eric — WR — 86 — Tulsa — 1987

A replacement player during the 1987 NFL players' strike; played in two games, catching five passes for 69 yards.

Brown, Larry — T — 79 — Miami (Fla.) — 1978-79

A ninth-round pick in the 1978 draft, Brown played in five games for the Chiefs.

Brown, Theotis — RB — 27 — UCLA — 1983-84

Came to the Chiefs from Seattle early in the 1983 season and made a big impact on the team's running game, gaining 467 yards and eight touchdowns. Ran for 337 yards and four touchdowns in 1984; caught 85 passes in that two-year period for 654 yards and two touchdowns. Brown suffered a heart attack in February of 1985 and wasn't able to return to the team. Moved successfully into radio, covering and commenting on the Chiefs. Played in 26 games.

Player	Position	Jersey(s) Worn	College	Year(s) Played

Browning, John DE 93 **West Virginia** **1996-2001**

A third-round pick in the 1996 draft, Browning's 1998 season was cut short by injury and he missed the entire 1999 season. Came back strong with a good season in 2000, recording six sacks and 71 tackles. His 2001 season was again cut short by injury. When healthy, Browning provides strength in the middle of the defensive line. In his six seasons he's totaled 209 tackles, 13.5 sacks and played in 57 games.

Brunson, Larry WR 83 **Colorado** **1974-77**

A versatile receiver, Brunson came to the Chiefs as a free agent; caught an 84-yard pass from Len Dawson for a touchdown in 1974; returned 71 punts for Kansas City, averaging 8.6 yards per return; also returned kickoffs; caught 98 passes for 1,723 yards and five touchdowns. Played in 53 games.

Bryant, Bob E 89 **Texas** **1960**

Caught five passes for the Texans in ten games.

Bryant, Trent CB 45 **Arkansas** **1982-83, 1987**

A free-agent signee, Bryant intercepted two passes and played in 28 games for the Chiefs. Returned in 1987 as a replacement player.

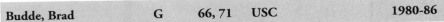

Buchanan, Buck DT 86 **Grambling** **1963-75**

see Chiefs in the Pro Football Hall of Fame

Budde, Brad G 66, 71 **USC** **1980-86**

Like his father, Brad Budde was a first-round pick (1980) and immediately made an impact on the offensive line. It was the first time in the league's history that a father and son had been chosen in the first round of the draft by the same team. Budde became a starter late in his rookie year and provided the Chiefs with solid line play for the next six seasons. Played in 92 games for the Chiefs.

Budde, Ed G 71 **Michigan State** **1963-76**

see Chiefs Hall of Fame

Burford, Chris E 88 **Stanford** **1960-67**

see Chiefs Hall of Fame

Burgmeier, Ted S 48 **Notre Dame** **1978**

Played in eight games for the Chiefs, returning four punts for 59 yards.

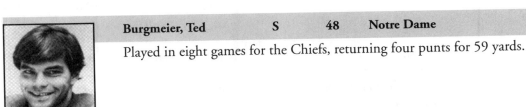

Player	Position	Jersey(s) Worn	College	Year(s) Played

Burks, Ray — LB — 59 — UCLA — 1977

Selected in the 12th round of the 1977 draft, Burks carried the ball once for 51 yards in 13 games with the Chiefs.

Burruss, Lloyd — S — 34 — Maryland — 1981-91

see Chiefs Hall of Fame

Bush, Lew — LB — 51 — Washington State — 2000-01

Signed as a free agent with Kansas City from the Chargers to fill the void left by Derrick Thomas's death, Bush provided strong run defense and started in eight games during the 2000 season. He finished the 2000 season with 33 tackles and one sack. Bush missed four games in 2001 because of an abdominal injury, but still started 11 times and totaled 42 tackles. For his career in Kansas City, Bush has 75 total tackles in 28 games.

Butler, Gary — TE — 82 — Rice — 1973

A second-round pick in the 1973 draft, Butler caught eight passes for 124 yards and two touchdowns. Played in 14 games.

Butler, Gerald — WR — 86 — Nicholls State — 1977

Signed with the Chiefs but never played in a game.

C

Cadrez, Glenn — LB — 51 — Houston — 2001

Signed with the Chiefs after playing nine seasons with the Jets and Broncos, and added good depth to the Chiefs linebacking corps. Cadrez started in five games, blocked a punt, partially blocked another punt and racked up 39 total tackles for the 2001 season. He's played in 16 games for the Chiefs.

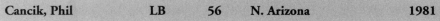

Cadwell, John — G — 61 — Oregon State — 1961

A replacement player during the 1987 NFL players' strike; played in four games for the Texans.

Cancik, Phil — LB — 56 — N. Arizona — 1981

Came to Chiefs from the Giants; played primarily on special teams; played in 16 games.

Cannon, Billy — TE — 80 — LSU — 1970

The AFL's first big-name star, Cannon came to Kansas City from Oakland for his final season. Originally a halfback, Cannon had switched to tight end with the Raiders, and that's what he played for the Chiefs. He caught seven passes for 125 yards in six games.

Player	Position	Jersey(s) Worn	College	Year(s) Played

Cannon, Mark — C — 70 — Texas-Arlington — 1989

Came to the Chiefs from Green Bay and filled in at center and on special teams. Played in 11 games.

Carlson, Dean — QB — 9 — Iowa State — 1972-74

On the active roster for three seasons, Carlson played in just one game, in 1974. Threw 15 passes and completed seven for 116 yards with one interception.

Carolan, Reg — E — 80 — Idaho — 1964-68

Came to the Chiefs from the Chargers and provided strong depth at tight end for five seasons. Caught 20 passes for 325 yards and four touchdowns. Played in Super Bowl I against the Packers and caught one pass. Played in 62 games.

Carruth, Paul Ott — RB — 30 — Alabama — 1989

Came to the Chiefs from the Packers and played in two games during the 1989 season.

Carson, Carlos — WR — 88 — LSU — 1980-89

see Other Chiefs Greats

Carter, Dale — CB — 34 — Tennessee — 92-98

see Other Chiefs Greats

Carter, M.L. — CB — 42 — Cal State-Fullerton — 1979-81

A free-agent signee, Carter was named to the *Football Digest* All-Rookie team in 1979; had two interceptions in the Chiefs' 1979 win at Oakland; finished injury-shortened career with three interceptions and played in 33 games.

Carter, Perry — CB — 22 — Southern Mississippi — 1995

Played in two games for the Chiefs.

Case, Frank — DE — 95 — Penn State — 1981

Selected in the 11th round of the 1981 draft, Case played in seven games, primarily on the special teams, before injuring his knee.

Cash, Keith — TE — 89 — Texas — 1992-96

Came to the Chiefs a "Plan B" free agent and became one of the most productive tight ends in the franchise's history. Best season was 1995 when he grabbed 42 passes for 419 yards; his touchdown reception from Joe Montana in the 1993 divisional playoff against Houston sparked the Chiefs to a come-from-behind win and advanced the team to its first-ever AFC championship game. Caught 111 passes in 59 games for 1,046 yards and nine touchdowns for Kansas City.

Player	Position	Jersey(s) Worn	College	Year(s) Played

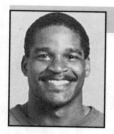

Cherry, Deron — S — 20 — Rutgers — 1981-91

see Chiefs Hall of Fame

Chilton, Gene — G/C — 62 — Texas — 1989

Played in 16 games for the Chiefs as a reserve offensive lineman.

Christopher, Herb — S — 41 — Morris Brown — 1979-82

Came to Kansas City as a free agent; Christopher was both a starter and nickel back during his career; best season was 1980 when he made 78 tackles and two interceptions. Played in a total of 50 games and had four interceptions.

Clark, Bruce — DE — 95 — Penn State — 1989

Played in 11 games as a backup on the defensive line.

Clark, Wayne — QB — 13 — U.S. International — 1975

Played in one game for the Chiefs.

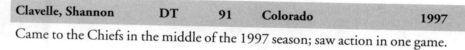

Clavelle, Shannon — DT — 91 — Colorado — 1997

Came to the Chiefs in the middle of the 1997 season; saw action in one game.

Clements, Tom — QB — 2 — Notre Dame — 1980

Performed in one game for the Chiefs, throwing 12 passes and completing seven for 77 yards. Also fumbled twice.

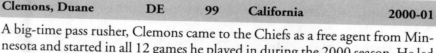

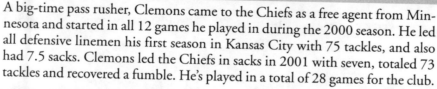

Clemons, Duane — DE — 99 — California — 2000-01

A big-time pass rusher, Clemons came to the Chiefs as a free agent from Minnesota and started in all 12 games he played in during the 2000 season. He led all defensive linemen his first season in Kansas City with 75 tackles, and also had 7.5 sacks. Clemons led the Chiefs in sacks in 2001 with seven, totaled 73 tackles and recovered a fumble. He's played in a total of 28 games for the club.

Clemons, Michael — RB/KR — 46 — William & Mary — 1987

A no. 8 pick in the 1987 draft (from the 1985 Willie Scott trade), Clemons was used primarily as a punt-return specialist, returning 19 punts for 162 yards. He also ran the ball twice for seven yards. Played in eight games.

Player	Position	Jersey(s) Worn	College	Year(s) Played

Cloud, Mike — RB — 34 — Boston College — 1999-2001

The Chiefs' second pick in 1999 draft, Cloud has played primarily on special teams his three seasons in Kansas City. He has shown a glimpse of his running talent, carrying the ball 72 times for 266 yards and two touchdowns. Cloud became the primary kick returner for the team in 2000 and returned 36 kickoffs an average of 21.6 yards per return. He has six career special team tackles and scored a touchdown on a blocked punt return. Cloud has played in 42 games for the Chiefs.

Coan, Bert — RB — 23 — Kansas — 1963-68

Acquired in a trade with San Diego, Coan became a principal component in the Chiefs' offense through the 1968 season. Was college teammate of Chiefs Hall-of-Famer Curtis McClinton; best season was 1966, rushing for 521 yards and seven touchdowns as the Chiefs won the AFL title and played in the first Super Bowl. Also threw a touchdown pass in '66; returned 31 kickoffs for the club during his career; finished with 1,249 yards rushing and 19 touchdowns; caught 38 passes for 315 yards. Played in 68 games.

Cocroft, Sherman — S — 22 — San Jose State — 1985-87

A valuable member of the Chiefs' special teams, Cocroft also played in nickel back situations on defense. He intercepted six passes, made three fumble recoveries and posted 71 tackles. Played in 44 games.

Coffman, Paul — TE — 84 — Kansas State — 1986-87

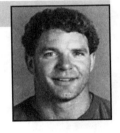

Came to Kansas City after a brilliant career at Green Bay, where he was a three-time Pro Bowler; provided valuable experience in a backup role for the Chiefs as they made the playoffs for the first time in 15 years in 1986; caught 17 passes for 117 yards and three touchdowns in 27 games for the Chiefs.

Cofield, Tim — LB — 54 — Elizabeth City State — 1986-88

An unheralded free agent, Cofield quickly moved into a starting position during his first training camp and registered five sacks his rookie season. Started five games in 1987; had a total of 8.5 sacks for the Chiefs and one interception in 43 games.

Colbert, Darrell — WR — 81 — Texas Southern — 1987-88

Played in 15 games over two seasons and caught four passes for 18 yards.

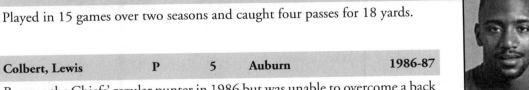

Colbert, Lewis — P — 5 — Auburn — 1986-87

Became the Chiefs' regular punter in 1986 but was unable to overcome a back injury early in the 1987 season and didn't punt for Kansas City again. An eighth-round pick by the Chiefs in 1986, Colbert played in 18 games and averaged 40.5 yards per punt.

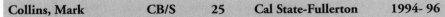

Collier, Tim CB 37 East Texas State 1976-79

Selected in the ninth round of the 1976 draft, Collier spent a lot of time on the field and started several games during his four seasons in Kansas City. Returned an interception 100 yards for a touchdown against the Raiders in 1977; intercepted nine passes in his career and played in 52 games.

Collins, Mark CB/S 25 Cal State-Fullerton 1994- 96

Came to Kansas City as a free agent from the Giants, and after playing one season at cornerback, made a successful switch to safety and was a key player in the Chiefs' 13-3 1995 season. Collins was known for his professionalism and team leadership. He intercepted nine passes, returned a fumble for a touchdown, and recorded four sacks during his three seasons in Kansas City. He played in a total of 46 games for the Chiefs.

Collins, Ray DT 71 LSU 1960-61

Joined the Texans in 1960 after being away from pro football since 1954; was the starting right tackle both seasons in Dallas; played in 27 games.

Collins, Todd QB 15 Michigan 1998-2001

The Chiefs claimed Collins on waivers from Buffalo prior to the 1998 season. Listed as the third quarterback on the roster for his first three seasons in Kansas City, Collins finally appeared in a game for the Chiefs in 2001. He completed three of four passes for 40 yards.

Colter, Jeff DB 48 Kansas 1987

Replacement during the 1987 NFL players' strike; Colter played in onegame.

Condon, Tom G 65 Boston College 1974-84

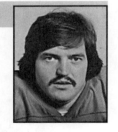

A tenth-round draft pick in 1974, Condon made the team his rookie season, primarily as a special teams player. Moved into the starting position at right guard in 1975 and held it through the 1984 season. His play on the line was steady and consistent, but more importantly, Condon was durable. He missed just 21 games during his career in Kansas City and played in a total of 147 games for the Chiefs.

Cooper, Louis LB 55 Western Carolina 1985-90

A solid defensive performer, Cooper signed with the Chiefs as a free agent and added strength to the linebacker corps during his time in Kansas City. Recorded 7.5 sacks and one interception in 79 games for the Chiefs.

Copeland, Danny S/KR 25 Eastern Kentucky 1989-90

Played in 30 games for the Chiefs as a defensive back and returned 26 kickoffs for an average of 17.9 yards per return.

Player	Position	Jersey(s) Worn	College	Year(s) Played

Corey, Walt   LB   56   Miami (Fla.)   1960-66

An original member of the Texans, Corey was the team's starting right-side linebacker for five seasons, and earned All-AFL honors in 1963. Intercepted four passes in his career; played in a total of 69 games for the franchise.

Cornelison, Jerry   T   74   SMU   1960-65

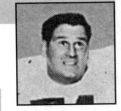

An original member of the Texans, Cornelison was the team's starting right tackle its first two seasons. Sat out the 1963 season and returned in 1964 for two more years. Played in 70 games for the franchise.

Craig, Reggie   WR   80   Arkansas   1975-76

Used primarily as a kick returner, Craig averaged 24.3 yards per kickoff return and caught one pass for ten yards in 15 games for the Chiefs.

Crawford, Keith   S   41   Howard Payne   1998

Came to the Chiefs from the Rams and made 11 special teams tackles in eight games during the 1998 season.

Criswell, Jeff   T   69   Graceland (Iowa)   1995-98

A free agent from the Jets, Criswell was the consummate team player, playing both guard and tackle on the offensive line; eventually settled in at left tackle and started there for two seasons. Was a big reason for the Chiefs' running success the four seasons he was on the offensive line. Played in the 1995 and 1997 playoff games; played in 60 games for the Chiefs.

Crockett, Ray   CB   39   Baylor   2001

A stellar 12-year veteran with the Lions and Broncos, Crockett provided stability in the Chiefs' defensive backfield throughout the 2001 season. He only picked off one pass for the club during the 2001 season, but his overall play was dependable and tough. Crockett finished his first campaign in Kansas City with 54 total tackles and played in 14 games.

Culp, Curley   DT   61   Arizona State   1968-74

see Other Chiefs Greats

D

Daney, George   G   60   Texas-El Paso   1968-74

The Chiefs' first-round draft pick in 1968, Daney played primarily on the special teams his first five seasons in Kansas City; was the starting right guard in '74. Scored a touchdown on a fumble recovery in 1969; played in 97 games for the Chiefs.

Player	Position	Jersey(s) Worn	College	Year(s) Played

Daniels, Calvin   LB   50   North Carolina   1982-85

A second-round pick by the Chiefs in 1982, Daniels was considered one of the best blitzers on the team; recorded nine sacks, two interceptions, and 168 tackles for the Chiefs; played in 57 games.

Daniels, Clemon   DB   36   Prairie View   1960

Played as a reserve defensive back for the Texans, Daniels also returned three punts for a 23.0 yard average and picked off three passes.

Davidson, Cotton   QB/P   19   Baylor   1960-61

The franchise's first starting quarterback, Davidson was able to make the most of his second chance at pro football and guided the Texans for two seasons before being traded to Oakland for the draft pick that ultimately brought Buck Buchanan to Kansas City. He threw for 4,919 yards, 32 touchdowns, and ran for 159 yards and two touchdowns. He was selected for the AFL All-Star game in 1961. Also served as the Texans' punter; had 123 punts for a 39.7 yard average. Played in 29 games for the Texans.

Davis, Anthony   LB   50   Utah   1994-98

Another good free-agent acquisition, Davis provided the Chiefs with outstanding play at the outside linebacker position after playing primarily on the special teams his first two seasons. Recorded 125 tackles in 1997; played in 68 games, and intercepted five passes while sacking the quarterback 12.5 times.

Davis, Dick   DE   86   Kansas   1962

Backup defensive end for the Texans, also played on the special teams. Played in 12 games.

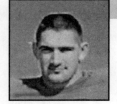

Davis, Ricky   S   40   Alabama   1977

Acquired from Tampa Bay on waivers, Davis started five games at safety; also played on special teams; played in a total of 13 games.

Davis, Willie   WR   84   Central Arkansas   1991-95

An improbable free-agent success, Davis moved up from the practice squad to become one of the Chiefs' premier receivers. Led the NFL with an average of 21 yards per reception in 1992; caught 52 passes for 909 yards and seven touchdowns in 1993; caught 51 passes, five for touchdowns in 1994; caught game-winning touchdown pass from Joe Montana on *Monday Night Football* against Denver in 1994; caught 172 passes for 3,014 yards and 20 touchdowns for Chiefs. Played in 79 games.

Dawson, Lake   WR   80   Notre Dame   1994-97

A third-round pick in the 1994 draft, Dawson spent four seasons in the Chiefs' receiving corps, making 103 receptions for 1,406 yards and ten touchdowns. He played in 43 games.

Player	Position	Jersey(s) Worn	College	Year(s) Played

| Dawson, Len | QB | 16 | Purdue | 1962-75 |

see Chiefs in the Pro Football Hall of Fame

| Dawson, Mike | NT | 73 | Arizona | 1984 |

Joined the Chiefs midway through the 1984 season; played in nine games and registered one sack.

| DeBerg, Steve | QB | 17 | San Jose State | 1988-91 |

Came to the Chiefs in a trade with Tampa Bay in 1988, and was Kansas City's main quarterback for four seasons. After stops in San Francisco, Denver, and Tampa Bay, DeBerg finally found the right club in the Chiefs. His expert play fakes fit perfectly with Marty Schottenheimer's run-oriented offense. Behind the strength of Kansas City's best team in decades, DeBerg put together a dream season in 1990. He passed for 3,444 yards and 23 touchdowns. "The best feeling in the world is when the ball's in the air and you know it's going to be caught," DeBerg said. He also completed 58 percent of his passes in 1990. He led the Chiefs to the playoffs in 1990-91. For his career in Kansas City, DeBerg passed for 11,873 yards and threw 67 touchdown passes. He played in 57 games for the Chiefs.

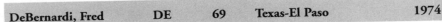

| DeBernardi, Fred | DE | 69 | Texas-El Paso | 1974 |

Joined Kansas City midway through the 1974 season and played in seven games.

| DeBruijn, Case | P | 5 | Idaho State | 1982 |

An eighth-round pick in the 1982 draft, DeBruijn played in one game for the Chiefs, punting five times for a 34.8 yard average.

| Delaney, Joe | RB | 37 | Northwestern Louisiana | 1981-82 |

see Other Chiefs Greats

| Del Rio, Jack | LB | 50 | USC | 1987-88 |

Kansas City sent a fifth-round 1988 draft pick to New Orleans for Del Rio; made 122 tackles with three sacks in 25 games for the Chiefs.

| Dennis, Pat | CB | 41 | Louisiana - Monroe | 2000-01 |

One of two fifth-round draft picks the Chiefs had in 2000, Dennis quickly established himself in the secondary, starting in 13 of 16 games. He picked off one pass, recovered two fumbles and made 70 tackles. Dennis started the 2001 season on the IR and was released after the first three games.

| Diamond, Charlie | T | 79 | Miami (Fla.) | 1960-63 |

Started at both left and right tackle on the offensive line, Diamond was an original Texan. Played in 51 games.

Player	Position	Jersey(s) Worn	College	Year(s) Played

Dickerson, Ron — WR — 23 — Arkansas — 1993-94

Used primarily to return kickoffs, Dickerson ran back a total of 32 kicks, averaging 22.2 yards per return. He played in 15 games.

Dickinson, Bo — FB — 32 — Southern Mississippi — 1960-61

Provided strong running off the bench; Dickinson rushed for 406 yards and caught 17 passes for 247 yards in his two seasons with Dallas; also scored six touchdowns. Played in 28 games.

DiGiacomo, Curt — G — 65 — Arizona — 1988

Came to Kansas City as a free agent from San Diego; played in 12 games.

DiMidio, Tony — T — 72 — West Chester — 1966-67

Selected by the Chiefs in the ninth round of the 1964 AFL draft; backup on offensive and defensive line; played in 26 games.

Dimmick, Tom — C — 55 — Houston — 1960

Backup on the offensive line; played in 13 games for the Texans.

Dirden, Johnny — KR — 80 — Sam Houston State — 1979

Played four games and returned seven kickoffs, averaging 22 yards per return.

Dishman, Chris — CB — 26 — Purdue — 1999

Dishman left the Redskins to sign with the Chiefs. The two-time Pro Bowler started all 16 games at left cornerback in 1999, and despite a couple of down games, Dishman had a great first season with Kansas City. He made 84 tackles, picked off five passes and recovered three fumbles. Dish became the first Chief to score two defensive touchdowns in a game since 1986 when he intercepted Oakland's Rich Gannon and returned it 47 yards for a score, and followed that with a 40-yard fumble recovery for another touchdown against the Raiders. Dishman also led the team with 22 passes defended.

Dixon, Al — TE — 84 — Iowa State — 1979-82

Came to Chiefs via free agency; released and reclaimed in 1980, Dixon won the starting tight end job for the 1981 season and held it through 1982. He caught 54 passes for 722 yards and five touchdowns. Played in a total of 39 games for Kansas City.

Dixon, Ernest — LB — 56 — South Carolina — 1998

Appeared in one game for the Chiefs late in the 1998 season.

Player	Position	Jersey(s) Worn	College	Year(s) Played

Dixon, Ronnie — DT — 90 — Cincinnati — 1998

Played in four games for the Chiefs.

Dohring, Tom — T — 71 — Michigan — 1992

An eighth-round pick in the 1991 draft, Dohoring played in three games for the Chiefs.

Dombroski, Paul — S — 46 — Linfield — 1980-81

Provided solid backup play for the Chiefs' secondary and special teams; intercepted two passes; played in 21 games for Kansas City.

Donaldson, Jeff — S — 42 — Colorado — 1990

Coming to Kansas City from Houston, Donaldson played in all 16 games for Kansas City during the 1990 season, sharing the free-safety position with Deron Cherry. He intercepted three passes.

Donnalley, Rick — C — 51 — North Carolina — 1986-87

Acquired by the Chiefs in a trade with Washington, Donnalley was the starting center in 1986 and part of 1987. He played in 22 games.

Dorsey, Larry — WR — 80 — Tennessee State — 1978

The Chiefs sent Wilbur Young to San Diego for Dorsey; caught nine passes for 169 yards and two touchdowns. He played in 16 games.

Dotson, Alphonse — DT — 79 — Grambling — 1965

A no. 1 pick in the 1965 Futures (also called Redshirt) Draft, Dotson was injured most of the 1965 season, but was activated for one game. Went to Miami in 1966.

Doubiago, Dan — T — 66 — Utah — 1987

A replacement player during the 1987 NFL players' strike; played in three games for the Chiefs.

Downing, Eric — DT — 79 — Syracuse — 2001

A third round pick in the 2001 draft, Downing played in 15 games and started nine times. His strong performance for the duration of the season was rewarded as his teammates awarded him the Mack Lee Hill Award as the club's outstanding rookie performer. Downing totaled 36 tackles for the season, and also added 1.5 sacks and three quarterback pressures.

Dozier, Cornelius — S — 26 — SMU — 1987

A replacement player during the 1987 NFL players' strike; played in two games for the Chiefs.

Player	Position	Jersey(s) Worn	College	Year(s) Played

Drayton, Troy — TE — 87 — Penn State — 2000

The veteran tight end came to Kansas City from the Dolphins. He played in 16 games in 2000, started once, and caught eight passes for 70 yards and two touchdowns.

Dressel, Chris — TE — 93 — Stanford — 1989

Played the first half of the 1989 season with Kansas City before going to the Jets; caught nine passes for 136-yards and one touchdown in seven games.

Dressler, Doug — RB — 41 — Chico State — 1975

Came to the Chiefs midway through the 1975 season; carried the ball three times for 16 yards and caught two passes for seven yards and one touchdown. Played in eight games.

Drougas, Tom — T — 76 — Oregon — 1974

Joined the Chiefs after the start of the 1974 season, coming from Denver. Played in seven games in a backup and special teams role.

Dumas, Troy — LB — 55 — Nebraska — 1995-97

A third-round draft pick in 1995, Dumas missed the 1995 season because of a knee injury; had one sack in 14 games.

Duncan, Randy — QB — 15 — Iowa — 1961

The Texans' backup quarterback in 1961, Duncan threw for 361 yards and one touchdown; played in 14 games.

Dunn, Jason — TE — 89 — Eastern Kentucky — 2000-01

A free agent from Philadelphia, Dunn played in 14 games in 2000, catching two passes for 26 yards.

Dyal, Mike — TE — 87 — Texas A&I — 1992-93

Came to Kansas City as a "Plan B" free agent; caught eight passes for 90 yards in 13 games.

Eatman, Irv — T — 75 — UCLA — 1986-90

A no. 8 pick in the 1983 draft, Eatman came to Kansas City after playing three seasons in the USFL. Played both left and right tackle; was a starter for three seasons (1986-89), and excelled in all phases of the game. Eatman played in 69 games for the Chiefs.

Player	Position	Jersey(s) Worn	College	Year(s) Played

Edwards, Donnie — LB — 59 — UCLA — 1996-2001

see Other Chiefs Greats

Elkins, Mike — QB — 10 — Wake Forest — 1989-90

A second-round pick in the 1989 draft, Elkins was injured for most of his rookie season; saw action in one game in 1989, completing one of two passes for five yards and an interception.

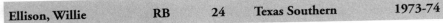

Elliott, Lin — K — 2 — Texas Tech — 1994-95

Came to the Chiefs from Dallas via free agency; made 49 of 60 field-goal attempts, but will always be remembered for missing three field goals in the Chiefs' 10-7 loss to Indianapolis in the 1995 Divisional Playoff. Scored a total of 211 points; played in 32 games.

Ellison, Willie — RB — 24 — Texas Southern — 1973-74

The Chiefs traded Bob Stein and a 1973 seventh-round draft choice to the Rams for Ellison; despite injuries, he was the team's second leading rusher in 1973 with 411 yards; rushed for a total of 525 yards in 15 games for the Chiefs and scored four touchdowns.

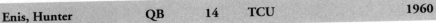

Elrod, Jimbo — LB — 57 — Oklahoma — 1976-78

The Chiefs' fifth-round pick in 1976, Elrod was a backup linebacker and special teams players. Intercepted one pass in 36 games.

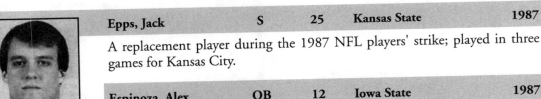

Enis, Hunter — QB — 14 — TCU — 1960

The Texans' backup quarterback their first season, Enis threw for 357 yards and one touchdown. Played in 14 games.

Epps, Jack — S — 25 — Kansas State — 1987

A replacement player during the 1987 NFL players' strike; played in three games for Kansas City.

Espinoza, Alex — QB — 12 — Iowa State — 1987

A replacement player during the 1987 NFL players' strike; played in one game for the Chiefs; hit nine of 14 passes for 69 yards with two interceptions.

Estell, Richard — WR — 84 — Kansas — 1987

A replacement player during the 1987 NFL players' strike; played in two games for the Chiefs, catching three passes for 24 yards.

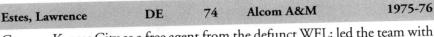

Estes, Lawrence — DE — 74 — Alcorn A&M — 1975-76

Came to Kansas City as a free agent from the defunct WFL; led the team with 5.5 sacks in 1976; played in 18 games.

Player	Position	Jersey(s) Worn	College	Year(s) Played

Evans, James — RB — 41 — Southern — 1987

A tenth-round draft pick in 1987, Evans played in two games for the Chiefs.

Evans, Mike — DE — 94 — Michigan — 1992

A fourth-round draft pick in 1992, Evans played in 12 games and had five tackles.

Everett, Eric — CB — 39 — Texas Tech — 1991

Came to the Chiefs as a free agent and played in 11 games.

F

Fada, Rob — G — 65 — Pittsburgh — 1985

Came to the Chiefs from Chicago and played in five games for Kansas City.

Farrier, Curt — DT — 70 — Montana State — 1963-65

Farrier was selected by the Chiefs in the tenth round of the 1963 AFL draft. Provided valuable backup to the defensive line; played in 27 games.

Favors, Greg — LB — 54 — Mississippi State — 1998

Selected in the fourth round of the 1998 draft, Favors started five of the last six games in the 1998 season; had two sacks in 16 games.

Feehery, Gerry — C — 64 — Syracuse — 1988

Came to the Chiefs from Philadelphia and played in four games.

Fields, Jaime — LB — 59 — Washington — 1993-95

A no. 4 draft pick in 1993, Fields was primarily a backup at linebacker and a special teams player. Missed the 1995 season; played in a total of 17 games.

Fields, Jitter — KR — 46 — Texas — 1987

Came to the Chiefs from the Colts; returned eight punts for an average of 20.1 yards per return with one touchdown. Played in five games.

Flores, Tom — QB — 12 — Pacific — 1969

The future head coach of the Raiders and Seahawks, Flores came to Kansas City as quarterback insurance in 1969 after Len Dawson was injured and Jackey Lee was lost for the season. Played in five games, threw one pass for a 33-yard touchdown.

Player	Position	Jersey(s) Worn	College	Year(s) Played

Flynn, Don — DB — 18 — Houston — 1960-61

An original Texan, Flynn was starter in the defensive secondary until he was sent to New York. Intercepted five passes, returning one for a touchdown; played in 20 games.

Fournet, Sid — G — 62 — LSU — 1960-61

An original Texan, Fournet resurrected his pro career in the AFL; played with Rams and Stellers from 1955-57; was the starting left guard the franchise's first two seasons; played in 28 games.

Fraser, Jim — LB — 51 — Wisconsin — 1965

Came to Kansas City from Denver; Fraser was a backup linebacker and special teams player; also punted three times for the Chiefs; played in 14 games.

Frazier, Cliff — DT — 61 — UCLA — 1977

Second-round pick by the Chiefs in the 1976 draft, Frazier was traded away to the Eagles and returned during the 1977 preseason; had 82 tackles and one sack; played in 14 games.

Frazier, Randy — LB — 95 — Morehead State — 1987

A replacement player during the 1987 NFL players' strike; played in three games for the Chiefs.

Frazier, Wayne — C — 66 — Auburn — 1966-67

Came to Chiefs from the Oilers in a trade; Frazier proved an important part of the Chiefs' 1966 AFL championship team, filling in at center; played in 21 games.

Frazier, Willie — TE — 83 — Arkansas AM&N — 1971-72

Came to the Chiefs midway through the 1971 season via a trade with Houston; caught 15 passes for 213 yards and five touchdowns; played in 22 games for Kansas City.

Frey, Dick — DE — 66 — Texas A&M — 1960

An original Texan, Frey was a backup on the defensive line; played in 14 games.

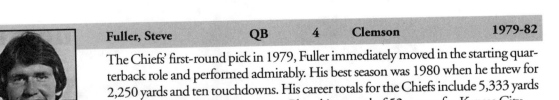

Fuller, Steve — QB — 4 — Clemson — 1979-82

The Chiefs' first-round pick in 1979, Fuller immediately moved in the starting quarterback role and performed admirably. His best season was 1980 when he threw for 2,250 yards and ten touchdowns. His career totals for the Chiefs include 5,333 yards passing and 22 touchdown passes. Played in a total of 52 games for Kansas City.

Player	Position	Jersey(s) Worn	College	Year(s) Played

Gagliano, Bob   QB   11   Utah State   1981-83

Came to Kansas City as a 12th-round pick in the 1981 draft; was on the roster three seasons but didn't play his rookie campaign; threw just one pass for the Chiefs and played in two games.

Gagner, Larry   G   79   Florida   1972

Signed as a free agent; played in seven games for the Chiefs.

Gaines, Clark   RB   21   Wake Forest   1981-82

Claimed on waivers from the Jets; carried the ball once for no gain and caught two passes for 17 yards. Played in ten games.

Gamble, Kenny   RB/DB   48   Colgate   1988-90

Selected in the tenth round of the 1988 draft, Gamble played primarily on the special teams. Ran the ball six times for 24 yards and one touchdown; returned 18 kickoffs and intercepted a pass. Played in 19 games.

Gammon, Kendall   TE   83   Pittsburg State   2000-01

Signed with Kansas City as an unrestricted free agent and handled all the long snapping duties for the Chiefs in 2000 and 2001. Gammon has played in 32 games for the club.

Gannon, Rich   QB   12   Delaware   1995-98

After sitting out the 1994 season because of a shoulder injury, Gannon signed with the Chiefs. He didn't play much in 1995 but made a relief appearance (replacing Steve Bono) late in the divisional playoff game with the Colts and led the offense to a game-tying field-goal attempt (which Lin Elliott missed). Gannon again saw limited duty in 1996 but played in nine games in 1997, starting in six. He threw for 1,144 yards and seven touchdowns that season, and when Grbac was injured again in 1998, Gannon's good performance fueled a quarterback controversy. He threw for 2,305 yards in 1998, ten of them for touchdowns. Also a great scrambler, Gannon rushed for 383 yards while quarterbacking the Chiefs. He left for Oakland following the '98 season. He played in 27 games for the Chiefs.

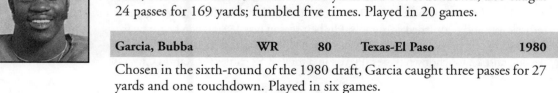

Gant, Earl   RB   23   Missouri   1979-80

Drafted in 1979 by the Chiefs in the fifth round, Gant was a backup running back; carried the ball 65 times for 228 yards and one touchdown; also caught 24 passes for 169 yards; fumbled five times. Played in 20 games.

Garcia, Bubba   WR   80   Texas-El Paso   1980

Chosen in the sixth-round of the 1980 draft, Garcia caught three passes for 27 yards and one touchdown. Played in six games.

Player	Position	Jersey(s) Worn	College	Year(s) Played

Gardner, Ellis — T/G — 75 — Georgia Tech — 1983

The Chiefs' sixth round pick in 1983, Gardner played in eight games as backup on the offensive line.

Garrett, Mike — RB — 21 — USC — 1966-70

see Chiefs Hall of Fame

Gaunty, Steve — WR — 83 — Northern Colorado — 1979

Caught five passes for 87 yards and one touchdown; returned 12 kickoffs and averaged 22.6 yards per return; played in nine games.

Gay, Matt — S — 49 — Kansas — 1994

Played in two games for the Chiefs.

Gehrke, Jack — WR — 17 — Utah — 1968

A tenth-round draft pick in 1968, Gehrke played in two games for the Chiefs.

George, Ron — LB — 55 — Stanford — 1998-2000

A free-agent signee from Minnesota, George played on the special teams, as well as playing a reserve role for the linebackers his first season in Kansas City. He played more at linebacker in 1999, but was still primarily a special teams performer. He's played in 32 games for the Chiefs.

Germaine, Joe — QB — 7 — Ohio State — 2001

Picked up from the Rams, Germaine was the Chiefs third quarterback for the 2001 season and did not see action in any games.

Getty, Charlie — T — 77 — Penn State — 1974-82

A no. 2 selection in the 1974 draft, Getty moved into the Chiefs' starting lineup, playing both guard and tackle; took over the right tackle position in 1978 and stayed there through 1982; never missed a game from 1974 through 1980; was always solid in both run and pass blocking; went to Green Bay before the start of the 1983 season; played in 119 games.

Getz, Lee — G — 71 — Rutgers — 1987

A replacement player during the 1987 NFL players' strike; played in two games for the Chiefs.

Gilliam, Jon — C — 65 — East Texas State — 1961-67

Signed with the Texans as a free agent in 1961 after unsuccessful tryouts with the Packers, Giants, and Cowboys; tried out at linebacker, but moved to center and took over the starting role for the Texans, where he remained for the next six seasons. Gilliam played in a total of 76 games for the franchise.

Player	Position	Jersey(s) Worn	College	Year(s) Played

Golub, Chris   S   47   **Kansas**   1977

Drafted in the seventh round of the 1977 draft, Golub played in one game for the Chiefs.

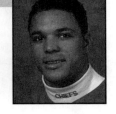

Gonzalez, Tony   TE   88   **California**   1997-2001

see Other Chiefs Greats

Goodburn, Kelly   P   2   **Emporia State**   1987-90

Signed as a free agent, Goodburn made the team after a couple of unsuccessful tries; was the Chiefs' punter through the first part of the 1990 season; best season was 1987 when he averaged 40.9 yards per punt; punted a total of 219 times, averaging 40.2 yards per punt; played in a total of 48 games.

Gossett, Jeff   P   7   **Eastern Illinois**   1981-82

Signed as a free agent halfway through the season, Gossett took over the team's punting duties and held them through the 1982 season. He averaged 40.4 yards per punt in 15 games.

Graham, Derrick   T   74   **Appalachian State**   1990-94

A fifth-round pick in the 1990 draft, Graham battled injuries throughout his time in Kansas City. Was very agile on the offensive line; played in 51 games for the Chiefs.

Graham, Tom   LB   56   **Oregon**   1974

Came to the Chiefs with Tom Drougas from Denver for two 1975 draft picks; played primarily on the special teams as well as backing up at the linebacker position. Played in eight games for the Chiefs.

Granderson, Rufus   T   75   **Prairie View**   1960

Played in six games for the Texans.

Gray, Carlton   CB   23   **UCLA**   1999-2000

Signed with Kansas City as a free agent, coming from the Giants; Gray played primarily on special teams and also saw action as a backup defensive back. He made five tackles and defended two passes. Gray played in 16 games in 1999.

Gray, Tim   S   46   **Texas A&M**   1976-78

The Chiefs sent Marvin Upshaw and Mike Sensibaugh to the Cardinals for Gray in 1976; Gray recovered two fumbles and returned them for touchdowns in 1977; had four quarterback sacks in 1977 as well; intercepted 12 passes in his career for Kansas City; his longest interception return was 61 yards against Denver. Played in 36 games for the Chiefs.

Grayson, Dave · DB · 45 · Oregon · 1961-64

Came to Kansas City as a free agent and played superbly in the defensive backfield before he was traded to Oakland following the 1964 season. Grayson was All-AFL in 1963-64; returned a kickoff 99 yards for a touchdown and also returned an interception 99 yards for a score; led the AFL in kickoff returns in 1961; intercepted a total of 19 passes for Chiefs; returned 84 kick-offs, averaging 26.6 yards per return; played in 55 games for the franchise.

Grbac, Elvis · QB · 11 · Michigan · 1997-2000

see Other Chiefs Greats

Green, Boyce · RB · 40 · Carson Newman · 1986

Came to Kansas City in a trade with Cleveland and was the team's starting halfback at the end of the 1986 season; ran for 314 yards and three touchdowns on 90 carries; caught 19 passes for 137 yards. His biggest play for the Chiefs was a 97-yard kickoff return in the playoff-clinching game against the Steelers. Played in a total of 16 games.

Green, Gary · CB · 24 · Baylor · 1977-83

see Other Chiefs Greats

Green, Trent · QB · 10 · Indiana · 2001

After a lengthy negotiation, the Chiefs traded their 2001 first round pick to the St. Louis Rams in exchange for Trent Green and a fifth round pick. The quarterback new head coach Dick Vermeil wanted more than any other, Green suffered through an up and down 2001 season as the Chiefs signal caller. He threw 24 interceptions and just 17 touchdown passes. The major positive for Green was his durability; he started all 16 games, finishing with 3,783 yards, the third highest total in Chiefs' history. Green completed 56.6% of his passes, and also ran for 158 yards. "The thing I am most proud of is what we have been able to accomplish," Green said of the 2001 season. "We have been able to accomplish a lot things, and I think we are building something really special."

Green, Woody · RB · 27 · Arizona State · 1974-76

The Chiefs' no. 1 draft choice in 1974, Green fought injuries throughout his career. Led the team in rushing in 1974 and 1975; his best game was in 1974 when he gained 146 yards on 23 carries against San Diego; his best season was 1975 when he ran for 611 yards and five touchdowns. Green rushed for 1,442 yards in his career and caught 58 passes for 562 yards. He scored 11 touchdowns and played in 28 games.

Greene, Ted · LB · 54 · Tampa · 1960-62

An original Texan, Greens was a backup at linebacker and provided strong play for the franchise during its three seasons in Dallas. He intercepted four passes in 32 games.

Player	Position	Jersey(s) Worn	College	Year(s) Played

Greene, Tom — QB — 14 — Holy Cross — 1961

Played in one game for the Texans.

Greene, Tracy — TE — 87 — Grambling — 1994

The Chiefs second seventh-round pick in the 1994 draft, Greene played in seven games, started in two, caught six passes for 69 yards, and scored one touchdown.

Griffin, Leonard — DE — 98 — Grambling — 1986-93

Selected in the third round of the 1986 draft by the Chiefs, Griffin was a steady performer on the defensive line throughout his career in Kansas City. Had 6.5 sacks in 1989 and totaled 16.5 for his career. Played in 103 games.

Griffin, Stephen — RB — 39 — Tennessee State — 1987

A replacement player during the 1987 NFL players' strike; played one game for the Chiefs and returned one kickoff for 16 yards.

Grow, Monty — S — 22 — Florida — 1994

A free-agent signee, Grow added good depth to the Chiefs' secondary and special teams. He played in 15 games, intercepting one pass and recovering one fumble.

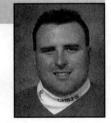

Grunhard, Tim — C — 61 — Notre Dame — 1990-2000

see Other Chiefs Greats

Grupp, Bob — P — 1 — Duke — 1979-81

Signed as a free agent, Grupp was brilliant as a rookie, averaging 43.6 yards per punt and being named to the Pro Bowl. Had 89 punts that season, including a 74-yarder. Punted a total of 214 times with an average of 40.9 yards per punt for his career; played 41 games.

Gunter, Michael — RB — 38 — Tulsa — 1984

Played in four games and ran the ball 15 times for 12 yards.

Hackett, Dino — LB — 56 — Appalachian State — 1986-92

see Other Chiefs Greats

H

Player	Position	Jersey(s) Worn	College	Year(s) Played

Hadley, David — CB — 23 — Alcorn — 1970-72

The Chiefs chose Hadley in the third round of the 1970 draft; played primarily on the special teams, intercepted one pass; played in 28 games.

Hadnot, James — RB — 48 — Texas Tech — 1980-83

Kansas City selected Hadnot in the third round of the 1980 draft; a strong runner, Hadnot was a capable fullback and gave the Chiefs good performances. His best game was a 106-yard-rushing effort against Seattle in 1981; ran for 1,029 yards in his career, scoring five touchdowns; caught 54 passes for 426 yards. Played in 43 games.

Hagy, John — S — 22 — Texas — 1991

Was on the team's roster but never played in a game.

Hall, Dante — RB — 20 — Texas A&M — 2000-01

Selected in the fifth round of the 2000 draft by the Chiefs, Hall played on special teams in five games. He returned 17 kickoffs for an average of 21.1 yards per return his rookie year, and also ran back six punts for 37 yards. Hall became the primary returner for the Chiefs in 2001, returning 32 punts and 43 kickoffs, including a 71-yard return against the Raiders on December 9, 2001. He has played in 19 games for Kansas City.

Hamilton, Andy — WR — 80 — LSU — 1973-74

The Chiefs got Hamilton in the fourth round of the 1972 draft; missed the 1972 season because of injuries; played primarily on the special teams; caught four passes for 60 yards in 15 games.

Hamilton, Rick — LB — 53 — Central Florida — 1994-95

Played in the Chiefs' final two games of the 1994 season.

Hamm, Bob — DE — 90 — Nevada-Reno — 1985

Came to Kansas City in a draft-day trade with Houston; played primarily as the fourth defensive lineman in passing situations; recorded 22 tackles and a sack in 14 games.

Hamrick, James — K — 4 — Rice — 1987

A replacement player during the 1987 NFL players' strike. He was two-for-two in field goals and four-for-four in extra points. Played in three games.

Hancock, Anthony — WR/KR — 82 — Tennessee — 1982-86

The Chiefs' first-round selection in the 1982 draft, Hancock possessed great speed, but was never able to mesh into the Chiefs' offensive schemes. His best season was 1983—he caught 37 passes for 584 yards and one touchdown. He also returned kickoffs and punts, averaging 20.0 yards per kickoff return and 6.8 yards per punt return. For his career, Hancock caught 73 passes for 1,266 yards and five touchdowns in 59 games.

Player	Position	Jersey(s) Worn	College	Year(s) Played

Hardison, Dee — NT — 93 — North Carolina — 1988

Signed as a free agent; played in seven games for the Chiefs.

Hargain, Tony — WR — 81 — Oregon — 1992

A "Plan B" free agent from San Francisco, Hargain caught 17 passes for 205 yards in 12 games.

Harrell, James — LB — 57 — Florida — 1987

Joined the Chiefs during the players' strike of 1987 and played in all three replacement games. After the strike ended, he rejoined the team after two weeks and played in the final eight games of the season, starting in two. Had 40 tackles and two fumble recoveries.

Harris, Bob — LB — 92 — Auburn — 1987

A replacement player during the 1987 NFL players' strike; played in three games for the Chiefs.

Harris, Corey — CB — 40 — North Alabama — 2001

A free agent signee, Harris played in four games on special teams and registered two tackles and a fumble recovery.

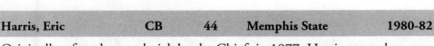

Harris, Eric — CB — 44 — Memphis State — 1980-82

Originally a fourth-round pick by the Chiefs in 1977, Harris spent three seasons in the CFL before coming to Kansas City in 1980. Won the Mack Lee Hill Award as the club's outstanding rookie in 1980; was a second-team All-AFC selection by UPI in 1981; intercepted seven passes in both 1980 and 1981; intercepted 17 passes during his time in Kansas City, returning one for a touchdown in 1982. Played in 39 games for the Chiefs.

Harris, Jimmy — DB — 44 — Oklahoma — 1960-61

An original Texan, Harris played for the Eagles and Rams before joining the new AFL team in 1960. Was the team's starter at safety both seasons he was with Dallas; intercepted four passes and played in 25 games.

Harris, Michael — C/G — 73 — Grambling — 1989

Played in three games for the Chiefs.

Harrison, Glynn — RB — 22 — Georgia — 1976

Signed with the Chiefs midway through the 1976 season; returned 13 kick-offs for an average of 21.4 yards per return; carried the ball 16 times for 41 yards; played in eight games.

Harry, Emile — WR — 86 — Stanford — 1986-92

Joined the Chiefs as a free agent; a clutch third-down performer, Harry's sure hands were counted on many times during his career to make the big catch; his 11 receptions against Cleveland in 1991 tied him for second-most in a game by a Chiefs receiver with Chris Burford and Kimble Anders. His best season was 1990 when he caught 41 passes for 519 yards and two touchdowns. For his career, Harry caught 149 passes for 1,999 yards and nine touchdowns. He played in 79 games for the Chiefs; went to the Rams after seven games in 1992.

Harts, Shaunard — S — 42 — Boise State — 2001

A seventh round selection in the 2001 draft, Harts played in three games and made two stops on special teams.

Harvey, James — G — 64 — Jackson State — 1987-88
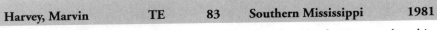

A replacement player during the 1987 NFL players' strike; played in four games for the Chiefs.

Harvey, Marvin — TE — 83 — Southern Mississippi — 1981

Selected in the third round of the 1981 draft by the Chiefs, Harvey played in seven games as a backup and special teams player.

Harvey, Stacy — LB — 59 — Arizona State — 1989
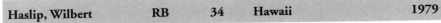

Played in nine games for the Chiefs.

Haslip, Wilbert — RB — 34 — Hawaii — 1979

Signed as a free agent, Haslip played in five games and ran the ball twice for one yard.

Hasty, James — CB — 40 — Washington State — 1995-2000
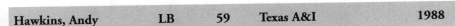

see Other Chiefs Greats

Hawkins, Andy — LB — 59 — Texas A&I — 1988
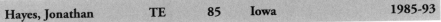

A free agent, Hawkins played in seven games for the Chiefs.

Hayes, Jonathan — TE — 85 — Iowa — 1985-93

Selected in the second round of the 1985 draft, Hayes became one of the more productive tight ends in the Chiefs' history and was particularly punishing with his blocking style, a key ingredient in the team's running game during his time in Kansas City. His best season was 1993 when he hauled in 24 pass receptions for 331 yards and one touchdown. He scored two touchdowns in the Chiefs' playoff-clinching win against the Broncos in 1990. For his career, Hayes caught 135 passes for 1,541 and 12 touchdowns in 136 games.

Player	Position	Jersey(s) Worn	College	Year(s) Played

Hayes, Wendell — RB — 38 — **Humboldt State** — 1968-74

Hayes came to the Chiefs from Denver in a trade before the 1968 season. He fit in perfectly with Hank Stram's small-back backfield and was a key component in the success of the running game. Hayes put together good back-to-back seasons in 1971 and 1972, running for 537 and 536 yards. But he always maintained he was a blocker, a team player. "I like to run, to score, but my game is different. It's blocking, and if I get 75 percent of my blocks, I figure I've had a good game." It was that kind of unselfish play that kept Hayes with the Chiefs for seven seasons. He ran for 2,560 yards and scored 23 touchdowns in 93 games for Kansas City.

Haynes, Abner — RB — 28 — **North Texas State** — 1960-65

see Chiefs Hall of Fame

Haynes, Louis — LB — 56 — **North Texas State** — 1982-83

Drafted in the fourth round in 1982, Haynes played in 11 games.

Headrick, Sherrill — LB — 69 — **Texas Christian** — 1960-67

see Chiefs Hall of Fame

Heard, Herman — RB — 44 — **Southern Colorado** — 1984-89

Heard came to the Chiefs in the third round of the 1984 draft and was a solid running back throughout his career, adjusting well to the roles three different head coaches asked him to perform. His combination of speed, balance, and durability enabled him to greatly contribute to the Chiefs' offense. In 1987 Heard posted an impressive 5.7 yards per carry average; 1987 was the when he collected the only 100-yard game of his career, a 107-yard effort against Seattle. For his career, he ran the ball 651 times for 2,694 yards and 13 touchdowns. He also caught 132 passes for 1,125 yards and three touchdowns. He played in 87 games and was a starter 50 times.

Helton, Darius — G — 62 — **North Carolina Central** — 1977

The Chiefs' fourth-round pick in 1977, Helton played in six games.

Herkenhoff, Matt — T — 60 — **Minnesota** — 1976-85

Kansas City's no. 4 pick in the 1974 draft, Herkenhoff played the 1974 season in the WFL before joining the Chiefs in 1975. He missed the 1975 season with ankle problems but became a starter by the third game of the 1976 season. He played in 47 straight games from 1976 through 1979, and 31 straight from 1981 through 1983. Was an excellent pass blocker. Played in a total of 125 games for the Chiefs.

Player	Position	Jersey(s) Worn	College	Year(s) Played

Hicks, Eric   DE   98   Maryland   1998-2001

After signing with the Chiefs as a free agent (he was the only rookie free agent to make the team), Hicks came into his own in the 1999 season and started all 16 games at left defensive end. He recorded 70 tackles, recovered two fumbles (one returned 44 yards for a touchdown against Minnesota) and made four sacks. His 2000 season was even better as he made 61 tackles, 14 sacks and one fumble recovery in just 13 games (he missed three games because of a knee injury). Hicks started all 16 games in 2001 and made 93 total tackles. His sack output dropped to just 3.5, but he forced three fumbles and recovered another. He's played in 48 games for the Chiefs and has 21.5 career sacks.

Hicks, Kerry   DE/DT   94   BYU   1996-97

Played in two games for the Chiefs.

Hicks, Sylvester   DE   75   Tennessee State   1978-81

Kansas City selected Hicks in the second round of the 1978 draft, and he fought the injury bug throughout most of his career. He was used primarily as a rush defender but also had 8.5 sacks in his career. He played in 43 games.

Hill, Dave   T   73   Auburn   1963-74

see Chiefs Hall of Fame

Hill, Greg   CB   23   Oklahoma State   1984-88

Originally coming to the Chiefs from Houston, Hill bounced back and forth between the Chiefs, Raiders, and Oilers. Was a valuable fifth defensive back for the Chiefs, intercepting nine passes and returning one for a touchdown (against Houston in 1986). Played in 78 games for the Chiefs.

Hill, Greg   RB   27, 29   Texas A&M   1994-97

Hill was the Chiefs' first-round pick in the 1994 draft. He was one of the fastest players in the NFL and was expected to take over the main running back duties from Marcus Allen. Never quite lived up to high expectations, but did provide solid running for Kansas City while he was with the club, and might have exploded to the top of the league if he had been given more chances to carry the ball. Ran for 575 yards his rookie year; best season was in 1996 when he averaged 4.8 yards per carry and gained 645 yards. Ran for a total of 2,428 yards for the Chiefs and scored 11 touchdowns. Also caught 38 passes for 323 yards. Played in 63 games.

Hill, Jim   DB   12   Sam Houston   1966

Came to the Chiefs as the last stop of a long career and played in three games.

Player	Position	Jersey(s) Worn	College	Year(s) Played
Hill, Kenny	S	41	Yale	1989

A free agent, Hill intercepted one pass and played in eight games.

Player	Position	Jersey(s) Worn	College	Year(s) Played
Hill, Mack Lee	RB	36	Southern (La.)	1964-65

see Chiefs Hall of Fame

Player	Position	Jersey(s) Worn	College	Year(s) Played
Hines, Jimmy	E	81	Texas Southern	1970

Played in one game for Kansas City.

Player	Position	Jersey(s) Worn	College	Year(s) Played
Hobgood-Chittick, Nate	DT	94	North Carolina	2001

Signed with the Chiefs after playing for both the Rams and 49ers in 2000. He saw action in ten games, starting once, and made 47 total tackles.

Player	Position	Jersey(s) Worn	College	Year(s) Played
Hodges, Eric	WR	89	Florida	1987

A replacement player during the 1987 NFL players' strike; played in one game for Kansas City.

Player	Position	Jersey(s) Worn	College	Year(s) Played
Holland, Darius	DT	99	Colorado	1998

Came to the Chiefs from Green Bay; played in six games before going to Detroit.

Player	Position	Jersey(s) Worn	College	Year(s) Played
Holle, Eric	DE	93	Texas	1984-87

Selected by the Chiefs in the fifth round of the 1984 draft, Holle provided solid play on the Chiefs' defensive line, mostly as a backup. He had 2.5 sacks in 56 games.

Player	Position	Jersey(s) Worn	College	Year(s) Played
Hollis, David	DB/KR	25	UNLV	1988

A replacement player during the 1987 NFL players' strike; played in two games for the Chiefs, returning two punts and six kickoffs.

Player	Position	Jersey(s) Worn	College	Year(s) Played
Holloway, Tony	LB	97	Nebraska	1987

A replacement player during the 1987 NFL players' strike; played in one game for the Chiefs.

Player	Position	Jersey(s) Worn	College	Year(s) Played
Holmes, Bruce	LB	57	Minnesota	1987

A 12th-round draft pick in 1987, Holmes played in three games for the Chiefs.

Holmes, Pat — DE — 74 — Texas Tech — 1973

Came to the Chiefs from Houston; played in ten games and intercepted one pass.

Holmes, Priest — RB — 31 — Texas — 2001

see Other Chiefs Greats

Holmes, Robert — RB — 45 — Southern (La.) — 1968-71

A 14th-round draft selection in 1968, Holmes overcame great odds and not only made the Chiefs' roster, but was voted the club's top rookie and won the Mack Lee Hill Award. "All I wanted was a chance to prove I could play," Holmes said. "The Tank" ran for 866 yards and seven touchdowns in '68. He followed with 612 rushing yards in 1969. For his career in Kansas City, Holmes carried the ball 408 times for 1,719 yards and 12 touchdowns. He played in a total of 48 games for the Chiefs before going to Houston in the middle of the 1971 season.

Holohan, Pete — TE — 89 — Notre Dame — 1991

Came to the Chiefs as a "Plan B" free agent; was used as a backup at tight end; caught 13 passes for 113 yards and two touchdowns. Played in 16 games.

Holston, Mike — WR — 84 — Morgan State — 1985

Joined the Chiefs midway through the 1985 season and played four games. Caught five passes for 51 yards.

Holub, E.J. — C/LB — 55 — Texas Tech — 1961-70

see Chiefs Hall of Fame

Homan, Dennis — WR — 21 — Alabama — 1971-72

Came to Kansas City from Dallas; played primarily on the special teams, returning 12 punts. Caught 14 passes for 182 yards and one touchdown. Played in 15 games.

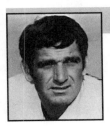

Hoppock, Doug — T — 79 — Kansas State — 1987

A replacement player during the 1987 NFL players' strike; played in three games for the Chiefs.

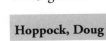

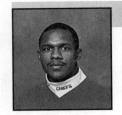

Horn, Joe   WR   84   Itawamba, J.C.   1996-99

A fourth-round pick by the Chiefs in 1996, Horn made it to the NFL the hard way, going to the CFL after finishing junior college, and then to Kansas City. Relegated to a backup and special teams role his first two seasons with the Chiefs, Horn finally got some playing time at wide receiver in 1998 and caught 14 passes for 198 yards and one touchdown. He followed with his best season in '99, catching 35 passes for 586 yards and six touchdowns. He's returned 20 kickoffs in his career, averaging 19.9 yards per return. Horn opted for free agency and left Kansas City for New Orleans following the 1999 season. He played in 49 games for the Chiefs.

Horton, Ethan   RB   32   North Carolina   1985

The Chiefs' first-round pick in 1985, Horton was one of the club's biggest disappointments. He never came close to reaching his projected potential, and after one poor season, the Chiefs released him. He remained the no. 2 back in 1985, but his receiving skills gained him more playing time. After his failure with Kansas City, he joined the Raiders and switched to tight end, a position that seemed to fit him more than running back. Carried the ball 48 times for 146 yards and three touchdowns; caught 28 passes for 185 yards and one touchdown. Played in 16 games for the Chiefs.

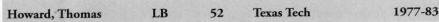

Houston, Bobby   LB   57   North Carolina State   1997

Played in five games for the Chiefs.

Howard, Thomas   LB   52   Texas Tech   1977-83

Selected by the Chiefs in the third round of the 1977 draft, Howard was one of the club's starting outside linebackers for six straight seasons. His career stats were impressive: 83 starts, 506 tackles, 17.5 sacks, five interceptions, and seven fumble recoveries, two for touchdowns. Howard started in 53 consecutive games; played in 95 games.

Howard, Todd   LB   53   Texas A&M   1987-88

The Chiefs' third-round selection in the 1987 draft, Howard was used on special teams and saw some action at linebacker. Played in 19 games.

Huarte, John   QB   7   Notre Dame   1969-71

The 1964 Heisman Trophy winner came to Kansas City when Len Dawson hurt his knee in 1969 but was never activated for a game. Made the squad in 1970. Threw just eight passes for the Chiefs, completing two. Played in two games.

Hudock, Mike   C   54   Miami (Fla.)   1967

Played in four games for the Chiefs.

Player	Position	Jersey(s) Worn	College	Year(s) Played

Hudson, Bob — LB — 61 — Clemson — 1960

Played in five games for the original Texans before going to Denver in the middle of the 1960 season. Had one interception.

Hudson, Doug — QB — 11 — Nicholls State — 1987

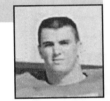

The Chiefs' seventh-round pick in the 1987 draft, Hudson played in one replacement game during the 1987 strike game, throwing one pass.

Hughes, Danan — WR — 83 — Iowa — 1993-98

Hughes was the Chiefs' seventh draft pick in 1993; he had great hands and was one of the best special teams players while he was with the Chiefs; caught 46 passes for 425 yards and four touchdowns; returned 35 punts for an average of 7.4 yards per return. Played in a total of 85 games for the Chiefs.

Hull, Bill — DE — 85 — Wake Forest — 1962

The Texans' fifth-round pick in 1962, Hull played in 14 games for the Texans.

Humphrey, Tom — C — 52 — Abilene Christian — 1974

Played in five games for the Chiefs; returned one kickoff for yards.

Hunt, Bobby — DB — 20 — Auburn — 1962-67

The Texans drafted Hunt in the 11th round of the 1962 draft, and it was one of the best selections the club ever made in the late rounds. His addition to the defense helped the franchise field one of the AFL's best secondaries. He played in Super Bowl I and was named to the AFL All-Star team in 1964. Hunt led the team in interceptions 1962-64, and tied with teammate Johnny Robinson for the league lead with 10 in 1966. He had 37 interceptions for his career in Kansas City, returning one for a touchdown. He played in 84 games for the franchise.

Hurston, Chuck — DE/LB — 85 — Auburn — 1965-70

Came to the Chiefs on waivers from Buffalo; was the teams' starting defensive end in 1966-67; switched to linebacker in 1968; played in Super Bowl I against the Packers and Super Bowl IV against the Vikings; played in a total of 84 games for the Chiefs.

Hyde, Glenn — C — 52 — Pittsburgh — 1987

Played in eight games for the Chiefs; recovered one fumble.

Player	Position	Jersey(s) Worn	College	Year(s) Played

Ingram, Byron G 60 Eastern Kentucky 1987-88

Played in 13 games for the Chiefs, returning two kickoffs for 16 yards.

Jackson, Billy RB 43 Alabama 1981-84

Kansas City selected Jackson in the seventh round of the 1981 draft; overshadowed by Joe Delaney his first two seasons, Jackson was a good runner and reliable receiver out of the backfield. Provided steady rushing numbers throughout his time in Kansas City. Best season was 1983 when he ran for 499 yards and caught 32 passes for 243 yards. Jackson had ten rushing touchdowns in 1981. He had 1,365 yards rushing for his career, caught 58 passes and scored 18 touchdowns. He played in 57 games.

Jackson, Charles LB 51 Washington 1978-84

The Chiefs picked Jackson up on waivers from Denver, and it proved to be a great move by the club. After spending most of his first three seasons on the specials teams, Jackson moved into the starting lineup at linebacker and stayed there for three seasons. Had five sacks, one interception and one touchdown on a fumble recovery in 86 games for the Chiefs.

Jackson, Charlie DB 40 SMU 1960

Played in three games for the Texans.

Jackson, Frank WR/RB 26 SMU 1961-65

Another successful late-round draft pick by the franchise, Jackson came to the Texans in the 19th round of the 1961 draft. Initially a running back, Jackson switched to flanker to beef up the injured receiving corps and never returned to the running back position. And he was a good halfback, gaining 386 yards his rookie season and 251 before switching to wide receiver in 1962. In his first full season at flanker, Jackson hauled in 50 passes for 785 yards and eight touchdowns. He followed with one of the best seasons a Chiefs receiver has ever had in 1964 by catching a then-team-record 62 receptions for 943 and nine touchdowns. For his career, Jackson caught 163 passes for 2,516 and 21 touchdowns. He also returned 47 punts. Jackson appeared in one AFL All-Star game and played in 70 games for the franchise before going to AFL expansion team Miami in 1966.

Jackson, Gerald S 38 Mississippi State 1979

Selected in the tenth round of the 1979 draft, Jackson intercepted one pass and recovered one fumble for the Chiefs in 16 games.

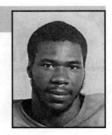

Jacoby, Mitch — TE — 85 — Northern Illinois — 1999

Came to the Chiefs in a trade with St. Louis; Jacoby played in six games in 1999, catching one pass for six yards and making two tackles on special teams.

Jakes, Van — DB — 22 — Kent State — 1983-84

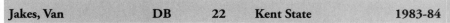

Made the Chiefs as a rookie free agent; played special teams and backup in the defensive secondary; played in 22 games for Kansas City.

Jamison, George — LB — 57 — Cincinnati — 1994-96

Came to the Chiefs as a free agent after spending seven seasons with the Lions; excellent at both pass and run coverage; best season for Kansas City was 1994 when he totaled 80 tackles, three fumble recoveries, and one sack; played in 32 games for the Chiefs.

Jankowski, Bruce — WR — 41 — Ohio — 1971-72

The Chiefs' tenth-round pick in 1971, Jankowski played in nine games and caught two passes for 24 yards.

Jaworski, Ron — QB — 7 — Youngstown State — 1989

Jaworski came to the Chiefs from Miami for the final year of his career. Played in six games for the Chiefs and threw for 385 yards and two touchdowns.

Jaynes, Dave — QB — 12 — Kansas — 1974

The Chiefs' third-round pick in 1974, Jaynes never met the high expectations the club had for him. He played in two games, threw two passes, one for an interception, and also had a fumble.

Jenkins, Keyvan — RB/KR — 41 — UNLV — 1988

Played in two games for the Chiefs and returned two kickoffs for 12 yards.

Jenkins, Trezelle — T — 74 — Michigan — 1995-97

The Chiefs' no. 1 draft pick in 1995, Jenkins was never able to adjust to the NFL and live up to the potential the Chiefs thought he had when they selected him. He had tremendous size (6' 7" and 317 lbs.), but never adjusted to the demands placed on an NFL offensive lineman. Jenkins played in nine games for the Chiefs.

Jeralds, Luther — DE — 89 — North Carolina College — 1961

Jeralds played in nine games for the Dallas Texans.

Johnson, Clyde — CB — 23 — Kansas State — 1997

Johnson played in 15 games for the Chiefs.

Player	Position	Jersey(s) Worn	College	Year(s) Played

Johnson, Curley — HB — 33 — Houston — 1960

A member of the original Texans, Johnson ran the ball 23 times for 43 yards and caught ten passes for 174 yards. He scored two touchdowns and played in 14 games.

Johnson, Dick — E — 85 — Minnesota — 1963

Johnson caught two passes for 17 yards and a touchdown while playing in five games for the Chiefs.

Johnson, Jack — DB — 32 — Miami (Fla.) — 1961

Played in one game for the Texans.

Johnson, Jimmie — TE — 45 — Howard — 1994

Played in seven games for the Chiefs and caught two passes.

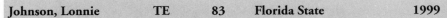

Johnson, Ken — DE — 97 — Knoxville — 1987

A replacement player during the 1987 NFL players' strike; played in two games for the Chiefs.

Johnson, Lonnie — TE — 83 — Florida State — 1999

Signed as a free agent from Buffalo, Johnson was the Chiefs' backup at tight end for the 1999 season. An excellent blocker, Johnson was also a good receiver. He played on special teams, making nine stops on kick coverage. He caught ten passes for 98 yards and one touchdown. Johnson started twice, and played in 14 games.

Johnson, Melvin — S — 35 — Kentucky — 1998

Came to the Chiefs in trade with Tampa Bay; provided depth in the secondary; played in seven games and had one sack.

Johnson, Reggie — TE — 85 — Florida State — 1996

Signed with the Chiefs as an unrestricted free agent; added depth and stability to the tight-end position for one season; caught 18 passes for 189 yards and one touchdown. Johnson played in 11 games.

Johnson, Sidney — CB — 45 — California — 1988

Played in 13 games for the Chiefs, primarily on the special teams.

Player	Position	Jersey(s) Worn	College	Year(s) Played

Johnson, Stone   WR   33   **Grambling**   1963 preseason

Selected by the Texans in the 14th round of the 1963 AFL draft, Johnson showed the promise of becoming an outstanding receiver. He had world-class speed and good hands, and had made the team going into the final preseason game of 1963. That game, played in Wichita, Kansas, against the Oilers, saw the end of Johnson's football career, and tragically, less than two weeks later, the end of his life. Johnson broke his neck in a game and died from complications following the injury. The Chiefs retired his jersey, No. 33, to honor his short time with the team.

Jolly, Ken   LB   52   **Mid-America Nazarene**   1984-85

A small college, free-agent success story, Jolley not only made the team as a rookie, but moved into the starting outside linebacker position the following season. He finished with 79 tackles in 1985 and played in a total of 32 games for the Chiefs.

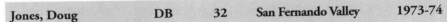

Jones, Bill   RB   43   **Southwest Texas State**   1990-92

Originally a 12th-round draft pick in 1989, Jones signed with the Chiefs as a free agent the following year. Played a big part in the success of the Chiefs' running game in 1990-92, leading the way for Barry Word and Christian Okoye. He only ran the ball 10 times, but had good hands, catching 35 passes for 240 yards and six touchdowns. Played in 38 games for Kansas City.

Jones, Doug   DB   32   **San Fernando Valley**   1973-74

Selected in the sixth round of the 1973 draft, Jones played on special teams and saw some action in the defensive secondary. Intercepted one pass in 18 games.

Jones, E.J.   RB   48   **Kansas**   1985

Jones signed as a free agent and provided a little depth in the backfield for the Chiefs. He played in five games and carried the ball 12 times for 19 yards. He also caught three passes.

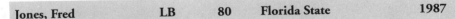

Jones, Fred   LB   80   **Florida State**   1987

A replacement player during the 1987 NFL players' strike; played in two games for the Chiefs.

Jones, Fred   WR   96   **Grambling**   1990-93

Drafted in 1990 in the fourth round, Jones gained a reputation for being one of the best blocking wide receivers in the NFL. He was also invaluable on the special teams, returning kicks and covering. He caught 36 passes for 466 yards and returned 12 punts and 23 kickoffs. He played 41 games.

Player	Position	Jersey(s) Worn	College	Year(s) Played

Jones, Hassan — WR — 81 — Florida State — 1993

Played in eight games for the Chiefs, catching seven passes for 91 yards.

Jones, Reggie — WR — 9 — LSU — 1997

Spent the entire 1997 season on injured reserve.

Jones, Rod — TE — 81 — Washington — 1987-88

Played in five games for the Chiefs, catching eight passes for 76 yards and one touchdown.

Jones, Victor — RB — 46 — LSU — 1994

Played in one game for the Chiefs.

Jones, Reggie — WR — 11 — LSU — 2001

Singed with the Chiefs late in the season and was inactive for two games.

Jozwiak, Brian — G — 73 — West Virginia — 1986-88

A first-round draft pick in 1986, Jozwiak fought injuries during his short career in Kansas City and was never able to achieve the results the club expected of a no. 1 choice. Jozwiak started as a tackle but later switched to guard. He played in 28 games for the Chiefs.

Junkin, Mike — LB — 93 — Duke — 1989

Played in five games for the Chiefs.

K

Kaiser, Jason — CB — 24 — Culver-Stockton — 1998

Played in one game for the Chiefs in 1998 and was on the practice squad most of the 1999 season.

Kauahi, Kani — C — 65 — Hawaii — 1992

Played in 16 games for the Chiefs.

Kearney, Jim — DB — 46 — Prairie View — 1967-75

see Other Chiefs Greats

Player	Position	Jersey(s) Worn	College	Year(s) Played

Kearney, Tim — LB — 50 — Northern Michigan — 1975

The Chiefs picked up Kearney on waivers from Cincinnati; was a backup at linebacker and a special teams player; played in 14 games for the Chiefs.

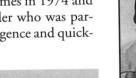

Keating, Tom — DT — 74 — Michigan — 1974-75

Acquired in a trade with Pittsburgh, Keating started in 12 games in 1974 and played in another nine the following season. A former Raider who was particularly hard on the Chiefs, Keating was known for his intelligence and quickness at the line. Played in 23 games for the Chiefs.

Keel, Mark — TE — 80 — Arizona — 1987

Came to the Chiefs midway through the 1987 season from Seattle; played in seven games and caught two passes for nine yards.

Kellar, Bill — WR — 82 — Stanford — 1978

The second of two seventh-round picks in 1978, Kellar played primarily on special teams. A knee injury ended his season. He played in five games for Kansas City.

Kelley, Ed — DB — 44 — Texas — 1961-62

A backup in the secondary, Kelley resurrected his career in the AFL after failing to make the Rams in 1955. Played in 15 games for the Texans.

Kelly, Bobby — T — 70 — New Mexico State — 1967

Played in three games for the Chiefs.

Kenney, Bill — QB — 9 — Northern Colorado — 1979-88

see Other Chiefs Greats

Kennison, Eddie — WR — 87 — LSU — 2001

Signed with the Chiefs as a free agent after leaving the Broncos midway through the 2001 season. Kennison added speed and experience at the wideout position, which enhanced the team's passing game the final month of the 2001 season. He caught 16 passes for 322 yards, and played in five games.

Keyes, Leroy — RB — 23 — Purdue — 1973

Played in three games for the Chiefs.

King, Bruce — RB — 46 — Purdue — 1985-86

A fifth-round draft pick in 1985, King was the Chiefs' starting fullback at the beginning of the 1985 season. Went to Buffalo after four games in 1986. Ran the ball 28 times for 83 yards and caught seven passes for 45 yards. King played in 20 games.

Player	Position	Jersey(s) Worn	College	Year(s) Played

Kinney, Jeff   RB   31   **Nebraska**   1972-76

The Chiefs' first-round pick in the 1972, Kinney came into the NFL after a brilliant career at Nebraska, and Coach Hank Stram had high hopes for him. He was never able to live up to his college standards, but did supply the Chiefs with good backup performances during his time in Kansas City. Kinney's best game was against Oakland in 1974, gaining 124 yards on the ground. For his career in Kansas City, he gained 810 yards rushing, caught 54 passes for 424 yards and scored five touchdowns. He played in 50 games.

Kirchbaum, Kelly   LB   62   **Kentucky**   1980

Played in one game for the Chiefs.

Kirchner, Mark   T/G   64   **Baylor**   1983

Came to the Chiefs on waivers from Pittsburgh; played in five games.

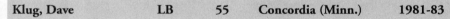

Klug, Dave   LB   55   **Concordia (Minn.)**   1981-83

A fourth-round draft pick in 1980, Klug played primarily on the special teams and was a backup linebacker; recovered a blocked punt in the end zone for touchdown against the Chargers in 1982; played in 26 games.

Knapp, Lindsay   G/T   65   **Notre Dame**   1993-94

The Chiefs' fifth-round draft pick in 1993, Knapp played in two games.

Koch, Pete   DE   74   **Maryland**   1985-87

Joined the Chiefs on waivers from the Bengals, played in all 16 games and collected two sacks. Became the starting defensive left end in 1986 and had a very good season, making 81 tackles and 5.5 sacks. Missed the second half of the 1987 season because of a knee injury and didn't play with Kansas City again. Played in a total of 54 games.

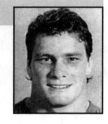

Koss, Stein   TE   80   **Arizona State**   1987

A replacement player during the 1987 NFL players' strike; played in two games and caught two passes for 25 yards.

Kragen, Greg   DT   71   **Utah State**   1994

Came to the Chiefs after putting in nine superb seasons with the Broncos. Played in 16 games as a backup defensive lineman.

Kratzer, Dan   WR   27   **Missouri Valley College**   1973

Played in one game for the Chiefs.

Player	Position	Jersey(s) Worn	College	Year(s) Played

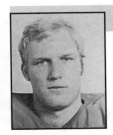

Kremer, Ken NT 91 **Ball State** **1979-84**

"Fuzzy" was a seventh-round draft pick by the Chiefs in 1979; had a solid career for Kansas City, providing excellent strength and stability up the middle; best season was 1981 when he had 61 tackles and eight sacks. For his career, Kremer had 22 sacks and one interception in 87 games. Kremer now owns a popular sports bar and grill in Kansas City.

Krieg, Dave QB 17 **Milton** **1992-93**

The long-time quarterback for the Seahawks came to the Chiefs as a free agent in 1992; had a very productive season in 1992 for Kansas City, but was replaced in the starting lineup by Joe Montana in 1993. Completed 335 of 602 pass attempts for 4,353 yards and 22 touchdowns for the Chiefs; also had a couple of rushing touchdowns. Krieg played in 28 games for Kansas City.

Krisher, Bill G 64 **Oklahoma** **1960-61**

An original Texan, Krisher got a second chance at professional football because of the AFL, and he made good on that chance. His play on the offensive line the Texans' first two seasons was very good, and he was selected both years for the All-AFL team. He played in a total of 27 games for Dallas.

Kubik, Brad G 67 **SW Missouri State** **1998-2000**

Was on the official team roster the last two games of 1998, but was listed as inactive for both games.

LaChapelle, Sean WR 18 **UCLA** **1996**

After failing to make the team in 1994 and '95, LaChapelle stuck with the club in 1996. He started eight games and pulled in 27 passes for 422 yards and two touchdowns. He played in a total of 12 games.

Lacy, Ken RB 40 **Tulsa** **1984-85, 87**

A free agent from the USFL, Lacy was the team's fourth leading rusher in 1984, but he fought injuries the rest of his career and played in just five games after the '84 season. He was a replacement player during the 1987 NFL players' strike. His total rushing yardage is 235 yards on 66 carries. He also caught 13 passes and scored four touchdowns. He played in 20 games.

Ladd, Earnie DT 99 **Grambling** **1967-68**

see Other Chiefs Greats

Player	Position	Jersey(s) Worn	College	Year(s) Played
LaGrand, Morris	RB	45	Tampa	1975

The Chiefs' sixth pick in the 1975 draft, LaGrand played primarily on special teams and carried the ball 13 times for 38 yards and a touchdown. He played in 11 games.

Lane, Garcia	CB/KR	48	Ohio State	1985, 87

The Chiefs' third pick in the 1984 supplemental draft, Lane was used to return kicks. He returned 43 punts for 381 yards and 15 kickoffs for 306 yards. He was also a replacement player during the 1987 NFL players' strike, and played in 17 games.

Lane, MacArthur	RB	42	Utah State	1975-78

The Chiefs traded a third-round pick in the 1976 draft to Green Bay for Lane. The big running back produced for the Chiefs, most notably with the pass receiving. He caught 66 passes in 1976 to lead the NFL, and also ran for 542 yards that season, tops on the Chiefs. He was the oldest running back in the league during his time with Kansas City, and while his overall numbers were down from his playing days in St. Louis and Green Bay, Lane was a valuable member of the Chiefs' offense. He finished his career in Kansas City with 1,209 yards rushing, 130 pass receptions, and nine touchdowns. Lane played in 42 games for the Chiefs.

Lane, Skip	CB/S	26	Mississippi	1984

Played in one game for the Chiefs.

Lanier, Willie	LB	63	Morgan State	1967-77

see Chiefs in the Pro Football Hall of Fame

Larpenter, Carol	G	67	Texas	1962

Played in two games for the Texans.

Lathrop, Kit	DE	70	Arizona State	1986

Came to the Chiefs from the USFL and was used in certain defensive alignments. Played in 17 games.

Lee, Jackey	QB	15	Cincinnati	1967-69

Joined the Chiefs from Houston with Ernie Ladd in exchange for Pete Beathard and the Oilers' no. 1 draft pick; was a capable backup at quarterback behind Len Dawson; completed 43 of 84 passes for 597 yards and five touchdowns; played in 14 games for the Chiefs.

Player	Position	Jersey(s) Worn	College	Year(s) Played

Lee, Willie — DT — 78 — Bethune-Cookman — 1976-77

The Chiefs' fifth choice in the 1976 draft, Lee racked up five sacks among his 67 tackles in 1977; scored a touchdown on a fumble recovery; played in 28 games.

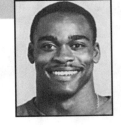

Lewis, Albert — CB — 29 — Grambling — 1983-93

see Other Chiefs Greats

Lewis, Garry — CB — 21 — Alcorn State — 1993

Played in one game for the Chiefs.

Lewis, Tahaun — CB — 21 — Nebraska — 1992

A "Plan B" free agent, Lewis played in nine games, primarily as a nickel back and on special teams.

Liggett, Bob — DT — 62 — Nebraska — 1970

The Chiefs picked Liggett in the 15th round of the 1970 draft. He played in seven games for Kansas City.

Lindstrom, Chris — DE — 60 — Boston University — 1987

A replacement player during the 1987 NFL players' strike; played in three games for the Chiefs.

Lindstrom, Dave — DE — 71 — Boston University — 1978-85

Picked up on waivers from San Diego, Lindstrom filled in as a starter on the defensive line frequently, subbing for Art Still and Mike Bell. He only missed three games from the time he joined the club until his retirement. He recorded 205 tackles, 13.5 sacks, and one fumble recovery; started 30 times in 118 games played.

Linger, Adam — C — 51, 62 — Illinois — 1983-86, 1988

A ninth-round pick in the 1983 draft, Linger served as the team's long snappe and backup center for most of his career. He spent the 1987 season with Buffalo, returned to Kansas City for the 1988 season and then returned to Buffalo where he played the next seven seasons. Played in a total of 76 games for the Chiefs.

Little, Dave — TE — 84 — Middle Tennessee — 1984

Played in ten games for the Chiefs and caught one pass for ten yards.

Player	Position	Jersey(s) Worn	College	Year(s) Played

Livingston, Mike   QB   10   SMU   1968-79

see Other Chiefs Greats

Lloyd, Jeff   NT   74   West Texas State   1978

Played in 16 games for the Chiefs.

Lockett, Kevin   WR   81   Kansas State   1997-2000

The Chiefs' second-round pick in the 1997 draft, Lockett came into his own in the 1999 season. After two seasons that saw him gain playing time gradually, Lockett grabbed 34 passes in '99 for 426 yards and two touchdowns. He had only 20 catches from his first two seasons. He has also returned eight punts and made 10 tackles on special teams. Lockett has played in 38 games for Kansas City.

Lohmeyer, John   DE   87   Emporia State   1973, 1975-77

A fourth-round draft pick in 1973, Lohmeyer came back from a crippling neck injury that forced him to miss all of the 1974 season. He filled in on the defensive line; played in a total of 41 games, scoring a safety and a touchdown.

Longmire, Sam   DB   15   Purdue   1976-78

Played in five games for the Chiefs.

Lothamer, Ed   DT   82   Mich. State   1964-69, 1971-72

The Chiefs' fourth-round pick in the 1964 draft, Lothamer was the starting left tackle on the defensive line from 1965 through 1968. His play was solid and consistent. He retired after the 1969 season but came back in 1971 for two more seasons as Curly Culp's backup. Lothamer played in a total of 88 games for the Chiefs.

Loveall, Calvin   CB   38   Idaho   1988

Played in four games for the Chiefs.

Lowe, Paul   RB   20   Oregon State   1968-69

One of the AFL's premier runners with San Diego, Lowe came to the Chiefs as running-back insurance the last two seasons of his career. He only carried the ball 11 times in two seasons and also returned five kickoffs. He played in eight games.

Player	Position	Jersey(s) Worn	College	Year(s) Played

Lowery, Nick   K   8   Dartmouth   1980-93

see Other Chiefs Greats

Lutz, David   G/T   72   Georgia Tech   1983-92

The Chiefs' second-round draft pick in 1983, Lutz was a mainstay on the offensive line for ten seasons. A powerful run blocker, he played his first six seasons at right tackle before making the switch to right guard, where he played his final four years. His blocking prowess led the way for three 1,000-yard rushers (Okoye twice and Word), and he was excellent at pass blocking. Lutz played on four playoff teams (1986, 1990-92) and appeared in a total of 139 games for the Chiefs before going to Detroit in 1993.

Lynch, Jim   LB   51   Notre Dame   1967-77

see Chiefs Hall of Fame

M

Maas, Bill   NT/DE   63   Pittsburgh   1984-92

see Other Chiefs Greats

Mack, Cedric   CB   40   Baylor   1992

Played one game for the Chiefs.

Maczuzak, John   DT   72   Pittsburgh   1964

Selected in the 22nd round of the 1963 draft, Maczuzak played in one game for the Chiefs.

Maddox, Bob   DE   75   Frostburg State   1975-76

Played in 14 games for the Chiefs.

Malone, Darrell   CB   42   Jacksonville State (Ala.)   1992

A sixth-round pick in the 1991 draft, Malone played in four games for the Chiefs.

Mandley, Pete   WR   89   Northern Arizona   1989-90

Signed with the Chiefs as a free agent after playing in Detroit five seasons; caught 42 passes for 573 yards and one touchdown; also returned 19 punts and five kickoffs; played in a total of 18 games.

Mangiero, Dino NT 74 Rutgers 1980-83

A free-agent signee, Mangiero started 12 times at nose tackle; for his career he played in 47 games, had 138 tackles, ten sacks and one interception.

Manuel, Sean TE 95 New Mexico State 1998

Was on the reserve list the entire 1998 season; never played in a game.

Manumaleuga, Frank LB 54 San Jose State 1979-81

A no. 4 draft pick in 1979, Manumaleuga's career was cut short by injuries; he was a starter at linebacker and intercepted six passes, returning one for a touchdown (against Seattle in 1980). He had 229 tackles in 35 games.

Manusky, Greg LB 51 Colgate 1994-99

Came to Kansas City as a free agent from Minnesota and has not only been one of the best special teams players in the franchise's history, but has consistently been among the NFL's elite covering kicks; great at finding the ball and covering fumbles; had never missed a game with the Chiefs, playing in 96 straight games.

Marsalis, Jim CB 40 Tennessee State 1969-75

see Other Chiefs Greats

Marshall, Henry WR 89 Missouri 1976-87

see Other Chiefs Greats

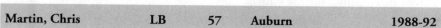

Marshall, Larry DB/KR 22 Maryland 1972-73, 1978

A 15th-round draft pick in 1972, Marshall had a sensational rookie season as a kick returner, averaging 28.3 yards per kickoff return. His second season was almost as good, as he averaged 27.9 per return. Returned 44 kickoffs and 53 punts in his career, and played in a total of 23 games.

Martin, Chris LB 57 Auburn 1988-92

Came to the Chiefs from Minnesota, Martin was the team's starting outside linebacker on the left side for four years. An aggressive defender, Martin was excellent at stopping the run, and sacked the quarterback 15 times. His best season for Kansas City was 1991 when he totaled 103 tackles and five sacks. Scored one touchdown in his career for the Chiefs. Played in 67 games for Kansas City.

Martin, Dave LB 58 Notre Dame 1968

Played in two games for the Chiefs.

Player	Position	Jersey(s) Worn	College	Year(s) Played

Martin, Don — CB — 47 — Yale — 1975

Came to the Chiefs as a free agent from New England and was the primary backup in the defensive secondary his one season in Kansas City; played in 14 games.

Martin, Eric — WR — 85 — LSU — 1994

A free agent from New Orleans, Martin caught 21 passes for 307 yards and one touchdown. He played ten games for the Chiefs.

Martin, Steve — DT — 90 — Missouri — 2000

Came to Kansas City from Philadelphia as an unrestricted free agent and played in all 16 games of the 2000 season in a reserve role. Totaled 27 tackles and recovered two fumbles.

Marts, Lonnie — LB — 51 — Tulane — 1991-93

Came to Kansas City as a free agent and displayed a knack for making big plays. A safety in college, Marts made the successful transition to linebacker for the Chiefs and was the top reserve for the linebacker corps and one of the top players on the special teams. Returned an interception 36 yards against Seattle for a touchdown in 1992. Recorded three sacks for the Chiefs and played in 47 games.

Maslowski, Mike — LB — 57 — Wisconsin-La Crosse — 1999-2001

A rookie free agent acquisition, Maslowski became the Chiefs' top special teams player in 1999, recording 23 stops in kick coverage. He also filled in as the team's long snapper for one game, and saw reserve duty at linebacker in another five games. Maslowski captained the special teams in 2000, and his outstanding play got better. He was named to *Sports Illustrated's* All-Pro team (special teams) and *USA Today's* All-Joe team. By the end of the 2000 season Maslowski was getting more and more playing time at linebacker, and finished the year with 59 tackles, and one fumble recovery. Appeared in just eight games in 2001 because of injuries, making ten tackles and one sack. He's played in 39 games for the Chiefs over three seasons.

Masters, Billy — TE — 84 — LSU — 1975-76

Came to the Chiefs from Denver; was originally drafted by the Chiefs in the third round of the 1967 draft; gave Kansas City two good years at tight end, catching 42 passes for 583 yards and six touchdowns. Masters played in 24 games for the Chiefs.

Matthews, Steve — QB — 15 — Memphis State — 1994-96

The Chiefs' seventh-round draft pick from the 1994 draft, Matthews, while on the Chiefs' active roster, never played in a game.

Matusak, John — DT — 79 — Tampa — 1974-75

A great underachiever with the Chiefs, Matusak came to Kansas City from Houston for Curly Culp and a first-round draft choice, in what could be considered one of the team's worst trades. Went to Oakland from Kansas City and became the star the Oilers and Chiefs thought he would be. Scored one touchdown for the Chiefs in 22 games.

Player	Position	Jersey(s) Worn	College	Year(s) Played

Mays, Jerry   DT   75   SMU   1961-70

see Chiefs Hall of Fame

McAlister, Ken   LB   94   San Francisco   1984-87

A prized free-agent pickup, McAlister had a great 1984 season, making 72 tackles, four sacks, and two interceptions. Missed the entire 1985 season with torn knee ligaments and only played in four more games for Kansas City. He played in a total of 19 games.

McCabe, Jerry   LB   92   Holy Cross   1988

Played in three games for the Chiefs.

McCann, Jim   P   5   Arizona State   1975

Was the Chiefs' punter the final three games of the 1975 season, filling in for the injured Jerrel Wilson. Punted the ball 14 times for a 35.2 yard average.

McCarthy, Mickey   TE   81   TCU   1969

The Chiefs' fourth-round draft pick in 1968, McCarthy played in three games.

McCleary, Norris   DT   71   East Carolina   2000-01

A free agent signee, McCleary joined the Chiefs active roster late in the 2000 season and played in three games, recording two tackles. He appeared in ten games in 2001 and made seven tackles.

McClinton, Curtis   RB   32   Kansas   1962-69

see Chiefs Hall of Fame

McDaniels, Pellom   DE   77   Oregon State   1993-98

Signed as a free agent, McDaniels was one of the Chiefs' most valuable defensive players during his time in Kansas City; capable of playing any position on the defensive line; was a valuable member of the Kansas City community, giving much of himself in a variety of different projects. His best season was 1997 when he started six games, made 38 tackles and recorded 3.5 sacks. McDaniels played in a total of 74 games for the Chiefs.

McElroy, Reggie   T   70   West Texas State   1993

Played in eight games as a backup offensive lineman for the Chiefs.

Player	Position	Jersey(s) Worn	College	Year(s) Played

McGlockton, Chester   DT   75   Clemson   1998-2000

The massive McGlokton came to the Chiefs as a free agent from the Raiders. His first season with the Chiefs was shortened by six games because of back problems, but McGlockton came back after surgery and performed very well. His 1999 season was stellar, as he continually plugged the middle on runs and harassed quarterbacks every game. He totaled 81 tackles in 1999, sacked the quarterback 1.5 times, recovered a fumble, forced a fumble, and intercepted a pass against the Colts. McGlockton registered 4.5 sacks in 2000 to go along with his 70 stops, but was released from the Chiefs after the season was concluded. He played in 41 games for Kansas City.

McGovern, Rob   LB   50   Holy Cross   1989-90

The Chiefs' tenth-round draft pick in 1989, McGovern excelled on the special teams and contributed with strong play at the linebacker position. He blocked a punt out of the end zone against Dallas to score a safety in 1989; played in a total of 27 games for the Chiefs.

McKinney, Odis   S   21   Colorado   1985

Played in five games for the Chiefs.

McKnight, Ted   RB   22   Minnesota-Duluth   1977-81

A waivers acquisition from Oakland, McKnight was the Chiefs' leading rusher in 1979-80. He suffered a severe knee injury in 1981 and was never able to return. McKnight ran for 627 yards in 1978, 755 in 1979 and 693 in 1980. He exploded for an 84-yard touchdown run in 1979 against Seattle and gained 147 yards that day, his best individual game effort. He was used for kickoff returns in 1977 and had one return of 70 yards. His pass-catching skills were also superb, as he caught 38 passes in 1979 and 1980. For his career, he gained 2,344 yards rushing, caught 99 passes for 717 yards, and scored 23 touchdowns. He played in 65 games for the Chiefs.

McLean, Ron   NT   62   Cal State-Fullerton   1988

Played in six games for the Chiefs.

McManus, Danny   QB   14   Florida State   1988

The Chiefs' 11th-round draft pick in 1988, McManus was active for seven games during the 1988 season but never saw any playing time.

McMillan, Erik   S   24   Missouri   1993

Played in one game for the Chiefs.

Player	Position	Jersey(s) Worn	College	Year(s) Played

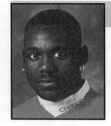

McMillian, Mark — CB — 29 — Alabama — 1997-98

"Mighty Mouse" signed with the Chiefs as a free agent, coming from the Saints. He was used primarily as a third defensive back in 1997 and made the most of his playing time, picking off an AFC-best eight passes, returning three for touchdowns. He moved into the starting spot in 1998, but was unable to match his brilliant '97 season, making three interceptions. He played in 32 games for Kansas City.

McNair, Todd — RB — 48 — Temple — 1989-93, 1996

An eighth-round draft pick in 1989, McNair was a dynamic back who excelled in third-down situations and on special teams. He made at least 30 receptions his first four seasons in Kansas City. His best rushing season was 1993 when he gained 278 yards and scored two touchdowns; his best receiving stats were compiled in 1990 when he caught 40 passes for 507 yards and two touchdowns. Also returned kickoffs. Played for Houston in 1994-95 and returned to the Chiefs in 1996. Gained 667 yards rushing in his career for the Chiefs, caught 186 passes for 1,856 yards and scored six touchdowns. McNair played in 90 games for the Chiefs.

McNeil, Pat — RB — 45 — Baylor — 1976-77

A 17th-round draft pick in 1976, McNeil ran the ball eight times for 26 yards and caught two passes for 33 yards. He played in 12 games.

McRae, Jerrold — WR — 83 — Tennessee State — 1978

The Chiefs' fifth-round draft pick in 1978, McRae played in four games for Kansas City.

McVea, Warren — RB — 6 — Houston — 1969-73

The Chiefs acquired McVea in a trade with Cincinnati before the start of the 1969 season, and he became one of the most productive of Hank Stram's scat backs on the Super Bowl champion team. He gained 500 yards rushing and scored seven touchdowns in 1969, and his 80-yard touchdown run against the Bengals broke open a tight game. Also returned kickoffs. For his career, McVea rushed for 1,053 yards and caught 17 passes for 94 yards. He scored ten touchdowns and played in 33 games.

Meisner, Greg — DE — 69 — Pittsburgh — 1989-90

Came to Kansas City as a "Plan B" free agent from the Rams; played a backup role on the defensive line; Played in 28 games and recorded 1.5 sacks for the Chiefs.

Mercer, Mike — K — 15 — Northern Arizona — 1966

Came to Kansas City after the start of the 1966 season and took over the team's place-kicking duties. Mercer played an important role in the Chiefs' first Super Bowl team, scoring 93 points and making 20 of 26 field goals. He made one of two field goals in Super Bowl I. Mercer played in ten games for the Chiefs.

Player	Position	Jersey(s) Worn	College	Year(s) Played

Merz, Curt — G/DE — 64 — Iowa — 1962-68

Joined the Texans as a free agent after playing in Canada and played on the 1962 AFL championship team. Played offensive guard and tackle, as well as the defensive line before he became a starting guard on the offensive line in 1964. Merz was one of the better pass blockers on the line during his time in Kansas City. He also played for the 1966 AFL champion Chiefs and in the first Super Bowl against the Packers. He played in a total of 92 games for the franchise.

Meyers, Jerry — DE — 79 — Northern Illinois — 1980

Played in two games for the Chiefs.

Mickell, Darren — DE — 92 — Florida — 1992-95

The Chiefs' second pick in the 1992 supplemental draft, Mickell was an outstanding pass rusher and was very good at stripping the ball. He became a starter at defensive end in 1994 and finished that season with seven sacks and four forced fumbles. Finished his time in Kansas City with 14 sacks; he went to New Orleans in 1996. Mickell played in 45 games for the Chiefs.

Miller, Bill — E — 82 — Miami (Fla.) — 1962

The Texans' second-round draft selection in 1962, Miller caught 23 passes for 277 yards. He played in 14 games for the Texans.

Miller, Cleophus — RB — 30 — Arkansas AM&N — 1974-75

Signed as a free agent, Miller was a backup running back for the 1974 season and the first part of 1975 before going to Cleveland. He ran for 186 yards, caught 14 passes for 149 yards, and returned 14 kickoffs in 1974. Miller played in 20 games for the Chiefs.

Miller, Paul — DE — 86 — LSU — 1960-61

The Texans' starting left end their first two seasons, Miller was another former NFLer who made it in the AFL. He played in 28 games and recovered one fumble for Dallas.

Milo, Ray — S — 27 — New Mexico State — 1978

Played in one game for the Chiefs.

Mincy, Charles — S — 42 — Washington — 1991-94

Mincy was the Chiefs' fifth-round draft pick in 1991 and was an important part of the secondary during his tenure in Kansas City. Possessing a knack for being around the ball and making big plays, Mincy picked off 12 passes for the Chiefs during his career, returning two for touchdowns. He also recovered a fumble for a touchdown. His best season was 1992 when he accumulated 96 tackles and had four interceptions. Mincy played in a total of 48 games for the Chiefs.

| **Minnis, Marvin** | **WR** | **81** | **Florida State** | **2001** |

The Chiefs' second selection in the third round of the 2001 draft, Minnis was big contributor to the team's offense during his rookie campaign. Nicknamed "Snoop," he caught 33 passes for 511 yards, including a 56-yarder against the Broncos that set up the game-winning field goal. Snoop scored one touchdown and played in 13 games, starting 11 times.

| **Mitchell, Willie** | **DB** | **22** | **Tennessee State** | **1964-71** |

A long-time member of the Chiefs' secondary, Mitchell was a regular at cornerback for four seasons and played on both Super Bowl teams, contributing greatly to the team's championship successes. Nicknamed "Top Cat," Mitchell also returned punts, running one back for a touchdown in 1965. He picked off five passes in 1968, and finished his career with 16, returning three for touchdowns. For his career, he returned 56 punts for an average of 10.1 yards per return. He played his entire career in Kansas City, 87 games in all.

| **Montagne, Dave** | **WR** | **87** | **Oregon State** | **1987** |

A replacement player during the 1987 NFL players' strike; played in three games for the Chiefs and caught five passes for 47 yards.

| **Montana, Joe** | **QB** | **19** | **Notre Dame** | **1993-94** |

see Other Chiefs Greats

| **Moon, Warren** | **QB** | **1** | **Washington** | **1999-2000** |

Moon came to the Chiefs from Seattle as a free agent and was the team's backup quarterback for the 1999 season. Having amassed more than 49,000 yards passing in his career, Moon tallied just 20 for the Chiefs, and only threw three passes. He played in one game.

| **Moorman, Mo** | **G** | **76** | **Texas A&M** | **1968-73** |

The Chiefs' first-round pick in 1968, Moorman moved into the starting guard position his rookie season and stayed there for six seasons before a knee injury prematurely ended his career. Known as an outstanding blocker with great second effort and quickness, Moorman was a key part of the Chiefs' running and passing game on the 1969 world championship team. He played in a total of 72 games for the Chiefs.

| **Moreau, Frank** | **RB** | **46** | **Louisville** | **2000** |

Kansas City selected Moreau with their fourth pick in the 2000 draft, and the rookie back didn't disappoint. He was third on the team in carries with 67 to gain 179 yards, and was tops with four rushing touchdowns. His longest run was for 22 yards against Denver. Moreau played in 11 games for the Chiefs.

Morgado, Arnold RB 21 Hawaii 1977-80

A free agent, Morgado made the most of the Chiefs' rushing offense in the late 1970s and gave the club some excellent runs off the bench. He also excelled on the special teams. His best rushing effort was against San Diego in 1978 when he gained 115 yards on 29 carries. He gained 593 yards and scored seven touchdowns in 1978 for his best season, and finished his career with 956 yards rushing and 16 touchdowns. He played in 52 games.

Moriarty, Larry RB 32 Notre Dame 1986-88

Came to the Chiefs from Houston and provided excellent depth at the running back position during his time in Kansas City. Played in a total of 31 games for the Chiefs and ran for 284 yards. He scored one touchdown and also returned kicks.

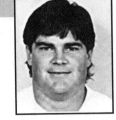

Morris, Bam RB 39 Texas Tech 1998-99

The Chiefs acquired Morris from Chicago, and despite several troubling episodes with the law throughout his career, the big, bruising runner played well, and during his two seasons with the Chiefs, remained trouble free. Morris provided the team with strong and powerful running. His best effort was 137 yards rushing against Dallas in 1998. He scored 11 touchdowns with Kansas City and rushed for a total of 895 yards in 22 games. Morris retired from pro football following the 1999 season.

Morris, Donnie Joe RB 22 North Texas State 1974

Played in three games for the Chiefs.

Morris, Michael C 68 NE Missouri State 1989

Played in five games for the Chiefs.

Morris, Sylvester WR 84 Jackson State 2000

The first wide receiver selected by the Chiefs in the first round of the draft since 1982, Morris more than lived up to the high expectations the club had for him. "Cat" caught a Chiefs' rookie record 48 passes (breaking Chris Burford's record of 46 in 1960) for 678 yards. Twice he had more than 100 receiving yards in a game, and scored three touchdowns against the Chargers. Morris also completed a 31-yard pass to Derrick Alexander against the Rams. He played in a total of 15 games, and was the starting third wideout 14 times. He missed the entire 2001 season because of a knee injury.

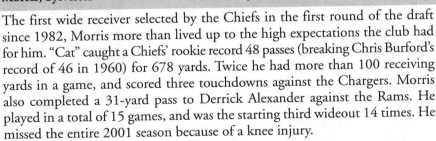

Moten, Gary LB 53 SMU 1987

A replacement player during the 1987 NFL players' strike; played in one game for the Chiefs.

Player	Position	Jersey(s) Worn	College	Year(s) Played

Mumphrey, Lloyd   DE   91   Miss. Valley State   1987

A replacement player during the 1987 NFL players' strike; played in three games for the Chiefs.

Murphy, James   WR   80   Utah State   1981

Came to Kansas City as a free agent; caught two passes for 36 yards and returned 20 kickoffs for an average of 22.9 per return. He played in ten games.

Murray, Eddie   K   2   Tulane   1992

One of the all-time great kickers in league history, Murray filled in for Nick Lowery in one game for the Chiefs. He kicked one field goal.

N

Napier, Walter   DT   76   Paul Quinn   1960-61

Nicknamed "Buffalo," Napier was an original member of the Texans and the team's starting left defensive tackle in 1960. He played in a total of 20 games for the Texans.

Nash, Kenny   WR   85   San Jose State   1987

A replacement player during the 1987 NFL players' strike; played in one game for the Chiefs and caught two passes for 22 yards.

Nelson, Mark   T   70   Bowling Green   1987

A replacement player during the 1987 NFL players' strike; played in one game for the Chiefs.

Nelson, Teddy   CB   49   UNLV   1987

A replacement player during the 1987 NFL players' strike; played in three games for the Chiefs.

Newton, Tim   DT   96   Florida   1993

Came to the Chiefs from Tampa Bay; was an important backup on the defensive line in 1993; recorded 22 tackles, recovered two fumbles, and made one sack. Played in 16 games.

Nicholson, Jim   T   70   Michigan State   1974-79

Came to Kansas City in trade with the Rams; Nicholson was both a starter and a backup during his career and showed versatility by switching back and forth from the left and right side of the line. He played in a total of 72 games for Kansas City.

Nix, Doyle — DB — 25 — SMU — 1961

Came to Dallas from San Diego and was a solid backup in the Texans' defensive backfield. Played in 11 games and intercepted three passes.

Nott, Mike — QB — 7 — Santa Clara — 1976

Played in one game for the Chiefs and completed four of ten passes for 46 yards. Also punted once for 35 yards.

Nottage, Dexter — DT — 94 — Florida A&M — 1997

Played in one game for the Chiefs.

Nunnery, R.B. — DT — 68 — LSU — 1960

Played in six games for the Texans.

O

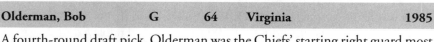

Oates, Brad — T — 72 — Brigham Young — 1980

Played in one game for the Chiefs.

Odom, Ricky — S — 38 — USC — 1978

A seventh-round draft pick in 1978, Odom played in eight games before going to the 49ers.

Okoye, Christian — RB — 35 — Azusa Pacific — 1987-92

see Chiefs Hall of Fame

Olderman, Bob — G — 64 — Virginia — 1985

A fourth-round draft pick, Olderman was the Chiefs' starting right guard most of his rookie season. Played in 16 games for the Chiefs.

Olenchalk, John — C/LB — 63 — Stanford — 1981-82

Played in ten games for the Chiefs.

Oliver, Muhammed — CB — 26 — Oregon — 1993

Played in two games for the Chiefs.

Player	Position	Jersey(s) Worn	College	Year(s) Played

Olsen, Orrin — C/G — 52 — BYU — 1976

The Chiefs' eighth-round pick in the 1976 draft, Olsen spent his one season in the NFL primarily on special teams, and also played center and guard. He's the youngest brother of NFL Hall-of-Famer Merlin Olsen. He played in 14 games for the Chiefs.

O'Neal, Leslie — DE — 91 — Oklahoma State — 1998-99

A productive sack artist, O'Neal joined the Chiefs as a free agent from the Rams. O'Neal fought through nagging and painful injuries his first season with the Chiefs to start in 13 games. Originally slated to rotate in on passing situations, O'Neal responded to the team's injury problems on the defensive line and played almost full time. He racked up 64 tackles, recovered three fumbles and made 4.5 sacks in 1998. His 1999 season was almost as good, as he made 5.5 sacks and started in another ten games. He has played in 32 games for the Chiefs.

Oriard, Mike — C — 50 — Notre Dame — 1970-73

The Chiefs' fifth-round pick in the 1970 draft, Oriard was an excellent backup for the offensive line. He also played on the special teams and appeared in a total of 42 games for the Chiefs.

Osiecki, Sandy — QB — 11 — Arizona State — 1984

Played in four games for the Chiefs, throwing 17 passes and completing seven for 64 yards.

Osley, Willie — DB — 47 — Illinois — 1974

A tenth-round pick in the 1973 draft, Osley played in three games for the Chiefs.

Otis, Jim — RB — 35 — Ohio State — 1971-72

The Chiefs acquired Otis in a trade with New Orleans, and he provided good blocking and powerful running off the bench for Kansas City. He only carried the ball 78 times in two seasons, gaining 276 yards, and caught 25 passes for 157 yards and two touchdowns. He went to St. Louis in 1973 and produced big rushing numbers, including a 1,000 yard season. He played in 23 games for the Chiefs.

Owens, Rich — DE — 97 — Lehigh — 2001

Signed with the Chiefs as an unrestricted free agent after spending the previous two seasons with the Miami Dolphins. Owens recorded 35 tackles and three sacks while playing in 16 games, including one start on the defensive line. He also played on special teams.

Player	Position	Jersey(s) Worn	College	Year(s) Played

| Paige, Stephone | WR | 83 | Fresno State | 1983-91 |

see Other Chiefs Greats

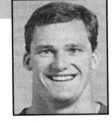

| Paine, Jeff | LB | 95 | Texas A&M | 1984-85 |

A no. 5 pick in the 1984 draft, Paine moved into the starting right outside linebacker spot at the end of his rookie season, but ligament damage to his right knee knocked him out. He played in 12 games in 1985 but never returned to his rookie season level of play. Had one sack and played in 26 games for the Chiefs.

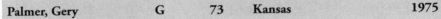

| Palewicz, Al | LB | 57 | Miami (Fla.) | 1973-75 |

An eighth-round draft pick in 1973, Palewicz was used primarily on special teams and as a backup outside linebacker. He played in 36 games for the Chiefs.

| Palmer, Gery | G | 73 | Kansas | 1975 |

Played in two games for the Chiefs.

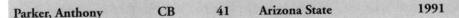

| Palmer, Paul | RB | 26 | Temple | 1987-88 |

The Chiefs' no. 1 pick in the 1987 draft, Palmer made a big splash as a kick returner his rookie season, returning two kicks for touchdowns and averaging 24.3 yards on 38 returns to lead the AFC. He only carried the ball 24 times in 1987, but saw more playing time in 1988, gaining 452 yards. But Palmer was never able to become the playmaker the Chiefs envisioned when they drafted him, and he left the club following the 1988 season. For his career he gained 607 yards rushing, caught 57 passes and scored six touchdowns in 27 games for Kansas City.

| Parker, Anthony | CB | 41 | Arizona State | 1991 |

Played in two games for the Chiefs.

| Parker, Glenn | G/T | 62 | Arizona | 1997-99 |

After quickly becoming one of the team's most versatile and proven players since arriving from Buffalo in 1997, Parker was the first offensive lineman in the franchise's history to win the team MVP award (following the 1998 season). Parker started at three different positions on the offensive line and his ability to adapt to new situations greatly helped the Chiefs' running and passing attack. He brought a great amount of playoff experience to Kansas City from Buffalo, where he played in four Super Bowls. Parker played in 42 games for the Chiefs.

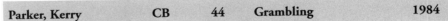

| Parker, Kerry | CB | 44 | Grambling | 1984 |

Came to the Chiefs from the CFL and was used as a backup at cornerback. Parker played in a total of 15 games for Kansas City.

Player	Position	Jersey(s) Worn	College	Year(s) Played

Parker, Larry   WR   80   USC   1999-2001

The Chiefs' number four selection in the 1999 draft, Parker saw duty in ten games his rookie season, with almost all of his playing time coming on special teams. Parker played sparingly at the wideout his second season; he caught three passes for 41 yards. He returned 10 punts for a 9.9 yards per return average, and 15 kickoffs for a 20.2 yards per return average. Parker saw more action at wide receiver in 2001, catching 15 passes for 199 yards and two touchdowns. He's played in a total of 38 games for Kansas City in three seasons.

Parker, Robert   RB   43   BYU   1987

A replacement player during the 1987 NFL players' strike; gained 150 yards rushing and scored one touchdown in three games for the Chiefs.

Parks, Nate   T   72   Stanford   1997

The Chiefs' seventh-round pick in the 1997 draft, Parks was on the team's roster the entire 1997 season but was never active for a game.

Parrish, Don   NT   61   Pittsburgh   1978-82

A free agent pickup by the Chiefs, Parrish proved to be a great acquisition and gave Kansas City five productive seasons on the defensive line. He won the Mack Lee Hill Award as the team's top rookie in 1978, and had a great season in 1979, starting all 16 games, making 74 tackles and five sacks. He finished his career in Kansas City with 13.5 sacks and played in 71 games.

Parten, Ty   DT   91, 97   Arizona   1997-2000

Signed as a free-agent, Parten played every position on the defensive line and gave the Chiefs rugged performances as well as contributed to the special teams. He started six games in 1998 and played in a total of 33 games for Kansas City.

Patton, Marvcus   LB   53   UCLA   1999-2001

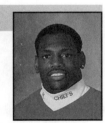

Patton signed with the Chiefs as a free agent, coming from Washington. In his three seasons with the Chiefs, the 12-year veteran has been everything the Chiefs had hoped he would be—a superior talent who is also committed to winning. Patton rang up 135 tackles with 6.5 sacks and three fumble recoveries in 1999, a performance that won him team MVP honors for the season. He followed with 143 stops in 2000, intercepted a couple of passes (returning one for a touchdown) and recovered a fumble. Patton was named defensive captain for the Chiefs in 2001, and the veteran responded with another good season, recording 138 tackles, three sacks, and two interceptions. He has played in 48 games for Kansas City.

Player	Position	Jersey(s) Worn	College	Year(s) Played

Paul, Whitney DE/LB 53 Colorado 1976-81, 1986

The Chiefs' no. 10 pick in the 1976 draft, Paul played his first two seasons at defensive end before switching to linebacker. He was productive at both positions. Paul had great seasons in 1978 and 1979, making 84 tackles and eight sacks in '79. He left for New Orleans following the 1981 season and returned to play one more year for the Chiefs in 1986. His career totals in Kansas City include two touchdowns scored on fumble recoveries and eight interceptions in 100 games.

Payton, Eddie KR 34 Jackson State 1978

Payton came to Kansas City in a trade with Detroit (for John Brockington) and provided the Chiefs with one great season as a return specialist. He is the older brother of NFL great Walter Payton. He averaged 11.4 yards per punt return and 25.8 yards per kickoff return in 14 games for the Chiefs.

Pearson, Aaron LB 96 Mississippi State 1986-88

Kansas City's 11th pick in the 1986 draft, Pearson started 19 times at inside and outside linebacker. His 1988 season was his best, as he made 74 tackles in 16 games. He played in 43 games and made 148 tackles for the Chiefs.

Pearson, Barry WR 85 Northwestern 1974-76

Came to the Chiefs from the Steelers for an eighth-round pick in the 1975 draft. Pearson possessed great hands and the ability to get open. His best game was against the Raiders in 1975, catching six passes for 103 yards and one touchdown. Finished his career with 63 receptions for 995 yards and four touchdowns. He played in 36 games for the Chiefs.

Pearson, Jayice CB 24 Washington 1986-92

A free-agent signee, Pearson's presence in the Chiefs' secondary was invaluable. He was a tough backup to the cornerback position and always a major contributor to the special teams, scoring a touchdown on a blocked punt in 1989. He finished with four interceptions and four sacks, and played in 90 games for the Chiefs.

Peay, Francis T 75 Missouri 1973-74

Came to Kansas City from Green Bay for Aaron Brown; was a solid backup for the offensive line; played in 19 games for the Chiefs.

Pelluer, Steve QB 11 Washington 1989-91

Came to the Chiefs from Dallas in the middle of the 1989 season; saw limited playing time as Steve DeBerg's backup; threw 52 passes and completed 28 for 315 yards and one touchdown; also ran for 143 yards and two scores; he played in 18 games.

Penn, Chris — WR — 81 — **Tulsa** — 1994-96

The Chiefs' third-round draft pick in 1994, Penn waited through two relatively inactive seasons before logging a lot of playing time in 1996. He caught 49 passes that year for 628 yards and five touchdowns. Penn also returned kicks, averaging 10.6 yards per punt return in 1996. He played in 26 games for Kansas City.

Pennington, Durwood — K — 1 — **Georgia** — 1962

Played three games for the Texans, scoring 19 points (two field goals and 13 extra points).

Perkins, Horace — CB — 20 — **Colorado** — 1979

Made the Chiefs as a free agent and spent the 1979 season as a backup at left cornerback and special teams player; played in 16 games for the Chiefs.

Perriman, Brett — WR — 85 — **Miami (Fla.)** — 1997

A big free-agent signee from Detroit, Perriman was a disappointment, catching just six passes while fighting injuries. He went to Miami after playing in just five games.

Perry, Michael Dean — DT — 95 — **Clemson** — 1997

Played in one game for the Chiefs.

Peterson, Bill — LB — 55 — **San Jose State** — 1975

Signed as a free agent after playing in the short-lived WFL; started nine games at left outside linebacker and played in a total of 14 games for the Chiefs.

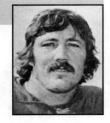

Peterson, Cal — LB — 50 — **UCLA** — 1979-81

Signed as a free agent, Peterson was a creditable replacement at linebacker while he was with the Chiefs. He also performed on the special teams. Peterson played in 43 games for Kansas City.

Peterson, Todd — K — 2 — **Georgia** — 2000-01

Signed with Kansas City as a free agent and took over the kicking duties for the remaining 11 games of the 2000 season. Peterson made 15 of 20 field goal attempts and all 25 extra point attempts to finish the season with 70 points. His 2001 season was even better as he made 27 of 35 attempts, and hit 27 of 28 PATs. His longest field goal was made from 51 yards. Peterson has played in 27 games for the Chiefs.

Petry, Stan — CB — 45 — **TCU** — 1989-91

A number four pick in the 1989 draft, Petry played in nickelback situations and on the special teams. Picked off three passes and returned one for a touchdown in 1990. He played in 34 games for the Chiefs.

Player	Position	Jersey(s) Worn	College	Year(s) Played

Phillips, Joe | DT | 75 | SMU | **1992-97**

Phillips signed with the Chiefs as a free agent from San Diego and established himself in the middle of the team's defensive line as a powerful force. His combination of strength and quickness forced many teams to double-team him in their blocking schemes, allowing other members of the defense to make plays. He was also as durable as he was consistent, missing just five games during his time in Kansas City. He totaled 14 sacks for the Chiefs, recovered three fumbles, and scored one safety. Phillips played in a total of 91 games for Kansas City.

Pickens, Bruce | CB | 39 | Nebraska | **1993**

Played in three games for the Chiefs.

Pietrzak, Jim | C | 62 | Eastern Michigan | **1987**

A replacement player during the 1987 NFL players' strike; played in two games for the Chiefs.

Pippens, Woodie | RB | 41 | Thiel College | **1987**

A replacement player during the 1987 NFL players' strike; played in two games for the Chiefs; ran the ball three times for 16 yards and caught two passes for 12 yards.

Pitts, Frank | WR | 25 | Southern (La.) | **1965-71**

see Other Chiefs Greats

Ply, Bobby | DB | 14 | Baylor | **1962-67**

Selected in the fifth round of the 1962 draft, Ply gave up playing quarterback and became a valuable member of the Chiefs' secondary. He was used mainly as a backup and special teams player, but he played often and intercepted three passes in a game against Denver in 1962, and then picked off four the following week against San Diego. Played both safety and cornerback, and finished with nine interceptions in his career. Ply played in 77 games for the franchise.

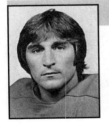

Podolak, Ed | RB | 14 | Iowa | **1969-77**

see Chiefs Hall of Fame

Pope, Daniel | P | 13 | Alabama | **1999**

A rookie free agent in 1999, Pope ousted veteran Louie Aguiar and took over as the Chiefs' punter. Pope set a Chiefs single-season record by punting 101 times. He averaged 41.8 yards per punt and landed 20 kicks inside the 20-yard line. He played in 16 games.

Player	Position	Jersey(s) Worn	College	Year(s) Played

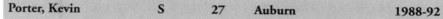

Popson, Ted — TE — 48 — **Portland State** — **1997-98**

Joined the Chiefs as a free agent from the 49ers and provided solid play at the tight end position his two seasons in Kansas City. He caught 35 passes for 320 yards and two touchdowns in 1997. His 1998 season was cut short by injuries, and he wasn't able to come back for the 1999 season. His career totals for the Chiefs were 48 receptions for 410 yards and two touchdowns. He played in 25 games.

Porter, Kevin — S — 27 — **Auburn** — **1988-92**

The Chiefs' third-round pick in the 1988 draft, Porter was the team's starting safety from 1989 through the 1991 season. He was a big hitter and especially good at providing run support. He picked off one pass, recovered two fumbles, and made 1.5 sacks. He played in 76 games for the Chiefs.

Porter, Lewis — E — 26 — **Southern (La.)** — **1970**

Played in five games for the Chiefs; carried the ball twice for 21 yards and caught one pass for 29 yards.

Potter, Steve — LB — 58 — **Virginia** — **1983**

Picked up on waivers from the Dolphins, Potter served as a backup linebacker and special teams player for the Chiefs. He intercepted one pass and played in 16 games.

Powers, Clyde — S — 29 — **Oklahoma** — **1978**

Played in one game for the Chiefs.

Prater, Dean — DE — 79 — **Oklahoma State** — **1982-83**

A free-agent signee, Prater backed up Art Still and Mike Bell at defensive end. He played in 18 games for the Chiefs.

Pricer, Bill — FB — 33 — **Oklahoma** — **1961**

Played in six games for the Texans and ran the ball five times for 13 yards.

Proby, Bryan — DT — 67 — **Arizona State** — **1995**

The Chiefs' sixth-round pick in 1995, Proby played in three games.

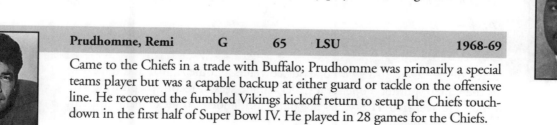

Prudhomme, Remi — G — 65 — **LSU** — **1968-69**

Came to the Chiefs in a trade with Buffalo; Prudhomme was primarily a special teams player but was a capable backup at either guard or tackle on the offensive line. He recovered the fumbled Vikings kickoff return to setup the Chiefs touchdown in the first half of Super Bowl IV. He played in 28 games for the Chiefs.

Player	Position	Jersey(s) Worn	College	Year(s) Played

Pruitt, Mike — RB — 43 — Purdue — 1985-86

Pruitt joined the Chiefs midway through the 1985 season and promptly became the team's starting fullback. He finished that season with 366 rushing yards, and continued to be productive the following year with 448 yards rushing. He also caught 15 passes and finished his time in Kansas City with 814 yards rushing and four touchdowns.

Pupunu, Alfred — TE — 85 — Weber State — 1997

Played in one game for the Chiefs.

Radecic, Scott — LB — 97 — Penn State — 1984-86

Drafted by the Chiefs in the second-round of the 1984 draft, Radecic moved into the starting lineup as the team's left inside linebacker. He returned an interception for a touchdown his rookie season (against Seattle), and finished his time in Kansas City with four picks. He also had four sacks, and was one of the top tacklers on the defense his last two seasons with the Chiefs. Radecic went to Buffalo following the 1986 season. He played in 48 games for Kansas City.

Randle, Ervin — LB — 55 — Baylor — 1991-92

Came to Kansas City for a fifth-round pick in the 1992 draft from Tampa Bay; Randle was a strong defender against the run in a backup role for the team's linebackers. He played in 20 games for the Chiefs.

Ransom, Derrick — DT — 95 — Cincinnati — 1998-2001

The Chiefs' no. six pick in the 1998 draft, Ransom played a reserve role on the defensive line at the tackle position his first three years in Kansas City. The 2001 season proved to be his breakout year, though, and he started all 16 games. Ransom recorded 76 tackles, registered three sacks and recovered one fumble his first season as a starter. He has played in 43 games for the Chiefs.

Rasley, Rocky — G — 66 — Oregon State — 1975

Came to the Chiefs from New Orleans; Rasley was one of the primary starters at guard on the offensive line his one season in Kansas City; went to the 49ers the following year. He played in 11 games for the Chiefs.

Reamon, Tommy — RB — 21 — Missouri — 1976

Came to the Chiefs as a free agent and provided good depth at running back while returning kicks; Reamon carried the ball 103 times for 314 yards and four touchdowns. He also returned one kickoff for a touchdown. He played in 11 games for Kansas City.

Player	Position	Jersey(s) Worn	College	Year(s) Played

Reardon, Kerry — CB — 15 — Iowa — 1971-76

Drafted by the Chiefs in the sixth round of the 1971 draft, Reardon spent the majority of his career at cornerback, but also played safety. Reardon also returned kicks and averaged 25.7 yards per return in 1971. He fought through injuries throughout his career, missing games each season until his last. Picked off five interceptions in 1976 and finished with 14 for his career. Reardon played in 58 games for the Chiefs.

Reed, Tony — RB — 32 — Colorado — 1977-80

Reed was the Chiefs' no. 2 pick in the 1977 draft. He had a good rookie season, but his second year with Kansas City was a great one. Reed carried the ball 206 times in 1978 for 1,053 yards, an average of 5.1 yards per carry. He also scored six touchdowns and caught 48 passes for another 483 a yards. At the time it was the second-highest season rushing total in Chiefs' history. He had five 100-yard games in his career, finished with 2,184 yards rushing and ten touchdowns. Reed played in 56 games for the Chiefs.

Reese, Jerry — S — 31 — Oklahoma — 1979-80

Reese made the Chiefs as a free-agent and battled for a starting position his two seasons in Kansas City. He injured his knee midway through the 1979 season. Returned in 1980 and played in 14 games. He played in 21 games for his career.

Reynolds, Al — G — 60 — Tarkio — 1960-67

An original member of the Texans, Reynolds made the team as a free agent and was a starter on the offensive line from 1961-64. He played for the 1962 and 1966 AFL Championship teams, providing quality depth when he wasn't a starter. Reynolds was an excellent blocker and very good at pulling for sweep plays. He played in a total of 98 games for the franchise.

Rice, Andrew — DT — 58 — Texas Southern — 1966-67

A backup for the defensive line, Rice played in 18 games for the Chiefs.

Richardson, Gloster — WR — 30 — Jackson State — 1967-70

Originally drafted in the seventh round of the 1965 draft, Richardson didn't make the team until 1967. A backup receiver, he made the most of his playing time and was one of the Chiefs' most explosive receivers. Richardson caught just 12 passes in 1967, but he averaged 26 yards a catch and scored two touchdowns. His best season was 1968 when he pulled in 22 passes, averaged 22.5 yards per catch and scored six touchdowns. He was also a quality special teams player. Richardson played in 51 games for the Chiefs.

Player	Position	Jersey(s) Worn	College	Year(s) Played

Richardson, Tony — RB — 49 — Auburn — **1995-2001**

see Other Chiefs Greats

Ricketts, Tom — G — 64 — Pittsburgh — **1993**

Played in three games for the Chiefs.

Ricks, Lawrence — RB — 42 — Michigan — **1983-84**

Played in 17 games as a backup halfback, running the ball 23 times and returning five kickoffs.

Ricks, Michael — WR — 85 — Stephen F. Austin — **2000-01**

Signed as a free agent from San Diego during the 2000 season, Ricks saw action in one game on special teams and was inactive for nine contests. Saw action in all 16 games in 2001 and caught 18 passes for 252 yards and one touchdown. He also blocked a punt for a safety. Ricks has played in 17 games for the Chiefs.

Riley, Victor — T — 66 — Auburn — **1998-2001**

The Chiefs first round draft pick in 1998, Riley became a starter on the offensive line in his second game and quickly showed he had the stuff necessary to become a great NFL lineman. His agile and athletic movements on the line are surprising for his huge size. Riley started the first five games of the 2001 season before suffering a broken fibula against the Steelers, but returned for the final two games of the season. He has played in a total of 55 games for Kansas City.

Rison, Andre — WR — 89 — Michigan State — **1997-99**

The five-time pro bowler made a big impact on the Chiefs his first season with the team in 1997, catching 72 passes for 1,092 yards and seven touchdowns. His production dropped a lot after that season, but he was a big-play receiver who could make clutch catches. He became the 11th player in league history to catch at least 700 passes in 1999. Rison dubbed himself "Spider Man" upon his arrival in Kansas City, and gave the Chiefs the big-play, go-to receiver they had been lacking. For his career in Kansas City, Rison caught 133 passes for 1,852 yards and 12 touchdowns. He played in 45 games for the Chiefs.

Roberts, Alfredo — TE — 87 — Miami (Fla.) — **1988-90**

A no. 8 pick in the 1988 draft, Roberts was a punishing blocker and excellent backup at the tight end position. He caught 29 passes for 278 yards and one touchdown. He played in 48 games for the Chiefs.

Player	Position	Jersey(s) Worn	College	Year(s) Played

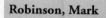

Robinson, Johnny — S/HB — 42 — LSU — 1960-71

see Chiefs Hall of Fame

Robinson, Mark — S — 30 — Penn State — 1984-87

The Chiefs selected Robinson in the fourth round of the 1984 draft. He was a hard hitter and played nickel back in pass situations for the Chiefs' secondary. He recorded 2.5 sacks, intercepted three passes, and played in 48 games for Kansas City.

Roche, Brian — TE — 85 — San Jose State — 1998

Roche played in four games for the Chiefs.

Rochester, Paul — DT — 72 — Michigan State — 1960-63

An original member of the Texans, Rochester was the team's starting defensive tackle in 1961-62 and was named to the AFL All-Star game in 1961. A strong and tough lineman, he was called "Cuddles" by his teammates because of his baby face. Rochester played in 48 games for the franchise.

Rogers, Steve — T — 77 — BYU — 1987

A replacement player during the 1987 NFL players' strike; played in three games for the Chiefs.

Rogers, Tracy — LB — 52 — Fresno State — 1990-96

Signed as a free agent, Rogers was a standout special teams player and short yardage performer. He was a starter at inside linebacker in 1993; his versatility allowed him to play the outside position as well, and he was a valuable member of the Chiefs' defense for seven seasons. He blocked a punt and recovered it for a touchdown against the Giants in 1992. His best overall season was 1993 when he totaled 94 tackles and two fumble recoveries. He played in 75 games for the Chiefs.

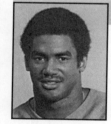

Rome, Stan — WR — 87 — Clemson — 1979-82

The Chiefs' 11th-round draft pick in 1979, Rome was a backup at wide receiver and special teams player. His best season was 1981 when he pulled in 17 passes for 203 yards and one touchdown. For his career, Rome caught 22 passes. He played in 42 games.

Romeo, Tony — E — 80 — Florida State — 1961

Played in 14 games for the Texans, catching seven passes for 89 yards.

Roquemore, Durwood — CB — 38 — Texas A&I — 1982-83

The Chiefs' sixth-round draft pick in the 1982 draft, Roquemore was a quality backup in the defensive secondary and started three games in 1983. He returned an interception for a touchdown against the Giants in 1983, and finished with five picks during his time in Kansas City. He played in 24 games.

Player	Position	Jersey(s) Worn	College	Year(s) Played

Rosdahl, Hatch — DE — 76 — Penn State — 1964-66

Came to the Chiefs from Buffalo in the middle of the 1964 season; an extremely versatile player, Rosdahl played on both the offensive and defensive lines. He played in 32 games for the Chiefs.

Rose, Donovan — CB — 27 — Hampton Institute — 1980

Played in seven games for the Chiefs.

Ross, Kevin — CB — 31 — Temple — 1984-93, 1997

see Chiefs Hall of Fame

Ross, Louis — DE — 75 — South Carolina State — 1975

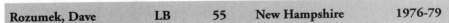

Played in one game for the Chiefs.

Rourke, Jim — G — 70 — Boston College — 1980-84, 1986

A free-agent signee, Rourke was a reserve offensive linemen and could play guard, tackle, and center. Spent the 1985 season with New Orleans, but came back to the Chiefs in 1986. He played in 64 games for Kansas City.

Rozumek, Dave — LB — 55 — New Hampshire — 1976-79

Selected by the Chiefs in the 15th round of the 1976 draft, Rozumek was the starting right inside linebacker in 1978 and also performed on special teams. Racked up 113 tackles in '78 and also picked off two passes. He played in a total of 45 games for Kansas City.

Rucker, Keith — DT — 96 — Ohio Wesleyan — 1997

Was on the Chiefs roster but never played in a game.

Rudnay, Jack — C — 58 — Northwestern — 1970-82

see Chiefs Hall of Fame

Rush, Bob — C — 53 — Memphis State — 1983-85

The Chiefs acquired Rush in a trade with the Chargers. He was the starting center for three seasons and was a great stabilizer for the offensive line. His presence led to better passing blocking and also bolstered the running game. Rush played in a total of 47 games for the Chiefs.

Player	Position	Jersey(s) Worn	College	Year(s) Played

Sadowski, Troy   TE   87   **Georgia**   1991

A "Plan B" free agent, Sadowski was a punishing blocker and was used as a backup at tight end. He played in 14 games for the Chiefs.

Saleaumua, Dan   DT   97   **Arizona State**   1989-96

see Other Chiefs Greats

Sally, Jerome   NT   70   **Missouri**   1988

Played in three games for the Chiefs.

Samuels, Tony   TE   86   **Bethune-Cookman**   1977-80

A fourth-round draft pick by the Chiefs in 1977, Samuels was primarily used on special teams and extra blocking situations in addition to his backup tight end duties. He caught 33 passes for 419 yards and two touchdowns in his career with the Chiefs. He played in 50 games.

Sanders, Clarence   LB   50   **Cincinnati**   1978, 1980

A free agent, Sanders was a special teams player and backup linebacker. He made 44 tackles in 1978 and also recovered a fumble. Sanders played in 17 games for the Chiefs.

Sauerbrun, Todd   P   5   **West Virginia**   2000

Came to Kansas City as an unrestricted free agent and handled the team's punting and kickoff duties for the 2000 season. Punted 82 times and averaged 44.6 yards per punt, and landed 28 of them inside the 20-yard line. Also made nine special teams tackles in 16 games for the Chiefs.

Saxon, James   RB   21, 45   **San Jose State**   1988-91

The Chiefs selected Saxon in the sixth round of the 1988 draft, and he made an immediate impact, winning the Mack Lee Hill Award as the team's top rookie. Saxon finished his initial campaign with 236 yards rushing and two touchdowns. He was also a big contributor on the special teams. Saxon finished his career in Kansas City with 497 yards rushing and five touchdowns. He played in 54 games for the Chiefs.

S

Player	Position	Jersey(s) Worn	College	Year(s) Played

Saxton, James — HB — 10 — Texas — 1962

The Texans' tenth-round draft pick in 1962, Saxton was a reserve halfback and kick returner. He ran the ball three times, caught five passes for 64 yards and returned three punts for an average of 46.3 yards per return. Saxton played in 13 games.

Scott, Todd — S — 47 — Southwestern Louisiana — 1997

Scott played in ten games as a backup for the secondary and on special teams.

Scott, Willie — TE — 81 — South Carolina — 1981-85

Scott was the Chiefs' no. 1 choice in the 1981 draft; he started slowly his rookie season because of a finger injury, but played in all 16 games, and caught five passes, one for a touchdown. He was the starting tight end by his third season and caught 29 passes, six for touchdowns. Scott was also an excellent blocker. He pulled in 75 passes for 682 yards in his career, and also scored 11 touchdowns. He played in 72 games.

Seals, George — DT — 67 — Missouri — 1972-73

Seals signed as a free agent with the Chiefs before the third game of the 1972 season; the Chiefs sent their no. 1 pick in the 1973 draft to the Bears to secure his services. He was used as a backup on the defensive line and also on the special teams. Seals played in 24 games for Kansas City.

Sellers, Goldie — DB — 20 — Grambling — 1968-69

Acquired in a trade with Denver, Sellers was a valuable reserve who excelled on special teams, returning punts and kickoffs. He returned a punt 76 yards against Boston in 1968, and picked off three passes in 1968. Sellers also scooped up a fumbled kickoff against the Bengals and ran 20 yards for a touchdown. He played in 28 games for the Chiefs.

Sensibaugh, Mike — S — 20 — Ohio State — 1971-75

The Chiefs selected Sensibaugh in the eighth round of the 1971 draft. He moved into the starting safety position in 1972, replacing Johnny Robinson, and picked off eight passes that season. Sensibaugh was a very good open-field tackler and maintained a high level of play during his time in Kansas City. He finished his Chiefs career with 20 interceptions before going to St. Louis in 1976. Sensibaugh played in 65 games for the Chiefs.

Seurer, Frank — QB — 10 — Kansas — 1986-87

Seurer played in nine games as a backup quarterback. He completed 26 of 55 passes for 340 yards.

Shaw, Dennis — QB — 12 — San Diego State — 1978

A backup quarterback, Shaw was on the Chiefs' roster, but never played in a game.

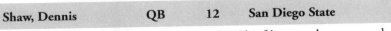

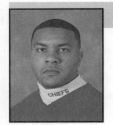

Shehee, Rashaan — RB — 22 — Washington — 1998-99

The Chiefs' no. 3 pick in the 1998 draft, Shehee showed signs of becoming a brilliant broken field runner in 1999 but was slowed by injuries to his hip, knee and ankle. He possessed great breakaway speed and quickness, and despite playing in just eight games in 1999, proved he could compete in the NFL. Shehee ran for 86 yards against the Chargers and scored his first career touchdown against the Lions. For his career, Shehee gained 295 yards rushing and caught 28 passes for another 136 yards. He played in 25 games for the Chiefs.

Shields, Billy — T — 70 — Georgia Tech — 1985

Played in two games for the Chiefs.

Shields, Will — G — 68 — Nebraska — 1993-2001

see Other Chiefs Greats

Shorthose, George — WR — 80 — Missouri — 1985

Played in three games for the Chiefs.

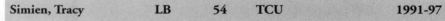

Siglar, Ricky — T — 66, 72 — San Jose State — 1993-96, 1998

Siglar came to the Chiefs a free agent from the 49ers after missing the 1991 and 1992 seasons. He was a starter on the offensive line—mostly at right tackle—34 times. Siglar was an athletic and powerful presence on the line and was a big part of the Chiefs' outstanding running game; his downfield blocking technique was one of the best on the team. Siglar played in 66 games for the Chiefs.

Simien, Tracy — LB — 54 — TCU — 1991-97

A free-agent acquisition from the WFL, Simien was a durable, powerful run-stopper in the middle of the Chiefs defense for seven seasons. He averaged almost 100 tackles per year, and was the Chiefs' leading tackler from 1992 through 1995, just the third Chief in the team's history to lead the club four years in a row (Spani and Cherry were the other two). For his career, Simien played in 109 games, picked off four passes, and recorded four sacks.

Simmons, Bob — G — 73 — Texas — 1977-83

Claimed off waivers from New Orleans, Simmons was a mainstay on the Chiefs' offensive line for seven seasons, and was a starter five of those seasons. Although primarily a guard, he played tackle several times when needed. His versatility was a plus for the team. Simmons played in a total of 88 games for Kansas City.

Player	Position	Jersey(s) Worn	College	Year(s) Played
Simmons, Wayne	LB	56	Clemson	1997-98

Simmons came to the Chiefs in a mid-season trade with the Packers in 1997 and immediately stepped into a starting role in the linebacker corps. He reputation as one of the meanest, hardest-hitting linebackers served well on the Chiefs defense until the Monday night game blowup with the Broncos in 1998, which saw the Chiefs' defense flagged five times for roughness and unsportsman like play on one Bronco drive. For his part in the Chiefs' disreputable play, Simmons was released from the team days later. He played in a total of 20 games for Kansas City and had 3.5 sacks.

Simons, Keith	DT	72	Minnesota	1976-77

One of three third-round picks selected by the Chiefs in the 1976 draft, Simons was a part-time starter on the defensive line. He had 1.5 sacks in his career and played in a total of 20 games.

Sims, Tom	NT	95	Pittsburgh	19 91-92, 1996

A no. 6 draft pick in the 1990, Sims was a backup on the defensive line. He missed his entire rookie season because of an ankle injury but returned and was valuable in his backup role for the 1991-92 seasons. He had three sacks in his career with the Chiefs and played in a total of 27 games.

Slaughter, Webster	WR	85, 88	San Diego State	1995

Slaughter came to the Chiefs with a reputation as a big-play receiver and gave the team one good season. Usually used in a backup role, Slaughter became one of the go-to guys, and made several big plays throughout the 1995 season. He caught 34 passes for 514 yards and four touchdowns in 16 games for the Chiefs.

Smith, Chris	RB	47	Notre Dame	1986-87

A free agent, Smith played in four games for Kansas City, running the ball 26 times for 114 yards; was a replacement player during the 1987 NFL players' strike.

Smith, Eric	S	27	SMU	1987

A replacement player during the 1987 NFL players' strike; was on the Chiefs' roster but never played in a game.

Smith, Dave	WR	70	Indiana (Pa.)	1973

Played in two games for the Chiefs.

Smith, Fletcher	DB	17	Tennessee A&I	1966-67

An eighth-round selection in the 1966 draft, Smith was used on special teams and as an extra back in the defensive secondary, and picked off six passes in 1967. He also kicked a couple of extra points in 1966. He played in 24 games for Kansas City before going to the expansion Bengals in 1968.

Player	Position	Jersey(s) Worn	College	Year(s) Played

Smith, Franky — T — 72 — Alabama A&M — 1980

Played in four games for the Chiefs.

Smith, Jeff — RB/KR — 42 — Nebraska — 1985-86

The Chiefs drafted the Cornhusker star in the tenth round of the 1985 draft. Smith was an all-purpose back who returned kicks, ran well, and was excellent at catching passes. He compiled 1,270 all-purpose yards in 1986 and won the Mack Lee Hill Award in 1985 after running up 929 all-purpose yards. Smith averaged 4.2 yards per carry and caught 51 passes for 356 yards. He scored a total of eight touchdowns and played 28 games.

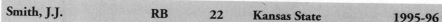

Smith, Jeff — C/G — 65 — Tennessee — 1996-99

A seventh-round pick in the 1996 draft, Smith has been versatile and valuable to the Chiefs' offensive line. A backup and special teams player, Smith has filled in at guard and center. He's played in 31 games and started five different times over the course of his career.

Smith, J.J. — RB — 22 — Kansas State — 1995-96

A free-agent acquisition, Smith was inactive for the entire 1995 season, and on injured reserve for the 1996 season.

Smith, J.T. — WR — 86 — North Texas State — 1978-84

Smith came to the Chiefs as a free agent, quickly proved his worth to the club and became one of the best non-drafted players in the team's history. He was a spectacular punt returner and also a top-notch receiver. He earned a spot on the AFC Pro Bowl team in 1980 for his returns. He returned 40 punts that season, averaging 14.5 yards per return, and scored two touchdowns. He returned a punt 88 yards against the Raiders in 1979. Smith's best pass receiving numbers were made in 1981, when he hauled in 63 passes for 852 yards and two touchdowns. He was slowed a bit by injuries his last three seasons in Kansas City, and moved on to the Cardinals in 1985. He caught 167 passes in his career, scored 12 touchdowns, and returned 220 punts. Smith played in a total of 89 games for the Chiefs.

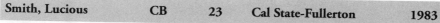

Smith, Lucious — CB — 23 — Cal State-Fullerton — 1983

Came to the Chiefs in a trade with the Rams before the start of the 1983 season and immediately became a starter. He picked off a John Elway pass and ran it back 58 yards for a touchdown and finished the season with three picks. He also forced a fumble and had 53 tackles in his lone season for Kansas City. Smith played in 16 games.

Smith, Michael — WR — 83 — Kansas State — 1992

Played in two games for the Chiefs.

Smith, Neil — DE — 90 — Nebraska — 1988-96

see Other Chiefs Greats

Smith, Noland — KR — 1, 46 — Tennessee State — 1967-69

see Other Chiefs Greats

Smith, Sid — T — 70 — USC — 1970-72

The Chiefs' no. 1 pick in the 1970 draft, Smith never advanced past being used in a backup role and on specialty teams. He was valuable as a backup and played in a total of 42 games for Kansas City.

Snipes, Angelo — LB — 52 — West Georgia — 1987-89

Came to the Chiefs from the Chargers; finished the 1988 season as one of the starting outside linebackers. Snipes finished 1988 with 35 tackles. For his career, he intercepted one pass and had three sacks in 21 games.

Snow, Percy — LB — 59 — Michigan State — 1990-92

The Chiefs' no. 1 pick in the 1990 draft, Snow showed great promise his rookie season, totaling 69 tackles and making two sacks. He had established himself as an intense, physical player and won the Mack Lee Hill Award as the team's top rookie. But a motor scooter accident in the 1991 training camp—Snow broke his ankle—all but ended his career. He missed all of the 1991 season and was never able to reach the high level of play he displayed in his first season. He played in a total of 30 games for the Chiefs.

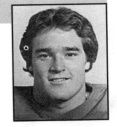

Spani, Gary — LB — 59 — Kansas State — 1978-86

see Other Chiefs Greats

Spann, Gary — LB — 94 — TCU — 1987

A replacement player during the 1987 NFL players' strike; played in two games for the Chiefs.

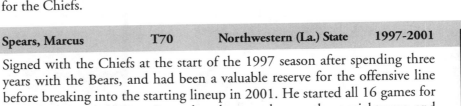

Spears, Marcus — T70 — Northwestern (La.) State — 1997-2001

Signed with the Chiefs at the start of the 1997 season after spending three years with the Bears, and had been a valuable reserve for the offensive line before breaking into the starting lineup in 2001. He started all 16 games for the first time in his career. Spears has also seen duty on the special teams, and played in a total of 55 games for Kansas City.

Spikes, Jack — FB/K — 30 — TCU — 1960-64

see Other Chiefs Greats

| **Stams, Frank** | LB | 55 | **Notre Dame** | 1995 |

Played in one game for the Chiefs.

| **Stargell, Tony** | CB | 45 | **Tennessee State** | 1996 |

A free-agent signee, Stargell came to Kansas City in the middle of the season. He played in eight games for the Chiefs, started in four and had one interception.

| **Staysniak, Joe** | G | 72 | **Ohio State** | 1992 |

Played in six games as a backup lineman for the Chiefs.

| **Stedman, Troy** | LB | 94 | **Washburn** | 1988 |

A seventh-round pick in the 1988 draft, Stedman played in five games for the Chiefs.

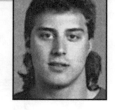

| **Stein, Bob** | LB | 66 | **Minnesota** | 1969-72 |

The Chiefs' fifth-round draft pick in 1969, Stein was a special teams player and backup linebacker throughout his time in Kansas City. He recovered a fumbled punt in the Chiefs' 1969 playoff contest against the Jets that sealed the win. He intercepted one pass in his career and played in 50 games for the Chiefs.

| **Steinfeld, Al** | C | 69 | **C.W. Post** | 1982 |

Played in seven games for the Chiefs.

| **Stenerud, Jan** | K | 3 | **Montana State** | 1967-79 |

see Chiefs in the Pro Football Hall of Fame.

| **Stensrud, Mike** | NT/DE | 67 | **Iowa State** | 1988 |

Signed as a free agent, Stensrud filled in on the defensive line, starting in five of the 13 games he played in. Had 2.5 sacks, 38 total tackles and an interception.

| **Stephens, John** | RB | 21 | **Northwestern (La.) State** | 1993 |

Came to Kansas City from Green Bay in the middle of the 1993 season. Stephens carried the ball six times for 18 yards. He played in seven games.

| **Stephens, Santo** | LB | 53 | **Temple** | 1993 |

A free agent, Stephens appeared in 16 games for the Chiefs, primarily as a special teams player.

Player	Position	Jersey(s) Worn	College	Year(s) Played

Stevens, Matt   QB   1   UCLA   1987

Replacement during the 1987 NFL players' strike, Stevens played in three games for the Chiefs, completing 32 of 57 passes for 315 yards and one touchdown.

Still, Art   DE   67   Kentucky   1978-87

see Chiefs Hall of Fame.

Stills, Gary   LB   56   West Virginia   1999-2001

A number three draft pick by the Chiefs in 1999, Stills played in two games his rookie season. He played primarily on special teams in 2000 and 2001, recording 35 career special teams tackles. Stills has appeared in a total of 24 games for Kansas City.

Stockemer, Ralph   RB   21   Baylor   1987

Played in two games for the Chiefs, carrying the ball once for two yards and catching one pass for four yards.

Stone, Jack   T   70   Oregon   1960

A first-round pick by the Texans, Stone played in 14 games as a backup and special teams player.

Story, Bill   G   62   Southern Illinois   1975

Originally a ninth-round pick in the 1973 draft, Story eventually came to the Chiefs from the defunct WFL. He played in 14 games, primarily on special teams, but filled in on the offensive line as well.

Stover, Smokey   LB   35   Northeast Louisiana   1960-66

An original Texan, Stover was a mainstay on the franchise's defense for seven seasons. A member of the first Super Bowl team, Stover was a backup the last part of his career. A solid player, his contribution to the Chiefs' success was his consistency. He finished his career with seven interceptions and played in a total of 98 games for the franchise.

Stowers, Tommie   RB   48   Missouri   1994

Played in one game for the Chiefs.

Stoyanovich, Pete   K   10   Indiana   1996-2000

Came to Kansas City in a trade with the Dolphins. Stoyanovich was regarded as one of the best kickers in the NFL, and his first four seasons with the Chiefs were highly productive. His best overall season with the Chiefs was 1997, which saw him drill 26 of 27 field goal attempts, the biggest a 54-yard line drive as the game ended to defeat the Broncos. For his career in Kansas City, Stoyanovich made 92 of 115 field goal attempts, an accuracy rate of 80 percent. Stoyanovich was released by the club five games into the 2000 season. He made 163 of 164 extra point attempts, and scored a total of 442 points. Stoyanovich played in 69 games for the Chiefs.

Player	Position	Jersey(s) Worn	College	Year(s) Played

Strada, John TE 87 William Jewell 1974

Played in 11 games as a backup tight end and special teams performer. He caught one pass for 16 yards.

Stradford, Troy RB 25 Boston College 1991

Played in ten games for the Chiefs, primarily as a kick returner. Ran back 22 punts for an average of 6.8 yards per return, and 14 kickoffs for an average of 20.9 yards per return.

Stroud, Morris TE 83 Clark 1969-74

A third-round pick in the 1969 draft, Stroud was one of the tallest players in the NFL. His 6-foot-10 frame was intimidating for opposing secondaries, and he possessed a lot of speed for a man his size. An outstanding blocker, Stroud also made several big plays. His best season was 1971 when pulled in 22 passes for 454 yards and one touchdown. He caught 54 passes for his career and scored seven touchdowns. Stroud played in 69 games for the Chiefs.

Stryzinski, Dan P 4 Indiana 2001

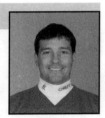

When he signed with the Chiefs as an unrestricted free agent, Stryzinski was widely regarded as one of the top punters—if not the best—in the NFL at placing the ball with deadly accuracy. The 12-year veteran had a fine inaugural year with Kansas City, punting the 73 times for a 40.8 yard average pick punt. Stryzinski punted himself into the Chiefs' record book against the Raiders on September 9, 2001, with a 76-yard punt, the longest of his career and the longest in the history of the Chiefs franchise. He had 27 punts inside 20 yard line (two shy of the Chiefs team record) and just five touchbacks. He played in 16 games.

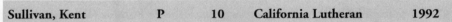

Studdard, Les C 64 Texas 1982

The Chiefs' tenth-round draft pick in 1981, Studdard played in nine games as a backup center.

Sullivan, Kent P 10 California Lutheran 1992

Played in one game for the Chiefs, punting six times for an average of 41.2 yards per punt.

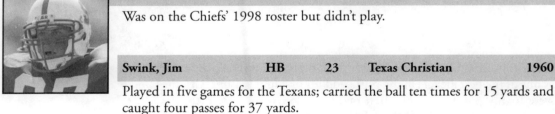

Swanson, Pete G/T 73 Stanford 1998

Was on the Chiefs' 1998 roster but didn't play.

Swink, Jim HB 23 Texas Christian 1960

Played in five games for the Texans; carried the ball ten times for 15 yards and caught four passes for 37 yards.

Player	Position	Jersey(s) Worn	College	Year(s) Played

Swoopes, Patrick   NT   67   **Mississippi State**   1991

Played in four games for the Chiefs.

Szott, Dave   G   79   **Penn State**   1990-99

see Other Chiefs Greats

Tait, John   T   76   **BYU**   1999-2001

The Chiefs number draft pick in 1999, Tait had problems hammering out his contract and joined the team late. But he played in 12 games his rookie season, started in three, and displayed the kind of physical skill and talent expected of a number one pick. Tait started in 15 games in 2000 and showed potential to become one of the better linemen on the team. He started all 16 games for the first time in his career in 2001 and was a big reason for the rushing success of Priest Holmes. He's played in a total of 43 games for the Chiefs.

Talton, Ken   RB   45   **Cornell**   1980

Played in two games for the Chiefs.

Tamm, Ralph   G   64   **West Chester**   1997-99

Signed as a free agent, Tamm provided the Chiefs with solid play as the team's long snapper. He scored one touchdown and played in 48 games for Kansas City.

Tate, Willy   TE   80   **Oregon**   1998

Played in one game for the Chiefs.

Taylor, Jay   CB   27   **San Jose State**   1993-95

Came to Kansas City in a trade with the Cardinals; Taylor was an excellent bump and run corner, and was the team's third cornerback. He played in 32 games for the Chiefs and picked off two passes.

T

Player	Position	Jersey(s) Worn	College	Year(s) Played

Taylor, Kitrick — WR/KR — 82 — Washington State — 1988

A fifth-round draft selection in 1987, Taylor was the Chiefs' primary punt returner, running back 29 kicks for an average of 6.4 yards per return. He also caught nine passes for 105 yards. Taylor played in a total of 16 games for the Chiefs.

Taylor, Otis — WR — 89 — Prairie View — 1965-75

see Chiefs Hall of Fame

Taylor, Roger — T — 76 — Oklahoma State — 1981

The Chiefs' third-round selection in the 1981 draft, Taylor played in 13 games.

Taylor, Steve — S — 48 — Kansas — 1976

A sixth-round draft pick in 1976, Taylor saw most of his playing time on the specials teams. He started one game and played in 14 games for the Chiefs.

Terrell, Marvin — G — 63 — Mississippi — 1960-63

Selected with the first batch of players in the AFL's first draft, Terrell fought through two injury-plagued seasons and then earned a starting spot at left guard. His outstanding play in the 1962 season earned him a spot on the AFL West All-Star team. Played the first season in Kansas City; Terrell played in a total of 38 games for Kansas City.

Terry, Doug — S — 24, 25, 32 — Kansas — 1992-95

An unheralded free agent, Terry made the Chiefs with a hard-hitting, aggressive style of play. He was a key player on special teams and in the defensive secondary, and was fearless with his hitting. One of his best hits came against the Oilers in 1995 when he drilled Oiler running back Todd McNair to force a fumble that was returned for a game-winning touchdown. Terry started ten games in the secondary, had two career interceptions, recovered three fumbles, forced four fumbles and made 108 tackles. He played in 57 games for Kansas City.

Thomas, Bill — RB — 43 — Boston College — 1974

Came to the Chiefs from Houston and was used as kick returner. Thomas returned 25 kickoffs for an average of 22.8 yards per return. He played in 14 games for the Chiefs.

Thomas, Carlton — CB — 38 — Elizabeth City College — 1987

A replacement player during the 1987 NFL players' strike; played in four games for the Chiefs.

Player	Position	Jersey(s) Worn	College	Year(s) Played

Thomas, Charlie — KR — 49 — Tennessee State — 1975

A free-agent signee, Thomas returned 12 punts for 112 yards and 22 kickoffs for 516 yards. He played in seven games for the Chiefs.

Thomas, Chris — WR — 87 — Cal Poly – San Luis Obispo — 2001

Signed with the Chiefs as a free agent from the Rams. Thomas played in ten games for Kansas City, starting five times. He caught 19 passes for 247 yards and one touchdown. Thomas also played on special teams.

Thomas, Derrick — LB — 58 — Alabama — 1989-99

see Chiefs Hall of Fame

Thomas, Emmitt — CB — 18 — Bishop College — 1966-78

see Chiefs Hall of Fame.

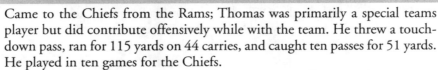

Thomas, Gene — FB — 45 — Florida A&M — 1966-67

Came to the Chiefs as a free agent and saw limited duty in the backfield. He played on special teams, returning a few kicks. Thomas played in a total of 28 games for the Chiefs, rushed for 186 yards, caught 13 passes for 99 yards, and scored four touchdowns.

Thomas, Jewerl — RB — 31 — San Jose State — 1983

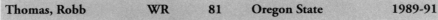

Came to the Chiefs from the Rams; Thomas was primarily a special teams player but did contribute offensively while with the team. He threw a touchdown pass, ran for 115 yards on 44 carries, and caught ten passes for 51 yards. He played in ten games for the Chiefs.

Thomas, Ken — RB — 35 — San Jose State — 1983

The Chiefs' no. 7 pick in the 1983 draft, Thomas switched from playing defensive back in college to running back in the NFL. He was used more as a receiver out of the backfield during his time with Kansas City and caught 30 passes for 254 yards and a touchdown. He rushed for 55 yards and played in a total of 14 games.

Thomas, Robb — WR — 81 — Oregon State — 1989-91

A no. 6 pick in the 1989 draft, Thomas had great hands and deceptive speed. He was the Chiefs' leading receiver in 1990-91 and started 14 games in that period. He finished his career in Kansas City with 92 receptions for 1,148 yards and seven touchdowns. He also played in three playoff contests and made five grabs for 34 yards. Thomas played in a total of 39 games for the Chiefs.

Thomas, Todd — C — 62 — North Dakota — 1981

A fifth-round draft choice by Kansas City, Thomas served as the team's deep snapper for the 1981 season. He played in 15 games.

Thompson, Arland — G — 58 — Baylor — 1987

A replacement player during the 1987 NFL players' strike; played in three games for the Chiefs.

Thompson, Bennie — S — 46 — Grambling — 1992-93

Came to Kansas City as a "Plan B" free agent and gave the Chiefs two hard-hitting seasons. A special-teams standout, Thompson also picked off four passes in 1992, and registered 1.5 sacks. He played in a total of 32 games for the Chiefs.

Thompson, Del — RB — 39 — Texas-El Paso — 1982

A fifth-round draft pick in 1982, Thompson played in six games and ran the ball four times for seven yards.

Thompson, Ernie — RB — 45 — Indiana — 1993

A free-agent acquisition, Thompson served as the backup fullback throughout the 1993 season. A blocker, he ran the ball just 11 times and caught four passes. He played in 16 games.

Thompson, Leroy — RB — 44 — Penn State — 1995

Came to the Chiefs from the Patriots and played primarily on special teams. He carried the ball 28 times for 73 yards and also caught six passes. He played in a total of 16 games for the Chiefs.

Thornbladh, Bob — LB — 50 — Michigan — 1974

An 11th-round pick in the 1974 draft, Thornbladh was a backup at linebacker and special teams player. He played in 14 games for the Chiefs.

Thorp, Don — DE — 71 — Illinois — 1988

Played in three games for the Chiefs.

Tolliver, Billy Joe — QB — 8 — Texas Tech — 1997

Came to Kansas City quarterback insurance when Elvis Grbac was injured in the 1997 season. Played in three games for the Chiefs and threw one pass.

Tongue, Reggie — S — 25, 41 — Oregon State — 1996-99

The Chiefs' no. 2 draft pick in 1996, Tongue developed into one of the team's premier defensive players during his four years in Kansas City. He was also excellent on the specials teams, registering 60 stops. Tongue totaled 380 tackles in his Chiefs career, picked off two passes, and scored after taking a lateral from Donnie Edwards against Baltimore in 1999. Great at the safety blitz, Tongue sacked the quarterback 6.5 times. He forced seven fumbles and recovered four, returning one for a touchdown against the Chargers. He played in 63 games for the Chiefs; Tongue signed with Seattle following the 1999 season.

Player	Position	Jersey(s) Worn	College	Year(s) Played

Trahan, John — WR — 83 — USC — 1987

A replacement player during the 1987 NFL players' strike; played in three games for the Chiefs and caught four passes for 40 yards.

Traylor, Keith — DT — 94 — Central Oklahoma — 1995-96

The Chiefs originally signed Traylor before their playoff game against the Steelers in January, 1994; he was inactive for that game and was waived a week later. After sitting out the 1994 NFL season, Traylor re-signed with the Chiefs and played in the WFL in the spring of 1995. He made the Chiefs in 1995 and was a major part of the team's defense the next two seasons, backing up at tackle. He played in 31 games and had 2.5 sacks before leaving for Denver in 1997.

Trosch, Gene — DE — 74 — Miami (Fla.) — 1967-69

The club's no. 1 draft pick in 1967, Trosch was used as a backup on the defensive line and special teams. He missed the entire 1968 season. Played in a total of 27 games for Kansas City.

Tyrer, Jim — T — 77 — Ohio State — 1961-73

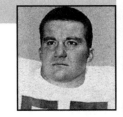

see Chiefs Hall of Fame

U

Upshaw, Marvin — DE — 81 — Trinity — 1970-75

The Chiefs traded a no. three draft pick to the Browns to acquire Upshaw, and the big defensive end gave Kansas City six solid seasons on the defensive line. He had seven sacks in 1974 and was as efficient at stopping the run as he was rushing the passer. Upshaw intercepted two passes in his career and scored one touchdown. He played in a total of 67 games for the Chiefs.

V

Valerio, Joe — T — 73 — Pennsylvania — 1991-95

The Chiefs selected Valerio in the second round of the 1991 draft, and the Ivy Leaguer became a popular player among the Kansas City fans. He spent the majority of his career as a backup tackle, center, and long snapper, but was also a highly effective offensive weapon in goal-line situations. Lining up as a third tight end, Valerio caught four passes—all for touchdowns—three from Joe Montana and one from Steve Bono. He also performed well on special teams. Valerio played in 61 games for the Chiefs.

Vanover, Tamarick — KR/WR — 87 — Florida State — 1995-98

see Other Chiefs Greats

Player	Position	Jersey(s) Worn	College	Year(s) Played

Vaughn, Jon   RB   21   Michigan   1994

Signed as a free agent late in the 1994 season, Vaughn handled the kickoff returns the last month of the season. Returned 15 kicks for 25.7 yard average, and returned one 91 yards for a touchdown against the Dolphins. He played in three games for the Chiefs, plus the playoff game against Miami.

Villa, Danny   G   72   Arizona State   1993-96

Came to the Chiefs as an unrestricted free agent. Villa was backup guard on the offensive line and also performed long snaps. His experience added much to the Chiefs' line; he was able to play left or right guard. Villa played in a total of 59 games for Kansas City.

Vitali, Mark   QB   6   Purdue   1977

On the Chiefs' roster in 1977, Vitali never played in a game.

Vlasic, Mark   QB   13   Iowa   1991-92

Came to the Chiefs as a "Plan B" free agent from San Diego. He started one game in 1991, and played in a total of six games. He completed 28 of 44 passes for 316 yards and two touchdowns.

W

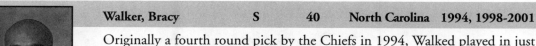

Wade, Charlie   WR   84   Tennessee State   1977

Played in five games for the Chiefs.

Waldrop, Rob   DT   98   Arizona   1994

Played in three games for the Chiefs.

Walker, Bracy   S   40   North Carolina   1994, 1998-2001

Originally a fourth round pick by the Chiefs in 1994, Walked played in just two games before being released. After stints with Cincinnati and Miami, he signed again with the Chiefs midway through the 1998 season. Excellent on special teams, Walker has also been used in the secondary in 1999-01 and started one game. He made 13 special team tackles in 1999, 2000, and again in 2001, and has played in a total of 56 games for Kansas City.

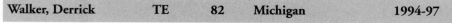

Walker, Derrick   TE   82   Michigan   1994-97

Came to Kansas City as a free agent from San Diego. Walker was a devastating blocker and reliable pass catcher. He greatly bolstered the team's running attack and made some big receptions as well. He caught 75 passes for 720 yards and four touchdowns. Walker played in a total of 58 games for the Chiefs.

Player	Position	Jersey(s) Worn	College	Year(s) Played

Walker, James — LB — 54 — Kansas State — 1983

Played in four games for the Chiefs.

Walker, John — DT — 98 — Nebraska-Omaha — 1987

A replacement player during the 1987 NFL players' strike; played in three games for the Chiefs.

Walker, Wayne — P — 68 — Northwestern Louisiana — 1967

The Chiefs' 13th-round pick in the 1966 draft, Walker played in four games and punted 19 times for a 38.7 yard average.

Wallace, Steve — T — 70, 74 — Auburn — 1997

Came to the Chiefs from the 49ers and played in ten games as a backup on the offensive line.

Walters, Rod — G — 76 — Iowa — 1976, 1978-80

The Chiefs' no. 1 draft pick in 1976, Walters was a reserve for the offensive line for most of his career in Kansas City. A knee injury forced him to miss the 1977 season, and he was never able to move past the reserve role. Walters played in a total of 52 games for the Chiefs.

Walton, Riley — TE — 88 — Tennessee State — 1987

A replacement player during the 1987 NFL players' strike; played in two games for the Chiefs.

Walton, Wayne — G/T — 72 — Abilene Christian — 1973-74

The Chiefs traded a fifth-round draft pick to the Giants for Walton. He played well on the offensive line, and had earned a starting spot in 1974 when a knee injury ended his season, and ultimately, his career. He played in a total of 23 games for the Chiefs.

Warfield, Eric — CB — 44 — Nebraska — 1998-2001

The Chiefs' no. seven pick in the 1998 draft, Warfield has shown he can handle NFL receivers and provide excellent coverage. He became a starter in 2001. He's also been effective on the special teams, making 30 stops in five seasons. Warfield picked off three passes in 1999, and another four in 2001, returning one 51 yards for a touchdown against Oakland. He has made 123 tackles in his career, and played in 57 games for the Chiefs, starting 20 times.

Warner, Charley — DB — 25 — Prairie View — 1963-64

Warner had great speed and served as a kick returner in 1963 and the first part of 1964. He averaged 23.9 per return in 1963 and ran back a total of 16 kicks in his career. He also returned 13 punts and picked off one pass. Warner played in a total of 19 games for the Chiefs.

Washington, Brian — S — 29, 48 — Nebraska — 1995-96

Came to the Chiefs as a free agent from the Jets and added solid, aggressive play to the Chiefs secondary. He returned an interception 74 yards for a touchdown against the Raiders in the 1995 AFC West division-clinching game. Finished his career in Kansas City with six interceptions. He played in a total of 31 games for the Chiefs.

Washington, Charles — DB — 46 — Cameron — 1990-91

A "Plan B" free agent, Washington missed ten games in 1990 but came back and was impressive at times in the Chiefs secondary throughout the 1991 season. He had one interception, blocked a punt against Cleveland in 1990 and also against Miami in the 1990 playoff game. He played in a total of 22 games for the Chiefs.

Washington, Tim — CB — 42 — Fresno State — 1982

Played in one game for the Chiefs.

Waters, Brian — C — 54 — North Texas — 2000-01

A free-agent signee, Waters played in five games on special teams for the Chiefs his first season with the club. He saw action on the offense in all 16 games in 2001, starting one game at center and seven at left guard. Waters has played in 22 games for the Chiefs.

Watson, Tim — S — 26 — Howard — 1993-95

A free-agent signee, Watson played in nine games for the Chiefs, plus two playoff contests.

Weathers, Clarence — WR — 80 — Delaware State — 1989

Came to the Chiefs early in the 1989 season and caught 17 passes for 192 yards in a backup role at wide receiver. He played in 11 games.

Webster, David — DB — 21 — Prairie View — 1960-61

An original Texan, Webster was a standout in the Dallas secondary in the team's first two seasons. He picked off six passes in 1960 and returned two for scores. He grabbed another five in 1961 to finish his career with 11. He also scored a touchdown on a fumble recovery. Webster played in a total of 28 games for the franchise.

Webster, Mike — C — 53 — Wisconsin — 1989-90

Webster concluded his Hall-of-Fame career in Kansas City after playing 13 seasons in Pittsburgh. A nine-time pro bowler with the Steelers, Webster helped solidify the Chiefs offensive and provided valuable leadership. He played in 25 games for Kansas City.

Werner, Clyde   LB   54   Washington   1970-74, 1976

The Chiefs' second-round draft pick in 1970, Werner was used as a special teams player and fill-in at linebacker. He missed the entire 1975 season with a torn Achilles tendon but returned for one more season in 1976. Werner had two interceptions in his career and played in a total of 63 games.

Wesley, Greg   S   25   Arkansas Pine Bluff   2000-01

The Chiefs' third round selection in the 2000 draft, Wesley moved into the starting safety position his rookie season and has started every game since. He picked off two passes in 2000 and 2001, and was third on the team in total tackles in 2001 with 126. He's also recorded three sacks in his career. Wesley has played in 32 games.

Wesson, Ricky   CB   25   SMU   1977

A free agent, Wesson spent his one season in Kansas City as a backup for the defensive secondary. He also returned seven kickoffs for an average of 18.7 yards per return. Wesson played in 14 games.

West, Robert   WR   26   San Diego State   1972-73

Signed by the Chiefs after he was released by Dallas, West played well for Kansas City in a reserve role. He caught nine passes for 165 yards and two touchdowns in 1972, and added a third score on a fumble recovery. West finished his two-year stay in Kansas City with 13 catches for 230 yards. He played in 19 games.

Wetzel, Ron   TE   87   Arizona State   1983

A fourth-round draft pick in the 1983 draft, Wetzel was used in short-yardage situations as a blocker. He played in 16 games.

Whitaker, Danta   TE   82   Mississippi Valley State   1990

Whitaker cam to Kansas City as a free agent and was used on special teams and triple tight-end formations. He caught two passes for 17 yards and a touchdown. Whitaker played in 16 games.

White, Walter   TE   81, 88   Maryland   1975-79

Claimed off waivers from the Steelers, White was one of the best pass-catching tight ends the Chiefs have ever had. His outstanding play in 1975, his rookie season, earned him the Mack Lee Hill Award. His best season was 1976, when he hauled in 47 passes for 808 yards and seven touchdowns, and he followed with 48 catches in 1977. He finished his career with 163 receptions for 2,396 yards and 16 touchdowns. White played in a total of 63 games for the Chiefs.

White, William   S   35   **Ohio State**   1994-96

White came to the Chiefs in a trade with Detroit, adding brains and fundamentals to the team's secondary. He was a big contributor to the team's 13-3 season in 1995, making 70 tackles in as a part-time starter. White had four interceptions and one sack in his career for the Chiefs and played in a total of 43 games.

Whitehurst, David   QB   15   **Furman**   1984

Was on the Chiefs' roster in 1984, but never played in a game.

Whitmore, David   S   41   **Stephen F. Austin**   1993-94

Came to Kansas City as part of the Joe Montana deal with San Francisco. Whitmore missed most of the 1993 season because of a knee injury, but played in a backup and special teams role the following season. He appeared in 18 games for the Chiefs.

Wickert, Tom   G   66   **Washington State**   1977

Played in five games for the Chiefs.

Wiegman, Casey   C   62   **Iowa**   2001

Signed with the Chiefs as an unrestricted free agent after spending the previous four seasons with the Bears. Wiegman missed the 2001 season opener because of an appendectomy, but started all 15 games the rest of the season at the center position.

Willard, Jerrott   LB   57   **California**   1998

The Chiefs' fifth-round draft pick in 1995, Willard played in one game.

Williams, Dan   DE   92   **Toledo**   1997, 1999-2000

A free agent from Denver, Williams had a great season in 1997, making 72 stops and racking up 10.5 sacks. The powerful end sat out the entire 1998 season because of a contract dispute, but returned in 1999 to play in 14 games, make 51 tackles, 5 sacks, and recover two fumbles. Williams recorded 55 tackles, had 7.5 sacks and recovered a fumble in just 11 games in 2000, missing the last part of the season because of a thigh injury. He was also responsible for 96 quarterback pressures in his three seasons with the Chiefs. Williams was released from the team after the start of the 2001 season. He played in a total of 40 games for Kansas City.

Player	Position	Jersey(s) Worn	College	Year(s) Played

Williams, Harvey　　RB　　22, 44　　LSU　　**1991-93**

The Chiefs' no. 1 draft selection in 1991, Williams appeared to have the the necessary stuff to make him the team's top back for several seasons. But after a good rookie campaign that saw him gain 447 yards on the ground, Williams' production tailed off the next two seasons, and following the 1993 campaign, he left for Oakland. His best game with the Chiefs was a 103-yard rushing effort against Buffalo in 1991. He finished his career in Kansas City with 858 yards rushing and four touchdowns. He also caught 28 passes and returned 48 kickoffs. Williams played in a total of 35 games for the Chiefs.

Williams, Jerrol　　LB　　44　　Purdue　　**1994**

Signed as a free agent, Williams played in six games as a backup at linebacker. He had 0.5 sacks.

Williams, Lawrence　　KR/WR　　40　　Texas Tech　　**1976-77**

A free-agent acquisition, Williams was primarily a kick returner for the Chiefs. He returned 25 kicks in 1976 for an average of 27.5 yards per return. He also scored a rushing touchdown, and caught eight passes for 103 yards. Williams played in 18 games for the Chiefs.

Williams, Mike　　RB/TE　　80　　New Mexico　　**1979-81**

The Chiefs' eighth-round draft pick in 1979, Williams ran for 261 yards and a touchdown his rookie season but was moved to tight end in 1980. He was used mostly as a blocker, and an injury to his knee ended his career in 1981. Williams finished with four touchdowns and played in 33 games.

Williams, Robert　　CB　　40　　Baylor　　**1993**

Williams was on the Chiefs' roster but didn't play in a game.

Williams, Robert　　CB　　46　　North Carolina　　**1998-99**

A fifth-round pick in 1998, Williams was used primarily on special teams but played in the defensive backfield and registered 0.5 sack. He played in 17 games for the Chiefs.

Williams, Sammy　　G　　72　　Oklahoma　　**1999**

Played in one game for the Chiefs in 1999.

Williams, Tyrone　　DE　　96　　Wyoming　　**2000-01**

Came to Kansas City from Philadelphia three games into the 2000 season. He made 14 tackles and 1.5 sacks in 10 games for the Chiefs. Started the 2001 campaign with the Redskins and returned to Kansas City for the final seven games of the season. Made seven stops on defense and four special teams tackles in 2001 for the Chiefs. He has played in 17 games for the club.

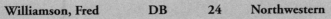

Williamson, Fred — DB — 24 — Northwestern — 1965-67

The "Hammer," Williamson was one of the most controversial players the Chiefs ever had because of his violent, forearm-to-head tackles. While his tactics were intimidating, he was susceptible to getting burned in the secondary. The Chiefs acquired Williamson from the Raiders for Dave Grayson. Williamson picked off 11 passes and returned one for a touchdown. He will always be remembered for talking about dropping the "hammer" on Green Bay before Super Bowl I and then being knocked out of the game himself. Since concluding his career with the Chiefs, Williamson has starred in several movies, including *M*A*S*H*.

Willis, Donald — G — 60 — North Carolina A&T — 2000-01

Made the team as a backup lineman, and also performed on special teams. Willis played in 16 games for the Chiefs, starting twice (once at center, once at right guard). Played in 14 games in 2001, starting four times at left guard. Willis has played in 30 games for the Chiefs.

Wilson, Eddie — QB/P — 12 — Arizona — 1962-64

Selected in the third round of the 1962 AFL draft by the Texans, Wilson served as Len Dawson's backup for three seasons, and as the team's punter in 1962. He completed 70 of 140 passes for 994 yards and four touchdowns. His best game was against the Patriots in 1963; he completed 20 of 32 passes for 258 yards and two touchdowns in that game. As a punter, Wilson averaged 35.12 yards per punt. He played in 42 games for the franchise.

Wilson, Jerrel — P — 44 — Southern Mississippi — 1963-77

see Chiefs Hall of Fame

Wilson, Mike — G — 67 — Dayton — 1975

The Chiefs signed Wilson late in the 1975 season, and he started in three games at left guard. He played in a total of four games for the Chiefs.

Winters, Frank — G/C — 65 — Western Illinois — 1990-91

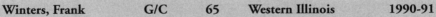

A "Plan B" free agent, Winters was a valuable addition to the Chiefs' offensive line. He played both guard and center, and also handled the team's long snaps. Winters played in a total of 32 games for the Chiefs.

Wolf, James — DT — 73 — Prairie View — 1976

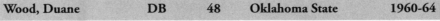

Came to the Chiefs as a free agent and started in seven games in 1976. He had one sack and played in a total of 14 games for Kansas City.

Wood, Duane — DB — 48 — Oklahoma State — 1960-64

An original Texan, Wood was one of the team's top defensive players in its first five years of existence. He had deceptive speed and excellent coverage skills, which led to 20 interceptions for the franchise. Wood ran one of the picks back for a touchdown in 1960 and scored another touchdown in 1963. After coming to the Texans from Canada, he played in a total of 65 games for the franchise.

Player	Position	Jersey(s) Worn	College	Year(s) Played

Woodard, Ray — DE — 70 — Texas — 1987

Came to the Chiefs from Denver in the middle of the 1987 season. He played in six games.

Wooden, Terry — LB — 90 — Syracuse — 1997

Came to Kansas City as a free agent after spending seven seasons with the Seahawks. His experience and consistency added much to the Chiefs' linebacker corps. He started eight games at right outside linebacker in 1997 and recorded 41 tackles, two sacks, and a fumble recovery. He played in the Chiefs playoff loss to the Broncos on January 4, 1998. Wooden appeared in a total of 15 games for the Chiefs.

Woods, Jerome — S — 21, 31 — Memphis — 1996-2001

The Chiefs' no. 1 draft pick in 1996, Woods has become an excellent NFL safety. He is a hard-hitting, tough player with intimidating talent and an extremely high threshold for pain. He had a great year in 2001, racking up 115 total tackles to go with his three interceptions. Through the 2001 season, Woods has accumulated 562 total tackles, forced eight fumbles, and picked off 12 passes. He also has four career sacks. Woods returned 25 kickoffs in 1996 for an average of 23.2 yards per return. He has played in 95 games for the Chiefs.

Word, Barry — RB — 23 — Virginia — 1990-92

After setting out the 1989 season, Word came to Kansas City as a free agent and astonished the team with his running prowess. After overcoming personal problems and being given a chance to properly show his talent, he became just the sixth Chiefs' running back to gain 1,000 yards in a season, netting 1,015 in 1990. He followed up with 684 rushing yards in 1991 and 607 yards in 1992. Word scored 12 touchdowns for the Chiefs, four in each season he was with the club. He played in a total of 44 games for Kansas City.

Word, Mark — DE — 67 — Jacksonville State — 1999

A rookie free agent in 1999, Word played in six games.

Worthen, Naz — WR — 84 — North Carolina State — 1989-90

Worthen was the Chiefs' third-round draft pick in 1989. The speedy wideout was used as a kick returner during his two seasons in Kansas City and caught just five passes. He returned 44 punts for an average of 7.1 yards per return, and 16 kickoffs for an average of 21.2 yards per return. Worthen played in 19 games for the Chiefs.

Wright, Elmo — WR — 17 — Houston — 1971-74

see Other Chiefs Greats

Player	Position	Jersey(s) Worn	College	Year(s) Played

Wright, Felix — S — 24 — Drake — 1993

Appeared in the 1993 postseason for the Chiefs.

Wyatt, Kevin — CB — 23 — Arkansas — 1987

A replacement player during the 1987 NFL players' strike; played in two games for the Chiefs and returned two punts and five kickoffs.

Yakavonis, Ray — NT — 92 — Eastern Stroadsburg State — 1983

Played in two games for the Chiefs.

Young, Michael — WR — 85 — UCLA — 1994

Played in two games for the Chiefs.

Young, Wilbur — DE — 99 — William Penn — 1971-77

Young was the second pick by the Chiefs in the 1971 draft, and his presence on the Chiefs' defensive line was a major plus for the team during his time in Kansas City. He totaled 12.5 sacks in 1976 and eight in 1973 for his best two seasons. Young returned an interception 52 yards for touchdown in 1974, and he also had another pick in 1971. He played in a total of 94 games before going to San Diego in 1978.

Zamberlin, John — LB — 61 — Pacific Lutheran — 1983-84

Picked up on waivers from New England, Zamberlin was a backup inside linebacker and special teams player. He played in 22 games for the Chiefs.

Zaruba, Carroll — DB — 46 — Nebraska — 1960

Taken in the first AFL draft, Zaruba played in seven games for the Texans.

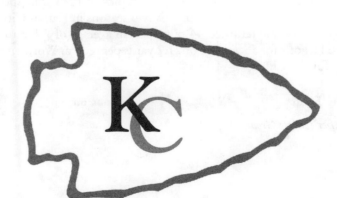

KANSAS CITY CHIEFS
Head Coaches

Year	Coach	Record	Pct.
1960-74	Hank Stram	124-76-10	.614
1975-77	Paul Wiggin	11-24-0	.314
1977	Tom Bettis	1-6-0	.143
1978-82	Marv Levy	31-42-0	.425
1983-86	John Mackovic	30-34-0	.469
1987-88	Frank Gansz	8-22-1	.274
1989-98	Marty Schottenheimer	101-58-1	.631
1999-2000	Gunther Cunningham	16-16	.500
2001-	Dick Vermeil	6-10	.375

Hank Stram

1960-74
Record: 124-76-10

The "Little General" stalked the Chiefs' sidelines for 15 seasons, carrying his trademark—a rolled-up game plan—as he led his team to many victories. He was highly innovative, both on offense and defense, adding several new wrinkles to the world of pro football.

Hank Stram was the coach, and, as much as any one person could be, is responsible for the great success the franchise enjoyed during his time with the club, including two Super Bowl appearances and one world championship. But he also was aware of what made that success possible.

"Any way you slice it, you win because of people," Stram said. "You win because of the way these people express their God-given talent. The biggest challenge we have is to win the battle within ourselves, and the biggest battle is to get the most out of our ability. That's what coaching is all about: to make your people express their talent."

A graduate of Purdue University, where he was a football and baseball letterman, Stram started his coaching career as an assistant at his alma mater. He then moved to SMU, Notre Dame, and Miami (Florida) before becoming the Texans' head coach in the AFL's inaugural season of 1960. Stram was an immediate winner in Dallas and led the team to the 1962 AFL championship.

On offense, Stram developed the moving quarterback pocket, which allowed the quarterback to roll side to side with pass protection in front of him. He also added the tight end I formation, in which the tight end would line up in the backfield before shifting to either side of the line. His most notable innovation on defense was the "stack," which lined up the linebackers directly behind the down lineman, and made a variety of defensive options available. Many other pro teams copied this defense.

Also know as "Dapper," Stram dressed for success and demanded the same from his players.

"This is my team," Stram said of the Chiefs in 1970. "We do things my way. That's it. If you can't accept that, you can't play here."

"He is the man. There is no in-between," Buck Buchanan said of his longtime coach. "But you talk to him and he puts the men on the field who should be there. I've never seen anyone who wants to win as much as he does."

"They understand me," Stram said of his players. "But it takes a while. They have to see things, not just hear me talk about them."

"His strongest point is his loyalty," Johnny Robinson said of Stram. "I've never seen a player get a bad deal from him."

Stram led the Dallas Texans to two winning seasons, and, after a losing mark during the club's first year in Kansas City, led the Chiefs to 10 straight non-losing records. The Chiefs' Super Bowl IV win over Minnesota was the highlight of his career, but he also fielded very good teams in 1966, 1968, and 1971. Stram was named AFL Coach of the Year twice by the Associated Press, in '66 and '68.

After the Chiefs finished with a losing mark in 1974—poor draft choices and age finally caught up with the team—Lamar Hunt reluctantly fired Stram, who had posted a winning percentage of .614. Stram coached for two years for the Saints following his departure from Kansas City. He was elected to the Chiefs Hall of Fame in 1986.

Hank Stram and his Hall of Fame quarterback, Len Dawson. (Topeka Capital-Journal)

Coach Stram and his ever-present, rolled-up program. (Kansas Collection, U. of Kansas)

Paul Wiggin

1975-77
Record: 11-24-0

Following the only head coach a team has ever had wasn't going to be easy. And as Hank Stram's successor, Paul Wiggin inherited an aging group of veterans and untested young players.

"We will have to do the best we can," Wiggin said of his situation with the Chiefs. "We have some rebuilding to do here, but I don't think this team is in such dire straits that we have to bring in a lot of youth and take our lumps for a while. Now, I don't see us in the Super Bowl yet, either. If this team was going to the Super Bowl, I wouldn't be here."

An All-American at Stanford, Wiggin spent 11 seasons (1957-1967) as a defensive end with the Cleveland Browns, and was a starter in the Pro Bowl in 1965 and 1967. After retiring as a player in 1968, Wiggin became the defensive line coach for the San Francisco 49ers, and in 1974 was promoted to defensive coordinator. He came to the Chiefs with a very strong recommendation from Dick Nolan, the 49ers head coach.

Despite the overall lack of talent on the Chiefs his first season, the team was competitive. Wiggin notched his first head coaching win in a 42-10 blowout victory over Oakland. The Chiefs then won five of their next seven games, including a 34-31 upset of that year's NFC Champion Dallas Cowboys on Monday Night Football. The team finished the season with a four-game losing streak and a record of 5-9.

"I'm not going to make any rash predictions," Wiggin said before the 1976 season, "but we'll be better both offensivly and defensively." Unfortunately, the Chiefs weren't any better, and again finished with a 5-9 record.

A poor start to the 1977 season spelled Wiggin's doom, and following a 44-7 blowout loss to Cleveland, he was fired. The Chiefs had a 1-6 record at the time of his dismissal. His final record with the Chiefs was 11 wins, 24 losses, and no ties. Tom Bettis took over the team for the remainder of the season.

Wiggin was the defensive coordinator for the New Orleans Saints in 1978-79, and then took the head coaching position at Stanford from 1980-1983. He worked on the 1984 Los Angeles Olympic Committee in 1984 before joining the Minnesota Vikings in 1985. He has remained with the Vikings since then, acting in many different capacities on and off the field.

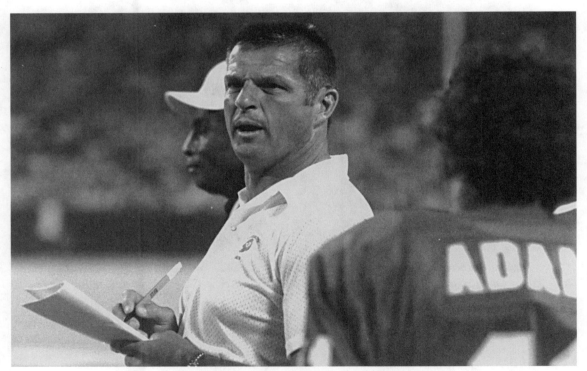

Paul Wiggin (Kansas Collection, U. of Kansas)

Tom Bettis

1977
Record: 1-6-0

When Paul Wiggin was fired midway through the 1977 season, Tom Bettis was given control of the club.

"The circumstances were not very good," Bettis said of his short head coaching stint with the Chiefs. "If I had it to do over again, I probably wouldn't do it."

Bettis had been an assistant coach with Kansas City for 11 and a half seasons. When Wiggin was hired as the Chiefs head coach, Bettis remained on the staff.

"Tom was a large part of the defense that won the world championship here," Wiggin said of Bettis, who helped develop the formidable Chiefs defense on the 1969 Super Bowl championship team.

An All American linebacker at Purdue, Bettis was a first round draft choice of the Green Bay Packers in 1955. He played with the Packers until 1961, and finished with the Bears in 1963. Bettis joined the Chiefs coaching staff in 1966 and remained with the team through the 1977 season. Although he wasn't comfortable taking the head coaching spot after Wiggin was let go, Bettis remained with the team out of loyalty to the many players he had coached during his time with the Chiefs.

The Chiefs won in his first game as head coach, defeating Green Bay 20-10. It was the only game the team won under his guidance. There was some talk of making him the permanent head coach, but in the end it was decided to get an outsider, Marv Levy. Bettis left the Chiefs following the 1977 campaign, but came back for one season as an assistant under Frank Gansz in 1988.

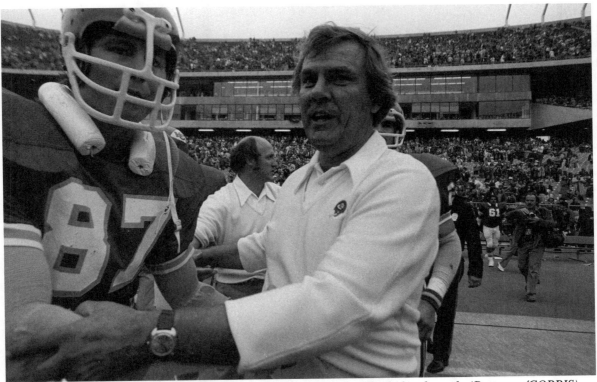

Tom Bettis is congratulated after his first and only win as the Chiefs' head coach. (Bettmann/CORBIS)

Marv Levy

1978-82
Record: 31-42-0

"Expect rejection but expect more to overcome it."

Marv Levy's career as the head coach of the Kansas City Chiefs reflected his own words. Dealt a bad hand—the Chiefs were 2-12 the year before Levy took over the team—when he first started with the Chiefs as Paul Wiggin's full-time successor. Levy led his team through a slow, gradual rebuilding process, winning small victories and drafting quality players. He managed just one winning season out of five, but his coaching performance in Kansas City was as good as any other coach's in the franchise's history.

Levy's coaching credentials were long and impressive before he came to the Chiefs. He was the head coach at the University of New Mexico in 1958-59, the University of California from 1960-63, and at William and Mary from 1964-68. Levy became the special teams coach for the Eagles in 1969, and had stints with the Rams and Redskins before taking over as the head coach for Montreal in the Canadian Football League.

To overcome the initial low talent level and overall lack of NFL experience on his first Chiefs team, the Harvard-educated Levy installed a winged-T offense that produced a powerful running game. As a team, the Chiefs ran for almost 3,000 yards in 1978. The running offense was designed to control the clock, keep the Chiefs in competition, and instill toughness in the offense. The unbalanced attack did those things, but the Chiefs won just four times that season.

"Our style is simple but not easy, roll up your sleeves and play good, solid football," Levy said at the beginning of his coaching stint with the Chiefs. "We want to develop a quality football team that is going to last. Our goal is to win the Super Bowl and win it again and again."

Levy pulled back on the running game the following season—Kansas City gained less than 2,000 yards on the ground—but the passing game remained sub par. Still, the Chiefs won seven games, the most since 1973. They won eight games in 1980, and with the emergence of superstar rookie running back Joe Delaney and a much improved defense, Kansas City finished at 9-7 in 1981. Great things were expected of the 1982 Chiefs, but the players' strike and a rash of injuries to key players short-circuited the club. The Chiefs finished 3-6, and the poor record finished Levy. Levy and Chiefs GM Jim Schaff were not getting along, and Levy was fired shortly after the season ended. His overall record with Kansas City was 31-42-0.

After serving as head coach of the USFL's Chicago Blitz, a front office job with Montreal in CFL, and even some time the broadcasting booth, Levy became the head coach for the Buffalo Bills in 1986. He put together an impressive string of AFC Championship teams in the early 1990s, making four straight appearances in the Super Bowl.

On August 4, 2001, Marv Levy was inducted into the Pro Football Hall of Fame.

"In 1978 Lamar Hunt, an NFL legend, hired me to coach the Kansas City Chiefs and players like Tom Condon, Fuzzy Kremer and Joe Delaney," Levy said in his induction speech. "I will always value my association with Lamar and the fine people in Kansas City."

Hall of Fame coach Marv Levy (Kansas Collection, U. of Kansas)

John Mackovic

1983-86
Record: 30-34-0

"Success is a journey, not a destination."

John Mackovic spoke those words shortly after becoming the Chiefs' head coach in 1983, but his four-year trip to success ended abruptly. After doing what no other coach with the Chiefs had been able to do since the days of Hank Stram—take the team to the playoffs—Mackovic's reward was to be fired. His irregular departure from the club was one of the worst chapters in the history of the Chiefs organization.

Just 39-years old when the Chiefs hired him, Mackovic had been the head coach at his alma mater, Wake Forest, and he came to Kansas City after serving as an assistant with the Dallas Cowboys for two years.

"The key to football today is the passing game," Mackovic said joining the Chiefs, and he worked to upgrade Kansas City pass offense.

One of Mackovic's first decisions with the Chiefs was to select Todd Blackledge, Penn State's All-American quarterback, with the team's 1983 first round draft pick. With the tragic death of Joe Delaney, Mackovic went into his first season with a depleted running game, and Kansas City finished 6-10 in 1983. But Bill Kenney passed for more than 4,300 yards and the team showed signs of being competitive at the end of the year.

A slight improvement to 8-8 in 1984 was followed by another disappointing 6-10 record in 1985.

"I think you learn more every year," Mackovic said following the 1985 season. "We went through some things that were tougher than anything we had gone through here." Mackovic shook up his coaching staff before the 1986 season; one of the changes was to bring in Frank Gansz as the special teams coach.

The Chiefs responded to the new coaches, and behind the incredible season-long efforts of the special teams, earned the club's first playoff berth since 1971. But Mackovic was never able to completely connect with his players, and the success of 1986 was credited more to Gansz than to him. Responding to player complaints and requests, Lamar Hunt fired Mackovic in January, 1987, and made Frank Gansz the head coach. The Chiefs reverted to their losing ways in the two seasons following Mackovic's departure.

Mackovic later coached at the University of Illinois and the University of Texas. He has also been an analyst at ESPN in recent seasons.

John Mackovic (Kansas Collection, U. of Kansas)

Frank Gansz

1987-88
Record: 8-22-1

Frank Gansz was a special teams guru, a master at using the kicking game to change momentum or control a football game. As the Chiefs' assistant head coach in charge of special teams in 1986, Gansz inspired results that led to the team's first playoff berth in 15 seasons. His special teams corps blocked or deflected a Chiefs' record ten kicks and scored five touchdowns that season, and also scored a touchdown in the playoff loss to the Jets. It was no secret that the Chiefs had lived or died on their special teams throughout the season, and Gansz also received most of the credit for the overall turnaround in the team's attitude and winning performance.

Frank Gansz (Kansas Collection, U. of Kansas)

The 1986 season was Gansz's second go around as the team's special teams coach—he was also on Marv Levy's staff in 1981-82—and following the playoff loss to the Jets he resigned his coaching position.

"I just feel at this time," said Gansz of his resignation, "it is necessary to prove what I feel I am able to contribute on the offensive side of the ball." In other words, he wanted to be a head coach.

The scenario that followed was one of the strangest, ugliest moves in the history of the franchise.

Lamar Hunt also placed a great deal of the Chiefs' success in 1986 on Gansz's shoulders, and he met informally with eight Chiefs players following the resignation. The meeting—some called it a mini revolt—seemed to seal the fate of head coach John Mackovic, who was fired the next day. Gansz was named as the Chiefs new head coach two days later.

"I'm really excited about this, I really am," Hunt said of Gansz. "Frank has outstanding leadership qualities. He's ready to make the move from an assistant's job to a head coaching job."

The move was supposed to be the final step back to the Super Bowl for the Chiefs. Gansz had the players' respect, and his hands-on leadership seemed to be an essential ingredient in winning. Instead, Gansz's head coaching stint in Kansas City proved to be a disaster.

Gansz had always held himself up as a fighter pilot, an image embraced by his team and the public alike. After the start of the 1987 season, it was learned that he had "enhanced" his flying credentials, and didn't possess the flying background he said he had. The truth of his time in the Air Force was a blow to the Chiefs team moral, who suffered through a dismal, strike-plagued season in 1987. They finished with just four wins.

Things weren't any better in 1988 as Kansas City again finished with four wins. Gansz was fired shortly after the end of the 1988 season by Carl Peterson, who had just taken over as the Chiefs' President and General Manager. His total record as the Chiefs head man was 8-22-1.

Most recently, Gansz was the special teams coach for the Super Bowl Champion St. Louis Rams in 1999 under present Chiefs coach Dick Vermeil.

Marty Schottenheimer

1989-98
Record: 101-58-1

The architect of smashmouth football, Marty Schottenheimer used a pounding running game and turnover-oriented defense to transform Kansas City back into a dominant, winning football team. The Chiefs had just two winning seasons in the 10 years before Schottenheimer's arrival; they didn't have a losing year again until his final season, 10 years later.

"He is, without a doubt, the fiercest competitor I have ever known," Chiefs president Carl Peterson said of Schottenheimer. And with Peterson's guidance, Schottenheimer excelled. After just missing the play-

Marty Schottenheimer, shown here in a discussion with an official during the 1989 season, turned the Chiefs' fortunes around immediately his first season as head coach. (Kansas Collection, U. of Kansas)

offs in 1989, his first season, Schottenheimer led the Chiefs to six straight playoff appearances. Kansas City won the AFC West three times during his tenure, and won a total of 101 games.

"The best way to establish a position of excellence in the NFL is to expect it," Schottenheimer said when hired. He more than lived up to his words.

An All-American linebacker at the University of Pittsburgh, Schottenheimer spent six seasons with the Buffalo Bills, then 10 years as an assistant with the Portland Storm of the WFL, and then time with the Giants, Lions, and Browns. He became the Browns' head coach midway through the 1984 season. Schottenheimer took the Browns to the playoffs four times, and twice to the AFC championship game. It was the Chiefs' good fortune that Schottenheimer left the Browns following the 1988 season. He was the first head coach the Chiefs had ever hired who had previously been a head coach in the NFL.

The one item missing from Schottenheimer's list of accomplishments is a championship, and his overall record in the playoffs with the Chiefs is a poor three wins, seven losses. His 1995 team finished with a 13-3 record, tops in the NFL, but lost its first playoff game at Arrowhead Stadium to Indianapolis, 10-7. The 1997 Chiefs also finished 13-3, and again lost their first playoff game, this time to the Broncos, 14-10.

Schottenheimer remained upbeat after the losses, but it was apparent the lack of postseason success wore him down.

"I will not feel sorry for myself," Schottenheimer said after the Chiefs' loss to Denver in the 1997 playoffs. "I do not believe in self-pity."

In his final season as the Chiefs' head coach, Schottenheimer lost control of his team six games into the season, and the club nose-dived out of playoff contention and finished 7-9, the only losing season he ever experienced in his NFL career. Schottenheimer resigned shortly after the season.

After a brief stint with ESPN, Schottenheimer returned to coaching in 2001 and led the Washington Redskins to an 8-8 record. Fired following the season, he was immediately hired to lead the San Diego Chargers in 2002.

Marty Schottenheimer (Alan Barzee)

Gunther Cunningham

1999-2000
Record: 16-16

A lifetime assistant coach, Gunther Cunningham finally grabbed a top coaching position when he became the Chiefs' eighth head coach on January 22, 1999.

"Gunther has earned this," Chiefs president Carl Peterson said when he hired Cunningham. "I have every confidence that he's going to take this next step. He's prepared himself for this for a long time, and prepared himself well. And again, probably the most important aspect is I know how players respond to him."

As the Chiefs' defensive coordinator from 1995-98, Cunningham put together one of the NFL's top defenses, leading the league in scoring defense in 1995 and 1997. The Chiefs won 13 games both of those seasons. Cunningham came up through the ranks and worked at four different colleges before going to the CFL for one season. He was an assistant for the Colts, Chargers and Raiders before joining the Chiefs in 1995. Despite losing the season finale that would have put the Chiefs in the playoffs, 1999 was a successful year for the rookie coach (a 9-7 record). The turmoil and losing habits of the previous season were gone, and there was every indication Cunningham would be a good head coach.

"He knows how to command and create discipline," Peterson said of his new head coach in 1999. "Overall, he's a leader, and that's obviously something you look for in a head coach."

"I was trying to develop a blood and guts football team," Cunningham said of his Chiefs team after the 1999 season. "I think we're starting to get closer and closer [to that]. I think the Chiefs are about toughness."

The Chiefs and Cunningham suffered tremendous emotional setbacks when Derrick Thomas passed away in February, 2000, and his loss left a huge void in team leadership. Cunningham waffled a bit after the Chiefs dropped the opening game of the 2000 season to Indianapolis, telling his players he was considering quitting. He quickly withdrew the remarks, but was unable to gain proper control afterwards. He switched the offense to a total passing game after a 3-3 start, but the defense was lacking and the team still limped to the end of the season with a 7-9 record. Carl Peterson decided changes needed to be made, and he started with the head coach.

On January 5, 2001, Gunther Cunningham was fired at the Chiefs' head coach. He spent the 2001 season as the linebackers coach for the Tennessee Titans.

Gunther Cunningham's first-ever head coaching job was with the Chiefs in 1999. (Alan Barzee)

Gunther Cunningham (Alan Barzee)

Dick Vermeil

2001-

On January 12th, 2001, Chiefs President Carl Peterson announced what he had wanted to 13 years earlier when he hired his first head coach for the Chiefs. Dick Vermeil was the ninth head coach in the franchise's history.

"He's had a philosophy that he's fine-tuned and refined," Peterson said of his new head coach and long-time friend. "He can do it statistically; he can do it philosophically. He has such a wealth and depth of background and experience that players know that he's right. If players do the things that he would like them to do in the fashion that he wants them to do it then we've got a chance for success."

"Sooner or later, it was probably going to happen that Carl and I would be back together again, rejoined and initiate a new crusade," Vermeil said of working again with Peterson. "Every time we've done it, we've been successful, from a Rose Bowl Championship to a NFC Championship to a loss in the Super Bowl."

The longstanding relationship between the Vermeil and Peterson relationship started in 1974 when Vermeil was named the head coach at UCLA. Peterson served as receivers coach and an administrative assistant. In 1975, Vermeil led the Bruins to their first Rose Bowl appearance in 10 seasons, and UCLA defeated the number one ranked team in the country, Ohio State. Vermeil is the only head coach to win both the Rose Bowl and the Super Bowl.

Vermeil became the head coach of the Philadelphia Eagles in 1976, and Peterson served as the club's receivers and tight ends coach. In 1977, Peterson was named Philadelphia's Director of Player Personnel. The Eagles made the playoffs for the first time in 18 seasons, and in 1980 won the NFC and spot in the Super Bowl.

Vermeil's coaching career began at Stanford in 1965, and in 1969 he became the first-ever special teams coach in NFL history for the Los Angeles Rams working under George Allen. After shifting back and forth between the Rams and UCLA, Vermeil became the head coach of the Bruins in 1974. He was a color analyst for television broadcasts of college and pro football games between his head coaching stints at Philly and St. Louis.

"He defiantly puts all of his trust and faith in you when you are out there on the field," the Chiefs' Pro Bowl running back Priest Holmes said of Vermeil during the 2001 season. "That is something you cannot take back. I think he possesses all of the intangibles as a head coach."

Vermeil has a penchant for making a winning impact on his teams after taking the head coaching spot. He inherited an Eagles squad that hadn't had a winning season in ten years. In his third season as head coach, the Eagles made the playoffs. In 1997, Vermeil took over a St. Louis team that had endured seven straight losing seasons, and three years later the Rams were World Champs. Twice Vermeil has been honored as the NFL's Coach of the Year.

The Chiefs got off to a poor start in 2001, Vermeil's 11th season as an NFL coach, winning just once in their first seven games. A new offense, defense, quarterback and overall philosophy was slow to take hold among the players. But the second half of the season the players showed improvement and a better grasp of Vermeil's coaching techniques. The Chiefs finished at 6-10.

"When we were 1-6, he has been there before so he knows how to handle it," Tony Gonzalez said of Vermeil and the Chiefs' poor start to the 2001 season. "He knows what to do and what not to do. He has handled it well. He has come in and made a lot of changes. It is more of a relaxed environment."

With his first season as the Chiefs head coach complete, Vermeil reflected on possible turning points in the season and the mental toughness of his players.

"I don't think there is one game that all of a sudden determines the season unless you're very, very fragile and you're going down," Vermeil said in his final press conference following the 2001 season. "I can name some in past opportunities, but here I can't name any one specific game. I think beating the Raiders in the opener would have been a huge boost, but I can't tell you we would have won the next week. I don't have the strong feeling because this football team is not as fragile mentally as the first-year football teams I've been around before. They're deeper than that. I think they continued to give good effort and believed they could win."

Dick Vermeil (Alan Barzee)

All-Time
Assistant Coaches

Abernethy, Rick	1979-82	Long, Billy	2001
Adolph, Dave	1993-94, 99	Lowe, Woodrow	1995-98
Arians, Bruce	1989-92	Mann, Richard	1999-2000
Ball, Russ	1989-98	Matthews, Billie	1987-88
Beake, John	1968-74	Mauck, Carl	1986-88
Beckman, Ed	1987-88	McCarthy, Mike	1993-98
Bettis, Tom	1966-77, 88	McCulley, Pete	1983-86
Brazil, Dave	1984-88	Mills, Chuck	1966
Bresnahan, Tom	1981-82	Mudd, Howard	1989-92
Brewster, Darrell "Pete"	1964-73	O'Boyle, Tommy	1966-74
Bunting, John	1993-96	Ortmayer, Steve	1975-77
Carson, Bud	1983	Pagna, Tom	1978-79
Catlin, Tom	1960-65	Parker, Roberto	1997-98
Christiansen, Jack	1977	Peete, Willie	1983-86
Cignetti, Frank Jr.	1999	Pendry, Joe	1989-92
Clements, Tom	2000	Pratt, Tom	1963-77,
Corey, Walt	1971-74, 78-86		89-94, 2000
Costello, Vince	1975-76	Raye, Jimmy	1992-2000
Cottrell, Ted	1981-82	Redding, Dave	1989-97
Cowher, Bill	1989-91	Roach, Dick	1978-80
Cunningham, Gunther	1995-98	Robinson, Greg	2001
Dalton, Kay	1978-82	Ross, Bobby	1978-81
Daniel, Dan	1983-85	Rossley, Tom	1999
Dungy, Tony	1989-91	Rowen, Keith	1999-2001
Erv Eatman	2001	Roy, Alvin	1968-72
Edwards, Herman	1993-94	Rust, Rod	1978-82, 88
Erkenbeck, Jim	1989-91, 95-98	Saunders, Al	1989-98, 2001
Fish, Jeff	1999-2000	Saxon, James	2001
Franklin, Chet	1975-77	Schnelker, Bob	1975-77
Galbraith, Marty	1985	Schottenheimer, Brian	1998
Gansz, Frank	1981-82, 86	Schottenheimer, Kurt	1989-2000
Gansz, Frank Jr.	2001	Sefcik, George	1988
Ghilotti, Bob	1962-63	Shaw, Willie	2000
Gibbs, Alex	1993-94	Shea, Terry	2001
Giunta, Peter	2001	Shell, Art	1995-96
Graber, Doug	1983-86	Smith, Homer	1987
Hackett, Paul	1993-98	Solari, Mike	1997-2000
Hairston, Carl	1995-96, 2001	Spencer, Joe	1975-80
Hatley, Mark	1987	Stock, Mike	1995-2000
Helm, J.D.	1982-88	Vechiarella, Jim	1983-85
Hewgley, C.T.	1983-88	Verduzco, Jason	2001
Hostler, Jim	2000	Vitt, Joe	2000-2001
Hughes, Ed	1960-62	Waller, Ron	1978-82
Humenuik, Rod	1983-84	Wallis, Darvin	1989-2001
Hurd, Jeff	1998-2001	Walsh, Bill	1960-74
James, Lionel	1998	Williamson, Richard	1983-86
Joiner, Charlie	2001	Wilson, Eddie	1974
Karmelowicz, Bob	1997-2001	Wood, Richard	1987-88
Lavan, Al	1999-2000	Young, John Paul	1986-87
Lawrence, Don	1980-82, 87-88	Zook, Ron	1999

KANSAS CITY CHIEFS
Stadiums

The home stadium of a professional football franchise can be an image-defining structure. The Kansas City Chiefs have used three playing fields in their 42-year existence, and each one provided a different type of identity for the club. The crowds, or lack of them, shaped the stadium around the teams and in many instances, especially in the past decade, became as much a part of the team as any star player. A winning team is a key ingredient to bringing in fans, although that wasn't the case when the franchise was in Dallas. Empty seats remained the standard for the first few seasons the team played in Kansas City, but once a winning team was established, Chiefs fans busted down the gates.

The Cotton Bowl

For three seasons the Texans played in the Cotton Bowl, and almost every home game was played before thousands and thousands of empty seats. The team shared the stadium with the NFL's Cowboys, which effectively split the city's fan base. Despite the Texans' two winning seasons and league championship, they were fighting a losing war; the empty seats and competition from the NFL eventually led to Lamar Hunt's decision to move the team to Kansas City.

The stadium is located on the Texas State Fairgrounds. The Cowboys played in the Cotton Bowl through the 1970 season, and Southern Methodist University still uses the stadium today as their home field. The Texans' final game in the Cotton Bowl was on December 16, 1962, against the San Diego Chargers. A small crowd of 18,384 saw the eventual AFL champions win, 26-17.

Stadium Information
Opened: 1930—An upper deck was added in 1948-49
Largest Texans Crowd: September 2, 1960, vs. Houston (preseason)—51,000
Smallest Texans Crowd: December 10, 1961, vs. Denver—8,000
Capacity: 75,504
Texans' Regular-Season Record at the Cotton Bowl: 15-6-0 (.714)

The Cotton Bowl (Kansas City Chiefs)

Municipal Stadium

The Chiefs' first home field in Kansas City, Municipal Stadium, housed some of the franchise's best teams. A baseball stadium that was first opened in 1923, the stadium was originally called Muehlebach Stadium (1923-37), later Ruppert Stadium (1938-42) and Blues Stadium (1943-54). It was re-named Municipal Stadium after an upper deck was added in 1955 when the Philadelphia A's major-league baseball team moved to town.

Kansas City's first NFL franchise, the Kansas City Blues (1924)/Cowboys (1925-26), used Muehlebach Stadium as their home field from 1924-26 but strangely didn't have any home games in 1925 and only two in 1926. The team was dropped from the NFL following the 1926 season when the league went from 22 teams to 12.

The Chiefs played their first game at Municpal Stadium on August 9, 1963, before a paltry crowd of 5,721 spectators and defeated the Buffalo Bills, 17-13. But by the end of the decade, the old stadium rocked with exuberance and excitement and was filled to near-capacity or sold out every game. Municipal had a certain blue-collar flavor about it that the players loved. During games, both teams used the same sideline in front of the Wolfpack bleachers that ran from left field to center, an advantage for the Chiefs who were used to the strange arrangement. The team's mascot, the horse Warpaint, circled the field regularly during games when the team scored. The Chiefs lost just three times during their final four regular seasons at the stadium and were undefeated at home in 1971.

The scoreboard at Municipal Stadium (Kansas Collection, U. of Kansas)

"I loved that old stadium," Otis Taylor said of Municipal. "All the guys who played there loved it. It gave us an advantage. The whole neighborhood was special. I missed it after we moved to Arrowhead."

The Chiefs' final game at Municipal Stadium was on December 25, 1971, in the AFC divisional playoff game against the Miami Dolphins. The only playoff game ever held at Municipal is the longest game ever played in the history of the NFL, and the Chiefs lost the famous contest in double overtime, 27-24, after 82 minutes and 40 seconds of play. It was a sad ending for the stadium, and the Chiefs were unable to transfer their winning tradition to Arrowhead Stadium when they began play there the following year.

Stadium Information
Opened: 1923—An upper deck was added in 1954-55
Largest Chiefs Crowd: October 24, 1971, vs. Washington—51,989
Smallest Chiefs Crowd: August 9, 1963, vs. Buffalo (preseason)—5,721
Capacity: 49,002 in 1971
Chiefs' Regular-Season Record at Municipal Stadium: 44-16-3 (.698)

A sellout crowd at Municipal Stadium in 1966 (Kansas City Star)

Arrowhead Stadium

It was an untested idea. No city in the country had ever built a two-stadium sports complex, but when the Jackson County voters approved a bond to build the Truman Sport Complex in 1967, Kansas City would become the first. A 78,000-seat football stadium and a 41,000-seat baseball stadium, set side by side, were planned and would give Kansas City the finest stadiums in the country.

"We were so far ahead of our time," the Chiefs' Jack Steadman said. "Now every city in the country wants what we did in 1972."

"I don't remember anyone sitting down and saying that this was going to be the concept of the future," said Joe McGuff, former sports editor of the *Kansas City Star*. "There was great discussion about the problems of multipurpose stadiums. That was one of the arguments used to justify the two-stadium concept."

"It really is fantastic to realize how farsighted Kansas City was in the planning of the dual stadiums at the crossroads of two interstates," Chiefs owner Lamar Hunt said. "The concept of two stadiums was absolutely 100 percent right. Other stadiums being built then were in the range of 55,000 to 58,000 seats and dual-purpose-type stadiums."

After sorting through possible location sites, finalizing details and suffering through major construction delays, Arrowhead Stadium opened on August 12, 1972. The Chiefs defeated the St. Louis Cardinals, 24-14, before 78,190 spectators.

The complex was originally designed to have a rolling roof that would cover both Arrowhead and Royals Stadium. The roof was dropped, though, because of cost overruns. For the first 23 years the Chiefs played in Arrowhead, tartan turf was the playing surface. The stadium was switched to natural grass before the 1994 season.

(Alan Barzee)

The team took several seasons to feel comfortable in the new stadium, though, and after posting five wins at Arrowhead in 1973, it didn't have a winning record at home until 1981. The Chiefs enjoyed tremendous success at the stadium throughout the 1990s, posting a record of 65-15 at home, and had 76 consecutive sellouts through the 1999 season. The large crowds and intense noise levels have provided the Chiefs with a distinct home-field advantage and made Arrowhead Stadium one of the most feared places to play throughout the NFL.

"Our fans have been conditioned to make noise ever since they opened the place in 1972," Chiefs director of public relations Bob Moore said. "The organization has always made a big thing of it, and every coach that's come through here has tried to take advantage of it."

The stadium remains one of the finest in the league. The Chiefs have provided several upgrades to Arrowhead—video boards, computerized scoreboard, new seats, refurbishing the locker rooms and offices—to ensure the it remains one of the league's best facilities.

Stadium Information
Opened: 1972
Largest Chiefs Crowd: November 5, 1972, vs. Oakland—82,094
Smallest Chiefs Crowd: December 18,1983, vs. Denver—11,377
Capacity: 79,451 (approximately)
Chiefs' Regular-Season Record at Arrowhead Stadium (through the 2001 season): 134-94-1 (.587)

Arrowhead Stadium, home of the Chiefs (Kansas City Star)

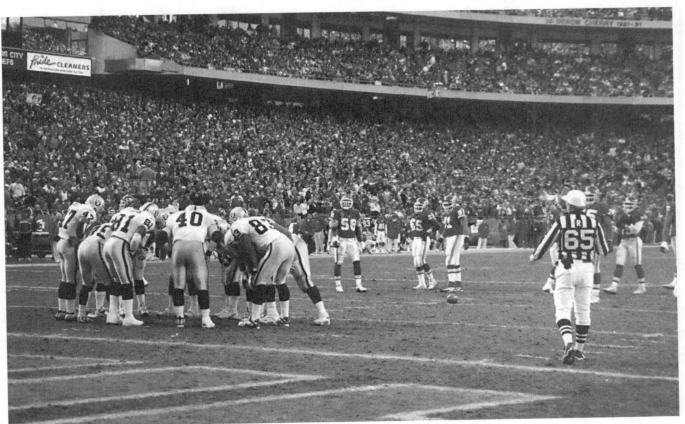

The Chiefs enjoyed a substantial home field advantage at Arrowhead throughout the 1990s. (Alan Barzee)

Grass replaced Arrowhead's AstroTurf surface before the 1994 season. (Alan Barzee)

Arrowhead's Home Field Advantage

• The Chiefs sold out 92 consecutive games through the 2001 season, including four playoff contests dating back to the '91 season.

• The Chiefs led the NFL in attendance six of the last eight seasons (1993-2001) and ranked second in the AFC and fourth in the NFL in paid home attendance.

• The Chiefs have topped the 560,000 mark in home attendance for 12 straight seasons and have attracted over 600,000 fans from 1993 through the 2001 season.

• Starting in 1988, the Chiefs are 54-3 (.947) at Arrowhead when the club scores 21 points or more.

• The Chiefs own a 40-16 (.771) record at Arrowhead Stadium since 1995. Denver is the only AFC team with a better home record over that same span at 45-11 (.804).

KANSAS CITY CHIEFS
Playoff Game Summaries

1968 AFL Divisional Playoff Game

December 22, 1968
Raiders 41, Chiefs 6
Oakland-Alameda County Coliseum (54,444)

Humiliation in defeat. When the Kansas City Chiefs took to the rain-softened field to play the Oakland Raiders for the AFL Western Division title, they expected a tight, hard-fought battle that resembled many of the two teams' clashes the past three seasons. Instead, the game was realistically over before the first 15 minutes had been played.

"We came a long way to end it like this," Chiefs end Reg Carolan said after the game. A very bad ending.

Oakland 41, Kansas City 6.

"Once you get them (the Chiefs) down, they don't stick to their game plan," Oakland defensive end Ike Lassiter said. "They seem to panic."

Oakland quarterback Daryle Lamonica hit touchdown passes of 24, 23, and 44 yards in the first period, and then applied the clincher late in the second period, a 54-yard bomb to Fred Biletnikoff to put the Raiders up 28-6 at the half. The Chiefs never recovered.

Chiefs coach Hank Stram said the Raiders were great, but had nothing to say about the performance of his team, which sputtered, stalled, and made mistake after mistake throughout the game. Len Dawson threw four interceptions, and the running game, the strong point of the offense, was shut down by the Raiders' aggressive defense and netted only 70 yards. The Raiders played mistake free and totaled 454 yards of total offense.

"Something like this is just a part of football," Raider head man Al Davis said of the game. "The Chiefs are a great team. We just got off on top, and the Chiefs had to go away from their game plan."

"You played awfully well," Chiefs owner Lamar Hunt told Davis. "In fact, I've never seen you play better. You really waxed us."

The win advanced the Raiders to the AFL championship game, where they met the Jets in New York. The Chiefs went home.

KANSAS CITY	0	6	0	0	—	6
OAKLAND	21	7	0	13	—	41

RAIDERS   – Biletnikoff, 24-yard pass from Lamonica (Blanda kick).
RAIDERS   – Wells, 23-yard pass from Lamonica (Blanda kick).
RAIDERS   – Biletnikoff, 44-yard pass from Lamonica (Blanda kick).
CHIEFS   – **Stenerud, 10-yard field goal.**
CHIEFS   – **Stenerud, 8-yard field goal.**
RAIDERS   – Biletnikoff, 54-yard pass from Lamonica (Blanda kick).
RAIDERS   – Wells, 35-yard pass from Lamonica (Blanda kick).
RAIDERS   – Blanda, 41-yard field goal.
RAIDERS   – Blanda, 40-yard field goal.

Team Statistics	Raiders	Chiefs
First Downs	22	13
Total Net Yards	454	312
Rushes/Net Yards	30/118	24/70
Net Passing	336	242
Pass Attempts/Completions	39/19	36/17
Had Intercepted	0	4
Sacked/Yards Lost	1/11	1/11
Punts/Average	5/45.4	6/50.3
Penalties/Yards	1/5	4/49
Fumbles/Lost	1/0	2/0

Rushing
CHIEFS   – **Holmes 13-46; Garrett 6-5; Hayes 3-10; Dawson 2-9.**
RAIDERS   – Dixon 10-13; Smith 13-74; Hagberg 4-12; Banaszak 3-19.

Receiving
CHIEFS   – **Pitts 5-56; Taylor 4-117; Garrett 4-31; Richardson 3-57; Holmes 1-(-8).**
RAIDERS   – Biletnikoff 7-180, 3 TDs; Wells 4-93, 1 TD; Smith 5-25; Cannon 2-15; Dixon 1-7.

Passing
CHIEFS   – **Dawson 17-36-253, 0 TDs, 4 INTs.**
RAIDERS   – Lamonica 19-39-345, 5 TDs, 0 INTs.

Interceptions
CHIEFS   – **None.**
RAIDERS   – Hopkins 1-7; Wilson 1-14; Conners 1-5; Brown 1-0.

Field Goals
CHIEFS   – **Stenerud (10) (8) 39S.**
RAIDERS   – Blanda (41) (40).

The Oakland Raiders' Fred Biletnikoff clutches a 20-yard pass as the Chief's Goldie Sellers puts the stop on him. (Bettmann/CORBIS)

1969 AFL Divisional Playoff Game

December 20, 1969
Chiefs 13, Jets 6
Shea Stadium (62,977)

KANSAS CITY	0	3	3	7	—	13
NEW YORK	3	0	0	3	—	6

JETS	— J. Turner, 28-yard field goal.
CHIEFS	— Stenerud, 23-yard field goal.
CHIEFS	— Stenerud, 25-yard field goal.
JETS	— J. Turner, 7-yard field goal.
CHIEFS	— Richardson, 19-yard pass from Dawson (Stenerud kick).

Facing the defending world champions in the first round of the AFL playoffs, the Chiefs used an inspired goal-line stand and a quick striking passing game to dethrone the New York Jets and advance to the final AFL championship game.

Kansas City left the Big Apple with a hard-fought win, 13-6.

"We have never played a greater game in a clutch situation than we did today," Hank Stram said of the Chiefs' effort. He's probably right.

Holding to a precarious 6-3 lead in the third quarter, the Jets had a first-and-goal at the Chiefs' one-yard line after a pass interference call on Kansas City cornerback Emmitt Thomas.

"I just said a little prayer," Chiefs middle linebacker Willie Lanier said. "We knew we had to do it. Every man gave as much as he could." And Lanier went crazy. He pleaded, shouted, screamed, and begged his teammates to stop the Jets. He cried.

"It was the way he did it—tears in his eyes, teeth gnashing," Jerry Mays said of Lanier. And the defense responded.

Jet running back Bill Mathis was stopped for no gain on first down. Matt Snell lost half a yard. On third down, Joe Namath faked a pitch to Snell, faked a handoff to Mathis and turned to the right. Bobby Bell picked up Snell, the intended receiver on the play. Namath was rushed and got off a poor pass that fell at Snell's feet. Jets kicker Jim Turner then kicked a field goal to tie the score.

The Chiefs then raced down the field in two plays, a 61-yard pass play to Otis Taylor from Len Dawson, and then a 19-yard scoring strike to Gloster Richardson. The Chiefs had a 13-6 lead and protected it the rest of the game. Namath hit on just 14 of 40 pass attempts, and the Chiefs intercepted three passes in the final quarter to seal the win.

"I'm exhausted," Chiefs linebacker Jim Lynch said afterwards. "Not so much from playing, but from the emotion. This was great victory. We have a fantastic bunch of guys on this team."

Team Statistics	Jets	Chiefs
First Downs	19	14
Total Net Yards	235	276
Rushes/Net Yards	22/87	30/99
Net Passing	148	177
Pass Attempts/Completions	40/14	27/12
Had Intercepted	3	0
Sacked/Yards Lost	2/16	2/24
Punts/Average	5/37.2	6/33.5
Penalties/Yards	3/15	5/63
Fumbles/Lost	1/1	0/0

Rushing
CHIEFS — Garrett 18-67; Hayes 10-32; McVea 1-0; Holmes 1-0.
JETS — Snell 12-61; Boozer 3-14; Mathis 6-11; Namath 1-1.

Receiving
CHIEFS — Holmes 1-29; Taylor 2-74; Hayes 5-46; Pitts 1-(-6); Arbanas 2-39; Richardson 1-19, 1 TD.
JETS — Lammons 3-37; Sauer 5-61; Boozer 1-10; B. Turner 2-25; Snell 1-9; Mathis 1-4; Maynard 1-18.

Passing
CHIEFS — Dawson 12-27-201, 1 TD, 0 INTs.
JETS — Namath 14-40-164, 0 TDs, 3 INTs.

Interceptions
CHIEFS — Marsalis 2-42; Thomas 1-0.
JETS — None.

Field Goals
CHIEFS — Stenerud 47S (23) 44WR 47 WL (25).
JETS — Turner (28) (7).

Emmitt Thomas (18) breaks up a pass during the 1969 divisional playoff at New York. (Topeka Capital-Journal)

Johnny Robinson, left, and Jim Marsalis celebrate during the Chiefs' playoff win over the Jets. Marsalis intercepted two passes in the game. (Topeka Capital-Journal)

1971 AFL Divisional Playoff Game

December 25, 1971
Dolphins 27, Chiefs 24 (2 OT)
Municipal Stadium (50,374)

Ed Podolak cried and Curley Culp slammed helmets into walls. Jan Stenerud stared blankly as he answered reporters' questions, and Hank Stram fought to maintain control over his emotions. The Kansas City Chiefs had just played in the longest game in the history of pro football with the Miami Dolphins. And they lost. Garo Yepremian's 37-yard field after 82 minutes and 40 seconds of playing time ended the Christmas Day playoff contest and made the Dolphins 27-24 winners.

"It's a shame to fight that hard, play that well, and not win," Hank Stram said following the game. "But it boils down to kicks. They made theirs. We didn't. We got a super return from Ed Podolak, and we had our chance to put the game away. We didn't do it."

Until Yepremian's kick, the Chiefs had never trailed in the game.

It was unseasonably warm in Kansas City for late December, 59 degrees at kickoff. The Chiefs scored 10 points in the first quarter on a Stenerud field goal and a seven-yard touchdown pass from Len Dawson to Podolak. Miami evened the score in the second period, and the two teams were tied at the half.

But the Chiefs lost a great opportunity to score a touchdown midway through the second quarter. Set to run a fake field goal, Stenerud was to get the snap and run. With two blockers in front of him, it would have been an easy touchdown. But long snapper Bobby Bell didn't think Stenerud was ready for the ball and snapped instead to holder Dawson. Improvising, Stenerud kicked the ball and just missed the field goal. Miami tied the score just before the half ended.

The teams traded touchdowns in the third and fourth quarters, Kansas City scoring on touchdown runs by Jim Otis and Podolak, and the Dolphins coming back to tie each time. But after Miami's touch-

down that knotted the score at 24 all with 1:42 remaining in regulation, Podolak returned the kickoff 78 yards to Miami's 22-yard line.

"The blockers opened up the middle perfectly," Podolak said of his return. "There was only one man there, Yepremian, and when I had to dodge him I had to slow down a little." He was forced out of bounds, but the Chiefs were in position to make the game-winning score. After three running plays to run down the clock, Stenerud came in to win the game. He missed the 31-yard attempt wide right.

"I have the worst feeling anyone could have," Stenerud said of his missed kicks and poor performance in the game. "I have no idea what I'm going to do now. I feel like hiding, I don't feel like playing football. It's a shame guys play like hell, like our team did, and lose because of a missed field goal. It's unbearable. It's totally unbearable."

The game went into overtime.

"That sudden death is horrifying," Dawson said. "One bad break, and you're out of the game."

Kansas City moved into field-goal range on their possession of the overtime, but Stenerud's kick was blocked. The two teams battled each other evenly for the duration of the overtime until Miami fullback Larry Czonka broke a run of 29 yards to the Kansas City 36-yard line. Three plays later, Yepremian made the game-winning field goal. After five and a half quarters of football, the Chiefs were eliminated from the playoffs.

Podolak had played the game of his life, accumulating 350 yards of total offense in running, receiving, and returning kicks.

"He just had kind of a magical day," Chiefs linebacker Jim Lynch said of Podolak's performance. "I don't think there had been another one like it."

"When it's happening," Podolak said a few minutes later, "you are just playing. But it seems everything happened just right, everything clicked that day." Losing the game, as Podolak's tears indicated afterward, was much more important than good statistics.

"It's tough to take, to lose this way," Stram said. "It has to be the toughest loss we've ever had. It's just incredible."

As the ball sails away from Miami kicker Garo Yepremian's foot, the Chiefs' Him Kearney (46) turns to watch the Chiefs' season end. The 37-yard field goal ended the longest game in the history of the NFL. (Kansas Collection, U. of Kansas)

MIAMI	0	10	7	7	0	3—27
KANSAS CITY	10	0	7	7	0	0—24

CHIEFS	**– Stenerud, 24-yard field goal.**
CHIEFS	**– Podolak, 7-yard pass from Dawson (Stenerud kick).**
DOLPHINS	– Csonka, 1-yard run (Yepremian kick).
DOLPHINS	– Yepremian, 14-yard field goal.
CHIEFS	**– Otis, 1-yard run (Stenerud kick).**
DOLPHINS–	Klick, 1-yard run (Yepremian kick).
CHIEFS	**– Podolak, 3-yard run (Stenerud kick).**
DOLPHINS–	Fleming, 5-yard pass from Griese (Yepremian kick).
DOLPHINS	– Yepremian, 37-yard field goal.

Team Statistics	Dolphins	Chiefs
First Downs	22	23
Total Net Yards	407	451
Rushes/Net Yards	43/144	44/213
Net Passing	263	238
Pass Attempts/Completions	35/20	26/18
Had Intercepted	2	2
Sacked/Yards Lost	0/0	1/8
Punts/Average	6/40.0	2/51.0
Penalties/Yards	5/26	6/44
Fumbles/Lost	1/0	3/2

Rushing

CHIEFS — **Hayes 22-100; Podolak 17-85, 1 TD; Wright 2-15; Otis 3-13, 1 TD.**

DOLPHINS — Klick 15-56, 1 TD; Csonka 24-86, 1 TD; Griese 2-9; Warfield 2-(-7).

Receiving

CHIEFS — **Podolak 8-110, 1 TD; Hayes 3-6; Wright 3-104; Taylor 3-12; Frazier 1-14.**

DOLPHINS — Warfield 7-140; Fleming 4-37, 1 TD; Klick 3-24; Twilley 5-58; Mandich 1-4.

Passing

CHIEFS — **Dawson 18-26-246, 1 TD, 2 INTs; Podolak 0-0-0, 0 TDs, 0 INTs.**

DOLPHINS — Griese 20-35-263, 1 TD, 2 INTs.

Interceptions

CHIEFS — **Lanier 1-17; Lynch 1-0.**

DOLPHINS — Johnson 1-0; Scott 1-13.

Sacks

CHIEFS — **None.**

DOLPHINS — Fernandez 0.5; Riley 0.5.

Field Goals

CHIEFS — **Stenerud (24) 29WR 31WR 42B.**

DOLPHINS — Yepremian (14) (37) 52WL.

1986 AFC Wild Card Playoff Game

December 28, 1986
Jets 35, Chiefs 15
Giants Stadium (69,307)

It was a short ride after such a long wait. The Chiefs played in their first playoff game in 15 years, and barely had time to take in their surroundings. After Kansas City jumped to a quick 6-0 lead, the New York Jets took off and brought the Chiefs back to earth, and then coasted to an easy 35-15 win.

"They outplayed us today; they outcoached us today," John Mackovic said of the playoff contest. "We did not make the plays we felt we could make." The Jets made almost all of their plays.

New York running back Freeman McNeil ran through the Chiefs' defense for 135 yards and two touchdowns. Jets quarterback Pat Ryan completed just enough of his passes to balance their running game, and the Jets' defense added three turnovers to the mix.

"Give the credit to the Jets," Mackovic said, "and the way they played every portion of the game. We didn't give our best effort, but maybe the Jets didn't let us."

Despite Kansas City's 67-yard drive that led to their first-quarter touchdown, Chiefs quarterback Todd Blackledge had a miserable game before he was replaced by the ailing Bill Kenney. On the ground, the Chiefs gained just 67 yards. Kansas City scored their second touchdown on a blocked punt by Albert Lewis in the fourth quarter, and then added a safety. Once again, the special teams had outscored the offense.

"To get here and be happy with that may satisfy some people," Chiefs nose tackle Bill Maas said of the game, "but it doesn't satisfy me."

"I told our guys we ought to hold our heads high and go out the door without being embarrassed," Mackovic said.

The Chiefs had ended their playoff drought, but the way they played against the Jets was very similar to the performances that had kept them away from the postseason for so long.

KANSAS CITY	6	0	0	9	—	**15**
NEW YORK	7	14	7	7	—	**35**

CHIEFS – J. Smith, 1-yard run (kick failed) (9-67).
JETS – McNeil, 1-yard run (Leahy kick) (13-75).
JETS – McNeil, 1-yard pass from Ryan (Leahy kick) (12-47).
JETS – Toon, 11-yard pass from Ryan (Leahy kick) (8-62).
JETS – McArthur, 21-yard interception return (Leahy kick).
CHIEFS – **Lewis, blocked punt recovery in end zone (Lowery kick).**
JETS – Griggs, 6-yard pass from Ryan (Leahy kick). (7-61).
CHIEFS – **Safety, Jennings runs out of end zone.**

Team Statistics	Jets	Chiefs
First Downs	19	15
Total Net Yards	306	241
Rushes/Net Yards	36/165	20/67
Net Passing	141	174
Pass Attempts/Completions	23/16	37/20
Had Intercepted	0	2
Sacked/Yards Lost	2/12	2/3
Punts/Average	4/29.0	3/41.3
Penalties/Yards	8/54	1/5
Fumbles/Lost	1/0	2/1

Rushing
CHIEFS – **Blackledge 4-33; Green 8-15; J. Smith 4-12, 1 TD; Moriarty 2-7; S. Paige 1-(-1); Heard 1-1.**
JETS – McNeil 31-135, 1 TD; T. Paige 2-3; Ryan 2-30; Jennings 1-(-3).

Receiving
CHIEFS – **Marshall 6-72; Green 5-7; Moriarty 1-16; Coffman 3-12; Carson 2-43; Smith 2-12; Heard 1-15.**
JETS – Toon 4-48, 1 TD; Shuler 4-28; McNeil 3-16, 1 TD; Walker 2-45; Sohn 1-11; Griggs 1-6, 1 TD; Alexander 1-(-1).

Passing
CHIEFS – Blackledge 12-21-80, 0 TDs, 1 INTs; Kenney 8-16-97, 0 TDs, 0 INTs.
JETS – Ryan 16-23-153, 3 TDs, 0 INTs.

Interceptions
CHIEFS – None.
JETS – McArthur 1-21; Carter 1-12.

Sacks
CHIEFS – **Hackett 1.0; Maas 1.0.**
JETS – Lyons 1.0; Gastineau 1.0.

Field Goals
CHIEFS – None.
JETS – None.

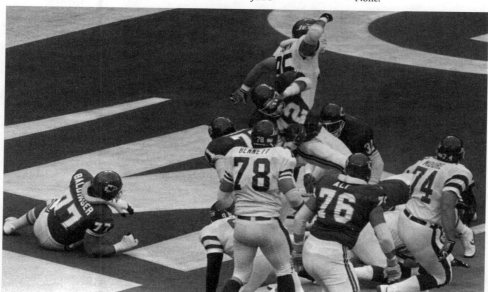

Kansas City running back Jeff Smith (42) fights his way into the end zone in the first quarter of the 1986 wild card game with the Jets in New York. (Bettmann/CORBIS)

1990 AFC First Round Playoff Game

January 5, 1991
Dolphins 17, Chiefs 16
Joe Robbie Stadium (67,276)

Nick Lowery's 52-yard field-goal attempt in the final minute of play fell a few feet short, and so did the Chiefs. After leading the Miami Dolphins 16-3 going into the fourth quarter, Kansas City gave up 14 points, losing a game they should have won, 17-16.

And the Chiefs' best season in almost two decades came to a premature end.

"It's tough to have the year end like this," Chiefs quarterback Steve DeBerg said.

"There is a lot of disappointment in here," Chiefs coach Marty Schottenheimer said after the game, "but what I told our team is that I want them to leave the disappointment in the locker room."

Kansas City's failure to score a second touchdown and a highly questionable holding call during their last drive added up to defeat. And the defense, which held the Dolphins at bay for three quarters, melted under Dan Marino's fourth-quarter assault. Marino tossed two touchdown passes in the final stanza to lead Miami's comeback.

Three times the Chiefs were in prime position to take control of the game if they scored a touchdown, and three times they had to settle for a field goal. The controversial holding penalty, which was called on Dave Szott with just under two minutes remaining in the games, nullified a Christian Okoye run that would have given the Chiefs a first down on the Miami 15-yard line. Instead, they were moved back to the 37, which proved to be just out of Lowery's kicking range.

"In the big game, it is the team that beats itself that loses more often than not," DeBerg said. "But they had to score a touchdown, and they did it. They had to stop us, and they did it."

Stephone Paige (83) had a great game against the Dolphins, catching 8 passes for 142 yards. He also scored the Chiefs' only touchdown. (Topeka Capital-Journal)

CHIEFS	– Lowery, 38-yard field goal (4-8).
DOLPHINS	– T. Paige, 1-yard pass from Marino (Stoyanovich kick) (10-66).
DOLPHINS	–Clayton, 12-yard pass from Marino (Stoyanovich kick) (11-85).

Team Statistics	Dolphins	Chiefs
First Downs	23	15
Total Net Yards	311	367
Rushes/Net Yards	32/98	24/103
Net Passing	213	264
Pass Attempts/Completions	30/19	30/17
Had Intercepted	0	1
Sacked/Yards Lost	2/8	1/5
Punts/Average	3/39.7	4/35.0
Penalties/Yards	2/22	4/35
Fumbles/Lost	2/2	0/0

Rushing
| CHIEFS | – Word 9-13; Okoye 13-83; McNair 2-7. |
| DOLPHINS | – S. Smith 20-82; Logan 7-17; T. Paige 1-2; Marino 4-(-3). |

Receiving
| CHIEFS | – S. Paige 8-142, 1 TD; R. Thomas 1-15; Roberts 2-26; Harry 2-59; McNair 3-22; Hayes 1-5. |
| DOLPHINS | – T. Paige 5-30, 1 TD; Clayton 5-66, 1 TD; Duper 3-36; Edmunds 2-49; S. Martin 1-7; Jensen 1-11; S. Smith 2-22. |

Passing
| CHIEFS | – DeBerg 17-30-269, 1 TD, 1 INT. |
| DOLPHINS | – Marino 19-30-221, 2 TDs, 0 INTs. |

Interceptions
| CHIEFS | – None. |
| DOLPHINS | – Williams 1.0. |

Sacks
| CHIEFS | – N. Smith 1.5; Cooper 0.5. |
| DOLPHINS | – Griggs 1.0. |

Field Goals
| CHIEFS | – Lowery (27) (25) (38) 52S. |
| DOLPHINS | – Stoyanovich (58) 57S. |

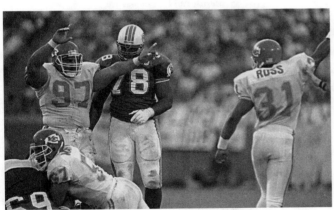
Dan Saleaumua and Kevin Ross celebrate a Dolphins turnover. (Topeka Capital-Journal)

KANSAS CITY	3	7	6	0	—	16
MIAMI	0	3	0	14	—	17

CHIEFS	– Lowery, 27-yard field goal (9-28).
DOLPHINS	– Stoyanovich, 58-yard field goal (9-40).
CHIEFS	– S. Paige, 26-yard pass from DeBerg (Lowery kick) (4-61).
CHIEFS	– Lowery, 25-yard field goal (11-63).

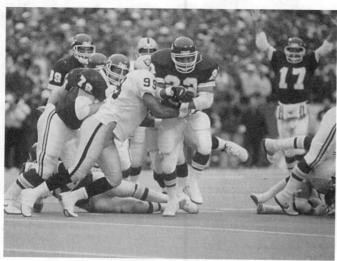

Barry Word (23) pounded the Raiders' defense for 130 rushing yards. (Kansas Collection, U of Kansas)

December 28, 1991
Chiefs 10, Raiders 6
Arrowhead Stadium (75,827)

The Chiefs fought through injuries, squandered opportunities, but ultimately defeated the Raiders and won the club's first postseason game since Super Bowl IV.

"It was another typical Chiefs-Raiders football game," coach Marty Schottenheimer said after the game. "Two evenly matched teams; it comes down to the fourth quarter. We were able to get some things done in the fourth quarter, and as a result, we won."

The Chiefs collected six turnovers, and harassed, rushed, and pummeled the Raiders' rookie quarterback Todd Marinovich throughout the game. They also lost five defensive starters through the course of the game to injuries.

"We had a bunch of young guys step up and guys play hurt," Bill Maas said. "I was proud of being associated with them."

Barry Word rushed for 130 of the Chiefs' 204 total yards, and Steve DeBerg hit Fred Jones on an 11-yard touchdown pass with just over five minutes left in the first half. The Chiefs never trailed in the game, but a couple of Nick Lowery field goal misses made the game a little closer than it should have been.

"I told him, 'Nick, those are gone (the missed kicks),'" Schottenheimer said of his pep talk to Lowery. "You can't do anything about them. We need you to make a winner in the ballgame, and you'll step up and deliver." Lowery made the game's final three points with more than ten minutes remaining. The Chiefs' defense made the score stand up.

The win was the third time the Chiefs beat the Raiders in 1991, and advanced the club to the AFC divisional playoff game against the Buffalo Bills.

LOS ANGELES	0	3	3	0	—	**6**
KANSAS CITY	0	7	0	3	—	**10**

CHIEFS	– F. Jones, 11-yard pass from DeBerg (Lowery kick) (1-11).
RAIDERS	– Jaeger, 32-yard field goal (10-65).
RAIDERS	– Jaeger, 26-yard field goal (11-62).
CHIEFS	– Lowery, 18-yard field goal (13-61).

Team Statistics	Raiders	Chiefs
First Downs	16	16
Total Net Yards	276	204
Rushes/Net Yards	30/152	39/131
Net Passing	124	73
Pass Attempts/Completions	23/12	14/9
Had Intercepted	4	1
Sacked/Yards Lost	2/16	2/16
Punts/Average	1/20.0	2/46.0
Penalties/Yards	9/75	3/20
Fumbles/Lost	2/2	2/1
Possession Time	29:28	30:32

Rushing
CHIEFS – Word 33-130; Williams 2-4; Okoye 1-2; DeBerg 3-(-5).
RAIDERS – S. Smith 3-6; Allen 7-39; N. Bell 20-107.

Receiving
CHIEFS – R. Thomas 3-18; B. Jones 2-25; Word 1-8; Birden 1-18; F. Jones 2-20, 1 TD.
RAIDERS – Gault 1-11; Brown 4-45; Horton 3-59; Allen 1-4; Fernandez 2-12; S. Smith 1-9.

Passing
CHIEFS – DeBerg 9-14-89, 1 TD, 1 INT.
RAIDERS – Marinovich 12-23-140, 0 TDs, 4 INTs.

Interceptions
CHIEFS – Cherry 2-46; Everett 1-23; Marts 1-7.
RAIDERS – Lott 1-35.

Sacks
CHIEFS – Martin 1.0; D. Thomas 1.0.
RAIDERS – Davis 2.0.

Field Goals
CHIEFS – Lowery 33WL 47S (18).
RAIDERS – Jaeger (32) (26).

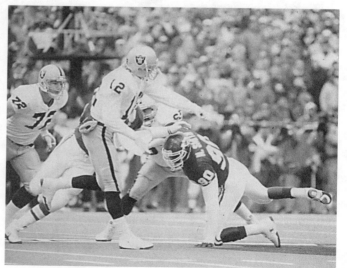

Raider quarterback Todd Marinovich feels the pass-rushing heat of Neil Smith (90). (Kansas Collection, U. of Kansas)

1991 AFC Divisional Playoff Game

January 5, 1992
Bills 37, Chiefs 14
Rich Stadium (80,182)

It wasn't as close as the lopsided score suggests. The Buffalo Bills drilled the Kansas City Chiefs out of the playoffs and advanced to the AFC championship game. For the Chiefs, the 37-14 defeat brought the realization that they still had a way to go before they could truly compete for a spot in the Super Bowl.

"When you are up against it in the playoffs, you have to play at your best or near your best," Chiefs coach Marty Schottenheimer said. "A failure to do that is generally going to bring you the result we had today."

The Chiefs were never in the game and didn't move the ball at all until they were behind 24-0.

"It's difficult to express the frustration you feel in losing a playoff game," Schottenheimer said. "The biggest thing that happened is we never put any pressure on Buffalo."

The Bills had 448 yards of total offense, the Chiefs a mere 213. And the rushing game, one of Kansas City's strengths, was able to produce only 77 yards.

"I think we're a good football team," Schottenheimer continued in his assessment of the game. "(But) we didn't play well today."

KANSAS CITY	0	0	7	7	—	**14**
BUFFALO	7	10	7	13	—	**37**

BILLS — Reed, 25-yard pass from Kelly (Norwood kick) (8-80).
BILLS — Reed, 53-yard pass from Kelly (Norwood kick) (4-69).
BILLS — Norwood, 33-yard field goal (9-39).
BILLS — Lofton, 10-yard pass from Kelly (Norwood kick) (3-36).
CHIEFS — Word, 3-yard run (Lowery kick) (4-43).
BILLS — Norwood, 20-yard field goal (14-68).
BILLS — Norwood, 47-yard field goal (4-2).
BILLS — Davis, 5-yard run (Norwood kick) (6-33).
CHIEFS — F. Jones, 20-yard pass from Vlasic (Lowery kick) (8-75).

Team Statistics	Bills	Chiefs
First Downs	29	14
Total Net Yards	448	213
Rushes/Net Yards	46/180	24/77
Net Passing	268	136
Pass Attempts/Completions	35/23	29/14
Had Intercepted	3	4
Sacked/Yards Lost	1/5	1/10
Punts/Average	3/33.3	7/40.3
Penalties/Yards	6/40	10/59
Fumbles/Lost	0/0	0/0
Possession Time	34:09	25:51

Rushing
CHIEFS — Word 15-50, 1 TD; Williams 8-24; McNair 1-3.
BILLS — T. Thomas 22-100; Kelly 1-2; Davis 19-75, 1 TD; Reed 1-6; Reich 3-(-3).

Receiving
CHIEFS — McNair 5-52; R. Thomas 1-1; B. Jones 1-2; F. Jones 3-31, 1 TD; Birden 2-19; Barnett 1-20; Hayes 1-21.
BILLS — McKeller 5-34; Reed 4-100, 2 TDs; Lofton 3-34, 1 TD; Beebe 6-77; Edwards 1-7; T. Thomas 4-21.

Passing
CHIEFS — DeBerg 5-9-22, 0 TDs, 0 INTs; Vlasic 9-20-124, 1 TD, 4 INTs.
BILLS — Kelly 23-35-273, 3 TDs, 3 INTs; Reich 0-0-0.

Interceptions
CHIEFS — Everett 1-15; Cherry 1-1; Marts 1-12.
BILLS — Jackson 2-6; L. Smith 1-0; Hicks 1-0.

Sacks
CHIEFS — D. Thomas 1.0.
BILLS — L. Smith 1.0.

Field Goals
CHIEFS — None.
BILLS — Norwood (33) (20) (47).

John Alt (Markus Boesch/Allsport)

1992 AFC First Round Playoff Game

January 2, 1993
Chargers 17, Chiefs 0
Jack Murphy Stadium (58,278)

The Chiefs defeated the San Diego Chargers twice in the regular season, but when it mattered most, when it really *counted*, Kansas City couldn't find its offense and again made an early exit from the playoffs. After a scoreless first half, the Chargers dominated the third and fourth quarters to win, 17-0.

"The inability to run the ball more effectively . . . some sacks, (the lack of) some big plays on defense," Chiefs coach Marty Schottenheimer said of his team's poor performance. "Those kind of analyses have to be made in more depth."

The Chiefs gained 61 yards rushing, a total for them that almost always spells defeat. Quarterback Dave Krieg threw two interceptions; Kansas City never really came close to scoring throughout the game, while San Diego pounded the middle of the Chiefs' defensive line for 192 yards rushing.

"For some strange reason, each year you say, 'This is the year. This is the year. This is the year it's going to happen,'" the Chiefs' Kevin Ross said. "It hasn't happened. Is something wrong?"

"We have not been able to do the things that we have set as our very specific goals," Schottenheimer said of his team's failure in the play-offs. "Until we do that, we're always going to be frustrated."

Hints were made about re-vamping the team for the 1993 season and addressing the stagnant offensive problems that plagued Kansas City throughout the season.

KANSAS CITY	0	0	0	0	—	**0**
SAN DIEGO	0	0	10	7	—	**17**

CHARGERS   – Butts, 54-yard run (Carney kick) (4-74, 1:57).
CHARGERS   – Carney, 34-yard field goal (4-9, 2:03).
CHARGERS   – Hendrickson, 5 yard run (Carney kick) (11-91, 5:32).

Team Statistics	Chargers	Chiefs
First Downs	18	17
Total Net Yards	342	251
Rushes/Net Yards	35/192	19/61
Net Passing	150	190
Pass Attempts/Completions	23/14	34/16
Had Intercepted	0	2
Sacked/Yards Lost	5/49	7/43
Punts/Average	6/44.2	8/45.0
Penalties/Yards	5/44	7/62
Fumbles/Lost	2/1	2/1
Possession Time	29:46	30:14

Rushing
CHIEFS   **– Williams 12-35; McNair 3-18; Krieg 2-4; Word 2-4.**
CHARGERS   – Bernstine 1-3; Butts 15-119, 1 TD; Humphries 1-0; Bieniemy 13-38; Harmon 4-27; Hendrickson 1-5, 1 TD.

Receiving
CHIEFS   **– Birden 4-78; McNair 4-35; Davis 3-30; Williams 1-11; Cash 1-5; Hargain 2-46; M. Smith 1-28.**
CHARGERS   – N. Lewis 1-39; Walker 3-60; Brennan 1-8; Bieniemy 1-(-4); Butts2-17; Miller 2-58; Harmon 4-21.

Passing
CHIEFS   **– Krieg 16-34-233, 0 TD, 2 INTs.**
CHARGERS   – Humphries 14-23-199, 0 TDs, 0 INTs.

Interceptions
CHIEFS   **– None.**
CHARGERS   – Carrington 1-40; O'Neal 1-3.

Sacks
CHIEFS   **– Thomas 1.5; A. Lewis 1.0; Bayless 1.0; N. Smith 1.0; Griffin 0.5.**
CHARGERS   – Grossman 2.5; O'Neal 2.0; Lee 2.0; Winter 0.5.

Field Goals
CHIEFS   **– None.**
CHARGERS   – None.

The Chiefs had problems running against the Chargers throughout the game. Todd McNair (48) ran for 18 yards in the game. (San Diego Chargers)

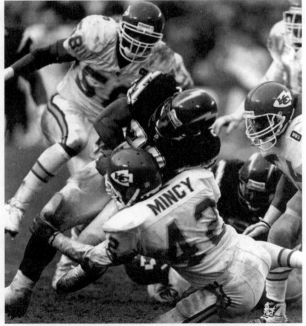

Derrick Thomas (58) and Charles Mincy (42) wrap up a Charger running back. San Diego ran almost at will against the Chiefs, gaining 192 yards for the game. (San Diego Chargers)

1993 AFC First Round Playoff Game

January 8, 1993
Chiefs 27, Steelers 24 (OT)
Arrowhead Stadium (74,515)

Holder Bryan Barker (4) and Nick Lowery watch as the game-winning field goal sails through the uprights. (Kansas Collection, U. of Kansas)

The Chiefs' special teams came up with the biggest play of the game, and Joe Montana took advantage to lead Kansas City to a come-from-behind win over the Pittsburgh Steelers. Keith Cash broke through to make an improbable punt block and give the Chiefs' offense the ball at the Steelers' nine-yard line. Montana hit Tim Barnett with a seven-yard, fourth-down TD pass 46 seconds later to tie the game. Nick Lowery's 32-yard field goal four minutes into the overtime period won the game, 27-24.

"We found a way to win," Chiefs coach Marty Schottenheimer said. "That's the name of the game. It's been an ingredient missing from the Chiefs' playoff formula in the past."

"Everybody's keying on Albert (Lewis)," Cash said of his blocked punt. "Albert went inside and two men followed him. I had one man to beat."

It looked like this was going to be another first-round playoff loss for the Chiefs. Montana struggled in the first half, and when the Steelers scored with 4:11 left in the game to go up 24-17, it looked like the Chiefs were beaten. The block and late touchdown pass gave the Chiefs the chance they needed to win.

"When I saw that, what a sigh of relief I felt," Neil Smith said of the Chiefs' last touchdown. "My whole season was relying on that one play."

The Steelers got the ball first in the overtime and moved to midfield before being forced to punt. Montana led a 66-yard drive that set up Lowery's winning kick.

"When all is said and done, and Joe finishes his career as a player in three or four years, they'll talk about him as one of the greatest quarterbacks in history," Schottenheimer said. "Certainly not the least of that is his ability to organize late-game victories."

The win sends the Chiefs to Houston to play the Oilers in the second round of the playoffs.

PITTSBURGH	7	10	0	7	0—24	
KANSAS CITY	7	0	3	14	3—27	

STEELERS – Cooper, 10-yard pass from O'Donnell (Anderson kick) (9-66, 5:00).

CHIEFS – Birden, 23-yard pass from Krieg (Lowery kick) (7-75, 2:21).

STEELERS – Mills, 26-yard pass from O'Donnell (Anderson kick) (6-51, 0:37).

CHIEFS – Lowery, 23-yard field goal (11-49, 5:11).

CHIEFS – Allen, 2-yard run (Lowery kick) (9-80, 5:18).

STEELERS – Green, 22-yard pass from O'Donnell (Anderson kick) (9-74, 4:47).

CHIEFS – Barnett, 7-yard pass from Montana (Lowery kick) (4-9, 0:46).

CHIEFS – Lowery, 32-yard field goal (11-66, 5:59).

Team Statistics	Steelers	Chiefs
First Downs	21	28
Total Net Yards	369	401
Rushes/Net Yards	35/97	33/125
Net Passing	272	276
Pass Attempts/Completions	42/23	44/29
Had Intercepted	0	0
Sacked/Yards Lost	3/14	4/23
Punts/Average	7/38.3	6/44.8
Penalties/Yards	5/40	5/25
Fumbles/Lost	1/0	0/0
Possession Time	34:58	36:05

Rushing
CHIEFS – Allen 21-67, 1 TD; Anders 5-27; Montana 4-13; McNair 2-9; Jones 1-9.
STEELERS – L. Thompson 25-60; Hoge 6-27; Stone 3-11; O'Donnell 1-(-1).

Receiving
CHIEFS – Cash 7-56; Birden 6-72; 1 TD; Allen 4-29; Anders 3-30; Barnett 3-30, 1 TD; Davis 2-47; Hayes 2-11; Hughes 1-15; McNair 1-9.
STEELERS – Graham 7-96; Mills 4-60, 1 TD; Hoge 3-43; Stone 3-36; L. Thompson 3-4; Green 2-37, 1 TD; Cooper 1-10, 1 TD.

Passing
CHIEFS – Montana 28-43-276, 1 TD, 0 INTs; Krieg 1-1-23, 1 TD, 0 INTs.
STEELERS – O'Donnell 23-42-286, 3 TDs, 0 INTs.

Interceptions
CHIEFS – None.
STEELERS – None.

Sacks
CHIEFS – N. Smith 2.0; Bayless 1.0.
STEELERS – G. Williams 3.0; Lloyd 1.0.

Field Goals
CHIEFS – Lowery (23) 43WR (32).
STEELERS – Anderson (30).

Joe Montana and Marty Schottenheimer discuss strategy during the Chiefs' 1993 playoff game with Pittsburgh. (Kansas Collection, U. of Kansas)

1993 AFC Divisional Playoff Game

January 16, 1993
Chiefs 28, Oilers 20
Astrodome Stadium (64,011)

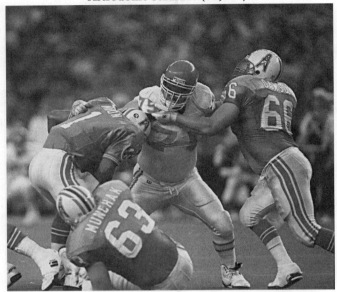

Joe Philips sacks the Oilers' Warren Moon. (Topeka Capital-Journal)

Montana Magic. After falling behind for the second straight week in a playoff game, Joe Montana rallied his teammates and led the Chiefs to 21 fourth-quarter points and a 28-20 upset win over the Houston Oilers. The victory sent Kansas City to its first-ever AFC championship game.

"He's a tremendous source of confidence for whoever lines up with him," Chiefs coach Marty Schottenheimer said of Montana after the game. "Guys who have been there can make a difference. They can lift the others around them to a different level." Montana completed 22 of 38 passes for 299 yards and three touchdowns. He also had two interceptions.

It was the defense, though, that made the comeback possible. The Chiefs sacked Oilers quarterback Warren Moon nine times in the game, forcing him to lose two fumbles.

"It was just the intensity of the players," Chiefs defensive coordinator Dave Adolph said of his defensive unit. "They just wanted to win the darn game." Kansas City was successful with its blitz of Moon throughout the game.

After trailing 10-0 at the half, Montana hit Keith Cash with a seven-yard strike to pull the Chiefs within three points. After an Oilers field goal with just under ten minutes remaining in the game, Montana led a 71-yard drive, aided by a 39-yard pass interference penalty, and hit J.J. Birden with the go-ahead touchdown. Marcus Allen's 21-yard touchdown run with 1:55 remaining in the game closed out the scoring. The Chiefs had the win and a shot at the Super Bowl. They met the Bills in Buffalo for the conference championship.

"I am really proud of this team and especially the offensive line," Chiefs center Tim Grunhard said. "This was one of the best defenses in the league."

KANSAS CITY	0	0	7	21	—	28
HOUSTON	10	0	0	10	—	20

OILERS — Del Greco, 49-yard field goal (4-8, 1:13).
OILERS — Brown, 2-yard run (Del Greco kick) (11-80, 6:30).
CHIEFS — **Cash, 7-yard pass from Montana (Lowery kick) (7-71, 3:30).**
OILERS — Del Greco, 43-yard field goal (4-1, 1:59).
CHIEFS — **Birden, 11-yard pass from Montana (Lowery kick) (2-71, 0:59).**
CHIEFS — **Davis, 18-yard pass from Montana (Lowery kick) (3-12, 0:42).**
OILERS — Givins, 7-yard pass from Moon (Del Greco kick) (9-80, 4:09).
CHIEFS — **Allen, 21-yard run (Lowery kick) (6-79, 1:40).**

Team Statistics	Oilers	Chiefs
First Downs	19	18
Total Net Yards	277	354
Rushes/Net Yards	14/39	18/71
Net Passing	238	283
Pass Attempts/Completions	43/32	38/22
Had Intercepted	1	2
Sacked/Yards Lost	9/68	2/16
Punts/Average	5/48.6	5/45.0
Penalties/Yards	3/63	7/51
Fumbles/Lost	7/2	0/0
Possession Time	35:42	24:18

Rushing
CHIEFS — **Allen 14-74, 1 TD; Krieg 2-(-2); Anders 1-0; Montana 1-(-1).**
OILERS — Moon 3-22; Brown 11-17.

Receiving
CHIEFS — **Birden 6-60, 1 TD; Davis 5-96, 1 TD; Cash 4-80, 1 TD; Barnett 2-24; McNair 2-9; Allen 1-12; Hayes 1-9; F. Jones 1-9.**
OILERS — Jeffires 9-88; Givins 7-63, 1 TD; Wellman 6-80; Duncan 6-49; Brown 4-26.

Passing
CHIEFS — **Montana 22-38-299, 3 TDs, 2 INTs; Krieg 0-0-0.**
OILERS — Moon 32-43-306, 1 TD, 1 INT.

Interceptions
CHIEFS — **Mincy 1-12.**
OILERS — Jackson 1-14; Hoage 1-0.

Sacks
CHIEFS — **Lewis 2.0; D. Thomas 2.0; B. Thompson 2.0; Phillips 2.0; N. Smith 1.0.**
OILERS — Fuller 1.0; Lathon 1.0.

Field Goals
CHIEFS — **None.**
OILERS — Del Greco (49) (43).

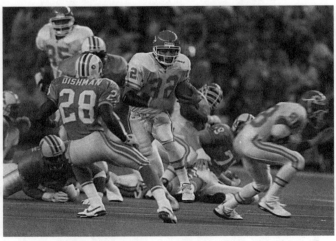

Marcus Allen ran for 74 yards in the Chiefs' win. (Topeka Capital-Journal)

1994 AFC First Round Playoff Game

December 31, 1994
Dolphins 27, Chiefs 17
Joe Robbie Stadium (67,487)

The Chiefs' two big playmakers, Joe Montana and Marcus Allen, had uncharacteristic turnovers in the fourth quarter and ruined any chance Kansas City had to pull the game out. The Chiefs lost to the Dolphins, 27-17.

"It was disappointing," Allen said of the loss after the game. "We tried to come back, but the mistakes killed us."

"In the playoffs it is a matter of making plays," Chiefs coach Marty Schottenheimer said. "The margin of error is narrower in the playoffs."

Trailing 27-17, Montana threw an interception when the Chiefs had first and goal at the Miami five-yard line early in the fourth period. Allen fumbled on the Chiefs' next possession. Miami then ran the clock down, killing any further chance the Chiefs might have at a comeback, and made the ten-point lead stand up for the win.

Montana passed for 314 yards and two touchdowns in the games, and Allen ran for 64 yards, but Montana wasn't happy with his play, and summed up his performance, as well as the Chiefs', "When you lose, it doesn't matter how well you played."

KANSAS CITY	14	3	0	0	—	**17**
MIAMI	7	10	10	0	—	**27**

CHIEFS	– **D. Walker, 1-yard pass from Montana (Elliott kick) (11-80, 6:28).**
DOLPHINS	– Parmalee, 1-yard run (Stoyanovich kick) (10-72, 6:12).
CHIEFS	– **Anders, 57-yard pass from Montana (Elliott kick) (4-83, 1:40).**
DOLPHINS	– Stoyanovich, 40-yard field goal (7-35, 3:25).
CHIEFS	– **Elliott, 21-yard field goal (12-69, 6:03).**
DOLPHINS	– R. Williams, 1-yard pass from Marino (Stoyanovich kick) (13-80, 5:50).
DOLPHINS	– Fryar, 7-yard pass from Marino (Stoyanovich kick) (6-64, 3:02).
DOLPHINS	– Stoyanovich, 40 yard field goal (10-59, 4:48).

Team Statistics	Dolphins	Chiefs
First Downs	22	24
Total Net Yards	381	414
Rushes/Net Yards	31/132	23/100
Net Passing	249	314
Pass Attempts/Completions	29/22	37/26
Had Intercepted	0	1
Sacked/Yards Lost	1/8	0/0
Punts/Average	3/43.3	2/40.0
Penalties/Yards	6/50	4/15
Fumbles/Lost	0/0	3/1

Rushing
CHIEFS – **Allen 14-64; Anders 5-17; Hill 2-14; Montana 2-5.**
DOLPHINS – Parmalee 18-57, 1 TD; Spikes 9-49; McDuffie 1-19; Marino 2-4; Craver 1-3.

Receiving
CHIEFS – **Anders 6-103, 1 TD; Allen 5-49; Birden 4-56; Cash 3-38; D. Walker 3-27, 1 TD; Dawson 3-21; Hill 1-11; Davis 1-9.**
DOLPHINS – Fryar 6-71; Craver 4-35; Parmalee 2-34; Jackson 2-29; M. Williams 2-28; McDuffie 2-25; Saxon 2-24; Miller 1-10; R. Williams 1-1.

Passing
CHIEFS – **Montana 26-37-314, 2 TDs, 1 INT.**
DOLPHINS – Marino 22-29-257, 2 TDs, 0 INTs.

Interceptions
CHIEFS – **None.**
DOLPHINS – Brown 1-24.

Sacks
CHIEFS – **Thomas 1.0.**
DOLPHINS – None.

Field Goals
CHIEFS – **Elliott (21).**
DOLPHINS – Stoyanovich (40) (40).

The Dolphins' Dan Marino, center, ripped the Chiefs' defense for 257 passing yards and two touchdowns. (Miami Dolphins)

INDIANAPOLIS	0	7	3	0	—	**10**
KANSAS CITY	7	0	0	0	—	**7**

January 7, 1996
Colts 10, Chiefs 7
Arrowhead Stadium (77,594)

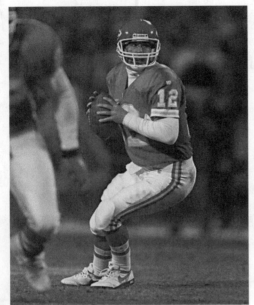

Rich Gannon took over at quarterback
in the fourth quarter. (Topeka Capital-Journal)

CHIEFS	– Dawson, 20-yard pass from Bono (Elliott kick) (5-62, 2:28).
COLTS	– Turner, 5-yard pass from Harbaugh (Blanchard kick) (18-77, 8:40).
COLTS	– Blanchard, 30-yard field goal (9-35, 4:35).

Team Statistics	Colts	Chiefs
First Downs	16	15
Total Net Yards	249	281
Rushes/Net Yards	39/147	28/129
Net Passing	102	152
Pass Attempts/Completions	27/12	33/16
Had Intercepted	1	3
Sacked/Yards Lost	2/10	0/0
Punts/Average	6/36.5	4/36.8
Penalties/Yards	6/38	3/29
Fumbles/Lost	4/0	1/1

Rushing

CHIEFS	– **Allen 21-94; Gannon 2-19; Anders 5-16.**
COLTS	– Warren 20-76; Harbaugh 9-48; Crockett 6-12; Humphrey 4-11.

Receiving

CHIEFS	– **Anders 7-44; Dawson 4-70, 1 TD; Allen 2-21; Slaughter 2-10; Walker 1-7.**
COLTS	– Dawkins 4-37; Bailey 2 –37; Warren 2-18; Turner, 1 TD;Crockett 2-5.

Passing

CHIEFS	– **Bono 11-25-122, 0 TDs, 3 INTs; Gannon 5-8-30, 0 TDs, 0 INTs.**
COLTS	– Harbaugh 12-27-112, 1 TD, I INT.

Interceptions

CHIEFS	– **Collins 1-0.**
COLTS	– Daniel 1-13; Corvatt 1-10; Ambrose 1-2.

Sacks

CHIEFS	– **Booker 1.0; N. Smith 1.0.**
COLTS	– None.

Field Goals

CHIEFS	– **Elliott 35WR 39WL 42WL.**
COLTS	– Blanchard 47S (30) 49S.

This was supposed to be the year. An NFL-best 13-3 record, home-field advantage for the playoffs, and a rock-solid defense. But the Chiefs found a way to lose against the Indianapolis Colts, like they had so many times in previous playoff games. Quarterback Steve Bono threw three costly interceptions, and kicker Lin Elliott missed three field goals in the bitter cold conditions, the final attempt in the waning seconds of the game that would have tied the score. Once again the Chiefs were losers.

It couldn't be true, but it was. Colts 10, Chiefs 7.

"You can't tell by the result," Elliott said after the game, "but I felt like I was going to get the job done."

"We had a golden opportunity," Neil Smith said of the Chiefs' playoff setup. "With the home-field advantage and everything, this seemed like it would be our season. But you've got to win the ballgames."

With the score tied 7-7, Colts kicker Gary Blanchard kicked a 30-yard field goal late in the third period to put the Colts ahead, 10-7. Blanchard also missed two field goals. The Colts had tied the score in the second quarter with an impressive 18-play, 77-yard drive.

Schottenheimer replaced Bono with Rich Gannon late in the game, and Gannon led the last-ditch drive that ended with Elliott's third miss. Gannon just missed connecting with Lake Dawson on what would have been the game-winning touchdown before the final attempt by Elliott.

"I tried to stretch out as much as I could and get the ball," Dawson said of the play. "It was one of those things when it was fingertips away."

"I understand the nature of our business, and I'm disappointed we haven't done better in the playoffs," Shottenheimer said. "The most disappointing thing is we had created home-field advantage, and it got away."

The Chiefs' held the Colts to 249 total yards, but failed to make the big play when needed.

"This hasn't set in yet," Dale Carter said. "We were all planning on playing some more games. Now you don't even know what you are going to be doing the next couple of weeks."

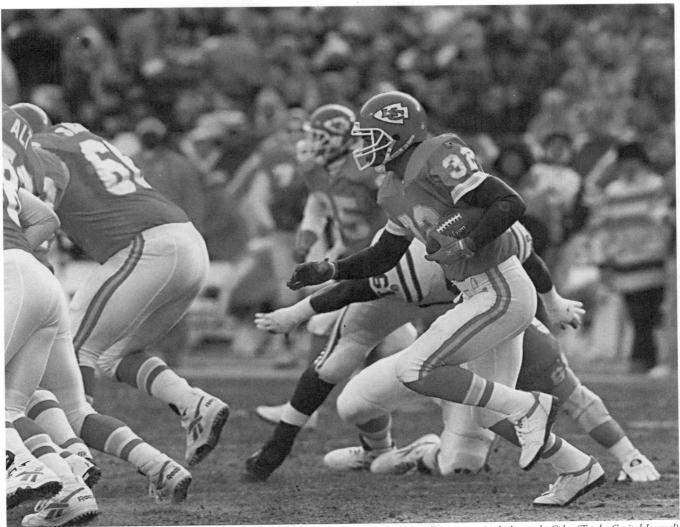

Marcus Allen gained 94 yards on 21 rushing attempts for the Chiefs. The veteran running back also caught two passes in the loss to the Colts. *(Topeka Capital-Journal)*

Lin Elliott kicks and then watches as he misses his third field goal attempt of the game. This final kick would have tied the score in the final minute of the fourth quarter. *(Topeka Capital-Journal)*

1997 AFC Divisional Playoff Game

January 4, 1998
Broncos 14, Chiefs 10
Arrowhead Stadium (76,965)

One last drive to win the game, one last play to propel the Chiefs past the Denver Broncos and into the AFC championship game. Elvis Grbac, improvising because he couldn't hear his coach on his helmet radio, passed to Lake Dawson on the goal line, and watched with the rest of the 76,965 fans as the ball dropped harmlessly to the ground. The Chiefs had lost to the Broncos, 14-10.

"Guys are in shock. After this game, you're going to come to a fork in the road," Chiefs center Tim Grunhard said after the game. "You're either going to cry and moan about it, or you're going to go to the other side of the road and be a champion."

Three plays earlier in the game made the last drive necessary. A questionable call in the end zone that took a touchdown reception away from Tony Gonzalez, a missed field goal, and a botched fake field goal kept the Chiefs from taking control of the game. Kansas City shut down the Broncos offense throughout the game, held them to 272 total yards, and recovered two fumbles. Denver quarterback John Elway led a 49-yard scoring drive to take the lead late in the fourth quarter. Terrell Davis scored from one yard out with 2:38 left in the game to put the Broncos ahead 14-10. Grbac then led the Chiefs down the field for one more chance at the win.

"I didn't get it done," Grbac said of the Chiefs' failed final drive. "We didn't make the plays when we had to. I take the blame for that." He finished the game with 260 yards passing and a touchdown.

"I just knew we were going to score," Schottenheimer said of the final drive. "I mean, I just knew we were going to get in there." It didn't happen, though.

"I will not feel sorry for myself," Schottenheimer continued. "I do not believe in self-pity. And I have such a distaste for people who do. I think it's wrong. I really do."

" 'Could have, would have, should have,' is not the thing you want to say year after year," Chiefs fullback Kimble Anders said. "But we sure have been saying it a lot."

DENVER	0	7	0	7	—	**14**
KANSAS CITY	0	0	10	0	—	**10**

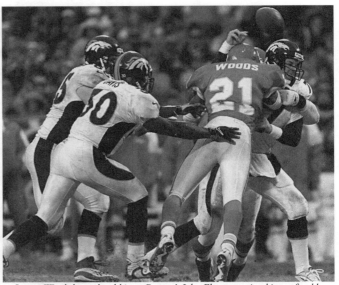

Jerome Woods lays a hard hit on Denver's John Elway, causing him to fumble. (Topeka Capital-Journal)

BRONCOS	– T. Davis, 1-yard run (Elam kick) (8-65, 4:51).
CHIEFS	**– Stoyanovich, 20-yard field goal (11-67, 5:18).**
CHIEFS	**– Gonzalez, 12-yard pass from Grbac (Stoyanovich kick) (4-65, 1:35).**
BRONCOS	– T. Davis, 1-yard run (Elam kick) (6-49, 2:38).

Team Statistics	Broncos	Chiefs
First Downs	16	18
Total Net Yards	272	303
Rushes/Net Yards	32/109	24/77
Net Passing	163	226
Pass Attempts/Completions	19/10	37/24
Had Intercepted	0	0
Sacked/Yards Lost	1/7	4/34
Punts/Average	6/36.2	5/46.4
Penalties/Yards	8/64	7/65
Fumbles/Lost	4/2	2/0
Possession Time	28:54	31:06

Rushing

CHIEFS	**– Allen 12-37; Grbac 4-22; Anders 3-9; Bennett 3-4; Aguiar 1-3; Hill 1-2.**
BRONCOS	– Davis 25-101, 2-TDs; Griffith 4-9; Loville 2-0; Elway 1-(-1).

Receiving

CHIEFS	**– Rison 8-110; Popson 5-26; Gonzalez 3-26, 1 TD; Dawson 2-20; Anders 2-4; Horn 1-50; Hughes 1-13; Allen 1-8; Vanover 1-3.**
BRONCOS	– McCaffrey 3-56; Sharpe 2-33; R. Smith 2-19; Carswell 1-26; Green 1-19; T. Davis 1-17.

Passing

CHIEFS	**– Grbac 24-27-260, 1 TD, 0 INTs.**
BRONCOS	– Elway 10-19-170, 0 TDs, 0 INTs.

Interceptions

CHIEFS	**– None.**
BRONCOS	– None.

Sacks

CHIEFS	**– Woods 1.0.**
BRONCOS	– N. Smith 2.0; A. Williams 2.0.

Field Goals

CHIEFS	**– Stoyanovich 44WL (20)**
BRONCOS	– None.

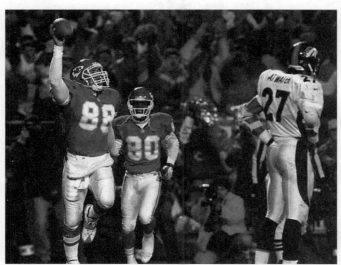

Tony Gonzalez (88) celebrates after catching a 12-yard touchdown pass from Elvis Grbac in the third quarter. Lake Dawson (80) looks on. (Topeka Capital-Journal)

KANSAS CITY CHIEFS
AFL and AFC
Championship Games

The Chiefs' franchise has played in four league (or conference) championship games—one as the Dallas Texans and three as the Chiefs. All four games were played on the opposing team's field. While three of the four games had a trip to the Super Bowl as an added prize, the 1962 AFL championship game has become a classic in pro football history, and greatly elevated the stature of the then-still young American Football League.

The Chiefs' record in championship games is 3-1.

1962 AFL Championship Game

Texans 20, Oilers 17 (2 OT)
December 23, 1962
Jeppesen Stadium (37,981)

In gray, misty Jeppesen Stadium, the Dallas Texans' Abner Haynes calmly called the coin toss before the start of the first sudden-death overtime in the AFL's short history. The Texans and Houston Oilers had battled to a 17-17 tie after regulation in a game that had been dominated by the Texans in the first half and by the Oilers in the second. Dallas blocked a late field-goal attempt by the Oilers' George Blanda to force the overtime.

Haynes won the toss and made his call.

"We'll kick to the clock," Haynes said. His teammate E. J. Holub walked off the field in anger and disgust. Haynes had inadvertently chosen to kick off into the brisk wind.

"The players were excited and tugging at Abner," Stram said later. "He just didn't understand the option. It was a mistake you don't like to make, but there was no use crying over it."

Despite selecting two options instead of one (the officials declared Dallas had chosen to kick off, the Oilers had chosen to have the wind at their back), the Texans held off Houston throughout the fifth period, making two big interceptions to stop drives. After the teams traded sides at the start of the sixth quarter, Dallas marched into field-goal position. Jack Spikes' run of 19 yards was the big play of the drive. Kicker Tommy Brooker set up for the game-winning field goal four plays later.

"Lenny [Dawson] told everyone to be quiet in the huddle, because noise might make me nervous," Brooker said. "We called timeout so I could clean the mud from my shoe—I didn't want that for an alibi if I missed. Then I just waited and kept my eyes on the ground. I knew Lenny would place the ball right for me because he's the best at that." Then Brooker reassured his teammates.

"Don't worry about it," he said. "It's all over now." Brooker's kick was straight and true. The Texans were the 1962 AFL champs. The game lasted 77 minutes and 54 seconds.

"We'll kick to the clock." Abner Haynes (28) has just uttered the words that gave Houston the ball and the wind at its back at the start of overtime in the 1962 AFL championship game. (Chris Burford)

Tommy Brooker calmly kicks the game-winning field goal to end the '62 championship game after almost 78 minutes of play. (Chris Burford)

Happy Texans carry Tommy Brooker off the field following his field goal that won the 1962 AFL Championship for Dallas. (Tommy Brooker)

"I never took my eyes off the ground until after the kick," Brooker said. "Then I looked up and saw the ball going through the uprights."

Houston's two-year reign as the league champion had ended.

The Texans, bloodied, muddied, and bruised from the then-longest game in the history of pro football (the record is now the Chiefs-Dolphins 1971 playoff game), pranced and danced around the locker room, swigging and spraying champagne. Spikes had rushed for 77 yards and was named the game's MVP. Haynes had scored two touchdowns. The defense, which had played so big in the fifth quarter, had picked off five passes.

"I'll always remember that locker-room celebration," Dawson said years later. "They gave every guy a bottle of champagne, and guys were running around pouring it on each other. E. J. [Holub] was going crazy. He was cutting everyone's neckties [including Lamar Hunt's]."

"I've never seen a team fight for a win like this one did today," Stram said afterwards. "None of us ever will forget it."

Less than two months later, Hunt announced the team was moving to Kansas City.

It was a happy Dallas locker room after the Texans defeated Houston, 20-17 in overtime to win the 1962 AFL Championship. (Chris Burford)

DALLAS	3	14	0	0	0	3	—	**20**
HOUSTON	0	0	7	10	0	0	—	**17**

TEXANS	– **Brooker, 16-yard field goal**
TEXANS	– **Haynes, 28-yard pass from Dawson (Brooker kick)**
TEXANS	– **Haynes, 2-yard run (Brooker kick)**
OILERS	– Dewveall, 15-yard pass from Blanda (Blanda kick)
OILERS	– Blanda, 31-yard field goal
OILERS	– Tolar, 1-yard run (Blanda kick)
TEXANS	– **Brooker, 25-yard field goal**

Team Statistics	Oilers	Texans
First Downs	21	19
Total Net Yards	359	237
Rushes/Net Yards	30/98	54/199
Net Passing	261	38
Pass Attempts/Completions	46/23	14/9
Had Intercepted	5	0
Sacked/Yards Lost	0/0	6/50
Punts/Average	3/39.3	8/31.2
Penalties/Yards	6/50	6/42
Fumbles/Lost	0/0	2/1

Rushing

TEXANS	– **McClinton 24-70; Spikes 11-77; Dawson 5-26; Haynes 14-26, 1 TD.**
OILERS	– Tolar 15-78, 1 TD; Cannon 11-37; Smith 2-3.

Receiving

TEXANS	– **Haynes 3-45, 1 TD; Spikes 2-24; Arbanas 2-21; Bishop 1-(-6); McClinton 1-4.**
OILERS	– Henningan 3-37; Tolar 1-8; McLeod 5-70; Cannon 6-54; Dewveall 6-59, 1 TD; Jamison 1-(-9); Smith 1-6.

Passing

TEXANS	– **Dawson 9-14-88, 1 TD, 0 INTs.**
OILERS	– Blanda 23-46-261, 1 TD, 5 INTs.

Interceptions

TEXANS	– **Robinson 2-50; Holub 1-43; Grayson 1-20; Hull 1-23.**
OILERS	– None.

Field Goals

TEXANS	– **Brooker (16) 33WL (25).**
OILERS	– Blanda 47WL (31).

1966 AFL Championship Game

Chiefs 31, Bills 7
January 1, 1967
War Memorial Stadium (42,080)

Brass Ring-Super Bowl bound!

The Kansas City Chiefs displayed their high-powered offense and stifling defense to win an impressive victory against the Buffalo Bills, 31-7, and capture the AFL championship. The win sent the Chiefs to Los Angeles, where they took on the NFL's powerful Green Bay Packers in the Super Bowl, pro football's new championship game.

"I thought our defense was fantastic, and Lenny [Dawson] gave us great direction," Chiefs coach Hank Stram said after the game. "His leadership and passing attest to his ability."

The big play of the game, the turning point, really, came late in the first half, when Chiefs safety Johnny Robinson picked off a pass at the goal line and returned it 72 yards to the Buffalo 28-yard line. Mike Mercer booted a 32-yard field goal before the half to put Kansas City up, 17-7. Robinson's play provided a big 10-point swing and gave the Chiefs an overwhelming momentum going in at the half.

"We had blitz on . . . and I read pass. Kemp [Buffalo's quarterback] looked like he was going to go to the weak side with it, but apparently nobody was open," Robinson said of the big interception. "I dropped off [my man]. It was right on my fingertips. I thought I was going to drop it."

The Chiefs scored two touchdowns in the first half on two 29-yard passes from Dawson to Fred Arbanas and Otis Taylor.

"It was a quick post pattern," Taylor said of his touchdown reception. "I thought after I caught the ball I could make the end zone, but then I got a lick. But nothing was going to keep me from going in for the score."

"Our game plan was to pass first and run second," Stram said. "The field was bad, but we had made our minds up to go with this game plan and we stayed with it."

Otis Taylor stretches for one of his five receptions during the Chiefs' 31-7 win over Buffalo in the 1966 AFL Championship. (Topeka Capital-Journal)

Mike Mercer booted a 32-yard field goal in the second quarter to extend the Chiefs' lead over the Bills to 17-7. (Topeka Capital-Journal)

The Chiefs' Mike Garrett scored two fourth-quarter touchdowns on runs of one and 18 yards to put the game away. Garrett was the leading rusher for the Chiefs with 39 yards. Dawson hit 16 of 24 passes for 227 yards.

The Chiefs' defense, the collective stars of the game, held the Bills to 255 total yards and intercepted two passes, as well as recovering two fumbles.

The locker room was a wild celebration afterwards, players shouting and spraying champagne everywhere.

"We brought a championship to Kansas City," a happy Jim Tyrer said. The team presented the game ball to Hank Stram.

"It's been a long season," Andy Rice said in the midst of the hoopla. "And we did what we set out to do. We took it to them, baby."

"The Hammer!" shouted Fred Williamson. "We got the hammer!"

"It was a supreme effort," Stram said of his team's play.

The Chiefs' next test would be the Green Bay Packers of the NFL. Teams from the two leagues had never met before on the field. When asked how he thought the Chiefs would do against the NFL powerhouse, Bills quarterback Kemp was complementary.

"They have a fine football team," Kemp said. "They have a good running game, their passing is versatile, and they play well defensively. They're going to surprise a lot of people."

"We'll be up and ready to go in two weeks," Chiefs wideout Chris Burford said.

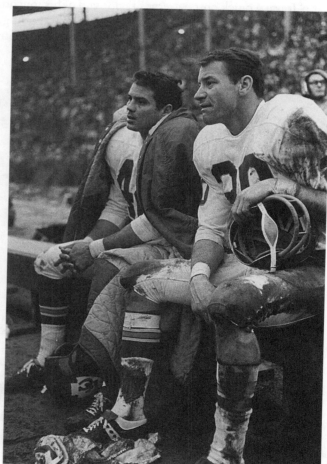

Johnny Robinson and Bobby Hurt take a break from action during the game. (Topeka Capital-Journal)

```
KANSAS CITY    7   10   0   14   —   31
BUFFALO        7    0   0    0   —    7
```

CHIEFS — **Arbanas, 29-yard pass from Dawson (Mercer kick)**
BILLS — Dubenion, 69-yard pass from Kemp (Lusteg kick)
CHIEFS — **Taylor, 29-yard pass from Dawson (Mercer kick)**
CHIEFS — **Mercer, 32-yard field goal**
CHIEFS — **Garrett, 1-yard run (Mercer kick)**
CHIEFS — **Garrett, 18-yard run (Mercer kick)**

Team Statistics	Bills	Chiefs
First Downs	9	14
Total Net Yards	255	277
Rushes/Net Yards	13/40	33/113
Net Passing	215	164
Pass Attempts/Completions	27/12	24/16
Had Intercepted	2	0
Sacked/Yards Lost	4/38	7/63
Punts/Average	8/39.3	6/42.3
Penalties/Yards	3/23	4/40
Fumbles/Lost	3/2	1/0

Rushing
CHIEFS — **Dawson, 5-28; Garrett 13-39, 2 TDs; McClinton 11-38; Coan 2-6; G. Thomas 2-2.**
BILLS — Carlton 9-31; Burnett 3-6; Kemp 1-3.

Receiving
CHIEFS — **Garrett 4-16; Arbanas 2-44, 1 TD; Taylor 5-78; Burford 4-76; McClinton 1-13.**
BILLS — Burnett 6-127; Dubenion 2-79, 1 TD; Carlton 1-5; Bass 2-26; Crockett 1-16.

Passing
CHIEFS — **Dawson 16-24-227, 2 TDs, 0 INTs.**
BILLS — Kemp 12-27-253, 1 TD, 2 INTs.

Interceptions
CHIEFS — **Robinson 1-72; E. Thomas 1-26.**
BILLS — None.

Field Goals
CHIEFS — **Mercer (32) 49S**
BILLS — None.

1969 AFL Championship Game

January 4, 1970
Chiefs 17, Raiders 7
Oakland-Alameda County Coliseum (54,544)

It was payback time, and the Chiefs made the Raiders pay. After losing seven of the previous eight games to their top rival, Kansas City won when it mattered most, capturing the final AFL championship game, 17-7. The win sent the Chiefs to their second Super Bowl.

"It's hard for me to tell you how we all feel right now," Hank Stram said after the game, "and how it feels to triumph in a season like this after we've endured hardships, even agony." The Chiefs had battled problems throughout the season. Len Dawson's knee injury and the death of his father, the loss of two close games to the Raiders in the regular season, and then the survival of a great defensive game with the New York Jets in the divisional playoff two weeks before the title game.

"There have been so many close calls, so many players out, and on top of that we didn't win the division," Chiefs owner Lamar Hunt said. "But this team came back. This team—the Kansas City Chiefs—won the championship."

"It's about time," Chiefs linebacker Bobby Bell said of the win. "We played our hearts out out there."

A supreme effort by the Chiefs' defense was the difference. Oakland completed just 17 of 45 passes, threw four interceptions, and gained a mere 233 yards of total offense. The defensive line, led by the magnificent play of Aaron Brown, harassed, hit, and pummeled Raiders quarterback Daryle Lamonica the whole game, at one point forcing him out of action.

"We were able to get to Lamonica today because the field was in better shape this time," Brown said of his pass rush. "For the first time this year, I wasn't bothered by nagging injuries."

Oakland scored first on a three-yard touchdown run late in the first quarter, after moving the ball effectively throughout the period. But George Blanda missed two field goal attempts, and the Chiefs finally established some offense. Wendell

Robert Holmes, right, dances into the end zone to give the Chiefs a 13-7 lead over the Raiders in the third quarter of the '69 AFL Championship. (Bettmann/CORBIS)

Robert Holmes rushed for 35 yards and caught two passes in the 1969 AFL Championship game. (Kansas Collection, U. of Kansas)

Hayes scored on a one-yard touchdown run in the second quarter, and the teams were tied at the half, 7-7.

Blanda missed another field goal early in the second half. Midway through the third quarter, the Chiefs were faced with a third-and-four from their own 2-yard line. Throwing from the end zone, Dawson laid out a pass on the right sideline, and Otis Taylor pulled it in for a 35-yard gain. It was the biggest play of the game for Kansas City.

"Otis wasn't the primary receiver on the third-down, goal-line pass completion," Dawson said. I was looking for (Robert) Holmes coming across the middle, but he got banged. I was in the end zone, and I couldn't wait much longer, so I threw it so it would have gone out of bounds if he didn't catch it. It was a great catch."

"I didn't know if I caught it over my head or on what side of me," Taylor said of the reception.

The catch sparked the Chiefs, and six plays later, Holmes barreled into the end zone to give the Chiefs the lead. A sequence of recovered fumbles by the Raiders and interceptions by the Chiefs followed in the fourth quarter. Emmitt Thomas' 62-yard interception return set up a field goal by Jan Stenerud, and the Chiefs made the 10-point lead stand up for the win—and the championship.

"It has great meaning," Hunt said quietly after the game. "It's the last AFL championship to be won, and we won it. We had some bad spots, but I can't complain about the final score. We have a lot to be proud of. Looking back over the years we've spent in the AFL, we've won three championships. That's more than any other team."

The Chiefs had earned the championship the hard way, failing to win their division but beating two great teams on the road. Not everyone was impressed with the team, though, least of all the Raiders.

"I don't think the Chiefs will be a good representative for the AFL," the Raiders' Jim Otto said of the Chiefs' chances to win the Super Bowl. "I never did like Kansas City. I guess that's the reason I feel that way."

But the Chiefs were going back to the Super Bowl, back to avenge one of the worst losses in the franchise's history. It was a sweet ending to a long, hard season.

"This victory today is a tribute to a great bunch of people," Stram said. "I told them back in training camp that I thought they had the ability to be champions."

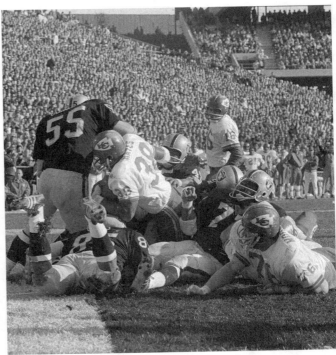

Wendell Hayes plows into the end zone for the Chiefs' first touchdown. (Bettmann/CORBIS)

```
KANSAS CITY—   0    7    7    3   —   17
OAKLAND—       7    0    0    0   —    7
```

RAIDERS – Smith, 3-yard run (Blanda kick)
CHIEFS – Hayes, 1-yard run (Stenerud kick)
CHIEFS – Holmes, 5-yard run (Stenerud kick)
CHIEFS – Stenerud, 22-yard field goal

Team Statistics	Raiders	Chiefs
First Downs	18	13
Total Net Yards	233	207
Rushes/Net Yards	28/79	39/86
Net Passing	154	121
Pass Attempts/Completions	45/17	17/7
Had Intercepted	4	0
Sacked/Yards Lost	4/37	1/8
Punts/Average	6/48.5	8/42.8
Penalties/Yards	5/45	5/43
Fumbles/Lost	1/0	5/4

Rushing
**CHIEFS – Holmes 18-14, 1 TD; Garrett 7-19; Hayes 8-35;
McVea 3-13; Dawson 3-5.**
RAIDERS – Dixon 12-36; Smith 12-31, 1 TD; Banaszak 2-8; Todd 2-4.

Receiving
CHIEFS – Taylor 3-62; Holmes 2-16; Pitts 1-41; Arbanas 1-10.
RAIDERS – Smith 8-86; Sherman 3-45; Cannon 2-22; Wells 1-24;
Banaszak 2-13; Dixon 1-1.

Passing
CHIEFS – Dawson 7-17-129, 0 TDs, 0 INTs.
RAIDERS – Lamonica 15-39-167, 0 TDs, 3 INTs;
Blanda 2-6-24, 0 TDs, 1 INT.

Interceptions
CHIEFS – Thomas 2-69; Marsalis 1-23; Kearney 1-17.
RAIDERS – None.

Sacks
CHIEFS – Brown 3; Culp 1.
RAIDERS – Davidson 1.

Field Goals
CHIEFS – Stenerud 52S (22).
RAIDERS – Blanda 52S 39WR 40WR.

1993 AFC Championship Game

January 23, 1994
Bills 30, Chiefs 13
Rich Stadium (76,642)

It was a wild, hectic experience in the playoffs, but the Kansas City Chiefs' Super Bowl dream died.

There was no Montana magic in Buffalo.

After pulling off come-from-behind wins in both of their previous playoff games, the Chiefs found the Bills too formidable a roadblock and lost the AFC championship game, 30-13. Joe Montana, the architect of the comeback wins, spent most of the second half on the sideline with a concussion he suffered early in the third period. The win gave the Bills their fourth-straight AFC championship.

"This issue today was that up front they did a job on us," Chiefs coach Marty Schottenheimer said. That translates into the running game for each team. Buffalo pounded the Chiefs on the ground, running the ball 46 times for 229 yards. Kansas City ran the ball just 21 times for 52 yards.

The Bills scored first midway through the first quarter on a 12-yard run by Thurman Thomas. Kansas City cut the lead to 7-6 on two Nick Lowery field goals before the period ended. The second field goal was set up when Buffalo fumbled the kickoff following the first field goal. The Chiefs started at the Bills' 24-yard line, but couldn't get into the end zone. Buffalo scored the next three times it had the ball to increase its lead to 20-6.

With 1:56 left in the first half, Montana led the Chiefs the length of the field to the Buffalo 5-yardline. But instead of pulling closer, the Chiefs saw Montana's second-and-goal pass slip through Kimble Anders' hands for an interception at the goal line.

"That's the worst thing that could have happened, seeing the guy pick it off," Anders said of the costly interception. "If it had hit the ground, we'd still have the opportunity to score."

Montana took the hit that knocked him out of the game on the Chiefs' fourth play of the third quarter. Dave Krieg took over and played quarterback the rest of the game.

"Dave came in and played his guts out," Chiefs center Tim Grunhard said. "Just like we knew he would."

Krieg led the Chiefs on a 14-play, 90-yard drive to pull the Chiefs within a touchdown at 20-13. Marcus Allen scored the touchdown from one yard out.

"We felt very confident we had a chance to win. I felt that, too," Krieg said of the touchdown drive that put the Chiefs back in the game. "Obviously, this team has the ability to come back."

It was as close as the Chiefs would get the rest of the day. The Bills scored on their next two possessions to put the game away.

"It's more disappointing to lose in this game than to not have made the playoffs at all," Montana said after the game. He was still feeling the effects of the concussion. "If you don't make the playoffs, you can just sort of write the whole thing off."

"There's a frustration and a disappointment that goes with any defeat, especially one that ends your season," Schottenheimer said. "Yet I think they would be doing themselves a great disservice as players and as people if they were to walk out of there with their heads down. We had a very good season—albeit not what we were after."

"I would say that they should be proud of everything they have accomplished," Marcus Allen said. "And I think that taste in our mouth should bring us back next year."

The Chiefs' run in the playoffs had ended; there would be no Super Bowl for the Chiefs in 1994. But despite the loss, the team played the way it was capable of playing in the postseason. Their season was a success, something they hadn't been able say in the past after playoff losses.

"What can you say right now?" Chiefs defensive tackle Dan Saleaumua said. "It's over. But it was a heck of a ride."

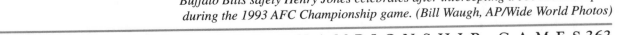

Buffalo Bills safety Henry Jones celebrates after intercepting a Joe Montana pass during the 1993 AFC Championship game. (Bill Waugh, AP/Wide World Photos)

KANSAS CITY	6	0	7	0	—	**13**
BUFFALO	7	13	0	10	—	**30**

BILLS — T. Thomas, 12-yard run (Christie kick)
CHIEFS — Lowery, 31-yard field goal
CHIEFS — Lowery, 31-yard field goal
BILLS — T. Thomas, 3-yard run (Christie kick)
BILLS — Christie, 23-yard field goal
BILLS — Christie, 25-yard field goal
CHIEFS — Allen, 1-yard run (Lowery kick)
BILLS — Christie, 18-yard field goal
BILLS — T. Thomas, 3-yard run (Christie kick)

Team Statistics	Bills	Chiefs
First Downs	30	22
Total Net Yards	389	338
Rushes/Net Yards	46/229	21/52
Net Passing	160	286
Pass Attempts/Completions	27/17	52/25
Had Intercepted	0	2
Sacked/Yards Lost	0/0	4/3
Punts/Average	4/33.3	6/40.8
Penalties/Yards	2/10	6/29
Fumbles/Lost	1/1	1/0
Time of Possession	30:40	29:20

Rushing
CHIEFS — Allen 18-50, 1 TD; Anders 2-1; Montana 1-1.
BILLS — T. Thomas 33-186, 3 TDs; K. Davis 10-31; Kelly 2-3; Reed 1-8.

Receiving
CHIEFS — Cash 6-87; W. Davis 5-57; Birden 4-60; Allen 2-36; McNair 2-33; Hayes 2-14; E. Thompson 1-12; Hughes 1-11; Anders 1-7; Szott 1-6.
BILLS — Reed 4-49; Brooks 4-34; Metzelaars 4-29; T. Thomas 2-22; Beebe 2-19; McKeller 1-7.

Passing
CHIEFS — Montana 9-23-125, 1 INT; Krieg 16-29-198, 1 INT.
BILLS — Kelly 17-27-160.

Interceptions
CHIEFS — None.
BILLS — H. Jones 1-15; J. Williams 1-0.

Sacks
CHIEFS — None.
BILLS — Talley 1; B. Smith 1; Hansen 1; Wright 1.

Field Goals
CHIEFS — Lowery (31) (31).
BILLS — Christie (23) (25) (18).

KANSAS CITY CHIEFS
Super Bowls

Green Bay Packers vs. Kansas City Chiefs

AFL-NFL World Championship Game (Super Bowl I) – January 15, 1967
Packers 35, Chiefs 10
Los Angeles Memorial Coliseum (63,036)

It was appropriate that Lamar Hunt's Kansas City Chiefs won the AFL title in 1966. After forging the start of the new league just seven years earlier, Hunt's team—and new league—were part of what would soon become the greatest single-day sporting event in world.

For six seasons the NFL and upstart AFL had warred off the field for playing talent, but a negotiated peace in the summer of 1966 had brought an end to all that. Now the two leagues would face each other in a game, the AFL-NFL World Championship game; each team had the extra responsibility of playing not just for themselves, but for their respective leagues. The AFL had endured name-calling—the NFL mockingly called it the "Mickey Mouse League,"—and hoped to earn respect for the whole league with a good showing in the game.

Kansas City had waltzed through the AFL during the 1966 season and were considered the best representative the baby league could offer. But the old-guard NFL had the Green Bay Packers, already being called at the time of the game the greatest team of all time. It's a label that has stuck and lasted for 35 years.

A war of words circled the two teams before the game, and the Chiefs' Fred Williamson, who called himself "The Hammer" for his smashing forearm tackles, shot off the most rounds. He said he thought the Chiefs were afraid of the Packers and in a state of awe. He said he was trying to snap his teammates out of being intimidated; instead he angered them and perked up the Packers.

"Lombardi, the mystique, even the idea that maybe this was the greatest team of all time—sure, that was on our mind," Chiefs safety Johnny Robinson said years after the game. "Were we in awe? I think apprehension would be a better word." The Packers were 13 ½ point favorites.

Pomp and celebration filled the field of the Los Angeles Memorial Coliseum during pre-game activities. Glee clubs, floats, bands and astronauts adorned the floor of the stadium. Two networks, NBC and CBS, were broadcasting the game to one of the largest television audiences ever. Still, the 90,000-seat stadium was only two-thirds full. This first Super Bowl game was a novelty, not yet a passionate national holiday.

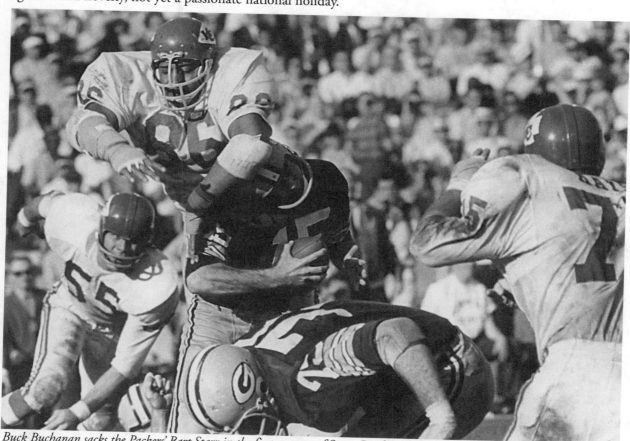

Buck Buchanan sacks the Packers' Bart Starr in the first quarter of Super Bowl I. (Kansas Collection, U. of Kansas)

The temperature was in the mid-70s when Kansas City kicked off to start the game. The Packers picked up a first down before punting. The Chiefs also picked up a first down before punting. Then the Packers got rolling. They moved 80 yards on six plays and scored, Packers quarterback Bart Starr hitting Max McGee from 19 yards out for the touchdown. McGee would become the story of this game, playing for the injured Boyd Dowler and burning the Kansas City secondary throughout the game.

"Three big plays by McGee, all on weak-side blitzes," Johnny Robinson said. "There's nobody to jam McGee, so he comes in the middle clean."

Kansas City responded, though, and moved down the field. Mike Mercer missed a 40-yard field goal wide right to end the threat. But the Chiefs held the Packers to a three-and-out situation and took over again at their own 34. Len Dawson led the team 66 yards in six plays, a 31-yard pass to Otis Taylor was the key play in the drive. Dawson hit Curtis McClinton in the end zone to tie the score. The two teams traded scores before the end of the half—a touchdown for the Packers and a field goal for Kansas City. Green Bay led at the intermission, 14-10.

"At halftime I felt pretty darn good," Lamar Hunt recalled of the game. "We had more yards and more first downs than the Packers, and we were moving the ball on them." Kansas City took the field for the start of the second half with high hopes and optimism.

It looks bad, but Chris Burford (88) didn't lose his head on this play. The Chiefs' veteran receiver had a good game against the Packers, catching 4 passes for 67 yards. (Chris Burford)

"I sincerely felt we could win," Chiefs coach Hank Stram said of his feeling at the start of the third quarter. "And I think our people felt that way, too."

Three minutes into the second half, the game turned.

Facing a third and five at their own 49-yard line, Dawson called for a pass to tight end Fred Arbanas. In the face of the Packers' blitz, Dawson floated a lame-duck pass out to the left flat, and Green Bay's Willie Wood picked it off and returned it to the Kansas City five-yard line. Elijah Pitts scored on the next play. The Chiefs were down by only 11 points, but their confidence was shot, and realistically, so was any chance they had to win the game.

"He should have taken the sack," Mike Garrett said of Dawson's costly interception. "I was yelling, 'Don't do it! Don't do it!'"

"I wish I had thrown a better pass," Dawson said of the play. "I wish I had done anything except what I did. If I had thrown it outside we don't catch it, but neither do they." Kansas City never made it farther than the Green Bay 44-yard line the rest of the game.

The Packers scored again in the third period and added a final touchdown in

Green Bay's Elijah Pitts is wrapped up by the Chiefs' Bobby Bell. (Chris Burford)

the fourth to make the final score 35-10. Fred Williamson, who predicted his "Hammer" was going to drop on the Packers, was knocked out in the fourth quarter when he caught a knee to the helmet. He had to be helped from the field.

"Yeah, we shoved them around for a while," E. J. Holub said of the Packers. "But we were just so young. They cashed in on every mistake we made." The Chiefs had just one turnover, the big interception by Wood. But they were unable to move on the Packers in the second half and finished the game with 239 yards of total offense. Green Bay had 358 yards.

"They just beat us, that's all," Stram said after the game. "The interception has to be the turning point in the game. You don't like to think one play can make that much difference, but it seemed to."

As far as the NFL was concerned, Mickey Mouse had been squashed. Vince Lombardi was not very complimentary of the Chiefs or the AFL.

"Kansas City is a good football team," Lombardi said of the Chiefs after the game. "But their team doesn't compare with the top National Football League teams. I think Dallas is a better team . . . I'd have to say NFL football is tougher."

"I'm still not convinced they're a better football team than we are," Dawson said after the game. "I think we played a lot of fine football and no one can take that away from us. We started out in the first half and did a fine job. If we had played the second half the way we did the first half we could have won."

Chiefs owner Lamar Hunt was realistic in his observation of the game.

"Green Bay was superior," Hunt said. "They were definitely the superior team today."

"I think we probably did what people expected," Jerry Mays said of the Chiefs' performance in the game. "We made a mistake and lost our poise. They were a great football team, Green Bay was, but I am sure the difference between us is not in the score."

The first Super Bowl was in the books, and it had gone accordingly for the NFL. The baby league representative had proved its inferiority, but Stram preferred to look at the game's result in another light, maybe the proper light.

"It wasn't anything we didn't do, or try to do; it was that their execution was perfect," Stram said. "It took exceptional timing between Starr and his receivers, and they got it. It took great pass blocking, and they got that."

Kansas City lost to a great, great football team, but it didn't change the hurt or stop the "Mickey Mouse League" accusations. If anything, they increased. Three years later, in Super Bowl IV, the Chiefs would exact a revenge of sorts, not just for themselves, but for the entire AFL.

KANSAS CITY	0	10	0	0	—	**10**
GREEN BAY	7	7	14	7	—	**35**

PACKERS — McGee, 37-yard pass from Starr (Chandler kick).

CHIEFS — McClinton, 7-yard pass from Dawson (Mercer kick).

PACKERS — Taylor, 14-yard run (Chandler kick).

CHIEFS — Mercer, 31-yard field goal.

PACKERS — Pitts, 5-yard run (Chandler kick).

PACKERS — McGee, 13-yard pass from Starr (Chandler kick).

PACKERS — Pitts, 1-yard run (Chandler kick).

Team Statistics	Packers	Chiefs
First Downs	21	17
Total Net Yards	358	239
Rushes/Net Yards	33/130	19/72
Net Passing	228	167
Pass Attempts/Completions	24/16	32/17
Had Intercepted	1	1
Sacked/Yards Lost	3/22	6/61
Punts/Average	4/43.3	7/45.3
Penalties/Yards	4/40	4/26
Fumbles/Lost	1/0	1/0

Rushing

CHIEFS — Coan 3-1; Dawson 3-24; Garrett 6-17; McClinton 6-16; Beathard 1-14.

PACKERS — Pitts 11-45, 2 TDs; Taylor 16-53, 1 TD; Anderson 4-30; Grabowski 2-2.

Receiving

CHIEFS — Burford 4-67; Arbanas 2-30; Carolan 1-7; Garrett 3-28; McClinton 2-34, 1 TD; Taylor 4-57; Coan 1-5.

PACKERS — Dale 4-59; Fleming 2-22; McGee 7-138; Pitts 2-32.

Passing

CHIEFS — Dawson 16-27-211, 1 TD, 1 INT; Beathard 1-5-17, 0 TD, 0 INTs.

PACKERS — Starr 16-23-250, 2 TDs, 1 INT; Bratowski 0-1-0, 0 TDs, 0 INTs.

Interceptions

CHIEFS — Mitchell 1-0.

PACKERS — Wood 1-50.

Field Goals

CHIEFS — Mercer 40WR (31)

PACKERS — None.

Play-by-Play Account of Super Bowl I

Green Bay wins the toss and elects to receive. Kansas City kicks off, and defends the west goal.
Smith kicks off to Adderly on the GB5, who runs to the GB25, 20-yard return (Bell).

First Quarter

Green Bay

1-10	GB25	Taylor at right guard for 4 yards. (Rice)
2-6	GB29	Pitts around left side for 5 yards (Robinson)
3-1	GB34	Taylor at left tackle for 3 yards and FD (Mitchell) – first down
1-10	GB37	Starr pass intended for McGee, incomplete.
1-10	GB37	Starr, back to pass, rushed and dropped by Buchanan for 10-yard loss
2-20	GB27	Starr, back to pass, rushed by Mays and Bell for 5-yard loss
3-25	GB22	Chandler punt taken by Garrett on KC28, returned to KC37. 50-yard punt, 9-yard return.

11:55 Kansas City

1-10	KC37	Dawson pass to Burford, caught out of bounds and incomplete.
2-10	KC37	Garrett on draw at middle, then cuts to right for 4 yards. (Kostenik, Jordan).
3-6	KC41	Dawson pass complete to Burford for 11 yards (Jeter) – first down
1-10	GB48	Garrett at left side for 1 yard. (Jordan)
2-9	GB47	Delay of game penalty on Chiefs, 5 yards
2-14	KC48	Dawson pass to Burford, caught out of bounds and incomplete.
3-14	KC48	Dawson pass intended for Taylor, incomplete.
4-14	KC48	Wilson punt to D. Anderson on GB5, returned to GB20. 47-yard punt, 15-yard return.

9:10 Green Bay

1-10	GB20	Pitts around right end for 3 yards. (Williams, Hunt)
2-7	GB23	Starr quick pass over the middle complete to Fleming for 11 yards (Hunt, Bell) – first down.
1-10	GB34	Starr, under pressure, passes complete to Pitts for 22 yards (Bell) – first down
1-10	KC 44	Taylor starts wide to left, dropped by Holub for 5-yard loss.
2-15	KC49	Starr pass complete to Dale for 12 yards (Williamson)

3-3	KC37	Starr pass complete to McGee on the KC19 and carried in for a 37-yard score.

Time left in first quarter: 3:56.
Chandler, kick good (80 yards on 6 plays)
Green Bay 7, Kansas City 0

Chandler kicks off to Garrett on KC1, returned to KC24. 23 yard return. Penalty on Chiefs for holding (DiMidio), 11-yard penalty.

5:54 Kansas City

1-10	KC13	Dawson, back to pass, then runs for 7 yards. (Nitschke)
2-3	KC20	Dawson short pass complete to Garrett for 3 yards (Jordan, Aldridge) – first down
1-10	KC23	Dawson pass intended for Burford incomplete, but Jeter ruled as interfering, 5-yard penalty – first down
1-10	KC28	McClinton in the middle for 4 yards (Kostelnik)
2-5	KC32	Dawson pass complete to Arbanas for 18 yards (Caffey)
1-10	KC50	Garrett through left guard for 9 yards (Caffey)
3-1	GB41	Dawson, back to pass, then runs up middle for 2 yards (Nitschke) – first down
1-10	GB39	Garrett wide to right for 1-yard loss (Robinson)
2-11	GB40	Dawson long pass intended for Burford, incomplete (Woods)
3-11	GB40	Dawson pass complete to Carolan for 7 yards (Nitschke)
4-4	GB35	With Dawson holding, Mercer 40-yard field-goal attempt is wide to north (right) and no good

1:34 Green Bay

1-10	GB20	Taylor at right tackle for 3 yards (Buchanan)
2-7	GB23	Packers at line of scrimmage as quarter ends

END OF FIRST QUARTER
First Quarter Score: Packers 7, Chiefs 0

Second Quarter

Green Bay

2-7	GB23	Starr pass intended for McGee, incomplete
3-7	GB23	Starr pass intended for Dale, incomplete – penalty declined
4-7	GB23	Chandler punt to KC32, Thomas returned to 34 for 2 yards (45-yard punt)

Kansas City

1-10	KC34	Dawson pass complete to Garrett on 35, ran to GB49 for 17 (Wood) – first down
1-10	GB49	Coan – left guard to 46 for 3 (Aldridge)
2-7	GB46	McClinton middle to 40 for 6 (Aldridge)
3-1	GB40	Coan – left tackle to 38 for 2 (Caffey) – first down
1-10	GB38	Dawson pass complete to O. Taylor to 7 for 31 (Brown) – first down
1-G	GB7	Dawson pass complete to McClinton for touchdown

Time left in second quarter: 10:40
Mercer, kick good (66 yards on 6 plays)
Green Bay 7, Kansas City 7

Smith kicks off to GB2 and Anderson returned to GB27 for 25 (Corey).

Green Bay

1-10	GB27	Pitts – left guard to 33 for 6 (Rice)
2-4	GB33	Taylor – left tackle to 36 for 3 (Hurston, Bell)
3-1	GB36	Starr pass complete to Dale for touchdown, illegal procedure (5-yard penalty puts ball on 32—illegal procedure was called because an interior lineman moved)
3-5	GB32	Starr pass complete to McGee to 42 for 10 (Robinson) – first down
1-10	GB42	Starr pass intended for Dale, incomplete (Mitchell defending)
2-10	GB42	Starr pass intended for Pitts, incomplete (Holub defending)
3-10	GB42	Starr pass complete to Dale to KC43 for 15 (Robinson) – first down
1-10	KC43	Taylor – left end to 40 for 3 (Mitchell)
2-7	KC40	Pitts in middle to 38 for 2 (Headrich, Rice)
3-5	KC38	Starr pass complete to Fleming to 27 for 11 (Robinson) – first down
1-10	KC27	Taylor in middle to 24 for 3 (Buchanan)
2-7	KC24	Pitts on draw in left side no gain (Rice, Buchanan)
3-7	KC24	Starr pass complete to Pitts to 14 for 10 (Holub) – first down
1-10	KC14	Taylor – Sweep to left in for touchdown.

Time left in second quarter 10:23
Chandler, kick good (73 yards in 13 plays) 4:31
Green Bay 14, Kansas City 7

Chandler kicks off to KC6 and Garrett returns to 26 for 20-yard return (Hathcock).

Kansas City

1-10	KC26	Dawson thrown for loss of 8 on 18 attempting to pass (Jordan)
2-18	KC18	Dawson pass complete to Arbanas to 30

		for 12 (Nitschke) Arbanas injured
3-6	KC30	Dawson pass complete to Taylor to 41 for 11 (Adderly) – first down
1-10	KC41	Dawson pass complete to Burford to GB 32 for 27 yards (Robinson) –first down
1-10	GB32	Garrett in middle to 30 for 2 (Nitschke)
2-8	GB30	McClinton fumbled and recovered for loss of 2 to 32
3-10	GB32	Dawson screen pass to Garrett to 24 for 8 (Robinson, Nitschke)
4-2	GB24	Mercer field goal from 31 – good

Time left in second quarter: 0:54
74 yards in 8 plays
Green Bay 14, Kansas City 10

Smith kicks off to GB6 and Adderly returned to 26 for return of 20 (Mays, Stover).

Green Bay

1-10	GB26	Pitts – right tackle to 33 for 7 (Bell)

END OF SECOND QUARTER
Green Bay 14, Kansas City 10

Willie Mitchell defends the Packers' Carroll Dale. Fred "The Hammer" Williamson looks on. (Bettmann/CORBIS)

Third Quarter

Chandler kicks off to KC13 and Coan returned to 29 for 16 (Mack).

Kansas City

1-10	KC29	Dawson on keeper – right end to 44 for 15, ran out of bounds – first down
1-10	KC44	McClinton – right guard to 47 for 3 (Kostelnik)
2-7	KC47	Garrett – in middle to 49 for 2 (Aldridge)
3-5	KC49	Wood intercepted Dawson pass intended for Arbanas on GB45 and ran to 5 for return of 50 yards (Garrett)

Green Bay

1-G   KC5   Pitts – left tackle for touchdown
Time left in third quarter: 12:33
Chandler, kick good
Green Bay 21, Kansas City 10

Chandler kicks off to KC 1-yard deep in end zone to Coan, returned to 30 for a 31-yard return (Weatherwax).

Kansas City

1-10	KC30	Dawson pass intended for Taylor, incomplete – fell short
2-10	KC30	Dawson pass complete to Taylor to 41 for 11 (Adderely) – first down
1-10	KC41	McClinton – in middle to 45 for 4 (Aldridge)
2-6	KC45	Dawson pass complete to Coan to 50 for 5 (Caffey)
3-1	KC50	Coan lost 4 to 46 (Caffey)
4-5	KC 46	Wilson punt to GB25, downed by Holub

Green Bay

1-10	GB25	Pitts – right tackle to 37 for 12 (Williamson) – first down
1-10	GB37	Starr dropped for loss of 7 on 30 (Holub)
2-17	GB30	Starr pass complete to McGee to 44 for 14 (Mitchell)
3-3	GB44	Taylor – left end to 46 for 2 (Headrick, Thurston)
4-1	GB46	Chandler punt to GB19, Garrett returned to 27 for an 8-yard return (Curry).

Kansas City

1-10	KC27	Dawson pass intended for Burford, incomplete (Jeter defending)
2-10	KC27	Dawson dropped for loss of 14 to 13, holding on KC declined
3-24	KC13	Dawson dropped for loss of 11 to 2 (Jordan, Davis, Kostelnik)
4-35	KC2	Wilson punt to KC45 and Anderson returned to 41 for 4 but Packers clipping, 15-yard penalty to GB44

Green Bay

1-10	GB44	Pitts – left end to 42, loss of 2 (Holub, Rice)
2-12	GB42	Starr pass complete to McGee to KC47 for 11 (Mitchell)
3-1	KC47	Taylor – left tackle to 43 for 4 (Headrick) – first down
1-10	KC43	Starr pass intended for Dale, incomplete. Dale fell down (Williamson defending)
2-10	KC43	Starr pass complete to Taylor to 44, loss of 1 (Bell)
3-11	KC44	Starr pass complete to McGee to 28 for 16 (Hunt, Bell) – first down

1-10	KC28	Taylor in middle to 25 for 3 (Buchanan)
2-7	KC25	Taylor on draw – left guard to 21 for 4 (Robinson)
3-3	KC21	Taylor – left end to 13 for 8 (Bell) – first down
1-10	KC13	Starr pass complete to McGee in end zone.

Time left in third quarter: 0:51
Chandler, kick good   (56 yards on 10 plays)
Green Bay 28, Kansas City 10

Chandler kicks off to KC2 and Coan returned to 17, return of 15 (Hathcock)

Kansas City

1-10	KC17	McClinton in middle to 18 for 1 (Jordan)

END OF THIRD QUARTER
Green Bay 28, Kansas City 10

Fourth Quarter

Kansas City

2-9	KC18	Dawson pass intended for McClinton, almost picked off by Wood
3-9	KC18	Dawson pass intended for Taylor, incomplete (Adderly)
4-9	KC18	Wilson punt taken by D. Anderson on GB41, returned to GB46. 41-yard punt, 6-yard return (Ply)

Green Bay

1-10	GB47	Taylor at left guard for 3 yards (Buchanan)
2-7	GB50	Starr long pass intended for McGee, is intercepted by Willie Mitchell on the KC 11, no return

Kansas City

1-10	KC11	Dawson pass complete to McClinton with diving catch for 27 yards (Wood) – first down
1-10	KC38	Dawson pass complete to Taylor for 4 yards (Adderly)
2-6	KC42	Dawson pass complete to Burford for 12 yards (Jeter) – first down
1-10	GB46	Dawson long pass intended for Taylor, incomplete in end zone. Penalty on Chiefs for illegal procedure, 5 yards
1-15	KC49	Dawson, back to pass, dropped by Davis for 10-yard loss
2-25	KC39	Dawson pass intended for Taylor, broken up by Adderly
3-25	KC39	Dawson pass intended for Garrett, broken up by B. Brown at line
4-25	KC39	Wilson punt goes into the end zone for 61-yard punt

Green Bay

1-10	GB20	Starr pass complete to Dale for 25 yards (Mitchell) – first down
1-10	GB45	Starr pass complete to McGee for 37 yards (Mitchell) – first down
1-10	KC18	Taylor in the middle for no gain (Mays)
2-10	KC18	Starr pass complete to Dale for 7 yards (Mitchell)
3-3	KC11	Pitts through right tackle for 6 yards (Robinson) – first down
1-5	KC5	Taylor at left guard for 3 yards (Headrick)
2-2	KC2	Taylor around left end for 1 yard (Robinson)
3-1	KC1	Pitts rolls off of left side for 1 yard and score.

Time left in fourth quarter: 6:23
Chandler kick, good (80 yards on 8 plays)
Green Bay 35, Kansas City 10

Chandler kicks off to Coan on goal line, returned to KC 25. 25-yard return (Mack)

Kansas City

1-10	KC25	Beathard at quarterback. Beathard pass complete to Burford for 17 yards (Jeter) – first down
1-10	KC42	Beathard, back to pass, then runs for 14 yards (Nitschke, Jeter) – first down
1-10	GB44	Beathard pass intended for Garrett, incomplete (Adderly)
2-10	GB44	Illegal procedure on Chiefs, 5 yards
2-15	GB49	Beathard, back to pass, dropped by B. Brown for 11-yard loss
3-26	KC40	Beathard pass intended for Burford, broken up by Jeter
4-26	KC40	Wilson punt taken by Wood with fair catch on GB 18. 42-yard punt

Green Bay

1-10	GB18	Bratkowski at quarterback. D. Anderson around left end for 13 yards (Holub) – first down
1-10	GB31	Grabowski fumbles when hit by Holub, and Skoronski recovers for Packers. No gain
2-10	GB31	D. Anderson around right end for 3 yards (Williamson – who is hurt on play) Time out Kansas City
3-7	GB34	Bratkowski long pass intended for Dale, incomplete (Mitchell, Robinson)
4-7	GB34	D. Anderson punt rolls dead on KC23. 43-yard punt

Kansas City

1-10	KC23	Beathard long pass intended for Taylor, incomplete (Adderly)
2-10	KC23	(2:00) Beathard, back to pass, dropped by Nitschke for 7-yard loss
3-17	KC16	(1:46) Beathard pass intended for Burford, high and incomplete
4-17	KC16	(1:24) Wilson punt taken by Wood on the GB30, returned to GB28 54-yard punt, 2-yard return. Clipping Packers, 15-yard penalty

Green Bay

1-10	GB13	(1:12) Grabowski in the middle for 2 yards (Buchanan)
2-8	GB15	(0:43) D. Anderson around right end for 10 yards (Mays) – first down
1-10	GB25	(0:29) D. Anderson cuts in at left end for 4 yards (Holub) as game ends

Final Score: Green Bay 35, Kansas City 10

Kansas City Chiefs vs. Minnesota Vikings

Super Bowl IV – January 11, 1970
Chiefs 23, Vikings 7
Tulane Stadium - New Orleans, LA (80,562)

The clock wound down in Tulane Stadium, ticking away the final seconds of Super Bowl IV that would make the Kansas City Chiefs the champions of the football world. Excitement covered the entire team and organization.

"This is a much greater thrill than anything that has ever happened," Kansas City Chiefs owner Lamar Hunt said after his team had easily disposed of the Minnesota Vikings, 23-7. "This is it."

Super Bowl IV was also the last time the AFL was represented in a game. The ten-year old league, conceived and founded by Hunt, was no more following the game, its ten teams joining the NFL. Kansas City wore patches on its jerseys to commemorate the upstart league and its success, and their dominating performance in the game proved the AFL was truly on even ground with the much older league.

The Chiefs subdued a powerful NFL opponent to claim the Super Bowl trophy. And what made the victory sweeter still was the MVP performance of Chiefs quarterback Len Dawson, who played brilliantly despite a great amount of the turmoil and controversy that surrounded him throughout the week leading up to the game.

Five days before the game, NBC broke a story that a special Justice Department task force was conducting the "biggest gambling investigation of its kind ever." Seven pro football players and one college coach were going to be called to testify on their relationships with known gamblers, most notably Donald "Dice" Dawson of Detroit. Len Dawson was one of the named players. Lenny had met Dice Dawson 10 years earlier while playing for Pittsburgh and had received phone calls from him twice in the past year, one concerning his knee injury and the other about the death of his father. He had never had any business dealings with him. Dawson's teammates were rightfully upset at the alleged gambling association.

"We're angry as hell the story came out the way it did," Chiefs defensive end Jerry Mays said.

"Lenny is too smart to get mixed up in something like this," Mike Garrett said. "To me there's nothing to it and it doesn't bother me at all."

"You've got to believe in something and I believe in Lenny," Ed Budde said.

After reading a statement to the press, Dawson tried to go about his business of preparing for the Minnesota Vikings. The NFL champs had had an impressive season and were listed as a 13-point favorite to beat the Chiefs. But in the days leading up to the game, Chiefs Coach Hank Stram put together a game plan that would shut down the Vikings' strengths and exploit their weaknesses.

"We had to control their defensive ends and throw in front of their cornerbacks," Stram said of the plan after the game. On the defensive side of the ball, the Chiefs keyed on Viking quarterback Joe Kapp, a tough, rugged leader who made up for a lack of overall quarterbacking skills with desire, scrambling and moxie.

Len Dawson shook off gambling allegations and performed brilliantly in Super Bowl IV, earning MVP honors. (Topeka Capital-Journal)

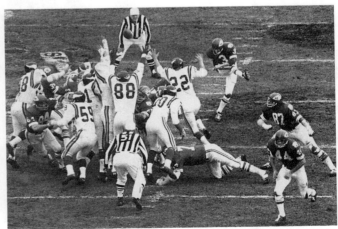

Jan Stenerud boots one of his three field goals in Super Bowl IV. (Bettmann/CORBIS)

"We wanted to try to keep Kapp in the pocket as much as we could," Stram continued of the Chiefs' game plan. He didn't think the distraction of the gambling allegations against Dawson would hurt the team.

"Our people have played with a great deal of toughness and determination all year. This is so important when you have to cope with the adversity we have experienced."

It was overcast and wet in Tulane Stadium when Kansas City's Jan Stenerud kicked off to start the game. Minnesota held the ball for four minutes and moved to the Kansas City 38-yard line, but the Chiefs held. A poor punt gave Kansas City the ball at their own 17. A 20-yard pass to Frank Pitts helped the Chiefs move the ball into Viking territory, and when the drive stalled, Stenerud came in a booted a 48-yard field goal to give Kansas City a 3-0 led. The Chiefs scored on their new possession as well, this time with 32-yard field goal. With ten minutes left in the second quarter, Stenerud connected again to put the Chiefs up 9-0. Pitts ran a reverse sweep for 19 yards to help set up the third field goal.

"I can hardly remember the game, I was so tense," Stenerud said his field goals. "I don't enjoy games when things get too close down to the end."

"We break 'em down with these threes and then we get on the board with some big ones," Stram crowed on the sideline following the third field goal.

On the ensuing kickoff, Minnesota's Charlie West misjudged the ball and fumbled. The Chiefs' Remi Prudhomme fell on the loose ball at the Minnesota 19-yard line. Five plays later, Chiefs faced a third and goal at the five-yard line.

Mike Garrett scampers through the Vikings' line to score the Chiefs' first touchdown in Super Bowl IV. (Bettmann/CORBIS)

"Sixty-five toss power trap." Stram sent the now famous play in, and Mike Garrett scampered past the Vikings' Alan Page and into the end zone for the game's first touchdown.

The Chiefs led at the half, 16-0.

"When we defeated the Jets, we were two weeks away from our goal," Stram addressed his team at halftime, referring to the playoff win over New York. "When we defeated Oakland [in the AFL title game], we were one week away. Now we are only 30 minutes from being champions of the world. Go out there and give it everything you've got."

Minnesota tried to make a game of it in the third, and after Kansas City punted, the Vikings mounted their only good drive of the game. Moving 69 yards in ten plays, Minnesota scored on a four-yard run by Dave Osborne to cut the lead to 16-7.

On their next possession, the Chiefs got a big first down on another reverse sweep by Pitts. Following a 15-yard penalty on the Vikings, Dawson threw a little hitch pass to his right for Otis Taylor. The big receiver made a spectacular move to break a tackle by the Vikings' Earsell Mackbee. He pranced down the sideline, faked out Karl Kassulke, and swept into the end zone.

"I got hit on the left side and spun out. Then I hit the last guy downfield with my hand," Taylor said of his touchdown play at the end of the third quarter. "I always try to punish a pass defender just as he does me. I wanted to score that touchdown because I remembered how Minnesota came back to beat the Rams and I felt we needed to continue to keep scoring today."

Taylor's great play put the Chiefs up 23-7.

"Even after Otis scored, I kept thinking that we'd still have to contain their offense, and I was right," Buck Buchanan said. "We did it, too, didn't we?"

The Chiefs' defense brutalized the Vikings the rest of the game, intercepting two of his passes and then knocking him out of the game. Len Dawson came out of the game with just more than a minute remaining to receive a well-deserved ovation. Two plays later the Chiefs were the champions of the world.

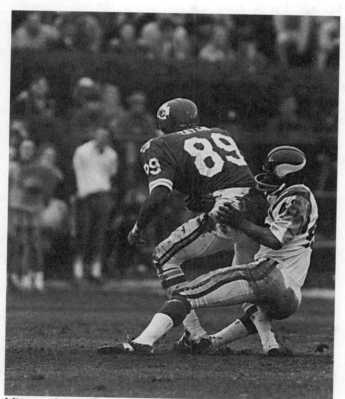

Minnesota's Earsell Mackbee can't hold on to Otis Taylor, and the Chiefs' gifted receiver busts loose for a 46-yard touchdown pass play that sealed the game for Kansas City. (Topeka Capital-Journal)

"I thought the first Super Bowl was the greatest, but this is so much more," Taylor said. I think more than anything I'm happy for Lenny. That guy has been under so much pressure this week with this gambling dirt—but I guess he showed everybody who the number-one quarterback was out there today, didn't he?"

For his performance, hitting 12 of 17 passes for 122 yards and a touchdown, Dawson was named the game's MVP. He tried not dwell on the gambling allegations afterwards.

"No, the gambling thing didn't give me any extra incentive," Dawson said. "How could it? I approached this game as a big game, as an opportunity to be the best. You don't need outside motivation."

And then the phone call for Dawson from President Nixon.

"The world looks up to pro football players for courage," President Nixon said to Dawson.

"Thank you, Mr. President," replied Dawson. "We try to exemplify the best in professional football . . . but it wasn't me, it was the whole team that did it."

"I thought Lenny showed the great toughness he possesses as a leader and a quarterback," Stram said of his quarterback. "I thought it was great the way he expressed his ability today after what happened earlier in the week."

The victory was also a retribution of sorts of the Chiefs, who never really got over the loss to the Green Bay Packers in the first Super Bowl.

"Winning a game like this is a big thing because if you win you don't have to explain anything," Dawson said. "We've been explaining our Green Bay game [losing Super Bowl I] for three years."

The Chiefs' locker room was excited and crowded following the win, but the players didn't display any out-of-control behavior. Hank Stram expected no less of his men.

"We have to win with grace and class," Stram said. "That's part of our program. Even though that wasn't expressed the last time we played in the Super Bowl, we are not going to deviate from our beliefs."

The Chiefs were the champions of the world and gave the AFL a big going away present. No more Mickey Mouse League, just Super Bowl champions. E. J. Holub, the Chiefs' veteran center, might have summed up the victory better than anyone in the crowded room of celebration.

"Whooooo-ey," he brayed.

MINNESOTA	0	0	7	0	—	7
KANSAS CITY	3	13	7	0	—	**23**

CHIEFS	– Stenerud, 48-yard field goal.
CHIEFS	– Stenerud, 32-yard field goal.
CHIEFS	– Stenerud, 25-yard field goal.
CHIEFS	– Garrett, 5-yard run (Stenerud kick).
VIKINGS	– Osborn, 4-yard run (Cox kicks).
CHIEFS	– Taylor, 46-yard pass from Dawson (Stenerud kick).

Team Statistics	Vikings	Chiefs
First Downs	13	18
Total Net Yards	239	273
Rushes/Net Yards	19/67	4/151
Net Passing	172	122
Pass Attempts/Completions	28/17	17/12
Had Intercepted	3	1
Sacked/Yards Lost	3/27	3/20
Punts/Average	3/37.0	4/48.5
Penalties/Yards	6/67	4/47
Fumbles/Lost	3/20	0/0

Rushing

CHIEFS – **Garrett 11-39, 1 TD; Holmes 5-7; Pitts 3-37; Dawson 3-11; Hayes 8-31; McVea 12-26.**

VIKINGS – Osborn 7-15, 1 TD; Brown 6-26; Kapp 2-9; Reed 4-17.

Receiving

CHIEFS – **Garrett 2-25; Pitts 3-33; Taylor 6-81, 1 TD; Hayes 1-13.**

VIKINGS – Osborn 2-11; Beasler 2-41; Brown 3-11; Henderson 7-111; Reed 2-16; Washington 1-9.

Passing

CHIEFS – **Dawson 12-17-142, 1 TD, 1 INT; Livingston 0-0-0.**

VIKINGS – Kapp 16-25-183, 0 TDs, 2 INTs; Cuozzo 1-3-16, 0 TD, 1 INT.

Interceptions

CHIEFS – **Lanier 1-9; Robinson 1-9; Thomas 1-6.**

VIKINGS – Krause 1-0.

Sacks

CHIEFS – **Mays 1; Buchanan 1; Brown 1.**

VIKINGS – Winston 1; Marshall 1; Eller 1.

Field Goals

CHIEFS – **Stenerud (48) (32) (25).**

VIKINGS – Cox 56S.

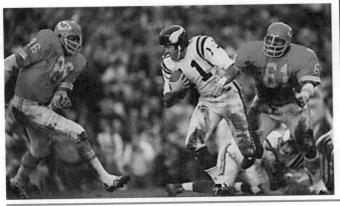

Buck Buchanan (86) and Curley Culp (61) zero in on Vikings' quarterback Joe Kapp. The Chiefs' defense harassed and punished Kapp throughout the game. (Topeka Capital-Journal)

Play-by-Play Account of Super Bowl IV

First Quarter

Stenerud kicks off to the end of the end zone, no return.

14:55 Minnesota

1-10	M20	Osborn runs left tackle for 2 yards (Thomas)
2-8	M22	Kapp passes to Osburn, left side, 10 yards (Raniar) – first down
1-10	M32	Brown runs left center, gets 3 to the 35 (Lynch)
2-7	M35	Kapp passes to Beasley, middle, 26 yards to KC39 – first down
1-10	K39	Osborn runs left tackle, gets 1 yard (Kearney)
2-9	K38	Kapp passes to Brown, right flat, for 1-yard loss (Mays)
3-10	K39	Kapp's pass for Beasley off his fingertips (Kearney)
4-10	K39	Lee punts out of bounds, KC17 (22-yard punt)

10:58 Kansas City

1-10	K17	Holmes runs left tackle for 3 yards (Hilgenberg)
2-7	K20	Dawson passes to Garrett, left side, 17 yards (Shareckman) – first down
1-10	K37	Holmes runs left guard, gets 3 (Page)
2-7	K40	Garrett at right guard for 4 yards (Larson)
3-3	K44	Dawson passes to Pitts, left side, 20 yards (Hilgenberg) – first down
1-10	M36	Dawson, back to pass, thrown for 8-yard loss (Winston)
2-18	M44	Garrett runs left tackle on draw for 3 yards (Page)
3-15	M41	Dawson's pass for Garrett, broken up (Page)
4-15	M41	Stenerud kicks 48-yard field goal

Chiefs 3, Vikings 0

Stenerud kicks off to the end of the end zone, no return (West).

6:17 Minnesota

1-10	M20	Brown gets 3 yards up middle, draw (Culp)
2-7	M23	Kapp, back to pass, thrown for 6-yard loss (Mays)
3-13	M17	Brown sweeps left for 10 yards (Buchanan)
4-3	M27	Lee punts to KC28, 45-yard punt. No return by Mitchell. But KC penalized 15 yards roughing the kicker – first down

1-10	M42	Kapp passes to Brown, right, 1 yard (Kearney)
2-9	M43	Kapp passes to Osborn, left, for 1 yard (Lynch)
3-8	M44	Kapp passes to Henderson, right, 6 yards (Marsalis, Kearney)
4-2	M50	Lee punts into the end zone (50-yard kick)

3:18 Kansas City

1-10	K20	Dawson passes to Pitts, middle, 20 yards (Krauss) – first down
1-10	K40	Dawson passes to Taylor, right flat, 9 yards (Krauss)
2-1	K49	Garrett runs left guard, 3 yards (Larson) – first down
1-10	M48	Garrett runs right tackle, gets 5 yards (Warwick)
2-5	M43	Holmes, on draw, loses 5 yards (Page)

END OF FIRST QUARTER

Chiefs 3, Vikings 0

Second Quarter

Kansas City

3-10	M48	Dawson pass to Pitts incomplete, pass interference call on Sharockman at the 31, 17-yard penalty – first down
1-10	M31	Dawson passes to Taylor, right, 7 yards (Mackbee)
2-3	M24	Holmes runs right guard, loses 1 (Winston)
3-4	M25	Dawson pass for Taylor broken up in end zone (Mackbee)
4-4	M25	Stenerud kicks 32-yard field goal.

Chiefs 6, Vikings 0

Stenerud kicks off to the 13, West returns 19 to the 32 (Dancy).

13:10 Minnesota

1-10	M32	Deborn runs left guard no gain (Culp)
2-10	M32	Kapp passes to Henderson 16 yards, fumbles, Robinson recovers and returns 2 yards to the Viking 46.

11:48 Kansas City

1-10	M46	Garrett loses 1 at right tackle (Page)
2-11	M47	Dawson's pass deep for Taylor intercepted by Krauss at 7, no return (Taylor)

11:09 Minnesota

1-10	M7	Osborn gets 3 at right guard (Buchanan)
2-7	M10	Kapp's long pass for Washington broken up (Thomas)
3-7	M10	Vikings penalized 5 yards, delay of game
3-12	M5	Kapp's long pass for Grim incomplete (Marsalis)
4-12	M5	Lee punts 39 yards to the 44, no return Garrett (Tingalhoff)

10:05 Kansas City

1-10	M44	Pitts sweeps right for 19 to the 25 (Mackbee) – first down
1-10	M25	Vikings penalized 5 yards, offside
1-5	M20	Dawson keeps at middle, no gain (Larson)
2-5	M20	Hayes gets 1 yard at left guard
3-4	M19	Hayes on left guard draw, gets 2 yards (Hilgenberg)
4-2	M17	Stenerud kicks 25-yard field goal.

Chiefs 9, Vikings 0

Stenerud kicks off to the 11, West fumbles, Prudhomme recovers for KC, 19-yard line.

7:21 Kansas City

1-10	M19	Dawson back to pass, loses 8 (Marshall)
2-18	M27	Hayes runs middle on draw, gains 13 (Winston)
3-5	M14	Dawson passes to Taylor right, 10 yards (Mackbee) – first down
1-G	M4	Garrett runs left center, loses 1 (Marshall)
2-G	M5	Dawson keeps at middle, no gain (Dickson)
3-G	M5	Garrett runs left guard, 5 yards and touchdown – first down

Stenerud, kick good (6 plays 19 yards)
Chiefs 16, Vikings 0

Stenerud kicks off to the 5, West returns 27 yards to the 32 (Prudhomme).

Minnesota

1-10	M32	Kapp passes to Henderson up middle, 27 yards (Prudhomme) – first down
1-10	K41	Kapp's pass for Reed incomplete (Lanier)
2-10	K41	Kapp, back to pass, sacked, loses 8 yards (Buchanan)
3-18	K49	Kapp's pass for Henderson broken up (Marsalis)
4-18	K49	56-yard field goal attempt is short, McVea returns 17 yards to 24 (Tingelhoff)

3:20 Kansas City

1-10	K24	McVea runs left guard, loses 1 (Warwick, Page)

2-11	K23	McVea runs right on pitchout, gains 2 (Page, Winston)
3-9	K25	(2:00) McVea sweeps right, 9 yards (Eller) – first down
1-10	K34	(1:33) Pitts sweeps right, end-around, 11 yards (Eller) – first down
1-10	K45	(1:27) Dawson passes to Taylor right, 3 yards (Mackbee)
2-7	K48	(1:00) Hayes runs middle, gets 3 yards (Warwick, Winston)
3-4	M49	(:49) Dawson's pass for McVea broken up (Hilgenberg)
4-4	M49	(:44) Wilson punts 34 yards to the 15, Grim fair catches, but KC penalized 5 yards, illegal procedure
4-9	M46	(:38) Wilson punts 36 yards, dead on the 10

:23 Minnesota

1-10	M10	Kapp's long pass for Washington incomplete (Thomas)
2-10	M10	(:06) Kapp keeps up middle, for 2 yards (Buchanan) as half ends.

END OF SECOND QUARTER

Chiefs 16, Vikings 0

Third Quarter

Cox kicks off to the end zone, 3 yards deep, Hayes returns 18 yards to 15 (Harris).

14:52 Kansas City

1-10	K15	McVea sweeps left for 5 yards (Marshall)
2-5	K20	Sawson passes to Taylor right, 6 yards (Mackbee) – first down
1-10	K26	Garrett gets 6 yards at right tackle (Winston)
2-4	K32	Hayes at right guard, loses 2 (Hilgenberg)
3-6	K30	Dawson passes left to Garrett, 8 yards (Sharockman) – first down
1-10	K38	Dawson pass for Richardson broken up by Mackbee
2-10	K38	Dawson passes to Hayes, screen left, 3 yards (Marshall)
3-7	K41	Dawson passes to Arbanas, 8 yards, but KC penalized 22 yds, holding
3-29	K19	Garrett sweeps left. center, gets 6 yards (Warwick)
4-23	K25	Wilson punts to the 20, West returns 11 yards, 55-yard punt

Minnesota

1-10	M31	Osborne gains nothing at left tackle (Culp)
2-10	M31	Kapp passes left to Beasley, 15 yards (Kearney) – first down

The reverse proved to be a big play for the Chiefs in Super Bowl IV. Frank Pitts, far right, with an escort from Ed Budde (no. 71), ripped the Minnesota defense three times for good yardage. Pitts' first down run in the third quarter set up Otis Taylor's touchdown reception two plays later. (Topeka Capital-Journal)

1-10	M46	Osborne runs right guard, gets 2 yards (Lanier, Buchanan)
2-8	M48	Kapp, back to pass, runs right center, 7 yards, (Bell, Lanier)
3-1	K45	Osborne runs left tackle, for 1 yard (Lanier, Kearney) – first down
1-10	K44	Brown at left guard, gets 8 yards (Bell)
2-2	K32	Kapp pases to Brown, left, 11 yards (Buchanan) – first down
1-10	K25	Kapp passes to Henderson, right, 9 yards (Marsalis)
2-1	K16	Kapp passes to Reed, left side, 12 yards (Kearney) – first down
1-g	K4	Osborne runs right tackle for 4 yards, touchdown

Cox, kick good (69 yards on 10 plays)
Chiefs 16, Vikings 7

Cox kicks off to KC 2-yard line, Hayes returns 16 yards to the 18 (Hackbart).

4:24 Kansas City

1-10	K18	Garrett runs left guard, gets 5 yards (Hilgenberg)
2-5	K23	Hayes runs draw, right guard for 6 yards (Warwick)– first down
1-10	K29	Garrett runs right guard for 4 yards (Hilgenberg)
2-6	K33	Dawson passes to Pitts left flat, 3 yards (Sharockman), but Chiefs penalized 5 yards, illegal procedure
2-11	K26	Hayes runs draw, right guard, for 4 yards (Warwick)
3-7	K32	Pitts sweeps right center for 7 yards (Mackbee) – first down
1-10	K39	Dawson overthrows Pitts long (Sharockman), but Vikings penalized 15 yards, personal foul – first down
1-10	M46	Dawson passes to Taylor on the Vikings 41, breaks 2 tackles and goes 46 yards for a touchdown.

Stenerud, kick good (82 yards on 6 plays)
Chiefs 23, Vikings 7

Stenerud kicks off to the 4, returned 33 yards to the 37 (Mitchell)

Minnesota

1-10	M37	Brown runs left tackle for 1 yard (Buchanan, Brown)
2-9	M38	Osborne for 9 yards (Marsalis) –first down third quarter ends

END OF THIRD QUARTER

Chiefs 23, Vikings 7

Fourth Quarter

Minnesota

1-10	M7	Osborn sweeps left center, for 4 yards (Lanier)
2-6	K49	Redd runs left guard, for 3 yards (Lanier)
3-3	K46	Kapp's pass for Beasley is intercepted by Lanier at the 34, returned 9 yards to the 43 (Vellone).

13:46 Kansas City

1-10	K43	Dawson's pass to Pitts, left, loses 7 (Sharockman)
2-17	K36	McVea runs left guard, gains 4 yards (Warwick, Winston)
3-13	K40	McVea sweeps left center on pitchout, gains 1 yard (Hilgenberg)
4-32	K41	Wilson punts 59 yards into end zone

11:29 Minnesota

1-10	M20	Kapp passes left to Reed, 2 yards, but Vikings penalized 10 yards, half-distance, illegal receiver downfield
1-20	M10	Kapp's long pass for Henderson incomplete (Margalis)
2-20	M10	Kapp passes to Henderson for 28 yards, right (Marsalis) – first down
1-10	M38	Kapp's pass for Beasley intercepted by Robinson for 9-yard return to 49 (Orin)

10:22 Kansas City

1-10	K49	McVea runs left center, 1-yard loss (Warwick)
2-11	K48	McVea sweeps left center for 4 yard gain (Sharockman)

3-7	M48	McVea runs left tackle, gets nothing (Hilgenberg)
4-7	M48	Wilson punts to the 12 – West returns 7 to the 19 (Belser) – 36-yard punt

7:52 Minnesota

1-10	M19	Kapp passes left to Washington, 9 yards (Thomas)
2-1	M28	Reed sweeps left center, loses 2 to the 26 (Brown)
3-3	M26	Kapp passes right to Reed, 4 yards (Bell) – first down
1-10	M30	Kapp, back to pass, loses 13 (Brown), fumbles, Vellone recovers
2-23	M17	(Cuozzo quarterbacking) Reed runs right guard for 15 yards (Thomas)
3-8	M32	Cuozzo passes to Henderson, middle, 16 yards (Kearney) – first down
1-10	M48	4:15 Cuozzo overthrows Washington out of bounds
2-10	M48	Cuozzo's pass for Henderson intercepted by Thomas at 28, returned 6 to the Chiefs 34 (Brown)

4:00 Kansas City

1-10	K34	Dawson back to pass, sweeps left center for 11 yards (Hilgenberg) – first down
1-10	K45	Hayes runs left tackle, loses 1 yard (Warwick)
2-11	K44	McVea runs right center, no gain (Winston)
3-11	K44	(2:00) Dawson, back to pass, runs right center, loses 4 (Eller), but Vikings are penalized 15 yards, personal foul – first down
1-10	M45	(1:53) McVea runs left center, gains 4 yards (Marshall)
2-6	M41	(1:10) (Livingston quarterbacking) – Hayes runs left tackle, gain 4 yards (Warwick)
3-2	M37	(:30) Holmes runs right tackle for 6 yards (Warwick) as clock runs out.

Final Score: Chiefs 23, Vikings 7

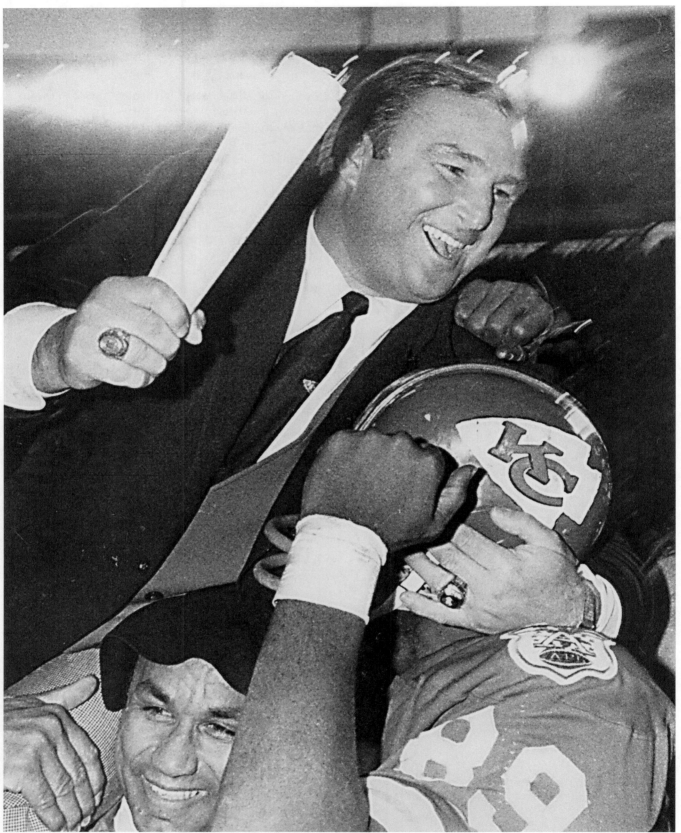

The victor! Hank Stram receives a ride off the field after the Chiefs defeated Minnesota to win Super Bowl IV. (Bettmann/CORBIS)

KANSAS CITY CHIEFS
All-Time Draft Selections

1960 AFL Draft

November 22, 1959 (First Selections)
December 2, 1959 (Second Selections)

When the AFL held its first draft, half of the teams still didn't have complete front offices or coaching staffs in place. In an effort to make the draft fair for all eight teams, the scouting reports and talent evaluations from each club were made available to all franchises. Each team received a territorial pick that would grant the rights of a local or regional college star that would not only be a main component of the team, but also to help gain recognition and sell tickets in the team's area. The Texans' territorial pick was SMU quarterback Don Merridith.

After the territorial picks were completed, the remaining top eight players at each position were selected and then drawn from a box by each club. At the time, most players still played both offense and defense; only the offensive positions were used. This process was used until a full 33 rounds, os selections, had been made by each club.

To increase each team's initial base of players, a second draft was held ten days later using the same system as before. Each team received and 20 playeers. In each draft, the players are listed aphabetically, not in the order they were chosen.

First Selections

Jack Atcheson, E, Western Illinois; George Boone, T, Kentucky; **Chris Burford, E, Stanford;** Earl Ray Butler, T, North Carolina; Gail Cogdill, E, Washington State; James Crotty, HB, Notre Dame; Gary Ferguson, T, Southern Methodist; Tom Glynn, C, Boston College; Gene Gossage, T, Northwestern; Jim Heineke, T, Wisconsin; William Jerry, T/G, South Carolina; John Kapele, T, Brigham Young; Louis Kelley, RB, New Mexico State; Gilmer Lewis, T/G, Oklahoma; John Malmberg, T/G, Knox College; Arvie Martin, C, Texas Christian; Don Meredith, QB, Southern Methodist; Tom Moore, HB, Vanderbilt; Ola Murchison, E, Pacific; Bob Nelson, C, Wisconsin; Jim Norton, E, Idaho; Warren Rabb, QB, Louisiana State; Howard Ringwood, HB, Brigham Young; **Johnny Robinson, HB, Louisiana State;** John Saunders, FB, Kentucky; Glenn Shaw, FB, Kentucky; Gordon Speer, HB, Rice; Jack Stone, G, Oregon; Marvin Terrell, G, Mississippi; Emery Turner, G, Purdue; Joe Vader, E, Kansas State; Carroll Zaruba, HB, Nebraska.

Second Selections

Grady Alderman, T/G, Detroit; Herman Alexander, T/G, Findlay (Ohio); Taz Anderson, HB, Georgia Tech; Jim Beaver, T/G, Florida; *Bill Beck, T/G, Gustavus Adolphus; Gary Campbell, HB, Whittier (Calif.); Vernon Cole, QB, North Texas State; Toby Deese, T/G, Georgia Tech; Carl Dumbald, T/G, West Virginia; Charles Elizey, C, Southern Mississippi; Tom Gates, HB, San Bernardino (Calif.); Austin Gonsoulin, HB, Baylor; Clark Holden, HB, Southern California; [MARK: first name not listed] DeWitt, T/G, Georgia; Bill Thompson, C, Georgia; Billy Tranum, E, Arkan-sas; Jim Vickers, E, Georgia; Larry Ward, E, Lamar Tech; Paul Winslow, HB, North Carolina College; *Doug Pat Brown, T/G, Fresno State.

1961 AFL Draft

Jerry Mays (Kansas Collection, U. of Kansas)

November 23, 1960 (Rounds 1-6)
December 5 (Rounds 7-30)

The AFL used the same draft format as the NFL for the first time—teams selected in an inverse order of finish in the standings. Also, each team was allowed to protect two players within its geographical territory the first two rounds, again to help with fan recognition and ticket sales.

1. ***E.J. Holub, C, Texas Tech***
2. Bob Lilly, T, Texas Christian
3. Jim Tyrer, T, Ohio State
4. Claude Mooman, E, Duke
5. ***Jerry Mays, DT, Southern Methodist***
6. Choice to Los Angeles.
7. ***Fred Arbanas, TE, Michigan State***
8. *John O'Day, T, Miami*
9. Dick Mills, T, Pittsburgh
10. Jerry Daniels, E, Mississippi
11. Marvin Tibbetts, HB, Georgia Tech
12. *Paul Hynes, HB, Louisiana Tech*
13. Glynn Gregory, HB, Southern Methodist
14. ***Curtis McClinton, RB, Kansas***
15. *Roy Lee Rambo, G, Texas Christian*
16. Aaron Thomas, E, Oregon State
17. *Jarrell Williams, HB, Arkansas*
18. Ron Hartline, RB, Oklahoma
19. *Frank Jackson, HB, Arkansas*
20. *Bob Lane, E, Baylor*
21. *Dick Thornton, QB, Northwestern*
22. *Ed Sharockman, HB, Pittsburgh*
23. *Lou Zivkovich, T, New Mexico State*
24. Pat Dye, G, Georgia
25. Pay Ramsey, QB, Adams State
26. *Danny House, HB, Davidson*
27. Bob Schloredt, QB, Washington

28. Bill Stine, G, Michigan
29. *Lonnie Caddell, RB, Rice
30. *Cedric Price, E, Kansas State*

1962 AFL Draft

December 2, 1961 (Rounds 1-25)
December 16 (Rounds 26-34)
   Two days after the AFL held its draft, the NFL held its draft, which included many players not chosen by the AFL teams. To emain competitive with the NFL, the AFL held a second draft, rounds 26-34, to choose future picks.
1. Ronnie Bull, HB, Baylor
2. *Bill Miller, E, Miami (Fla.)*
3. *Eddie Wilson, QB, Arizona*
4a. Charles Hinton, T, North Carolina College
4b. Irv Goode, C, Kentucky
5a. Bobby Plummer, T, Texas Christian
5b. *Bobby Ply, QB, Baylor*
6. Al Hinton, T, Iowa
7. No choice
8. Larry Bowie, T, Purdue
9. Marshall Shirk, T, UCLA
10. *James Saxton, HB, Texas*
11. **Bobby Hunt, QB, Auburn**
12a. Guy Reese, T, Southern Mississippi
12b. Bobby Lee Thompson, HB, Arizona
14. *Bookie Bolin, G, Mississippi
15. *Dave Graham, E, Virginai
16. Pettis Norman, E, Johnson C. Smith
17. **Tommy Brooker, E/K, Alabama**
18. Joe Carollo, T, Notre Dame
19. Lee Welch, HB, Mississippi
20. Mike Samcheski, G, Lehigh
21. *Kent Martin, T, Wake Forest*
22. *Jim Bernhardt, T, Linfield (Ore)*
23. *Russ Foret, T, Georgia Tech*
24. Pat Trammell, QB, Alabama
25. John Burrell, E, Rice
26. *Walt Rappold, QB, Duke*

1963 AFL Draft

Buck Buchanan (Kansas Collection, U. of Kansas)

Decmeber 1, 1962
1a. (from Oakland) **Buck Buchanan, DT, Grambling**
1b. **Ed Budde, G, Michigan State**
2. Walter Rock, T, Maryland
3. Don Brumm, T, Purdue
4. Daryl Sanders, G, Ohio State
5. John Campbell, E, Minnesota
6. Choice to Buffalo.
7. **Bobby Bell, LB, Minnesota**
8. John Sklopan, HB, Southern Mississippi
9. Jan Barrett, E, Fresno State
10. *Curt Farrier, T, Montana State*
11a. (from Oakland) Ron Goodwin, HB, Baylor
11b. **Jerrel Wilson, P, Southern Mississippi**
12. Choice to New York
13. Choice to Houston
14a. (from Oakland) *Stone Johnson, HB, Grambling*
14b. *Preacher Pilot, HB, New Mexico State*
15. *Joe Auer, HB, Georgia Tech*
16. Mel Profit, E, UCLA
17. Billy Moore, QB, Arkansas
18. *Bill Freeman, T, Southern Mississippi*
19. Bruce Starling, HB, Florida
20. *Lowell Vaught, T, SW Louisiana*
21. *Ernie Boghetti, T, Pittsburgh*
22. *John Maczuzak, T, Pittsburgh*
23. Bob Yaksick, HB, Rutgers
24. **Dave Hill, T, Auburn**
25. *John Hughes, LB, Southern Methodist

1964 AFL Draft

November 30, 1963
1. *Pete Beathard, QB, Southern California*
2. Billy Martin, E, Georgia Tech
3. Ken Kortas, T, Louisville
4. **Ed Lothamer, T, Michigan State**
5. Choice to Buffalo.
6a. (from Buffalo) Duke Carlisle, DB, Texas
6b. Joe Don Looney, RB, Oklahoma
7. John Simon, E, Notre Dame
8. Hal Bledsole, WR, Southern California
9. Tony Dimidio, T, West Chester State
10. Clay Stephens, E, Notre Dame
11. Tommy Crutcher, LB, Texas Christian
12. Jake Adams, E, Virginia Tech
13a. (from Houston) Orville Hudson, C, East Texas State
13b. Jay Wilkinson, HB, Duke

1964 AFL Redshirt Draft

1. Paul Costa, HB, Notre Dame
2. Jim Snowden, HB, Notre Dame
3. Roger Staubach, QB, Navy
4. Jack Peterson, T, Omaha
5. Jerry Knoll, T, Washington

6. *Jerry Lamb, E, Arkansas*
7a. (from Denver) Bob Hohn, HB, Nebraska
7b. Sandy Sands, E, Texas
8. Bob Burrows, T, East Texas State
9. Dick Evers, T, Colorado State
10. *Bud Abell, E, Missouri*
11. Robert Young, T, Howard Payne
12. Jerry McClurg, T, Colorado
13. Phil Zera, HB, St. Joseph's

1965 AFL Draft

*Frank Pitts, Otis Taylor and Gloster Richardson
(Topeka Capital-Journal)*

November 28, 1964
1. Gale Sayers, RB, Kansas
2a. (from Buffalo) Jack Chapple, G, Stanford
2b. *Ron Caveness, LB, Arkansas*
3. Mike Curtis, LB, Duke
4a. **(from Buffalo) Otis Taylor, WR, Prairie View**
4b. **Frank Pitts, WR, Southern**
5. Smith Reed, HB, Alcorn A&M
6. *Mickey Sutton, DB, Auburn*
7. **Gloster Richardson, WR, Jackson State**
8. *Danny Thomas, QB/K, Southern Methodist*
9. Joe Ceme, C, Northwestern
10. *Bob Howard, DB, Stanford*
11. *Al Piriano, T, Wisconsin*
12. *Mike Cox, LB, Iowa State*
13. *Robert Bonds, DB, San Jose State*
14. *Fred Dotson, DB, Wiley*
15. Dave Powless, B, Illinios
16. Stan Irvine, T, Colorado
17. Don Croftcheck, LB, Indiana
18. Jerry Smith, TE, Arizona State
19. Mike Alford, C, Auburn
20. Bill Symons, HB, Colorado

1965 AFL Redshirt Draft

November 28, 1964
This was a separate 12-round draft for future player considerations.
1. *Alphonse Dotson, DT, Grambling*
2. Frank Cornish, DT, Grambling
3. Henry Carr, WR, Arizona State
4. Steve Cox, T, South Carolina

5. John Thomas, E, Southern California
6. John Wilbur, G, Stanford
7. Bill Moore, HB, Mississippi State
8. Roosevelt Ellerbe, DB, Iowa State

1966 AFL Draft

Mike Garrett (Kansas Collection, U. of Kansas)

November 28, 1965
1. **Aaron Brown, DE, Minnesota**
2. *Francis Peay, T, Missouri*
3. Walt Barnes, T, Nebraska
4. *Elijah Gipson, HB, Bethune-Cookman*
5. Doug Van Horn, G, Ohio State
6. John Osmond, C, Tulsa
7. Charles Gogolak, K, Princeton
8. *Fletcher Smith, DB, South Carolina State*
9. Dick Smith, DB, Northwestern
10. *Fred Dawston, DB, South Carolina State*
11. *Willie Ray Smith, WR, Kansas*
12. Bill Bonds, DB, McMurry
13. *Wayne Walker, K, NW Louisiana*
14. Charles Harraway, RB, San Jose State
15. Bruce Van Dyke, G, Missouri
16. Tom Barington, RB, Ohio State
17. Walt Garrison, RB, Oklahoma State
18. Hal Seymour, DB, Florida
19. Bob Dunlevy, E, West Virginia
20. **Mike Garrett, RB, Southern California**

1966 AFL Redshirt Draft

November 28, 1965
1. George Youngblood, DB, Cal State Los Angeles
2. Robert Tickens, T, Nebraska
3. **Jan Stenerud, K, Montana State**
4. Dan Berry, HB, California
5. Lynn Senkbell, LB, Nebraska
6. Kick Reding, DB, NW Louisiana
7. Dill Ogle, T, Stanford
8. *Mel Myricks, DB, Washburn*

1967 Draft

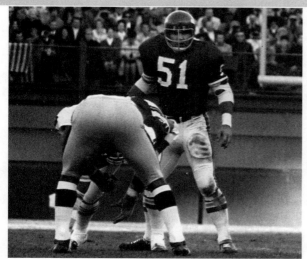

Jim Lynch (Kansas Collection, U. of Kansas)

March 14, 1967

This was the first combined AFL-NFL draft.

1. Gene Trosch, DT, Miami
2a. **Jim Lynch, LB, Notre Dame**
2b. **Willie Lanier, LB, Morgan State**
3. **Billy Masters, TE, Louisiana State**
4. Ron Zememann, G, East Texas State
5. Choice to Buffalo for previous considerations.
6. Noland Smith, KR/WR, Tennessee State
7. Richard Erickson, G, Stout State
8. Thomas Altmeier, T, Luther
9. Ed Pope, DT, Jackson State
10. Choice to Houston for Wayne Frazier.
11. William Braswell, G, Auburn
12a. Richard Kolowski, G, Wake Forest
12b. Kent Iashley, WR, Oklahoma State
13. Lenwood Simmons, RB, Edward Waters
14. John Bishop, G, Delta State
15. Denny Capponi, HB, Xavier
16. Charlie Noggle, QB, North Carolina State
17. David Lattin, TE, Texas Western

1968 Draft

January 30 & 31, 1968

1a. **Maurice (Mo) Moorman, G, Texas A&M**
1b. **George Daney, G, Texas-El Paso**
2. **Mike Livingston, QB, Southern Methodist**
3. Choice to Denver for Curley Culp.
4. Mickey McCarty, TE, Texas Christian
5. Choice to Buffalo for Remi Prudhomme.
6. Choice to Cincinnati in expansion draft.
7. Sam Grezaffi, DB, Louisiana State
8. Lindon Endsley, DE, North Texas State
9. Mac McClure, LB, Mississippi
10. Jack Gehrke, QB, Utah
11. Tom Mosewicz, DE, Tulane
12. Bobby Johns, DB, Alabama
13. Jim Kavanagh, WR, Boston College

14. **Robert Holmes, RB, Southern**
15. Bill Chambless, C, Miami (Fla.)
16. Pat Talburt, T, SW Missouri State
17. Wesley Williams, RB, Texas Southern

1969 Draft

Jim Marsalis (Kansas Collection, U. of Kansas)

January 28 & 29, 1969

1. **Jim Marsalis, CB, Tennessee State**
2. **Ed Podolak, RB, Iowa**
3. **Morris Stroud, TE, Clark (Ga.)**
4. **Jack Rudnay, C, Northwestern**
5. Bob Stein, LB, Minnesota
6. John Pleasant, RB, Alabama State
7. Tom Nettles, WR, San Diego State
8a. Clanton King, T, Purdue
8b. Maurice LeBlanc, RB, Louisiana State
9. Dan Klepper, G, Nebraska-Omaha
10. John Sponheimer, DE, Cornell
11. Skip Wupper, TE, C.W. Post
12. John Lavin, LB, Notre Dame
13. Rick Piland, G, Virginia Tech
14. Al Bream, CB, Iowa
15. Leland Wilson, T, Rice
16. Uriel Johnson, CB, Prairie View
17. Ralph Jenkins, CB, Tuskegee

1970 Draft

January 27 & 28, 1970

1. Sid Smith, T, Southern California
2. Clyde Werner, LB, Washington
3a. Billy Bob Barnett, DE, Texas A&M
3b. David Hadley, CB, Alcorn A&M
4. Choice to Cincinatti for Warren McVea.
5. Mike Oriard, C, Notre Dame
6. Robert Hews, DT/DE, Princeton
7. Clyde Glosson, WR, Texas-El Paso
8. Fred Barry, CB, Boston University
9. Charley Evans, TE, Texas Tech
10. Bob Stankovich, G, Arkansas
11. Bil O'Neal, RB, Grambling
12. Rodney Fedorchak, G, Pittsburgh
13. Troy Patridge, DE, Texas-Arlington

14. Glenn Dumoni, RB, American International
15. Bob Liggett, DT, Nebraska
16. Randy Ross, LB, Kansas State
17. Rayford Jenkins, S, Alcorn A&M

1971 Draft

January 28 & 29, 1971
1. **Elmo Wright, WR, Houston**
2a. **Wilbur Young, DT, William Penn**
2b. Scott Lewis, DE, Grambling
3. Choice to Cleveland for Marvin Upshaw.
4. David Robinson, TE, Jacksonville State
5. Mike Adamie, RB, Northwestern
6. **Kerry Reardon, CB, Iowa**
7. Choice to New Orleans for Jim Otis.
8a. **Mike Sensibaugh, S, Ohio State**
8b. Rick Telander, S, Northwestern
9. Alvin Hawes, T, Minnesota
10. Bruce Jankowski, WR, Ohio State
11. Nate Allen, CB, Texas Southern
12. Tony Esposito, RB, Pittsburgh
13. Chuck Hixson, QB, Southern Methodist
14. Bruce Bergey, TE, UCLA
15. Mike Montgomery, CB/S, SW Texas State
16. Darrell Jansonius, G, Iowa State

1972 Draft

February 1 & 2, 1972
1. **Jeff Kinney, RB, Nebraska**
2. Choice to New England for pervious considerations.
3. Choice to Houston for Willie Frazier.
4a. Andy Hamilton, WR, Louisiana State
4b. Choice to New Orleans for Charles Williams.
5. Milton Davis, DE/LB, Texas-Arlington
6. John Kahler, DT, Long Beach State
7. Dean Carlson, QB, Iowa State
8. Scott Mahoney, G, Colorado
9. Dave Taylor, T, Weber State
10. Richard Ruppert, T, Hawaii
11. Elbert Walker, T, Wisconsin
12. Mike Williams, DT, Oregon
13. Tyler Hellams, DB, South Carolina
14. Dave Chaney, LB, San Jose State
15. Larry Marshall, DB, Maryland
16. Bob Johnson, DE, Hanover
17. Ted Washington, LB, Mississippi Valley

1973 Draft

January 30 & 31, 1973
1. Choice to Chicago for George Seals.
2a. Gary Butler, TE, Rice
2b. Choice to Los Angeles for Willie Ellison.
3. Paul Krause, T/G, Central Michigan

4a. John Lohmeyer, DE, Emporia State
4b. Choice to Los Angeles for Pete Beathard.
5. Fred Grambau, DE, Michigan
6. Doug Jones, DB, San Fernando Valley State
7. Donn Smith, C, Purdue
8. Al Palewicz, LB, Miami (Fla.)
9. Bill Story, G, Southern Illinois
10. Willie Osley, CB, Illinois
11. Choice nullified.
12. Tom Ramsey, DT, Northern Arizona
13. Paul Mettallo, CB, Massachusetts
14. Albert White, WR, Fort Valley State
15. Choice to Buffalo for pervious considerations.
16. Wilbur Grooms, LB, Tampa
17. Clayton Korver, DE/TE, Southern Methodist

1974 Draft

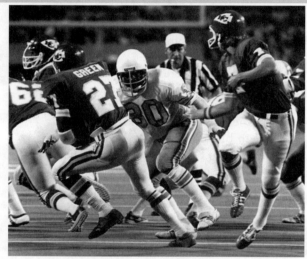

Woody Green (Kansas Collection, U. of Kansas)

January 29 & 30, 1974
1. **Woody Green, RB, Arizona State**
2. **Charlie Getty, T, Penn State**
3. Dave Jaynes, QB, Kansas
4. **Matt Herkenhoff, T, Minnesota**
5. Choice to N.Y. Giants for Wayne Walton.
6. Jay Washington, RB, Clemson
7. LeRoy Hegge, DE, South Dakota (Springfield)
8. Choice to N.Y. Jets for Gerry Philbin
9. J.J. Jennings, RB, Rutgers
10. **Tom Condon, G, Boston College**
11. Bob Thornbladh, RB, Michigan
12. Carl Brown, WR, West Texas State
13. Norm Romagnoli, LB, Kentucky State
14. Frank Pomarico, G, Notre Dame
15. Lem Burnham, LB, U.S. International
16. Barry Beers, G, William & Mary
17. Dave Langner, KR, Auburn

1975 Draft

January 28 & 29, 1975
1. Choice to Houston for John Matuszak.
2. Elmore Stephens, TE, Kentucky
3. Cornelius Walker, DT, Rice
4. Choice to Denver for Tom Graham.
5. Choice to Los Angeles for Jim Nicholson.
6a. Morris LaGrand, RB, Tampa
6b. Dave Wasick, DE, San Jose State
7. Choice to Houston for Bill Thomas.
8a. Choice to Pittsburgh for Barry Pearson.
8b. Wayne Hoffman, T, Oklahoma
9. Choice to Cleveland for Bob Briggs.
10. Choice to Denver for Tom Drougas.
11. Dale Hegland, G, Minnesota
12. James Rackley, RB, Florida A&M
13. John Snider, LB, Stanford
14. Gene Moshler, G, Vanderbilt
15. Choice to Pittsburgh for Tom Keating.
16. Mark Petersen, DE, Illinois
17. Mike Bulino, S, Pittsburgh

1976 Draft

Henry Marshall (Alan Barzee)

April 8 & 9, 1976
1. Rod Walters, G, Iowa
2. Cliff Frazier, DT, UCLA
3a. **Keith Simons, DT, Minnesota**
3b. Choice to Green Bay for MacArthur Lane.
3c. **Gary Barbaro, S, Nicholls State**
3d. **Henry Marshall, WR, Missouri**
4. Choice to Cincinnati for Ken Avery.
5a. **Willie Lee, DT, Bethune-Cookman**
5b. Jimbo Elrod, LB, Oklahoma
6a. Steve Taylor, CB, Kansas
6b. Bob Gregolunas, LB, Northern Illinois
6c. Calvin Harper, T, Illinois State
7. Rod Wellington, RB, Iowa

8. Orrin Olsen, C, Brigham Young
9. **Tim Collier, CB, East Texas State**
10. **Whitney Paul, DE, Colorado**
11. Bob Squires, TE, Hastings
12. Harold Porter, WR, SW Louisiana
13. Joe Bruner, QB, NE Louisiana
14. Rick Thurman, T, Texas
15. **Dave Rozumek, LB, New Hampshire**
16. Dennis Anderson, DB/P, Arizona
17. Pat McNeil, RB, Baylor

1977 Draft

May 3 & 4, 1977
1. **Gary Green, CB, Baylor**
2. **Tony Reed, RB, Colorado**
3. **Thomas Howard, LB, Texas Tech**
4a. **Mark Bailey, RB, Cal State Long Beach**
4b. **Tony Samuels, TE, Bethune-Cookman**
4c. Darlus Helton, G, North Carolina Central
4d. **Eric Harris, DB, Memphis State**
5. Choice to Pittsburgh for Tommy Reamon.
6a. Rick Burleson, DE, Texas
6b. Andre Herrera, RB, Southern Illinois
7. Chris Golub, S, Kansas
8a. Ron Olsonoski, LB, College of St. Thomas
8b. Waddell Smith, WR, Kansas
9a. Derrick Glanton, DE, Bishop
9b. Dave Green, T, New Mexico
10. Mark Vitali, QB, Purdue
11. Maurice Mitchell, WR, Northern Michigan
12. Raymond Burks, LB, UCLA

1978 Draft

May 2 & 3, 1978
1. **Art Still, DE, Kentucky**
2. **Sylvester Hicks, DT/DE, Tennessee**
3. **Gary Spani, LB, Kansas State**
4a. Danny Johnson, LB, Tennessee State
4b. Pete Woods, QB, Missouri
5a. Jerrold McRae, WR, Tennessee State
5b. Dwight Carey, DT, Texas-Arlington
5c. Robert Woods, WR/KR, Grambling
6. Choice to Chicago with 5d choice for 4b choice.
7a. Ricky Odom, DB, Southern California
7b. Bill Kellar, WR, Stanford
8. John Henry White, RB, Louisiana Tech\
9. Larry Brown, T, Miami (Fla.)
10. Earl Bryant, DE/DT, Jackson State
11. Ray Milo, S, New Mexico State
12. Willie Brock, C, Colorado

1979 Draft

Mike Bell (Kansas Collection, U. of Kansas)

May 3 & 4, 1979
1a. **Mike Bell, DE, Colorado State**
1b. **Steve Fuller, QB, Clemson**
2. Choice for Houston for Steve Fuller.
3. Choice to L.A. Rams for Stan Johnson.
4. **Frank Manumaleuga, LB, San Jose State**
5. Earl Grant, RB, Missouri
6. Robert Gaines, WR, Washington
7. **Ken Kremer, DE, Ball State**
8a. **Mike Williams, RB, New Mexico**
8b. Robert Brewer, G, Temple
9a. James, Folston, TE, Clemson
9b. Joe Robinson, T, Ohio State
10a. Michael DuPree, LB, Florida
10b. Gerald Jackson, S, Mississippi State
10c. Larry Willis, WR, Alcorn State
11. Stan Rome, WR, Clemson
12. Michael Forrest, RB, Arkansas

1980 Draft

Carlos Carson (Alan Barzee)

April 29 & 30, 1980
1. **Brad Budde, G, USC**
2. Choice to Houston for Steve Fuller.
3. **James Hadnot, RB, Texas Tech**
4. Dave Klug, LB, Concordia
5a. **Carlos Carson, WR, Louisiana State**
5b. Dan Pensick, DE, Nebraska
5c. Choice to Detroit for Larry Tearry

6a. Bubba Garcia, WR, Texas-El Paso
6b. Larry Heater, RB, Arizona
7. Choice to L.A. Rams with Walter White for '80 6b choice and '81 third-round choice.
8. Sam Stepney, LB, Boston University
9. Tom Donovan, WR, Penn State
10. Rob Martinovich, T, Notre Dame
11. Dale Markham, NT, North Dakota
12. Mike Brewington, LB, East Carolina

1981 Draft

Willie Scott (Kansas Collection, U. of Kansas)

April 28 & 29, 1981
1. **Willie Scott, TE, South Carolina**
2. **Joe Delaney, RB, NW Louisiana**
3a. Marvin Harvey, TE, Southern Mississippi
3b. Roger Taylor, T, Oklahoma State
3c. **Lloyd Burruss, DB, Maryland**
4. Ron Washington, WR, Arizona State
5. Todd Thomas, T/C, North Dakota
6. Dock Luckie, NT, Florida
7. **Billy Jackson, RB, Alabama**
8. David Dorn, WR, Rutgers
9. Tony Vereen, DB, SE Louisiana
10. Les Studdard, G, Texas
11. Frank Case, DE, Penn State
12. Bob Gagliano, QB, Utah State

1982 Draft

April 27 & 28, 1982
1. **Anthony Hancock, WR, Tennessee**
2. **Calvin Daniels, LB, North Carolina**
3. Choice to St. Louis for exchange for first-round positions.
4a. Louis Haynes, LB, North Texas State
4b. Stuart Sheridan, LB, Virginia
5. Del Thompson, RB, Texas-El Paso
6. Durwood Roquemore, S, Texas A&I
7. Greg Smith, NT, Kansas
8. Case deBrujin, WR, Miami (Fla.)
9. Lyndie Byford, T, Oklahoma
10. Larry Brodsky, WR, Miami (Fla.)
11. Bob Carter, CB, Arizona
12. Mike Miller, S, SW Texas State

1983 Draft

Todd Blackledge (14) (Kansas Collection, U. of Kansas)

April 26 & 27, 1983
1. **Todd Blackledge, QB, Penn State**
2. **David Lutz, T, Georgia Tech**
3. **Albert Lewis, CB, Grambling**
4. Ron Wetzel, TE, Arizona State
5. **Jim Arnold, P, Vanderbilt**
6. Ellis Gardner, T, Georgia Tech
7a. Ken Thomas, RB, San Jose State
7b. Daryl Posey, RB, Mississippi College
8. **Irv Eatman, T, UCLA**
9. Adam Lingner, C, Illinois
10. Mark Shumate, NT, Wisconsin
11. Dwayne Jackson, DE, South Carolina State College
12. Kenny Jones, T, Tennessee

1984 Draft

Bill Maas (Kansas Collection, U. of Kansas)

May 1 & 2, 1984
1a. **Bill Maas, NT, Pittsburgh**
1b. **John Alt, T, Iowa**
2. **Scott Radecic, LB, Penn State**
3. **Herman Heard, RB, Southern Colorado**
4. Mark Robinson, S, Penn State
5a. Eric Holle, DE, Texas
5b. Jeff Paine, LB, Texas A&M
6. Rufus Stevens, WR, Grambling
7. **Kevin Ross, CB, Temple**
8. Randy Clark, S, Florida

John Alt (Alan Barzee)

9a. **Scott Auer, G/T, Michigan State**
9b. Dave Hestera, TE, Colorado
10. Al Wenglikowski, LB, Pittsburgh
11. Bobby Johnson, RB, San Jose State
12. Mark Lang, LB, Texas

1984 Supplemental Draft

June 5, 1984

A supplemental draft was held for players who were eligible for the NFL, but were contracted to another league (USFL). This draft gave NFL teams the selected players should they ever become free agents.
1. Mark Adickes, T, Baylor
2. Lupe Sanchez, DB, UCLA
3. Garcia Lane, DB, Ohio State

1985 Draft

April 30 & May 1, 1985
1. Ethan Horton, RB, North Carolina
2. **Jonathan Hayes, TE, Iowa**
4. **Bob Olderman, G, Virginia**
5. **Bruce King, RB, Purdue**
6. John Bostic, CB, Bethune-Cookman
7a. Vincent Thompson, DE, Missouri Western
7c. Choice to Washington for undisclosed '86 choice.
8. Ira Hillary, WR, Southern California
9. Mike Armentrout, S, Southwest Missouri
10. Jeff Smith, RB, Nebraska
11. Chris Jackson, C, Southern Methodist
12. Harper LeBel, C, Colorado State
Choices 5b and 6b sent to Houston in Bob Hamm trade.

1986 Draft

April 29 & 30, 1986
1. Brian Jozwiak, T, West Virginia
2. **Dino Hackett, LB, Appalachian State**
3. **Leonard Griffin, DE, Grambling**
4a. **Tom Baugh, C, Southern Illinois**
4b. Chas Fox, WR, Furman
5. Choice to San Diego in '83 Bob Rush Trade.
6a. Ken Hagood, RB, South Carolina
6b. Choice to Washington for Rick Donnalley.
7. Choice to Cleveland for Boyce Green.
8. **Lewis Colbert, P, Auburn**
9. Gary Baldinger, NT/DE, Wake Forest
10. Isaac Readon, NT, Hampton Institute
11. **Aaron Pearson, LB, Mississippi State**
12. Traded to Buffalo in 8th-round transaction.

1987 Draft

April 28 & 29, 1987
1. **Paul Palmer, RB, Temple**
2. **Christian Okoye, RB, Azusa Pacific**
3. Todd Howard, LB, Texas A&M
4. Choice to Houston in second-round trade.
5. Kitrick Taylor, WR/KR, Washington State
6. Choice to Houston in '86 Larry Moriarity trade.
7. Doug Hudson, QB, Nicholls State
8. Michael Clemons, RB/KR, William & Mary
9. Randy Watts, DE, Catawba
10. James Evans, RB, Southern University
11. Craig, Richardson, WR/KR, Eastern Washington
12. Bruce Holmes, LB, Minnesota

1988 Draft

April 24 & 25, 1988
1. **Neil Smith, DE, Nebraska**
2. Choice to Detroit in first-round trade.
3. **Kevin Porter, DB, Auburn**
4. J.R. Ambrose, WR, Mississippi
5. Traded to New Orleans for Jack Del Rio in '87.
6. James Saxon, RB, San Jose State
7. Troy Stedman, LB, Washburn
8. **Alfredo Roberts, TE, Miami (Fla.)**
9. Azizuddin Abdur-Ra'oof, WR, Maryland
10. Kenny Gamble, RB, Colgate
11. Danny McManus, QB, Florida State
12. Traded to Buffalo for Charles Romes in '87

1989 Draft

Derrick Thomas (Alan Barzee)

April 23 & 24, 1989
1. **Derrick Thomas, LB, Alabama**
2. Mike Elkins, QB, Wake Forest
3. Naz Worthen, WR, North Carolina State
4. Stan Petry, CB, TCU
5. Choice to Cleveland for LB Mike Junkin.
6. **Robb Thomas, WR, Oregon State**
7. Ron Sancho, LB, Louisiana State
8a. Bryan Tobey, RB, Grambling
8b. Todd McNair, RB, Temple
9. Jack Phillips, S, Alcorn State
10. Rob McGovern, LB, Holy Cross
11. Marcus Turner, CB, UCLA
12. **Bill Jones, RB, Southwest Texas State**
Obtained 8b from Buffalo in '88 Art Still trade.

1990 Draft

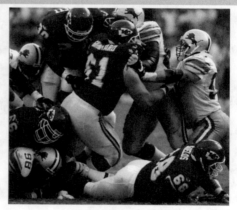

Tim Grunhard (Alan Barzee)

April 22 & 23, 1990
1. **Percy Snow, LB, Michigan State**
2. **Tim Grunhard, C, Notre Dame**
3. Choice to Dallas in '89 Steve Pelluer trade.
4. Fred Jones, WR, Grambling
5a. **Derrick Graham, T, Appalachian State**
5b. Ken Hackemack, DT, Texas

6. Tom Sims, DT, Pittsburgh
7. **David Szott, G, Penn State**
8. Choice to Buffalo in '88 Art Still trade.
9. Michael Owens, RB, Syracuse
10. Craig Hudson, LB, Wisconsin
11. Ernest Thompson, RB, Georgia Southern
12. Tony Jeffery, WR, San Jose State
Obtained 5b from Buffalo in '88 Art Still trade.

1991 Draft

April 21 & 22, 1991
1. Harvey Wiliams, RB, Louisiana State
2. Joe Valerio, T, Pennsylvania
3. **Tim Barnett, WR, Jackson State**
4. Choice to Dallas in '89 Steve Pelluer trade.
5. **Charles Mincy, DB, Washington**
6. Darrell Malone, DB, Jacksonville State
7. Bernard Ellison, CB, Nevada
8. Tom Dohring, T, Michigan
9. Robbie Keen, P/K, California
10. Eric Ramsey, DB, Auburn
11. Bobby Olive, WR, Ohio State
12. Ron Shipley, G/T, New Mexico

1992 Draft

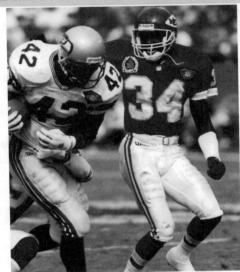

Dale Carter (Alan Barzee)

April 26 & 27, 1992
1. **Dale Carter, DB/KR, Tennessee**
2. Matt Blundin, QB, Virginia
3. Choice to Dallas in second-round trade.
4. Mike Evans, DT, Michigan
5. Traded to Tampa Bay for Ervin Randle in '91.
6. Tony Smith, WR, Notre Dame
7. Erick Anderson, LB, Michigan
8. Jim Jennings, G/C, San Diego State
9. Jay Leeuwenburg, C, Colorado
10. Jerry Ostroski, G, Tulsa
11. Doug Rigby, DE, Wyoming
12. Corey Williams, DB, Oklahoma

1993 Draft

Will Shields (Alan Barzee)

April 25 & 26, 1993
1. Traded to San Francisco for Joe Montana, David Whitmore and 49ers third-round pick in '94.
2. Used in '92 supplemental draft to select DE Darren Mickell from Florida.
3. **Will Shields, G, Nebraska**
4. Jaime Fields, LB, Washington
5. Lindsay Knapp, G/T, Notre Dame
6. Darius Turner, RB, Washington
7. Danan Hughes, WR, Iowa
8. Traded to Phoenix for Jay Taylor.

1994 Draft

Greg Hill (Alan Barzee)

April 24 & 25, 1994
1. **Greg Hill, RB, Texas A&M**
2. **Donnell Bennett, RB, Miami (Fla.)**
3a. **Lake Dawson, WR, Notre Dame**
3b. **Chris Penn, WR, Tulsa**
4. Bracy Walker, S, North Carolina
5a. James Burton, CB, Fresno State
5b. Rob Waldrop, DT, Arizona

6. Anthony Daigle, RB, Fresno State
7a. Steve Matthews, QB, Memphis State
7b. Tracy Greene, TE, Grambling

Obtained 3a from San Francisco with Joe Montana and David Whitmore for the Chiefs first-round pick in '93. Obtained 5a from Minnesota for Barry Word in '93. Obtained 7a from L.A. Rams for Chris Martin in '93.

1995 Draft

April 22 & 23, 1995
1. Trezelle Jenkins, T, Michigan
2. Traded to Philadelphia along with a sixth-round pick in '96 in exchange for Victor Bailey and a fourth-round pick in '95.
3a. **Tamarick Vanover, WR, Florida State**
3b. Troy Dumas, LB Nebraska
4. Choice to San Francisco in '93 Steve Bono trade.
4. Steve Stenstrom, QB, Stanford
5a. Mike Pelton, DT, Auburn
5b. Jerrott Willard, LB, California
6a. Bryan Proby, DT, Arizona State
6b. **Tom Barndt, DT/C, Pittsburgh**
1. Choice to Tampa Bay in '93 Darren Anderson trade.

Obtained 3b, a fourth-round pick (used on Stenstrom) and a fourth-round pick in '96 from Jacksonville in exchange for trading first-round draft position in '95. The fourth-round pick obtained from Philadelphia in second-round Victor Bailey trade was subsequently traded to New England for their highest third-round selection in '96. The sixth-round pick obtained from Jacksonville in first-round trade was subsequently traded to Carolina for their highest sixth-round pick in '96.

1996 Draft

April 20 & 21, 1996
1. **Jerome Woods, DB, Memphis**
2. **Reggie Tongue, DB, Oregon State**
3. **John Browning, DE, West Virginia**
4. **Donnie Edwards, LB, UCLA**
5. Joe Horn, WR, Itawamba, J.C.
6. Dietrich Jells, WR, Pittsburgh
7a. Ben Lynch, C, California
7b. Jeff Smith, C, Tennessee
7c. Darrell Williams, DB/KR, Tennessee State

Obtained a fourth-round selection (98th overall used on Edwards) and a seventh-round selection in '97 from Miami in exchange for the Chiefs two fourth-round draft picks (113th overall) and (125th overall). Obtained a fifth-round selection (135th overall used on Horn) from Arizona in exchange for the Chiefs two fifth-round picks (162nd overall). Pick 7c was a compensatory selection from the NFL for '95 free agent losses.

Tony Gonzalez (Alan Barzee)

April 19 & 20, 1997
1. **Tony Gonzalez, TE, California**
2. Kevin Lockett, WR, Kansas State
3. Choice to Houston in first-round trade.
4. Pat Barnes, QB, California
5a. Choice to Miami in '96 Pete Stoyanovich trade.
5b. June Henley, RB, Kansas
6. Isaac Byrd, WR, Kansas
7a. Traded to Pittsburgh for Brentson Buckner
7b. Nate Parks, OT, Stanford

Obtained Houston's first-round pick (13th overall used on Gonzalez) and fourth-round pick (110th overall used on Barnes) in exchange for the Chiefs first-round pick (18th overall), fourth-round pick (116th overall) as well as the Chiefs picks in the third (81st overall) and sixth rounds (181st overall). Chiefs sixth-round selection (195th overall used on Byrd) was a compensatory selection from the NFL for '96 free agent losses.

1998 Draft

April 18 & 19, 1998
1. **Victor Riley, OT, Auburn**
2. Choice to Oakland in compensation for restricted free agent DT Chester McGlockton.
3. Rashaan Shehee, RB, Washington
4. Greg Favors, LB, Mississippi State
5a. Robert Wiliams, CB, North Carolina
5b. Choice to Green Bay in '97 Wayne Simmons trade.
6. **Derrick Ransom, DT, Cincinnati**
7a. **Eric Warfield, CB, Nebraska**
7b. Ernest Blackwell, FB, Missouri

Obtained Chicago's fifth-round pick (128th overall used on Williams) for WR Chris Penn in '97 trade. Traded original fifth-round pick (150th overall) to Green Bay for LB Wayne Simmons in '97. Pick 7b was a compensatory selection from the NFL for '97 free agent losses.

1999 Draft

John Tait (Alan Barzee)

April 17 & 18, 1999
1.   **John Tait, OT, BYU**
2.   Mike Cloud, RB, Boston College
3a. Gary Stills, LB, West Virginia
3b. Larry Atkins, S, UCLA
4.   Larry Parker, WR, USC
5.   Choice to Chicago in '98 Bam Morris trade.
6.   Choice to Tampa Bay in '98
Obtained Miami's second-round pick (54th overall used on Cloud), a third-round pick (84th overall used on Atkins) and a sixth-round pick in '00 in exchange for the Chiefs second-round pick (43rd overall) in '99.

2000 Draft

April 15 & 16, 2000
1.   **Sylvester Morris, WR, Jackson State**
2.   William Bartee, CB, Oklahoma
3.   **Greg Wesley, S, Arkansas Pine Bluff**
4.   Frank Moreau, RB, Louisville
5a. Dante Hall, RB/KR, Texas A&M
5b. **Pat Dennis, CB, Louisiana-Monroe**
6.   Darnell Arnold, OT, Boston College
7.   Desmond Kitchings, WR/KR, Furman
Second pick in the fifth round was a compensatory selection.

2001 Draft

April 21 & 22, 2001
3a. **Eric Downing, DT, Syracuse**
3b. **Marvin Minnis, WR, Florida State**
4a. Monty Beisel, DE, Kansas State
4b. George Layne, FB, TCU
5a. Billy Baber, TE, Virginia
5b. Derrick Blaylock, RB, Stephen F. Austin
6.   Alex Sulsted, G, Miami (Ohio)
7a. Shaunard Harts, S, Boise State
7b. Terdell Sands, DT, UT-Chattanooga
Sent first round pick to St. Louis in compensation for Trent Green, sent second-round pick to St. Louis in compensation for Dick Vermeil, pick 3b (used on Marvin Minnis) from Washington in compensation for Marty Schottenheimer, pick 4b (used on George Layne) obtained from Jacksonville in exchange for G Brenden Stai in 2000, pick 5b (used on Derrick Blaylock) obtained from St. Louis in trade for QB Trent Green, pick 7b (used on Terdell Sands) compensatory selection for free agent losses in 2000.

2002 Draft

April 20 & 21, 2002
1.   Ryan Sims, DT, North Carolina
2.   Eddie Freeman, DE/DT, UAB
4.   Omar Easy, FB, Penn State
5.   Scott Fujita, LB, California
7.   Maurice Rodriguez, LB, Fresno State
Traded first round pick (eighth overall), third round pick and sixth round pick in 2003 to Dallas for first round pick for sixth overall pick (used for Ryan Sims).

2002	Ryan Sims
2001	Traded to St. Louis
2000	Sylvester Morris
1999	John Tait
1998	Victor Riley
1997	Tony Gonzalez
1996	Jerome Woods
1995	Trezelle Jenkins
1994	Greg Hill
1993	Traded to San Francisco
1992	Dale Carter
1991	Harvey Williams
1990	Percy Snow
1989	Derrick Thomas
1988	Neil Smith
1987	Paul Palmer
1986	Brian Jozwiak
1985	Ethan Horton
1984	Bill Mass, John Alt
1983	Todd Blackledge
1982	Anthony Hancock
1981	Willie Scott
1980	Brad Budde
1979	Mike Bell, Steve Fuller
1978	Art Still
1977	Gary Green
1976	Rod Walters
1975	Traded to Houston
1974	Woody Green
1973	Traded to Chicago
1972	Jeff Kinney
1971	Elmo Wright
1970	Sid Smith
1969	Jim Marsalis
1968	Mo Moorman, George Daney
1967	Gene Trosch
1966	Aaron Brown
1965	*Gale Sayers
1964	Pete Beathard
1963	Buck Buchanan, Ed Budde
1962	*Ronnie Bull
1961	E.J. Holub
1960	*Don Meredith

*Signed with NFL

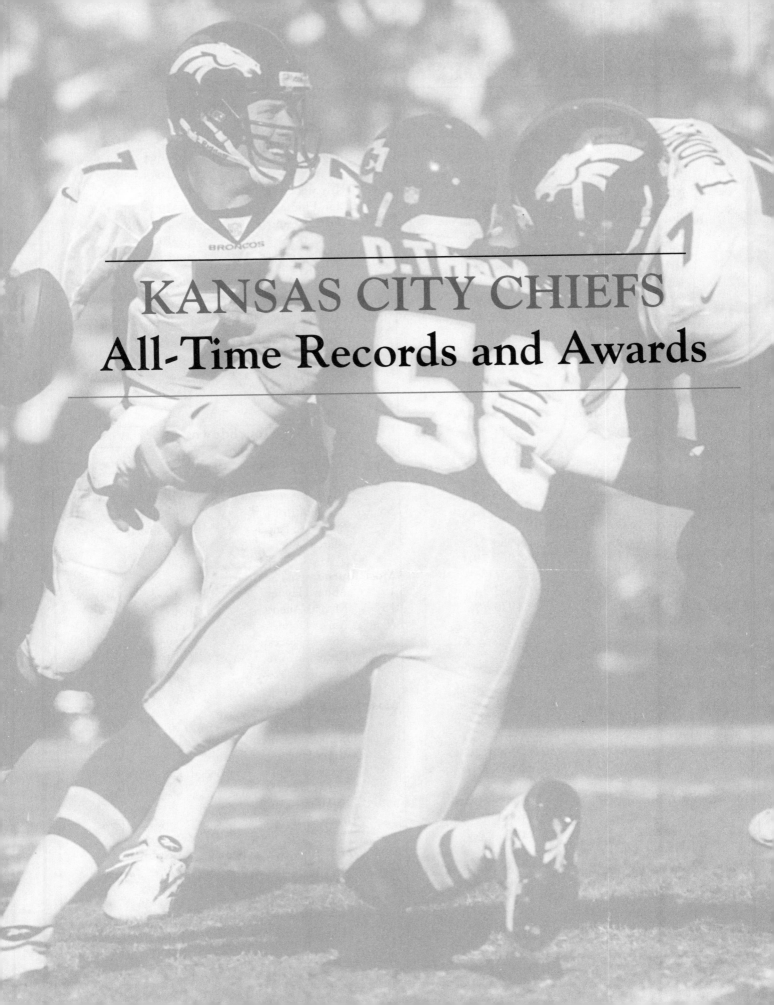

KANSAS CITY CHIEFS
All-Time Records and Awards

Individual Records

Service

Most Seasons, Active Players
15	Jerrel Wilson	1963-77
14	Len Dawson	1962-75
	Ed Budde	1963-76
	Nick Lowery	1980-93
13	Jim Tyrer	1961-73
	Buck Buchanan	1963-75
	Emmitt Thomas	1966-78
	Jan Stenerud	1967-79
	Jack Rudnay	1970-82
	John Alt	1984-96
12	Johnny Robinson	1960-71
	Dave Hill	1963-74
	Bobby Bell	1963-74
	Mick Livingston	1968-79
	Henry Marshall	1976-87

Most Games Played, Career
212	Nick Lowery	1980-93
203	Jerrel Wilson	1963-77
186	Jan Stenerud	1967-79
182	Len Dawson	1962-75
181	Buck Buchanan	1963-75

Most Consecutive Game Played
188	Nick Lowery	1980-92
186	Jan Stenerud	1967-79
180	Jim Tyrer	1961-73
166	Buck Buchanan	1963-74
144	Jack Rudnay	1970-79

Scoring

Most Point, Career
1,466	Nick Lowery	1980-93
1,231	JanStenerud	1967-79
360	Otis Taylor	1965-75
348	Abner Haynes	1960-64
332	Chris Burford	1960-67

Most Points, Season
139	Nick Lowery	1990
129	Jan Stenerud	1968
119	Jan Stenerud	1969
116	Jan Stenerud	1970
	Nick Lowery	1963
115	Nick Lowery	1981
	Pete Stoyanovich	1998

Most Seasons, 100 or More Points
*11	Nick Lowery	1981, 1983-86, 1988-93
5	Jan Stenerud	1967-71
2	Lin Elliott	1994-95
	Pete Stoyanovich	1997-98
1	Jack Spikes	1960
	Abner Haynes	1962

*NFL RECORD

Most Points, Game
30	Abner Haynes vs. Oakland	Nov. 26, 1961
24	Frank Jackson vs. Denver	Dec. 10, 1961
	Abner Haynes vs. Boston	Sept. 8, 1962
	Frank Jackson vs. San Diego	Dec. 13, 1964
	Bert Coan vs. Denver	Oct. 23, 1966

Touchdowns

Most Touchdowns, Career
60	Otis Taylor	1965-75
58	Abner Haynes	1960-64
55	Chris Burford	1960-67
49	Stephone Paige	1983-91
47	Marcus Allen	1993-97

Most Touchdowns, Season
19	Abner Haynes	1962
15	Marcus Allen	1993
13	Abner Haynes	1961
12	Abner Haynes	1960
	Chris Burford	1962
	Christian Okoye	1989

Most Touchdowns, Game
5	Abner Haynes vs. Oakland	Nov. 26, 1961
4	Frank Jackson vs. Denver	Dec. 10, 1961
	Abner Haynes vs. Boston	Sept. 8, 1962
	Frank Jackson vs. San Diego	Dec. 13, 1964
	Bert Coan vs. Denver	Oct. 23, 1965
3	13 Time—Last;	
	Barn Morris vs. San Diego	Nov. 22, 1998

Most Consecutive Games Scoring Touchdowns
7	Marcus Allen	1993
5	Chris Burford	1962
	Curtis McClinton	1965-66
	Otis Taylor	1966
	Mike Garrett	1967-1969

Points After Touchdown

Most Points After Touchdown Attempted, Career
483	Nick Lowery	1980-93
409	Jan Stenerud	1967-79
149	Tommy Brooker	1962-66

Most Points After Touchdown Attempted, Season
46	Tommy Brooker	1964
45	Jan Stenerud	1967
44	Nick Lowery	1983

Most Points After Touchdown Attempted, Game
8	Tommy Brooker vs. Denver	Sept. 8, 1963
	Mike Mercer vs. Denver	Oct. 23, 1966

Most Points After Touchdown Made, Career
479	Nick Lowery	1980-93
394	Jan Stenerud	1967-79
149	Tommy Brooker	1962-66

Most Points After Touchdown Made, Season
46	Tommy Brooker	1964
45	Jan Stenerud	1967
44	Nick Lowery	1983

Most Points After Touchdown Made, Game
8	Tommy Brooker vs. Denver	Sept. 8, 1963
	Mike Mercer vs. Denver	Oct. 23, 1966
7	Cotton Davidson vs. Denver	Dec. 10, 1961
	T. Brooker vs. N.Y. Titans	Nov. 11, 1962
	Jack Spikes vs. Denver	Dec. 8, 1963
	Tommy Brooker vs. Houston	Nov. 28, 1965

Most Consecutive Points After Touchdown
197	Nick Lowery	1983-89
155	Jan Stenerud	1968-73
149	Tommy Brooker	1962-66

Highest Points After Percentage, Career (200 PATs)
99.17	Nick Lowery (479-483)
99.33	Jan Stenerud (394-409) 1967-79

Field Goals

Most Field Goals Attempted, Career
436	Jan Stenerud	1967-79
410	Nick Lowery	1980-93
87	Tommy Brooker	1962-66

Most Field Goals Attempted, Season
44	Jan Stenerud	1971
42	Jan Stenerud	1970
40	Jan Stenerud	1968

Most Field Goals Attempted, Game
7	Jan Stenerud vs. Buffalo	Dec. 19, 1971
6	Tommy Brooker vs. San Diego	Dec. 16, 1962
	Jan Stenerud	6 times
	Last; vs. Washington	Oct. 10, 1976

Most Seasons Leading League, Field Goals Made
3	Jan Stenerud	1967, 1970, 1975

Most Field Goals Made, Career
329	Nick Lowery	1980-93
279	Jan Stenerud	1967-79
70	Pete Stoyanovich	1996-98

Most Field Goals Made, Season
34	Nick Lowery	1990
30	Jan Stenerud	1968, 1970
27	Jan Stenerud	1969
	Nick Lowery	1988
	Pete Stoyanovich	1998
26	Jan Stenerud	1971
	Nick Lowery	1981
	Pete Stoyanovich	1997

Most Field Goals Made, Game
5	Jan Sternerud vs. Buffalo	Nov. 2, 1969
	Jan Sternerud vs. Buffalo	Dec. 7, 1969
	Jan Sternerud vs. Buffalo	Dec. 19, 1969
	Nick Lowery vs. L.A. Raiders	Sept. 12, 1985
	Nick Lowery vs. Cincinnati	Nov. 13, 1988
	Nick Lowery vs. Chicago	Dec. 29, 1990
	Nick Lowery vs. Denver	Sept. 20, 1993
4	Tommy Brooker vs. San Deigo	Dec. 16, 1962
	Mike Mercer vs. N.Y. Jets	Nov. 27, 1966
	Lin Elliott vs. Seattle	Dec. 24, 1995
	Jan Stenerud	10 times
	Nick Lowery	8 times
	Pete Stoyanovich	2 times

Most Consecutive Games Scoring Field Goals
16	Jan Stenerud	1969-70
12	Pete Stoyanovich	1997-98
11	Jan Stenerud	1968-69
	Jan Stenerud	1971-72
	Nick Lowery	1985-86

Most Consecutive Field Goals Made
22	Pete Stoyanovich	1997-98
21	Nick Lowery	1990-1991
16	Jan Stenerud	1969

Longest Field Goal

58	Nick Lowery vs. Washington	Sept. 18, 1983
	Nick Lowery vs. L.A. Raiders	Sept. 12, 1985
57	Nick Lowery vs. Seattle	Sept. 14, 1980
55	Jan Stenerud vs. Denver	Oct. 4, 1970
54	Jan Stenerud vs. Houston	Sept. 9, 1967
	Jan Stenerud vs. Denver	Oct. 5, 1969
	Jan Stenerud vs. San Francisco	Dec. 6, 1971
	Nick Lowery vs. L.A. Raiders	Nov. 26, 1983
	Nick Lowery vs. Detroit	Nov. 26, 1987
	Pete Stoyanovich vs. Denver	Nov. 16, 1997
53	Pete Stoyanovich vs. Seattle	Nov. 8, 1998
52	Jan Stenerud	4 times
	Eddie Murray vs. Pittsburgh	Oct. 25, 1992
	Nick Lowery	8 times
	Pete Stoyanovich vs. St. Louis	Oct. 26, 1997

HIGHEST FIELD GOAL PERCENTAGE, CAREER
(Minimum 100 made)

80.2	Nick Lowery (329-410)	1980-93
64.0	Jan Stenerud (279-436)	1967-79

Highest Field Goal Percentage, Season

96.3	Pete Stoyanovich (26-27)	1997
91.9	Nick Lowery (34-37)	1992
91.6	Nick Lowery (22-24)	1992
88.9	Nick Lowery (24-27)	1985

Most Field Goals, No Misses, Game

5	Jan Stenerud vs. Buffalo	Nov. 2, 1969
	Jan Stenerud vs. Buffalo	Dec. 7, 1969
	Nick Lowery vs. L.A. Raiders	Sept. 12, 1985
	Nick Lowery vs. Chicago	Dec. 29, 1990
	Nick Lowery vs. Denver	Sept. 21, 1993

Most Field Goals, 50 or More Yards, Career

20	Nick Lowery	1980-93
12	Jan Stenerud	1967-79

Most Field Goals, 50 or More Yards, Season

4	Nick Lowery	1980
3	Nick Lowery	1985
	Nick Lowery	1988

Most Field Goals, 50 or More Yards, Game

*2	Nick Lowery vs. Seattle	Sept. 14, 1980
	Nick Lowery vs. New Orleans	Sept. 8, 1985
	Nick Lowery vs. Detroit	Nov. 26, 1987

*NFL RECORD

Safeties

Most Safeties, Career

3	Derrick Thomas	1989-98

2	Bill Maas	1984-92
	Dan Saleaumua	1989-96
	Joe Phillips	1992-97
1	Buck Buchanan	1963-75
	Rob McGovern	1989-90

Most Safeties, Season

1	Buck Buchanan	1968
	Willie Lanier	1974
	John Lohmeyer	1976
	Ed Beckman	1978
	Dino Hackett	1988
	Albert Lewis	1988
	Bill Maas	1988, 1990
	Rob McGovern	1989
	Dan Saleaumua	1991, 1996
	Derrick Thomas	1994, 1997, 1998
	Joe Phillips	1997

Rushing

Most Seasons Leading League

1	Albert Haynes	1960
	Christian Okoye	1989
	Priest Holmes	2001

ATTEMPTS

Most Attempts, Career

1,246	Christian Okoye	1987-92
1,158	Ed Podolak	1969-77
932	Marcus Allen	1993-97
792	Abner Haynes	1960-64
762	Curtis McClinton	1962-69

Most Attempts, Season

370	Christian Okoye	1989
327	Priest Holmes	2001
245	Christian Okoye	1990
236	Mike Garrett	1967
234	Joe Delaney	1981
225	Christian Okoye	1991

Most Attempts, Game

38	Christian Okoye vs. Green Bay	Dec. 10, 1989
37	Christian Okoye vs. Seattle	Nov. 5, 1989
35	Barry Word vs. L.A. Raiders	Dec. 22, 1991
33	Christian Okoye vs. Dallas	Oct. 22, 1989
	Marcus Allen vs. L.A. Raiders	Dec. 24, 1994

YARDS GAINED

Most Yard Gained, Career

4,897	Christian Okoye	1987-92
4,451	Ed Podolak	1969-77

3,837	Abner Haynes	1960-64
3,698	Marcus Allen	1993-97
3,246	Mike Garrett	1966-70

Most Yards Gained, Season

1,555	Priest Holmes	2001
1,480	Christian Okoye	1989
1,121	Joe Delaney	1981
1,087	Mike Garrett	1967
1,053	Tony Reed	1978
1,049	Abner Haynes	1962
1,031	Christian Okoye	1991
1,015	Barry Word	1990

Most Yard Gained, Game

200	Barry Word vs. Detroit	Oct. 14, 1990
193	Joe Delaney vs. Houston	Nov. 15, 1981
192	Mike Garrett vs. N.Y. Jets	Nov. 5, 1967
170	Christian Okoyo vs. Dallas	Oct. 22, 1989
169	Mike Garrett vs. Denver	Dec. 17, 1967

Most Games, 100 or More Yards, Career

14	Christian Okoye	1987-92
12	Abner Haynes	1960-65
11	Ed Podolak	1969-77
7	Mike Garrett	1966-70
	Barry Word	1990-92
	Priest Holmes	2001
5	Tony Reed	1977-80
	Joe Delaney	1981-82

Most Games, 100 or More Yards, Season

8	Christian Okoye	1989
7	Priest Holmes	2001
5	Joe Delaney	1981
4	Abner Haynes	1962
	Mike Garrett	1967

Most Consecutive Games, 100 or More Yards

1981	Joe Delaney	Oct. 4 – Oct. 18,
1989	Christian Okoye	Sept. 24 – Oct. 8,
1989	Christian Okoye	Oct. 22 – Nov. 5,

Longest Run from Scrimmage

84 (TD)	Ted McKnight vs. Seattle	Sept. 30, 1979
82	Joe Delaney vs. Denver	Oct. 18, 1981
80 (TD)	Abner Haynes vs. N.Y. Jets	Nov. 29, 1964
	Warren McVea vs. Cincinnati	Oct. 26, 1969
77 (TD)	Mike Garrett vs. Houston	Oct. 30, 1966

AVERAGE GAIN

Highest Average Gain, Career (400 attempts)

4.84	Abner Haynes (792-3,837)	1960-64
4.44	Ted McKnight (528-2,344)	1977-81
4.41	Mike Garrett (736-3,246)	1966-70

Highest Average Gain, Season (100 attempts)

6.03	Ted McKnight (104-627)	1978
5.61	Abner Haynes (156-875)	1960
5.45	Mike Garrett (147-801)	1966

Highest Average Gain, Game (10 attempts)

12.25	Ted McKnight vs. Seattle (12-147)	Sept. 30, 1979
11.58	Ed Podolak vs. Denver (12-139)	Dec. 6, 1970
	Abner Haynes vs. Oakland (14-158)	Nov. 26, 1961

TOUCHDOWNS

Most Touchdowns Rushing, Career

44	Marcus Allen	1993-97
40	Christian Okoye	1987-92
39	Abner Haynes	1960-65
34	Ed Podolak	1969-77

Most Touchdowns Rushing, Season

13	Abner Haynes	1962
12	Christian Okoye	1989
	Marcus Allen	1993
11	Marcus Allen	1997
10	Billy Jackson	1981

Most Rushing Touchdowns, Game

4	Abner Haynes vs. Oakland	Nov. 26, 1961
3	Jack Spikes vs. Houston	Oct. 1, 1961
	Abner Haynes vs. Boston	Sept. 8, 1962
	Bert Coan vs. Denver	Oct. 23, 1966
	Ed Podolak vs. Detroit	Nov. 25, 1971
	Ed Podolak vs. Cleveland	Dec. 12, 1976
	Billy Jackson vs. Oakland	Oct. 25, 1981
	Marcus Allen vs. Seattle	Dec. 5, 1993
	Donnell Bennett vs. Philadelphia	Sept. 27, 1998
	Bam Morris vs. San Diego	Nov. 22, 1998

Most Consecutive Games Rushing for TDs

5	Mike Garrett	1967
4	Abner Haynes	1960
	Jack Spikes	1960-61
	Warren McVea	1969
	Ted McKnight	1981
	Theotis Brown	1983-84
	Christian Okoye	1989
	Bam Morris	1998

Passing

Most Seasons Leading League

| 4 | Len Dawson | 1962, 1964, 1966, 1968 |

PASS RATING

Highest Pass Rating Career (1,00 attempts)
83.2	Len Dawson	1962-75
81.6	Steve DeBerg	1988-91
77.1	Bill Kenney	1979-88

Highest Pass Rating, Season (Qualifiers)
101.9	Len Dawson	1966
98.9	Len Dawson	1968
98.4	Len Dawson	1962
96.3	Steve DeBerg	1990

ATTEMPTS

Most Passes Attempted, Career
3,696	Len Dawson	1962-75
2,430	Bill Kenney	1979-88
1,751	Mike Livingston	1968-79
1,616	Steve DeBerg	1988-91
1,075	Steve Bono	1994-96

Most Passes Attempted, Season
693	Bill Kenney	1983
547	Elvis Grbac	2000
526	Trent Green	2001
520	Steve Bono	1995
499	Elvis Grbac	1999
493	Joe Montana	1994
444	Steve DeBerg	1990
438	Steve Bono	1996

Most Passes Attempted, Game
55	Joe Montana vs. San Diego	Oct. 9, 1994
	Steve Bono vs. Miami	Dec. 12, 1994
54	Joe Montana vs. Denver	Oct. 17, 1994
	Steve Bono vs. San Diego	Sept. 29, 1996
52	Bill Kenney vs. Denver	Oct. 30, 1983
50	Bill Kenney vs. Buffalo	Nov. 30, 1986
	Steve DeBerg vs. Cleveland	Nov. 24, 1991
	Rich Gannon vs. Jacksonville	Nov. 9, 1997

COMPLETIONS

Most Passes Completed, Career
2,115	Len Dawson	1962-75
1,330	Bill Kenney	1979-88
934	Steve DeBerg	1988-91
912	Mike Livingston	1968-79
594	Steve Bono	1994-96

Most Passes Completed, Season
346	Bill Kenney (603 att.)	1983
326	Elvis Grbac (547 att.)	2000
299	Joe Montana (493 att.)	1994
296	Trent Green (526 att.)	2001
294	Elvis Grbac (499 att.)	1999
293	Steve Bono (520 att.)	1995
258	Steve DeBerg (444 att.)	1990

Most Passes Completed, Game
39	Elvis Grbac vs. Oakland	Nov. 5, 2000
37	Joe Montana vs. San Diego	Oct. 9, 1994
34	Joe Montana vs. Denver	Oct. 17, 1994
33	Steve Bono vs. Miami	Dec. 12, 1994
31	Bill Kenney vs. San Diego	Dec. 11, 1983
30	Steve DeBerg vs. Cleveland	Nov. 24, 1991
29	Steve Bono vs. N.Y. Giants	Sept. 10, 1995
	Steve Bono vs. Cleveland	Sept. 24, 1994

Most Consecutive Passes Completed
15	Len Dawson vs. Houston	Sept. 9, 1967
	Bill Kenney vs. San Diego (13)	Sept. 12, 1983
	Bill Kenney vs. Washington (2)	Sept. 18, 1983

COMPLETION PERCENTAGE

Most Seasons Leading League
*8   Len Dawson   1962, 1964-69, 1975
*NFL RECORD

Most Consecutive Seasons Leading League
*6   Len Dawson   1964-69
*NFL RECORD

Highest Completion Percentage, Career (1,000 Attempts)
57.97	Steve DeBerg (1,616-934)	1988-91
57.22	Len Dawson (3,696-2,115)	1962-75
54.73	Bill Kenney (2,430-1,330)	1979-88

Highest Completion Percentage, Season (Qualifiers)
66.43	Len Dawson (140-93)	1975
60.95	Len Dawson (310-189)	1962
60.74	Joe Montana (298-181)	1993

Highest Completion Percentage, Game (20 attempts)
80.95	Dave Krieg vs. N.Y. Jets (21-17)	Nov. 29, 1992
80.95	Trent Green vs. Denver (21-17)	Dec. 16, 2001
80.77	Trent Green vs. Washington (26-21)	Sept. 30, 2001
79.17	Len Dawson vs. Pittsburgh (24-19)	Nov. 15, 1970
78.26	Steve Bono vs. Seattle (23-18)	Sept. 3, 1995

YARDS GAINED

Most Yards Gained, Career
28,507	Len Dawson	1962-65
17,277	Bill Kenney	1979-88
11,873	Steve DeBerg	1988-91

| 11,295 | Mike Livingston | 1968-79 |
| 10,643 | Elvis Grbac | 1997-2000 |

Most Yards Gained, Season

4,348	Bill Kenney	1983
4,169	Elvis Grbac	2000
3,783	Trent Green	2001
3,444	Steve DeBerg	1990
3,283	Joe Montana	1994
3,121	Steve Bono	1995

Most Yards Gained, Game

435	Len Dawson vs. Denver	Nov. 1, 1964
411	Bill Kenney vs. San Diego	Dec. 11, 1983
397	Bill Kenney vs. New Orleans	Sept. 8, 1985
395	Steve DeBerg vs. Denver	Sept. 17, 1990
393	Joe Montana vs. Denver	Oct. 17, 1994

Most Games, 300 or More Yards Passing , Career

15	Bill Kenney	1979-88
9	Len Dawson	1962-75
5	Steve DeBerg	1988-91

Most Games, 300 or More Yards Passing , Season

7	Bill Kenney	1983
4	Joe Montana	1994
2	Cotton Davidson	1960
	Len Dawson	1964
	Bill Kenney	1984, 1985, 1987
	Steve DeBerg	1990
	Dave Krieg	1992
	Steve Bono	1994

Most Consecutive Games, 300 or More Yards Passing, Season

4	Bill Kenney	1983
2	Joe Montana	1994
	Steve Bono	1994

Long Pass Completion (All TDs)

93	Mike Livingston vs. Miami	Oct. 19, 1969
	(to Otis Taylor for 79 yards, lateral to Robert Holmes for 14 yards)	
92	Len Dawson vs. Denver (to Tommy Brooker)	Nov. 18, 1962
	Len Dawson vs. Oakland (to Gloster Richardson)	Nov. 3, 1968
90	Len Dawson vs. Houston (to Frank Pitts)	Nov. 17, 1968
	Steve DeBerg vs. San Deigo (to J.J. Birden)	Nov. 18, 1990

AVERAGE GAIN

Most Seasons Leading League

| 3 | Len Dawson | 1962, 1966, 1969 |

Highest Average Gain, Career (1,000 attempts)

7.71	Len Dawson (3,696-28, 507)	1962-75
7.35	Steve DeBerg (1,616-11,873)	1988-91
7.11	Bill Kenney (2,430-17,277)	1979-88

Highest Average Gain, Season (Qualifiers)

| 9.42 | Len Dawson (224-2,109) | 1968 |
| 8.90 | Len Dawson (284-2,527) | 1966 |

Highest Average Gain, Game (20 attempts)

15.76	Steve DeBerg vs. New England (21-331)	Dec. 2, 1990
12.82	Len Dawson vs. Denver (22-282)	Dec. 19, 1965
12.48	Bill Kenney vs. Oakland (23-287)	Oct. 11, 1981

TOUCHDOWNS

Most Seasons Leading League

| *4 | Len Dawson | 1962, 1963, 1965, 1966 |

*NFL RECORD

Most Touchdown Passes, Career

237	Len Dawson	1962-75
105	Bill Kenney	1979-88
67	Steve DeBerg	1988-91

Most Touchdown Passes, Season

30	Len Dawson	1964
29	Len Dawson	1962
28	Elvis Grbac	2000
26	Len Dawson	1963-1966
24	Len Dawson	1967
	Bill Kenney	1983

Most Touchdown Passes, Game

6	Len Dawson vs. Denver	Nov. 1, 1964
5	Len Dawson vs. Boston	Sept. 25, 1966
	Len Dawson vs. Miami	Oct. 8, 1967
4	Len Dawson	6 times
	Bill Kenney	4 times
	Last; vs. Chicago	Nov. 1, 1967

Most Consecutive Games, Touchdown Passes

| 14 | Len Dawson | Oct. 3, 1965 - Oct. 8, 1966 |
| 12 | Len Dawson | Sept. 8, 1962 - Dec. 2, 1962 |

HAD INTERCEPTED

Most Consecutive Passes, None Intercepted

| 233 | Steve DeBerg | 1990 |
| 202 | Rich Gannon | 1997-98 |

Most Passes Had Intercepted, Career

178	Len Dawson	1962-75
86	Bill Kenney	1979-88
83	Mike Livingston	1968-79

Most Passes Had Intercepted, Season

23	Cotton Davidson	1961
19	Len Dawson	1963
	Bill Kenney	1983
17	Len Dawson	1962, 1967

Most Interceptions, Game

6	Todd Blackledge vs. L.A. Rams	Oct. 20, 1985
5	Cotton Davidson vs. Houston	Oct. 16, 1960
	Len Dawson vs. Oakland	Nov. 23, 1969
	Mike Livingston vs. Pittsburgh	Oct. 13, 1974
	Bill Kenney vs. San Diego	Sept. 20, 1981
	Steve DeBerg vs. San Diego	Sept. 24, 1989

Most Attempts, No Interceptions, Game

45	Bill Kenney vs. L.A. Raiders	Oct. 9, 1983
	Steve DeBerg vs. Denver	Sept. 17, 1990
43	Bill Kenney vs. Houston	Oct. 23, 1983
	Rich Gannon vs. Denver	Dec. 6, 1998
41	Todd Blackledge vs. Houston	Nov. 11, 1984
	Steve Bono vs. San Diego	Oct. 9, 1995
	Rich Gannon vs. Dallas	Dec. 13, 1998

LOWEST PERCENTAGE, PASSES HAD INTERCEPTED

Lowest Percentage, Passes Had Intercepted, Career (1,000 att.)

3.09	Steve DeBerg (1,616-50)	1988-91
3.54	Bill Kenney (2,430-85)	1979-88
4.74	Mike Livingston (1,751-83)	1968-79

Lowest Percentage, Passes Had Intercepted (Season Qualifiers)

0.90	Steve DeBerg (444-4)	1990
1.69	Rich Gannon (543-6)	1998
1.83	Joe Montana (493-9)	1994

Times Sacked (Compiled since 1972)
Times Sacked, Career

195	Bill Kenney	1979-88
132	Mike Livingston	1968-79
120	Steve Fuller	1979-82

Times Sacked, Season

49	Steve Fuller	1980
48	Dave Krieg	1992
41	Bill Kenney	1983
37	Steve Fuller	1979

Times Sacked, Game

10	Steve Fuller vs. Baltimore	Nov. 2, 1980
8	Steve Fuller vs. Pittsburgh	Dec. 5, 1982

Pass Receiving

Pass Receptions
Most Seasons Leading League

1	MacArthur Lane	1976

Most Pass Receptions, Career

416	Henry Marshall	1976-87
410	Otis Taylor	1965-75
391	Chris Bradford	1960-67
377	Stephone Paige	1983-91
354	Kimble Anders	1991-98

Most Seasons, 50 or More Pass Receptions

5	Kimble Anders	1994-98
4	Chris Burford	1961, 1963-64, 1966
	Otis Taylor	1966-67, 1971-72
3	Carlos Carson	1983-84, 1987
	Stephone Paige	1986, 1988, 1990
2	Frank Jackson	1963-64
	Henry Marshall	1983-84
	Willie Davis	1993-94

Most Pass Receptions, Season

93	Tony Gonzalez	2000
80	Carlos Carson	1983
78	Derrick Alexander	2000
76	Tony Gonzalez	1999
73	Tony Gonzalez	2001
72	Andre Rison	1997
68	Chris Burford	1963
67	Kimble Anders	1994
66	MacArthur Lane	1976

Most Pass Receptions, Game

12	Ed Podolak vs. Denver	Oct. 7, 1973
11	Chris Burford vs. Buffalo	Sept. 22, 1963
	Emile Harry vs. Cleveland	Nov. 24, 1991
	Kimble Anders vs. N.Y. Giants	Sept. 10, 1995
	Tony Gonzalez vs. New England	Dec. 4, 2000
10	Chris Burford vs. Boston	Oct. 12, 1962
	Chris Burford vs. Buffalo	Oct. 13, 1963
	Frank Jackson vs. N.Y. Jets	Nov. 29, 1964
	Chris Burford vs. Boston	Sept. 25, 1966
	Otis Taylor vs. Cincinnati	Oct. 15, 1972
	Ed Podolak vs. Houston	Sept. 29, 1974
	Stephone Paige vs. Denver	Sept. 17, 1990
	J.J. Birden vs. Miami	Dec. 12, 1994
	Kimble Anders vs. Denver	Nov. 16, 1998
	Tony Gonzalez vs. Denver	Sept. 24, 2000
	Tony Gonzalez vs. Carolina	Dec. 10, 2000

Most Consecutive Game, Pass Receptions

83	Stephone Paige	Nov. 17, 1985 – Sept. 29, 1991
46	Ed Podolak	Oct. 22, 1970 – Dec. 21, 1975
44	Carlos Carson	Dec. 20, 1981 – Sept. 12, 1985
	Tony Gonzalez	Dec. 7, 1997 – Nov. 26, 2000
37	Otis Taylor	Nov. 21, 1965 – Oct. 27, 1968
	Otis Taylor	Sept. 20, 1970 – Nov. 19, 1972

YARDS GAINED

Most Yards Gained, Career

7,306	Otis Taylor	1965-75
6,545	Henry Marshall	1976-87
6,360	Carlos Carson	1980-89
6,341	Stephone Paige	1983-91
5,525	Chris Burford	1960-67

Most Seasons, 1,000 or More Yards

3	Carlos Carson	1983-84, 1987
2	Otis Taylor	1966, 1971
1	Stephone Paige	1990
	Andre Rison	1997
	Tony Gonzalez	2000
	Derrick Alexander	2000

Most Yards Gained, Season

1,391	Derrick Alexander	2000
1,351	Carlos Carson	1983
1,297	Otis Taylor	1966
1,203	Tony Gonzalez	
1,110	Otis Taylor	1971
1,092	Andre Rison	1997
1,078	Carlos Carson	1984
1,044	Carlos Carson	1987
1,021	Stephone Paige	1990

Most Yards Gained, Game

309	Stephone Paige vs. San Diego (8 receptions)	Dec. 22, 1985
213	Curtis McClinton vs. Denver (5 Reception)	Dec. 19, 1965
206	Stephone Paige vs. Denver (10 Receptions)	Sept. 17, 1990
197	Carlos Carson vs. San Diego (9 Receptions)	Oct. 25, 1987
190	Otis Taylor vs. Pittsburgh (6 Receptions)	Oct. 18, 1971

Most Games, 100 or More Yards, Career

20	Otis Taylor	1965-75
18	Carlos Carson	1980-88
12	Chris Burford	1960-67
	Derrick Alexander	1998-2000

Most Games, 100 or More Yards, Season

6	Otis Taylor	1966
	Carlos Carson	1983
	Derrick Alexander	2000
	Tony Gonzalez	2000
4	Chris Burford	1961
	Carlos Carson	1984
	Carlos Carson	1987

Most Consecutive Games, 100 or More Yards Pass Receiving, Season

3	Frank Jackson	1964
	Otis Taylor	1966
	Willie Davis	1992

Longest Pass Receptions (All TDs)

92	Tommy Brooker vs. Denver (from Len Dawson)	Nov. 18, 1962
	Gloster Richardson vs. Oakland (from Len Dawson)	Nov. 3, 1968
90	Frank Pitts vs. Boston (from Len Dawson)	Nov. 17, 1968
	J.J. Birden vs. San Diego (from Steve DeBerg)	Nov. 18, 1990
89	Otis Taylor vs. Miami (from Len Dawson)	Nov. 13, 1966
86	Stephone Paige vs. New England (from Steve DeBerg)	Dec. 2, 1990

AVERAGE GAIN

Highest Average Gain, Career (200 receptions)

18.12	Carlos Carson (351-6,360)	1980-89
17.82	Otis Taylor (410-7,306)	1965-75
16.82	Stephone Paige (377-6,341)	1983-91

Highest Average Gain, Season (24 receptions)

22.36	Otis Taylor (58-1,297)	1966
21.93	Stephone Paige (43-943)	1985
21.83	Frank Pitts (30-655)	1968

Highest Average Gain, Game (3 receptions)

42.00	C. McClinton vs. Denver (5-213)	Dec. 19, 1965
40.00	J. Robinson vs. N.Y. Titans (3-120)	Oct. 2, 1960
39.67	Otis Taylor vs. Denver (3-119)	Dec. 14, 1968

TOUCHDOWNS

Most Touchdowns, Career

57	Otis Taylor	1965-75

| 55 | Chris Burford | 1960-67 |
| 49 | Stephone Paige | 1983-91 |

Most Touchdowns, Season

12	Chris Burford	1962
11	Otis Taylor	1967
	Stephone Paige	1986
10	Stephone Paige	1985

Most Touchdowns, Game

4	Frank Jackson vs. San Diego	Dec. 13, 1964
3	Chris Burford vs. Oakland	Sept. 23, 1962
	Chris Burford vs. Boston	Sept. 25, 1966
	Otis Taylor vs. Denver	Dec. 17, 1967
	Otis Taylor vs. N.Y. Jets	Nov. 16, 1969

Most Consecutive Games, Touchdown Receptions

| 5 | Chris Burford | Sept. 8, 1962 – Oct. 12, 1962 |
| | Otis Taylor | Oct. 23, 1966 – Nov. 20, 1966 |

Interceptions By

Most Seasons, Leading League

| 2 | Johnny Robinson | 1966, 1970 |
| | Emmitt Thomas | 1969, 1974 |

Most Interceptions By, Career

58	Emmitt Thomas	1966-78
57	Johnny Robinson	1960-71
50	Deron Cherry	1981-91
39	Gary Barbaro	1976-82
38	Albert Lewis	1983-93

Most Interceptions By, Season

12	Emmitt Thomas	1974
10	Johnny Robinson	1966
	Bobby Hunt	1966
	Johnny Robinson	1970
9	Emmitt Thomas	1969
	Deron Cherry	1986

Most Interceptions By, Game

*4	Bobby Ply vs. San Diego	Dec. 16, 1962
	Bobby Hunt vs. Houston	Oct. 4, 1964
	Deron Cherry vs. Seattle	Sept. 29, 1985
3	Bobby Ply vs. Denver	Dec. 9, 1962
	Johnny Robinson vs. Baltimore	Sept. 28, 1970
	Albert Lewis vs. Atlanta	Dec. 8, 1985
	Lloyd Burruss vs. San Diego	Oct. 19, 1986
	Albert Lewis vs. Atlanta	Sept. 1, 1991

*NFL RECORD

Most Consecutive Games, Passes Intercepted By

| 6 | Eric Harris | 1980 |

YARDS GAINED

Most Yards Gained, Career

938	Emmitt Thomas (58 INTs)	1966-78
771	Gary Barbaro (39 INTs)	1975-82
741	Johnny Robinson (57 INTs)	1960-71
688	Deron Cherry (50 INTs)	1981-91
674	Bobby Hunt (37 INTs)	1962-67

Most Yards Gained, Season

274	Mark McMillian (8 INTs)	1997
228	Bobby Hunt (6 INTs)	1963
214	Emmitt Thomas (12 INTs)	1974
193	Lloyd Burruss (5 INTs)	1986
165	Gary Barbaro (8 INTs)	1977
163	Gary Barbaro (10 INTs)	1980

Most Yards Gained, Game

121	Lloyd Burruss vs. San Diego (3 INTs) Oct. 19, 1986
108	Bobby Ply vs. San Diego (4 INTs) Dec. 16, 1962
102	Gary Barbaro vs. Seattle (1 INT) Dec. 11, 1977
100	Tim Collier vs. Oakland (1 INT) Dec. 18, 1977
99	Dave Grayson vs. N.Y. Titans (1 INT) Dec. 17, 1961
	Kevin Ross vs. San Diego (1 INT) Sept. 6, 1992

Longest Interception Return (All TDs)

102	Gary Barbaro vs. Seattle	Dec. 11, 1977
100	Tim Collier vs. Oakland	Dec. 18, 1977
99	Dave Grayson vs. N.Y. Titans	Dec. 17, 1961
	Kevin Ross vs. San Diego	Sept. 6, 1992
87	Mark McMillian vs. San Diego	Dec. 14, 1997
80	David Webster vs. Oakland	Oct. 9, 1960

TOUCHDOWNS

Most Touchdowns, Career

6	Bobby Bell	1963-74
5	Emmitt Thomas	1966-78
	Jim Kearney	1967-75
4	Lloyd Burruss	1981-91

Most Touchdowns, Season

*4	Jim Kearney	1972
3	Lloyd Burruss	1986
	Mark McMillian	1997
2	Emmitt Thomas	1974
	Charles Mincy	1992

*NFL RECORD

Most Touchdowns, Game
| *2 | Jim Kearney vs. Denver | Oct. 1, 1972 |
| | Lloyd Burruss vs. San Diego | Oct. 19, 1986 |

* NFL RECORD

Punting

Most Seasons Leading League
*4	Jerrel Wilson	1965, 1968, 1972-73
1	Bob Grupp	1979
	Jim Arnold	1984

* NFL RECORD

PUNTS

Most Punts, Career
1,014	Jerrel Wilson	1963-77
421	Louie Aguiar	1994-98
284	Jim Arnold	1983-85
272	Bryan Barker	1990-93
219	Kelly Goodburn	1987-90

Most Punts, Season
99	Lewis Colbert	1986
98	Jim Arnold	1984
93	Jim Arnold	1983, 1985

Most Punts, Game
11	Bob Grupp vs. Baltimore	Sept. 2, 1979
	Jim Arnold vs. San Francisco	Nov. 17, 1985
	Kelly Goodburn vs. Cleveland	Nov. 19, 1989
	Louie Aguiar vs. San Diego	Nov. 18, 1994
10	Jerrel Wilson vs. N.Y. Jets	Sept. 18, 1965
	Jerrel Wilson vs. Denver	Oct. 6, 1974
	Kelly Goodburn vs. N.Y. Jets	Oct. 2, 1988

Longest Punt
76	Dan Stryzinski vs. Oakland	Sept. 9, 2001
74	Bob Grupp vs. San Diego	Nov. 4, 1979
72	Jerrel Wilson vs. San Diego	Sept. 29, 1963
70	Jerrel Wilson vs. Denver	Oct. 11, 1964
	Jerrel Wilson vs. Buffalo	Oct. 18, 1964
	Jerrel Wilson vs. Houston	Nov. 28, 1968

AVERAGE YARDAGE

Highest Average, Career (200 Punts)
43.57	Jerrel Wilson (1, 014-44,185)	1963-77
42.59	Louie Aguiar (421-17,930)	1994-98
42.02	Jim Arnold (284-11,934)	1983-85

Highest Average, Season (Qualifiers)
46.06	Jerrel Wilson (63-3,132)	1965
45.53	Jerrel Wilson (80-3,642)	1973
45.10	Jerrel Wilson (63-2,841)	1968

Highest Average, Game (4 punts)
56.40	Jerrel Wilson vs. Boston (5-282)	Oct. 11, 1970
55.60	Louie Aguiar vs. Arizona (5-278)	Oct. 1, 1995
54.75	Jerrel Wilson vs. Boston (4-129)	Oct. 3, 1965

PUNTS HAD BLOCKED

Most Consecutive Punts, None Blocked
377	Louie Aguiar	1994-98
256	Jerrel Wilson	1968-71
233	Jim Arnold	1983-85

Punts Had Blocked, Career
12	Jerrel Wilson	1963-77
2	Bob Grupp	1979-81
	Jim Arnold	1983-85
	Bryan Barker	1990-93

Punts Had Blocked, Season
| 2 | Jerrel Wilson | 1974 |
| | Jim Arnold | 1985 |

Punts Had Blocked, Game
| 2 | Jim Arnold vs. Denver | Oct. 27, 1985 |

Punt Returns

PUNT RETURNS

Most Punt Returns, Career
220	J.T. Smith	1979-84
130	Tamarick Vanover	1995-98
86	Ed Podolak	1969-77
83	Dale Carter	1992-95
71	Larry Brunson	1974-77

Most Punt Returns, Season
58	J.T. Smith	1979
51	Tamarick Vanover	1995
50	J.T. Smith	1981
43	Garcia Lane	1980
40	J.T. Smith	1980

Most Punt Returns, Game
8	Ed Podolak vs. San Diego	Nov. 10, 1974
7	J.T. Smith vs. Baltimore	Sept. 2, 1979
	J.T. Smith vs. N.Y. Giants	Oct. 21, 1979

YARDS GAINED

Most Seasons Leading League
| 2 | J.T. Smith | 1979-80 |

Most Yards Gained, Career

2,322	J.T. Smith	1979-84
1,303	Tamarick Vanover	1995-98
787	Dale Carter	1992-96
739	Ed Podolak	1969-77
609	Larry Brunson	1974-77

Most Yards Gained, Season

612	J.T. Smith	1979
581	J.T. Smith	1980
540	Tamarick Vanover	1995
528	J.T. Smith	1981
398	Dale Carter	1992

Most Yards Gained, Game

141	J.T. Smith vs. Oakland	Sept. 23, 1979
130	Tamarick Vanover vs. New Orleans	
		Dec. 21, 1997
123	J.T. Smith vs. Baltimore	Nov. 2, 1980
	Jitter Fields vs. Denver	Oct. 18, 1987
110	Goldie Sellers vs. Boston	Nov. 17, 1968

Longest Punt Return (All TDs)

88	J.T. Smith vs. Oakland	Sept. 23, 1979
86	Dale Carter vs. Seattle	Nov. 22, 1992
	Tamarick Vanover vs. San Diego	
		Oct. 9, 1995
85	Jitter Fields vs. Denver	Oct. 18, 1987
82	Tamarick Vanover vs. New Orleans	
		Dec. 21, 1997

AVERAGE YARDAGE

Most Seasons Leading League

1	Abner Haynes	1960
	Noland Smith	1968
	Ed Podolak	1970
	J.T. Smith	1980

Highest Average, Career (50 returns)

11.11	Noland Smith (53-589)	1967-69
10.87	Abner Haynes (54-587)	1960-64
10.55	J.T. Smith (220-2,322)	1979-84

Highest Average, Season (Qualifiers)

15.36	Abner Haynes (14-215)	1960
15.00	Noland Smith (18-270)	1968
14.79	Johnny Robinson (14-207)	1960

Highest Average, Game (3 returns)

28.67	Mike Garrett vs. Buffalo (3-86)	Sept. 11, 1966
	Noland Smith vs. N.Y. Jets (3-86)	Sept. 15, 1968
27.50	Goldie Sellers vs. Boston (4-110)	Nov. 17, 1968
27.00	Ed Podolak vs. Denver (3-81)	Oct. 4, 1970

TOUCHDOWNS

Most Touchdowns, Career

4	J.T. Smith	1979-84
2	Tamarick Vanover	1995-98

Most Touchdowns, Season

2	J.T. Smith	1979, 1980
	Dale Carter	1992

Most Touchdowns, Game

1	15 times, Last:	
	Tamarick Vanover vs. New Orleans Dec. 21, 1997	

Kickoff Returns

KICKOFF RETURNS

Most Kickoff Returns, Career

168	Tamarick Vanover	1995-98
84	Dave Grayson	1961-64
68	Noland Smith	1967-69
64	Anthony Hancock	1982-86
62	Jeff Smith	1985-86

Most Kickoff Returns, Season

51	Tamarick Vanover	1997
43	Tamarick Vanover	1995
41	Noland Smith	1967
	Tamarick Vanover	1998

Most Kickoff Returns, Game

*9	Noland Smith vs. Oakland	Nov. 23, 1967
	Paul Palmer vs. Seattle	Sept. 20, 1987

*NFL RECORD

YARDS GAINED

Most Yards Gained, Career

4,213	Tamarick Vanover	1995-98
2,231	Dave Grayson	1961-64
1,822	Noland Smith	1967-69
1,309	Abner Haynes	1960-64
1,292	Paul Palmer	1987-88

Most Yards Gained, Season

1,308	Tamarick Vanover	1997
1,148	Noland Smith	1967
1,095	Tamarick Vanover	1995
956	Tamarick Vanover	1998
923	Paul Palmer	1987

Most Yards Gained, Game

251	Jon Vaughn vs. Miami	Dec. 12, 1994
244	Noland Smith vs. San Diego	Oct. 15, 1967
221	Paul Palmer vs. Seattle	Sept. 20, 1987

Longest Kickoff Return (All TDs)

*106	Noland Smith vs. Denver	Dec. 17, 1967
99	Dave Grayson vs. Denver	Sept. 7, 1963
	Tamarick Vanover vs. Seattle	Sept. 3, 1995
97	Boyce Green vs. Pittsburgh	Dec. 21, 1986
	Tamarick Vanover vs. Denver	Oct. 27, 1996

*NFL RECORD

AVERAGE YARDAGE

Most Seasons Leading League

1	Dave Grayson	1961

Highest Average, Career (50 returns)

26.79	Noland Smith (68-1,822)	1967-69
26.56	Dave Grayson (84-2,231)	1961-64
25.17	Abner Haynes (52-1,309)	1960-64

Highest Average, Season (Qualifiers)

29.71	Dave Grayson (18-535)	1962
28.31	Dave Grayson (16-453)	1961
28.30	Larry Marshall (23-651)	1972

Highest Average, Game (3 returns)

44.33	Paul Palmer vs. Seattle (3-133)	Dec. 27, 1987
40.67	Noland Smith vs. San Diego (6244)	Oct. 15, 1967
40.33	L. Williams vs. Cincinati (3-121)	Nov. 21, 1976

TOUCHDOWNS

Most Touchdowns, Career

4	Tamarick Vanover	1995-98
2	Paul Palmer	1987-88

Most Touchdown, Season

2	Paul Palmer	1987
	Tamarick Vanover	1995

Most Touchdowns, Game

1	12 times
	Last; Tamarick Vanover vs. Buffalo Sept. 14, 1997

Fumbles

Most Fumbles, Season

16	Steve Fuller	1980
15	Len Dawson	1964

Most Fumbles, Game

*7	Len Dawson vs. San Diego	Nov. 15, 1964
	*NFL RECORD	

OPPONENT FUMBLES RECOVERED

Most Opponent Fumbles Recovered, Career

18	Derrick Thomas	1989-98
17	Dan Saleaumua	1989-96
15	Bobby Bell	1963-74
	Willie Lanier	1967-77
	Deron Cherry	1981-91
14	Jim Lynch	1967-77

Most Opponent Fumbles Recovered, Season

6	Deron Cherry	1988
	Dan Saleaumua	1990
5	Dan Saleaumua	1989
4	Bill Andrew	1977
	Tim Gray	1977
	Gary Spani	1980

Most Opponent Fumbles Recovered, Game

*3	Charles Jackson vs. Pittsburgh	Sept. 6, 1981

*NFL RECORD

Longest Return After Fumble Recovered, Yards

100 (TD)	Chris Martin vs. Miami	Oct. 13, 1991

Combined Net Yards Gained

(Rushing, receiving, interceptions returns, punt returns, kickoff returns and fumble returns)

ATTEMPTS

Most Attempts, Career

1,559	Ed Podolak	1969-77
1,288	Christian Okoye	1987-92
1,095	Abner Haynes	1960-65

Most Attempts, Season

389	Priest Holmes	2001
372	Christian Okoye	1989
286	Mike Garrett	1967
277	Ed Podolak	1973

Most Attempts, Game

38	Christian Okoye vs. Green Bay	Dec. 10, 1989
37	Christian Okoye vs. Seattle	Nov. 5, 1989
36	Abner Haynes vs. Denver	Oct. 30, 1960
35	Barry Word vs. L.A. Raiders	Dec. 22, 1991
34	Woody Green vs. N.Y. Giants	Nov. 3, 1974

YARDS GAINED

Most Yards Gained, Career

8,442	Abner Haynes	1960-65
8,178	Ed Podolak	1969-77
7,467	Otis Taylor	1965-75

Most Yards Gained, Season

2,169	Priest Holmes	2001
2,100	Abner Haynes	1960
1,897	Tamarick Vanover	1995
1,865	Abner Haynes	1961

Most Yards Gained, Game

309	Stephone Paige vs. San Diego	Dec. 22, 1985
276	Abner Haynes vs. San Diego	Oct. 20, 1963
265	Abner Haynes vs. Oakland	Sept. 27, 1964

Sacks

(Sacks have been compiled since 1973)

Most Sack, Career

119.5	Derrick Thomas	1989-98
86.0	Neil Smith	1988-96
72.5	Art Still	1978-87
51.0	Mike Bell	1979-85, 1987-91
40.0	Bill Maas	1984-92

Most Sacks, Season

20.0	Derrick Thomas	1990
15.0	Neil Smith	1993
14.5	Art Still	1980
	Art Still	1984
	Neil Smith	1992
	Derrick Thomas	1992

Most Sacks, Game

*7.0	Derrick Thomas vs. Seattle	Nov. 11, 1990
6.0	Derrick Thomas vs. Oakland	Sept. 6, 1998
4.0	Wilbur Young vs. San Diego	Oct. 19, 1975
	Art Still vs. Oakland	Oct. 5, 1980
	Derrick Thomas vs. Buffalo	Oct. 7, 1991
	Derrick Thomas vs. San Diego	Nov. 8, 1992
	Neil Smith vs. L.A. Raiders	Oct. 3, 1993

*NFL RECORD

Tackles

Most Tackes, Career

999	Gary Spani	1978-86
992	Art Still	1978-87
927	Deron Cherry	1981-91
827	Kevin Ross	1984-93, '97
742	Donnie Edwards	1996-2001
728	Derrick Thomas	1989-99

Most Tackes, Season

157	Gary Spani	1979
153	Gary Spani	1981
151	Deron Cherry	1988
	Donnie Edwards	1998
	Donnie Edwards	2000
149	Gary Spani	1980

Miscellaneous

Longest Return of Blocked Field Goal

78 (TD)	Lloyd Burruss vs. Pittsburgh	Dec. 21, 1986
65 (TD)	Kevin Ross vs. Cincinnati	Dec. 6, 1987

Team Records

Games Won

Most Consecutive Game Won
7	1968-69, 1969, 1995
6	1968, 1997
5	1961-62, 1966-67, 1971, 1984-85

Most Consecutive Games Won, Start of Season
4	1996
3	1962, 1966, 1994, 1995

Most Consecutive Games Won, End of Season
6	1997
5	1968
3	1960, 1963, 1966, 1967, 1971, 1972, 1984, 1986

Most Consecutive Home Games Won
11	1997-98
10	1968-69, 1995-96
9	1970-71, 1994-95
8	1997

Most Consecutive Road Games Won
9	1966-67, 1994-95
6	1967-68, 1968-69, 1971-72

Games Lost

Most Consecutive Games Lost
9	1987
8	1975-76
7	1985

Most Consecutive Games Lost, Start of Season
5	1977
4	1976, 1980
3	1975

Most Consecutive Games Lost, End of Season
6	1977
4	1975
3	1996

Most Consecutive Home Games Lost
8	1974-75
7	1975-76
6	1977-78

Most Consecutive Road Games Lost
8	1978-79, 1985-86
6	1988
5	1961, 1975-76, 1984, 1987, 1998

Scoring

Most Points, Season
448	1966
408	1967
389	1962

Fewest Points, Season
176	1982 (9 games)
225	1977
231	1973

Most Points Scored, Game
59	vs. Denver	Sept. 7, 1963
56	vs. Denver	Oct. 23, 1966
54	vs. St. Louis	Oct. 22, 2000
52	4 times; Last vs. Denver	Oct. 29, 1967

Most Points, Both Teams, Game
99 (OT)	Kansas City (48) vs. Seattle (51)	Nov. 27, 1983
88	Denver (39) vs. Kansas City (49)	Nov. 1, 1964
	KC (54) vs. St. Louis	Oct. 22, 2000

Fewest Points, Both Teams, Game
3	Kansas City (0) vs. Tampa Bay (3)	Dec. 16, 1979
9	Cleveland (6) vs. Kansas City (3)	Sept. 4, 1988
12	Kansas City (3) vs. Miami (9)	Oct. 20, 1974
	St. Louis (6) vs. Kansas City (6)	Nov. 22, 1970

Most Points, Shutout Victory, Game
48	vs. N.Y. Jets	Dec. 22, 1963
41	vs. Miami	Oct. 8, 1967
34	vs. Boston	Dec. 11, 1960
	vs. Houston	Nov. 26, 1989
	vs. Cleveland	Sept. 30, 1990

Fewest Points, Shutout Victory, Game
14	vs. Baltimore	Sept. 2, 1979
16	vs. Denver	Dec. 6, 1970
17	vs. L.A. Chargers	Sept. 25, 1960

Most Consecutive Games Scoring
179	1963-76
124	1994-current
91	1987-92
60	1979-84
52	1960-63, 1976-79

Touchdowns

Most Touchdowns, Season
55   1966
50   1962
49   1964, 1967

Fewest Touchdowns, Season
17   1982 (9 games)
23   1973
24   1988

Most Touchdowns, Game
8   vs. Denver   Sept. 7, 1963
        vs. Denver   Oct. 23, 1966
7   9 times; Last vs. St. Louis   Oct. 22, 2000

Most Touchdowns, Both Teams, Game
13   Kansas City (7) vs. Seattle (6)Nov. 27, 1983 (OT)
12   Denver (5) vs. Kansas City (7)   Nov. 1, 1964
        KC (7) vs. St. Louis (5)   Oct. 22, 2000

Most Consecutive Games Scoring Touchdowns
96   1963-70
64   1997 - 2001
52   1960-63
33   1976-78

Points After Touchdown

Most Points After Touchdown, Season
48   1966
47   1962
46   1964

Fewest Points After Touchdown, Season
17   1982 (9 times)
21   1973
23   1988

Most Points After Touchdown, Game
8   vs. Denver   Sept. 8, 1963
        vs. Denver   Oct. 23, 1966

Fields Goals

Most Field Goals Attempted, Season
44   1971
42   1970
40   1968

Fewest Field Goals Attempted, Season
17   1964
18   1977
22   1979

Most Field Goals Attempted, Game
7   vs. Buffalo   Dec. 19, 1971
6   7 times; Last vs. Denver   Dec. 16, 2001

Most Field Goals Attempted, Both Teams, Game
10   Kansas City (7) vs. Buffalo (3)   Dec. 19, 1971
        Kansas City (5) vs. San Diego (5)   Oct. 29, 1972
        Kansas City (6) vs. Denver (4)   Dec. 16, 2001

Most Field Goals Made, Season
34   1990
30   1968, 1970
27   1969, 1988, 1997, 1998, 2001

Fewest Field Goals Made, Season
7   1961
8   1963, 1964
12   1979

Most Field Goals Made, Game
5   vs. Buffalo   Nov. 2, 1969
        vs. Buffalo   Dec. 7, 1969
        vs. Buffalo   Dec. 19, 1971
        vs. L.A. Raiders   Sept. 12, 1985
        vs. Cincinnati   Nov. 13, 1988
        vs. Chicago   Dec. 29, 1990
        vs. Denver   Sept. 20, 1993

Most Field Goals Made, Both Teams, Game
8   Kansas City (5) vs. Buffalo (3)   Dec. 19, 1971
7   Buffalo (2) vs. Kansas City (5)   Dec. 7, 1969
        Kansas City (4) vs. Denver (3)   Dec. 16, 2001

Most Consecutive Games Scoring Field Goals
16   1970
11   1968-69, 1971-72, 1985-86
10   1980-81

Safeties

Most Safeties, Season
3   1988, 1997

Most Safeties, Game
1   16 times; Last vs. Oakland   Sept. 6, 1998

First Downs

Most First Downs, Season

324	2001
322	1991, 1994
321	2000
315	1981, 1997
314	1983

Fewest First Downs, Season

163	1982 (9 games)
183	1970
208	1973

Most First Downs, Game

32	vs. Houston	Oct. 24, 1965
31	vs. Oakland	Nov. 5, 2000
30	vs. L.A. Raiders	Dec. 22, 1991
29	vs. N.Y. Giants	Nov. 3, 1974
	vs. Denver	Oct. 24, 1976
	vs. Seattle	Nov. 22, 1981
	vs. San Diego	Sept. 20, 1981
	vs. Seattle	Sept. 28, 1997
	vs. Washington	Sept. 30, 2001

Fewest First Downs, Game

4	vs. Tampa Bay	Dec. 16, 1979
7	vs. Boston	Oct. 23, 1964
	vs. Oakland	Dec. 12, 1970
8	10 times; Last vs. Miami	Oct. 11, 1987

Most First Downs, Both Teams, Game

62	KC (31) vs. Oakland (31)	Nov. 5, 2000
59	Seattle (33) vs. Kansas City (26)	Nov. 27, 1983 (OT)
58	Denver (34) vs. Kansas City (24)	Nov. 18, 1974

Most First Downs, Rushing, Season

160	1978, 1981
130	1969, 1997

Fewest First Downs, Rushing, Season

71	1982 (9 games)
79	1985
83	1970, 1983, 1986

Most First Downs, Rushing, Game

20	vs. Houston	Oct. 1, 1961
18	vs. Oakland	Oct. 20, 1968
	vs. Seattle	Nov. 22, 1981
	vs. Detroit	Nov. 28, 1996
16	8 times; Last vs. Buffalo	Oct. 7, 1991

Fewest First Downs, Rushing, Game

0*	vs. Cincinatti *NFL RECORD	Nov. 24, 1974
	vs. Pittsburgh	Nov. 10, 1985
	vs. L.A. Raiders	Dec. 6, 1992
	vs. Denver	Oct. 27, 1996
1	7 times; Last vs. Denver	Nov. 16, 1998

Most First Downs, Passing, Season

211	1994
208	1983
207	2000
180	1993

Fewest First Downs, Passing, Season

79	1982 (9 games)
86	1970
89	1968

Most First Downs, Passing, Game

23	vs. Oakland	Nov. 5, 2000
21	vs. Dallas	Nov. 20, 1983
	vs. Denver	Oct. 17, 1994
19	vs. Denver	Nov. 1, 1964
	vs. N.Y. Jets	Nov. 16, 1969
	vs. Denver	Oct. 30, 1983
	vs. Miami	Dec. 12, 1994
	vs, Washington	Sept. 30, 2001

Fewest First Downs, Passing, Game

1	vs. Oakland	Oct. 20, 1968
	vs. Houston	Sept. 10, 1978
	vs. Tampa Bay	Dec. 16, 1979
2	4 times; Last vs. Seattle	Dec. 17, 1978

Most First Downs, Penalty, Season

33	1996, 1998
29	1966, 1978, 1984
28	1979

Fewest First Downs, Penalty, Season

4	1969
8	1965
9	1973

Most First Downs, Penalty, Game

9	vs. L.A. Raiders	Oct. 3, 1993
7	vs. L.A. Raiders	Sept. 17, 1989
	vs. Seattle	Oct. 17, 1996
5	6 times; Last vs. San Diego	Nov. 22, 1998

Net Yards Gained Rushing and Passing

Yards Gained
Most Yards Gained, Season
5,692 1994
5,673 2001
5,614 2000
5,596 1983
5,321 1991, 1999

Fewest Yards Gained, Season
2,498 1982 (9 games)
3,536 1973
3,577 1970

Most Yards Gained, Game

615	vs. Denver	Oct. 28, 1966
566	vs. Detroit	Oct. 14, 1990
551	vs. Buffalo	Sept. 30, 1962
546	vs. Washington	Sept. 30, 2001
542	vs. Houston	Oct. 24, 1965
537	vs. San Diego	Dec. 11, 1983

Fewest Yards Gained, Game

62	vs. Oakland	Nov. 8, 1963
80	vs. Tampa Bay	Dec. 16, 1979
104	vs. Buffalo	Oct. 29, 1973
106	vs. Oakland	Dec. 8, 1973
121	vs. Denver	Oct. 4, 1970
	vs. Oakland	Dec. 12, 1970

Most Yards Gained, Both Teams, Game
1,013 Kansas City (537) vs. San Diego (476)
           Dec. 11, 1983
986 KC (513) vs. Oakland (473) Nov. 5, 2000
968 San Diego (532) vs. Kansas City (436)
           Dec. 22, 1985
962 Kansas City (431) vs. Seattle (531)
           Nov. 27, 1983 (OT)

Fewest Yards Gained, Both Teams, Game
323 Kansas City (178) vs. N.Y. Jets (145) Nov. 7, 1971
335 Houston (91) vs. Kansas City (244) Oct. 12, 1969
338 Oakland (276) vs. Kansas City (62) Nov. 8, 1963

Most Consecutive Games, 400 or More Yards Gained
4 1976
3 1974, 2000

Most Consecutive Games, 300 or More Yards Gained
10 1966-67, 1989
7 1981, 1991
6 1961-62, 1964-65, 1984-85

Plays

Most Plays, Season
1,098 1994
1,074 1983
1,059 1995

Fewest Plays, Season
573 1982 (9 games)
775 1970
831 1968

Most Plays, Game

91	vs. Cincinnati	Sept. 3, 1978
86	vs. N.Y. Giants	Nov. 3, 1974
	vs. Seattle	Sept. 28, 1997
85	vs. Jacksonville	Nov. 9, 1997

Fewest Plays, Game

38	vs. Oakland	Dec. 12, 1970
	vs. Tampa Bay	Dec. 16, 1979
41	vs. San Diego	Oct. 7, 1962
42	vs. Oakland	Dec. 8, 1973

Rushing Attempts

Most Rushing Attempts, Season
663 1978
610 1981
569 1979

Fewest Rushing Attempts, Season
269 1982 (9 games)
383 2000
387 1983
400 1963

Most Rushing Attempts, Game

69	vs. Cincinnati	Sept. 3, 1978
60	vs. Oakland	Oct. 20, 1968
57	vs. Seattle	Nov. 5, 1989

Fewest Rushing Attempts, Game

9	vs. Oakland	Nov. 5, 2000
11	vs. New England	Oct. 11, 1998
12	vs. Oakland	Dec. 8, 1973
	vs. Denver	Oct. 27, 1996
	vs. Atlanta	Dec. 24, 2000
14	vs. San Diego	Sept. 29, 1963
	vs. Pittsburgh	Nov. 10, 1985
	vs. L.A. Raiders	Dec. 6, 1992

Most Rushing Attempts, Both Teams, Game
102   Kansas City (52) vs. San Diego (50)
                                     Nov. 12, 1978 (OT)
100   Denver (59) vs. Kansas City (41) Sept. 24, 1978

Fewest Rushing Attempts, Both Teams, Game
37   Houston (16) vs. Kansas City (21) Dec. 16, 1990
40   Kansas City (17) vs. Buffalo (23)   Dec. 12, 1965

Yards Gained

Most Yards Gained, Rushing, Season
2,986   1978
2,633   1981
2,407   1962

Fewest Yards Gained, Rushing, Season
943   1982 (9 games)
1,254 1983
1,465 2000
1,468 1986

Most Yards Gained, Rushing, Game
398   vs. Houston   Oct. 1, 1961
380   vs. Denver   Oct. 23, 1966
320   vs. Buffalo   Sept. 30, 1962
313   vs. Cincinnati   Oct. 26, 1969
310   vs. Detroit   Oct. 14, 1990

Fewest Yards Gained, Rushing, Game
0   vs. Denver   Dec. 19, 1965
14   vs. New England Oct. 11, 1998
17   vs. Boston   Nov. 18, 1960
      vs. L.A. Raiders   Dec. 6, 1992

Most Yards Gained, Rushing, Both Teams, Game
502   Houston (104) vs. Texans (398)   Oct. 1, 1961
       Oakland (218) vs. Texans (284) Nov. 26, 1961
479   Detroit (228) vs. Kansas City (251) Nov. 23, 1975

Fewest Yards Gained, Rushing, Both Teams, Game
75   Kansas City (20) vs. Houston (55) Sept. 29, 1974
105   Boston (78) vs. Kansas City (27) Nov. 17, 1968
111   Dallas Texans (108) vs. San Diego (3)
                                      Nov. 19, 1961
       Kansas City (48) vs. San Diego (63) Oct. 13, 1985

Average Gain

Highest Average Gain, Rushing,
5.18   1966
5.03   1962
4.97   1961

Lowest Average Gain, Rushing, Season
3.24   1983
3.39   1980
3.40   1986

Touchdowns

Most Touchdowns, Rushing, Season
24   1960
23   1961
22   1981

Fewest Touchdowns, Rushing, Season
3   1982 (9 games)
6   1972
7   1987

Most Touchdowns, Rushing, Game
5   vs. Denver   Oct. 23, 1966
4   10 times; Last vs. Detroit   Oct. 14, 1990

Most Touchdowns, Rushing, Both Teams, Game
7   Boston (3) vs. Texans (4)   Sept. 8, 1962
      Kansas City (4) vs. Denver (3)   Oct. 10, 1965

Passing Attempts

Most Passes Attempts, Season
641   1983
615   1994
593   1984

Fewest Passes Attempted, Season
264   1982 (9 games)
270   1968
289   1970

Most Passes Attempts, Game
59   vs. Dallas   Nov. 20, 1963
55   vs. San Diego   Oct. 9, 1994
      vs. Miami   Dec. 12, 1994
54   vs. Denver   Nov. 16, 1986
      vs. Denver   Oct. 17, 1994
      vs. San Diego   Sept. 29, 1996
      vs. San Diego   Nov. 24, 1996
53   vs. Oakland   Nov. 5, 2000

Fewest Passes Attempted, Game
3   vs. Oakland   Oct. 20, 1968
6   vs. Oakland   Dec. 13, 1969
10   vs. Denver   Sept. 24, 1978

Most Passes Attempts, Both Teams, Game

100	Tampa Bay (54) vs. Kansas City (46)	
		Oct. 28, 1964
95	Kansas City (54) vs. San Diego (41)	Sept. 29, 1996
90	Kansas City (59) vs. Dallas (31)	Nov. 20, 1983
	Kansas City (41) vs. San Diego (49)	Dec. 11, 1983

Fewest Passes Attempted, Both Teams, Game

26	Kansas City (6) vs. Oakland (20)	Dec. 13, 1969
	Kansas City (13) vs. Tampa Bay (13)	Dec. 16, 1979
27	Houston (13) vs. Kansas City (14)	Sept. 10, 1978

Completions

Most Passes Completed, Season

369	1983
366	1994
342	2000
305	1984, 1998

Fewest Passes Completed, Season

145	1982 (9 games)
154	1970
156	1968

Most Passes Completed, Game

39	vs. Oakland	Nov. 5, 2000
37	vs. San Diego	Oct. 9, 1994
34	vs. Denver	Oct. 17, 1994
33	vs. Dallas	Nov. 20, 1983
	vs. Miami	Dec. 12, 1994

Fewest Passes Completed, Game

2	vs. Oakland	Oct. 20, 1968
	vs. Oakland	Dec. 13, 1969
5	7 times; Last vs. Seattle	Dec. 17, 1978

Most Passes Completed, Both Teams, Game

62	Kansas City (31) vs. San Diego (31)	Dec. 11, 1983
55	San Diego (32) vs. Kansas City (23)	Oct. 14, 1984
	Tampa Bay (29) vs. Kansas City (26)	Oct. 28, 1984

Fewest Passes Completed, Both Teams, Game

11	San Diego (1) vs. Kansas City (10)	Sept. 20, 1998
12	Kansas City (7) vs. Tampa Bay (5)	Dec. 16, 1979
13	Kansas City (2) vs. Oakland (11)	Dec. 13, 1969
	Boston (5) vs. Kansas City (8)	Oct. 11, 1970

Yards Gained

Most Yards Gained, Passing, Season

4,388	2000
4,341	1983
3,960	1994
3,863	2001
3,568	1984

Fewest Yards Gained, Passing, Season

1,555	1982 (9 games)
1, 660	1979
1,719	1970

Most Yards Gained, Passing, Game

474	vs. Oakland	Nov. 5, 2000
406	vs. San Diego	Dec. 11, 1983
395	vs. New Orleans	Sept. 8, 1985
393	vs. Denver	Oct. 17, 1994
391	vs. Dallas	Nov. 20, 1983
383	vs. Denver	Nov. 1, 1964

Fewest Yards Gained, Passing, Game

-22	vs. Oakland	Nov. 8, 1963
15	vs. Seattle	Sept. 30, 1979
16	vs. Oakland	Oct. 20, 1968
18	vs. Denver	Oct. 4, 1970
20	vs. New Orleans	Dec. 21, 1997

Most Yards Gained, Passing, Both Teams, Game

782	Kansas City (406) vs. San Diego (376)	
		Dec. 11, 1983
716	Kansas City (474) vs. Oakland (242)	Nov. 5, 2000
698	Kansas City (229) vs. Oakland (469)	Nov. 3, 1968

Fewest Yards Gained, Passing, Both Teams, Game

67	Kansas City (22) vs. Tampa Bay (45)	Dec. 16, 1979
81	Houston (47) vs. Kansas City (34)	Sept. 10, 1978

Times Sacked

(Complied since 1962)

Most Times Sacked, Season

57	1980
53	1975
50	1986

Fewest Times Sacked, Season

19	1994
21	1978, 1991, 1995
22	1990

Most Times Sacked, Game

10	vs. Baltimore	Nov. 2, 1980
8	vs. Pittsburgh	Dec. 5, 1982
	vs. L.A. Raiders	Dec. 12, 1982

Most Times Sacked, Both Teams, Game

13	Cleveland (11) vs. Kansas City (2)	Sept. 30, 1984
	Houston (7) vs. Kansas City (6)	Sept. 21, 1986

Completion Percentage

Most Consecutive Seasons Leading League, Completion Percentage
4*   *NFL RECORD   1966-69

Highest Completion Percentage
60.56   (322-195)   1962
59.54   (435-259)   1989
59.51   (366-615)   1994

Lowest Completion Percentage, Season
44.36   (399-177)   1961
47.61   (439-209)   1960
48.90   (409-200)   1965

Touchdowns

Most Touchdowns, Passing, Season
32   1964
31   1966
30   1963
29   1983, 2000

Fewest Touchdowns, Passing, Season
7   1978, 1979
10   1973, 1982 (9 games)
11   1974, 1977

Most Touchdowns, Passing, Game
6   vs. Denver   Nov. 1, 1964
5   5 times; Last vs. San Diego   Sept. 17, 2000

Most Touchdowns, Passing, Both Teams, Game
8   Denver (2) vs. Kansas City (6)   Nov. 1, 1964
        Kansas City (4) vs. San Diego (4) Dec. 11, 1983

Passes Had Intercepted

Most Passes Had Intercepted, Season
27   1961
26   1977
25   1974

Fewest Passes Had Intercepted, Season
5   1990
8   1982 (9 games)
10   1993, 1994, 1997

Most Passes Had Intercepted, Game
7   vs. Pittsburgh   Oct. 13, 1974
6   vs. Seattle   Nov. 4, 1984
        vs. L.A. Raiders   Oct. 20, 1985

Most Passes Had Intercepted, Both Teams, Game
9   Miami (6) vs. Kansas City (3)   Nov. 13, 1966
8   7 times; Last; Seattle (5) vs. Kansas City (3)
Sept. 29, 1985

Punting

Most Season Leading League (Average Distance)
6*   1968, 1971-73, 1979, 1984   *NFL RECORD

Most Consecutive Seasons Leading League
3   1971-73

Most Punts, Season
99   1986
98   1984
95   1985

Fewest Punts, Season
38   1982 (9 games)
54   1962
57   1991

Most Punts, Game
11   vs. N.Y. Jets   Sept. 18, 1965
        vs. Baltimore   Sept. 2, 1979
        vs. San Francisco   Nov. 17, 1985
        vs. Cleveland   Nov. 19, 1989
        vs. San Diego   Nov. 13, 1994
10   vs. Denver   Oct. 6, 1974
        vs. Oakland   Oct. 5, 1980
        vs. N.Y. Jets   Oct. 2, 1988
        vs. San Diego   Nov. 26, 2000

Fewest Punts, Game
0   vs. L.A. Raiders   Dec. 22, 1991
        vs. Carolina   Dec. 10, 2000

AVERAGE YARDAGE

Highest Average Distance, Punting, Season
45.53   (80-3,642)   1973
45.26   (65-2,942)   1968
44.85   (66-2,960)   1972

Lowest Average Distance, Punting, Season
36.06   (54-1,947)   1962
38.53   (70-2,697)   1981
38.67   (81-3,132)   1990

Punt Returns

Most Seasons Leading League (Average Return)
5   1960, 1968, 1970, 1979-80

Most Punt Returns, Seasons
58   1979, 1995
50   1981
45   1978

Fewest Punt Returns, Seasons
15   1982 (9 games)
26   1961, 1963
27   1962

Most Punt Returns, Game
8   vs. San Diego   Nov. 10, 1974
7   vs. N.Y. Giants   Oct. 21, 1979

Most Punt Returns, Both Teams, Game
15   Baltimore (9) vs. Kansas City (6)   Sept. 2, 1979

YARDS GAINED

Most Yards, Punt Returns, Season
612   1979
581   1980
561   1995

Fewest Yards, Punt Returns, Season
126   1972
129   1982 (9 games)
150   1971

Most Yards, Punt Returns, Game
141   vs. Oakland   Sept. 23, 1979
131   vs. Boston   Dec. 11, 1960
123   vs. Baltimore   Nov. 2, 1980
         vs. Denver   Oct. 18, 1987
118   vs. Denver   Dec. 19, 1965

AVERAGE YARDS RETURNING PUNTS

Highest Average, Punt Returns, Season
15.03   (33-496)   1960
14.53   (40-581)   1980
14.52   (31-450)   1968

Lowest Average, Punt Returns, Season
4.35   (29-126)   1972
4.69   (32-150)   1977
6.56   (36-236)   1977

TOUCHDOWNS RETURNING PUNTS

Most Touchdowns, Punt Returns, Season
2   1968, 1979, 1980, 1992
1   1960, 1965, 1966, 1987, 1995, 1997

Most Touchdowns, Punt Returns, Game
2   13 times; Last vs. New Orleans   Dec. 21, 1997

Most Touchdowns, Punt Returns, Both Teams, Game
2*   Kansas City (1) vs. Buffalo (1)   Sept. 11, 1966
         *NFL RECORD

Kickoff Returns

Most Kickoff Returns, Season
70   1987, 2000
66   1996
64   1976

Fewest Kickoff Returns, Season
31   1973
34   1982 (9 games)
37   1962

Most Kickoff Returns, Game
10   vs. Oakland   Nov. 2, 1967
         vs. Seattle   Sept. 20, 1987
9   vs. Pittsburgh   Nov. 10, 1985

YARDS GAINED

Most Yards, Kickoff Returns, Season
1,567   1996
1,538   1976
1,465   1961

Fewest Yards, Kickoff Returns, Season
722   1992
723   1982 (9 games)
725   1973

Most Yards, Kickoff Returns, Game
251   vs. Miami   Dec. 12, 1994
245   vs. San Diego   Oct. 15, 1967
236   vs. Pittsburgh   Nov. 10, 1985

AVERAGE YARDAGE

Highest Average, Kickoff Returns, Season
27.64   (53-1,465)   1961
26.59   (41-1,090)   1969
25.81   (37-955)   1962

Lowest Average, Kickoff Returns, Season

16.52	(56-925)	1988
17.04	(46-784)	1990
17.20	(54-929)	1983

TOUCHDOWNS

Most Touchdowns, Kickoff Returns, Season

2	1987, 1995
1	1961, 1963, 1967, 1969, 1986, 1994, 1996, 1997

Most Touchdowns, Kickoff Returns, Game

1	12 times; Last vs. Buffalo	Sept. 14, 1997

Fumbles

Most Fumbles, Season

42	1980

Fewest Fumbles, Season

13	1982 (9 games)
17	1995, 1996
19	2001
21	1966, 1988, 1994, 1997

Most Fumbles, Game

10*	vs. Houston
	*NFL RECORD

Most Fumbles, Both Teams, Game

14*	Kansas City (10) vs. Houston (4) Oct. 12, 1969

*NFL RECORD

Fumbles Lost

Most Fumbles Lost, Season

24	1981, 1987
21	1965, 1977

Fewest Fumbles Lost, Season

4	1982 (9 games)
8	1967, 1991

Most Fumbles Lost, Game

6	vs. Houston	Oct. 12, 1969

Turnovers

(Number of times losing the ball
on interceptions and fumbles)

Most Turnovers, Season

47	1977
46	1981

Fewest Turnovers, Season

12*	1982
19	1990
	*NFL RECORD

Most Turnovers, Game

9	vs. Buffalo	Oct. 17, 1965
	vs. Pittsburgh	Oct. 13, 1974
8	vs. San Diego	Sept. 20, 1981

Most Turnovers, Both Teams, Game

16	Houston (9) vs. Kansas City (7) Oct. 12, 1969

Penalties

Fewest Penalties, Season

43	1982 (9 games)
52	1963

Most Penalties, Seaon

158*	1998
127	1994
122	1993, 1996

*NFL RECORD

Fewest Penalties, Game

0	vs. Buffalo	Oct. 2, 1966
	vs. Oakland	Dec. 8, 1974
1	16 times; Last vs. San Diego	Sept. 28, 1991

Most Penalties, Game

17	vs. Seattle	Nov. 8, 1998
15	vs. San Diego	Sept. 20, 1998
14	vs. Atlanta	Sept. 18, 1994
	vs. Denver	Oct. 17, 1994

Fewest Penalties, Both Teams, Game

1	Buffalo (1) vs. Kansas City (0) Oct. 2, 1986

Most Penalties, Both Teams, Game

30	Kansas City (17) vs. Seattle (13) Nov. 8, 1998
25	Kansas City (11) vs. Denver (14) Sept. 20, 1993
24	Kansas City (13) vs. L.A. Raiders (11) Oct. 9, 1983
	L.A. Raiders (12) vs. Kansas City (12)
	Sept. 16, 1984
	L.A. Raiders (14) vs. Kansas City (10)
	Dec. 13, 1987
	Kansas City (14) vs. Atlanta (10) Sept. 18, 1994
	Kansas City (14) vs. Denver (10) Oct. 17, 1994
	San Diego (9) vs. Kansas City (15) Sept. 20, 1998

Yards Penalized

Fewest Yards Penalized, Season

371	1982 (9 games)
515	1974

Most Yards Penalized, Season
1,304* 1998
*NFL RECORD

Fewest Yards Penalized, Game
0	vs. Buffalo	Oct. 2, 1966
	vs. Oakland	Dec. 8, 1974
5	7 times; Last vs. Denver	Dec. 7, 1986

Most Yards Penalized, Game
154	vs. Oakland	Nov. 1, 1970
152	vs. Seattle	Nov. 8, 1998
141	vs. San Diego	Oct. 25, 1987

Fewest Yards Penalized, Both Teams, Game
| 10 | Boston (0) vs. Kansas City (10) | Nov. 17, 1968 |
| | Oakland (10) vs. Kansas City (0) | Dec. 8, 1974 |

Most Yard Penalized, Both Teams, Game
259	Kansas City (141) vs. San Diego (118)	
		Oct. 25, 1987
258	L.A. Raiders (132) vs. Kansas City (126)	
		Sept. 16, 1984

Defense

SCORING

Fewest Points Allowed, Season
170	1968
177	1969
184	1982 (9 games)

Most Points Allowed, Season
388	1967
376	1976
367	1983

Most Points Allowed, Game
51	vs. Seattle	Nov. 27, 1983 (OT)
50	vs. Buffalo	Oct. 3, 1976
49	vs. Oakland	Nov. 5, 2000
45	vs. San Diego	Oct. 15, 1967
	vs. Pittsburgh	Nov. 7, 1976
	vs. Seattle	Nov. 4, 1984
	vs. Miami	Dec. 12, 1994

Fewest Touchdowns Allowed, Season
18	1968
19	1969
21	1971

Most Touchdowns Allowed, Season
51	1976
45	1987
44	1975, 1983, 1998

Most Touchdowns Allowed, Game
7	vs. Buffalo	Oct. 3, 1976
	vs. Oakland	Nov. 5, 2000
6	10 times; Last vs. Miami	Dec. 12, 1994

FIRST DOWNS

Fewest First Downs Allowed, Season
170	1982 (9 games)
181	1969
200	1965

Most First Downs Allowed, Season
344	1987
336	1985
335	1984

Fewest First Downs Allowed, Game
5	vs. Oakland	Dec. 7, 1997
6	vs. Boston	Sept. 21, 1969
	vs. Boston	Oct. 11, 1970
	vs. Chicago	Dec. 29, 1990
7	9 times; Last vs. San Diego	Sept. 20, 1998

Most First Downs Allowed, Game
35	vs. San Diego	Oct. 19, 1986
34	vs. Denver	Nov. 18, 1974
	vs. Cleveland	Oct. 30, 1977

Fewest First Downs Allowed, Rushing, Season
52	1968
53	1969
67	1965

Most First Downs Allowed, Rushing, Season
169	1977
162	1988
149	1975

Fewest First Downs Allowed, Rushing, Game
0	vs. Houston	Dec. 4, 1960
	vs. Buffalo	Dec. 3, 1967
	vs. Denver	Oct. 3, 1971
	vs. Oakland	Dec. 3, 1995
	vs. Oakland	Dec. 7, 1997
1	13 times; Last vs. Denver	Dec. 17, 2000

Most First Downs Allowed, Rushing, Game
| 21 | vs. Pittsburgh | Nov. 7, 1976 |
| 19 | vs. Cleveland | Oct. 30, 1977 |

Fewest First Downs Allowed, Passing, Season
92	1982 (9 games)
95	1973
111	1969, 1970

Most First Downs Allowed, Passing, Season

202	2000
192	1984
184	1985, 1996
179	1980

Fewest First Downs Allowed, Passing, Game

0*	vs. Houston *NFL RECORD	Oct. 9, 1988
	vs. San Diego	Sept. 20, 1998
2	5 times; Last vs. Houston	Sept. 10, 1978

Most First Downs Allowed, Passing, Game

25	vs. Denver	Nov. 18, 1974
22	vs. Cincinnati	Dec. 6, 1987

Fewest First Downs Allowed, Penalty, Season

9	1982 (9 games)
11	1964
13	1980

Most First Downs Allowed, Penality, Season

56*	1998 *NFL RECORD
36	1993
33	1987

*NFL RECORD

Most First Downs Allowed, Penality, Game

7	vs. Denver	Nov. 16, 1998
6	6 times; Last vs. Denver	Nov. 16, 1997

Net Yards Allowed Rushing and Passing
Yards Allowed
Fewest Yards Allowed, Season

2,733	1982 (9 game)
3,163	1969
3,575	1973

Most Yards Allowed, Season

5,658	1985
5,639	1987
5,625	1984

Fewest Yards Allowed, Game

86	vs. Seattle	Dec. 24, 1995
91	vs. Houston	Oct. 12, 1969
93	vs. Oakland	Dec. 7, 1997
100	vs. Boston	Sept. 21, 1969
105	vs. Boston	Dec. 14, 1963
	vs. Boston	Oct. 11, 1970

Most Yards Allowed, Game

563	vs. Houston	Dec. 16, 1990
542	vs. N.Y. Jets	Oct. 2, 1988 (OT)
539	vs. Oakland	Nov. 3, 1968
	vs. Oakland	Oct. 3, 1977

PLAYS ALLOWED

Fewest Plays Allowed, Season

556	1982 (9 games)
808	1969
813	1971

Most Plays Allowed, Season

1,159	1984
1,126	1985
1,102	1981

Fewest Plays Allowed, Game

39	vs. Houston	Oct. 22, 1967
	vs. Oakland	Dec. 7, 1997
40	vs. Cincinnati	Oct. 13, 1968
	vs. Boston	Sept. 21, 1969

Most Plays Allowed, Game

97	vs. N.Y. Jets	Oct. 2, 1988 (OT)
95	vs. San Diego	Oct. 19, 1986
91	vs. Chicago	Nov. 8, 1981

RUSHING ATTEMPTS ALLOWED

Fewest Attempts Allowed, Rushing, Season

279	1982 (9 games)
316	1969
343	1967

Most Attempts Allowed, Rushing, Season

634	1977
609	1988
601	1978

Fewest Attempts Allowed, Rushing, Game

11	vs. New Orleans	Sept. 4, 1994
	vs. Oakland	Dec. 3, 1995
12	vs. N.Y. Jets	Nov. 27, 1966
13	vs. New England	Dec. 2, 1990
	vs. L.A. Raiders	Dec. 22, 1991

Most Attempts Allowed, Rushing, Game

65	vs. Buffalo	Oct. 29, 1973
62	vs. Tampa Bay	Dec. 16, 1979
61	vs. Oakland	Dec. 8, 1973
	vs. Chicago	Nov. 8, 1981

YARDS ALLOWED

Fewest Yards Allowed, Rushing, Season

980	1960
1,066	1982 (9 games)
1,091	1969

Most Yards Allowed, Rushing, Season
2,971   1977
2,861   1976
2,712   1975

Fewest Yards Allowed, Rushing, Game
-27   vs. Houston   Dec. 4, 1960
3   vs. San Diego   Nov. 19, 1961
8   vs. Oakland   Dec. 3, 1995

Most Yards Allowed, Rushing, Game
330   vs. Pittsburgh   Nov. 7, 1976
322   vs. Cleveland   Oct. 30, 1977
299   vs. New Orleans   Sept. 26, 1976

TOUCHDOWNS ALLOWED

Fewest Touchdowns Allowed, Rushing, Season
4   1968
6   1969, 1971
7   1982 (9 games), 1995

Most Touchdowns Allowed, Rushing, Season
24   1975, 1976
23   1977, 1988
22   1998

Most Touchdowns Allowed, Rushing, Game
5   vs. Pittsburgh   Nov. 7, 1976
4   5 times; Last vs. Miami   Oct. 11, 1987

PASSING ATTEMPTS ALLOWED

Fewest Pass Attempts Allowed, Season
262   1982 (9 games)
324   1973
325   1975

Most Pass Attempts Allowed, Season
596   1995
586   1984
576   1985

Fewest Pass Attempts Allowed, Game
9   vs. N.Y. Jets   Nov. 7, 1971
     vs. Oakland   Dec. 8, 1974
10   vs. L.A. Raiders   Sept. 16, 1973
     vs. San Diego   Dec. 18, 1988
12   vs. Philadelphia   Oct. 22, 1972
     vs. Buffalo   Oct. 29, 1973
     vs. L.A. Raiders   Nov. 28, 1982

Most Pass Attempts Allowed, Game
65   vs. San Diego   Oct. 19, 1986
61   vs. Seattle   Sept. 29, 1985
60   vs. Oakland   Oct. 5, 1980

COMPLETIONS ALLOWED

Fewest Pass Completions Allowed, Season
155   1982 (9 games)
157   1973
175   1977

Most Pass Completions Allowed, Season
332   1985
329   1984, 1995
312   1993

Fewest Pass Completions Allowed, Game
1   vs. San Diego   Sept. 20, 1998
3   vs. Houston   Oct. 22, 1967
     vs. N.Y. Jets   Nov. 7, 1971
     vs. Oakland   Dec. 8, 1974
4   vs. San Diego   Nov. 2, 1986
     vs. Houston   Oct. 9, 1988

Most Pass Completions Allowed, Game
37   vs. San Diego   Dec. 22, 1985
     vs. San Diego   Oct. 19, 1986
34   vs. L.A. Raiders   Sept. 12, 1985

YARDS ALLOWED

Fewest Yards Allowed, Passing, Season
1,619   1973
1,667   1982 (9 games)
2,010   1970

Most Yards Allowed, Passing, Season
3,662   1990
3,645   1984
3,626   1981

Fewest Yards Allowed, Passing, Game
-19   vs. San Diego   Sept. 20, 1998
9   vs. N.Y. Jets   Nov. 7, 1971
12   vs. Oakland   Dec. 8, 1974

Most Yards Allowed, Passing, Game
499   vs. Houston   Dec. 16, 1990
469   vs. Oakland   Nov. 3, 1968
459   vs. Denver   Nov. 18, 1974

TOUCHDOWNS ALLOWED

Fewest Touchdowns Allowed, Passing, Season
10   1969
11   1971, 1973
12   1982 (9 games), 1988

Most Touchdowns Allowed, Passing, Season

25	1964, 1976, 1980, 1987, 2000
23	1994
22	1974, 1979, 1985

Most Touchdowns Allowed, Passing, Game

4	7 times: Last vs. Oakland	Nov. 5, 2000

SACKS

Most Seasons Leading League

4	1960, 1965, 1969, 1990

Most Sacks, Season

60.0	1990
54.0	1997
51.0	2000
50.0	1984, 1992
48.0	1969

Fewest Sacks, Season

15.0	1982 (9 games)
22.0	1976

Most Sacks, Game

11.0	vs. Cleveland	Sept. 30, 1984
10.0	vs. Oakland	Sept. 6, 1998
9.0	vs. Buffalo	Nov. 2, 1969
	vs. Seattle	Nov. 11, 1990

MOST OPPONENT YARDS LOST

Attempting to Pass, Season

439	1968

FEWEST OPPONENT YARDS LOST

Attempting to Pass, Season

120	1982 (9 games)
157	1988

INTERCEPTION BY

Most Consecutive Seasons Leading League

5	1966-70

Most Passes Intercepted By, Season

37	1968
33	1960, 1962, 1969

Fewest Passes Intercepted By, Season

11	1987
12	1982 (9 games), 1994
13	1998

Most Passes Intercepted By, Game

7	vs. San Diego	Dec. 8, 1968
6	6 times; Last vs. Seattle	Dec. 9, 1984

Most Consecutive Games, One or More Interceptions By

23	1967-69
18	1966-67

RETURN YARDS

Most Yards Returning Interceptions, Season

596	1969
578	1967
567	1986

Fewest Yards Returning Interceptions, Season

140	1987
161	1976
166	1988

Most Yards Returning Interceptions, Game

142	vs. L.A. Raiders	Oct. 28, 1991
136	vs. Seattle	Dec. 11, 1977

TOUCHDOWNS

Most Touchdowns Returning Interceptions, Season

6	1992
5	1972, 1974

Most Touchdowns Returning Interceptions, Game

2	vs. Denver	Oct. 1, 1972
	vs. Denver	Dec. 19, 1982
	vs. San Diego	Oct. 19, 1986
	vs. Denver	Dec. 27, 1992

MOST TOUCHDOWNS RETURNING

Interceptions, Both Teams, Game

4*	Seattle (4) vs. Kansas City (0)	Nov. 4, 1984
	*NFL RECORD	
3	Kansas City (2) vs. San Diego (1)	Oct. 19, 1986

Opponent Interceptions

Yard Gained

Most Yards Interception Returns Opponents, Season

688	1984

Most Yards Interception Returns Opponents, Game

325*	vs. Seattle	Nov. 4, 1984
	*NFL RECORD	

TOUCHDOWNS

Most Touchdowns
Returning Interceptions Opponent, Season
7   1984

Most Touchdowns
Returning Interceptions Opponent, Game
4*   vs. Seattle   Nov. 4, 1984
         *NFL RECORD

PUNT RETURNS

Fewest Opponent Punt Returns, Season
22   1982 (9 games)
26   1962

Most Opponent Punt Returns, Season
60   1984

Most Opponent Punt Returns, Game
9   vs. Cincinnati   Nov. 24, 1974

Fewest Yards Allowed, Punt Returns, Season
190   1991

Most Yards Allowed, Punt Returns, Season
702   1977

Most Yards Allowed, Punt Returns, Game
170   vs. San Diego   Sept. 26, 1965

Lowest Average Allowed, Punt Returns, Season
6.37   (46-293)   1981

Highest Average Allowed, Punt Returns, Season
15.36   (22-338) (9 games)   1982
14.93   (29-433)

Most Touchdowns Allowed, Punt Returns, Season
2   1982, 1990

KICKOFF RETURNS

Fewest Opponent Kickoff Returns, Season
40   1973

Most Opponent Kickoff Returns, Season
84   1966

Fewest Yards Allowed, Kickoff Returns, Season
794   1982 (9 games)
958   1977

Most Yards Allowed, Kickoff Returns, Season
2,045*   *NFL RECORD   1966

Most Yards Allowed, Kickoff Returns, Game
289   vs. Denver   Sept. 7, 1963

Lowest Average Allowed, Kickoff Returns, Season
18.00   (71-1,278)   1986

Highest Average Allowed, Kickoff Returns, Season
25.78   (40-1,031)   1973

Most Touchdowns Allowed, Kickoff Returns, Season
2   1988, 1989

Fumbles

Fewest Opponent Fumbles, Season
16   1971
18   1982 (9 games)

Fewest Opponent Fumbles Recovered, Season
7   1971
8   1966

Most Opponent Fumbles, Season
42   1981
40   1975

Most Opponent Fumbles Recovered, Season
26   1994
25   1990

Turnovers

Fewest Opponent Turnover, Season
22   1982 (9 games)
27   1996
28   1987

Most Opponent Turnovers, Season
51   1983
49   1962, 1968, 1986

Most Opponent Turnover, Game
9   vs. Houston   Oct. 28, 1962
         vs. Houston   Oct. 12, 1969
         vs. St. Louis   Oct. 2, 1983

Best Turnover Ratio, Season
+26   (45 takes/27 gives)   1990
+22   (49 takes/27 gives)   1968

Worst Turnover Ratio, Season
-13   (28 takes/41 gives)   1987
-11   (33 takes/41 gives)   1989

Opponent Single Game Individual Records

Pass Attempts
58   Mark Hermann, San Diego   Dec. 22, 1985

Pass Completions
37   Mark Hermann, San Diego   Dec. 22, 1985

Passing Yards (Games with 400+ Yards)
527   Warren Moon, Houston   Dec. 16, 1990
445   Charley Johnson, Denver   Nov. 18, 1974
413   Pete Beathard, Houston   Sept. 9, 1968
400   John Elway, Denver   Dec. 6, 1998

Touchdown Passes
5   George Blanda, Houston   Oct. 24, 1965

Interceptions Thrown
6   John Hadl, San Diego   Dec. 8, 1968

Long Pass
90   Norm Johnson to Rich Upchurch, Denver
Sept. 21, 1975

Pass Receptions
14   Kellen Winslow, San Diego   Dec. 11, 1983

Receiving Yards
245   Haywood Jeffires, Houston   Dec. 16, 1990

Touchdown Receptions
3   Bob Chandler, Buffalo   Oct. 3, 1976
    Kellen Winslow, San Diego   Dec. 11, 1983
    Shannon Sharpe, Denver   Dec. 12, 1993

Rushing Attempts
39   O.J. Simpson, Buffalo   Oct. 29, 1973
     Ricky Bell, Tampa Bay   Dec. 16, 1979
     Marion Butts, San Diego   Dec. 17, 1989

Rushing Yards (Games with 200+ Yards)
217   Gary Anderson, San Diego   Dec. 18, 1988
214   Greg Pruitt, Cleveland   Dec. 14, 1975
207   Curt Warner, Seattle   Nov. 27, 1983 (OT)

Rushing Touchdowns
3   Jon Keyworth, Denver   Nov. 18, 1974
    Greg Pruitt, Cleveland   Dec. 14, 1975
    Pete Banaszak, Oakland   Dec. 21, 1975
    Walter Payton, Chicago   Nov. 13, 1977
    Curt Warner, Seattle   Nov. 27, 1983 (OT)
    Marcus Allen, L.A. Raiders Nov. 25, 1990
    Rodney Hampton, N.Y. Giants Dec. 19, 1992
    Terrell Davis, Denver   Dec. 6, 1998

Long Run
87   Paul Lowe, San Diego   Sept. 10, 1961

Interceptions Made
3   David Fulcher, Cincinnati   Oct. 1, 1989

Long Interceptions Return
101   Tony Greene, Buffalo   Oct. 3, 1976

Long Punt Return
95   Johnny Bailey, Chicago   Dec. 29, 1990

Long Kickoff Return
100   Nemiah Wilson, Denver   Oct. 8, 1966

Long Punt
83   Chris Norman, Denver   Sept. 23, 1984

Long Field Goal
55   John Kasey, Seattle   Jan. 2, 1994

Times Sacked
11   Paul McDonald, Cleveland   Sept. 30, 1984

Touchdowns On Interception Returns
2   Dave Brown, Seattle   Nov. 4, 1984

Fumbles
6   Dave Krieg, Seattle   Nov. 5, 1989

Post-Season: Individual Records

Service

Most Games Played, Career

10	John Alt
	Tim Grunhard
	Dave Szott
	Derrick Thomas
9	Dan Saleaumua
	Tracy Simien
	Neil Smith
8	Len Dawson
	Jonathan Hayes
	Nick Lowery
	Johnny Robinson
	Kevin Ross
	Jim Tyrer
	Jerrel Wilson

Scoring

POINTS

Most Points, Career

37	Nick Lowery (8 games – 7 FGs, 14 PATs)
35	Jan Stenerud (5 games – 9 FGs, 8 PATs)
18	Mike Garrett (6 games – 3 TDs)
	Marcus Allen (6 games – 3 TDs)

Most Points, Game

12	Abner Haynes vs. Houston	Dec. 23, 1962
	Mike Garrett vs. Buffalo	Jan. 1, 1967
	Ed Podolak vs. Miami	Dec. 25, 1971
11	Jan Stenerud vs. Minnesota	Jan. 11, 1970

TOUCHDOWNS

Most Touchdowns, Career

3	Marcus Allen (6 games)
	Mike Garrett (6 games)

Most Touchdowns, Game

2	Abner Haynes vs. Houston	Dec. 23, 1962
	Mike Garrett vs. Buffalo	Jan. 1, 1967
	Ed Podolak vs. Miami	Dec. 25, 1971

POINTS AFTER TOUCHDOWN
Most Points After Touchdown, Career

14	Nick Lowery (8 games – 15 Att.)
8	Jan Stenerud (5 games – 8 Att.)
5	Mike Mercer (2 games – 5 Att.)

Most Points After Touchdown, Game

4	Mike Mercer vs. Buffalo (4 Att.)	Jan. 1, 1967
	Nick Lowery vs. Houston (4 Att.)	Jan. 16, 1994

Most Points After Touchdown, No Misses, Career

8	Jan Stenerud (5 games)

FIELD GOALS

Most Field Goals Attempted, Career

17	Jan Stenerud (5 games – 17 Att.)
12	Nick Lowery (8 games – 12 Att.)

Most Field Goals Attempted, Game

5	Jan Stenerud vs. N.Y. Jets	Dec. 20, 1969
4	Nick Lowery vs. Miami	Jan. 5, 1991

Most Field Goals, Career

9	Jan Stenerud (5 games – 17 Att.)
8	Nick Lowery (8 games – 12 Att.)

Most Field Goals, Game

3	Jan Stenerud vs. Minnesota	Jan. 11, 1970
	Nick Lowery vs. Miami	Jan. 5, 1991

Longest Field Goal

48	Jan Stenerud vs. Minnesota	Jan. 11, 1970
38	Nick Lowery vs. Miami	Jan. 5, 1991
32	Mike Mercer vs. Buffalo	Jan. 1, 1967
	Jan Stenerud vs. Minnesota	Jan. 11, 1970
	Nick Lowery vs. Pittsburgh	Jan. 8, 1994

Rushing

ATTEMPTS

Most Attempts, Career

100	Marcus Allen (6 games)
61	Mike Garrett (6 games)
59	Barry Word (4 games)

Most Attempts, Game

33	Barry Word vs. L.A. Raiders	Dec. 28, 1991
24	Curtis McClinton vs. Houston	Dec. 23, 1962
22	Wendell Hayes vs. Miami	Dec. 25, 1971

Highest Average, Game (4 punts)
50.3   Jerrel Wilson vs. Oakland (302-6) Dec. 22, 1968
46.4   Louie Aguiar vs. Denver (232-5)   Jan. 4, 1998

Punt Returns

Most Punt Returns, Career
10   Mike Garrett (6 games)
7   Danan Hughes (6 games)

Most Punt Returns, Game
4   Mike Garrett vs. Oakland   Jan. 4, 1970
     Tamarick Vanover vs. Indianapolis Jan. 7, 1996

YARDS GAINED

Most Yards Gained, Career
84   Danan Hughes (6 games)
63   Mike Garrett (6 games)

Most Yards Gained, Game
42   Danan Hughes vs. Houston   Jan. 16, 1994
31   Danan Hughes vs. Pittsburgh Jan. 8, 1994

Longest Punt Return
35   Danan Hughes vs. Houston   Jan. 16, 1994
27   Mike Garrett vs. Buffalo   Jan. 1, 1967

Average Yardage
Highest Average, Career (10 returns)
6.3   Mike Garreet (6 games: 11-73)

Highest Average, Game (3 returns)
14.0   Danan Hughes vs. Houston (3-42) Jan. 16, 1994
10.3   Danan Hughes vs. Pittsburgh (3-31)   Jan. 8, 1994

TOUCHDOWNS

Most Touchdowns
None

Kickoff Returns

Most Kickoff Returns, Career
10   John Stephens (3 games)
5   Bert Coan (2 games)
     Noland Smith (1 game)
     Tamarick Vanover (2 games)

Most Kickoff Returns, Game
5   Noland Smith vs. Oakland   Dec. 22, 1968
     John Stephens vs. Buffalo   Jan. 23, 1994

YARDS GAINED

Most Yards Gained, Career
194   John Stephens (3 games)
154   Ed Podolak (1 game)

Most Yards Gained, Game
154   Ed Podolak vs. Miami   Dec. 25, 1971
89   John Stephens vs. Buffalo   Jan. 23, 1994
72   John Stephens vs. Pittsburgh Jan. 8, 1994

Longest Kickoff Return
78   Ed Podolak vs. Miami   Dec. 25, 1971
35   Bert Coan vs. Buffalo   Jan. 1, 1967
34   John Stephens vs. Pittsburgh Jan. 8, 1994

AVERAGE YARDAGE

Highest Average, Career (10 returns)
19.9   John Stephens (3 games: 10-199)

Highest Average, Game (3 returns)
51.3   Ed Podolak vs. Miami (3-154)   Dec. 25, 1971
24.0   John Stephens vs. Pittsburgh (3-72)   Jan. 8, 1994
23.0   Tamarick Vanover vs. Denver (3-69)   Jan. 4, 1998

TOUCHDOWNS

Most Touchdowns
None

Combined Net Yards Gained

(Rushing, receiving, interceptions returns, punt returns, kickoff returns and fumble returns)

ATTEMPTS

Most Attempts, Career
147   Marcus Allen (6 games)
88   Mike Garrett (6 games)

Most Attempts, Game
34   Barry Word vs. L.A. Raiders Dec. 28, 1991
30   Ed Podolak vs. Miami   Dec. 25, 1971

YARDS GAINED

Most Yards Gained, Career
541   Marcus Allen (6 games)
481   Otis Taylor (7 games)

Most Yards Gained, Game
350   Ed Podolak vs. Miami   Dec. 25, 1971
142   Stephone Paige vs. Miami   Jan. 5, 1991

Sacks

Most Sacks, Career
7.5   Derrick Thomas (10 games)
6.5   Neil Smith (9 games)
5.0   Aaron Brown (6 games)

Most Sacks, Game
3.0   Aaron Brown vs. Oakland   Jan. 4, 1970
2.0   Five times; By five players
        Last: Four players vs. Houston   Jan. 16, 1994

Post-Season: Team Records

Scoring

POINTS

Most Points, Game

31	vs. Buffalo	Jan. 1, 1967
28	vs. Houston	Jan. 16, 1994
27	vs. Pittsburgh	Jan. 8, 1994

Most Touchdowns, Game

4	vs. Buffalo	Jan. 1, 1967
	vs. Houston	Jan. 16, 1994
3	Twice: Last: vs. Pittsburgh	Jan. 8, 1994

FIRST DOWNS

Most First Downs, Game

28	vs. Pittsburgh	Jan. 8, 1994
24	vs. Miami	Dec. 31, 1994
23	vs. Miami	Dec. 25, 1971

Fewest First Downs, Game

13	vs. Oakland	Dec. 22, 1968
	vs. Oakland	Jan. 4, 1970
14	Four times; Last: vs. Buffalo	Jan. 5, 1992

Net Yards Gained Rushing and Passing

YARDS GAINED

Most Yards Gained, Game

451	vs. Miami	Dec. 25, 1971
414	vs. Miami	Dec. 31, 1994
401	vs. Pittsburgh	Jan. 8, 1994

Fewest Yards Gained, Game

204	vs. L.S. Raiders	Dec. 28, 1991
207	vs. Oakland	Dec. 20, 1969
213	vs. Buffalo	Jan. 5, 1992

RUSHING ATTEMPTS

Most Attempts, Game

54	vs. Houston	Dec. 23, 1962
44	vs. Miami	Dec. 25, 1971
41	vs. Minnesota	Jan. 11, 1970

Fewest Attempts, Game

18	vs. Houston	Jan. 16, 1994
19	vs. Green Bay	Jan. 15, 1967
	vs. San Diego	Jan. 2, 1993

YARDS

Most Yards, Game

213	vs. Miami	Dec. 25, 1971
199	vs. Houston	Dec. 23, 1962
151	vs. Minnesota	Jan. 11, 1970

Fewest Yards, Game

52	vs. Buffalo	Jan. 23, 1994
61	vs. San Diego	Jan. 2, 1993
70	vs. Oakland	Dec. 22, 1968

TOUCHDOWNS

Most Touchdowns, Game

2	vs. Buffalo	Jan. 1, 1967
	vs. Oakland	Jan. 4, 1970

PASSING ATTEMPTS

Most Passes Attempted, Game

52	vs. Buffalo	Jan. 23, 1994
44	vs. Pittsburgh	Jan. 8, 1994
37	vs. Miami	Dec. 31, 1994
	vs. Denver	Jan. 4, 1998

Fewest Passes Attempted, Game

14	vs. Houston	Dec. 23, 1962
	vs. L.A. Raiders	Dec. 28, 1991
17	vs. Oakland	Jan. 4, 1970
	vs. Minnesota	Jan. 11, 1970

COMPLETIONS

Most Completions, Game

29	vs. Pittsburgh	Jan. 8, 1994
26	vs. Miami	Dec. 31, 1994
25	vs. Buffalo	Jan. 23, 1994

Fewest Completions, Game

7	vs. Oakland	Jan. 4, 1970
9	vs. Houston	Dec. 23, 1962
	vs. L.A. Raiders	Dec. 28, 1991

YARDS

Most Yards, Game

314	vs. Miami	Dec. 31, 1994
286	vs. Buffalo	Jan. 23, 1994

Fewest Yards, Game

38	vs. Houston	Dec. 23, 1962
73	vs. L.A. Raiders	Dec. 28, 1991
121	vs. Oakland	Jan. 4, 1970

TIMES SACKED

Most Times Sacked, Game

7.0	vs. Buffalo	Jan. 1, 1967
	vs. San Diego	Jan. 2, 1993
6.0	vs. Houston	Dec. 23, 1962
	vs. Green Bay	Jan. 15, 1967

TOUCHDOWNS

Most Touchdowns, Game

3	vs. Houston	Jan. 16, 1994
2	Three times; Last: vs. Miami	Dec. 31, 1994

INTERCEPTIONS THROWN

Most Interceptions Thrown, Game

4	vs. Oakland	Dec. 22, 1968
	vs. Buffalo	Jan. 5, 1991
3	vs. Indianapolis	Jan. 7, 1996

INTERCEPTIONS BY

Most Interceptions By, Game

5	vs. Houston	Dec. 23, 1962
4	vs. Oakland	Jan. 4, 1970
	vs. L.A. Raiders	Dec. 28, 1991

PENALTIES

Most Penalties, Game

10	vs. Buffalo	Jan. 5, 1992
7	Three times; Last: vs. Denver	Jan. 4, 1998

Fewest Penalties, Game

1	vs. N.Y. Jets	Dec. 28, 1986
3	Twice; Last: vs. Indianapolis	Jan. 7, 1996

YARDS PENALIZED

Most Yards Penalized, Game

65	vs. Denver	Jan. 4, 1998
63	vs. N.Y. Jets	Dec. 20, 1969
62	vs. San Diego	Jan. 2, 1993

Fewest Yards Penalized, Game

5	vs. N.Y. Jets	Dec. 28, 1986
15	vs. Miami	Dec. 31, 1994
20	vs. L.A. Raiders	Dec. 28, 1991

FUMBLES

Most Fumbles, Game

5	vs. Oakland	Jan. 4, 1970
3	vs. Miami	Dec. 25, 1971

Most Fumbles Lost, Game

4	vs. Oakland	Jan. 4, 1970
2	vs. Miami	Dec. 25, 1971

TURNOVERS

Most Turnovers, Game

4	vs. Oakland	Dec. 22, 1968
	vs. Oakland	Jan. 4, 1970
	vs. Miami	Dec. 25, 1971
	vs. Buffalo	Jan. 5, 1992
	vs. Indianapolis	Jan. 7, 1996

Defense

SCORING

Fewest Points Allowed, Game

6	vs. N.Y. Jets	Dec. 20, 1969
	vs. L.A. Raiders	Dec. 28, 1991

Most Points Allowed, Game

41	vs. Oakland	Dec. 22, 1968
37	vs. Buffalo	Jan. 5, 1992
35	vs. Green Bay	Jan. 15, 1967
	vs. N.Y. Jets	Dec. 28, 1986

Fewest Touchdowns Allowed, Game

0	vs. N.Y. Jets	Dec. 20, 1969
	vs. L.A. Raiders	Dec. 28, 1991

Most Touchdowns Allowed, Game

5	vs. Green Bay	Jan. 15, 1967
	vs. Oakland	Dec. 22, 1968
	vs. N.Y. Jets	Dec. 28, 1986

FIRST DOWNS

Fewest First Downs Allowed, Game

9	vs. Buffalo	Jan. 1, 1967
13	vs. Minnesota	Jan. 11, 1970
16	Three times; Last: vs. Denver	Jan. 4, 1998

Most First Downs Allowed, Game

30	vs. Buffalo	Jan. 23, 1994
29	vs. Buffalo	Jan. 5, 1992
23	vs. Miami	Jan. 5, 1991

Net Yards Gained Rushing and Passing

Fewest Yards Allowed, Game

233	vs. Oakland	Jan. 4, 1970
235	vs. N.Y. Jets	Dec. 20, 1969
239	vs. Minnesota	Jan. 11, 1970

Most Yards Allowed, Game

454	vs. Oakland	Dec. 22, 1968
448	vs. Buffalo	Jan. 5, 1992
407	vs. Miami	Dec. 25, 1971

RUSHING ATTEMPTS

Fewest Attempts, Game

13	vs. Buffalo	Jan. 1, 1967
14	vs. Houston	Jan. 16, 1994
19	vs. Minnesota	Jan. 11, 1970

Most Attempts, Game

46	vs. Buffalo	Jan. 5, 1992
	vs. Buffalo	Jan. 23, 1994
43	vs. Miami	Dec. 25, 1971

YARDS ALLOWED

Fewest Yards Allowed, Game

39	vs. Houston	Jan. 16, 1994
40	vs. Buffalo	Jan. 1, 1967
67	vs. Minnesota	Jan. 11, 1970

Most Yards Allowed, Game

229	vs. Buffalo	Jan. 23, 1994
192	vs. San Diego	Jan. 2, 1993
180	vs. Buffalo	Jan. 5, 1992

TOUCHDOWNS ALLOWED

Most Touchdowns Allowed, Game

3	vs. Buffalo	Jan. 23, 1994
2	Twice; Last: vs. Denver	Jan. 4, 1998

PASSING ATTEMPTS

Fewest Attempts, Game

19	vs. Denver	Jan. 4, 1998
23	vs. N.Y. Jets	Dec. 28, 1986
	vs. L.A. Raiders	Dec. 28, 1991
	vs. San Diego	Jan. 2, 1993

Most Attempts, Game

46	vs. Houston	Dec. 23, 1962
45	vs. Oakland	Jan. 4, 1970
43	vs. Houston	Jan. 14, 1994
40	vs. N.Y. Jets	Dec. 20, 1969

COMPLETIONS

Fewest Completions Allowed, Game

10	vs. Denver	Jan. 4, 1998
12	vs. Buffalo	Jan. 1, 1967
	vs. L.A. Raiders	Dec. 28, 1991
	vs. Indianapolis	Jan. 7, 1996

Most Completions Allowed, Game

32	vs. Houston	Jan. 16, 1994
23	vs. Houston	Dec. 23, 1962
	vs. Buffalo	Jan. 5, 1992
	vs. Pittsburgh	Jan. 8, 1994

YARDS ALLOWED

Fewest Yards Allowed, Game

102	vs. Indianapolis	Jan. 7, 1996
124	vs. L.A. Raiders	Dec. 28, 1991
141	vs. N.Y. Jets	Dec. 28, 1986

Most Yards Allowed, Game

336	vs. Oakland	Dec. 22, 1968
272	vs. Pittsburgh	Jan. 8, 1994
263	vs. Miami	Dec. 25, 1971

TOUCHDOWNS ALLOWED

Most Touchdowns Allowed, Game

5	vs. Oakland	Dec. 22, 1968
3	Three times; Last: vs. Pittsburgh	Jan. 8, 1994

SACKS

Most Sacks, Game

9.0	vs. Houston	Jan. 16, 1994
5.0	vs. San Diego	Jan. 2, 1993
4.0	vs. Oakland	Jan. 4, 1970
	vs. Buffalo	Jan. 1, 1967

INTERCEPTIONS BY

Most Interceptions By, Game

5	vs. Houston	Dec. 23, 1962
4	vs. Oakland	Jan. 4, 1970
	vs. L.A. Raiders	Dec. 28, 1991

AFL All Star and Pro Bowl Selections

AFL All-Star Game

Selected Texans/Chiefs played for the Western Division Team

1960

No All-Star game was played following the AFL's inaugural season.

1961

Mel Branch, DE
Chris Burford, WR
Cotton Davidson, QB
Jon Gilliam, C
Abner Haynes, RB
Sherrill Headrick, LB
E.J. Holub, LB
Bill Krisher, G
Paul Rochester, DT
David Webster, DB
Buck Buchanan, DT

1962

Fred Arbanas, TE
Mel Branch, DE
Reg Carolan, WR
Jerry Cornelison, T
Len Dawson, QB
Dave Grayson, DB
Abner Hayes, RB
Sherrill Headrick, LB
E.J. Holub, LB
Jerry Mays, DE
Curtis McClinton, RB
Marvin Terrell, G

1963

Fred Arbanas, TE
Mel Branch, DE
Ed Budde, G'Walter Corey, LB
Jim Fraser, LB
Dave Grayson, DB
Johnny Robinson, S
Jim Tyrer, T
Duane Wood, DB

1964

Fred Arbanas, TD
Bobby Bell, LB
Tommy Brooker, K
Buck Buchanan, DT
Len Dawson, QB
Jim Fraser, LB
Dave Grayson, DB
Abner Haynes, RB
Mack Lee Hill, RB
E.J. Holub, LB
Bobby Hunt, DB
Jerry Mays, DE
Johnny Robinson, S
Jim Tyrer, T

1965

Fred Arbanas, TE
Bobby Bell, LB
Buck Buchanan, DT
Sherrill Headrick, LB
E.J. Holub, LB
Frank Jackson, WR
Jerry Mays, DE
Johnny Robinson, S
Jim Tyrer, T

1966

Bobby Bell, LB
Buck Buchanan, DT
Ed Budde, G
Len Dawson, QB
Mike Garrett, RB
Sherrill Headrick, LB
E.J. Holub, LB
Jerry Mays, DeE
Curtis McClinton, RB
Johnny Robinson, S
Jim Tyrer, T

1967

Fred Arbanas, TE
Bobby Bell, LB
Buck Buchanan, DT
Ed Budde, G
Len Dawson, QB
Mike Garrett, RB
Jerry Mays, DE
Curtis McClinton, RB
Johnny Robinson, S

1968

Buck Buchanan, DT
Ed Budde, G
Len Dawson, QB
Willie Lanier, LB
Jim Lynch, LB
Jerry Mays, DE
Johnny Robinson, S
Jan Stenerud, K
Emmitt Thomas, CB
Jim Tyrer, T

1969

Buck Buchanan, DT
Ed Budde, G
Curley Culp, DT
Len Dawson, QB
Robert Holmes, RB
Willie Lanier, LB
Mike Livingston, QB
Jim Marsalis, CB
Jan Stenerud, K
Jim Tyrer, T

AFC-NFC Pro Bowl Game

Selected Chiefs played for the AFC Team

1970

Buck Buchanan, DT
Ed Budde, G
Curley Culp, DT
Willie Lanier, MLB
Jan Stenerud, K
Otis Taylor, WR
Emmitt Thomas, CB
Jim Tyrer, T
Jerrel Wilson, P

1971

Buck Buchanan, DT
Ed Budde, G
Curley Culp, DT
Len Dawson, QB
Willie Lanier, MLB
Jan Stenerud, K
Otis Taylor, WR
Emmitt Thomas, CB
Jim Tyrer, T
Jerrel Wilson, P

1972

Bobby Bell, LB
Willie Lanier, MLB
Otis Taylor, WR
Emmitt Thomas, CB
Jerrel Wilson, P

1973

Willie Lanier, MLB
Jack Rudnay, C

1974

Willie Lanier, MLB
Jack Rudnay, C
Emmitt Thomas, CB

1975

Willie Lanier, MLB
Jack Rudnay, C
Jan Stenerud, K
Emmitt Thomas, CB

1976

Jack Rudnay, C
Jan Stenerud, K

1979

Bob Grupp, P
Jack Rudnay, C

1980

Art Still, DE
Gary Barbaro, S
J.T. Smith, KR

1981

Gary Barbaro, S
Joe Delaney, RB
Gary Green, CB
Nick Lowery, K
Art Still, DE

1982

Gary Barbaro, S
Art Still, DE
Gary Green, CB

1983

Carlos Carson, WR
Deron Cherry, S
Gary Green, CB
Gill Kenney, QB

1984

Deron Cherry, S
Art Still, DE

1985

Deron Cherry, S

1986

Lloyd Burruss, S
Deron Cherry, S
Bill Maas, NT

1987

Carlos Carson, WR
Deron Cherry, S
Albert Lewis, CB
Bill Maas, NT

1988

Deron Cherry, S
Dino Hackett, LB
Albert Lewis, CB

1989

Albert Lewis, CB
Christian Okoye, RB
Kevin Ross, CB
Derrick Thomas, LB

1990

Albert Lewis, CB
Nick Lowery, K
Kevin Ross, CB
Derrick Thomas, LB

1991

Christian Okoye, RB
Neil Smith, DE
Derrick Thomas, LB

1992

John Alt, T
Nick Lowery, K
Neil Smith, DE
Derrick Thomas, LB

1993

Marcus Allen, RB
John Alt, T
Joe Montana, QB
Neil Smith, DE
Derrick Thomas, LB

1994

Dale Carter, CB
Neil Smith, DE
Derrick Thomas, LB

1995

Kimble Anders, FB
Steve Bono, QB
Dale Carter, CB
Dan Saleaumua, DT
Will Shields, G
Neil Smith, DE
Derrick Thomas, LB

1996

Kimble Anders, FB
Dale Carter, CB
Will Shields, G
Derrick Thomas, LB

1997

Kimble Anders, FB
Dale Carter, CB
James Hasty, CB
Andre Rison, WR
Will Shields, G
Derrick Thomas, LB

1998

Will Shields, G

1999

Will Shields, G

2000

Will Shields, G
Tim Grunhard, C
James Hasty, CB
Tony Gonzalez, TE

2001

Will Shields, G
Elvis Grbac, QB
Tony Gonzalez, TE

2002

Priest Holmes, RB
Will Shields, G
Tony Gonzalez, TE

40th Anniversary Team

Mack Lee Award Recipients

Offense

WR	Otis Taylor	1965-75
WR	Carlos Carson	1980-89
TE	Fred Arbanas	1962-70
T	Jim Tyrer	1961-73
T	John Alt	1984-96
G	Ed Budde	1963-76
G	Will Shields	1993-99
C	Jack Rudnay	1969-82
QB	Len Dawson	1962-75
FB	Christian Okoye	1987-92
RB	Ed Podolak	1969-77

Defense

DE	Art Still	1978-87
DE	Neil Smith	1988-96
DT	Buck Buchanan	1963-75
DT	Jerry Mays	1961-70
LB	Willie Lanier	1967-77
LB	Bobby Bell	1963-74
LB	Derrick Thomas	1989-99
CB	Emmitt Thomas	1966-78
CB	Albert Lewis	1983-93
S	Deron Cherry	1981-91
S	Johnny Robinson	1960-71

(As selected by Lamar Hunt and Lamar Hunt, Jr.)

Year	Recipient
1966	Mike Garrett, RB
1967	Jan Stenerud, K
1968	Robert Homes, RB
1969	Jim Marsalis, CB
1970	Jack Rudnay, C
1971	Elmo Wright, WR
1972	Larry Marshall, WR
1973	Gary Butler, TE
1974	Woody Green, RB
1975	Walter White, TE
1976	Gary Barbaro, S
1977	Gary Green, CB
1978	Don Parrish, NT
1979	Bob Grupp, P
1980	Eric Harris, CB
1981	Lloyd Burruss, S
1982	Les Studdard, C
1983	David Lutz, T
1984	Kevin Ross, CB
1985	Jeff Smith, RB
1986	Dino Hackett, LB
1987	Christian Okoye, RB
1988	James Saxon, RB
1989	Derrick Thomas, LB
1990	Percey Snow, LB
1991	Tracy Simien, LB
1992	Willie Davis, WR
1993	Will Shields, G
1994	Lake Dawson, WR
1995	Tamarick Vanover, WR/KR
1996	Reggie Tongue, S
1997	Tony Gonzales, TE
1998	Victor Riley, OT
1999	Mike Maslowski
2000	Greg Wesley
2001	Eric Downing

All-Time AFL Team
1960-1969

Offense

Lance Alworth, San Diego Chargers	Wide Receiver
Don Maynard, New York Jets	Wide Receiver
Fred Arbanas, Kansas City Chiefs	Tight End
Ron Mix, San Diego Chargers	Tackle
Jim Tyrer, Kansas City Chiefs	Tackle
Ed Budde, Kansas City Chiefs	Guard
Billy Shaw, Buffalo Bills	Guard
Jim Otto, Oakland Raiders	Center
Joe Namath, New York Jets	Quarterback
Clem Daniels, Oakland Raiders	Running Back
Paul Lowe, San Diego Chargers	Running Back

Defense

Jerry Mays, Kansas City Chiefs	End
Gerry Philbin, New York Jets	End
Houston Antwine, Boston Patriots	Tackle
Tom Sestak, Buffalo Bills	Tackle
Bobby Bell, Kansas City Chiefs	Linebacker
George Webster, Houston Oilers	Linebacker
Nick Buoniconti, Boston Patriots	M-Linebacker
Willie Brown, Oakland Raiders	Cornerback
Dave Grayson, Oakland Raiders	Cornerback
Johnny Robinson, Kansas City Chiefs	Safety
George Saimes, Buffalo Bills	Safety

Specialists

George Blanda, Oakland Raiders	Kicker
Jerrel Wilson, Kansas City Chiefs	Punter

(Chosen by AFL Members of the Hall of Fame Selection Committee)

Most Valuable Player Award

(As voted by Chiefs' players)

1979	Gary Barbaro, S
1980	Art Still, DE
1981	Joe Delaney, RB
1982	Gary Green, CB
1983	Bill Kenney, QB
1984	Art Still, DE
1985	Lloyd Burruss, S
1986	Albert Lewis, CB
1987	Carlos Carson, WR
1988	Deron Cherry, S
1989	Christian Okoye, RB
1990	Steve DeBerg, QB
1991	Derrick Thomas, LB
1992	Neil Smith, DE
1993	Marcus Allen, RB
1994	Derrick Thomas, LB
1995	Marcus Allen, RB
1996	Mark Collins, S
1997	Andre Rison, WR
1998	Glenn Parker, G/T
1999	Marvcus Patton, LB
2000	Derrick Alexander, WR
2001	Priest Holmes, RB

Sources

AFL to Arrowhead, by Mark Stallard

The American Football League: A Year-By-Year History, 1960-1969, by Ed Gruver

American Football League recruiting brochure, 1961

Arrowhead: Home of the Chiefs, by Michael McKenzie

Championship, Jerry Izenberg

Chiefs Rivalries, by The Kansas City Star

Confessions of a Dirty Ballplayer, by Johnny Sample with Fred Hamilton and Sonny Schwartz

Dallas Morning News

Dallas Texans game programs, 1960-62

Dallas Texans Team Videos, 1960, 1962

Great Teams Great Years – Dallas Cowboys, by Jeff Meyers

Great Teams Great Years – Kansas City Chiefs, by Dick Connor

Hail to the Chiefs, by Bob Gretz

A History of the Kansas City Chiefs Football Club, by Wade Moyer and Bill Althaus

Kansas City Chiefs, by Loren Stanley

Kansas City Chiefs game programs, 1963-2001

Kansas City Chiefs Media Guides, 1963-2001

Kansas City Chiefs Post Season Media Guides, 1999-2001

Kansas City Chiefs Team Yearbooks, 1968-1972, 1997-2000

Kansas City Chiefs Team Videos, 1964, 1966-1971, 1999-2000

Kansas City Star

KCChiefs.com

Jim Otto: The Pain of Glory, by Jim Otto with Dave Newhouse

Len Dawson: Superbowl Quarterback, by Larry Bortstein

Marcus, by Marcus Allen with Carlton Stowers

New York Times

NFL.com

NFL-AFL Illustrated Digest – Official 1969 Edition, by Don Smith and Ed Croke

The NFL's Official Encyclopedia History of Professional Football

Pro Football Hall of Fame Research Library – Player files

Pro Football Heroes Today, by Berry Stainback

Professional Football's Greatest Games, by Paul Michael

The Official NFL Encyclopedia, by Beau Riffenburgh

Raiders Forever: Stars of the NFL's Most Colorful Team Recall Their Glory Days, by John Lombardo

Sport Magazine

The Sporting News

Sporting News American Football League Guides, 1964-1969

The Sports Encyclopedia: Pro Football, by David S. Neft, Roland T. Johnson, Riach Cohen & Jordan Deutsch

The Sports Encyclopedia: Pro Football - 17th Edition, by David S. Neft, Richard Cohen & Rick Korch

Sports Illustrated

The Story of Football, by Robert Leckie

The Super Bowl, published by Simon & Schuster

Super Bowl I game program

Super Bowl I & IV highlight videos, NFL Films

Super Bowl IV game program

Super Bowl play-by-play game logs provided by Kansas City Chiefs

Super Bowl Sunday: The Day America Stops, edited by Matt Fulks

They're Playing My Game, by Hank Stram with Lou Sahadi

Total Football, by Bob Carroll, Michael Gershman, David Neft & John Thorn

Total Football II by Bob Carroll, Michael Gershman, David Neft & John Thorn

Warpaths: The Illustrated History of the Kansas City Chiefs, Alan Hoskins

We Came of Age: A Picture History of the American Football League, by Jack Orr

Wichita Eagle

Winning It All, by Joe McGuff

Player and Lamar Hunt drawings courtesy of Bob Carroll
Pg. 1 photo courtesy of Orlin Wagner, AP/World Wide Photos
Pg. 315 photo courtesy of Transcendental Graphics

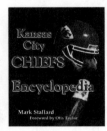

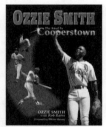

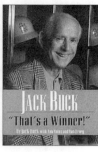

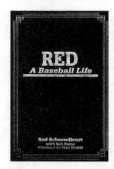